St. Louis Community College

Library

5801 Wilson Avenue
St. Louis, Missouri 63110

Trial
by Fire

Trial by Fire

THE TRUE STORY OF A WOMAN'S ORDEAL AT THE HANDS OF THE LAW

Gerry Spence

WILLIAM MORROW AND COMPANY, INC.
NEW YORK

Library of Congress Cataloging-in-Publication Data

Spence, Gerry.
  Trial by fire.

  Includes index.
  1. Pring, Kim—Trials, litigation, etc. 2. Penthouse
(New York, N.Y.)—Trials, litigation, etc. 3. Trials
(Libel)—Wyoming—Cheyenne. I. Title.
KF228.P76S63   1986   345.73´0256   86-2432
ISBN 0-688-06075-7   347.305256

Printed in the United States of America

First Edition

1   2   3   4   5   6   7   8   9   10

BOOK DESIGN BY VICKI HARTMAN

To my darling, Imaging, who, by being free,
has delivered me.

ACKNOWLEDGMENTS

It is frightening to be lost in a forest of one's own making, and one is desperate for someone who is intimately familiar with such a strange and lonely place to join him and help him find his way through it—to find his way out into the sunshine again where things can be clearly seen—where things make sense. I am grateful for Imaging's kind forebearance when, having come to rescue me, she was accused often of leading me deeper into darker places, and it was then that her gentleness prevailed like a kindly attendant in an asylum who brings the sweet light of sanity to the mad—the state, from time to time, of all those who attempt to write. None but the masochistic, the stupid, or the also mad would dare be truthful with the writer concerning his work in progress, or his completed work for that matter, unless, of course, there is great love, and it is that rare gift from Imaging that I now acknowledge. The giving has too often been painful. I have only wishes that it will have all been worth it.

And why my friend John Scott Turner should have also willingly engaged me, why he should have taken me on in a hand-to-hand battle for simple clarity of expression, for clean statements of thought, why he should have fought so relentlessly for pages that did more than merely blot up, soak up my raging, my passion and should have been willing to expend that great energy and suffer those frequent injuries in arguing me down time and time again as only a superior lawyer could have when the only reward was that his friend, me, should not be utterly embarrassed with the presentation of some indefensible document—that also is not merely the expression of great caring, but the proof of it, for which I am beholden.

My friend Sandra Lambert looked at every word on every page and often sat by me like a music teacher asking her pupil to hear the notes he plays and to make them better, to strike the discords and to add the more pleasant phrases, and to be aware of the accursed redundancies of note and rhythm. Her devotion to the cause of my literacy has been, I fear, more bathed in hope than established in the results herein. Yet should one come onto an occasional triumphant phrase, it is to her that the credit must be given, for she wished to make a writer of me for selfless reasons that speak most generously of her nature as a teacher and a friend.

My secretary, Rosemary McIntosh, laid her weary eyes time and again on every word in this book in perpetual proof that I can neither spell nor punctuate—that as to both I am beyond learning. She never gave up. She has nurtured this manuscript in my hands and in the publisher's and is without a doubt the mother of it—all of which simply says that any man who has enjoyed the devoted assistance that has been bestowed on me has also been deprived of all excuses.

Kim Pring kindly agreed to let me republish the memory of her trial by fire with the hope that this book might present some truth, perhaps might tell a story worth telling, might create an awareness of certain genetic evils in the law as it pertains to women, and perhaps, although she never said so, that the pain she suffered might not be wasted, that it might, instead, be converted into something positive and worthy. I have never known a more courageous young woman nor one who wished more for the well-being of her fellowman than Kim Pring. She has asked that I, for her, acknowledge the great love and support she received from her parents, Norman and Mary Jayne Pring, of Cheyenne, Wyoming.

INTRODUCTION

Letting go is so frightening. I used to suffer a recurrent nightmare in which I dangled on a small slab of rock by my fingertips, the treacherous canyon floor thousands of feet below staring up maliciously, a mad river roaring in laughter, deaf to all but itself. The rock I clung to joined in the evil conspiracy, cutting away first at the flesh and then at the bone. There weren't many choices. I could clutch and bawl and slobber like a steer in the slaughter chute, scream and struggle against it until I was drowned in the panic and my fingers finally gave way, and then I could clinch my eyes against the horror of it and descend into the hideous night, leaving a trail of terror to mark my passing, or—yes, it is quite possible—once having accepted that all hope of rescue had vanished, I could gently release my grip and enjoy the trip down—floating free, taking in the sights as they flashed by, laughing lightly, for—can't you see?—I can fly.

I always experience that frightful feeling at letting go when the bailiff leads the jury away to decide my case. I want to holler one last argument after them, to shout one last word that will surely seal their verdict, and then the door to the jury room shuts and the bailiff sits down beside it to guard the jury from intrusion, and there is that awful silence, and it is too late. I have lost control. I think of all those things I should have said and didn't, and vice versa. How could I have forgotten? I had planned the case for months, tested each word, not just once. And as I turned away to gather up my empty books and foolish files, I knew I was nothing but a miserable fop, fit to serve mankind best by hiding myself in some desolate, godforsaken place until my time had come. And then I should go quietly.

So it was also with the release of this manuscript. I felt it all again, the terrible ripping loose, the sense of hurtling into the dark and the dreadful—my case now out of control before this multitude of jurors

9

I took no part in choosing. They chose me. But worst of all it was the piteous waste, the futility of the lonely wrangle with words, the writing and rewriting until the damnable words were worn smooth, the exasperation at creating a single thought—and then the horrid truth—not a word was a worthy word, not a thought, a real thought, and worse still, my case, as presented, would please no one. But I had to let go.

In the first place, I had no intention of writing a book from any illuminated position about women or women's rights. I was not an enlightened feminist, nor did I particularly wish to be. I set out to write about a compelling jury trial and the subsequent appeals from which I wished to illustrate the deplorable state of the law. That my client was a woman—indeed, a very pleasant and pretty one—was incidental. I have represented many women, even famous ones, and should I choose to write about the predicament of the modern woman seeking justice, I would not have chosen this one to symbolize the cause. I mean, how plainly preposterous that I should be moved to concern myself with what *Penthouse* magazine published concerning one blond-headed, blue-eyed Wyoming baton twirler, much less write a book about it that would greedily devour these precious several years. One can glance in almost any direction at this bitter, blistered world of ours and find infinitely more compelling cases and causes, more deserving victims to write about than Kim Pring, Miss Wyoming of 1978.

There is a time for all cases to be over. Yet such a time never came for me in the Miss Wyoming case. There were petulant, haunting, undefined urgings inside me wishing to take form, to be born, but why and what they were I didn't know. I simply felt their presence the way a woman must feel new life growing in her belly. Then as if by a witch's touch I was given the gift, or the curse, as you may judge, and the circumstances began to drop out of fate's basket in proper order and at exactly the correct time.

I know now that it all actually started long before I had even heard of Kim Pring's case, when my pawky, precocious friend, the famous criminal trial attorney from Milwaukee, Jim Shellow, introduced me to the *Malleus Maleficarum, The Witches' Hammer,* the evil old tome by which millions of women were persecuted, tortured, and burned as witches in the two and a half centuries following its publication in 1487. With uncanny insight and more courage than an intelligent lawyer should display, Shellow sometimes cited the *Malleus* to judges whose righteous breath, whose zeal and fervor for respite against some poor wretch before them was in perfect harmony with the pernicious spirit by which witches were persecuted—it being obvious to Shellow, as, quite frankly, it is to me, that the witch trial, under the force of the same blind and bigoted judiciary that does not care a whit for the human spirit, is a common occurrence in the courtroom today—that nothing really changes, least of all that mean spirit of arrogant authority that craves to wield its malevolent power over those helpless wretches, those caught in the clutches of the state and charged with crimes, or those who are injured—the maimed, the defamed, the forgotten and the damned who pound at the doors of the judiciary begging for justice.

As I studied the *Malleus,* that foul, superstitious legal authority that had rotted its way up through the miseries and ignorance of the Dark Ages, I discovered from what vile flanks our law was spawned. Our law, our blessed, sacred law, spent its early youth in those hideous times following the publication of the *Malleus,* when the smell of millions of innocent women burning at the stake and the sound of their screaming into the night, of their flesh sizzling in the Christ-fires, scorched the nostrils and blistered the eyes and perverted the minds of our fathers, yes, during those times the men of history have wished to hide from themselves and their children, dark times that culminated in the hanging of the innocent goodwives at Salem in 1692. Our law was dragged through that history, was soaked in it, and absorbed it, so that today, should a woman dare come before our law seeking justice, what is offered is all that any system based on precedent has to offer—namely, a hash of leftovers from past iniquities. When a woman comes to court to defend herself, she must still struggle in the shadows of the Dark Ages.

I began to have those tiniest insights that, like a seedling grown to a tree, I could no longer uproot. One day I realized I must know, fully know, this new emerging woman I saw rising out of the ashes of her sisters, this brash, confrontive revolutionary I had so carefully circumvented these many years. And I knew I must join her—for my sake. For no one who is fettered to those he holds captive is ever, himself, free.

I tell you I worked at it. It was painful. It was sometimes even degrading to discover my own inherent prejudices, to view the vast borders of my ignorance, to recognize the persistence of my accursed chauvinism. There were bitter arguments with many women. My

sister, ten years younger, was always leagues ahead of me on any social issue. There were frightful, full-faced confrontations with
women lawyers from which I always left feeling angry and ragged.
Often I felt guilty. I also felt lonely.

I plead for understanding. It is hard for such a man as I, born in the
wilds of Wyoming, a man educated here, who has lived all of his life
in this place of hard-bitten, ill-bred barbarians who make the Marl-
boro man look like an Avon lady—it was, I say, a severe, perhaps impossible mandate imposed on me that I should burst out one glorious
morning as a full-fledged, born-again feminist, correctly and permanently sensitized to the rights and feelings of the new woman.

I was taught different platitudes—the party lines of all Wyoming
men of my generation. We liked to brag that, after all, ours was the
Equality State, the first state to grant women suffrage, and like other
men of our age, we insisted with all due ardor that we respected
women so long as women respected us, and stayed in their place. But
we never went so far as to insist that this "place" was solely in the
home, drowning in wet diapers and squawling kids. Our more liberated Wyoming view was born of necessity, for we sure as hell
needed them on the end of an irrigation shovel or on a buck rake
during haying, and, by God, they could get up in the middle of the
night like the rest of us and pull a calf out of an old cow having trouble and down in two feet of March snow.

We were proud of our women, mostly because they could raise the
kids and cook the meals and keep the house, and do a man's work on
top of it. But all of that didn't mean they should take all of this
women's liberation business too seriously. They were already free—
to work their butts to the bone, to work until they came in looking
like a bunch of scraggly critters trapped in Hell's Canyon all winter
without feed, and after supper, after the dishes were done, they were
free to jump under the conjugal covers and absorb whatever sexual
delights their brutish and hair-triggered husbands might wish to
serve up, in response to which they were expected to convince him
he was, and always had been, the world's greatest gift to women.

Our women in Wyoming had rights, all right. To prove it, there's a
statue in front of the capitol building in Cheyenne of Esther Hobart
Morris, the first Wyoming woman to hold public office, the mother of
women's suffrage in Wyoming, they say. She was a justice of the
peace at South Pass City, population 460, for eight and a half
months. On her first court day she is said to have taken the bench

wearing a calico gown, worsted breakfast shawl, green ribbons in her hair, and a green necktie. She was acclaimed as "the terror of all rogues, and to afford infinite delight to all lovers of peace and virtue," but she was definitely not nominated for another term.[1]

The most telling argument made for women's suffrage, adopted by Wyoming's first legislature in 1869, was that it gave to the stable, married man two votes over the one of the single trash who otherwise, by their very numbers, might have taken over the territory. It wasn't until 1892 that Wyoming gave women the right to convey their property without the consent of their husbands, and by 1871 those judges who were said to be more in tune with the times prohibited women from serving on juries, holding that service by women on juries was not an adjunct of suffrage. They should be home with the kids, not gallivanting around in jury rooms with strangers.

It is therefore a miracle of at least small proportions that one immersed in such frontier versions of women's rights, a native son of the Equality State, should take any position as to women and women's rights except one most likely to avoid trouble with these snappish, querulous, ineffable, new-age females—to pay the necessary lip service to their avowed cause, to be sure (for they argue from certain logical premises) to consciously edit from one's language in their presence words such as "gals" and "chicks," but to otherwise stay as far away as possible from the front of that revolution lest one get injured. Such is, I fear, the pose most men of my generation have taken.

But one day (perhaps I began to realize it when my agent told me, after having read the first ten chapters of this book, that I was a budding feminist), I was nevertheless (I despise the word) converted, and like any new convert, I wished to be loved by the flock. I especially wanted this book to be lauded by women. I wanted them to say, "Here is a country lawyer who has proven that even the most petrified of sexists, a man paralyzed from birth in his own chauvinism, can overcome this most crippling of disabilities and walk again." But I fear most women will hate me, the younger ones especially. They will give a man like me no quarter—no, none, for no living generation better represents the archenemy of the new woman than mine.

Despite careful editing, I fear I have been unable to fully conceal the persistent remnants of my previous sexist attitudes, which always expose themselves to women like some miserable old flasher whenever I lose my concentration. Their roots, like the damnable Canadian thistle that threatens a good stand of hay, go deep, go beyond surface weeding, and new sprouts keep popping up to my dismay and despair. Despite the fact that it has taken a lifetime to become who we are, they expect us, these new women, to rub the old callouses from our souls overnight. Even a snake takes a full season to shed his hide, and the new one looks exactly like the one it replaced.

And I also know that the judges—especially the judges—and the scholars, too, will hate me, for they worship a different set of myths than I. I am also no legal scholar. They will surely see me as an uncouth ruffian, for Christ's sakes, whose views, perhaps occasionally amusing, are to be taken as merely parochial. But I have always confessed that. I am, indeed, a country lawyer who has learned more from the mountain creatures, from the desperate reservation Indians, the crippled, the wasted, and the damned who are my clients, from the old cowhands whose stringy wisdom is born of hard lives lived in desolate places, from the squawk of the magpies, the simple affection of my dogs, and the innocent truths spoken by my children, than I ever learned from all the judges and professors and the sages of the law, who would, if they could, educate me to embrace high mental axioms instead of people.

I shudder to think whatever will become of me now, after having demanded my own First Amendment rights to speak as truthfully as I know how. I must appear before these judges for the rest of my days. I must make my poor pleas on behalf of my clients (who never did the judges any slight) before these men who will never forget—who will never forgive. Judges have eternal memories. Only a grand fool would have done it, I admit.

I believe that our beloved right to freedom of speech carries with it a corresponding duty to use it responsibly, that the greatest threat to the First Amendment is not the limitations the law purportedly places on free speech, such as the duty not to maliciously libel each other, but that the real danger is the unbridled *abuse* of the right to free speech. I cannot agree to any form of censorship, not even of the rankest pornographers. Yet, strangely, the media is only too willing to sacrifice its own credibility for fear that any attack on pornography will, in some strange way, curtail the legitimate media's rights as well, as if we are incapable of killing the ticks on the dog's back without killing the dog. We in a free society, and with reasonably good success, have always been able to identify those who are the enemies of society and those who are not, and in order to protect our other freedoms, we have never advocated a prohibition against the capture of those who murder, rob, and rape us.

I insist that the media use its freedom responsibly in the same manner the rest of us are required to temper the exercise of our other freedoms, failing which the media, too, must pay damages to those it injures. The media has no special status, no particular privilege to do harm merely because it wields such mammoth power. On the contrary, because of its great power, the media has a special duty not to release it against the relatively powerless individual without first having been reasonably careful in doing so. We require no greater care of a child with his hunting rifle.

I experience no right-wing religious fervor concerning the First Amendment but instead see that great freedom as an essential, yes, even the most necessary tool of liberty to be correctly and intelligently used by the people to preserve their democratic way of life. I am, I fear, therefore automatically disqualified from becoming a member in good standing of those absolutist First Amendment clubs that nowadays abound and would permit the press to ravage as it pleases.

In sum, I have succeeded marvelously in at least one thing— within these pages I have been able to raise the hackles on the hides of multitudes—of both sexes and of many persuasions. I have not gone far enough for many modern women and I still reveal a level of consciousness too crude to warrant my total acceptance by them. I will be taken as a traitor by my own chauvinist compadres. Those of the legal community, who for thirty-five years have been my peers, will think me mad, and most judges only too eager to certify it. The world of literature will certainly continue to make no room for the likes of me. They guard their membership with a certain fussiness that would have excluded me from the beginning anyway. The very press I depend upon for the survival of this effort will undoubtedly be hostile and will see the simplest mention of this book as giving aid and comfort to the enemy—all of which puts me back hanging on that thin, rocky ledge looking down into that terrible abyss, knowing I cannot hang on much longer, that I must let go of this. Now. Silently, without the screaming, without the terror in my heart—if only I could enjoy the fall. If only I could fly.

—GERRY SPENCE

Jackson Hole, Wyoming

1

"Are you a virgin, Miss Pring?"

The young woman sat stiff and straight and silent, facing her inquisitor. The tendons in her neck protruded, her eyes were covered with a colorless glaze, bulging, like someone engaged in mortal struggle. I doubted that she actually saw the *Penthouse* lawyer who had been so vehement in his argument to the magistrate. His questioning of Kim Pring, the former Miss Wyoming, was precisely, faithfully, in accordance with law. I stood up to object. This was no witch's trial. But the magistrate, clutching a heavy volume in his hands, motioned me back to my seat. He peered intently into the book. I knew of its predecessor—that most venerated medieval treatise which once lay on the bench of every judge and every magistrate, the *Malleus Maleficarum*, the "ultimate, irrefutable, unarguable authority"[1] on the prosecution of witches, that decreed "common justice demands the accused not be condemned to death unless she is convicted by her own confession."[2]

How else could you see Kim Pring but as a witch? Had she not committed her vulgar, her worse than vulgar, act before the world, committed fellatio on the fool until he was actually levitated—until by her lurid sorcery he was made to rise, his arms and head thrown back in a delight bestowed only by those who possess the power of the devil?

I tried to interrupt the interrogation again.

"Here, Kim, would you like a sip of water?" There was pitifully little I could do to delay the torture. I started toward the witness stand with the glass, but her eyes were steadfast on her interrogator. The magistrate motioned me back to my seat, and the lawyer for *Penthouse* thrust the question at her again.

"Are you a virgin, Miss Pring?"

No man would be asked such a question. No judge would permit such a scurrilous interrogation. Even if the question were allowed—a preposterous presumption—and should a man actually assert his virginity—an equally ludicrous likelihood—his answer would not be taken in his favor but, instead, as a concession that he was either dead or daft.

The magistrate, however, had ruled that *Penthouse* had begun its interrogation completely within its rights. The question, and those I knew would follow, were intended to expose the woman's most private facts, to strip her bare of her innermost secrets. I thought of the *Malleus*, how it suggested that the interrogation begin with "light torture at first" and how, too, at the outset, the *Penthouse* attorney, a man referred to by His Honor as "Mr. Daichman," had asked only that one forthright question to which he now demanded an answer.

The *Malleus* prescibed simple procedures designed to assure the successful trial of any witch. "While the officers are preparing for the questioning, let the accused be stripped, and her clothes searched for any instruments of witchcraft sewn therein, for they often make such instruments, at the instruction of devils, out of the limbs of unbaptized children."[3] Naked, women were most likely to confess their crimes. The *Malleus* reported: "The Inquisitor of Como has informed us ... in 1485, he ordered 41 witches to be burned, after they had been shaved all over."[4]

Kim Pring had been called to the witness stand in the United States District Court in Cheyenne, Wyoming, on the twenty-seventh day of September, 1980, nearly five hundred years after the *Malleus* first appeared, that authority said to be "among the most important, wisest, and weightiest books in the world."[5] The publication acquired special acclaim and dignity from the famous bull of Pope Innocent VIII, *Summis desiderantes affectibus*, of December 9, 1484, and charged Europe's judges with the solemn duty of combating the Society of Witches.[6] Over the two and a half centuries following its publication it is estimated that no less than a million women were burned at the stake, some responsible authorities estimating as many as nine million, mostly women, died in the fires.[7] One authority even argues that the enormity of the atrocity could be compared only to the Holocaust.[8]

Since those shadowy centuries and out of those abominable beginnings, the trials of innocent women, in one form or another, have continued. Although in America the last of the witches were hanged at Salem in 1692, the command of that malignant manifesto, the *Malleus Maleficarum,* has persisted like a virulent germ. Of course, I do not argue that we have made no progress in our search for truth, or that the pain of the trial of this woman, Kim Pring, in any real way achieved that state of abject horror of those times when terror froze the townspeople, when the smell of the burning flesh of women filled their nostrils and the screams of the condemned sizzling at the stake shattered the silence of the night. Those were, indeed, the dark ages: the diabolical times when men of power, the holy fathers of the Church, the landed, the wealthy, the great men of medicine joined to do their duty by the book, the *Malleus.* Under the holy hand of the Church they organized their inquisitions, accused and tried and burned the midwives and the magic healers of the poor whose crimes were often only the administration of herbs and roots and ancient potions gathered from the blessed Mother Earth. They tried and burned the earthy sensuous daughters of the forest squatters, for they too were obviously witches. Had they not seduced the pious fathers in their dreams and stolen the semen from their bodies in the night? Had they not dedicated themselves to the devil, lain with him, made their bargains? Most who burned were women, the poor and the old and the helpless, the not-worth-mentioning except for the enormity of their wickedness. But then, as now, the women were tried by men, and by men's laws in accordance with those ancient rites (and rights), for as the *Malleus* proclaimed, was not witchcraft, practically without exception, a crime of women?

Daichman waited for Kim Pring to answer.

I heard the dreadful screaming of the woman, the deadly metallic clicking of the crank, the deep dull thudding of the executioner's fist against her naked white flesh, the heavy exhortations of the judge pleading with her to confess—confess in the name of Christ and the Blessed Virgin and the Holy Apostles, Peter and Paul—so, too, these sounds must have moved the officers of the court to their most ingenious improvisations, and those few who dared whisper that these were the sounds of the devil presiding over the court, like crows cawing over carrion, were often themselves prosecuted as the damnable, the accursed heretics.

So may it be.

Kim Pring sat at the southernmost edge of the bench, quite obviously out of reach of the magistrate. Daichman looked up, waiting for His Honor's order. The magistrate gave the sleeve of his robe nearest her a quick, smart, downward jerk so that his suit jacket was now fully covered. Then he brushed away a speck, and waited for the woman to speak.

The judges were warned in the *Malleus:* "They must not allow themselves to be touched physically by the witch, especially any contact of their bare arms or hands, but they must always carry about them some salt consecrated on Palm Sunday and some Blessed Herbs. For these can be enclosed together in Blessed Wax and worn around the neck," for their "wonderful protective virtue."[9] Even now some judges wear special pins on their lapels and certain gold rings on their fingers bearing the emblems of the secret organizations to which they belong, and some of our judges still wear the cross itself underneath their stiff white collars and their deadly black robes. The men of the law are holy men.

Kim Pring refused to answer Daichman. His Honor cleared his throat. The stubborn silence of the witch was always a serious detriment to justice. The *Malleus* gave advice. The judge "shall use his own persuasions and those of other honest men zealous for the faith to induce her to confess the truth voluntarily; and if she will not, let him order the officers to bind her with cords, and apply her to some engine of torture, and then let them obey at once, but not joyfully, rather appearing to be disturbed by their duty."[10] An eyewitness to the tortures of witches reported: "There are men who in this art exceed the spirit of hell. I have seen the limbs forced asunder, the eyes driven out of the head, the feet torn from the legs, the sinews twisted from the joints, the shoulder blades wrung from their place, the deep veins swollen, the superficial veins driven in, the victim now hoisted aloft, and now dropped, now revolved around, head undermost and feet uppermost. I have seen the executioner flog with the scourge, and smite with rods, and crush with screws, and load down with weights, and stick with needles, and bind around with cords, and burn with brimstone, and oil, and singe with torches."[11]

Word of the spectacle spread quickly. As the interrogation of Kim Pring mounted, the clerks and other employees around the courthouse began tiptoeing into the courtroom like people arriving late at church. Glancing at each other in slight embarrassment, they quickly, quietly, took seats near the back and leaned forward to listen. In a few minutes the room was already half full.

I had demanded that the proceedings be conducted in privacy, but the magistrate had ruled, "This courtroom is a public place," and the doors had been flung wide open. Then he looked out at the gathering audience, and, recognizing someone, gave a faint but friendly smile, and without even looking down at Kim Pring, he commanded, "Answer the question, Miss Pring."

The people strained farther forward to hear her answer, but she sat mute, shaking her head obstinately. Once she rubbed her eyes on the sleeve of her dress. I felt as if nothing had really changed, that we had learned nothing through the centuries. I felt helpless. I was helpless. I felt an urge to pull her down from the stand and run with her out into the safety of the streets of Cheyenne, out where people walked by with vacant eyes, where people thought justice was a natural right available to them like air, like water, where people believed that justice was the holy work of judges.

"I object to this entire line of inquiry," I shouted. That's all I could do. Never once did the magistrate look in my direction. Again he fixed his eyes on the book he grasped with both hands, a work grown thick with time, at the very core of which I knew lay the *Malleus Maleficarum.*

"Overruled," the magistrate said. His lips were pulled thin and he spoke through his teeth. "I've already heard your arguments, Mr. Spence." He looked down at the witness, and in a voice too shallow to carry feeling, he repeated his command. "Answer the question, Miss Pring." She stared silently out at the audience, then at the judge. She looked over at me for help. I could do nothing. Finally she shook her head.

I thought she was very brave.

When the witch on the rack still refused to confess, the officers of the court would start the slow cranking again until her hip joints began to give way, and there was a sickening snapping in her spine, and the muscles at her shoulders started to rip. Even then the accused often remained silent. Sometimes the officers of the court, patient men, finally grew weary of it, and one would say to the man at the crank, very quietly, respectfully, "When are you going to put a little pressure on this witch so we can be done with her and go home for supper?" Then the man at the crank would give a polite nod and another half turn to the crank for good measure, and in pursuit of his duty, he would deliver a heavy fist into the pit of the woman's stomach. An awful tearing could be heard, but still the woman would remain mute. The devil had taken her tongue. Following the further advice of the *Malleus*, the officers would wait until the morrow: "If, after being fittingly tortured she refuses to confess the truth, he [the magistrate] should have other engines of torture brought before her, and tell her that she will have to endure these if she does not confess. If then she is not induced by terror to confess, the torture must be continued on the second and third day. . . ."[12]

After work, and weary, the judge would plod home, giving the townsfolk kindly smiles as he passed by, and the townsfolk, of course, respected the judge, for he was their faithful servant committed to drive the plague of witches from the village. Judges were engaged in holy work.

For over thirty years I had seen women struggle under the heavy body of the law. There had been remarkable reforms, I admit. Their position in the jurisprudential pecking order had been spectacularly elevated so that one might nowadays count token women jurists, and many women had taken up the profession of law as well. I admit I had witnessed a reluctant lip service offered by the fathers of the law to women and to women's rights so that one was left with the clear impression there had been a minor revolution out of which women had emerged in the law as equals. But I observed it as more a matter of social politeness by men in power than the delivery of any substantial new rights to women, more as a well-behaved tolerance of the "new woman" in the law rather than any real commitment by men that their counterparts be truly equal.

But scars cannot be wished away, nor can the underlying damage once rendered to the flesh be denied. The remnant of that horrid history of women, however diminished, of that terrible trauma, however healed, remained as much a part of the law as if the infamous inquisitors, now subdued and genial, still reigned supreme—as if these thoroughly decent, ethical, agreeable men full of charm and social grace, elegant and disarming, still conducted the affairs of justice under the vestigial authority of that evil treatise, the *Malleus Malificarum*.

Perhaps I should never have brought this suit for Kim Pring, for I knew these men of court had just begun to exercise the power men have always wielded over women. My objections to the questions only confirmed what the magistrate knew—it was his right to subject her to this and I was helpless to stop him. My adversary would show her no mercy. There would be no mercy, not in war, not in a trial—for the trial of a case is war.

Finally Kim Pring spoke and what she said as a woman every man should have heard. She spoke to the magistrate in a clear enough voice, and the magistrate heard her, but his face didn't soften. He looked up quickly from his book and then went back to his reading. Surely his gift of dead ears was not given out of any perniciousness of his soul or insensitivity to her humanness. No. He was a man dedicated to the law, immersed in it, shackled by its precedents and therefore he could not hear the woman's words fill the courtroom as full as the screaming of any wretch on the rack.

For centuries judges have been warned against emotion. The law is without feeling, like the numb member of one stricken. The *Malleus* explained how judges must protect against feeling, especially for women, "for sometimes, with God's permission, they [the accused women] are able with the help of the devil to bewitch the Judge by the mere sound of the words which they utter, especially at the time when they are exposed to torture."[13] The temptation to respond with mercy to the cries and the screaming is only the work of the devil and must never be allowed to amend the logic of the law. The law is logic. No, it was not that the magistrate was different from other men; he had been born with his full share of compassion, and off the bench one could easily see he was quite human. It was only that he had been fully trained in the law, and at the bench the law had rendered him deaf.

I remember first seeing Kim Pring in the doorway of my office clutching an issue of *Penthouse* like a small girl caught with something nasty in her hand. Her mother stood behind her, as blond, almost as young-looking as she.

"Here, give that thing to me," I said, taking the magazine and motioning both women to a seat. Almost in unison they took opposite ends of the couch in front of me, crossed their legs in the same direction, folded their hands in their laps, and peered at me politely with small smiles. They were like two sisters waiting for something magical to happen; perhaps they waited to be touched with the magnanimity of the law they thought was in my power.

"I've already read this," I said, giving it a toss to the side of my desk. The magazine, trained by many readings, obediently flopped open to the first page of a story titled MISS WYOMING SAVES THE WORLD, BUT SHE BLEW THE CONTEST WITH HER TALENT.

The mother fidgeted on the couch, embarrassed to be in such a place where sin is confessed and scandal revealed. She looked down at her hands and squeezed them together as if they comforted each other. The woman's hide was as thin and translucent as the egg of a small bird and gave off the same pale and pearly gleam, especially at the cheekbones and across the outer edges of the forehead. Her hair was done up to give a careless appearance, a kind of happenstance bouffant, I supposed, and she'd tied a purple paisley scarf around her neck and tucked it down the front of a plain gray long-sleeved dress the way my own Methodist mother had dressed herself for church.

"That damn thing is obscene," I said. I slouched down in my chair, trying to look relaxed.

"We always love to come to Jackson Hole," the mother replied, wiggling on the couch like a bird trying to settle on her eggs, her face aglow. "It's beautiful here." She looked with distant eyes across the room and out my front window. "Cheyenne is so flat and dry and hot this time of year," she said, retaining that same imprinted smile— one I thought that might have remained perfect even when she slept.

"This damn thing is libelous," I said, motioning to the magazine.

"Well, I'd hope so," the mother said in her wee distant voice. She nodded her head in quick little birdlike affirmations.

"How did you react to this?" I asked the daughter.

"Well, it upset her terribly," the mother answered. But I kept my eyes on the younger woman. There was something extraordinarily sensual about her—sensual, I say, not classically beautiful. She was not a woman who had labored to make herself obvious in obvious places, not one who presented herself as beguilingly beddable or anything like that. At first glance she was in all ways an ordinary young woman—well-scrubbed, her fine, very blond hair hanging loosely past her shoulders and her blue eyes creating an impression of innocence and kindness. Yet it was likely a man would look at this woman a second time, and when he did, his focus would come naturally, irresistibly, to the mouth, and when she spoke he would find himself fascinated with the slow, easy movements of her ample lips.

Kim Pring had won the 1978 Miss Wyoming contest hands down, and her reign had continued through the summer of 1979. Even the judges claimed they had chosen her for her talent, not her looks; that was the thing in Wyoming—talent. At the county fairs we select cattle for their conformation—groom them up pretty, parade them around, and hang ribbons on them, after which they are sold to the highest bidder, and butchered. But in Wyoming we have always professed a certain pride in our women. Weren't we the first state to grant women suffrage, to recognize women as fully endowed members of the species, with the same rights as men? Therefore was it not fitting that we chose Miss Wyoming for her talent instead of her looks?

"I'll tell you, Mr. Spence," she said in a voice without the slightest seductive sound. It was more the clear, crisp voice of a boy. "I think something should be done about this. Those people at *Penthouse*—well, they are the lowest kind. I mean they are nothing but"—she struggled a moment—"they are nothing but smut peddlers. That's what they are. Smut peddlers." Then instantly the anger left her voice; she seemed dismayed. "How can they say such things about a person and get away with it?" She stopped to think of how she was going to phrase her argument. She looked determined. Her lips began to move slightly ahead of her words.

"I was the United States Grand National Twirling Champion," she said. "I've worked all my life for that title."

"She worked very hard," her mother said.

"And then in about three thousand words, or however many—I never took the time to count them—that magazine turned me into the world's greatest—" She pointed at the *Penthouse* flopped open on the desk in a pose worthy of its centerfolds. Now she was stopped by a mere word again. How should she say it in front of her mother and me? She looked at the prim, blond, smiling woman sitting next to her. She turned to me, and when I kept silent too, she said, "Well, you know what I mean."

"Fellatio," her mother said suddenly, sweetly.

"Yes, fellatio," Kim said.

Soon she was earnestly, anxiously, cautiously trying to explain it to me, as a farm girl might confess a rape to her father. "They turned me from a baton champion to a—well, I'm just going to say it—to a blowjob artist in just one little article in a magazine." She looked quickly again at her mother and then at me, and seeing neither of us had disintegrated, a look of amusement slowly appeared on her face. Finally she let out a small boyish chuckle and smiled at her mother with soft eyes. She liked her mother.

"Mother didn't even know what fellatio meant, did you mother?" she said.

"I did too," the mother answered, her mouth still stuck in that small smile. "I think they should be sued for a million dollars for saying that about Kim. And they lied to the whole world. Everybody," she said. "Just everybody." Her eyes seemed placid, even happy. For Christ's sakes, she looked like the Madonna, I thought. She glanced again at her folded hands. "You know, of course, that Kim was born with a clubfoot?"

"Oh, Mother," Kim said.

"Well, Mr. Spence, she was. Her foot was terribly deformed. It was all pulled back against her ankle, like this." She took her left hand and forced her right hand down toward the wrist. I could envision the young mother, perhaps eighteen or nineteen, holding her newborn in her arms with that grotesque foot, a young mother too stunned to know what to do or say, too much a mother not to clutch the child to her, but hiding that one foot inside her robe so that her baby appeared perfect. Then I thought she had sobbed like a child with a broken heart.

"Her father was in the air force, and right after Kim was born they stationed him overseas, so there was just Kim and me." The daughter said nothing, sensing, I supposed, it was her mother's clear right to speak. "I used to pull her foot out all the time—kept putting pressure on it, like the doctor said, and Kim would scream and—"

"Oh, Mother," Kim said, very gently, "do you have to give all the gory details?"

"Well, Mr. Spence might just as well know what we went through. At the time we were living at the base, and the doctors there put her in casts. We had to change them every week because a baby grows so fast, you know, and it hurt her. She was always crying, and finally my mother said I should stop it—that it was better to leave her crippled on the outside than to keep hurting the child and risk crippling her on the inside. But I wouldn't stop. No, I wouldn't stop. Nobody could stop me. And that poor child had to go to bed every night with her legs tied together on a steel frame, and then in the morning I'd have to massage her foot and—"

"Oh, Mother, please," Kim said, and I thought she was about to cry, not for herself but, like someone whose empathy was complete, for this woman with her painful memory. "Finally when she was five, we had to have her operated on. They cut the tendons on this side to shorten them where they had been stretched out and they lengthened them on the other side." She made her finger the knife and did dainty cutting motions on her wrist to show me the operation. "And the operation, thank God, was a success." She stopped when she discovered she had completed her story and waited for my response.

"That must have been very hard on such a young mother," I said.

"It was hard on her," Kim said. "She didn't have time for anybody but me. She could have been something special. I mean she is special, very special, but she was beautiful enough to be Miss America herself," Kim said. She gave her mother a proud look and I looked too, and I could see that Kim was right. "And she never did anything or went anywhere except with me, and Daddy was gone overseas a lot of the time, and there was just mother and me."

"I got her into baton twirling," the mother said. "She couldn't dance like the other girls, but she took right to baton twirling, and she practiced every day and I got her into contests, and she kept practicing and she began to win and the more she won, the harder she tried. Well, Mr. Spence, I always told Kim that if she was going to do something, she should be the best. And she was."

"She made all my costumes," Kim said.

"Yes, I still have them all—fifty-two of them hanging in the closet. You should have seen her, Mr. Spence. She was so cute."

"I was fat, Mother," Kim said.

"Well, she was just a little chubby is all, but she was as cute as a bug's ear. I took her everywhere, to all the contests. When she got to high school she was the head majorette for four years, and she was the head majorette at the University of Wyoming for four years too—all the time she was there—and one year the National Twirling Association sent her to Lima, Peru, to a big national festival and she won the competition at the Winter Carnival at St. Paul a lot of years—I can't even remember how many it was now, and for seven or eight years straight she won the competition at Notre Dame, and I got her special lessons from a nationally known instructor at Chicago," she said, finally running out of breath. "It cost us thirty dollars an hour for the lessons and we bought eight hours' worth, and once I took her to California for some more lessons from another instructor and we were there two days and—"

"Oh, Mother, please. Mr. Spence doesn't want to listen to all the details." But she spoke to her mother in that very kind and patient way, almost as if she were the mother.

"When Norman got back—that's my husband—he bought a '70 Malibu and he rebuilt it. He's very good at mechanics. He's good at anything he tries. Well, anyway, we just drove the wheels off of it. It had a hundred and twenty thousand miles on it when Norman traded it off for another old car. He likes to fix cars up. He goes out in the garage and works till all hours of the night." She looked down at her hands where she clutched a handkerchief.

"Well, you must be very proud of your daughter," I said, and then Rosemary, my secretary, came in about a call I had to make, which is what she does when I've been with a client too long. But the mother went right on.

"She won five regionals in one year, Mr. Spence. Probably any girl could have become the Women's Grand National Champion if she had practiced as hard as Kim did. You couldn't stop her. What she had, Mr. Spence, was the heart of a champion. That's what she had," she said.

"It was Mother who was the champion. She kept me at it," Kim said.

"But it was worth it," the mother said, still smiling faintly at the corners of her mouth. "Until this."

"I'll go over your case with my partners," I said, but Mrs. Pring wanted to know, please, couldn't we come to a decision on the case today because they'd driven all the way from Cheyenne to Jackson Hole to see me and I said, of course. I didn't think it would be a very difficult decision. I didn't like the case.

I watched them leave in a Toyota with a fresh paint job.

2

"That's a hell of a case," Eddie Moriarity said.

"Well, for Christ's sakes," I said. "Why? We got drawers jammed with cases begging for attention—people hurting, suffering. We're behind—"

"I like the case a lot," Schuster said. Robert Schuster was a Yaley with a big mop of blond hair flopped over a large head bulging with ponderous legalisms. He looked like a goddamned schoolboy and loved the pedantic. Sometimes he'd put on his judge-look, as I called it. He should have been a judge. When he argued he'd wrinkle up his forehead and begin to speak slowly, and his mouth would form each word carefully as if the words were bound for eternity.

Schuster put on his judge-look and began speaking. Once in a while his voice cracked, but I liked to listen to him. He was a good man and a smart man. He said very slowly, "The First Amendment guarantees the right to free speech, but there's no compelling public issue at stake in a story like this. What's at stake are merely Guccione's profits. It's a clear abuse of the Constitution when a publisher takes an innocent person, calls her a blowjob artist, holds her up to humiliation and embarrassment across the land, and then crawls behind the shield of the United States Constitution for protection while he rakes in the profits."

I thought, he is right—absolutely right! Some called Guccione the "King of Porn," but I knew him to be the chairman of the board of Penthouse International, its sole shareholder, and the publisher of *Penthouse* magazine. Whether the First Amendment was meant to give Guccione a license to sell his open-crotch shots of women and his X-rated letters in the "Penthouse Forum" seemed to me to be a moral issue, not a legal one—I'd leave that for the preachers to settle. But this was a case of libel.

Schuster looked grave and the fingers on his right hand twisted for a moment as if he were spastic, as if his mind had locked itself in final decision and his fingers had spasmed in sympathy. "It's a very serious abuse of the Constitution," he said, and then he gave me a small apologetic smile. Scholars, like judges, are expected to avoid the emotional.

"Yeah," Eddie said. "Abuse it and lose it."

"They throw these libel cases out as fast as they're filed," I said. "We'll never even get to a jury." More than half such cases in the federal courts are cast out by the judge before trial begins and for a variety of reasons that never quite match up case to case. But lawyers have been trained to accept the inconsistencies of judges as one accepts the unpredictablity of God, and the legal scholars labor away at making sense of the whole ridiculous tangle like some addled fisherman working hopelessly at the snarls in his line. It provides the legal scholars with work, and they write books that are good for business, and the confusion actually creates a certain charming mystique to this body of law. But to me it came down to one clearly discernible rule that brought all the cases into harmony, a rule of the jungle I call Baboon Law.

Baboons are deathly afraid of the leopard because he kills in the night while the baboons sleep, and they are essentially defenseless against this stronger deadly marauder. Upon his mere appearance in the territory, the whole pack may explode and scatter, thereby becoming his easy prey. Judges are no less afraid of the media and have ruled most consistently in any way they can in order to placate the leopard. They have delivered the First Amendment to the media and scattered their decisions all over the place, which, of course, makes the judges even more vulnerable and creates this body of work for the scholars. Perhaps I extend the analogy too far when I say the function of the scholars, like that of jackals, is to clean up after the slaughter.

"We'll never get the case to trial," I said.

"Don't tell me about Baboon Law," Schuster replied. He'd heard my simplistic arguments before and they usually amused him, but not now. "Leave the law to me." Then he laughed his kind of crackly laugh, and he looked over at me like a man determined to patronize a simple aborigine. "Trust me," Schuster said.

"*Penthouse* will run our asses around the country with depositions and motions and legal bullshit until we're broke or senile or both.

You know that, Schuster," I said. "Even if we get to a jury and win, we'll have to win again in the court of appeals—maybe even in the Supreme Court."

Eddie jumped in. "We can win it, Gerry," he said. "I got it figured out." He waited for me to ask him how.

I said, "You don't have to be a Yaley to understand what's going on here. The media think any, and I mean *any,* suit against them 'chills' their First Amendment rights—it's the Sparrow Doctrine." Schuster rolled his eyes and looked over at Eddie for comfort. They'd heard it all before. "I mean letting some little hick from the sticks, like Miss Wyoming, win against the media is like letting the sparrow kill the hawk, just once, and after that every fucking little sparrow secretly thinks he's a hawk killer, and there'd be no end to the sparrows' suing," I said. Schuster ground out a laugh again.

"Even if we won, we couldn't get a big enough verdict to pay our expenses," I said. "How much would any jury give some cutie pie who calls herself Miss Wyoming and parades her half-bare ass around and then claims she's been hurt—her poor psyche decimated—her good name destroyed because she thinks somebody was talking about her when they published this story about some fictional Miss Wyoming who gave great head. They'll say she's just hogging up good court time looking for one more little snatch of publicity."

"That's the Hog Rule, I suppose." Schuster laughed again.

"No, it's the Snatch Rule," Eddie said and laughed back. "But we can win it big, Gerry," Eddie said.

He had a certain barbaric wisdom he acquired growing up tough in tough times in Butte, Montana. The story goes that on their twelfth birthday the Irish boys in Butte went through a certain ceremony during which they had the left side of their mouths sewn shut so that they could talk only out of the right side, and say "Youse guys" and other such tough-sounding words, and, at the same time, were given a lifetime supply of white socks.

Eddie's father had hacked out a living for his family underground in the copper mines and then he had died in his early forties like any creature dies from having been trapped too long in mean places— "miner's lung disease," Eddie said. He'd left a widow and four Irish kids huddled together in a little house next to the railroad tracks under the entrance to the main mine shaft. Later Eddie had to go down into the mines himself, and he talked like a miner—thought like one most of the time—and sometimes when he erupted in anger, which could occur without warning, he looked like a miner fighting, scratching, clawing his way out of some deep deadly hole. Then nobody had better be in his way. As a lawyer Eddie still had a distrust for anybody who talked out of both sides of his mouth.

"We can lose it big too, Eddie," I said. "Pay me a couple hundred bucks an hour on the case and give me a book of blank checks like the *Penthouse* lawyers will have—then we can decide if we want this case. Who's going to meet the payroll and the rent next month?" Jesus Christ, I thought. They make their decisions like a couple of adolescents. That's why we send kids to war—they think they're immortal, invincible.

I looked over at Eddie. He was a reverent man, not a big man, but he had a powerful barrel chest and the sloping shoulders of a wrestler. He'd fought for the Montana Lightweight Wrestling Championship when he was just a ninety-eight-pound pup, grown physically into a middleweight, and as a man, as a lawyer, Eddie Moriarity was a heavyweight. I understood Eddie. He was a man full of passion, full of anger, and on the other side of that, a man bursting with tenderness as fragile as the blossom of the wild Irish rose. We called him the Sweet Irish Terror. Sometimes I thought he was the brightest among us, but he covered any hint of his genius with tough miner talk.

"The judges will never let us keep a big verdict even if we get one," I said. "You know the rule: Little people get little justice."

"I know," Eddie said, and finally he couldn't wait any more. His voice got high, and he dumped his words on me like a miner jerking the trip on an ore car and the words came tumbling out. "This time we can beat the judges," he began. "See—" He stopped because all his thoughts jammed up at once in his mouth. "Those judges are so fuckin' conservative—so fuckin' tight you couldn't drive a needle up their asses with a sledgehammer. But one thing!" His arms were flailing and his voice grew higher and he spoke faster. "One thing! We got 'em! We got 'em, see, because one thing the judges hate worse than people is pornography—those appeals court judges hate pornography. It makes 'em crazy like a fly in a dog's ear." Eddie stopped. He looked me in the eye to see if he'd come through.

"He's right," Schuster said. They stuck together when they wanted a case.

"Those old judges will forget how mean they feel about people once they get a good look at some a Guccione's closeup pussy shots," Eddie said. "They'll leave our verdict be, I tell ya. They got no choice. And when Guccione's lawyers start arguing the Constitution so he can sell that shit, it won't take those judges five seconds to decide the case in our favor."

"What about the Baboon Law?" I asked. "Those judges would rather put up with a fly in their ear than be eaten for supper by the media!"

Schuster aimed his right eye at me like he always does when he's ready to bear down on his argument. "The law is on our side. The judges can't get around this one. This woman, this Kim what's-her-name, was innocent and libeled, and if libel means anything at all in the law, then *this* is the case!"

Finally I turned my eyes away from Schuster. He was the one who was innocent I thought—a scholar's innocence. He'd been a poor kid from Casper, Wyoming, who'd made it with his mind. He'd been an honor graduate in law at the University of Wyoming and then he'd gone on to Yale, then Harvard, for a graduate degree. I didn't think much of the fancy eastern schools, and Schuster knew that. Sometimes I was mean to him about it.

I'd gone to the University of Wyoming at Laramie myself in the days when anybody could get into law school—and almost anybody could get out—only twenty-three in my class, I think. I wasn't resentful of Schuster's Ivy League legal education, although I think he thought otherwise. To me all law schools took the young and ruined them as warriors, but the elitist schools were the worst. The professors didn't train fighters. They duplicated themselves, timorous bookworms who could play the word games all right, but who couldn't run a spear through a witness with a sharp cross-examination or communicate the simplest idea to ordinary people. These kids were bright and bright-eyed enough when they entered law school, but when they graduated they were seriously impaired. In a profession whose very core is communication, the law schools, all of them, had dedicated themselves to destroying our God-given power to speak to each other simply, precisely—and to hear.

Schuster had escaped from the Ivy League, but not without damage, I thought, because nobody does. Yet Schuster had fought it through on his own with that great brain and his dogged persistence. He'd grown up without a father in the house. Later he got into the firm like a stray pup you can't chase off, and he'd taken me on as a father, and sometimes he drove me crazy like a kid does when he tests the old man, but I loved Schuster, and he knew it, and he was smart as hell.

"This is a country of law, not of jungle rules," he said looking at me, still seeming amused, and then he turned to Eddie and said, "And this case isn't going to turn on the intensity of the judge's anal spasms. Whether their sphincters are irrevocably cramped closed or not, they will decide this case on the law, and the law is clear. This is a case of pure libel. Pure libel! And judges are honorable men," he said, as if it were an afterthought. He aimed his right eye at me again. "Speaking of prejudice—you've already convicted the judges before they've had a chance to consider the case. Neither of you has bothered to review the cases on libel. I'll bet you haven't read a single authority in the last decade." Schuster looked first at Eddie and then at me, waiting for either of us to contest him.

Eddie shrugged his shoulders.

"You need to have a little faith in your own profession," Schuster said as if he were the father. "And in the law that makes this country what it is. You should avoid as much as possible that shallow cynicism of yours, and become lawyers. It's not enough to just be advocates—warriors, as you call yourselves." Schuster stopped.

"Well," I said, "I think there are a lot more important cases for us to try than this obscenity case." But Schuster argued back. It wasn't an obscenity case. It was libel—defamation—breach of privacy. Could the *Penthouse* people say anything they wanted to about anybody, thinly disguise it as fiction, and then claim constitutional protection for it?

"If they get away with this, they can write a story"—Schuster stopped to think and wrinkled up his forehead—"they could write a filthy, false story about your mother, change a fact or two, give her another name so they could claim it was fiction, and nobody could do anything about it. Yet they would have libeled your mother. Everybody would laugh at her. She would become a dirty public joke." Schuster knew how to get to me.

I knew they needed a case like this, one with a little sex appeal, an exciting case different from the kinds in which they struggled, like our case for the widow whose husband had been ground up in the pulpwood machinery and splattered on the wall where he worked, and all that was left of him was his picture on the piano. He was a good man, an innocent man—never hurt a soul, a loyal employee who had worked away his life for the company but who was as important to the company as any worn-out part. When his widow reached over in her sleep at night to touch him, what she touched was cold and empty, and she woke up and cried out, but no one heard her, and justice would be as empty as her bed if we couldn't beat the company lawyers.

And we had other cases, like the one for that nice kid who was paralyzed from the neck down. It would take about $100,000 a year to pay for special therapy and equipment and the constant care to keep him alive and even a little comfortable. If we lost, Lord knows what would happen to him. Nobody dared ask. According to the doctors and the insurance-company mortality tables, he was supposed to live another 63.71 years, and his father was dead and his mother worked as a clerk for J. C. Penney.

My younger lawyers didn't dare lose cases like those. I was proud of them. They took on the automobile companies, the utility companies, the big oil companies—didn't make any difference how big—they took them on, locked themselves into mortal combat against the best trial lawyers in the land because the big corporations, the insurance companies, own the majority of the great trial lawyers the way rich men usually own the fastest racehorses. The corporation lawyers were paid, win or lose. But widows and paralyzed kids can't pay you—which is something to be said for the contingency fee—you only get paid out of your winnings. We are still in the jungle. We are still a little tribe of hunters. We still have to kill to eat.

"We'll sue 'em for ten million," Eddie said. He jumped up and began pacing the floor in fast steps as though he wouldn't stop until I'd agreed to take the case.

But I had mixed emotions about the Pring case. I'd have to try it—put my guts in it and make it live. It wasn't enough that they loved the case. "You have to put it all in," I'd tell these young lawyers, "or don't get in in the first place, because if you don't care enough to put it all in, then how can you expect the jury to care? You can't win with just pretty oratory and a great cross-examination. Juries can tell. Juries are smart. If they think you're holding out on them, they'll hold out on you."

I used to think that killing anybody in the courtroom for any cause was all right, like the matador kills any bull. A bull is a bull and killing is killing. The matador doesn't hate the bull. He has no just cause to kill the animal, except that the killing is the end move in the game, a game with no moral constraints—only that the killing be done by the rules, artfully and with grace. I used to represent the insurance companies and the large corporations against the people, and won for them—couldn't bear to lose. The pain of losing was like having your belly slashed open so your insides all plopped out in a pile of offal in the courtyard, and you could feel the enemy dragging you around in the arena, your entrails filling with gravel, and you were helpless and dying. That's how losing felt to me, and I put it all in, everything I had—not so much to win, but so as not to lose, and the juries felt my energy. My passion engulfed juries, deluged them. Once I'd gone ten years without losing a jury trial.

But one day I quit representing those companies against the little people, because after a while winning began to hurt me as much as losing—to win for some soulless thing, some non-thing called a corporation, to win against the poor and the weak, against my own people, for Christ's sakes. I have a low pain threshold, and finally I couldn't stand the pain of it anymore.

Kim and her mother came back after lunch exactly on time. Rosemary let them into my office before I had decided how I was going to tell them. They sat there, both still smiling, waiting for me to say I'd take the case. I didn't want to disappoint my partners, or them, but it wasn't my kind of fight.

"Did you have a nice lunch?" I asked, getting ready.

"We went to the Wort and had hamburgers," Kim said, and she laughed. The mother didn't say anything, just turned that nice little smile on me and looked down at her hands and waited. The room grew quiet. I thought, well, if I don't take the case they can always find some lawyer somewhere who'll give it a run, and if she doesn't win, she'll still survive. Maybe she could get some mileage out of the damned thing, call a press conference, tell the reporters how much the article hurt her and how unkind it was of *Penthouse* to publish nasty things like that about a good Wyoming citizen, and she could talk about her life—maybe even get a feature story.

If I took the case it would be just my luck to find out that she had known all along the damned story was going to be published. Maybe she'd consented to it and it didn't come out the way she thought it would. Or maybe she was the best damn blowjob artist in the world, for Christ's sakes, which would probably turn out to be *Penthouse*'s defense. You never know what's in a case or what's behind it.

"Did you know whether or not any writer from *Penthouse* was at the pageant?" I asked.

"I never gave an interview to anybody," she said.

"How was your health before this article, Kim?" I asked.

"Fine," Kim said.

"Except for colds and the like and her foot, of course, she never had a sick day in her life," her mother said. "But I had to take her to the doctor after this." Unconsciously she grabbed at her throat.

"What kind of a doctor?" I asked.

"Our family doctor."

"Oh, Mother," Kim said. "Mr. Spence doesn't want to hear about that." She laughed.

"What did she go to the doctor for?" I asked.

"She couldn't sleep. And she wouldn't stop crying. It was awful. I couldn't comfort her. She'd just keep on crying."

"Oh, Mother."

"Well, it's true," her mother said.

"Why did this thing hurt you so badly, Kim?" I asked.

She thought a moment, shrugged her shoulders, and then she said, "I don't know, Mr. Spence. I don't know how to say it."

I looked closely at her eyes and I thought I saw the faint lines of hurt along the outer lids like you see on a person who's grown patient with his pain, like the old man's eyes at Safeway when I finally decided to stop killing in the courtroom for the insurance companies. Imaging and I were standing in the check-out line laughing, clowning around, happy, flushed with new love in a new marriage, and then I saw this crippled old man ahead of me. It wasn't right to be so happy in the presence of such obvious misery. I watched him labor to get his billfold from his hip pocket. He moved slowly to gather up his small sack of groceries—probably all he could afford—more than he could carry without pain. Then I saw his face. He was the man I'd just beaten.

He was entitled to win his case. I knew that. But I beat his lawyer. That was my job, wasn't it?

I represented the insurance company who insured this drunk who had run the red light because she was too plastered to see anything, including the old man. The jury never knew there was insurance—that's the way the law works—insurance companies hide behind the people they insure so it looked like this was some old greedy geezer who wasn't hurt very much and who was trying to make a fortune off this poor woman I'd dressed up like Apple Annie—in a silly old hat, scuffed, round-toed shoes, and a dress that must be half a century old. Poor thing.

Imaging sat in the back of the courtroom and watched me destroy the old man on the stand that day. She hated it.

It had been easy. He got angry right away; anybody would, I suppose, being treated like a thief when he knew he was in the right, when he knew it was I who was trying to steal justice from him. He fought back so hard he forgot how bad he hurt, and he looked mean, and I came off so reasonable, so just and right, for Christ's sakes, that the jurors didn't believe the old man, because all they could remember about him after the evidence was in was the mean part. People don't remember our good sides, and his lawyer hadn't shown the jury much.

I called a sweet-talking doctor with a long and impressive list of qualifications. He made a lot of money testifying for insurance companies, convincing juries that injured people weren't really hurt, and he made this jury believe the old man was faking it too. It was all fair, wasn't it? The old man could call his own doctor to the stand, but I made quick work of him on cross-examination. Anyway, his own doctor hated to testify, hated lawyers and trials, and the jury didn't think much of him either.

On the stand the insurance-company doctor looked sad like he didn't really want to testify against the old man, and he looked right into the eyes of the jurors and said, "There is no objective evidence of injury here." He gave the jury a small, knowing smile, "Nor of any pain." And the doctor was telling the truth. The patient can suffer excruciating pain the rest of his life, but you can never see pain or the terrible mangle of muscles and nerves on an X ray.

The old man tried to explain that he hurt so bad sometimes he wanted to lie down and give it all up, but the jury liked the doctor, and they knew that the world was full of phonies trying to fake it for a dollar. The old man's lawyer didn't have the skills to cross-examine my doctor, which was another reason the companies liked to use him. He could handle himself on "cross," as we say.

The old man's lawyer never gave the jury a chance to understand his client. The old man had worked at that damned refinery, hated every minute of it, counted the years, the months, finally the days until he could retire, when he and that woman who had stuck by him could enjoy the good life together. Then the blessed time had come. True, they weren't young anymore, but the few precious years they had belonged to them—not to the kids, not to the company, not to anybody but them. Finally they owned themselves, and they were going to go fishing and travel a lot in their camper, and Christ, I knew it was a terrible tragedy that nobody in the courtroom understood.

Then this drunk had robbed him of what was left, and now this sweet-talking doctor, yes, and this sweet-talking lawyer, me, were making a common liar of him and robbing him of justice too. It had been too much for the old man. His patience had worn too thin. The trial had humiliated him too much and he'd become too angry. What did he know about the art of persuasion? All he knew was that he hurt, and people who hurt are hard to like sometimes because they seem mean. It hadn't taken the jury long to find against him.

Then at Safeway the old man had turned around and he had seen me standing behind him. "How ya doin', Mr. Spence?" he asked. He looked friendly and had kind watery eyes like my grandfather Spence.

"Pretty good," I said. "How about you?"

"I'm gettin' by." He gave me a nice smile, and suddenly I felt a terrible gripping at my heart. Before he'd been an opponent. Now he was just a crippled old man, a man I'd cheated out of justice, and what I saw was that agony seeping out from behind those eyes, and I needed to say something to him. I didn't know what to say.

"I'm sorry about how your case came out," I finally said. That's all I could think of to say.

"Oh, don't think nothin' about it, Mr. Spence," he said. "You was only doin' your job." He smiled at me again, and I could feel that hurting at my heart. I carried his little sack of groceries to his rattle-trap of a pickup, and he thanked me. Thanked me, for Christ's sakes, and that was the last I ever saw of him.

The next morning I talked a lot about the old man to Imaging. I said, "Imaging, is that my job? Is that all my life is about—to beat some poor old man out of his just dues in a court of justice?" I had to get things straightened out.

I could see my old grandpa fighting his life away on that small farm in the rocks at the foot of the mountains in Colorado. All he had ever hoped for was something better for his kids, and my father had wanted the same for me. My people were the working people and my father would have laid it all down for any one of them. Now here I was, his son, the final product of generations of toil and sacrifice by poor people who wanted it better for their children, and the "better" had become this crafty lawyer who had learned how to beat his own people with clever words and right moves, a man who stole the poor man's just entitlement with his skill and delivered it to some insurance company the way a fucking spaniel brings back the dead bird and drops it at his master's feet. I was worse than that. I was a hired killer. I killed for the pure pleasure of it like some renegade coyote.

I had grown to love the taste of blood too much.

Suddenly I couldn't stand it any longer. The next morning I wrote a bunch of letters to the insurance companies I had represented. "Come get your files," I wrote them, and after that I took only the cases of the little people against the insurance companies and the big corporations and the banks.

Thank God, I was through proving myself as a trial lawyer. I didn't need this case for Miss Wyoming to prove anything. Life, damn this accursed aging, had become too dear to waste on challenges, too tender, too fragile to hold on to for even a moment, for if you grasped it, it disintegrated in your hands like a pretty blue Miller's moth, leaving only wiggling legs and broken wings. I tried not to infect my young warriors with such thoughts. Their time would come soon enough. But once I read them a poem, the last words of a great Blackfoot warrior. I wished for such eloquence myself, and for the knowledge of an ignorant savage.

> *What is life?*
> *It is the flash of a firefly in the night.*
> *It is the breath of buffalo in the wintertime.*
> *It is the little shadow which runs across the grass*
> *And loses itself in the sunset.*[1]

For an instant my own brave warriors looked like small boys gazing into the campfire. The fierce light was gone from their eyes, and they were silent. Eddie nodded and looked away. Schuster's brow was relaxed, and he seemed sweet and gentle, and I thought they understood my urgent feelings. I looked at their open, unlined faces, and I wondered how such caring men as these could be, like me, killers in the courtroom.

There were things I wanted to do, had to do—books to write to discover what I knew, and if I discovered I knew anything, to share it, the way a flower that has bloomed needs to spread its seeds, rare or common, in a good fall wind. I wanted to try cases that might slash new trails through the impenetrable judicial jungles, the territory of the great corporations where people get lost and many perish. I had things to do with the next five years this case could consume that were more important than fussing over what *Penthouse* did or didn't say about some disappointed beauty queen. Besides, wasn't it a purely exhibitionist pageant in which she had voluntarily packaged up her pretty parts and paraded them around in front of a nation of gawking voyeurs? I had better things to do.

It wasn't that I didn't enjoy looking at a pretty woman as much as the next man, but the whole affair made me actually physically retch. Bert Parks was too convincing playing the part of an aging eunuch entrusted with the nation's most beautiful virgins, and the virgins looked as if they'd all been punched out of the same machine, all with the same insipid smile stretching their poor faces so tight that an intelligent word could barely escape, all with the same perfect teeth gleaming away and the same wet lips and voices gurgling with happiness. The real contest was to discover which one, if any, could sing on key, and when the judges found one they were so grateful they forthwith crowned her Miss America while the band played that thoroughly repulsive song sung by Bert Parks, the essence of obscenity itself.

I even tried fantasizing the case; I made my final arguments to the jury, but nothing inside me stirred. Once I remembered that the week before Kim Pring had called me, I'd been in the barbershop and the barbers were laughing over that *Penthouse* article about Miss Wyoming.

"Well, Wyoming made the big time again," my barber said.

"Yeah," the other barber chimed in. "Guess she's the best. *The best.*" He went on snipping.

"How's that?" I asked.

"Well, Miss Wyoming can give you such a blowjob as will make ya rise right up off the floor, man," he said, and he laughed and slapped his leg. He laid my head down gently into the sink like I was being baptized. He was still laughing.

"Is that right?" I said. I wasn't interested.

"Yeah. Man, she oughta market that stuff, franchise it! But I'd sure save a little fer myself." He laughed again and gave my head a final squirt out of the hose. "Says she discovered her talent over at Colter Bay. Always figured them beauty queens really made it with their hidden talent." He gave the word "hidden" undue emphasis.

"Those judges are probably too old to appreciate *that* kind of talent," I said. "They're looking for a good strong woman who can help them in and out of bed."

"I don't know if ya ever get too old fer a good blowjob," the barber said, and then he concentrated on my head, and there was the sound of his shears. When I left I heard him say to the next customer getting into the chair, "Well, I see Wyoming made the big time again."

Maybe I'd forgotten. Maybe I'd grown insensitive to the perniciousness of slander. People had said untrue things about me for as long as I could remember, and I'll admit that it hurt me and I always felt helpless; the more you deny those damnable lies, the more people think they're true—protesting too much, you know. And it seems like the more innocent you are, the more damage they do to you.

I thought people who spread falsehoods about others were like the lepers the teacher told us about in Sunday school who believed the only way they could rid themselves of their horrible disease was to give it to somebody else, so they rubbed their sores on anybody and anything they could. The teacher said they were so desperate they'd even rub their sores on a person's wash hanging on the line.

One is helpless against the lie. It is the most cruel, the most foul and wicked weapon your enemies can use against you. But I had developed a certain thickening of the skin over the years—not to the extent that I couldn't be hurt, but hurt less, I suppose. Besides, I had come to realize that ever so occasionally, someone said something beautiful about me that also wasn't true, and I tried to tell myself that it all balanced out. But I knew it didn't.

I was having trouble believing that an article like this, filthy as it was, could hurt Kim Pring as she claimed—the emotional trauma, the doctor, the sudden transformation of the woman into a recluse. Then I thought, Christ, it really was a filthy article, but that's all it was. Maybe it wasn't *Penthouse* that had put that thin glaze of pain over her eyes. Maybe something else had happened to her I didn't know about.

"You understand, Kim, that truth is a defense to libel?"

She nodded.

"The *Penthouse* lawyers will dig up all the dirt they can against you. That's how they'll defend themselves. If you've got any skeletons in your closet they'll find 'em. They'll put you under oath." I said, "They'll be ruthless about it. You better give that some serious thought before you jump into a lawsuit against a bunch like that."

"She's got nothing to hide, Mr. Spence," her mother said. "Isn't that right, Kim?"

"Well, nothing much, Mother," Kim said, and then she laughed.

"How did other people react to this story?" I asked Kim.

"They thought it was funny," she said.

Everybody was silent for a long time, and I remembered how I laughed in the barbershop myself. I looked at Kim again. I could see the tears forming and her lips quivering and I thought, Oh, God, she's going to cry the way a hemophiliac bleeds—once she starts there'll be no stopping her. I can't stand it.

"Well, how do you know that people thought it was funny?" I asked Kim, trying to call on her mentally.

"Well, I didn't think it was funny, and nobody else I know thought it was funny either," her mother said. "And her grandparents certainly didn't think it was funny. Her grandfather is dying of cancer, you know." Oh, God, do I have to go through that too—her grandfather dying and all, and of cancer! Jesus!

"Well, Mother, that doesn't have anything to do with it," Kim said. She didn't cry, and when she spoke to her mother she still sounded kind. You can tell a lot about a woman by the way she treats her mother.

Then Kim Pring looked at me with those hurt eyes, and I could still hear them laughing at her in the barbershop. Maybe she wasn't a greedy, disillusioned ex–beauty queen. Maybe she was just an ordinary young woman who got caught up in the dreams of little girls and became an unwitting victim of *Penthouse*. Wasn't that a good enough cause? I mean, I didn't have to save the world, did I?

"And her grandfather has one last wish," her mother said. "He wants to live long enough to see this case go to a jury, and he says he wants Kim's name cleared so he can die in peace." God Almighty, spare me! "And that magazine made fun of Wyoming people. They just made the whole state look ridiculous," she said, still smiling. Please, dear Lord, have her stop. "They have no respect for anybody or anything. And people say you fight for little people like us, and—"

"Mrs. Pring, I'll—" She interrupted me before I could tell her I'd take the case.

"And people say you're the best, and we'd be so proud to have you represent us, and the State, and—" Spare me. I'll take it!

I'd always fought for freedom of the press, but this wasn't a case against the First Amendment. This was a case against that arrogant bunch at *Penthouse* who thought they had the right to say anything they wanted about anybody and sell it. They thought they had the God-given authority to take a young Wyoming woman like this and say her *real talent* was to give such wondrous blowjobs she could actually levitate men and then to drag in their profits out of the millions of laughs across the country—at her expense. I had begun to feel something. Maybe I could get into this case. Maybe it was my own arrogance that led me to be so disdainful of this young woman's struggle to become the best baton twirler in the world. What's the matter with that? She had accomplished her goal, hadn't she? Maybe that was more than I could say for myself. Who was I to judge people's goals? At least she had one, and she'd become the best. That's more than I could say for most. She was proud of what she'd done, and she had been hurt.

I looked at the open, innocent face of this woman. Suddenly, as if by some blazing apperception, I understood. Kim Pring was not dragging *Penthouse* into court. It was not her choice to sue. It was the other way around. *Penthouse* had made the charges against her to an entire nation—it was *Penthouse* who had desecrated and defiled her name, and by their charges, she was forced into the courtroom as surely as any woman accused of witchery. And I knew, as well, she was already convicted. They would torture her in the sanctioned ways of the law, until she confessed. No woman ever escapes.

"I'll take your case," I said.

"Thank you," the mother said, her smile no larger than before. Kim Pring said nothing. She looked down like a woman afraid to face the decision that had just been made—as if she didn't know for sure what she had bargained for, and, as I would discover soon enough, neither did I.

3

On November 15, 1979, I sued Penthouse International, Ltd., and Philip Cioffari, the author of the Miss Wyoming story, for $7 million in the United States District Court in Cheyenne, Wyoming, Kim's hometown. I alleged that the *Penthouse* story had "created the impression throughout the United States and Wyoming that Kim Pring, the plaintiff, was sexually promiscuous, depraved, unchaste and morally lacking," that the story injured her reputation, caused her grave mental, emotional, and physical pain and suffering, and that she had been greatly embarrassed and humiliated. I sought $2 million for the damages Kim had personally suffered and $5 million in damages to punish *Penthouse*—"punitive damages" as they are called in the law, damages for malicious injury inflicted on the victim of the libel.

Norman Roy Grutman of New York would defend, of course. He always represented *Penthouse* in libel suits, and by reliable accounts he was cunning, crafty, and tough. He would do whatever was necessary to win. His style was to attack straight on—everybody and everything—relentlessly. He gave no quarter until his opponent was subdued, prostrate, and begging for mercy, and having none, he gave none.

To Grutman I would be just another of that ignoble pack he had so often encountered in such suits—another greedy, bloodthirsty opportunist, a shifty shyster who flooded the courts with groundless suits, a man distinguished only by his scheming and conniving, his conspiring and contriving—who used whatever maneuvers, whatever machinations and devices his fertile but circuitous mind could concoct, and whose noodle head Grutman would no doubt sever with one easy swipe of his sword of facile words and skillful polemic. To Grutman I would be worse—for I was not even urban, not even civilized—a country bumpkin, the smallest of the small-time players

45

from some unlikely one-horse town called Jackson Hole. He would gladly take me on.

On January 4, 1980, Grutman filed an answer on behalf of his client setting forth his legal defenses—that the article, as fiction, was protected under the United States Constitution and that Kim was a public figure as defined in *New York Times* v. *Sullivan*, therefore requiring us to prove that *Penthouse* had been guilty of actual malice in publishing the article.

I began to wonder if I had made the dangers of a libel suit clear enough to Kim. Had she really understood they would attack her— not defend themselves? Did she know they would dig into every conceivable dark place in her past, sniff at the faintest rumor, and expose whatever they found? If they could, they would hold her up to the jury as nothing more than some insignificant trollop, and argue that a woman like Kim Pring wasn't hurt—that she was only using the courts to enrich herself at the expense of the publisher, a businessman who was, thank God, protected by the First Amendment. Therefore, Norman Roy Grutman would argue, the judge and jury should make short shrift of this avaricious shrew so that everybody could go home and get on with their lives and business.

It was Kim Pring who had sued *Penthouse*. Now, under the rules, she had to make herself available to Grutman for her deposition. She would be put under oath and Grutman would ask any and all the questions he chose of this woman who would be as helpless as any patient laid open on the operating table for the surgeon to pry and peek and poke around in at will.

On the second day of June 1980, Grutman served notice to take Kim's deposition. Now I began to worry. Would she hold up? What would Grutman discover about her that I didn't already know? Opponents always teach you things about your client.

Litigation isn't for the sweet and the tender. It is a tough, sordid, seamy business, and Kim was unsophisticated, a Wyoming woman without those veneered social graces from the finishing schools that save the elite from both others and themselves. She hadn't spent her life in a cedar closet, of course. Simply, she was like other girls who had grown up in Cheyenne, at the time. Then she'd gone on to the University of Wyoming at Laramie. She could play Miss America, all right, as small girls do, but you could tell right off that she was a woman without guile or pretenses. She would be easy prey for the likes of Norman Roy Grutman.

❖   ❖   ❖

Laramie and Cheyenne were separated by the Continental Divide, the rocky spine of America. The once-towering primal peaks, torn and jagged, now ground away smooth, ground to soil and sand by wind and weather over endless aeons, worn-out old peaks, still protruded from empty oceans' floors. A person could stand there on the gable of the continent with one foot pointing to the Pacific and the other to the Atlantic and spit into both oceans. That gave one a large sense of power.

These two towns, located on the nation's first transcontinental railroad, were established only fifty miles apart because in the old days the coal-burning steam engines had to stop to take on more water after having heaved and panted over that high summit at 8,640 feet. Laramie was established where there was plenty of water, on the banks of the Laramie River—a damn good trout stream besides. General Grenville M. Dodge had discovered the pass, "that ridge which led down to the plains without a break." Some claimed the general found the route when Indians on the horizon had frightened him and sent him, by lucky chance, down this natural chute to the plains below.

Now U.S. Interstate 80, the Lincoln Highway, crossed the summit a few miles to the east of the railroad and automobiles sped by the rocky outcroppings of Vedauvoo, an Indian name for those gnarled granite fingers clawing up from the stony stratum below. Where the highway burst over the summit a three-story-tall bust of Old Abe stared pensively out across the landscape that, on a clear day, stretched seventy miles before those bronze eyes, blinkless eyes whipped by winds so strong a good horse had to stand hard against them.

The town of Laramie clung to high, barren plains, 7,278 feet above the sea. Laramie had a campus of about 9,000 students—the majority, Wyoming kids—and the town had a permanent population of 24,000 hardy souls most of whom were connected to the university or the railroad, and some worked on the edge of town at the cement plant. Downtown Laramie was bleak, a collection of dilapidated old buildings, patched up and refaced. Lately even their facelifts had fallen. There were, of course, the gaudy, multifarious neon signs that clutch the buildings in every small town, that flash away as if the townspeople were mindless moths to be attracted thereby. But up Grand Avenue toward the university, the streets were lined with pretty old cottonwoods.

I was born in that desolate place, and when it came time for me to go to college, well, the university was just down the street. The idea that I might go to Harvard or Yale never entered my mind. Those places were as unreal, as nonexistent to me, as Oxford to an Irish urchin.

The wind never stops in Laramie. Never. We had to walk with squinted eyes against the blowing railroad cinders—black as black blowing snow—that formed piddling drifts in front of the whorehouse steps. Up on the second floor, the ladies worked into the early hours of the morning trying to deliver quid pro quo to the itchy, bushy-tailed college boys, most of whom were returning veterans from the Second World War, and the ladies listened like mothers to the sad tales of the railroad men, and sold the railroad men beer and a shot of whiskey after work, and sometimes the railroad men were good for "a short time," and sometimes a preacher or a banker would slip up the alley stairs early in the morning after everybody else had gone home. Underneath the whorehouses were the bars and cardrooms and a Chinese café or two run by the descendants of Chinese laborers who'd been imported to lay the tracks on the Union Pacific.

Any day in Laramie you could see the wind in whole pages of newspaper flying like drunken bats up the middle of Second Street, and in empty tin cans rolling, bouncing down the alleys, and in the wash standing out straight on clotheslines as if gravity had been shifted a quarter turn, and you could see the wind against the people who bent forward when they walked like beasts of burden against the plow. Yet the wind, having passed, remained, blew again, blew forever so that early in my life I made some connection between the wind of Laramie and eternity.

Outside the town, the wind lays the prairie grasses flat, and the limber pines grow crooked against it on the ridges of the bluffs. The ranches are miles apart as if the wind had tumbled them across vacant plains like empty shoeboxes until they'd caught momentarily on some small protrusion on the landscape. There the buildings had clung and weathered and leaned and swayed for Lord knows how long, or for how much longer. There, in that vast emptiness, large herds of pronghorn antelope turn their white rumps to flare in the wind, and mule deer hide in the gullies and washes, and badgers and jackrabbits huddle in holes, and the rattlesnakes slide into the cracked, dry earth and are safe from the wind, and beyond the prairies are the long mountains.

Nothing much has changed in Laramie since my day except for the new buildings on the campus—cheap, spare structures reflecting the new view that all, including the occupants, are disposable. The new buildings stand among the grand old sandstone edifices like barefoot hippies at a formal ball. And within, the boys and girls now live together, proof to the world that Wyoming, too, has modernized not only its physical plant but also its moral imperatives. With the advent of modern morals the whorehouses were abandoned and the ladies moved on, except one of the town's favorites who is said to have opened up a laundry. We are all the beneficiaries and the victims of the new virtues, of the pill and penicillin. Even the old coal-burners down on the Union Pacific had outlived their usefulness and had been replaced with modern diesels—that got rid of the cinders.

On Saturday afternoon Kim would put on her white majorette outfit trimmed in the gold and brown colors of the University of Wyoming, and she'd cock her cowboy hat in a jaunty angle at the back of her head, and with her blond hair flapping out in front, she'd prance and parade around at half time in the wind, sometimes even in the sudden bitter snowstorms that invaded those high plains when it was Indian summer everywhere else. She put on quite a show for the fans, and for her mother who faithfully duded up every Saturday in her own brown and gold costume and drove over the summit from Cheyenne to watch and to cheer in her small voice. Then after the game Kim went home with the family.

On most any Saturday afternoon in the fall, the good citizens of Wyoming descended on Laramie like fierce invaders to witness this spectacle, this war between those small armies gathered there to sweat and fight and, before the clock ran out, even to hate. We are a species who has learned to recognize the enemy not by his human fears or the longings of his human heart—which are always the same as our own—but by the color of the jersey he wears. We have been taught that it is blessed to kill those of the other color.

Now, for Kim Pring there was the serious business of survival. I spent hours getting her ready for the deposition. I explained the legal issues that would come up, and we reviewed the facts many times so that when she was attacked by Grutman her mind wouldn't suddenly go blank and her words come out in scattered, frightened, inaccurate fragments that he could hurl back at her at the time of the trial.

"Only answer the question he asks you," I warned. "Don't add anything. Don't volunteer anything." Her testimony would be taken down by the court reporter and later transcribed in black-and-white so there would be a written record. She'd be under oath. There'd be no escaping what she said; she'd be trapped in her own words forever, and lawyers know how to use words, innocent words, and make of them what they want. Even if there was but one small mistake, and everybody makes mistakes, Grutman would hurt her with it later in front of a jury. He'd say, "Do you remember when I took your deposition in Cheyenne last fall?"

"Yes, sir," she'd have to admit.

"Do you remember? Then you said—" and he'd read her answer from her deposition out loud in front of the jury, use it to contradict her, to make it appear as if she weren't telling the truth then, or now. I told Kim, "Be careful what you say. Take it easy and take it slow. I'm sending Gary Shockey with you to watch over you. He'll take care of you."

Gary Shockey was one of our bright young associates then, a partner now. He was tough and spoke straight, and if anybody could keep Grutman from hamstringing Kim, it was Shockey. "Just relax. Shockey won't let him hurt you," I said, like a surgeon reassuring his patient before the operation, and I gave her a little fatherly pat on the shoulder and she smiled back, like she wasn't afraid, and then Shockey hauled her off to the deposition, and later Shockey told me what happened.

Grutman had flown in from New York for Kim's deposition. It would be an unfair match—Grutman against this scared kid. Shockey said she looked real nice, like a college girl at her first job interview. She was wearing a navy-blue cotton dress and dark blue shoes to match and she had her hair done up on the top of her head so she'd look very businesslike and she put on a smile to cover her jitters.

Grutman began with a pleasant fatherly smile, trying to put his victim at ease—all the easier for the kill. She looked like a cornered pup.

"And where do you live, Miss Pring?" Grutman began.

Finally she answered, "I live with my parents, Norman and Mary Jayne Pring."

"Were you born on January twenty-fifth 1956?" Grutman asked.

"Correct," she said. That scared her worse because she must have realized the man had already investigated her. You could actually hear her breathing.

"Have you been married?"

"No."

"Are you a matriculating student?"

"I don't understand," she said, sounding as if he were accusing her of something nasty.

"Are you a student taking courses leading to a degree?" Grutman explained, patiently.

"Yes, I am."

"What degree is that?"

"General Business Finance."

"Besides being a student, do you have other jobs?"

"Yes, I am a baton-twirling instructor. I teach on the weekends, Friday evenings, all day Saturday, and sometimes Sunday."

"How much do you charge?"

"In 1977—seven-fifty an hour lesson, and in 1978, ten dollars an hour."

"Any other sources of income in 1979?"

"I worked for Husky Oil Company—as a log tester—the mother of one of my students got me the job there, and I drove a truck, worked on the pipeline—"

"You actually worked as a construction worker in building the pipeline?"

"Yes, I did."

"Did you do that as a union or nonunion employee?"

"Union." Grutman would try to keep union jurors off the case at the time of the trial.

"And what was your job status?"

"Laborer."

"How much were you paid an hour?"

"Eight-thirty an hour." Then she volunteered additional information. They always do, not because they don't want to follow my instructions but because honest people aren't used to holding things back. "I worked for Fleischli Oil in the Credit Department too—and they paid me three dollars an hour." Then she told Grutman she made $1,874.90 during her summer jobs in 1979, as shown on her income-tax withholdings before her summer jobs had been interrupted by her responsibilities as Miss Wyoming.

Grutman asked how she first heard of the Miss Wyoming article in *Penthouse*. He must have seen she was holding back her tears.

"I hope you understand that in all the questions I ask of you, Miss Pring, I am asking them because it is my job as a lawyer . . . that I am not casually prying into your personal life, and that I would not otherwise seek to do so."

Kim nodded. She said the first person who told her of the article was some lawyer in the East who phoned her saying he knew immediately that she was the subject of the *Penthouse* story, that it was nothing but "trash and filth," and if she wanted to get any modeling contracts she must clear her name. She was no longer interested in modeling, she said, but she began to cry.

"It is your testimony that you were so overcome by this telephone call that you began crying tears?"

"Yes," she answered. A lot of people called her. She named some of them for Grutman because he said he wanted the names. He always wanted the names and times and places. Several of her students began saying bad things about her, too, she said, and she was forced to drop them. And she had to see a doctor.

"What kind of doctor?"

"General practitioner," Kim said. She couldn't sleep. "I used to be extroverted," as she called it. She tried to explain, but she couldn't seem to make Grutman understand. She'd quit school—couldn't stand to face the people anymore. "I overheard people say things about me, and these things bothered me. I was very embarrassed."

What things? What people? "Did you go up and say, 'I'm not that person'?" Grutman demanded.

"No, I didn't. I left immediately."

"Is this disruption of sleep something you attribute to the article?"

"Yes."

"It's persisted for nearly a year?" Grutman asked.

"Yes."

Then she said she had gone to see a local lawyer in Cheyenne who advised her to see Gerry Spence about the case.

"Did you smoke?" Grutman asked.

"No."

"Did you partake of alcoholic beverages?"

"Never," she said.

"Not only spiritous liquors of a distilled nature, but those of a fermented nature as well?"

Shockey hollered, "Well, what's the difference?"

"I'm talking about the difference between beer and any sacramental wine," Grutman said.

"Never," Kim repeated in the record, matter-of-factly.

"I commend you." He toyed with her. "Without meaning any disparagement, you haven't been hiding your light under a bushel, have you?"

"Object to the form of that question," Shockey hollered, but Grutman ignored him.

"I mean, you have sought publicity, haven't you?"

"I don't know if I sought publicity, no," Kim said.

"You've entered contests?"

"Yes, for my own personal reasons."

"Those included an awareness that you would be seen by millions of people, isn't that true?"

"That's true," Kim admitted.

"You were hoping to become Miss America—to make something of yourself?"

"Yes."

"Become famous?" Grutman asked. "And you considered yourself an attractive person, did you not?"

The room was silent for a long time and finally she said quietly to Shockey, but out loud so the reporter got it down, "If he wants to know the truth—no." Then she turned to Grutman. "And you can ask anybody you want to."

"Well," Grutman said. "Well, now, when you appeared as a drum majorette, you didn't come in a hoop skirt, did you?"

"Object to the form of that question and innuendo," Shockey shouted.

"No," she said.

He persisted. She had "displayed herself" publicly in "skintight costumes," and there were pictures that "showed her naked legs," where her "physical attributes were prominently featured." But she tried to counter. They were just her majorette costumes like every twirler wears.

"I show you Exhibit D for identification—do you recognize that?" It was a picture of Kim in the costume she wore when she performed at the Miss America pageant. She had worn the same costume at the Grand National when she won the title. "And it shows your legs—"

"It's not as brief as the swimsuit your daughter probably wears," Kim said. Shockey told her not to volunteer. "Just answer whether it shows your legs; don't let the innuendo that he's making upset you. And if his questions are improper, I'll tell you not to answer."

Next Grutman pulled out a Peruvian publication called *Gente*, a magazine featuring Kim on the cover in her majorette costume. She and some other twirlers sponsored by the Jaycees had gone to Peru to perform.

"You posed for that picture?" Grutman asked.

"Yes."

"I mean, this picture features your thighs, your naked thighs, does it not?"

"Yes."

"And the costume is designed to accentuate your bosom, is it not?" What could she say? Later Grutman showed her *Penthouse*'s illustration of Miss Wyoming that accompanied its story—a woman with her head tipped back drinking in the phallic baton, her breast exposed where the paper swimsuit had been ripped away. "I invite your attention to the drawing of what is commonly called 'the nipple.' Do you see it?"

"Um-hm," Kim said.

"You'll notice that there is an area around the protuberance which is the nipple itself, which is biologically called the areola, that is the whole of the actual bud or nipple and the pink-colored tissue surrounding it. Looking at that, do you say that what is depicted there looks like your nipple and your areola?"

"I'm going to instruct her not to answer any questions about breasts, nipples, or anything like that," Shockey shouted.

"In the complaint you filed you claimed that you're not unchaste. Do you know the meaning of that word?"

"No, sir."

"It means you claim that you're a virgin."

"Just a minute. That's your definition," Shockey said. "Don't answer."

"Let me consult the dictionary," Grutman retorted. "Do you claim that you're a virgin?"

"Don't answer that," Shockey said.

"It goes directly to sexual promiscuity and chastity, which is the language of paragraph nine of the complaint. Do you withdraw that paragraph?" he asked Shockey. "I want to pursue the allegation," Grutman said. "I want to know, yes or no, does she claim to be a virgin?"

"Don't answer that question. It's none of his business," Shockey shouted.

"She's made it our business by filing this preposterous lawsuit!"

Grutman said, "The word *chastity* in the dictionary means an unruptured hymen, a virgin, someone who has not engaged in sexual intercourse. She's been in tears, so she said. I want to know, under oath, does she claim to be a virgin?"

"Don't answer that question," Shockey shouted again.

"We'll have to take that up with the court," Grutman said. "What do you mean by 'sexual promiscuity' as it appears in paragraph nine of the complaint?"

"Don't answer that question, Kim," Shockey instructed, and then he took her out of the room because she was shaking all over. Her shaking scared Shockey.

"I feel like he's trying to strip me naked," she said. It was hard for her to speak.

"Well, I won't let him. Don't worry, Kim," Shockey said.

"Well, I never had anybody talk to me like that," she said. She seemed to be suddenly struck with an uncontrollable chill. She couldn't stop the shaking. "I didn't know people could talk to you like that, especially in a court of law." Then she looked up at the serious young lawyer and said, "How can they do this to me? I didn't do anything to them."

"I know," Shockey said, suddenly feeling ashamed of the law, as if the law were incapable of responding to a human being, as if it had no feeling for the people it governed. It was as if justice were really blind—and deaf. Shockey told me later, "Justice couldn't hear her. And there wasn't anything I could do except tell her not to answer. It was like a woman being raped, and when she comes into court for justice, they'll rape her all over again."

Later Shockey tried to argue on the record that the *Penthouse* story created the *impression* among readers that Miss Pring was sexually promiscuous. He tried to point out that we made no claim one way or the other about whether Kim Pring was a virgin. That wasn't the issue. The issue was, did the article hurt her reputation?

"I don't know how many libel cases you have tried, Mr. Shockey, but in every case *truth* is an absolute defense," Grutman said.

Shockey said, "Well, if you'll admit that she's that person in the article—"

Grutman interrupted. "We will not! The issue is whether she is a *virgin* or whether she is not, whether she has slept with any of her boyfriends or not, and whether fellatio, or a 'blowjob,' is or is not something she has ever done," but Shockey wouldn't budge.

Later Grutman read to Kim from the *Penthouse* story itself. " 'He began to pour into her, and she thought she could feel his soul rising within her, his fountain rising at the same time so that she had to strain on her knees to keep it in place.' " Grutman said, "What is being described there is the sensation of the man in the story ejaculating into the girl's mouth. Correct?"

"Correct," Kim answered.

He read some more from the story. "Now you understand from that language what is described is that after having received his blowjob and ejaculating, the man in the story is levitating. Isn't that what the story is saying?"

"Yes, sir," Kim said.

"Now, Miss Pring, in the real world, do you know or have you heard of anyone who could ever levitate?"

"No, sir."

"Whether connected with a blowjob or otherwise?"

"Correct."

"And if you read this in this fictional story, would it not support the idea that this story was a fantasy?"

"I agree that the story is a fantasy to a certain extent," Kim said.

Grutman got her to admit that none of her friends believed the story to be true. And how could she be damaged if none of her friends believed the story to be true?

Then he said, "Don't you think that a reasonable person could infer from some of your routines and costumes that there is a significant element of sublimated or muted sexuality in what you're doing?"

"I feel that people are going to think whatever they want to think," Kim said, "but I try, personally, to make myself a clean-cut, traditional-type baton twirler. I've worked very hard, and I don't believe in sexual movements and things like that."

"Have you ever committed an act of osculation?"

"I don't know what that is," Kim said.

"Kissing," Grutman said with a fine sneer.

"If the whore of Babylon brought a libel suit claiming that she was a Vestal Virgin, I'm sure you would agree, in some shock, I'd have a right to demonstrate that she didn't serve in the temple of Diana but at someplace else; and in view of the conditions, there would be little doubt that your client's sexual practices and preferences would be highly germane. Now, I ask you, have you ever slept with anyone?"

"Objection," Shockey shouted again. "I instruct the witness not to answer the question."

"Have you ever performed oral sex or fellatio, as is classically described, on anyone?" Grutman asked.

"Same objection. I instruct her not to answer," and then Kim started shaking all over again, and Shockey was mad as hell. Later he asked me, "How can they treat someone like that?"

"A lawsuit is war," I said. "And Kim Pring was the enemy."

"I know," Shockey said. "But there are rules even in war."

"Damn few," I said. "The object of any war is to kill the enemy."

"I thought the object of the game was to render justice," but then Shockey knew better than that and looked away, sad.

Finally Grutman concluded his deposition because he said he could go no further in his questioning in face of Shockey's "obstructive instructions" to his client. He would ask the federal judge to order her to answer his questions.

"They are proper questions and you know it, Mr. Shockey," Grutman scolded. "They are fully pertinent to the defense. Certainly you concede that every litigant has the right to make his defense."

"Yeah," Shockey said. "But you aren't going to ask those questions."

Then Grutman had said, "Well, Mr. Shockey, we shall see."

4

When at war, one should know what the war is about and who his adversary is. I believe in the old proverb "Be thine enemy an ant, see him as an elephant." Who was this Robert C. Guccione? I used to tell my children bedtime stories about famous people, and then I'd say, "If you want to know *who* a person is, find out what that person *does.*" Guccione had been written up in numerous publications, lately gathered by Schuster. Guccione was no ant. He had created his own legends—as though the members of the media were his children at bedtime.

Once upon a time, Guccione told the press, he was living in England as a poor artist, poor as a church rat without enough money to even buy a ticket home. Then out of the blue one day the decided he was going to publish a magazine like *Playboy* right there in England. He talked a printer into making up thousands of prepublication brochures containing full-color photos of eight beautiful nudes on his promise to pay the printer from his first moneys on advance subscriptions. But the mailing list he had obtained contained the names of fourteen-year-old schoolboys and old-age pensioners and vicars, and soon all hell broke loose, which was great for Guccione.

"The screams went up all over the country," Guccione laughed. He always laughed when he told this part of the story.

"There were three separate parliamentary subcommittees formed to investigate me and stamp me out. I was heralded as the harbinger of a new wave of pornography which threatened to flood Britain. The Home Secretary tried to get me deported. I was on the news every day for months." Guccione loved it. "Six cops were assigned eight-hour shifts three times a day outside my house in Chelsea in London—it was some kind of technical rather than criminal summons," he explained. "They couldn't enter my premises, so they waited for me to come out"—silly old English and their servitude to propriety.

So Guccione stayed right there in the house and put out the first issue of *Penthouse*. His art director delivered the galleys to the publisher. The authorities bellowed; the public seethed and fumed, and the poor old bobbies marched up and down in front of his home waiting for him to appear. How could one choose a better set of parents for *Penthouse* than an offended English jurisprudence as the sire and an outraged British citizenry as the dam?

Ah, trouble and its sweet publicity! It made him! Guccione was quick to learn that simple formula for marketing success: The more one offends, the more one profits. *Penthouse* was an immediate success. The genius of Guccione was, in part, that he understood what people wanted, probably because he knew something of himself. If you give people what they want, package it up pretty, and make it easy for them to acquire, you will succeed. The stuffy old English devoured the new magazine like the starving at a smorgasbord. Guccione's fortune was assured. Then one day the genius unbuttoned his shirt to his navel, exposed his manly chest, bedecked himself with golden medallions, donned leather pants, and slipped on a pair of high-heeled French boots. He sure as hell had enough to get home on now—enough to launch *Penthouse* in America.

He worked hard at it—give the man credit. He lectured at any university that would have him; he enthralled the college boys. "I went everywhere. I asked and did TV, radio, even high-school newspaper interviews," he admitted. He was intelligent, flamboyant, charismatic, candid—he admitted he outright lifted the format of his publication from *Playboy*—and he was always grand. "Immediately, the magazine got off the ground because it's my personality as opposed to Hefner's," he said. The media could count on him for good copy and even alleged outrageous statements like "I think I had every whore on the Via Veneto and I never paid for one." Or he would say "My cock is exceptional"—things like that. He said he loved good pornography: "I got a bang out of *Deep Throat!*"

His view on women's rights was forthright and simple. "In the end women's lib is a lot of nonsense. I think their attitude toward equal employment is a sexist attitude. I pay no attention to sex." He sent beautiful women out to solicit the advertisers and paid them for what they produced the same as men.

How about his own need for sex? Here was this guy who actually went into a room alone with those naked women! Guccione said, "I'm different from the poor bastard who works in an office all day and gets to look at his secretary's legs or glimpses her thigh and sees a horny picture. That guy really suffers and *needs* it." Guccione said he had become "infinitely more selective" about his women—like a Wyoming herd bull, I thought, with his pick of heifers in the pasture.

He never tired of bragging that *Penthouse* was the first major national publication to show *pubic hair.*

Great stuff, pubic hair.

I could see him arguing *pro se* at the Pearly Gates.

"State your case," I heard Saint Peter say.

Then Guccione would flash a medallion in the old boy's eyes. "I was the first to show *pubic hair* to the American people," and when Saint Peter shook his head, sadly, slowly, I could hear Guccione offer the same argument he once laid on *Screw* magazine in an interview: "If I am going to be prosecuted by Christian ethics, I feel my defense would be that if God created it, then it had to be acceptable. Now I have seven firms of lawyers under my retainer and they all said, 'You're right. They can only prosecute you under God's law, and you've got the perfect defense because the pubic hair is not doing anything. *It's just there.*'"

Guccione's passion was money. "I love to build empires," he said. He'd discovered that the secret sexual longings of the American male could be exposed, packaged up prettily, and sold back to him. The American male provided an inexhaustible market for an extraordinary variety of fetishes. "I am sexually excited by the sight and smell of wet fish," a supposed contributor to one of Guccione's publications called *Variations* wrote. "I often purchase a fillet of wet fish, take it up to the bathroom (on the pretense of having a bath) and rub and caress my naked body with it. After doing this for several minutes, I have an ejaculation without having touched my penis."

He published letters lauding incest, one supposedly from a young woman. "I've had sex with several boys since I was sixteen, but the quality of the sex is a far cry from the love I get from my dad. I'd say that our loving sex has been very good." In defense of incest, one of his publications quoted Dr. Wardell Pomeroy, co-author of the Kinsey report: "Incestuous behavior between consenting adults in private is not society's concern." He published letters and articles on every conceivable sexual interest, including "urolagnia" and "coprolagnia." He published a magazine called *Forum Adviser* in which a mother allegedly wrote, "Last week I caught my sixteen-year-old daughter and her first cousin from Los Angeles having sex with our large, fifty-pound Malamute dog." He published letters describing every possible combination of group sex, letters recounting the romping and playing of homosexuals, the whips and chains of sadists—you name it.

"How can he publish all that shit?" Schuster said, pointing to boxes that filled half a room.

"Well, he doesn't force people to buy it," I answered. "He sells what people want, and that's what they want."

Guccione formed a company called Evelyn Rainbird, which offered dildos of various sizes, shapes, and colors, artificial vaginas, special stimulators to be inserted into every human orifice—the variety of products seemed endless. He sold pornographic films. He learned that anything sexual would sell if it was properly packaged and marketed. He made millions. He bought a mansion in New York and spent four million remodeling it. He gave interviews to *Money* magazine. The claims for his wealth reached as high as a hundred million. He launched *Viva* and *Omni* magazines. He formed a nuclear-energy company and bought hotels in Atlantic City. Whenever he was displayed in an unfavorable light, he sued. Whenever he was charged with having defamed others, he unleashed his pack of lawyers in defense.

He was charged with obscenity in various states and in Canada, and probably elsewhere, but the cases only enhanced his sales. We adore the forbidden and are excited by the censored. His magazine was sued by more than one woman who claimed she had been unlawfully used. One charged *Penthouse* had displayed her picture in a condom ad without her consent; another claimed the magazine had published lurid pictures of her accompanied with a text describing how she would make love night or day with any man who turned her on, and "if something gets torn, I love it." *Penthouse* tantalized its readers with quotes from her about her sexual preferences. But she charged that she was a married woman, that the descriptions were false and had been published without her authorization. Another woman alleged in a public document that "the defendant, Guccione, through trick and deceit, drugged her and assaulted her and 'carnally knew her without her consent and while she was unable to resist such defilement.' " The complaint was dismissed, but the resulting publicity must have been priceless.

Guccione told Michael Korda, author of *Power: How to Get It, How to Use It,* that he loved power. "Big companies *had me under their fucking knuckles!* Power gives you a new *weapon!*" Korda reported, "As Guccione talks about 'big companies,' his face changes—it swells with passion, the smile lines vanish and he seems to me, to be honest, a little frightening. 'I have absolute power. . . . As power corrupts, it also mellows. I'm very patriarchal to begin with.' "[1]

His mother was Sicilian, his father Italian and, whether intentionally or not, for some he created a Sicilian godfather image. At least one publication intimated he was involved with the Mafia. He sued. The New Jersey Gaming Commission refused to give him a license for his planned casino, and the *Orlando* (Florida) *Sentinel Star* published, as its quote of the week, Guccione's claim to the commission, "I'm 100 per cent clean." There was other litigation surrounding his Atlantic City deals. He kept good lawyers busy.

Finally Guccione had conversed as pretty as you please with Morley Safer to a national *60 Minutes* audience. He was decked out, as usual, in his gold costume jewelry. Safer had admitted that "in spite of appearances—the chest load of silver and gold pendants, the mansion off Fifth Avenue—Guccione is not your swinging, girlie publisher. He is a tough-minded businessman who just dresses for the part." He was gaining respectability in the business world where the final judgment of a man was derived from the bottom line of his financial statement. No one asked where the money came from because having money was intrinsically virtuous. Money was respectability, human worth. And Guccione had it.

Wasn't *Penthouse* offensive? Safer asked.

Guccione replied, calmly, reassuringly. His magazine represented the community of America. "You see—taking the Supreme Court dictum of community standards"—after all of Guccione's experience in the courts he was beginning to talk like a lawyer himself—"if . . . the biggest-selling newsstand magazine in the area, that is to say, *Penthouse,* isn't the community standard, what is?" It was a wrongheaded argument, I thought—measuring the morality of America by the number of copies *Penthouse* sold. "How does one determine the community standard, save by the greatest number of people buying a single product?" Guccione asked of twenty million Americans. He didn't need lawyers.

Then Safer charged: "But . . . what you're doing is hiding the most obscene smut behind the skirts of the First Amendment," and I thought, yes, that was the legal key to Guccione's empire. Cleverly, simply, he merely presented the obscenities of *Penthouse* in the company of the works of serious artists, writers, thinkers, investigative journalists, even politicians who, when the price was right, were willing to be published in his magazine and who, by doing so, took his magazine outside the definition of obscenity as handed down by the United States Supreme Court in *Miller* v. *California*. He placed his misty-lensed photos of gaping crotches, his "Penthouse Forum" letters, and his formula explicit sex stories in the company of the works of many of America's best-known names—John Chancellor, Henry Morgan, Mickey Spillane, Gore Vidal, Garson Kanin, Isaac Asimov, Pete McCloskey—hundreds of others. Since the magazine *"when taken as a whole"* did indeed contain *"works of serious literary, artistic, political and scientific value"* (the test in *Miller*), he was free to publish anything he chose, no matter how obscene the individual photograph or writing.

Lately he had taken to publishing a magazine called *Forum Letters* and made it legal by simply including excerpts from *Huckleberry Finn*. Who could say Mark Twain had no literary value? It is, after all, the *whole* package that must be judged in an obscenity case, and so long as there was something of redeeming value within, the whole could not be condemned.

"Judges protect the pornographers," I said.

"That's not so," Schuster said. We were having coffee in the atrium of our office. A couple of Canadian honkers flew over. "The judges are bound by the law," Schuster said.

"They're bound by the law like my ass is stuck to this chair," Eddie said, jumping up to make his point. "If the judges are bound by the law, how come they never agree on a goddamn thing? It's the same law, but they can't agree what it is. They're always changin' the law to suit 'em anyway." He sat down in another chair.

"I'll tell ya what that *Miller* test is like," Eddie hollered. "You see that garbage pail over there?" Schuster looked at the waste basket. It was full. Schuster gave him nothing—not even a nod. "Now if I put this little crumb of cookie down in there"—and he did—"the *Miller* test says because there's a little crumb down in there ya can eat, you gotta save the whole friggin' basket." Eddie laughed his high Irish laugh. "You see what I mean? That's the legal bullshit of the *Miller* test." He reached for another cookie out of the box and stuffed it in his mouth.

"The First Amendment protects our sacred rights," Schuster said.

"If you let the judges start censoring, pretty soon we'll lose everything. You see that mountain up there?" Schuster pointed up through the glass ceiling of the atrium to the mountain towering up above the roof of our office. "Now when that mountain is covered with sheet ice, it's treacherous. You don't want to start slipping, not even a little bit, because if you start slipping, you'll never be able to stop yourself, and you'll be dead before you're halfway to the bottom. That's what'll happen when you start letting First Amendment rights slip away." He looked satisfied with his argument.

"I agree." Eddie usually never gave an inch in an argument. "But if we don't do somethin', we're gonna suffocate in the garbage before we ever get to the mountain." He laughed again. They argued about complex legal questions that way because I insisted that if you couldn't actually *see* the law in your mind's eye, if you couldn't make it come alive in simple stories and analogies (as the Indians did with their legends), then you couldn't teach it to a jury, and that's because you probably didn't really understand it yourself. We were still only that small tribe of savages.

Eddie started another argument. "Guccione's got the judges where he wants 'em." Eddie waited for Schuster to bite.

"You'll never make me believe that," Schuster said.

"Well there's this boat, see, and it's out in the ocean, and it's got the media in it—I mean all them bastards, all the religious television stations, the holy rollers and all, the churchy papers and *Time* magazine is in the boat, and so is the good old *Reader's Digest* and the right- and the left-wingers—all the media's in the boat, and also in the same boat is old Guccione and all the other peddlers of pussy pictures. See?" There was a hush in Eddie's voice. Schuster got a disgusted look on his face. He knew the rest.

"Now this boat is out in the middle of the ocean, ya understand?" He waited for Schuster to agree but Schuster gave him nothing. "And somebody asks the judges to sink the boat to get rid of the pornographers. Now you tell me what judge is gonna do that. Like I said, the judges protect Guccione. He's got 'em where he wants 'em as long as he stays in the boat."

"You make the very point I'm arguing," Schuster said. "As soon as you start shooting at anybody in this boat called *The First Amendment*, we risk sinking the whole ship."

"That's because the judges are such poor fuckin' shots," Eddie said. "If they can't shoot any better than to sink the whole fuckin' boat, we better get rid of 'em." Then Schuster looked very serious and spoke quietly and I knew the argument was over and that what Schuster said was true. "No matter. The First Amendment doesn't protect libel. Never has."

But the right to free, open, and vigorous debate concerning public issues is the very soul of a great democracy. Thomas Jefferson had said it correctly: "Our liberty depends on the freedom of the press, and that cannot be limited without being lost." I thought of pornography more like the barnacles on the boat, not its passengers. Yet I could not abide censorship. I also fully agreed with the women who charged that pornography degrades their sex.

Yet everybody agrees, even the mainline pornographers, that there have to be limits. Do we permit "snuff movies"—those films that record the actual murder of some poor wretch whose life is sacrificed for a sex film? Do we permit the magazines to sell photos of sex with children? As the great judge asked, "Do we permit someone to cry fire in a crowded theater?" What are the limits? The history of censorship is full of examples of the ghastly seeds that inevitably grow to choke out our freedom. Whether it be the book burning of Hitler or Stalin or, in our own country, the banning of *Leaves of Grass, The Tropic of Capricorn,* and *Ulysses,* it was book burning just the same. The censor's fire knows no bounds.

If pornography represents a point of view in America, as it surely does, then the price of freedom is the toleration of a point of view we may find repugnant; yet another price is the pornographers' exploitation of the American male whose natural sexuality has been repressed, like a Chinese girl with little feet bound and crippled.

Eddie didn't want to give up the argument. "I'll tell you one thing," he said, looking very serious. "Those judges can't do what a good hound dog can do."

"Yeah?" Schuster said.

"Yeah. They can't tell a pussy from a polecat." Then he laughed until he made Schuster laugh too, and grabbed for one last cookie.

Guccione had answered Safer. No, *hard-core* obscenity didn't interest him, whatever *hard-core* was supposed to mean. Seemingly, therefore, soft-core obscenity was permissible. Like a cagey lawyer, he made nice distinctions and he never missed an argument. He claimed sexual explicitness had a therapeutic value.

"You know," Guccione said in a voice as authoritative as Almighty God, "that sort of guy is kept off the rooftops, kept from peeping in people's windows and invading the privacy of other citizens, and kept from committing crimes of rape and other sex acts." America was to thank Guccione for saving us from the misdeeds of the sexually perverted who, thanks to him, discharged their freakish passions over the pages of *Penthouse* instead. I doubted *Penthouse* ever prevented a single rape. I could argue it the other way, perhaps even prove it.

For a couple of bucks Guccione delivered a potpourri of sex from which every male could surely find something to his taste—Bondage and Bestiality and Voyeurism and Anal Sex and Incest and Masturbation and Group Sex and Troilism and Fellatio and Cunnilingus and Homosexuality and—the list went on. Each sexual category—call it deviant, laughable, pitiful, frightening, neurotic, natural, however one sees it—he openly presented each without judgment, each as fully acceptable as the other, each alleged that wonderfully erotic product of the good life in a world where all who dealt openly with their sexuality, no matter how bizarre, were the courageous sexual adventurers of the new age.

Despite Guccione's grandiose claims of having liberated the sexuality of the American male, I thought Erica Jong said it best: "The very proliferation of pornography shows that our society is not liberated sexually. . . . Today's pornography shows us in sharp relief the sickness of our society, the twisted attitudes toward sex that persist beneath the facade of gentility. The ugliness we see in it—the joyless, obsessional, humorless quality—is the ugliness and twisted puritanism that exists in America."[2]

Men and women living together lived alone. The American male never spoke of his deepest yearnings because they had been prejudged as deviant and freakish and evil, even insane. But in the "Penthouse Forum," and in his other publications like *Forum* and *Variations,* Guccione reassured the American male that there were others out there like him, that nothing was abnormal and he was not insane. Thank God for that. Thank God for *Penthouse.* It was worth the two dollars a month just to know you weren't alone in this world.

Women, too, lived lives empty of that magic connection between sex and love. Many nourished their lives from the pages of cheap romances and women's magazines and many more lived vicariously through the soaps. But they were as alone and dissatisfied as their men. Some men said they felt cuckolded by the handsome heroes on the television screen with whom their wives had secretly fallen in love, and women raged at pornography because it seemed to excite their husbands more than they. But men and women rarely spoke to each other about what they wanted from each other, rarely spoke of it to their closest friends, often not even to their shrinks.

Guccione and the other pornographers laid it all out in easy, slick, pretty pages for the American male. Five million men rushed to the newsstands each month for their monthly dose. Little wonder pornography had exploded into a $7 billion a year industry.[3] Jean Bethke Elshtain said, "If pornography is the marketing of fantasies, then we can assume, following Freud, that these fantasies provide something that is missing from real life. . . ."[4]

But pornography had not gone unchallenged in America. Women's groups formed to fight it. They were joined by the far right and the preachers. Women Against Pornography, an organization of vocal feminists, proclaimed that "the proliferation of images eroticizing the degradation, brutalization, and dehumanization of female bodies . . . contributes to a pervasive cultural devaluation of women." Andrea Dworkin, who often speaks deep truths, said in her book *Woman Hating*, "Our study of pornography, our living of life, tells us that though the witches are dead, burned alive at the stake, the belief in female evil is not, the hatred of female carnality is not. The Church has not changed its premises; the culture has not refuted those premises. It is left to us, the inheritors of that myth, to destroy it and the institutions based on it."[5] Guccione's empire had surely become one of those institutions.

The pornographers fought back and were joined by the American male who whimpered along, giving them his tacit, timid support. "Pornography helps us free ourselves from the puritanical attitudes about sex that have long dominated our society,"[6] Al Goldstein of *Screw* magazine said, and he said other allegedly wonderful things like "To me erection is its own best defense" and "Pornography can now serve as a celebration of human sexuality and an aid to sexual congress."[7] I recognized truths in those arguments as well.

The ragings of both sides were heard across the nation. It had all the sounds of war. Women who claimed they had been transformed into mere things by men and pornographers now launched their own attacks, and any man who had not joined them either out of conviction or intimidation was the enemy and as such was himself

objectified by women. It was, it is, war—with no room for understanding, nor time to discover the little children and the demons
within us all. There is no dialogue—only the furious denouncements,
the high screaming of the enraged combatants. No prisoners are
taken.

I thought men and women might begin with a simple hearing of
each other, but while the war raged between the women and their
men, the nation could hear Guccione endow *Penthouse* with the sacred status of art—ah, art!

"What you're saying is Larry Flynt publishes trash and Bob Guccione publishes art?" Safer asked. Guccione eagerly agreed, as if
Safer had reached over and put his finger on the very pulse of his
being. To me Flynt's *Hustler* and Guccione's *Penthouse* were the
same, maybe a difference in the wrapping, in the style, but the same.
He proclaimed, however, "If there were to be a definition [*sic*] between the two publications, it would have to be that [art], yes."

Then Guccione told Safer that *Hustler's* Larry Flynt wasn't persecuted because of the explicitness of his magazine but because of the
"dismemberment and the excrement and the scatological scenes—
that which one easily finds offensive, because I don't think that has
anything to do with sex," nor art, I supposed. Guccione protested to
Safer that *Penthouse* was different than *Hustler*, and that he was different from Flynt—the frog explaining his difference from the toad.

He said outlandish things to Safer before this national audience—
that there *should* be censorship. "But I'm now talking about real
hard-core porn; I'm not talking about the sort of magazine that I
publish or even the sort of thing that Flynt publishes, which although
I don't like it, is not hard-core. It is simply vulgar." I grew tired of
the silly distinctions and moral gradations, as if he, Guccione, were
invested with the power to draw that nice line where what was acceptable ended and what was to be censored began. In such a role he
became like all censors. He would begin his expurgations with those
residing one step below him, at least as he perceived it, and at a
place where his own profit projections were left undisturbed. But
while a nation listened to his endless chortling, the war between the
sexes raged on, and on, and no one heard the combatants.

No one heard the women say, "We don't want to be raped in the
streets and on the beaches and in the parking lots and in the working
places and in the courtrooms anymore. We don't want to be raped by
our husbands anymore. We don't want to be depicted in the pages of

Penthouse and *Hustler* as reveling in our rapes. We don't want to be beaten anymore, and hurt, and degraded. We will not suffer it anymore. We have had it for centuries and we have had enough."

No one heard the women say, "We don't want to be used as things for sale by pornographers. We don't want the pornographers to take us, to take our parts, and out of us create the mass of monthly erections and mind fucks our men have grown to crave like addicts crazy for a fix."

But as in all wars, both sides are victims—the men are also victims.

Little boys are victims. No one heard the little boys who cry out from all men, the little boys seduced in countless ways by their mothers—little boys raped in their minds and in their hearts by old grandmothers and schoolteachers with vaginas so virtuous, so pure, they have grown putrid to thought and touch and with minds so self-righteous they have grown ugly. They have been raped in their minds, these little boys, by the Sunday school teachers and the preachers and the religious prunes and prudes—they have raped little boys in their tender core and when the little boys become men, the men are already weary of such judgments because they are the same painful judgments we charge against ourselves.

Men are like poor weeds that have struggled too long to grow in the dark under some cruel rock. Yet men too, were born perfect. But we were taught by our mothers that everything sexual was ugly—nasty. Even the word was nasty.

"Do not say that word. Do not think that word," for the Ever Watching God, the Holy Voyeur, will know it if you even think that word.

We are tired of hiding ourselves from women. We are consumed with despair. How can we bear it any longer, women hating us so, and us hating ourselves. How can we endure it any longer, women seeing us as monsters and us believing it to be true? How can we stand this agony of being separated from the women whom we love, or being loved by them only for what we are not?

No one heard the men. "Our hunger for you is so urgent, but what we receive instead is the pornographer's pages, and after that we are as empty and lonely as ever. As time passes, our longing becomes disappointment and bitter words and we are forced even farther apart by the screechings and the cursing and the cruel slanders we hurl at one another, and the chasm between us grows greater, and we become even lonelier."

Strife stifles the air.

It is time for the war to end. We are all weary of it. Yet all I heard were the sounds of the warring and then the awful silence of lonely men and lonely women. And I also heard the laughter of Guccione and a host of pornographers who, like any profiteers in time of war, filled their coffers to overflowing.

In my own fantasies I heard a new dialogue. It was a dialogue between children, happy, free, excited, without judgments. It was a dialogue that released all of the demons who themselves became only little children again. It was a dialogue out of which new respect was born between the sexes, for they had heard and understood each other, and out of the dialogue a miracle had occurred—the resurrection of the innocent primal coupling of the sexes.

Who is at fault in this war? Who is guilty?

Let me plead both cases.

Before the Church, the top of the hand did not hate its own palm, nor did the eye stare back at itself in contempt. "Uncivilized" men in their foolish, primitive way, unpolluted by Holy Doctrine, knew nothing but to love the earth, for the earth was their mother, and they knew only to love their women, for they were themselves.

Was not the original sin the conviction of Eve and all of her daughters and sisters forever on false charges? Hear the charges of the Holy Church as recorded in the Bible and cited as final authority by the *Malleus* for the wickedness of women:

> The sin of Eve would not have brought death to our soul and body unless the sin had afterwards passed on to Adam, who was tempted by Eve, and not by the devil—therefore, she is more bitter than death.
>
> More bitter than death, again, because that is natural and destroys only the body; but the sin which arose from woman destroys the soul by depriving it of grace, and delivers the body up to the punishment for sin.
>
> More bitter than death, again, because bodily death is an open and terrible enemy, but woman is a wheedling and secret enemy.[8]

What God, worthy of worship, could levy such charges against the innocent and perpetuate such vile and eternal judgments against every unborn female child? When Eve was falsely charged and convicted, we ourselves were convicted, as was God. Those false charges took our women from us and we made witches of them, and we joined with the monks and the eunuchs of the Holy Church, and we persecuted women so that down through those dark centuries their burning at the stake may have been the most honest of our transactions with them. And now, lonely and separated from them and ourselves, we awaken in the morning clutching the pornographer's dead pages.

Is it not a pity to see men still joined with the Holy Church in their woman hating, to see men still embracing those repressive doctrines that make sexual cripples of us and have fathered a century of Freudian psychology? In this time of war, women have joined with the very institution that has dragged them to that low place from which they struggle so hard for their extrication. Have we not—both men and women—been like two curs chained together and, when the whip was laid to one of us, we ripped and tore at each other until we were both bloody and exhausted? Never once did we turn against our vicious master. It is time we join each other as we were meant to be joined, that we become whole again, that we renounce those who have separated us and exploited us.

It is a time to love again.

And when the men and the women did not speak to each other, the silence was filled with Guccione's great gasconades to Morley Safer: "I rather like the sort of thing I do, because it's more"—he searched for just the right word—"it's more mysterious and it's something that I can think about." Oh, God, I thought. What is mysterious about a full-in-the-face photo of some poor woman's rectum, which she's sold for a couple of thousand dollars, probably less, to the "discriminating lens of Guccione?" What is mysterious about the vaginal lips spread open, gaping helplessly out at millions? Who did he think we were? But Guccione continued to beat his drum to Safer about what he published. "It arouses me cerebrally as well as physically." I had no doubt he told the truth.

I set out to discover the chronic themes in *Penthouse* that might excite Guccione both cerebrally and physically. I advertised in the Denver *Post* for a complete collection of *Penthouse,* and when a faithful soul answered my ad, I rented it. I also gathered Guccione's so-called "Collectors' Edition," entitled "The Best of *Penthouse.*" It sold for two dollars and was a republication of selected letters from the "Penthouse Forum" in previous editions of the parent magazine. The editors claimed the letters were authentic, letters "reflecting the life-style of our readers." It contained an introduction by Albert Ellis, Ph.D., lauding the publication and pointing out the therapeutic advantages to be experienced from both writing and reading letters. "Read these letters thoughtfully, seriously, and select material that you might care to experiment with yourself," the good doctor prescribed. The introduction was the omnipresent verbiage included to provide some redeeming value, "when taken as a whole," and thus to avoid the judgment of obscenity under the *Miller* test of the Supreme Court.

I opened the pages to the section on "Domination," because sado-masochistic letters were usually a part of the "Penthouse Forum" 's pantry of plenty:

> She started tying me to the head of the bed . . . Then, getting up on her knees above me she told me to eat her. I took her luscious clit in my mouth and started sucking it. She cried out and writhed ecstatically. The feeling of bondage caused by the ropes tied around my hands, and the hot, sweet taste of her juices gave me one of the most mind-blowing sensations I've ever had. I kept going until she came, pushing my tongue deep into her . . . after a while she stopped crying and untied me. I held her gently in my arms and reached down to her legs. Just as I expected, there was the hot trickle of blood between her thighs.

The variations of the same theme made the Marquis de Sade seem unoriginal and dull. There was even a detailed exposition of how to train a man for female domination. After explaining the initial and intermediate steps, the female expert wrote:

> If I feel that the slave has progressed sufficiently, I begin to reduce the amount of genital stimulation. Simultaneously, I introduce the slave to further refinements, such as nipple clamps, horse riding, and the ability to respond to hand signals. For advanced training, I fasten the leash to the slave's balls only. This provides me with absolute control, since a slight tug on the leash tends to produce instant compliance with my commands. During this stage the slave is made to wear nipple clamps throughout the session. Genital stimulation is reduced to an absolute minimum, and the severity and frequency of whipping is increased, often being accomplished by a few sharp slaps of my hand, aimed directly at the penis. When a slave is able to take 40 lashes with the riding crop and ten penis slaps without whimpering or crying, I consider him to be fully trained.

As I thumbed these pages, I thought of similiar confessions of the infamous Marquis de Sade, and of those great names who had taken up his cudgel and became his apologists—Simone de Beauvoir, Dostoevski, Camus (who praised him as the one who undertook "the great offensive against a hostile heaven"), and even Baudelaire and Apollinaire who lauded his daring and revolutionary spirit. But perhaps the greatest monument to Sade that sprang to mind as I scanned "The Best of *Penthouse*" was raised by Sade to Sade himself and, I thought, to *Penthouse:* "Do not all passions require victims?"[9]

Yet one must not judge Guccione too quickly. Had he not, as he insisted, merely provided the American male with what he seemed to long for? Had he not fulfilled him, or so it would appear, in the cold smooth pages of *Penthouse* when he was otherwise left hungry and alone? Guccione furnished the American male with images of the nonexistent women, artfully propped up and propped open like corpses, all with the same glazed smile on their faces, and he also gave him something other than rejection and guilt. Month after month Guccione promised even more. And that was blessed in these days of deadly dreariness. But it was always the same—the same empty images, the same $2.50 nonliving substitutes for our living women. It was a time when the American male himself had been raped by the long mechanical penis of Robert C. Guccione's camera.

5

Norman Roy Grutman demanded protection for Guccione. He argued to Judge Brimmer in a conference call from New York that I should not be permitted to take Guccione's deposition. I listened from Wyoming, fascinated at the man's lofty, always eminently correct, language. He put me in mind of Boswell's Dr. Johnson. When he finally got down to it, what he said in plain English was that Guccione was busy in another court on July 7 and 8, 1980, and wouldn't show. Grutman was putting Judge Clarence A. Brimmer to his first test in the case, but I was told Grutman tested every judge. Before Judge Brimmer could rule, Grutman offered him a reasonable way out.

"I suggest, Your Honor, that Mr. Guccione's affidavit that he had nothing to do with this article, nothing to do with the author, nothing to do with the editing, is certainly entitled to some credence." Then he put his client in good company. "Surely the president of the telephone company or General Motors or of any substantial publishing company, if he had to be personally examined on deposition every time somebody brought a lawsuit, would have little time left to attend to the principal financial policy of his company."

Judge Brimmer was a veteran trial judge who was not easily put off.

"What is the name of the court and the name of the judge where Mr. Guccione is to attend?" Judge Brimmer asked.

"I am not counsel in that case," Grutman replied, sounding calm, in utter control. "It has to do with depositions being taken in a matter related to Mr. Guccione's other business concerns—relative to the construction of a hotel and casino complex in Atlantic City. If your Honor wishes me to get that information—" Then Grutman stopped and added, "I make that representation," as if that were all the proof the judge should need.

"You can't tell me the name of the court, or judge or clerk of that court?" the judge asked. Not right then he couldn't, Grutman admitted, and then the judge said the only reason he wanted to know was because he was going to call the judge and verify Grutman's claim because, "Frankly, I don't believe you—"

"Really?" Grutman said, incredulous.

"Because you omitted that information from Guccione's affidavit," the judge added.

"That is such a harsh remark—that you don't believe me," Grutman said.

"Didn't you know the contents of Mr. Guccione's affidavit?"

"No, I did not," Grutman said. "I presented the affidavit for his signature at a meeting that I had with him." The judge must have noticed it was Grutman whose signature and notary seal were clearly on the paper. I said nothing.

Then, as if he were about to pass sentence on a felon before the bar, the judge said, "Well, do you have anything else to say as to why these depositions shouldn't be taken?"

Grutman launched a new attack. "Before you leave that subject, Judge, I am very concerned about what I regard as an unexpected hostility from you—that you should tell me that you *disbelieve* what I tell you." Grutman's obvious move was to put Judge Brimmer on the defensive before he could announce his decision.

"Well, I find it hard to believe," the judge said, softening slightly.

"That's different from saying you disbelieve!"

"I find it hard to believe," the judge said. "and that is what I meant to say—that you, a skilled lawyer in this field, present an affidavit to his client couched in legal language, obviously prepared by a lawyer, and you knew that these other depositions were scheduled. As a careful lawyer, practicing in New York City, you would not have omitted from the affidavit the fact that Guccione had a prior engagement in connection with depositions in New Jersey."

"Your Honor—"

"That fact is not in the affidavit."

"I did not prepare the affidavit."

"I am sorry. One would have thought you might have checked it."

"But I told you I didn't." I thought of a boy railing at an intransigent father. The judge, a father himself, said, "Well, I believe that you didn't," but that only encouraged Grutman further.

"Your Honor has assumed that the lawyer who is speaking drafted the affidavit, and you assume that I possessed the knowledge which I now impart to you, and I ask Your Honor in a state of fair-mindedness, please, not to overlook the fact that you have misjudged me, and you have misjudged the affidavit and the client. The fact is that I have just told you this afternoon that on July seventh, Mr. Guccione has depositions which are scheduled in a case in New Jersey that has nothing to do with the magazine."

"Well, unfortunately," the judge said, trying to bring the matter to a close, "he is not going to be able to be there, because his deposition is going to be taken *in this case* in New York at the time stated. I have already reached that point."

But later Grutman attempted to open the matter again. "Your Honor, may I now be heard?"

"Mr. Grutman, I'm talking," the judge said. Then he began to speak of the pretrial conferences he intended to schedule in the case.

"Your Honor, may I raise one subject, please?"

"Mr. Grutman, please, don't interrupt me." The judge went on, but when he hesitated momentarily to catch his breath, Grutman pressed again.

"If you are finished, Your Honor, may I have a word?" But it was the same old argument. His client, Guccione, had to be elsewhere. He offered to bring Guccione in at night, but I objected. I had a right to question his client when I was fresh. The judge suggested Grutman bring Guccione in as early as 7:30 A.M., but Grutman objected to that. "I have no way of getting a video transcriber here before the sun gets up, but—"

"I understand your problem," the judge said. "Frankly, that really isn't anyone's problem but yours. It is your client who has created the problem."

"I beg to differ with the Court," Grutman said. His voice was sharp and affrontive. "I think it is the rule that *you* have laid down. . . . I have given you good and sufficient reason to—"

"Mr. Grutman, I am not accustomed to being talked to like that! As far as I am concerned," the judge continued, "you are not admitted in this court yet—and you may never be!" Grutman had no absolute right to practice in the federal court in Wyoming. The judge's message was he'd better behave, and his order was that Guccione and Cioffari, the author of the Miss Wyoming story, and the two *Penthouse* editors give their depositions in Grutman's office on Park

Avenue in New York City beginning on the seventh of July promptly at nine o'clock in the morning.

In New York the lawyers in Grutman's offices looked down on the small specks that were the people many stories below them. I have always said a lawyer's head should never be higher than the folks walking on the street. Sitting in high places gives lawyers high-headed ideas, which finally do them in. Grutman's receptionist didn't speak to me. I stood there looking around and she went back to her typing. These were showy spaces with modern paintings and black mirrors covering whole walls.

The receptionist must have known who I was, dressed in that hat and Levis and cowboy boots—no uniform for a respectable lawyer, I admit. Lawyers should appear competent whether they are or not. The receptionist looked me over with incurious eyes and finally, without a flicker in her face, she motioned me to follow her to a large anti-septic, glass-walled room. Inside, I felt isolated like some virulent germ.

The New York Bar, of which Norman Roy Grutman is an esteemed member, was accustomed to the likes of me—the poorly bred and barely educated who represent the common man and who are common themselves. As early as 1879 the president of the New York Bar was complaining that those representing the ordinary citizen were "seen in almost all our courts slovenly in dress, uncouth in manner and habit, ignorant even of the English language, jostling, crowding, vulgarizing the profession."[1]

Where was Guccione? Probably part of his plan was to be late. I hated being cooped up alone in this glass room like some poor fish in a bowl. I tried to get comfortable. I put my boots up on the large walnut conference table, leaned back, closed my eyes, and breathed deeply, trying to relax. Then the receptionist ushered in the court reporter and the television technician who would tape the proceedings on video. They set up their equipment and fiddled around as long as they could, but Guccione still hadn't arrived, and Grutman, presumably in his office, didn't show either. The place grew as soundless as an empty forest. Maybe I should leave.

Half an hour late. Grutman sure as hell didn't care if I left. It was part of the game. I'd come all the way from Wyoming to New York to cool my heels in his office. I could leave and complain to the judge, but after all the smoke cleared, I would be right back there again another day. Grutman would probably tell the judge that Guccione was detained—held up in the traffic—and I had abandoned the deposition—didn't have the courtesy to wait a few minutes for the man who was desperately trying to get there.

Finally I heard the distant sound of rattling chains, and the tap-tapping of steel heel plates with another set of heavy feet alongside. I didn't move—stayed with the boots propped up on the table and the eyes fixed to the ceiling. Grutman made his entry first. Close behind came Guccione, his gold medallions swinging, his pointed-toe French boots dainty and darling and his leather pants as slick and tight as a condom. Sullen, soggy-faced, Grutman swaggered silently to the other side of the table without acknowledging my presence. I tipped my chair back farther and sized them up.

Grutman, a man whose features could have been pleasant enough, scowled at me, looking more like a fleshy-faced friar of fifty than the immaculately dressed, quite extraordinary trial lawyer I would soon encounter.

I glanced at Guccione. He was above average in height, a man in his late forties with the dark complexion of his heritage, and he needed sun. His hair, obviously once black, had somewhat resisted recent attempts to be reddened. His face was handsome, with strong masculine lines that seemed to have gradually given in along the mouth and under his dark eyes to record the many years of the *dolce vita*. Guccione glowered, but he didn't look entirely evil.

Grutman glared at me like a schoolmaster at a disorderly pupil. He slapped his thick file down on the conference table, and everything jiggled, the table, his hefty jowls, his comfortable paunch, and with a deep and elegant voice he commanded, "Remove your boots from my table, Mr. Spence. You are only a lost savage, a crude aborigine—at best an uncouth bumpkin who comes to the city with a gaping mouth and the sensibilities of a bucolic. Dirty boots, too. Disgusting." My boots weren't too shiny. I lifted them up slowly and set my feet firmly on the floor and gave Grutman a nod and a friendly smile. "How ya doin', Norman?" I said. Guccione plunked down in a chair across from me and tried to stare me down.

"You know I dislike being called Norman," Grutman said. "You do that, of course, out of ill manners." I hadn't known he didn't like his name. "Let's get on with it, Mr. Spence," Grutman said.

"Swear the witness, Mr. Reporter," I said. Guccione slumped farther down in his chair, then begrudgingly he half raised his hand while the reporter administered the oath. "I'm Gerry Spence. I represent the plaintiff, Miss Pring." The video cameras were rolling. I gave Guccione a smile.

"Thank you," Guccione said sarcastically, inspecting me closely. I saw an amused look come over his face. I thought he was going to laugh out loud. I waited.

"Let's get on with the questions," Grutman said.

I began with cautious questions, easy questions, like what did Guccione instruct his editors to look for in articles being considered for publication?

"Libel!" Guccione said in mock concern.

"Why?" I asked. I wanted to see how Guccione would handle himself if given a little slack and an open-ended question.

"Because publishing companies are notoriously subjected to the greed and opportunistic attitudes of the public at large," he said. Then he put himself in the company of *Time* and *Life* and *The New York Times,* and although claiming not to have been sued as often as they, "It is something that befalls all of us," he said, assuming the role of spokesman for the entire publishing industry.

"Well, when you refer to the greed of the public at large, does that include the greed of your own personal eighty-million-dollar libel suit presently pending against *Hustler?*"

"That was *not* a matter of greed," he shouted. He lunged forward in his chair.

"It was an attack on *me* in the magazine. It was a magazine that suggested things about *me* as a person, as an individual, with descriptions of *me,* and a photograph of *me.*" *Hustler* had published a parody on Guccione—a photograph of his head superimposed on the naked body of a man engaged in a homosexual act—"buggery" was how Grutman later characterized it.

"Did whatever was portrayed of you hurt your feelings?" I asked.

"Don't answer that question," Grutman instructed.

"He's an expert on how he feels—"

"Preposterous, Mr. Spence," Grutman interrupted. "There had been a long history of personally identified, specific, unspeakable, monstrous accusations about Robert C. Guccione, in word, in photograph, and in illustration—so that the person being defamed was Robert Guccione. In my opinion, there is absolutely no factual or evidentiary basis on which you can pursue this as some kind of stilt on which to elevate your case, which the witness has characterized as being predicated by greed."

"How did you suffer any damages as a result of what *Hustler* published?"

"Don't answer that question," Grutman instructed. I tried the question again, because if Guccione suffered damages from the *Hustler* thing, then surely so did Kim Pring from the Miss Wyoming article.

"Did you suffer any hurt feelings?" I asked.

"Do not answer that question."

"Do you know anything about the business of hurt feelings—the business of suffering damages from libel?"

"Do not answer that question," Grutman said.

"Have you had any personal experience in this area?"

"Do not answer that question." I was making a record to show Judge Brimmer.

"As you define and understand libel, as a publisher, do you feel that a writing which holds a person up to ridicule—"

"Perhaps you didn't understand me," Grutman interrupted again, and carefully laid one well-manicured hand on the glassy surface of his table.

"I did understand," I said. Already the tactic was clear. They would never answer any question that might cause them a problem at the trial unless the judge ordered them to do so. They would jerk us back and forth between Wyoming and New York until we gave up or we were financially exhausted.

I wanted to know if he thought the photographs that appeared in *Penthouse* were artistic. But his answers included a long commercial for his new book of erotic photography, which he said had an introduction by Federico Fellini and would retail for $120. He said it was an art book.

"What is erotic photography?"

"Erotic photography is the kind of photography that you see in *Penthouse* magazine."

"Does that include open-crotch shots of women?" I could see Guccione damming up the anger.

"Sometimes, yes. Sometimes a photograph can be erotic when a girl is entirely dressed."

I pressed. "Do you consider those open-crotch photographs in *Penthouse* to be art?"

"Yes. The photographs that appear in *Penthouse* are artistic. If they weren't artistic they would not appear in *Penthouse*."

"What is artistic about an open crotch?" I asked.

"I object to this," Grutman interrupted, "and I instruct the witness not to answer. Yours is a libel suit, Mr. Spence, and has nothing to do with photographs."

Guccione's face was red. His jaws bulged like a man hanging by his teeth from a trapeze rope. Now he wouldn't admit even obvious facts. Was there a Miss Wyoming in the year 1978? How should he know? He wouldn't even admit the likelihood of a Miss Wyoming in that year or any other year, and Grutman was objecting to protect him. "I object to that as calling for speculation, since he doesn't know," Grutman said.

"Do you instruct him not to answer?"

"In view of his prior answer, certainly."

"How many times have you testified in libel actions?" I asked.

"Objection," Grutman said. "The witness is instructed not to answer."

"Now I want the record to show we will ask the court to order Mr. Guccione to come to Jackson, Wyoming, at your expense."

"That kind of intimidation is just part of your bullying tactics," Grutman shouted.

"I'm sorry you feel bullied," I said.

Neither Grutman nor Guccione would produce any information of prior or pending lawsuits against *Penthouse*. Instead, Grutman made long speeches about my improper tactics, and equally long speeches were launched at will by Guccione. Send a courier to the *Penthouse* offices for the case files, I suggested, but Grutman said I was incensing Guccione by such a request, and I said it was entirely immaterial to me whether Guccione was incensed or not. "The question is, will you or will you not send a courier?"

"We don't have a courier," Grutman said.

"I have no idea where the papers or documents may be," Guccione added. I would wait for him to find them, I replied. "We operate all over the United States and we operate all over the world. We have offices everywhere. And I have no knowledge, as of this moment, where such documents may be kept."

I turned to Grutman. Surely he had the case files right there in his office. "I don't have them ready at hand," Grutman said. "I have received no proper request by way of discovery."

At noon I made one last try at civility. Could Grutman recommend a good place close by for lunch? But Grutman said no such place existed, and closed his paneled door in my face.

I felt alone, like an old bull dumped off in a strange pasture. I knew nothing of Park Avenue, not much of New York. I'd been there before and wasn't really as much of a bumpkin as Grutman claimed, but I was a country lawyer, all right, and in the city I usually hung close to my hotel, did my business, and got the hell out as soon as I could.

I grabbed my briefcase and looked for the elevator. Then one of Grutman's young lawyers, who rode down with me and who had overheard me asking Grutman about a place to have lunch, timidly volunteered the name of a restaurant half a block away, but Grutman had been right; the food was bad.

After lunch, Guccione's deposition deteriorated further. He openly displayed his mounting anger. His voice came in nasty snarls. "Fifty percent of every question that you have asked today has been a statement—a derogatory statement about the magazine, about me, and about people associated with the magazine, let alone its readers."

"I think they have been truthful statements," I said. "Are you insulted that I call your magazine—"

Guccione's high, sudden screaming silenced me: "Are you capable of calling this magazine smut?"

"I think I *am* calling it smut," I said very quietly.

"By what criterion do you determine this magazine is smut!" He lunged forward in his chair again, his fists doubled.

"By his own bigotry, his own narrow-mindedness, by his own avaricious interests in attempting to muck you to satisfy himself and his predatory client," Grutman joined in. I could hear a pack of Wyoming coyotes after some poor old hound dog. There was nothing left to do. This deposition was going nowhere, and part of their game was to see if they could incite me into some sort of misconduct they might later use against me with the judge. "I'm not going to proceed further," I said. "I've taken as much abuse from you as I'm going to." I closed my files and stuffed them into my briefcase. It was 5:35 P.M. They knew what I was about. I would ask the judge to take supervisory control of the depositions.

"Come off it!" Grutman shouted, hoping to keep the wrangle going until something flared, something exploded.

"What abuse?" Guccione hollered. "You sit here insulting everybody!"

"Firing a fire hose at everyone!" Grutman added.

"There is no way I can proceed," I said. "You won't permit him to answer a question. You have instructed him on over half of the questions not to answer." Grutman's reply, of course, was that my questions were improper, and now Guccione himself demanded that I continue, but it was over. The weary reporter was putting away his machine, and the TV man was gathering up his equipment. We were all tired, and now off the record. I turned to Guccione, who was still seated across from me, and with a smile I held out my hand and said, "Well, Mr. Guccione, it's been a pleasure meeting you."

Guccione yelled, "How can you say such a thing?" He pulled his hand away. His dark face turned purple and the veins at his temples protruded. "How can you ask such questions?"

"Because he's a hypocrite," Grutman hollered. At that Guccione jumped up and stood over me and screamed down at me, "You are a fucking cunt!" He clenched both fists and was shaking. "I wouldn't give your girl or anyone else a fucking cent. You get shit! Do you understand?" His eyes were wild and he was still screaming, shaking. "If you weren't here, I'd punch you out."

I didn't move. All I needed was some small physical altercation with Guccione in Grutman's New York law office—like getting into a fistfight in another man's house; it would all be over no matter who started it. Cautiously, slowly, I picked up my pencil and began making a note about Guccione's outburst, but Guccione attacked—not me—my pencil. He grabbed the pencil from my hand, and broke it in two. He threw the pieces at the tabletop. They bounced across the table's rich surface.

I said nothing—barely breathed—never looked up at him—didn't move a hair.

The room was still—like the air after thunder.

Then Guccione stormed out followed by Grutman, and as Grutman stamped down the hall I could hear him hollering, "He's a hypocrite, a bigot, and a buffoon," and I listened to the rattling of Guccione's chains and the heavy sound of Grutman's feet, and when the sounds disappeared I picked up my things silently, and once outside, I hailed a cab.

"How ya doin'?" I said to the cab driver, shutting the door behind me. He didn't acknowledge me. He waited in silence. "Could you take me to the St. Moritz?" The driver flipped the flag down on the meter and hauled me like so much baggage to the correct address, where he waited for me to dump myself out. I paid him silently.

New York City is a lonely place for a country lawyer, especially at night. I hate sitting sad-faced and alone in a restaurant, looking silently out at the rest of the patrons as they gaily dine away. What do you do? Do you put a smile on your face like some idiot delirious with his own company? Sometimes I take something to read so I'll look too busy to have dinner with anyone, but most dining rooms are too dark to read in.

I passed by the newsstand to pick up a paper, and there was the current issue of *Penthouse* staring out from the rack, beckoning to the lonely men of America, to me. I had good reason to buy a copy, didn't I? I had to study my opponent. I was glad the woman behind the counter didn't recognize me—"Oh, Mr. Spence, I see you're a *Penthouse* fan. What part do you like best—the dirty letters or the dirty pictures?"

"Could you put this in a bag for me?" I asked the clerk. Think of the toll made on America's forests by five million paper bags covering five million *Penthouse* sales each month—all to protect us from small embarrassments.

I went to the coffee shop where a person could see to read, slipped the magazine out of the sack, and began flipping through the pages, skipping quickly by the full-page, full-color nudes for fear someone would look over and see me staring at such pornography in public.

I stopped at a full-page ad for *Caligula*, Guccione's multimillion-dollar X-rated film. I had read the news stories about the film's sordid history. Gore Vidal, the author of the screenplay, claimed he desperately wanted his name off the film. The papers reported Vidal had been paid $200,000 to write an original script, and although Vidal said he hadn't seen the movie, he claimed to have read "the dubbing script."

"I have a pretty fair idea of the sleazy porn Guccione has done with my screenplay. Every major releasing company has turned it down," Vidal asserted.

Guccione said the film version of Vidal's script had more heterosexual appeal, less perverted sex than Vidal's original.

"Every other scene is masturbation and bestiality," Vidal retorted, "so that dialogue is merely filler." He was threatening a million-dollar lawsuit because Guccione had changed his script. Guccione replied that was silly because Vidal hadn't even seen the film yet. As for the lawsuit, Guccione said, "I could care less. It just means more publicity for the movie," and they raged on at each other. It was the same old hype—the same old formula for success. Trouble and tumult were the foundation of Guccione's empire.

Caligula had been released in Rome in six cinemas, including the classy Holiday and Royal hardtops and had been ordered seized by the district attorney. Before that, *Caligula* was playing to packed houses. The district attorney claimed he found many scenes in the film "flagrantly obscene" and in no way related to the historical basis of the story.

"There are several minutes of extremely explicit sex. There is a lot of violence in the film. There is a lot of nudity," Guccione said. That should be enough to entice the American public. He'd sunk $16 million of his personal money into the production of the film, which he touted as a work of art. "I estimate the movie will make about one hundred million." Then Guccione proudly declared to the press, "I am not a publisher, or a photographer, or a filmmaker. I am first an innovator. I am a creator; that's the most interesting thing to me." Then he added, "There is no simulation in my movie," which meant, I guess, that if people came to see Caligula they could actually see people doing it. "The film is very faithful to history."

As far as I knew, the film had never come to Wyoming. Maybe never would. Maybe I should go see it—didn't have anything else to do—and maybe I should study my opponent. And on a lonely night in New York City.

The movie was showing on some dark side street. I didn't know where—the cab took me. I walked up to the window and paid a dead-faced ticket seller three times the going rate for a good show at home; as it turned out, I would have paid a lot more than that to have been spared the experience.

The picture started innocently enough with the young Caligula skipping through the woods after his sister, and when he caught her, there was incestuous sex right then and there before our eyes with up-close shots of the young woman's underparts. Next we were introduced to Tiberius Caesar and his "little fishes," nude adolescents who at his command dove in and out of his pool caressing his wretched, frail, scab-ridden old body.

The scenes were brutal, and often I found myself closing my eyes like a small boy seeing his first horror movie. Tiberius ordered a funnel forced down the throat of a hapless guard accused of drinking on the job and wine poured into his stomach until it nearly ruptured. His penis was tied off with a shoestring so no fluid could escape and then, during one of Tiberius's wanderings and while he spewed his mindless monologue, he absently reached out, as if he were merely flicking a fly off his sleeve, and emptied the poor man's body of both wine and entrails with one easy slash of his knife. The offal came slopping out as if a bulging bag were suddenly slit in our faces. Tiberius never paused in his speech, delivered amid explicit closeups of the nude women of court who made love to each other, babbling senselessly, sexually in tongues and enthralling us with their masturbatory skills.

Never before had so many freaks been gathered in one picture. Beautiful women were shown in closeup shots performing fellatio on poor misshapen dwarfs. It was as if Guccione commanded us to behold the special attraction of his sideshow—see those pitifully deformed souls, hands growing out of hands, heads out of heads, the horrid faces staring out without human expression, like grotesque statues standing on their own pedestals.

No virtue was permitted to survive in Guccione's movie, no beauty permitted to remain unspoiled. There was always the cutting, the stabbing, the slicing and hacking of the innocent, always alive, always screaming in their blood and their agony. See the blood dripping everywhere, hear the insane, incessant giggles of the naked ladies of court reaching out for the blood and eagerly wiping it on the inside of their thighs and on their lusty vaginas as if the blood had magical sexual powers. See the woman squatting over the body of the innocent victim. Dead now. Watch them urinate on his carcass—and the women laughing. The steady stench of sadism soon blotted out any fragrance of the erotic in the film.

Watch. Caligula laughs. He chases the servants from the kitchen so that alone he may render Caesar's gift. The bride is a virgin? What a rarity! We shall see.

Disrobe woman. Now Caligula spreads her legs and looks curiously inside while the hapless groom watches in horror. Caligula screams at the groom, "Look, damn you, look!" and then, mocking the lilt of a child curious over a flower, he inspects the bride again. Now he mounts her like a dog, and with a brutal thrust, and thrust again, he takes her hymen amid the tears and the blood.

Ah, the art!

Caligula reaches down and feigning the idiot with mouth open and head nodding, he mindlessly wipes the vagina of the bride and holding up his bloody finger for the groom to see, for us to see, he grins like any madman—a virgin!

Next he demands the groom assume the position, naked. Lubricating his fist with lard from the kitchen, he smashes it, huge finger ring and all, up the rectum of the groom, and there is more piteous screaming.

"Why are you doing this to me?" the victim asks. "I have always been loyal to you."

"That's just it," Caligula replies with a simpering smile and a fiendish laugh. "There is no loyalty in Rome. By being loyal you are a disloyal Roman." Caligula screeches in laughter again. Later we are shown the man's severed penis close up. Perhaps there is artistry in its bloody stump. Perhaps there is some genius of innovation in the guard tossing it to a dog that devours it before our eyes in massive bestial gulps.

Now Guccione demanded we accompany him in his descent. Watch while my Caligula makes love to his dead sister. Watch! See! I have him performing cunnilingus on that limp dead body. See his tongue cover the cadaver? Look closely because after this there is nothing left. Nothing! Nothing for art. Nothing—not even for the necrophile!

I left the theater sick and feeling guilty. I thought Guccione had been slighted by the critics. I thought he should have been crowned the new de Sade.

Later I found out *Variety* had reviewed Caligula. It called the movie "totally without merit, degrading human values and a disgrace to the film industry." But *Variety* also thought the film might make money: "It offers something for every appetite in pants or panties. It has a potential audience in flesh mag readerships and the Bob Guccione–Penthouse Films International presentation at the top of the credits is the link with millions of sex mag followers in America and elsewhere."

Ah, Art—what swill is sanctified in your name by men who never see the exquisite patterns in the gravel under their French-heeled boots.

"Art teaches nothing, except the significance of life," Henry Miller said.

Whatever life is, its requiem was played in *Caligula* by Guccione. Guccione's art reflected an age in which the living were committed to the dead, pledged and affixed to dead machines, glued to nonliving tubes and screens, their lives dedicated to nonliving corporate masters, where love and sex were merchandised to the new man from the lifeless pages of *Penthouse*. Guccione was a man of his time.

At the theater where *Caligula* was playing I had plunked down my dead money and then myself. I sat in a lonely seat next to rows of lonely seats. We had been strangers touching elbows, breathing what each exhaled, never speaking, never even nodding, as if our neighbors in the theater were also dead, rows of the dead, row on row at fifteen dollars a head. Guccione had delivered a simple message to America—alienated man speaking to his alienated audience—joy was gone, all human value was gone, life itself was gone—given over finally to a love of the dead.

Then, when the film was over, we had left the theater like a mob struck dumb, and we dispersed in all directions over the concrete and into the darkness, each to his separate cell.

6

In the morning I waited alone in Grutman's glass room for Cioffari to arrive for his deposition. Already he was half an hour late, then an hour. Still he didn't show. Then as I was packing up my briefcase, Cioffari came flying into the conference room like a molting rooster chased by a cur.

"Traffic," he panted. I had him sworn.

This man in his early forties—sallow, narrow-faced with thinning dark hair and glasses—looked more like a pawnshop clerk than a professor. He made certain easy admissions: He had attended high school at St. Michael's in the Bronx, then gone to Holy Cross College and taught creative writing at William Paterson College, a four-year public institution at Wayne, New Jersey. He also admitted writing certain formula sex stories for the "girlie magazines."

I said, "Well, Mr. Witness, other than what you have been told by your attorney, and prior to the time that you were sued in this case, I would like you to tell me what knowledge you had of defamation?"

"I don't understand the question."

"Well, I can't say it any clearer." I had the reporter read the question back.

"I've answered the question," Cioffari said.

"I want your statement on the record. You simply do not understand that question?"

"I don't understand the question."

"What is it that you don't understand about it?"

"That is argumentative," Grutman said. "Next question, please. Do not answer that question," he said to Cioffari.

"Well, I think we may have to apply to the court for assistance if a doctor of English can't understand a simple question." Then I asked if understanding the meaning of libel was part of the writing trade?

Grutman answered for him. "No, it is not, Mr. Spence. That is a legal concept. He is not a lawyer. He is a professor and an author."

"Have you ever heard anybody talk about libel and slander?"

"I don't understand the question," Cioffari said.

"You don't understand that question either?"

"No, I don't understand that question."

"You have never heard anybody talk about libel and slander? You do not know what that means . . . ?"

"Do not answer that question," Grutman directed Cioffari.

"Are you confused about whether or not you have ever heard anybody talk about libel and slander?"

No answer. Cioffari was sneering. I smiled back.

"Are you going to answer?" I asked.

"I don't understand what the question is."

Cioffari wrote stories for *Gallery*. "What kind of a men's magazine is *Gallery*?" I asked. I knew it was another girlie magazine with the omnipresent open crotches in full color staring expressionlessly out at the reader.

"I don't understand the question."

"You don't understand that question?"

"No, I don't."

"What kind of stories does it publish?"

Grutman was amused at my struggle, but I had to make a record to show the judge when I would ask him to order these witnesses to Wyoming for their depositions under the supervision of the court.

"I don't understand the question."

He also published in *Chic*, another girlie magazine.

"What kind of a story did you publish in *Chic*?"

"I don't understand the question."

"Is that all you have to say about it?"

No answer.

Finally, referring to the Miss Wyoming article, I asked, "Can you tell me how such a story as this came about in your mind?"

"Do not answer it," Grutman warned.

"Well," I said to Grutman, "I think the court will instruct him to answer that question, and if we have to come back a second time, it will be at your expense."

"I do not need your insulting, and your upbraiding and threatening the witness, which is what you have been doing the last hour. If you want to ask a question—you are not a freshman lawyer, Mr. Spence, and I ask you, please, not to act like one."

I repeated the last question. "Can you give me any information at all about how you came to the story?"

"I answered that question," Cioffari said.

"Answer it again," I insisted.

"No, he will not. That would be repetitious," Grutman said. Then he called in a secretary and ordered cold drinks for himself and Cioffari. The room was hot from the video floodlamps, and when the secretary returned, Grutman and Cioffari drank up. The rest of us, the reporter, the video operator, and I looked on, dry. I said nothing. Nothing to say.

I got into specifics. How was it that there were so many similarities between Kim Pring and Charlene, the main character in the Miss Wyoming article? For example, they both wore blue warm-up suits. "Did you happen to know what color warm-up suit Miss Wyoming wore?"

"I don't understand the question." I didn't want to play this game anymore—I would ask Judge Brimmer to order Cioffari to Wyoming. I called James Goode, chief editor of *Penthouse.*

Goode was a tall, gaunt, tight-hided man in his fifties with skin the color of an old newspaper. He looked as if he needed to be fed some meat and potatoes. He wore a mismatched coat and pants, no tie, and seemed friendly enough.

"Hot in here, isn't it?" I said.

"Yeah," he said. "Where do you get those white long-sleeved western shirts? Always wanted one."

"Got this one in Cheyenne," I said, starting to name the store.

Grutman interrupted. "I won't have you engaging in any conversation with my witness. Get on with your questions, Mr. Spence."

I asked Goode what investigation he'd made to be sure that the facts in the article couldn't be attributed to living persons, and the names of his investigators.

"I don't feel like answering," Goode said, leaning back and looking sleepily up to the ceiling.

"I don't think it's a matter of whether you *feel* like answering."

"Oh, I think it is, Mr. Spence," he said without lowering his gaze.

"Could you have checked to see if there was a real Miss Wyoming? Could you have done that?"

"I have already objected to your question. It contains a term which does not apply to what we're talking about," he said, sounding like a lawyer.

"Aren't you aware of the fact that people can be libeled, that people can be held up to ridicule and be hurt, whether the article is fictional or true?"

Grutman interrupted. "That's objected to, and the witness is instructed not to answer. It calls for a legal conclusion."

Goode said, "I don't believe, as an editor, we can invade the privacy of any real person in a fictional piece or short story."

"Would it be your position—just as a hypothetical case—that you could write a fictional story about the Reverend Billy Graham, have him commit cunnilingus to save the world in a fictional story, and thereby avoid any responsibilities?"

"That is objected to as being a hypothetical question," Grutman said. "He is here as a fact witness. That is not this case."

"Well, what would your opinion on that be as an editor?" I asked.

"His opinion on that is irrelevant. It has nothing to do with this case, Mr. Spence," Grutman said.

"Do you instruct him not to answer?"

"I believe that was my decision, yes," Grutman said.

"Could you publish a cartoon, a fictional cartoon, say, of Guccione, claiming in the cartoon that he had V.D. and get away with that because it's fiction?"—Guccione's suit against *Hustler*.

"Same objection," Grutman said. "Why don't you want to try this case, Mr. Spence, instead of some other that you're dreaming up?"

"Do you, from an editorial standpoint, know what libel is?"

"Objection . . . Even though you preface it by saying 'from an editorial standpoint,' what libel is in this case—"

"Don't get upset," I interrupted. "Don't shout." I smiled at Grutman, and he glared back. "I am not upset. I am clearing my voice." It would be futile to continue. I would take Goode to the judge as well.

At a break I wandered over to the secretary who had brought Grutman and Cioffari their cold drinks and asked her where I could get the same for the reporter, the cameraman, and me. When she volunteered, I gave her the change, but Grutman had pressed for the depositions to get started again before she'd returned. Robert Hofler, the senior editor, was waiting, Grutman said. Important people should not be kept waiting.

I thumbed through my papers and found Hofler's affidavit, which Grutman had filed to support his pending motion that our case be dismissed. The words Hofler had sworn to were obviously those of Grutman himself. The affidavit read in part, "I cannot understand how the plaintiff can seriously claim that the fictional 'Charlene' of the story is really her, and how the court can permit such a lawsuit to continue with its attendant expense and chilling effect upon the freedom of expression. . . . I strongly believe that the guarantees of our Constitution, if they are to mean anything, must surely protect the press from a lawsuit such as this." Hofler's signature was scrawled at the bottom. Hofler called the affidavit an "autobiography." I didn't think he had the slightest idea what he'd signed.

"Are these your words?" I pointed to the affidavit.

"No, those are not my words."

"Did you sign it under oath?"

"I don't know," he said. He was tall and slender and frail-looking; his boyish voice made word-sounds that turned up on the ends. I began to form my next question when there came a timid tapping at the door. It was the secretary who entered cautiously with our cold drinks.

Grutman confronted her. "What are you doing here?"

"I'm bringing Mr. Spence his refreshments."

"Who told you to do that?" he shouted again.

"Mr. Spence," she whispered.

"You take your orders from me!" Grutman yelled, and the woman nodded, set the drinks down, and hurried out of the room, shutting the door softly, very softly behind her. I went on questioning Hofler.

"As you read the article, weren't you on notice of the fact that this was an article that was, first of all, about a person referred to as Miss Wyoming?"

"I beg your pardon. I object to that. The document says otherwise," Grutman said.

"Are you instructing him not to answer?"

"Yes, sir." Then Grutman was off again: "It is a piece of pure fantasy, invention—it's fiction, and in the world of fiction it's imagination, and it is not amenable to truth or falsity, correctness or incorrectness, although you, for the purposes of lucre and your client's objectives in the case, would try to make it seem so."

I'd had enough. I left the office of Norman Roy Grutman.

I left New York.

Back in Wyoming, I filed my motion. Seven days later, Judge Brimmer called the matter up for hearing in Cheyenne, requiring the lawyers to appear in person. Now Grutman sat scowling over at me while a young associate arranged the contents of large file boxes like a fussy housewife, scampering here and there at Grutman's direction. Suddenly all the activity ceased and the place became quiet as a church as Judge Brimmer strode to the bench with giant steps for a man his size, steps longer than mine, and his feet hit the floor with resolution. He walked slightly pigeon-toed, Indian-like, I thought. He had grown up and practiced law in the small sheepman's town of Rawlins, Wyoming, one of those stops on the Union Pacific, 120 miles west of Laramie and another of those Wyoming towns isolated by thousands of square miles of lonely prairie. Judge Brimmer was a Wyoming man, no doubt of that. He'd run for governor as a Republican and after his defeat he'd taken the federal appointment to the district court bench. He'd been a competent lawyer, even a bit of a virtuoso, I thought. I'd been up against him in those days and his lawyering had given him the capacity to be a good trial judge.

The bailiff struck his gavel, everybody rose, and the bailiff declared court in session.

I began with a prayer that is never answered: "May it please the Court."

The judge, a man a few years my senior, maybe fifty-five, wore his sparse blond hair cut close to his head. He peered down first at Grutman and then at me through glasses that intensified his already penetrating dark eyes. He nodded for me to begin.

"Have you read the *Penthouse* article?" I inquired.

"I glanced at it, and it wasn't anything I wanted to read, but I know the general nature of it," the judge said.

I told the judge that Grutman had instructed Guccione a minimum of a hundred times not to answer my questions—and when he did answer they were only long, self-serving orations. "I wanted to know how many times Guccione has been sued and how *Penthouse* has dealt with these suits."

"How do you contend that that would lead to admissible evidence?" Judge Brimmer asked.

"Let me give you an example," I said. "In the back of *Penthouse* is a cartoon called 'Wicked Wanda'—a cartoon of a lesbian woman who, with her troupe of fellow lesbians, does many outrageous things. It is obviously fictional. The cartoon depicts President Kennedy and Kissinger and Guccione's competitor, Hefner, and many others behaving in startling ways with Wicked Wanda. The people depicted are all obviously public figures and were blatantly defamed.

"It's my contention this magazine, without any serious public issue, simply cloaks itself with First Amendment privileges to sell its smut to shock the public and reap the rewards. Over the fifteen-year history of the magazine there have been many lawsuits. Guccione says they have won them all. How? What has *Penthouse* learned from the anguish of these many people who have been defamed? He claims this magazine has the largest circulation of any men's magazine in the world. What kind of policy changes have developed as they were sued, as they heard people cry out? That deals with the question of malice."

"Here is the author. He has written four or five articles for *Penthouse* before, one for *Playboy,* and some for some other smut magazines. He has a Ph.D. and teaches in a Wayne, New Jersey, college.

"I asked him, 'Where did you go to school?' He said, 'I don't understand the question.' " I went over the record of unanswered questions and asked the Court to take supervisory control and require the witnesses to appear in Wyoming for their further depositions.

Without notes Grutman's argument rolled out as if it had been carefully prerecorded. I was astounded. "It is a source of personal displeasure to have to air before this court the fact that the depositions, which were taken in New York on July seventh and July eighth, were riddled with such acrimony and such disputatiousness. And as I say, Your Honor, I have tried cases against great lawyers, men of considerable legal acumen, but never in my experience have I ever encountered the kind of special rudeness, aggressiveness, overbearingness, and unpleasantness that may be Mr. Spence's hallmark, but which was the prevading spirit that permeated these depositions." He claimed he hadn't had time to review the depositions and asked for a continuance of the hearing.

"Oh, Counsel," Judge Brimmer said impatiently. "Move on to something else. . . . You were present at the depositions. You knew what you did and what your witnesses did. You heard them all. The simple issue is whether or not you permitted effective discovery to be made."

"I think the record reflects that I, acting as an attorney, was not capriciously or captiously seeking to thwart lines of inquiry and acting in any way that would be regarded as deliberately violative or defiant of a court order or of the spirit of the rules." Next he argued that the names of the investigators used by *Penthouse* might be trade secrets or areas of privacy.

"Counsel, you know that the name and the address of an investigator is not an industrial trade secret." The judge continued, "It is obvious that the witness did not answer the question here."

"You haven't read the magazine from what you have said?" Grutman asked.

"No, I have never seen a copy of it. I've seen copies in the newsstand, but I've never examined the magazine."

"Well, may I say, Your Honor, that this is the single largest-selling, sophisticated man's entertainment magazine on the newsstand in the world."

"That really doesn't have anything to do with the case," the judge said.

"Well, it has to do with the contents of what is in that magazine. The contents of that magazine is something more than 'crotch shots,' so characterized by Mr. Spence, or the 'Readers' Forum' about which Mr. Spence has had some searing comments.

"In that magazine are published articles of investigative journalism," Grutman said with great reverence in his voice, "which, as Mr. Guccione testified, are quoted more frequently in the *Congressional Record* than any other publication in the United States, including *The New York Times*, which—" He stopped short. "Your Honor smiles?"

"Anything can happen in Congress," the judge said. There was laughter from the audience, but Grutman continued unperturbed. Finally the judge stopped him again, "It looks to me like the depositions were a futility, that no information of any real value was uncovered, primarily because of your own actions in directing the witnesses not to answer the questions."

"I am shocked that Your Honor should say that," Grutman said. Then he attacked. He referred to my questions concerning Guccione's case against *Hustler* as "a barefaced reflection of the kind of prejudice, bias and bigotry and loaded dice that Mr. Spence is trying to create by presenting Mr. Guccione in this position, so that he can allude to his poor client." He never took his eyes from the judge. "Now, without making a poor pun, that is clearly a naked demonstration."

I whispered to Eddie, "Jesus Christ, listen to this guy!"

"Yeah!" was all Eddie said. I felt like a fighter watching his opponent display a frightful array of fancy moves in the gym.

"Mr. Spence is not trying the Miss Wyoming article, he is trying *Penthouse* magazine and its affluent publisher and other publications, which he believes conservative people in his community will not find to their liking and, therefore, building upon that unspoken, but very plain prejudice, he hopes to create a springboard for damages which are not legally cognizable."

He quoted Guccione. All great painters from Rembrandt to Caravaggio, from Leonardo da Vinci to Michelangelo, depicted women with open crotches.

"Let's not get into that," the judge said.

"I ask you, Your Honor," Grutman pleaded, "is that kind of cavalier, loose, deliberate kidney punch going to be justified by you, or will it be recognized by you, sir, as setting the kind of tone of insult, abuse, and arrogance which is what provoked the difficulty and acrimony in the depositions in the first place? I dare say, Your Honor, that kind of language from Mr. Spence is a demonstration that he is, as I think Montaigne said, 'a cock so vain he thinks the sun rises to hear him crow.'"

"Who the hell is this Montaigne?" Eddie whispered.

"Christ, don't ask me. I didn't go to Yale."

Grutman read the judge one of the questions I'd asked Guccione: "Would this story be funny if it were your daughter and she was Miss Wyoming and a baton twirler?" Grutman looked up at His Honor, his eyes blazing with indignation. "I instructed him not to answer," Grutman said.

He read another of my questions to Guccione: "Do you think a story suggesting that a simple country person like Miss Wyoming took a penis into her mouth and caused levitation tends to increase the sale of your magazine?" Grutman looked up at Judge Brimmer, shaking his head, his voice trembling with deep shock. "I objected to the form of that question."

He argued there was a difference between Guccione's case against *Hustler* and ours against *Penthouse*. "It had his [Guccione's] photographic likeness and it had the photograph of his girlfriend—so that there was no dispute. It *was* Mr. Guccione. The name on the door was 'Robert Guccione, Photographer.' And it had an abominable caption on it, with which I will not, in your courtroom, defile your ears, but it was *insecretable*."

"It was what, sir?" I asked.

Grutman turned to me in disdain, *"Insecretable."* He said the word slowly. "Worthy to be spat upon."

"Thank you," I said.

Now Grutman turned to Guccione's pencil-breaking episode. "It was not to my belief that anything had to be presented to this court, but since it has been—"

"Counsel said you condoned it," the judge said.

"I dispute that," Grutman said. "I do not condone the use of that kind of vocabulary, since it is not part of my particular diction."

"I wouldn't think so," the judge said.

"I do know the meaning of those words, Judge, as I think every man over the age of fourteen does, and I say to you now, looking at you man to man and lawyer to judge in the eye, that what Mr. Guccione said is not something I am proud of his having said, but it was provoked, incited, and induced by Mr. Spence."

The sound of Grutman's indignation filled the room. "I have been outside counsel to Mr. Guccione for approximately ten years. The experience of the Spence deposition has no comparison in any deposition in any court anywhere. Perhaps one of the things that you may take from that is the measure of acrimony that was engendered."

Grutman paused. Now his voice grew soft as eider and sweet as cider. "I am satisfied that I, for my part, and the witnesses who were called for my client, acted in absolute honesty and good faith. . . . We have sought to obey your orders and to abide by your orders, which did not mean that we were to lie prostrate and let Mr. Spence clang over us remorsefully like some machine."

The judge gave me five minutes to respond. I, too, spoke quietly. "Judge Brimmer, I just want to say to the Court that I think a man should appreciate his adversary, and I want the Court and Mr. Grutman to know that I appreciate mine.

"I don't believe I have ever seen such a man with such a gift for words. It is a beautiful gift. It has been an educational experience for me. I have heard words I have never heard before, Latin phrases, and French phrases, and words that are pretty and nice to listen to. I am not altogether sure what I really heard. The game is this: If the Court makes him answer two questions, there are twenty-five more he didn't have to answer.

"Well, I don't have anything more to say about it excepting, Your Honor, we didn't get discovery; we didn't have due process; we didn't get fair treatment; we didn't get any answers. It was a waste of time. It was a mockery. I think that Mr. Grutman has told you they have never lost a case. I think you are starting to see why."

Judge Brimmer said, "I am not fully sure in the case of Mr. Guccione if a further deposition is needed in view of his testimony that he really didn't know much about the case. I am inclined to think that written interrogatories might be able to get to the answers that are needed there.

"With regard to the other three, though, as I say, subject to further review, I will require the defendants to bring these three witnesses to Wyoming, for the purpose of their depositions, and I order that the United States magistrate, Mr. Beaman, preside over these depositions to prevent what happened in New York, and that the witnesses will be commanded to bring with them all of the necessary files and records, including all the records pertaining to all of those other suits, and I want them prepared to answer the questions so we only have to go through this one time."

Grutman had won. He had protected Guccione. That the others had to come to Wyoming was of little consequence. I could take the depositions of the *Penthouse* editors till hell froze over, and Grutman could care less. He had saved the king—at least for now.

Then Judge Brimmer called a recess, and Grutman walked happily out of the courtroom. For such a hefty man he walked with a very light and long-legged swagger.

7

With a courtly air Grutman waited, his hands crossed in front of him, the podium bare of notes, his physical bearing offering no hint of his renown as a trial man, nothing imposing, nothing splendid, no special bone structure in the face, no distinguished lines, not even a head of hoary hair. His shirt was starched as stiff as a nurse's cap and he wore a fine black silk tie. He had a farmer's red bandana in his lapel pocket. His gold cuff links showed from under the sleeve of his coat when he gave his arm a quick twist, the way a concert pianist does just before he begins to play, and his shoes shone like patent leather.

Once when Eddie came into court with his boots scuffed and dull, I said, "Eddie, you can tell a lawyer who attends to detail by the shine on his boots."

"Yeah," Eddie replied, "but which detail?"

I looked down at my own boots. They needed polish.

I saw the tailoring in Grutman's coat. In Wyoming the old-time morticians still wore black coats like Grutman's, and even though they handled the corpses in their workrooms like so many slabs of bull meat, they thought that wearing formal black at the funeral showed their respect for the dead. I looked at the judge's black robe and began to have dark feelings.

Grutman waited until the judge looked up from his file. Then he gave a quick nod and Grutman began.

"May it please the Court." Grutman gazed tranquilly up at Judge Brimmer. "Summary judgment should be granted in order to afford proper constitutional safeguards for the First Amendment rights for freedom of speech and press." His deep voice filled the room with the sounds of divine revelation. He paused to give his words a chance to register with His Honor. "Those words, Judge Brimmer, are yours." Grutman looked up at the judge as if he had made the checkmate move and was waiting for the judge to respond in any way he dared, but Judge Brimmer looked back with eyes that did not reveal the state of the judicial brain behind them.

I loved to hear good lawyers, although I'd rather hear them in somebody else's case. But still I marveled at Grutman who now argued that the Court should grant his motion for summary judgment and dismiss our case without a jury trial "because the record was quite barren of anything at all to submit to the jury." He said the facts revealed only a plaintiff with "an egocentric distaste for the magazine," that the story was a fictional story and had nothing whatever to do with Kimerli Jayne Pring. He held up *Penthouse* and waved it at the judge. "You may have found it prurient or insipid, tasteless or revolting, but if I may be permitted, in a parochial sense, to quote the language of the former presiding judge of my court, Judge Bernard Boteen, 'What is one man's amusement teaches another's doctrine.'

"What is there that can support a claim against the article, this brummagem trumped-up claim, when it is not about her, and when she knows it is fiction? Forgive me for raising my voice, Your Honor," he said. "It was the artist's own creative imagination that led him to conceive the idea of somehow relating the beauty and majesty of the Grand Tetons—which in French means 'big breasts'—with the fictional sexual exploits of the beauty pageant contestant." He smiled at the judge and nodded. Judge Brimmer did not smile back.

Fiction was protected under the First Amendment. "Besides if it wasn't fiction this Pring woman was a public figure," and he began enumerating the beauty pageants she had entered prior to the Miss America contest, including the Thirty-third National Sweet Corn Festival. Then Grutman spoke to the judge in a very confidential whisper. There was this Peruvian magazine called *Gente* that featured a full-cover photograph of Kim Pring "clad in a skimpy, skin-tight outfit." She had voluntarily posed for the photographs. "Kim Pring, abetted by her mother for seventeen years, thrust herself into every Miss-something-or-other contest conceivable to the minds of man. . . ." She was a public figure. Therefore, under *Gertz* v. *Welch,* it was her burden to prove the article was published against her with actual malice, and since there was none, her claim for punitive damages must also fall. With a sentimental look on his face, Norman Roy Grutman smiled up at Judge Brimmer and began his concluding story. "When I was a younger man, I was in the courthouse in New York when a person named George Lincoln Rockwell, head of an organization called the American Nazi Party, was creating an enormous tumult out in front of the building because he wanted to hold a parade and spew his noxious, hateful doctrine on the streets of New York. I stood in the corridor of the courthouse. The sun was slanting through the window, and I saw an old, obviously Jewish man. He had creased skin. He looked like a concentration-camp victim. He was obviously an Orthodox Jew, who wore a beard, and the curly things that those people have, and he was crying in impotent rage and pounding his head against the wall of the courthouse.

"His grandson was standing by his side tugging his sleeve, obviously born in America, and couldn't have been more than twelve, and he said to him, 'Zayde,' which I think means grandfather. 'Zayde, you have to let him speak. It's America.' And, Judge, I believe that with every fiber of my being! 'It's America!' You may not like *Penthouse* and you are free not to read it. Mr. Spence may not like it; Miss Pring may not like it; and many of the people in Wyoming may not like it; five million people buy it every month. We will stay as a free society so long as the channels of expression remain open. It's America, Judge, and this is a motion for summary judgment under the Federal Rules. . . . I respectfully ask on this record that the complaint be dismissed and summary judgment be granted for the defendant. Thank you, sir."

"Thank you, Mr. Grutman," Judge Brimmer said and called another recess.

I looked over at Grutman sitting unruffled and cool in his black coat, his face calm, his brow dry. I was up against a real lawyer; I knew that much. He was the most articulate creature of the court I'd ever encountered. His deep voice had captured me against my will and transported me for the moment to the vast halls of the House of Lords where I could just as well have been listening to the eloquent plea of some great barrister of old. His argument finished, he seemed utterly confident that he had converted His Honor to his point of view on the matter, and that no reasonable man could dispute such obvious truths. Now he peered at me with a small smug smile on his lips, as if challenging me to undo in the slightest the monument to logic and justice he had just constructed. I began to feel that dastardly twisting and stirring in my belly, that fear that has always been my constant companion in the courtroom.

I had no such treasure of artful phrases or polished rhetoric. I spoke the ordinary language of the people—plain words. I felt as if I were that same beginning lawyer I'd known thirty years before standing there, that fierce judge glaring down at me, and I could offer up nothing in defense of my position—I could say nothing because my damnable mind had frozen at the worst of all times, that mutinous mind that is so sprightly, so free and limber when nothing more is at stake than passing laughter at the supper table. Thirty years before, I had looked up at the judge to see the cold, formidable features of the law, and I could feel my face burning red and something in my mind locked tight. The judge stared down in silence, his dreadful glower steadily changing to disdain. I had felt terror and had been on the verge of panic. I looked down at my boots. For God's sake, they needed polish.

I glanced at Grutman. I thought he was going to laugh. I got up slowly, walked with deliberate steps to the podium, put down a large stack of notes and cases I had prepared for the occasion, and looked up at the judge who was again busy in his file. The entire case was at stake. If he accepted Grutman's position as correct, he would dismiss our case before a jury ever heard it.

I wish I could tell judges how frightened we lawyers really are, especially of judges. We are always at their mercy, and often it seems they have little. Our clients' cases survive at their whim. Look at us. We stand before the court stiff-legged, squeezing out our stifled words as if some invisible hand were at our throats.

Judges, sworn to do justice, have the identical power to deliver injustice, out of ignorance, or prejudice, or an evil heart, or in revolt against infantile enemies or childhood ghosts. Some bear a sadistic longing to wield power over the helpless, and their power is nearly infinite. For others, the idea of mercy has faded over the years, and these judges, immersed daily in the misery of humankind, find that their senses have dulled. They become oblivious to their own cruelty, and perform only their bounden duty the way a hangman, too, finally goes to work in the morning and comes wearily home at night. Your Honors, perhaps that poor lawyer you perceive as incompetent suffers from nothing more than a caring heart on which you have placed a lock of fear. I looked up at Judge Brimmer. He gave me that faint smile of his, and I realized he was a friendly man, and wanted to hear me.

"Your Honor, it is a very interesting phenomenon to see what has happened to the Supreme Court's desire to preserve our First Amendment rights. Men like Mr. Grutman come in here to peddle their wares, their miserable publications, claiming that to do so is in the furtherance of the great American tradition of free speech.

"I need to say to Your Honor that *Penthouse* is here not asking for freedom to speak. It wants to sell its crotch shots. It wants to sell its 'Forum' letters to America—on the *theory* of freedom of speech.

"Your Honor, it isn't freedom of speech. It is freedom to defame, it is freedom to sell this shocking, this sick product to America under the argument of constitutional government.

"I didn't hear Mr. Grutman tell Your Honor what the real theory was behind *New York Times* versus *Sullivan*. Let me read it to you." I opened the book. " 'We express,' says the Supreme Court, 'a profound national commitment to the principle that *debate on public issues* should be uninhibited, robust and wide open, and that such debate may well include vehement, caustic and sometimes unpleasant sharp attacks on government and public officials. . . . Criticism of government is at the very center of a constitutionally protected area of free discussion. . . .'

"And it couldn't have been a better decision for American people. It was a decision that America needed. The press has a right to be free. We need free criticism. We need uninhibited, robust, and wide-open editorial discussion about public issues that have to do with our continuation as a free nation where people can say what they believe. But to have the likes of Mr. Grutman come here and tell us today that this case is about an old Jewish man and his grandson who says 'This is America' is such a perversion, such a far cry from what the Supreme Court intended."

Nobody knows for sure who a "public figure" is, but stripping public figures of their right to be protected from defamation also poses serious problems to a free people. I quoted Professor Laurence Eldredge of Hastings College Law School: " 'One of the great needs in contemporary America is to encourage more good people to participate in government. . . . We want the people to speak out, to stand up and be counted on important issues . . .' and how seldom are they willing to say things publicly and give the general public the guidance which is needed. Do you know why? Because as Linus Pauling found out, if he said anything publicly they could defame him with impunity. As scientist after scientist, leading politician after politician has discovered, 'If I say anything I have thrust myself into the public arena. If I open my mouth in criticism I am therefore a target for every magazine, every publication, every crackpot who wishes to defame me under First Amendment rights.' " I was sweating.

"Unbridled defamation concerning matters of public concern was the tool the Nazis used in pre–World War II Germany to destroy important men and render useless what they said, men whose message desperately needed to be heeded. How much is freedom of speech really advanced by the constitutional rule which says, Once you speak out on a question of public interest you become fair game for the John Birch Society, for every venomous newspaper editor and for everyone else who wants to destroy you and the power of what you say?

"The fact that the verdict, which constitutes a public vindication, may impose large money damages on the defendant, plus the fact that the preparation of the trial of the case may be very expensive for the defendant, effectively deters the publication of many defamatory statements and thus enables an honorable man to go through life with a deserved good name unsullied . . . but the opposite was shockingly revealed in the outrageous conduct of the late notorious United States Senator Joseph R. McCarthy, as he ruthlessly uttered his venom in the protective halls of Congress."

I paused for a moment to catch my breath and to let the courtroom clear itself of the sounds of my voice. I could feel Grutman's energy stabbing at my back, but to turn and look would only cause the judge to look too. It was my chance to hold the court this one crucial time. The judge's face was relaxed and open. He was listening intently. I needed to say it well, to create those first good impressions of the case that would follow us throughout the coming trial—if, indeed, we could now survive Grutman's motion. I heard Grutman's young associate coughing.

"Your Honor," I said, "what has happened to this society? What has happened to the doctrine of *New York Times* versus *Sullivan* as attended to by the likes of Mr. Grutman who comes here to tell you that because his corporation is American it has the right to sell this stuff to American people?

"This is hardly the important public issue guaranteed immunity under our Constitution. What if we said to the framers of the Constitution: '*Penthouse* magazine wants to take one of your virgin Virginia lasses, a public figure, and describe in public print how she commits "blowjobs." ' That is the language contained in this article—how would they like that? Would they say such defamation is protected because she is a public figure or would they say, 'We did not give a license to sell defamation. We gave Americans the right to speak out freely on public issues'?

"It is a freakish ugly perversion which permits men like Mr. Grutman to give touching stories about an old Jew as he watches the Nazi parade in front of the courthouse, which he may or may not have attended.

"Now Miss Wyoming had no general fame, no general notoriety, no pervasive involvement in the affairs of society. This defamation had nothing to do with her office as Miss Wyoming. She wasn't arguing for the beauty of fellatio. She wasn't saying to the world, 'I believe in oral sex.' She wasn't even saying to the world, 'I'm a sexy figure.' All she said was 'I spent seventeen years trying to become the United States Grand National Twirling Champion.' What she did had nothing to do with fellatio, or sex, or levitation, or all the smut and ugliness that they wish to publish and to laugh about."

Something magical locked in. My mind gave way to its magic flow. I had forgotten my notes long ago. "I asked Mr. Guccione, 'Do you think the article is funny?' And his answer was yes. But what of the other side— 'Is it funny were it your daughter—were you the parent of Miss Wyoming, or the grandparent, or were you Miss Wyoming herself?' " I was pounding my glasses on the podium to emphasize the point when the frames broke in two. I looked at the useless pieces, tossed them aside on the clerk's table and began anew.

"On the cover of *Penthouse* it says, 'Miss Wyoming's Unique Talent.' It shows a picture of a bare-breasted woman with her posterior presented to the reader. It doesn't say that it's fiction, and if you were to turn to the masthead inside, it gives the name of Philip Cioffari, the author, and it says 'humor' not fiction. The article itself is entitled, 'Miss Wyoming Saves the World—But She Blew the Contest with Her Talent.' The implication, the innuendo, is clear. It shows Miss Wyoming with something in her mouth. There is a striking resemblance between the plaintiff and the woman illustrated in the magazine: she is obviously blond, as is Miss Wyoming. But she is portrayed wearing a ripped swimsuit, with a breast and the nipple fully exposed and there is nothing indicating it is fiction.

"Yet the original manuscript, which was delivered by the author's literary agent to *Penthouse,* contained the title 'Miss Wyoming Saves the World.' That was all—and the word 'fiction' was on the face of the original instrument when *Penthouse* bought the article. Later the word 'fiction' was *eliminated* from the magazine, and *they* added the ungodly language to the title: 'But She Blew the Contest with Her Talent.'

"Mr. Cioffari tells us it was his intent that such baton-stroking was a sexual act, a stroking of the male sex organ." He had at least admitted that much in his deposition. "In bold print are the words '*Would you blow the entire Soviet Central Committee to prevent a Third World War?*' Here is her answer, also in bold print: '*I would. I would,*' she thought.' The word 'blow' means to give fellatio.

"What would she do? What kind of a woman was Miss Wyoming? But that is all right, Your Honor, because 'this is America,' where an old Jewish man stands weeping and pounding his head against the wall."

The judge lowered his eyes, and began reading. Had I lost him? I waited for him to look up again from his desk. "Go ahead, Counsel," he said, and now he began thumbing through the file in front of him. I felt sick. I began searching my own file to retrieve the affidavit of Kim Pring.

I began reading Kim's affidavit aloud: " 'It has hurt me gravely to see the misery brought upon my friends, and the shame upon the Miss Wyoming Pageant and upon my relatives—to see my parents and grandparents go through the anguish and embarrassment that the article caused. My grandfather is afflicted with cancer—he suffers enough without this *Penthouse* story. My grandparents were so upset after reading the article that they spent the entire afternoon crying—they had never read such a perverted writing in their entire sixty years. This adds to my own pain and hurting.' " Then I said quietly to Judge Brimmer, "It is her grandfather's wish that he live to see his granddaughter vindicated for this smear upon her good name."

Some might understand the article to be fantasy, some not, I argued. "We are not all tested by the sophistication and the worldliness of the many-languaged Mr. Grutman. We are tested by what the ordinary people in Wyoming would conclude. Listen to this: 'Posed, Monte appeared more like a work of art than a Lizard, his private part extended without being rigid and arched in a downward curve like a spigot. She felt herself being drawn to it, and she did something she had never done to anyone.' " The judge was listening. He started to say something. Then, thinking better of it, he let me argue on.

" 'She drew his flesh into her'—consider Kim Pring's grandfather reading this, or her grandmother, or unsophisticated people, or farmers, or blue-collar workers, or even professors, or teachers, or lawyers who are reading—or judges—'she drew his flesh into her, not with her mouth alone but with her entire body, the deepest, most remote parts of her uniting in common effort, calling to him, worshipping side by side with her lips and tongue and the warm tube of her throat, all of her, body and soul, crying in harmony for nourishment.' " I read on while the judge was still focused on me. " 'Beyond the borders of his hips, her glazed eyes scaled the Tetons, pleading with the snow-tipped summit of the highest peak for she knew not what—strength, endurance, love?—that she might lift his soul (and her own) from despair. He began to pour into her—'

"I asked what Cioffari meant by that and he said he was simply 'having an orgasm in her mouth.' Would you have quit reading there?" I asked. "Would the average person quit reading there? Well, I say the article is malicious on its face. Why do I say that? Because every living human being knows that there is a real Miss America Pageant. There isn't anyone in the sound of my voice who doesn't know that, including Mr. Grutman. They knew there was an identifiable human being who held the office of Miss Wyoming and that someone would be hurt by it, but when I asked them, 'Well, do you think that simply because it's fiction there is no responsibility?' the answer was, from Mr. Grutman: 'Don't answer the question.'

"Who were they going to hurt? They knew they were hurting some Miss Wyoming. They knew they were saying that someone who held the office of Miss Wyoming gave fellatio—and they didn't care. That's the test for malice. They didn't care. They made no inquiry at all. That's why I say it was malice on its face.

"Fiction has never been protected by the law. If in the reader's eyes the plaintiff is understood to be the person intended, that's enough." I read the law to His Honor. " 'The fact that the author states that his work is exclusively one of fiction, and is in no way applicable to living persons, is not decisive if readers actually and reasonably understand otherwise. Such a statement, however, is a fact to be considered by the jury.' "

I glanced at Eddie to see how I was doing, but he gave me no sign. I looked up at the judge. He was waiting. The sweat was rolling down my forehead.

"Now I don't have a nice story to tell Your Honor about an old

Jewish man crying and pounding his head against a wall, but I, too, will say 'This is America!' and my client, Miss Wyoming, is an American citizen, and she, too, has rights. She has the right to be secure in her privacy. She has the right not to be defamed. She has a right to live a peaceful life and to go about her business without being held up in a smutty magazine to have her life ruined and her reputation smeared, to be ridiculed and laughed at and shamed. She has the right to have little girls all over the country who have looked up to her as a national champion continue to admire her, to see her as she is, a woman who worked at her skill seventeen years and is the best—not one who now gives fellatio to save the world—she has rights, too, Your Honor. That's what this lawsuit is about.

"I ask that this case be presented to a jury—that a jury be permitted to determine as reasonable people if there was such an identification of Kim Pring as to cause her damage. Thank you, Your Honor."

"Thank you, Mr. Spence," Judge Brimmer said.

Then Norman Roy Grutman rose in a very stately manner and walked to the podium like a good friend about to read a eulogy over the dead. He spoke in a quiet, lulling melodious voice of the legal struggles that had been carried on over such great literature as *Ulysses* and of *Oh! Calcutta!* and *Lady Chatterley's Lover* and *Forever Amber* and others. He said, "Your Honor, this is a gerry-built case. That's a pun. It is a case in which the plaintiff claims personality changes . . . and you will find that those were created by her counsel.

"This is a fanciful case—more fanciful than the imaginary article which is the subject of the lawsuit. I listened to the faint praise from Mr. Spence. I will conclude, Your Honor, if you will permit me, with a quotation from Shakespeare. 'Out, out, brief candle! . . . it is a tale told by an idiot, full of sound and fury, signifying nothing.' Thank you, sir."

Judge Brimmer said he would take the arguments and the briefs under advisement and give his decision at an early time, and then he turned to Norman Roy Grutman and smiled at him—smiled, for Christ's sakes.

"I am going to admit Mr. Grutman for the purposes of this case, and I apprehend, Mr. Grutman, that you will familiarize yourself with our local rules and obey them, and not be disruptive in the course of the trial or anything like that."

Norman Roy Grutman gave a long sweeping bow to His Honor and said, "Faithfully, I promise."

"That's fine." The judge seemed very pleased. "You are admitted."

"Thank you, Your Honor."

"Let's adjourn then to chambers," Judge Brimmer said as if we were now one big happy family.

Although it was late in the afternoon our work was only beginning. We would now argue the many motions that had piled up awaiting the judge's decision. Perhaps arguing them would be a waste of energy since the Court could, at his slightest whim, order our case dismissed. We followed the judge into his chambers like obedient children.

"You did good," Eddie said, but I knew he was only trying to soothe a boiling anxious belly.

"Have a seat, gentlemen," the judge said.

Eddie and I took chairs across from Grutman and his young associate. The judge allowed us to amend our complaint to demand fifty million dollars actual damages and a like sum as punitive damages—he ordered us to deliver Kim's personal scrapbooks to Grutman, and he said, "Let me say this: The road runs both ways. You have the same rights to have questions answered, Mr. Grutman, that Mr. Spence has." That was all the encouragement Grutman needed.

"That's the very next point," Grutman said, leaning forward over the desk in the direction of the judge. "The gravamen of the complaint made by Miss Pring is that Mr. Spence characterized her as an impeccably virtuous model of a woman. She is as pure as the driven snow. I realize that ordinarily this would probably be one of the most personal and searching questions, but I would like to have a physical examination conducted of Miss Pring, and I would like to know whether she is *virgo intacta* or not."

"What's that?" I asked.

"Whether her hymen has been ruptured—whether she is a virgin, or whether or not this virtuous lady is a stranger to coitus," Grutman answered speaking as if I weren't there.

"I tell you what I would like to do, Judge," I said in a whisper. "If that motion is granted I would dismiss my lawsuit, because I will not put my client through that for any amount of money. This Court should not even consider that kind of talk—anything to do with her private life has nothing whatever to do with this lawsuit. If he wants to get into her reputation, he can, but the results of a physical examination have nothing to do with reputation. I think that is the most heinous, unbelievable request I have ever heard." I couldn't think of any more words.

My God, I thought. The evil goes to the very genes of the law. We can never escape it. The evil is in the memory of the law, and the law never forgets. The *Malleus* reported: "The witches themselves have often been seen lying on their backs in the fields or the woods, naked up to the very navel, and it has been apparent from the disposition of those limbs and members which pertain to the venereal act and orgasm, as also from the agitation of their legs and thighs, that, all invisibly to the bystanders, they have been copulating with Incubus devils; yet sometimes, howbeit this is rare, at the end of the act a very black vapour, of about the stature of a man, rises up into the air from the witch."[1]

Let her open her legs before our physicians that they may peer in with pious eyes, and let them report to the court so justice may know, and then let the physicians speak to the jury so the whole world may know what the physicians saw.

"Don't worry," Eddie whispered. "Keep it cool. The judge won't go along with that shit." I looked at the judge. His face was of a man in dreadful conflict.

"I want to think about it," the judge said. "I am not going to decide that now."

But Grutman persisted. "Whether she has even been carnally known by anyone—that does not require an angiogram or any complex or painful examination. A physician can perform what I think euphemistically is called a routine internal examination, and we can be apprised whether or not she is what she professes to be, or whether she is something else."

"That is so humiliating I am sick to hear it," I shouted, pounding my fist on the judge's table.

"Sick?" Grutman asked. He held back a smile. "Sick?"

I thought if he laughed I might rip his head off. "It makes me sick," I said to the judge again. But the judge said nothing.

Grutman wasn't finished. He began quoting the allegations in our complaint. " 'The net effect of the aforementioned article was to create the impression throughout the United States and Wyoming that the plaintiff was sexually promiscuous, depraved, unchaste, and morally lacking.' Now we have looked up the word *unchaste*," Grutman said. "It is an issue. *Unchaste* means 'not virginal.' "

"Take it easy, Gerry," Eddie whispered. "He's trying to get to you."

"No," I said. "He's trying to get Kim." The judge pondered hard questions with deep roots. The *Malleus* also reported that when scandalous reports were circulated concerning the honor of Saint Cunegond, wife of Henry II, German king and Roman emperor in about the year 1000, she did not hesitate. Although it was said her husband could not for a moment suspect her purity, she insisted upon a trial by ordeal. "And having walked unhurt over the red-hot plough shares, publicly testified her innocence."[2]

Finally the judge said to Grutman, "Well, you can put your argument and authorities for such an examination in your memo and submit it to me." I began to speak. The judge turned to me. "I haven't allowed it yet. I am a little skeptical about it." He turned back to Grutman. "Let's wait and see what your law is."

I knew what the law was. He could order her to submit to a physical examination if he chose. There was clear authority for the same in the Federal Rules of Procedure and also in the *Malleus:* "And it should be begun in this way. While the officers are preparing for the questioning [preparing the engines of torture], let the accused be led to the penal cells and there stripped by honest women of good reputation,"[3] for the inquisitors knew from experience that when the witch was interrogated naked of all clothing, she lost the power of keeping her silence.

Grutman's argument was clear enough to me: If a woman can display no hymen, we may say what we wish against her, and should she raise her head in protest, we will say it is the head of a harlot. All that protects a woman to this very day is her hymen of virtue—Oh, holy *virgo intacta.*

It was suppertime. But Grutman wasn't finished. If the judge were to decide against Grutman on his motion to dismiss our case, then he wanted the constitutional question certified to the Tenth Circuit. That, of course, would delay the trial by at least two years. He was also reminding Judge Brimmer that if he didn't hold for *Penthouse* on the law, he would take the judge to the court of appeals.

I called Grutman on it. "That's the nicest little intimidation I've seen a lawyer hand a judge," I retorted. "He just said to you in effect, 'Judge, if you don't hold for me we are going to take you to the appellate court.' "

"No. No. No," Grutman said.

"No, that doesn't bother me," Judge Brimmer said.

"No. No," Grutman said again.

"That doesn't bother me a bit," the judge said again, "because I expect everything I do to be appealed," and then the judge set the date for the trial—Monday, November 17, 1980—provided, of course, that he didn't grant Grutman's motion for summary judgment first. That would be the easiest way for any judge to avoid the tortuous ordeal ahead.

When the conference was over, Norman Roy Grutman got up and leaned over to Judge Brimmer with extended hand. "Since we have met—I think that the air is cleared—I would like to shake the Court's hand and thank you very much for welcoming me to your court." He gave the Court a big smile.

"Thank you," the judge said, taking his hand and returning his own big Wyoming smile.

"Glad to meet you," Grutman said and laughed.

"Glad to meet you," Judge Brimmer said with his own good-natured laugh.

"Well, Judge, I guess I would like to shake your hand, too," I said, and the judge laughed again and shook my hand so that everybody had been touched by the Court, and then he reached over and grabbed the hand of Grutman's associate who had sat quietly through the entire proceeding. His name was Jeffrey Daichman and even now he did not join in the frivolities. As the judge extended his hand, Daichman shrugged his shoulders and extended his own.

"Why not?" Daichman said. "I am going back to New York."

"Well, today I'm gonna get 'em for you," I said to Kim Pring as we walked through the front door of the Federal Court House in Cheyenne. It was September 26, 1980, and I was about to retake the deposition of Philip Cioffari and the others as Judge Brimmer had ruled. "A little revenge might be in order."

Silently she stretched long stride for stride with me. Perhaps, I thought, the only justice she'd ever know would come from the bloodletting she was about to witness when I took Cioffari's deposition. But now she said nothing.

"Well, what do you want me to do to him?" I asked like the devoted champion. "I mean, would you like his parts on a platter—should I skin him out for you? Do you want him stuffed for hanging on the wall? What do you want?" I laughed again. Still Kim made no answer. But when the elevator door closed she had to look at me and I could see the sadness in her eyes.

"What's the matter, Kim?" I asked.

"I don't know," she said. "I don't really hate him."

For Christ's sakes, I thought. I can't handle Miss Jesus right now. I was trying to get psyched up for this battle and the fair lady doesn't hate the enemy! "Well, you don't need to hate him, exactly," I said. "But you might enjoy seeing him bleed a little for all he's put you through." We got off on the second floor and started down the long marble corridor toward the courtroom. "Revenge feels good sometimes," I said. She didn't say anything. I expected too much from her. What did she know about war? I could hear my own mother say, "You can't wash blood away with blood." What do mothers know about war?

Philip Cioffari arrived precisely on time with Jeffrey Daichman, alongside. They walked past us to their table without acknowledging our presence. Cioffari, pale and thin as ever, looked like a man trying not to look afraid. I knew the feeling. I felt a twinge of pity in my belly—below the sternum. There would be no escaping for Cioffari—he'd have to answer my questions under the supervision of the presiding magistrate, and it would be hard for Cioffari.

Who was this Cioffari? A poor professor, no doubt, merely trying to supplement his income. There is always the hope that when a man's little demons escape to the printed page they may magically take on the dignity of a creative work, perhaps even becoming cherished. Cioffari labored at his work in hopes that his writing might achieve that high and blessed status called art, but the risks are great when one attempts to fly to such airy places, for after having jumped over the cliff with a piece of intended artistic erotica, one may fail to take wing, and, Lord knows, all that remains when art has fallen flat is the ugly and obscene wreckage. Cioffari claimed he spent months at his stories—worried over every word—and I understood his grasping for that elusive muse. Art is a demon of its own.

Early in his career he had written "Rat Hunting in the Bronx," a story published in the *Michigan Quarterly* about a boy who, with his friend Allie, was killing rats in a filthy swamp at the edge of the city. Once, loitering underneath a bridge between kills, Allie showed the boy a magazine with pictures of naked women in it. Cioffari wrote, "All the ladies wore black stockings with garters and have an ugly dark spot between their legs. The worst one is of a lady with her legs spread wide apart. The dark spot is large and open, like a sore. I couldn't look at it," and I realized that his demons, too, were born of innocent times. Perhaps he wrote as Steinbeck says we all write, this autobiographical material hounding us until we get it said, and out of the system, and until we understand who we are and why.[1]

But how shall we ever know who we are and why? Even in this alleged sexually liberated age, it is too horrifying to unlock our closets and stand face to face staring down the frightening images within. Men will confide their infidelities to each other—even a murderer may share the horror of his bloody hands with a cellmate. But men will never tell each other about their private demons, for the most feared of all judgments is to be deemed a sexual pervert.

I called Cioffari to the stand—watched him spring up from beside Daichman and head toward the witness chair, saw him struggle to put dignity in his gait, holding his head slightly higher than necessary, walking a shade too fast, too vigorously, his hands swinging freely at his side with the affectation of a man determined to appear relaxed. He was the bull turned loose in the ring.

Like the matador, the trial lawyer both hates and loves the bull, and the killing is both brutal and exquisite, for in the letting of the fatal blood of the bull, the matador releases his own blood. With the power of death in his hands—never the power of life—the matador thrusts the sword to its hilt and the blood of life flows out until that one moment of miracle when the blood of life becomes the blood of death. But the matador is not in the fight to kill, not even to save himself, but to extract life from the living and to grasp it for that brief instant, that single drop of blood, and to thereby conquer death. Cioffari raised his hand to be sworn.

Ha, Toro!

We are a species obsessed with killing because we cannot understand life and are terrorized by death, and to diminish our fear we continue to create death because we cannot create life. I launched my attack without any decent introduction. Killing was in my genes.

"It [the rat-killing story] describes some of the open-crotch shots you've seen in *Penthouse,* isn't that true?" I asked. With the magistrate watching, Cioffari now understood the question.

"Yes, it does."

I read out loud from his story. " 'The dark spot is large and open, like a sore.' " He sat up straighter and tried to glare back, but suddenly he looked quickly away. I felt nothing for the man. He was not one of the species, not one of us, not a man with his own demons—he was the enemy, and I knew my art. "That's how the open-crotch shots might well appear to some children, as the ones you referred to in your story, isn't that true?" Daichman made no effort to stop me and finally Cioffari replied, his voice held back, high, strained.

"Well, to this particular boy in my story, that's the way it appeared to him, yes." How could he deny the boy?

I struck at him again. "Do you have children?"

"No, I do not."

"Are you married?"

"No, I am not."

"Have you been?"

"Yes. Once." He began to stiffen, but not from the questions alone. It was the bearing down with the eyes, the righteous, threatening tone of the voice, the physical stance of the assailant before the witness, the intimidating atmosphere in the courtroom, all other eyes upon the witness as well, so he could not hide. There was no escaping.

I read from "Either Way You Lose," an earlier story he'd written for *Penthouse* containing another tormenting autobiographical question: "Is it better to opt for a series of brief intense love affairs than settle for one mediocre long-term marriage?" Is it better to embrace the goat of lust or the lamb of love? The darling lamb matures into a common sheep, and the goat, to a foul-smelling beast. It is the way of all goats and all lambs.

Cioffari's story, of course, fit the *Penthouse* formula. He wrote, "I kissed her cunt softly—I licked her softly, my tongue sliding down into her long shaft. I sucked the flesh on her thighs in small mouthfuls." The ghost of de Sade made his early appearance in Cioffari's story, in the passages about "forcing her to come," and "I turned her over and shoved my hand roughly up into the crotch of her ass. . . . Her tight asshole was like a sheath, unwilling, holding out on me. I forced my cock down into the private darkness . . . I forced deeper. There was a terrible moan, and I felt her whole body tear, the ripping of flesh from flesh. . . . *Feel it, you crazy bitch. Feel it the way I do! Fuck you, Karen! Fuck you, you tight-assed bitch.* I plunged deeper to the very bottom of her, groveling for her love in the deepest, filthiest part of her."

Perhaps he was still a boy in the swamp, killing rats, where, as Cioffari had written, "if you aren't careful you can be sucked right down into it, into all the oozing darkness and muck, and maybe even die there." In the swamp, the filth and blood and sex and the horror of the killing were blended into one. "I hit it in the back," Allie said of the rat. "Hit it with your bat. . . . You ain't scared of a rat that's got an arrow in its ass, are ya?" And later Allie takes out some pictures he got from one of his father's magazines. They are pictures of naked people doing things to each other. Allie holds up one picture that shows a naked man lying on top of a naked lady. " 'That's what your parents do at night,' he says. 'They do not,' I say, and there were the pictures of ladies with their legs spread apart. 'I can't look at it.' 'That's a cunt,' Allie says. . . . I think of the rats running wild in the swamp. 'We better go back and hunt,' I say."

In the *Penthouse* story, Cioffari, still obsessed with the dark places of boyhood, metaphorical or real, himself a victim, as we all are victims, wrote in yet another story, "We fucked in the webbed shadows of the swamp."

"Do you think that the language is artistic?" I asked Cioffari. Daichman didn't move from his chair. I took a step toward Cioffari, and I could see his spine begin to stiffen.

"I think what is artistic is what is appropriate to evoke the proper emotion in a particular situation."

"Are you proud of that story?"

"I am proud of everything I do, in terms of my writing, because I work on it carefully, very carefully," and I knew he did; the competition for space in *Penthouse*—for space anywhere for that matter—was fierce for any writer. *Penthouse* paid Cioffari only $750 for one of his stories. For Christ's sakes, the shame of it—to permit a man to labor, to reveal himself, to lay it out plain for the world to see for such a sum! And how did the $750 paid for that five-page story, $150 a page, compare to the $35,000 Guccione received for a single page of advertising? How dear is art?

"Well, when one of your students says to you, 'Doctor Cioffari, what is art in writing?' what do you say?" He stared blankly back. The courtroom fell silent and I let the weight of it push down on the witness. Finally he shrugged his shoulders as if the question were nothing. He said he would ask the student the same question the student had asked him. Art created a subjective response, he said. But what if the reader's only subjective response was to engage in a masturbatory orgy—was that art? I asked. Cioffari shrugged his shoulders again.

The themes in his stories created repetitive patterns—young girls, older men, oral sex, and always the voyeur. In *Gallery* he wrote of a detective's passion, "squeezed dry from the surveillance of other husbands and wives." The detective in Cioffari's story found the missing girl and watched, and the *Penthouse* readers watched. "As she worked with her mouth, her hands slowly milked the base of the man's shaft. Several times she stopped to pull her hair to the side with her free hand." The detective took the missing girl himself, and when she shed her clothes in front of him and bared her small, quivering breasts she said, "You want me. The same way Daddy does."

In the story Cioffari called the girl "Angel," and the detective fell in love with Angel, but he was wounded in a gunfight over the child. "You crazy fuck," Angel said as the detective bled to death like the rats in the swamp, and the last words he heard as he died were the girl saying, "He's dead. The poor bastard's dead."

"That's what a voyeur does sexually, is watch somebody in order to get sexually aroused, isn't that true?" I asked.

Cioffari tried to fight back from the stand. "Yes. I don't know that that necessarily makes him a voyeur."

"Now both of these things [voyeurism and fellatio] are also involved in the Miss Wyoming story, are they not? You have a whole nation watching Miss Wyoming perform fellatio on television, isn't that true?"

"Yes," Cioffari admitted.

"I'm interested in knowing whether you also refer to both voyeurism and fellatio in 'Shattering,'" a story he'd written for *Chic* about a man listening through the walls and hearing the "grunts and groans, moans, giggles—the entire chorus of human sexual response," from which the man in Cioffari's story learned what he wanted from his wife. Cioffari wrote, "Clasping his hands around her [his wife's] neck he pulled her face between his legs. 'Jesus, Steven, no,'" the story read. "She twisted her face from side to side, but he held her until her mouth was pressed against him, and he went after her ruthlessly, and he didn't notice when he ceased being the hunter, and became like her, the prey; both of them being eaten alive, blood and bones and flesh, and then she came and the cry she gave was the cry that came through the walls every night of the summer, a cry that shattered and fell through every shade of pain and delight and said yes to everything in the world."

The Marquis de Sade had said it from his prison cell: "I've already told you: the only way to a woman's heart is along the path of torment. I know none other for sure."[2]

I tried very hard to get Cioffari to admit that this had been another story about force and voyeurism. "And doesn't he [the story's character] *force* his mate to perform fellatio on him in your story?" For the first time Daichman weakly objected, saying only that the story spoke for itself. The magistrate overruled.

"I would say, no," Cioffari said. "I don't think that necessarily means she is performing fellatio on him, no," and he denied that the story included scenes of voyeurism and fellatio. "I think that conclusion would be unreasonable from my point of view, yes," Cioffari said. "I always try to make my intent clear as I write."

The same themes reappeared in "Lady Chatterley's Last Stand," the story of a bigoted evangelist who believed that "the future of America depends upon the untainted and unsoiled purity of our women." The preacher ran a school for "virginettes" and had poked his finger into the hole alongside the water pipe where the plaster had fallen away until the hole was big enough that he could watch the little girls, one in particular who "held the forbidden bar [of soap] firmly and inserted its tapered head into her, sliding it in and out, the steady slippery motion like the movement of a hypnotist's chain . . . but the hairless crotch remained in his thoughts."

"When the minister looks through the hole into the shower—would you call that voyeurism?" I asked Cioffari.

"Oh, I think in the minister's case he is trying to police his school." The magistrate scowled down at the witness.

"Well, he watches naked little girls, and watches one of them masturbate, isn't that true?" I asked.

"No, no, no. No, that's incorrect. He does not watch them masturbate. They are washing themselves, and he is trying to determine who it is who is defiling his school." I looked at Cioffari for a long time and then decided to let his answer stand.

"Well, the little girl finally shows herself on top of the sky tower, isn't that right?"

"Yes, that's right."

"And when he goes up there the girl wants the minister to perform cunnilingus on her?" (" 'Eat me,' she said.")

"Yes."

"And then the girl falls off the tower and dies?"

"Yes."

Cioffari admitted he had actually gone to the pageant at Atlantic City when Kim Pring was also there, and he watched—but he insisted he saw only the last night. The Atlantic City paper had carried a prominent story about Kim. Under her picture were the words "Wowing the crowd with her magical baton routine is Kim Pring, Miss Wyoming." The story read: "A National Champion Baton Twirler from Wyoming was the crowd pleaser by far in Tuesday's competition. . . . Miss Pring began her number with two batons, changed to one and ended it flinging three high in the air. Showing the dexterity that earned her the U.S. Twirling Association National Grand Championship in Milwaukee last month, the 22-year-old from Cheyenne balanced a spinning baton on her back, neck, shoulders, and even in her mouth." It took no great creative skills to make the conversion of the baton to the phallus. The metaphor had already structured Cioffari's story for him.

"Do you deny ever seeing such a newspaper?" I asked.

"I deny it," he said.

"Do you deny that anybody ever told you that Miss Wyoming was a baton twirler?"

"Yes."

"Do you deny reading about her anywhere?"

"Yes."

"It was only a coincidence that Miss Wyoming turned out to be a baton twirler?"

"I don't know how else to explain it. I would say, yes, it's a coincidence," and so were all the other similarities between the story and the real Kimerli Jayne Pring. "That's my sworn testimony," Cioffari said. He began to slump in the witness chair. There was a long, sad silence in the room.

"I have no further questions, Mr. Cioffari," I said, and he raised himself at once from the witness chair and walked with quick steps to his seat beside Daichman like one who knew his way back in the dark.

At the recess I said to Kim in the hallway, "What did you think of Cioffari?"

"I don't know how he could say such things," she said.

"I know," I said, "but how did he come off as a person up there on the witness stand?" I wanted feedback. How would a jury see him?

"I'm prejudiced," Kim said. "But I didn't feel sorry for him, if that's what you want to know. You did sorta kill him, Mr. Spence," she said, "and I didn't feel too bad about it after all." She thought about it a minute more. "Actually I felt good about it." She gave her shoulders a shrug. "Yes, I felt very good about it." She laughed, mostly at herself, and then the laugh creases faded.

"It's sweet revenge," I said. "Some say revenge is part of justice."

"Well, anyway, he never should have written stuff like that," she said.

"Do you want me to kill the next witness for you? He's the chief editor of *Penthouse.*"

"I'll just put a hex on him myself and we can go home." She laughed and made small stabs at the air with her fingers. "Hex. Hex," she said. "May he be raped by every centerfold who's ever been in *Penthouse*—on every Thursday."

"You call that a hex? Some witch you are," I said. "And may he never once get it up," I added.

"That too," she said, and we laughed together.

9

After the recess I asked the Sweet Irish Terror, Eddie Moriarity, to do the honors on James Goode, editor in chief of *Penthouse*. I sat back in my chair to watch with pleasure, like a father seeing a son carry on the art. Now, in front of the magistrate, Goode behaved himself, answered the questions, and Eddie pressed the attack with the same intensity as the ferocious Irish Kid in Butte, Montana, fighting for the State Lightweight Wrestling Championship.

"The purpose of the magazine is to entertain the readers, isn't that correct?"

"Yes, it is."

"And the entertainment of readers increases the sale, isn't that also correct?" Eddie was already on a roll, his high piercing voice stabbing at the cornered Goode.

"Yes, it does."

"It doesn't make any difference to the publishers or editors of *Penthouse* that people are held up to ridicule for the purposes of entertaining their readers, and increasing the sales of the magazine, isn't that a fact?"

"Yes."

"Do you believe that the good name and reputation of a person should be protected against false or defamatory statements?"

"Yes, I do."

"Mr. Goode, if Kimerli Pring was, in fact, hurt by the August 1979 publication and the story contained in that publication was about Miss Wyoming, do you care?" Daichman objected but the magistrate overruled him.

"In answer to your question I see no reason why she should be hurt, because we did not name or identify her." Eddie restated the question—did he care?

Goode claimed he couldn't answer because the question presumed she was hurt, but the magistrate ordered him to answer, and Eddie held him to the fire—*did he care* if Kim Pring was hurt?

"I'd have some *mild* concern," he finally answered.

Kim whispered in my ear, "May he also drown in smut."

Eddie was still after him. "Prior to the time that you approved the article for publication, did you think about whether this article would, in fact, hurt Kimerli Pring?"

"No." That was an admission the jury could consider on the issue of malice.

"You gave no thought to it at all, is that correct?"

"None," Goode said as if it were his clear constitutional right not to think.

Then I called Robert Hofler, the senior editor, for the retake of his deposition. Hofler said *Penthouse* played heavily on themes of sex because sex was "interesting to our readers," and homosexual sex between women was also interesting to men; it appealed to their eroticism. I listened to the high, soft, plaintive voice of the man—watched his way of speaking—how he emphasized his points with delicate movements of his hands, and wondered how he could be in tune with the average American male. Perhaps it was I who had been too long in the wilderness of Wyoming, and in my absence a new breed of men I didn't recognize or understand had grown up around me.

Hofler admitted that the exposure of the female body had become more explicit during the seven years he had labored at *Penthouse*. To stimulate sales the ante had to be continuously raised, so lately the magazine published the "gesture series," photos of women obviously engaged in masturbation—well, it was pornography I thought, pure and simple. I didn't need to define it. As Judge Potter Stewart said, I knew it when I saw it.

Pornography did exactly what women complained it did—it degraded womanhood. Susan Brownmiller said it served to "distort the image of the group or class of people, to deny their humanity, to make them such objects of ridicule and humiliation [that was the key word—*objects*] that acts of aggression against them are viewed less seriously." She concluded, "In an age when women are putting forward their aspirations toward equality in a healthy, positive way, pornography is working to increase hostility toward women, and therefore to increase tensions between the sexes. I find this unbearable. . . ."[1]

I, too, found such tension unbearable; it set us apart from women and left us lonely, and pornography degraded men as well. Who could or would deny that? Pornography was *business*, and that seemed to justify it. I began to study this business. In the first place, why does the human male become sexually aroused by something so unalive as a two-dimensional symbol, by these cold and flat and lifeless pornographic photos of *Penthouse*? I saw the startling similarity between this strange phenomenon and the *necrophilic personality* described by Fromm in his *Anatomy of Human Destruction*. Fromm saw the *necrophilic personality* (to be distinguished from the grossly morbid necrophiliac who is obsessed with the love of dead bodies) as someone who "turns his interest away from life, persons, nature, ideas—in short from everything that is alive; he transforms all life into things, including himself, and the manifestations of his human faculties of reason, seeing, sharing, tasting, loving. Sexuality becomes a technical skill ('the love machine')."[2] Fromm used the term *necrophilious quality* to refer "to those individuals whose interest in artifacts has replaced their interest in what is alive, and who deal with technical matter in a pedantic and unalive way."[3] Fromm asserted, "The world of life has become a world of 'non-life'; persons have become 'non-persons,' a world of death."[4]

I thought of Guccione's Evelyn Rainbird Company. How could men take plastic blow-up dolls and the "Forum" letters of *Penthouse* to bed with them as substitute sex partners? Was the explanation to be discovered in the words of Fromm? "Joy, the expression of intense aliveness, is replaced in the *necrophilic personality* by fun or excitement." He said, "Whatever love and tenderness man has is directed toward machines and gadgets. The world becomes a sum of lifeless artifacts, from synthetic food to synthetic organs,"[5] including, I thought, those who cherished and cuddled and cooed over the cold pages of *Penthouse* in preference to the warm, living women of their own species.

From a marketing standpoint these two-dimensional women in Guccione's publications were much more easily converted to money than any live woman. A clever pimp could sell a woman only a few times a night, but Guccione could sell his girls to five million men each month. These women he claimed he loved—whose most private parts he made public to anyone who would pay him a couple of bucks for a look—could harm no one, safely stored away as they were, silent and dead in the pages of *Penthouse*. That, I thought, was the ultimate act of chauvinism—to convert real women to the nonliving for stacking and storing and sale from the shelves of America's newsstands.

Guccione spread his women out for inspection the way any good salesman displays his wares. There she was each month—pages of her—the new quintessential woman, that dead two-dimensional creature staring out at the lonely, frightened men of America, smiling seductively, all orifices opened wide and waiting, beckoning, this object that could never reject him as some pervert, never scorn him as some sexual freak, never harm him, never find him unworthy. And when the reader was through with her she disappeared quietly, faithfully, into the pages of *Penthouse.* Yet when it was over, the American male found himself as threatened, as frightened, as misunderstood, and as lonely as ever.

Hofler assured us that the Miss Wyoming article was humorous—in fact the scene where the man ejaculated in Miss Wyoming's mouth could be interpreted as funny. The jury would appreciate that, I thought. I looked over at Daichman. His head was down, his forehead pasty, his arms folded tightly across his chest.

"If the article in this case was read by someone who believed it to be about Miss Pring, do you believe that the article would, from the standpoint of an editor, hold her up to ridicule and shame?" The question asked for an admission by the witness that the article was defamatory.

Daichman, a bright and alert lawyer, jumped to his feet like a hen flushed from the nest. "Objection!"

"Overruled," the magistrate said. But Daichman's violent reaction to the question alerted the witness to the danger.

"No, I do not," Hofler said.

"Do you think there is any shame in giving a blowjob in the presence of a nationwide TV audience?"

"Not a blowjob where someone levitates off the floor, because it would be totally impossible." Someone in the audience snickered behind me.

"Do you think it would be shameful to be accused of that whether it's possible or not?"

"Objection. He has answered the question!" Daichman shouted.

"He answered the question," the magistrate ruled.

"Do you believe that the pictures in *Penthouse* of women with their vaginal parts exposed and their anuses square in the reader's face are artful?"

"Objection to the form of the question," Daichman shouted again.

"How else can I say it?" I asked.

"Do it the right way!" Daichman shouted once more.

"Tell me what is right."

"That's not my job, Mr. Spence."

"Thank you," I said.

The magistrate broke the clinch. "Overruled."

"Yes, I do," Hofler answered. Yes, everything in the magazine was artful, according to Hofler. I took him through the magazine page by page.

"Do you consider the picture with the woman fingering her clitoris at both the top and the bottom of page sixty-four artful?"

"Yes."

"Would you put your initials there, please?" The witness complied but his face began to redden.

"How about the picture on page sixty-seven, for example, in which the wet clitoris is shown—do you think that is artful?"

"Yes."

"And here is a lady sucking her finger. What does that suggest to you?"

"That she is sucking her finger," he blurted.

"Does it suggest anything else overtly sexual?"

"It could be a penis."

"Do you consider that artful?"

"Yes." His cheeks were as red as a turkey's.

"How about the picture where the vulva lips are spread on page—"

"Yes," the witness interrupted, eager to get it over with, and he initialed the page hurriedly.

"On page sixty-nine where the woman's anus is seen and the hair around the anus is apparent, is that artful?"

"Yes."

". . . and now you say that the Kim Pring article is artful."

"Uh-huh."

"Are you judging it more or less by the same standards that you are judging these pictures?"

"More or less, yes."

I showed him a series of pictures of two women engaged in homosexual acts. "How about this one," where one woman was squirting the other's vagina with a hose. "Do you think that is artful?"

"Yes."

"You don't think that's repulsive?"

"No, I really don't."

"Well, are they in good taste generally, in your opinion?"

"Yes."

"Thank you, sir," I said. Then I quoted Guccione: " 'The little voyeur in every man is only satisfied when invading someone's privacy.' Do you recognize that as a quote from Mr. Guccione?"

"I have never heard him make that statement before."

"Have you heard him make the statement that the business of *Penthouse* is 'the merchandising of sex'?"

"I have never heard that quote before."

"What do you think the responsibility of your magazine is to the American public that it so influences?"

"To be entertaining—to give them informative articles."

"Is that all?" I asked in disbelief.

Is the sole responsibility of one as powerful as Guccione merely to further goad the gonads to keep the money flowing?

Greed is a disease that is dangerous to the people and has become confused with freedom.

I saw little in the *Penthouse* philosophy beyond the acquisitive creed—little commitment to life, little allegiance to love of man, little genuine concern for art. Although Guccione had denied he was a missionary, few would doubt he used the immense power of the First Amendment with all the boundless energy of every zealot. To me, Guccione's mission was to plunder the repressed libido of the American male, to ransack it and loot it, to fleece and strip and rifle it until the American male delivered up his nuts on a platter. To me, his mission was to create the Great American Erection out of the body parts of women, to convert women into pussies and beavers and buttocks and breasts and opened mouths and gagging throats, and to sell the Great American Erection back to the men of America for a ransom.

By late afternoon the depositions of the *Penthouse* people were concluded. Now Daichman wanted his turn. During the recess I tried to explain it to her.

"Kim, they're going to try to pry into your private life," I said, "and there's probably nothing I can do to stop them." She sat listening closely while I tried to explain it. "It's like a case of rape. If the woman asks justice for a rape they'll rape her again in the courtroom. They'll smear her in any possible way."

"I've been expecting it," she said.

"Remember the questions Grutman asked you about being a virgin and Shockey wouldn't let you answer?" She nodded. "Well, they've filed a motion to compel you to answer those questions. Judge Brimmer is going to let the magistrate decide whether you have to answer or not, and I think he'll make you answer those questions," I said, "and if the magistrate orders you to answer they're going to pry into everything—every boy you ever kissed, every boy you petted—whatever you've done with any boy. Christ, whatever it is, they'll ask, and then they'll subpoena every one of the boys, and they'll ask them too. They'll ask for all the details."

"They're going to do that in the courtroom in front of everybody?"

"Yes," I said.

"You mean the newspaper can sit in there and print every question and every answer?" She looked stunned.

"The press claims its right under the same First Amendment. I don't think the magistrate will order the press out." She thought for a long time, biting first her top lip and then the bottom. She uncrossed her legs like a small girl and slid down in her chair in dejection. "Well, what am I supposed to do, Mr. Spence?" She looked open, vulnerable, defeated. "That isn't fair."

"The law isn't always fair, Kim." The law is like God.

"That means *Penthouse* can print whatever they want to about a person because if the person ever sues them they can ask the person all those personal things in public and embarrass a person so bad she'll never go near a court—I mean that isn't right."

What could I say?

"Well, I don't understand that." She stopped, then started again. "Who made those laws?"

"If you don't answer, the judge could throw your case out," I said.

"And everybody gets to watch?"

I didn't answer.

"That really preserves my rights of privacy, doesn't it?" She looked at me for a long time.

Then, like a kid who thinks his father is the toughest man in town, she said, "You're the best lawyer in the world. You can change the law."

"Well," I began thinking out loud, "if you don't answer, the judge can throw the case out and we can appeal."

"Could we get the law changed if we appealed?"

"If we could talk the Tenth Circuit Court into holding for us. But nobody talks the Tenth Circuit into very much."

"But there's a chance?"

"Yes," I said. "A small chance. But if we won in the Circuit Court, *Penthouse* would take us up to the United States Supreme Court."

"I'm not going to answer those questions then," she said as if she'd suddenly come to her decision. "I don't care what they do." She'd quit biting her lip. "It's none of their business." Her face suddenly burst into a big grin. "They'd be disappointed with my answer anyway. My sex life hasn't been anything to write home about." Then as suddenly she was serious again. "And we'll change the law!"

Tough old warriors aren't supposed to get teary.

"Okay, you've got a deal," I said. "Okay! We'll take this case all the way to the United States Supreme Court if we have to." I jumped up and slammed my fist down in the air. I felt it! "All the way!" Kim jumped up too and hugged me. I didn't care, and I hugged her back.

Then Daichman had begun arguing to the magistrate in Grutman style but in his own sharp voice. "We claim, Your Honor, that there are at least three legal reasons why we are entitled to venture into this area—really the heart of the lawsuit: If the plaintiff, Miss Pring, was in fact sexually promiscuous, was unchaste, she is not entitled to the same amount of damages that she would otherwise be entitled to as a virginous, lily-white type person—as she describes herself. Secondly, she claims to be chaste, and if she is not as she claims, this raises a clear question of credibility. Thirdly, truth is always a defense. If she is sexually promiscuous, then those allegations she claims are defamatory are *not* defamatory if they are true—and these matters are before the court only because the plaintiff herself has voluntarily elected to put these matters at the forefront of the case through her complaint. She cannot make the allegation of defamation and at the same time deprive us of our defenses, and as Judge Brimmer says, 'The road runs both ways—you have the same rights to have questions answered as Mr. Spence has.'"

I tried to persuade the magistrate that the law must be just—that the law should not allow *Penthouse* to further invade Kim Pring's privacy in defense of having robbed her of her privacy in the first place.

"The questions posed offend me, Your Honor," I said, "and if she must either answer or lose her case, I will ask to have her case dismissed, because the price of justice is too high. This is a tactic of theirs, Your Honor, because if all who are injured with such a libel as this must submit to further injury by such questions, no one will ever seek justice. She is put between a rock and a hard place," I said. "She must either give up her lawsuit as any decent person would, or suffer further insult. *Her personal life isn't an issue.*"

I told the magistrate that the *Penthouse* lawyers claimed the article was fiction and hence could not be about her. "Guccione has said, 'This is not an article about Kim Pring. This is fiction. This is not about any real person.'" If the article was not about a *real person*, why should they be permitted to seek information about her *real life* for a defense?

"I wouldn't permit my daughter, or my wife, or my friend, or any loved one to answer these questions. Kim has the same rights to dignity and to justice as any other person." I argued that reputation is not proven by actual fact but by what other people believe the facts to be.

"Take Mother Superior in the nunnery, for example. Her reputation is virginous. One cannot disprove her reputation by attempting to prove facts of some secret affair with the village priest. What she in fact *does* and what her reputation *is* may not be the same. The law is settled that evidence of specific acts of misconduct are not admissible to disprove a good reputation. If you were to change places with me, Your Honor, you wouldn't permit your client to answer these questions either."

But Daichman argued back. "The plaintiff doesn't have all the rights and the defendant none." He claimed I was attempting to compel the court to enforce a different set of rules for the plaintiff than for the defendant. "This was not a rape case," he cried. He accused me of appealing to the emotion and sympathy of the court. "He says he will drop the case if required to answer—I would say that is purely an improper gesture on the part of counsel. I am not a betting man, but I would bet that if this discovery were permitted, the plaintiff would not drop her case—that she would pursue it with vigor as Mr. Spence, as her advocate, has done since its inception."

"Yes," the magistrate Beaman began, delivering his decision. "Yes. The plaintiff is in this case by choice. She had the choice of not coming to the court." But didn't she have to defend the *Penthouse* charges against her or stand convicted of their defamation? Her name was all she had. She was not in court voluntarily—she had no choice.

It was too late for such picayune points. The magistrate clutched the book and spoke clearly, confidently, out of the authority of centuries. "Whether the answers solicited in the deposition as to her promiscuousness or chastity are admissible is not the issue. The defendants do have the right to *discover* such things."

"But I think if you require her to answer these questions, she will refuse," I warned quietly.

"If she refuses she is in contempt of court," the magistrate warned back.

I walked slowly toward the bench. When I was within a few feet of the man I said, "Then you can throw her in jail if you want to. I think she is prepared to go to jail—or you could dismiss her case. Your ruling is improper. The Tenth Circuit won't support it—I doubt that Judge Brimmer will—he may out of loyalty to you, but I doubt it. If you want to dismiss her action and throw her into jail, you can." I motioned to Kim. The judge looked over at her. She was biting her lips again.

The magistrate sat mute. Then Daichman stared menacingly at Kim, who sat next to me. The courtroom was filling with curious spectators. Kim looked awful.

"This is only a deposition—not a trial," I said to the magistrate. "The spectators—this should be conducted in private!"

"Well, I talked about that with Judge Brimmer, Mr. Spence," the magistrate said. "He informed me that anything that goes on in the courtroom is public—the door remains open. We will proceed. Miss Pring, take the stand," he commanded.

The rights of a witch are few. She must face her tormentors. It was the law. They would hoist her up on the rack once more for her confession.

Kim Pring took the stand and faced Daichman, who rushed now from his table clutching a handful of notes. Even before he arrived at the podium, he began his examination.

"Miss Pring, the questions I am about to ask you may be somewhat embarrassing. I am going to try to be as courteous and considerate as possible. I don't want to upset you; I just want to get answers." Perhaps he was concerned with his own discomfort. He cleared his throat.

"Are you a virgin, Miss Pring?"

10

The *Malleus Maleficarum, The Witches' Hammer,* was the bible of the witch trials in Europe. There were over thirty editions printed between 1487 and 1669, and it was the ultimate revered authority not only because of its papal blessing but because its authors were men of distinction. James Sprenger was dean of the Faculty of Theology at the University of Cologne, and Heinrich Kramer the prior of the Dominican House and a distinguished inquisitor. Academicians and clergy had once again joined hands. The *Malleus* was implicitly accepted by Catholic and Protestant legislatures alike. Next to the Bible, it was *the* book, the most widely read and acclaimed of all authorities.

Guccione claimed for *Penthouse* a similar influence over the minds of American men. The August 1979 issue, in which the Miss Wyoming article appeared, sold exactly 4,642,535 copies, and Guccione, Pope of The Church of the Sexually Oppressed, claimed five readers for each copy of this holy scripture—all in a single month.

The *Malleus* is perhaps the most unabashed journal of misogyny ever published. Even the writings of Sade pale in its presence, for the *Malleus* takes its authority not only from the Holy Scriptures but from ancient and classical literature as well, even from etymology. "Wherefore in the many vituperations that we read against women, the word 'woman' is used to mean the lust of the flesh."[1] The authors quoted Socrates and Cicero, the latter's *The Rhetorics:* "The many lusts of man lead them into one sin, but the one lust of woman leads them into all sins; for the roots of all woman's vice is avarice."[2] The *Malleus* said of women, "She is a liar by nature . . . and her voice is like the song of the sirens, who with their sweet melody entice the passersby and kill them," then quoted from Proverbs, "Her mouth is smoother than oil; that is, her speech is afterwards as bitter as absinthium."[3] Saint Bernard observed, "Their face is a burning wind, and their voice the hissing of serpents," and, the *Malleus* declared, "When it is said that her heart is a net, it speaks of the inscrutable malice which reigns in their hearts."[4]

The *Malleus* established the proofs for the prosecution of women as witches. All women were suspect, especially the aged, the poor, and the helpless, but none were safe from an accusation, and accusation was equivalent to death. Witches were women who had given in to the devil, had intercourse with him, and had become his slaves. They were responsible for every evil that might befall man—his sickness, his death, the deformities of his children, the failure of his crops or his libido. Therefore, the prosecution of witches was not only justified, even holy, it was obligatory, failing which man himself was subject to a charge of heresy and his own soul placed in jeopardy.

The *Malleus* outlined in detail the steps required in any trial of a witch. Of course, before she was burned her confession must be obtained, and it was no sin that trick and deceit, even torture, were used to extort it, for no sin except sorcery itself was a sin against the devil. She was to be stretched out on that horrid "engine of torture," the most private parts of her body, even those parts she had not closely inspected herself, pushed up for common scrutiny like a feature from the pages of *Penthouse* in full, vivid color. Nothing can be hidden from justice. It was the solemn duty of the judges to see, their duty to stretch her to the very soul where the guilt is squeezed out, an almost imperceptible groan at first, nothing more, then the desperate grunts and the urgent nodding of the head, the head nodding, nodding, faster, and finally the confession bursting out in one unrestrained scream after another so that it was plain to see, even to the woman on the rack, that she was, indeed, a witch. The procedures of the *Malleus* were tested, proven.

The magistrate opened the book once again and turned the pages rapidly but quietly so as not to disturb Daichman in his questioning. Kim's hands were seized to the arms of the witness chair, her knuckles protruding like distant peaks, her lips and the underlying muscles and tendons of her face and neck stretched tight. I saw the eager faces of the people gathered in the courtroom like a mob come to a hanging, come to savor the spectacle, to cherish the nasty snapping of the neck at the end of the bitter rope, come to be repulsed by the body's silly swinging. Yet we are not satisfied. Before death there must be an utter degradation of the condemned, like savages who smear dung on the body of the victim before the stoning. I looked up at the face of the magistrate but it told me nothing.

Kim's time had come.

Could she hold up under Daichman's interrogation and the magistrate's injunctions? If she faltered once, if she gave them one small innocuous answer in order to relieve the pressure for a moment's respite, it would all be over, for they would wedge in and tighten down on her, and the questions would come faster and harder in a frenzy for the kill. They would get very specific, of course. Every private act would be pushed up so close our eyes would blur and the smell of it would fill our nostrils. The crowd knew it, adored it. They waited.

"Do you want a drink of water, Kim?" I asked, interrupting Daichman's flow.

She didn't seem to hear me. Daichman began anew.

"I object to this whole line of inquiry," I interrupted again, but the magistrate overruled me without looking up from the book he was carefully studying. Now he closed his book respectfully, held it next to his chest, and dropped his chin to its edge as if to support his head. He peered down at the witness with the look of a man satisfied with his position. The magistrate was ready.

Now Daichman, sounding almost bored, asked the question again.

"Are you a virgin, Miss Pring?"

Andrea Dworkin had said, "Silence is what women have instead of speech. Silence is our dissent during rape unless the rapist, like the pornographer, prefers to *hurt me*, in which case we have no dissent. Silence is our moving persuasive dissent during battery unless the batterer, like the pornographer, prefers to *hurt me*."[5]

Yet the *Penthouse* lawyers had the right to defend their client. This woman was their adversary in an adversary system, and as the *Malleus* admonished, if the advocate fails to perform his duty forthrightly, "he would be more damnably guilty than the witches themselves."

Daichman waited patiently for Kim's answer. She turned to me, but all I could do was look back. Finally Daichman said, "I ask the court to direct the witness to answer the question."

"The witness will answer the question," the magistrate said. Kim looked up at His Honor, but he averted his eyes and stared out over the heads of the gathering audience. Perhaps he knew the warnings of the *Malleus* about how witches, getting first sight of the judge, "have been able so to alter the minds of the Judge or his assessors that they have lost all their anger against them and have not presumed to molest them in any way, but have allowed them to go free. . . ." The *Malleus* prescribed, "If it can be conveniently done, the witch should be led backwards into the presence of the judge and assessors [the predecessors of our jury]" in order that the judge might be relieved of seeing the pitiful face of the accused with those beseeching eyes looking up at him, because it was said in the *Malleus* that such eyes of a woman under torture were only the orbs of the devil and had the power to amend the mind of the judge.[6]

I knew if she even mumbled an answer to Daichman's first question it would all be over then and there that late afternoon in the courtroom of the United States District Court in Cheyenne, Wyoming.

"I refuse to answer," Kim said in a surprisingly clear strong voice. But Daichman pressed on.

"Miss Pring, have you ever performed fellatio?" I jumped up, but before I could say anything Kim gave her reply.

"I refuse to answer that question also."

"Miss Pring, this court is directing you to answer that question," the magistrate said, still gazing at the back wall. When Kim remained silent the magistrate suddenly looked down at her.

"I'm sorry. I won't answer that question," Kim said. It took courage to confront the law, and the judge is the law and we all must obey it. We are trained to accept authority, not to stand against it.

Now I whispered, "I object, Your Honor." Perhaps he could hear that better than the shouting, but the magistrate stared on as if his ear were tuned to the medieval echos of the *Malleus:* "One must not be too quick to subject a witch to examination [torture] . . ." because "unless, God, through a holy angel, compels the devil to withhold his help from the witch, she will be so insensible to the pains of torture that she will sooner be torn limb from limb than confess any of the truth."[7]

It was, of course, against such common acts of torture that the Fifth Amendment was added to the Constitution. But the people have no memory of those times.

"It is the order of this court that you answer these questions," the magistrate repeated.

"Miss Pring, have you ever had cunnilingus performed upon you?"

Daichman asked. My God! I jumped up again, and started toward Daichman. He looked quickly in my direction and froze. The magistrate, without a word, hit his gavel. It stopped me short. She was silently weeping, looking at me. I couldn't cut her down.

"I'm sorry. I refuse to answer that question," she sobbed.

She was clearly a witch—her magic stick, the baton—the spells she cast over whole audiences—now her refusal to answer—had she not laid curses on her enemies, her evil hexes?

Confess, witch.

The *Malleus* explains why some confess easily while others do not. It is because of "a natural hardness of heart; for some are soft-hearted, or even feeble-minded so that at the slightest torture they admit everything, even some things which are not true; whereas others are so hard that however much they are tortured the truth is not to be heard from them; and this is especially the case with those who have been tortured before, even if their arms are suddenly stretched and twisted."[8]

"The witness shall answer the question," the magistrate ordered again.

"These are very personal and very private questions that are only between myself and possibly my loved ones, and I refuse to answer any of these questions," Kim said. Then she began to cry quietly again, this time into her hands. She wiped her eyes and tried to stop the crying, tried to concentrate on her hands as if they alone were listening.

The magistrate motioned me to the bench.

"Off the record," he said in a very kind voice, "I hate this as much as you do. But I think the law is against you, Mr. Spence, and it's my duty, as painful as it is, to call it as I see it. I'm sorry, believe me, but she's got to answer these questions. Don't you think we could spare everybody a lot of trouble if she answered and got it over with?" His voice sounded reasonable. I hesitated and he continued. "Her answers aren't necessarily evidence that can be admitted at the trial. I don't need to tell you that. That will be up to Judge Brimmer. But as of now, this is discovery, and she has to answer Mr. Daichman's questions. Can't I call a recess here? Can't you talk to her, reason with her? Perhaps if you explained it." The *Malleus* advised, "Then let her be released again at someone's earnest request, and taken on one side, and let her again be persuaded. . . ."[9]

"No," I answered the magistrate at the bench in a loud enough whisper that Kim could hear. "She won't answer those questions, and I won't instruct her to do so. Can't you see what's happening here? This is a twentieth-century courtroom. This witness is being raped with the sanction of the court!" Then the magistrate shrugged his shoulders and nodded to Daichman to proceed.

The *Malleus* gave further instructions. "While she is being questioned about each several point, let her be often and frequently exposed to torture, beginning with the more gentle of them, for the judge should not be too hasty to proceed to the graver kind, and while this is being done, let the notary [equivalent to our court reporter] write all down, how she is tortured, and what questions are asked, and how she answers."[10] Now the court reporter's nimble fingers recorded it all.

"Miss Pring, are you chaste?" Daichman asked.

"I refuse to answer that question."

"You are ordered to answer the question," the magistrate said.

"I refuse to answer the question."

The magistrate stared out into the audience, his jaws now set, the skin at his temples stretched tight. Daichman stood stiff as a cross. The *Malleus* gave clear guidance. "If after being fittingly tortured she refuses to confess the truth, he [the judge] should have other engines of torture brought before her, and tell her she will have to endure these if she does not confess. If then she is not induced by terror to confess, the torture must be continued on the second or third day," and in the meantime, "the judge should take care that during that interval there should always be guards with her, so that she is never left alone, for fear lest the devil will cause her to kill herself."[11]

These judges, these executioners, these advocates themselves were men of honor. The town executioner, James Underwood, who was said to have presided over the burning of over seven hundred witches, was described as a quiet man, a citizen thought to be gentle and generous who did his job dispassionately and with competence. It is said he grew a garden, that he loved children, and that he lived to be ninety-four. He was in every way a respected humble public servant. The judges were the same—men who smiled kindly at the people they served, men in whom it was natural to repose great confidence, for they were learned men, scholars, Christian men.

I thought of pulling Kim down and dragging her out of the courtroom leaving the magistrate and Daichman staring there, but it would only give the magistrate grounds to hold me in contempt, and a lawyer in jail is good to no one, and there was no use asking for a recess.

Daichman waited for Kim to compose herself. I watched the magistrate. Women have always cried in court. They have cried there for centuries. They were crying in court before America was even discovered, crying in 1484, the year of the first edition of the *Malleus*. But the propensity of women to deceive with tears was well known, and even the *Malleus* provided an answer. "In passing sentence the Judge or priest may use some such method as the following in conjuring her to true tears if she be innocent, or in restraining false tears. Let him place his hand on the head of the accused and say: 'I conjure you by the bitter tears shed on the cross by our Savior the Lord JESUS Christ for the salvation of the world, and by the burning tears poured in the evening hour over His wounds by the most glorious Virgin MARY, His Mother, and by all the tears which had been shed here in this world by the Saints and Elect of God, from whose eyes He has now wiped away all tears, that if you be innocent you do now shed tears, but if you be guilty, that you shall by no means do so. In the name of the Father, and of the Son, and of the Holy Ghost, Amen.'[12]

"And it is found by experience," the *Malleus* instructed, "that the more they are conjured the less they are able to weep, however hard they may try to do so, or smear their cheeks with spittle."[13] Yet the *Malleus* finally admitted, "It may be objected that it might suit with the Devil's cunning, with God's permission, to allow even a witch to weep; since tearful grieving, weaving and deceiving are said to be proper to women."[14]

We have hated our women, oh, hated them through the centuries. It is like a deadly poison homogenized into the milk of every son. We have hated women out of the very scriptures of Christian love, hated them in the words of the apostle who denounced women as "evil of nature painted with fair colors." We have hated women in the dialogue of Valerius to Rufinus, who saw women as a monster of three forms: "Its face was that of a radiant and noble lion, it had the filthy belly of a goat, and it was armed with a virulent tail of a viper."[15] We have even argued that God hated women, for were it otherwise He would have created Eve out of her separate dust instead of from an imperfect rib of Adam, a rib bent in a contrary direction to man's, and "since through this defect, she is an imperfect animal, she always deceives."[16] Socrates spoke out of a marrow-deep malignancy against women. As to marrying them he said, "If you do not, you are lonely, your family dies out and a stranger inherits. If you do, you suffer perpetual anxiety, querulous complaints, reproaches concerning the marriage portion, the heavy displeasure of your relations, the garrulousness of mother-in-law, the cuckoldom and no certain arrival of her heir."[17] History cannot remember when we did not hate women.

The *Malleus Maleficarum* finally brought these classic arguments for the hatred of women into a single authoritative collection, and its immediate success, like that enjoyed by Guccione with the introduction of *Penthouse,* sprang from the same deep sexual roots. *Penthouse*'s pontifications lauded sexuality of almost every kind, while the *Malleus,* with equal passion, condemned all but the barest procreational sexuality as the lust of the devil.

Guccione and Pope Innocent VIII, with zealousness of similar intensity, fondled that forbidden subject from opposite points of view, but for identical purposes, to merchandise their respective dogmas, to enhance their positions of influence, and to reap the plenty of power. Guccione argued that *Penthouse* was the redeemer of man's libido by releasing his repressed demons, while the *Malleus* sought to protect man's soul from an original invasion by those same evil demons, and none dared declare any disbelief in the existence of witches. The *Malleus* decreed, "The question arises whether people who hold that witches do not exist are to be regarded as notorious heretics, or whether they are to be regarded as gravely suspect of holding heretical opinions. It seems that the first opinion is the correct one," and heretics, too, were burned at the stake.[18]

As the *Malleus* set forth the criteria by which the identification of a witch could be established, so *Penthouse* proclaimed its own sacred doctrines for what was to become acceptable as the new sexuality—whatever pleased man was glorified as individual taste, whatever aberrant fetish, whatever twisted compulsions—all were unreservedly lauded, and those who protested were held up as modern heretics whose petty minds and bigoted spirits stood in the way of the freeing of the sexuality of the new American male.

Daichman began anew. "Have you ever touched the male penis with any part of your body?" Kim sat silent.

"The court instructs you to answer the question," the magistrate ordered.

"I will refuse again."

Then, after Kim had refused to answer other questions, Daichman moved the magistrate that she be held in contempt of court, and her case be dismissed. The magistrate thought it over. Finally he spoke.

"Well, there is no such thing as contempt before a U.S. magistrate," he said. "It is contempt of *court*. I can only make my recommendations to Judge Brimmer. He must decide." The magistrate leaned back in his chair and folded his hands.

Then I walked to the bench and said, "I want the court to clearly understand that Miss Pring's refusal to answer is a moral and personal issue based upon her constitutional rights. I hope you make that clear to His Honor, Judge Brimmer—that it is only after serious thought and not out of any sense of disrespect to either you or Judge Brimmer or to the court that she refuses to answer these questions. She has a right to receive justice without a betrayal of her dignity." I helped Kim down from the witness chair. She could barely stand. She grabbed on to me and wept freely now, and I looked up at the magistrate.

"She has a right to justice without being raped in court." I looked at Daichman and the spectators as she sobbed, and I wondered if everyone felt satisfied. As I held her, the courtroom silently emptied.

"Come on, Kim," I said, "let's get the hell out of here." She was like a kid who had been crying too long, gasping in quick spasms, and she couldn't speak. I grabbed her by the hand and led her out of the courtroom. The door shut behind us noiselessly, muffling the last sounds of the *Penthouse* lawyers still lounging in their victory. Now Judge Brimmer would surely dismiss our case.

11

I glanced at Kim, her head down, her mouth set, her feet stamping the concrete. She'd stopped the sobbing, thank God for that. Then we both realized it was silly to be running down a peaceful street, and we stopped and stood staring at each other. You'd never know she'd been a beauty queen, and Lord knows what she saw when she looked at me. We were like children who had escaped the monster, laughing children in the gentle sun of Indian summer, and having understood it was all a bad dream, there was nothing to say, and she had driven off in her yellow Volkswagen. I watched her stop at the intersection on the yellow light, like any good citizen does before the light turns red.

I walked on down the street alone. I walked past small dilapidated houses with bare yards cooped up in sagging chicken-wire fences. An old man with a rumpled face sat on a broken porch soaking up the last of the sun. He stared smilelessly at me as I walked by. These days were the bright, the numbered days of fall—days of high schoolers, who now came bouncing, hollering, tramping, yelling at the light yellow air, one hopping backward. I moved over. The cars fled up the street in mindless frenzy to places from which other cars were fleeing. Daichman was in one, a man driving I'd not seen in court. The man was pounding the steering wheel, laughing, and Daichman was laughing too. I kicked a beer can on the sidewalk. Kick.

And rattle.

Kick hard again.

I saw a pack of dogs snarling and tearing at each other over the bloody carcass of a skinny bitch, lately in heat, smashed flat in the street, flat as the "girls of *Penthouse*" are flat on their hard slick pages. An adolescent dog sniffed at the corpse, nuzzled under its tail while the old dogs fought on. They ripped hunks of hide and hair from each other in terrible convulsions. The dead bitch bled silently from the mouth. The golden light of fall flickered and gleamed on the hair on the back of the humping adolescent. A yellow warbler flitted by. I found my car, and at the intersection I ran the yellow into the red in front of the high schoolers.

"Fuck you!" one hollered.

Back at my room the red message light was on. It had no rights over me. I flopped down on the bed and stretched out my aching body, like any weary beast after a fight. I stared up at the cottage cheese and glitter ceiling.

I'd fooled myself. Perhaps I'd taken this case out of my own story-book dreams and Grutman had been right. I could hear his talmudic voice now better than ever. "It is a case created by counsel out of the contrivance of his own fancy." I could imagine Guccione's laughter, and I could see the tortured face of Kim Pring.

This young woman knew nothing of the law. She had her own dreams of justice. I saw Justice standing there, a woman, for Christ's sakes, a blindfolded imbecile with those farcical scales hanging from her hand, weighing nothing, and when *Penthouse* asked Lady Justice that Kim Pring be stripped and stretched on her engines of torture, Lady Justice nodded her consent, and if rape be the taking of that which is private and not freely given, then when *Penthouse* asked to rape Kim in a court of justice, Lady Justice faithfully nodded again.

Justice is the daughter of History. Like any good child she is obedient to her father. His ways are hers—she loves the past, adores it, and thereby old sins become sacred. Justice also loves the dead; she named her stillborn child in honor of her father—she named it Precedent! How is it then we lay such cruel expectations on her—that she should deliver justice to the living?

The red message light kept blinking. It was Schuster wanting to know what had happened.

Back at Jackson I told Schuster, "I think Judge Brimmer is going to order Kim to answer those fucking questions, and I'll tell you one thing—Daichman has me figured wrong. The judge can dismiss this case before I'll put her through that again."

"Well, maybe it is the law," Schuster said, his brow wrinkled, his face worried. "The law is the law, you know."

"The law is not the law," I hollered. "The law is only what judges say it is. This trial is the worst fucking obscenity yet." I felt powerless. Schuster got up and began pacing too.

"That's right," Schuster said. "People have to take a stand some-time, and this is the time. If the judge orders her to answer those questions, we'll appeal. I'll write a hell of a brief."

I paced back and forth across the atrium, flailing the air. "When the appeal comes up we'll be looking up at those judges like a bunch of lepers wailing at the fucking gates of justice. We can cry and plead, and gnash our teeth till they're ground to the gums. To the judges it's just another opinion someone has to write, and they're al-ready two years behind. And for two years when I get up in the morning, I'll argue the case all over again in the mirror and wonder what they're doing with my case today, which will be lying on one of their desks under forty other cases where it's been for six months." I stopped to catch my breath. "You know who should be on television? The appellate courts—back in their secret chambers when they make their decisions—so the people can watch those judges play their games."

"Yeah," Schuster said.

"No," I said. "They'd be too boring to watch."

But we have to believe in the system whether the system is believ-able or not, like people believe in God. We have to believe in it.

I railed on. "Those judges will never let some poor Wyoming girl keep a lot of money. Judges aren't rich, and nobody else is going to get rich, by God. That's why we keep judges poor—so they won't let poor people get rich off the banks and corporations."

I was too hard on judges. But they'd been hard on me. I knew most judges tried to do the right thing. Most wanted to go home at night feeling good about themselves, but instead they probably went home hollering to their women about how the day went and how some other judge was fucking things up—stealing justice and playing games. I ought to feel sorry for them—locked up there like a bunch of monks in a monastery, stuck for life with each other. You can di-vorce your wife, but a judge can't divorce a fellow judge on his court. It's hell for a judge being cooped up forever with some bastard on the court he can't bear one minute longer, which probably accounts for their decisions being so dead and dull, so mean and so often against the people.

Once I looked up through the glass of the atrium roof and a crow flew over. Sometimes in the early fall the geese flew over instead. They were a better sign.

"It's all a silly game and it takes two to play a silly game," I said.

"We ought to get out of the case." Schuster didn't even answer. We couldn't get out of the case. I'd made my promises. "The only people who'll get rich in this case will be the *Penthouse* lawyers."

"Justice isn't getting rich," Schuster said.

"Well, justice is stopping *Penthouse,* and the only way to stop a corporation is to take a lot of their money—take their blood—bleed 'em. You know that."

"Yeah," Schuster said.

"You can't put corporations in jail."

Schuster didn't answer.

"You hit them with a big money verdict. Then off in the distance—as if the sound comes all the way from New York, you'll hear the most God-awful scream, and the sound will grow louder and louder, the most piteous, agonizing scream ever to fall on human ears, and you will know it's the scream of a giant corporation finally brought to justice because you took its money." I couldn't stop.

"Schuster, these characters from *Penthouse* are arguing to Judge Brimmer that if a woman ever had *any* sex they can libel her all they want—they can say she fucks chickens in church! The only person in the history of the law who would be immune under that logic would be the Virgin Mary, and that's not because she's the mother of Christ but because she didn't have any sex life."

"She wasn't a very well-rounded person," Schuster said.

"If the Virgin herself were on the stand they'd argue they had the right to go into the Immaculate Conception."

"I'd like to cross-examine the Holy Mother myself about that," Schuster said.

I hollered some more, and Schuster heard me out, and I paced another fifteen miles back and forth across the atrium, and we also argued back and forth, and finally we decided to file a motion asking Judge Brimmer for authority to amend our complaint to get rid of the words that were causing us all the trouble. Instead of alleging that the *Penthouse* story created the impression that Kim was "unchaste" and "promiscuous"—which invited *Penthouse* to prove she was, in fact, either or both, since truth is a defense—we could allege that "the *Penthouse* article created the impression that the plaintiff committed fellatio on her boyfriend and coach in the presence of a national television audience at the Miss America pageant." We could play the game too. They were only words. But a suit for libel is a war waged with words, about words, and people bleed and people are destroyed in these wars of words. "That should stop all that bullshit about *virgo intacta* and motions for physical examinations and all those goddamned questions," I said.

Daichman came screaming into court with a seventeen-page brief labeling our proposed amendment a "semantic sleight of hand in order to avoid and obstruct essential discovery in this action." He wrote, "Plaintiff's sexuality is very much at the forefront of this litigation and directly relevant to issues of mitigation of damages, credibility and truth." He sounded like a budding Grutman. He cited well-known cases holding that embarrassment alone is not a sufficient reason to deny a party legitimate discovery. "If she [Kim Pring] is truly ashamed of her past conduct, that is a problem created by no one but herself, for she never should have engaged in that conduct in the first place." Perhaps Daichman had been reading the *Malleus*. Five hundred years ago it decreed, "It is in the power of the human will either to accept such evil influences or to reject them, and this a man [and a woman] can always do by invoking the grace of God."[1] To languish in the loins of the devil is of our own choosing. The *Malleus* conceded that young girls were "more given to bodily lusts and pleasures," proclaiming the devil works through "their carnal desires" and through their "pleasures of the flesh."[2] But the power to resist is always available through the grace of God, and failing to resist the devil, she had, as Daichman said, none to blame but herself.

To further strengthen his argument, Daichman enfolded *Penthouse* within the sacred cloth of the Constitution. "If every plaintiff who brings a baseless lawsuit against a media defendant were to succeed in preventing legitimate discovery, that would encourage legal blackmail and impose an intolerable chilling effect upon First Amendment freedoms."

That afternoon I locked myself up in my own office, taped a DO NOT DISTURB sign on the door, took the phone off the hook, and composed forty-nine pages of carefully drawn questions for Guccione to answer. Even Grutman couldn't evade the questions. They quoted what Guccione had said about himself and his business and what others had said as revealed in the record of the public media, statements he could now either admit or deny "forthwith" as the judge had previously ordered.

Thirty days passed. No response—not a whisper from Grutman. Silence.

I filed a motion asking the judge to order Guccione to answer and the judge did, finding that if there had been valid objections they had been waived under federal procedure because Grutman had not filed timely objections.

Finally Grutman answered a few of my questions, but despite the judge's ruling that he had waived his objections, Grutman now objected anyway, claiming that the questions were "irrelevant, annoying, burdensome, improper and privileged and were not calculated to lead to discovery, or were overbroad."

"Christ Almighty, Schuster, did you see this?" I was shouting in the atrium again weeks after I had served the interrogatories. "Grutman says he doesn't have to answer my interrogatories."

"That doesn't surprise you, does it?" Schuster said.

"Well, but wait a minute. Listen! I've already been to New York to take the deposition of Guccione once—cost us five, six thousand after we paid the court reporters, the television cameraman, the hotel, the airplane, the—"

"Yeah, yeah," Schuster said.

"And Guccione didn't answer anything, right?"

"Right."

"We got nothing for our money—for our trouble. Then we have to go to Cheyenne and argue to the judge to make Guccione answer. That costs us too. They drag our asses clear across the state and we have more expense, hotel, air fare—"

"That's the game," Schuster said.

"Then the judge says they at least have to answer our written questions, and I sit down and carefully compose all these questions—"

"Yeah," Schuster said, starting back into his office.

"Wait a minute. Listen. The judge orders them to answer and they still don't. They file these fucking objections." I waved the papers at Schuster. "Grutman says the court's ruling requiring Guccione to answer 'results in an egregious burden which no civil litigant should be compelled to bear.' Listen to that—egregious! Who the hell can even say it? And he wants more time to answer. He's already had over thirty days and hasn't even tried to answer them!"

"Yeah," Schuster said. "Well, if anybody knows that game, you do. You've played it better yourself than any lawyer I ever knew." Schuster waited for me to admit it, and when I didn't say anything he turned and went back into his office.

Then Judge Brimmer entered another order. This time he ordered that Guccione needn't answer my questions inquiring into his alleged connections with organized crime, and alleged obscenity indictments in Canada, and a supposed pending warrant for Guccione's arrest in Fulton County, Georgia, and whether he was offended by being referred to as a "Pope-baiter," as some writer had called him, and other such pesky questions. I'd also asked questions about Guccione's experience with fellatio. If Kim was asked such questions about her sex life, then Guccione could tell us about his, but Judge Brimmer thought these seemed too personal and "perhaps constituted harassment rather than discovery." However, the judge ordered Guccione to answer the balance of the forty-nine pages "forthwith."

In about two weeks a few more answers dribbled in. Guccione voluntarily chose to answer two of the questions the judge had ordered out. He claimed he was offended at being called a "Pope-baiter," and didn't think there was still a warrant pending for his arrest in Fulton County, Georgia.

I had asked him many of the same questions Grutman forbade him to answer at his deposition in New York—did the doctored *Hustler* photograph, an obviously fictional parody depicting Guccione engaged in "buggery," as Grutman chose to call it, hurt him? Now he answered that the *Hustler* libels held him up to public scorn and ridicule, had damaged his reputation, and he said he was entitled to punitive damages because, he claimed, "*Hustler* acted recklessly, viciously, spitefully and with ill will." Yet from the beginning, Guccione claimed *Penthouse*'s Miss Wyoming story was also a fictional parody. How did his case against *Hustler* differ from Kim's against *Penthouse?* If he was hurt, wasn't she?

He admitted to seventeen suits that had been filed against *Penthouse,* ten of which were still pending, the others having been either settled or dismissed by court order. He also admitted that one woman, who claimed her picture had been used without authorization in a condom ad, had brought suit against *Penthouse* and that the case had ended in a verdict in her favor for $100,000. Pages of details were provided concerning this body of litigation from which it began to appear that suing and being sued was, indeed, a part of doing business at *Penthouse.*

"Hey, Schuster," I hollered again from the atrium. "Listen to this." I started reading some of Guccione's answers. "This guy's memory is worse than mine. He says he can't remember if he said 'The little voyeur in every man is only satisfied when invading someone's privacy.' That's a quote. And he says he doesn't remember saying 'The vagina is enjoying a vogue at the moment because it's like a brand-new toy—people never saw it before.' "

"Did he really say that?"

"It's a quote," I said. "And listen to this one: 'As soon as people know what the vagina is about, they'll be able to integrate it back into the woman again.' What do you think of that one?"

"Well, he's probably right," Schuster said.

"Yeah, but wouldn't you remember saying it?"

"If I said something that quotable I probably would," Schuster said.

"And listen. He said, 'All men are basically voyeurs, and all women exhibitionists,' but he doesn't remember saying that either."

"Well, he ought to at least take credit for his good quotes," Schuster said.

"We've spent all this time and money, and when the man's finally forced to answer he just says he doesn't remember. I could spend the rest of my life trying to get straight answers, and I'd get nothing—nothing until he wants to remember something that'll help his case. Then his memory will be like a mainframe computer."

"That's the game," Schuster said again as if that settled it once and for all. "The law's a game."

Guccione did admit that he used props in his photography "which give the reader the impression that he's peeping into a secret, forbidden, intimate moment and invading the privacy of the naked pet's life." If his chronic theme was to invade someone's privacy to provide erotic stimulus for his readers, I wanted to show he wouldn't hesitate to likewise invade Kim Pring's privacy. I got that much, anyway, and he admitted it was his policy to "constantly change, provoke, excite, and convince the reader that he will see something that he has never seen before." How could he deny that? The Miss Wyoming story was but one more step in *Penthouse*'s commitment to a continuous upping of the ante in fiction for the sexual thrill. No one could predict where it would all end. The lust for something more shocking, more obscene, for something harder and deeper, something crazier, something that would make each man's secret demons scream and dance—that was the open secret to the continued growth of *Penthouse*. Pornography is a growth industry.

Guccione couldn't remember saying his time was worth something like $40,000 a day nor that he'd told a national publication he was worth between $150 and $300 million. He didn't know the value of his Evelyn Rainbird business, which sold all those plain and fancy dildos and the rest of an ignominious assortment of "sexual aids," and he couldn't remember saying that the take on *Caligula* would be around $100 million, or that he had told the press after the movie had been banned in Massachusetts that it was hard to put a dollar figure on how that publicity would improve the film's total earnings. Trouble makes money. Neither could he remember whether he paid a million dollars for his mansion and had spent another three or four to renovate it, and he didn't know the value of his treasure trove of paintings by Picasso, Chagall, Degas, van Gogh, Renoir, and Matisse—it was all in the public press and the estimates of their worth was over $3 million, but Guccione couldn't say and wouldn't guess. Under oath his memory failed him.

"Schuster," I hollered. Schuster came popping out again, trying not to seem irritated. He had important deadlines to meet. He waited to see what was coming next. "If the system won't work in a case as clear as this, if all the legal maneuvers get in the way, all the lawyer games, if *Penthouse* wears us down so we can't even get our case prepared and into court, if we can't make this system work in a case like this, if the whole damned system has degenerated until this is just the usual course of business for Corporate America, well, we might just as well find it out, once and for all, because if justice is only this kind of game, I don't want to play it anymore."

"Don't act like this is all news to you," Schuster said. "Lawyering is a business too, and you've been pretty damned successful at playing those so-called games yourself."

"Maybe I'm getting old," I said.

Then Schuster was kind, as finally he always was, and said, "Maybe just wise. You'll feel better in the morning."

"Listen to me. If we're only pawns, just idealistic, glassy-eyed pawns as blind as Justice, if lawyers are used up by the courts, by the system to make it look like there are honest cases and sincere lawyers and worried, caring judges and innocent, compassionate juries and fair trials for every citizen, but if it's all just so much horseshit—if it's all an illusion like these fucking 'Penthouse girls,' if all we're really doing is providing fodder on the people's side of these cases so the game can go on, so the likes of *Penthouse* can do whatever it damn well pleases—well, maybe we better find out about it. I tell you I don't feel like playing these games anymore."

Schuster looked sad. "You've lost your faith. Try trusting your own profession."

"Is it worth trusting, Schuster?" He didn't answer. "Well, let's find out," I said. "Let's go all the way on this one."

"We go all the way on all of them," he said.

Then for some reason I couldn't think of anything more to say. "Why don't you turn the light on in there, Schuster?"

"It is on," he said and he disappeared into the dark again.

Then one day Judge Brimmer entered another order. He ruled we could amend our complaint and therefore "issues relating to the plaintiff's personal sex history *are and should be irrelevant.*" On his own motion he relieved Guccione from answering any interrogatories dealing with his personal sex life. "The same standard should apply to the plaintiff." The road runs both ways. Judge Brimmer had overruled the magistrate.

I called Kim and told her the good news.

"Thank you," was all she said and then there was a long silence. Maybe she couldn't think of anything else to say. Finally she said, "I knew we'd win. That will sure make my mother happy. She got sick over this."

For Christ's sakes, I should have trusted the law like Schuster said. I started to feel guilty. I loved the law. I'd devoted my whole life to the law. How could I have become so sour, so cynical? I must be getting stale.

"Hey, Schuster," I hollered out in the atrium.

"Yeah?" Schuster stuck his head out.

"We won." I handed him the judge's order, and he read each word carefully to make sure I was right. Then he gave me that wiseacre Yaley grin of his. "Well," I said, "we still have to get by Grutman's motion for summary judgment." Maybe the judge was just cleaning up his record before he threw the whole case out so the court of appeals wouldn't reverse him for making a woman answer a lot of dirty questions. That judge was no fool. We weren't in court yet. Over half of all libel cases filed in the federal system are thrown out by judges before a jury even hears them. Besides, as the old cowboy in these parts says, "Anytime things seem to be going better, you're probably overlookin' somethin'—important."

12

Rosemary McIntosh, looking pale as a fresh-plucked quail, eased into my office sideways and tiptoed toward me. No one tiptoes in the office, especially Rosemary. She looked sick like a daughter about to tell her father she has just wrecked the family car. Carrying an envelope in both hands, as if it were too weighty for one, she thrust it at me.

"I didn't want to tell you, Gerry," she began, "but I thought you ought to know as soon as possible. When I heard the piteous tone in her voice and saw her sad face and her merciful eyes I knew whom the letter was from. Every lawyer knows. We do not speak of it, not even to each other, but the heart starts to pound, the head grows light, and there is a sudden rush to the temples. Instantly I reviewed my multitudinous sins as a lawyer, and all the others as well. The hostile face of every brother of the bar burst into memory, for since Cain slew Abel, brothers have been the most treacherous of friends.

Grievance committees are feared—more than the judges of the court—more even than God himself, for God, they say, can hear a sinner and forgive, but nothing approaches so nearly a perfect vacuum as the heart of a member of the Grievance Committee. Moreover, they possess the terrible power to begin that abhorrent process by which a lawyer may be stripped of his license, without which a true lawyer becomes the walking dead.

What false charges lay within this pristine envelope? I ripped it open and extracted the crisp white letter. Grievance committees, always composed of the bluebloods of the bar, will decide whether the accused lawyer is to stand trial for the offense charged, and should they subject him to that frightening ordeal, the same committee will also become the prosecutor, the judge, and the jury. A common thief is entitled to be tried by an impartial jury of his peers. No murderer, no rapist, is put to trial behind secret doors by his enemies or those who may benefit the most by his conviction.

I was shaking. The dreadful epistle bore the date of November 12, 1980, and began: "The purpose of this letter is to lodge a formal complaint against Attorney Gerry Spence and to request an immediate inquiry and hearing concerning Mr. Spence's misconduct in a case pending before Judge Clarence Brimmer, entitled *Pring* v. *Penthouse*, C 79-351." It was signed "Norman Roy Grutman."

"Eddie," I hollered. Eddie came bursting out of his office into the atrium like a cock dumped into the ring looking for the other rooster.

"What's goin' on?" the Sweet Irish Terror hollered back. I handed him the letter, which he read a page at a time in a sweep powered by an intelligence his rough exterior belied. "Who does this son of a bitch think he is?" He shook the letter back at me. "I'll knock the son of a bitch's head right off his fuckin' shoulders. How does he come off with this bullshit?" Grutman charged I had violated every subdivision of the disciplinary rule in question and concluded, "This is no peccadillo or trifle to be lightly disregarded."

The complaint was about my having given an interview to *Rocky Mountain Magazine*. "Christ, I didn't know they were going to put a picture of Kim and me on the damned cover," I said. Grutman attached the story and the full-color cover, which revealed me staring out with the cold eyes of the gunfighter, wearing my big hat and fringed buckskin shirt, my jaw set, my hand hanging loosely at my side. Kim, blond, like something made out of marble and polished, was standing behind me, and behind both of us were the Tetons pushing up. It was a hell of a picture and the story was the lead story in the magazine; the caption in bold white across the deep blue of the Wyoming sky read:

GUNNING FOR JUSTICE

LEGENDARY LAWYER GERRY SPENCE AND A WYOMING BEAUTY QUEEN TAKE ON "PENTHOUSE" FOR $100,000,000

Grutman complained to the Grievance Committee: "Patently, the article could not have been written and, based on our investigation, was not written, except at the instigation of or with the cooperation and encouragement of Mr. Spence."

"What is this 'no mere peccadillo' shit or however you say it?" Eddie asked. I tried to explain. Tony Polk, a reporter from the *Rocky Mountain News* in Denver, had wanted to write a story, not about the case but about me, and I thought that might be all right—might give me a chance to say some things I thought the public and other lawyers should hear about this bloody business. Polk had also asked me some questions about the *Penthouse* case and I'd given him some general information, facts available in the records at the courthouse—that's all. But if I couldn't do any better job explaining this to the Grievance Committee than I did to Eddie, they'd have me for sure—they'd claim I was trying my case in the press, and Lord knows what else. Christ, they'd hang it on me.

And I'd been in battle against some of the committee members before—fought one of them thirty years ago in a suit I'd brought against Ford Motor Company for a young Chicano who, as a result of his ride in a new Ford automobile, ended tangled up in a barbed-wire fence along the side of the road permanently paralyzed from the waist down. Those were the days when I still had that fresh strut and I was mean. I'd also had bad trouble with another one of the members, also years before. His firm represented the bank, and I sued banks. There were the other usual committee members who represented banks and insurance companies, most of them leaders in the establishment bar. But before them, I knew I'd be like any person who tries to explain: The harder you try, the more guilty you seem, and if you don't explain, well, then you're guilty too.

"He's just tryin' to get ya all upset and your attention diverted from the case," Eddie said. "If he can get ya defendin' yerself against the bar he figures ya won't have enough left to fight the case." He thought a minute. "That's a pretty smart move—gettin' the Wyomin' Bar to help him fight. Fuck 'em."

"Yeah," I said. Eddie looked at my face and he knew what I was feeling—I play by the rules—their rules. The test of every true lawyer is whether he can win playing the rules, because if you can't, then a win isn't a win. It's just something that makes you sick.

I didn't say anything more—didn't know what to say—and then Eddie asked, "Do you want me to kick the shit out of him?" Then he laughed. It's hard for a hard-rock miner to tell you he loves you.

Practicing law is like an animal roaming in the forest—if you don't starve to death first, there's some bigger beast behind that rock or that tree waiting to tear you apart and rip your guts out and feed on you for a week. If your own clients don't get you, or the judges don't, then other lawyers will, especially if you're down. But I wasn't down.

In the quiet of my office I read Grutman's complaint. He wrote: "We believe Mr. Spence has escalated past flagrant improprieties to a point where he now requires appropriate professional discipline and censure.... After discounting Mr. Spence's self-proclaimed flamboyance and the eccentricity of his personal style, it is plain that, since the inception of the lawsuit in question, he has rambunctiously endeavored to create a circus-like atmosphere out of the Pring case, and to surround it with myth-making hoopla concerning himself.... The general metaphor that prevails throughout the article is that of a 'shoot out' with Mr. Spence depicted as the 'good guy in the white hat' and me and my client as the Eastern Establishment villains who are to be 'killed' in the denouement of the horse opera."

I could hear Grutman dictating the complaint, his voice finally dropping to a whisper when he said, "If Mr. Spence had done in England what he has done, or caused to be done in this article, he would be in prison and probably stripped of the right to practice law."

I wrote Norman Roy Grutman a nice letter. "I admire the lyrical literary quality of your grievance," I said. "When we come to the inevitable place in our confrontations which will permit us, we ought to sit and visit. I think we might enjoy it." Then I added a postscript: "This is no mere peccadillo or trifle lightly to be disregarded. Enclosed please find silver bullet." I taped a silver bullet to the letter and posted it. Then I wrote my apologies to the Grievance Committee that their valuable time had been diverted to this struggle. It was merely Grutman's tactic. He was defending by offending.

In the article I had confessed my fear of Grutman's great ability, telling the author that Grutman was, indeed, an extremely fast, articulate adversary, the best of the black-hat gunfighters I'd seen. The speed of his mind and his extraordinary imagination were such that he could keep a straight face before a United States district judge and with dignity and manner take that obscenity-laden magazine and magically transform it into a manual for every decent young American male to live by and, at the same time, portray Kim Pring as a shameful strumpet who'd sued this great journal out of ugly avarice and an insatiable yearning for publicity. I gave the devil his due.

Rocky Mountain Magazine wrote: "Spence knows he has a dangerous adversary in Norman Roy Grutman.... A thick, fleshy-faced man with thin hair and horn-rimmed glasses, a graduate of Yale and Columbia, he speaks with precision and eloquence. He dazzled Gerry Spence for nearly an hour that day in Cheyenne.... Grutman spoke extemporaneously, spicing his speech with phrases from the three foreign languages in which he's fluent. He used no notes and stumbled not at all. He was one of the finest speakers Spence had ever heard. . . ."[1] It was all true.

Polk continued: "Spence returned to Jackson feeling disappointment and dread, like a gunfighter who knows he must face a man he isn't sure he can beat. The scuttlebutt at the federal courthouse in Cheyenne is, in the words of one clerk, that 'Gerry Spence has met his match.' In the days after the Cheyenne hearings, Spence's mood was dark. He had seen the movie *Caligula* which was produced by Guccione, and he kept wondering what kind of a man could expend so much power and money to produce a film of such hideous inhumanity, such demented debauchery, with its scenes of incest, necrophilia and rape. He also kept rehashing in his mind his confrontation with Grutman, hearing the eloquence in his opponent's speech like a recurring nightmare."[2] That was also true.

Grutman's position was that it is unethical for a lawyer to speak his piece in the public press on the merits of a pending case. I agreed with him, and I hadn't. But Grutman told a reporter for the *Rocky Mountain News:* "This case [Kim's against *Penthouse*] is a contrivance dreamed up by plaintiff apparently as a publicity stunt or an effort to extract money from a large corporation."[3] Later, Grutman complained to the Grievance Committee about my having sent him the silver bullet. "You will observe," he pointed out to the committee, "that there was affixed to it [the letter] a silver bullet. Either Mr. Spence is deranged or he thinks he is the 'Lone Ranger.' In any event, the bullet, together with the letter, attest to the menace and grandiosity which Mr. Spence exudes and which has given rise to the grievance I have submitted to you." He made a production of my picture on the cover. "Mr. Spence is bedecked in his finest 'gunslinger' garb, consisting of a Wyatt Earp cowboy hat and fringed jacket."

The Gerry Spence story in *Rocky Mountain Magazine* was the ground from which Grutman would now launch a new series of diverting attacks intended not only to intimidate me but to sop up my energy and the court's as well. I thought his tactic was to create massive smokescreens, and generally to raise all kinds of hell in side issues, and even before the grievance matter was concluded, Grutman filed a motion to change the place of the trial to the United States District Court for the District of New Jersey.

New Jersey! He wanted to move the war more than a thousand miles from home, drag our asses and those of our witnesses to a foreign forest because of one insignificant, innocent article that said more complimentary things about him than me. He was hollering at the top of his lungs, quoting from the story at length, charging not only that I had promoted it, but that the local atmosphere had been so poisoned against the defendants they could not possibly receive a fair trial in Wyoming, referring to what he now called "that startling and blatant instance of advance pretrial publicity."

By the end of December 1980, over a year after the case had begun, there were nineteen pending motions before the court, creating a file over a foot thick and causing one to speculate whether the case was being tried by the pound. Among the undecided pending matters still remained *Penthouse*'s motion for summary judgment.

"You know, Schuster," I said one day, "I think we're in deep trouble. Grutman is making good moves. He's taken the offensive away from us. A lawyer should never be on the defense in any case. That's a cardinal rule, especially for the plaintiff. Always be on the offense, never on the run—always attack. We're on the run, Schuster. I don't like it. I'm not in the practice of running. If Grutman can make the judge sick enough of this case—he has to rule on every one of those motions—he might grant Grutman's motion to move it to New Jersey just to get rid of the whole mess. I can hear the judge thinking: 'I don't need to spend the rest of my life wrestling with those New York lawyers over a bunch of crap like this. As fast as I decide something, they dump in a new batch of motions until a man could drown in them. Who wants to drown in all that crap? Let some judge back east take care of his own. I don't need it.'"

"It's going to be all right," Schuster said with a kindly smile. "The judge can handle it." He walked over and began to reach his hand out for my shoulder and then hesitated. Finally he patted me gently like a doctor reassuring a hypochondriac.

Within a few weeks Grutman filed a motion demanding a gynecological examination of Kim. We countered, asking for a mental examination of Guccione. The United States Supreme Court had held that the state of mind of the writer might be inquired into on the issue of malice. Why not the publisher? We were prepared to argue that a mental examination of Guccione might well lead to the discovery of relevant evidence for the trial pertaining to "the state of mind of Guccione in connection with his editorial processes," and thereafter both sides filed numerous motions seeking every conceivable advantage and sanction provided by the rules of procedure, each side trying to maintain the advantage, each trying to gain the initiative in a war of paper.

Grutman had made good moves, and further, he was ripping huge holes in our finances. How much of his money is a lawyer supposed to gamble on behalf of his client? A doctor doesn't advance his patient's hospital bills hoping the client can survive the operation and pay him back. Grutman was making it hard for us to meet the costs he was running up with these tactics. But Grutman and I saw one thing alike—a good lawyer should take the initiative.

On December 15, 1980, Grutman dropped his bomb, which was intended to make the fallout too dirty and the landscape too desolate and depressing for Judge Brimmer to survive as judge in the case. Grutman filed his motion to disqualify Judge Brimmer as the presiding judge. The grounds stated were that "Judge Brimmer has a personal bias and prejudice against the defendants." It was a bomb, all right, because now Judge Brimmer had to pass judgment on himself, the hardest of all judgments for any honest man to make.

No man, judge or not, relishes admitting any such accusations as bias and prejudice, and in this case Judge Brimmer certainly wouldn't enjoy making any concessions to some fancy-talking New Yorker. Moreover, if Judge Brimmer took himself off the case, the entire proceeding would be derailed because he would have to find another judge from another district to come in, and that would take time and cause further serious delay.

To support his motion to disqualify Judge Brimmer, Grutman had attached an affidavit undoubtedly authored by Grutman himself but signed by Guccione. It began: "It is with great reluctance the defendants have been compelled to resort to a disqualification motion in order to protect their constitutional right to due process and a fair trial. I sincerely believe that Judge Brimmer is a highly qualified, able and learned jurist and presume that he dispenses impartial and evenhanded justice in every other case that comes before him. . . .

"In this case, it appears that without being aware of it, Judge Brimmer has drawn upon his own personal emotional feelings and moral attitudes which have caused him to act in a manner contrary to his own fine sense of judicial responsibility. . . .

"With all due respect to Judge Brimmer, I believe that he has manifested a personal bias and prejudice toward the defendants because of the forthright and often explicit way in which *Penthouse* magazine deals with matters of a sexual nature."

The preliminary bowing and curtsies finished, Grutman now

struck boldly at His Honor: "Judge Brimmer's conduct since the inception of the action has reflected neither fairness, impartiality, patience nor restraint. Instead, from the very outset, he has made rulings which have been consistently unfair to the defendants." Then followed twenty pages of diatribe, as though *Penthouse* were throwing the boiling oil over the wall on the enemy after which it also threw over every other thing lying loose, the garbage, the garbage cans—the lids—everything. He claimed the judge had attacked both Grutman and Daichman, that the judge had rushed Grutman into an abbreviated time schedule in the case, had made unwarranted findings that they had "thwarted discovery," that the judge had, "without any basis in fact," called Norman Roy Grutman a liar. Guccione's affidavit further accused the judge of having improperly required Guccione, a non-party, to answer interrogatories which were "horrendously offensive, obnoxious and voluminous," the judge having required Guccione to answer "utterly irrelevant and immaterial questions," these "preposterous interrogatories" having been served in violation of the Federal Rules. It was all under oath—Guccione's—and was filed in the public record.

Grutman attacked Judge Brimmer for having overruled the magistrate's order that Kim be required to answer their questions about her private sex life. It was as if Grutman had taken up the venerable arguments of the *Malleus* itself. The good and the Christian were entitled to the confession of witches. How could the judge have ordered that woman down from the rack? "This is likely the only libel action in the history of Anglo-Saxon jurisprudence where a plaintiff alleges defamation of her reputation, but the defendants are precluded by the court from challenging her reputation. . . . The effect of this inexplicable ruling is to prevent the defendants from defending themselves, and to create an irrebuttable presumption of virtue and chastity in this plaintiff."

Again the affidavit complained about the story in *Rocky Mountain Magazine.* "The entire article is written with a western theme that focuses around this lawsuit as a shootout at the O.K. Corral with Mr. Spence and his client on the side of right and virtue and the defendants and their lawyer on the side of evil and injustice. Spence is lauded as 'the imposing westerner, champion of the little guy' and 'the only lawyer in Wyoming whose name is a household world'; his client, of course, is sympathetically portrayed as 'a sweet, wholesome woman' with 'blonde curly hair, wide cheeks and a ready white smile' who was 'born with a clubfoot' and resorted to baton twirling as a 'good therapy after corrective surgery.' I am belittled as a 'paunchy middle-aged man in the skintight silk shirt whose medallions and chains jangled against his bare chest' and Mr. Grutman is characterized as my 'legal hired gun.'

"The carnival atmosphere engendered by plaintiff's publicity ploy is typified by the concluding paragraph of the article: '[Spence] will slouch toward his rendezvous with Grutman, Guccione and his personal destiny, armed with the murderous talents of earlier western gunmen and secure in his belief that the killing he must do will make the world a better place to live in. The myth of the West lives.' "

Then Grutman analyzed the court's rulings on the various motions of the parties, concluding that Judge Brimmer favored the plaintiff over *Penthouse* in a numerical count of his rulings, as if justice were portrayed in the court file only when both sides have won and lost equally. The affidavit concluded, "It is with both the greatest of reluctance and respect for the court that we make the instant motion," but how does one respect any court guilty of such charges?

I walked out into the atrium and hollered at Eddie and Schuster.

Schuster said, "I've looked at Grutman's motion and his motion is insufficient in law. The precedents are clear. You can't get rid of a judge merely because you don't like his rulings."

"He made another pretty good move," I said. "Either the judge will grant his motion just to get rid of this case or, if he refuses to step down, Grutman will take him to the Tenth Circuit Court of Appeals and the case could get stuck up there for Lord knows how long."

Eddie laughed like an Irish urchin wrestling out back with some other young ruffian. "But this time he made a crack and got his own ass caught in it. He's gonna lose in the Circuit and then he's gonna have ta come back here and try this case in front of the same judge he's insulted—gonna have ta face the same bear he bit in the butt."

"Well, boys," I said, "I beg to disagree. Grutman made another no-lose move. Even if Judge Brimmer doesn't take himself off the case, and even if Grutman loses in the Circuit, he still wins, because when the case comes back to Judge Brimmer for trial, the judge will have to lean over backwards to prove he's *not* prejudiced."

But I hadn't convinced them. They worked in the system too, and had to believe in it. Maybe it was enough for them that the system worked occasionally, the way a slot machine pays off once in a while to keep the players coming back.

* * *

On December 31, 1980, Judge Brimmer filed his order disposing of all nineteen pending motions. He ruled for us on *Penthouse*'s motion for summary judgment. He also overruled almost all the other motions of both parties, proving that the road still ran both ways. He pointed out that he himself, *sua sponte*—on his own motion—had relieved Guccione from answering interrogatories that were of a personal nature and "with respect to the balance of Guccione's interrogatories," the judge wrote, "while so many of them are answered, 'I don't remember,' or 'I'm not certain,' or 'I don't know' that one becomes skeptical of the bona fides of deponent in submitting such answers, yet the court is not convinced that at this stage it would materially assist in preparation of the case for trial to require further answers."

He overruled Grutman's motion to change the place of trial to New Jersey finding that "as of June 30, 1980, that District had 3,220 civil and 241 criminal cases pending while this court, as of November 30, 1980, has 251 civil cases and 33 criminal cases pending divided between two District Judges. It is unthinkable and in fact at least frivolous, if not silly, to request this court to add this case to the burden of the overworked judges of the District of New Jersey." Then the judge quoted from one of our affidavits that showed the total circulation of *Rocky Mountain Magazine* in the four Wyoming counties from which our jury would be selected was 556 copies as compared to a total population of those same counties of 82,632. "The Court is of the opinion that it is unlikely that the members of this jury panel will have either read the article concerning plaintiff's counsel, Mr. Spence, in the November-December issue of *Rocky Mountain Magazine* or will have been influenced in any way by it."

Would Judge Brimmer get off the case? He found that he knew none of the parties; he was not a subscriber to any of the publications of the defendants; he had never read *Penthouse* magazine previously and therefore maintained no feelings of antagonism and bias against the defendants. The Court found that the complaint of *Penthouse* "really boils down to a complaint by defendants' counsel that he didn't get to have his way. While it is natural for unsuccessful counsel to grumble over adverse rulings, a motion for disqualification on that account is not only astounding but is also bad precedent. In each instance, I have decided the pretrial matters as I have seen and understood them, without keeping 'score' as to how many rulings were for either side. . . . The Court will note that from the very first conference telephone call in this case, Mr. Grutman has evidenced a willingness to reargue matters decided by the Court and to aggressively and disputatiously reassert his positions. That may be the way to do it in New York, although I doubt it, but such conduct is not customary in Wyoming and has required the court many times to 'turn the other cheek' out of a sense of patience with him. I do not think that I have been anything less than fair, impartial and tolerant of the actions of Grutman and Daichman and believe that there are not many judges in the country who would have been that tolerant. I suspect that these oft-repeated charges of harshness and bias are part of a trial strategy designed to get the court to 'lean the other way' to prevent repetition of them, and I do not care to do so."

The Court found Guccione's affidavit was legally insufficient because it showed no factual basis for any claims of personal bias or prejudice stemming from an extrajudicial source other than what the Court had learned from participation in the case. "At best the claims of bias and prejudice are conclusory only."

Judge Brimmer cited many cases and quoted from them at length and finally ended his order by saying, "It is indeed true that this court has not regarded the conduct of counsel as correct and proper. Defendants' counsel has intentionally thwarted and delayed discovery. Plaintiff's counsel has sought to bring in the case extraneous issues concerning the view and morality of the publisher of *Penthouse*. Defendants' counsel were remiss in failing to file a timely objection to interrogatories. . . . The Court does not intend to let Messrs. Grutman, Daichman or Spence direct the course of this case, nor will the Court bow to their attacks and serve at their will. The motion to disqualify must be denied. . . . The Court anticipates that Messrs. Grutman and Daichman will endeavor to appeal the ruling on the motion for disqualification by a writ of mandamus, and the Court, by combining that ruling with the other procedural matters, hopes to give the Court of Appeals a more accurate and true picture of what has really been happening in the administration of this case."

Judge Brimmer was correct. He'd seen it all coming as clearly as we, and he'd stood by his guns. Eddie and Schuster were right. When the judge got his hair up he was intransigent as hell. Then, as everybody predicted, Grutman promptly took Judge Brimmer to the Court of Appeals on a writ of mandamus, a lawyer's fancy way of asking the court for its order commanding Judge Brimmer to step down.

The case was now in the hands of the yet greater gods.

13

On January 22, 1981, Grutman for *Penthouse* sued Judge Brimmer in the Tenth Circuit Court of Appeals in Denver in a case entitled *Penthouse International, Ltd., and Philip Cioffari, Petitioners*, v. *Clarence A. Brimmer, United States District Judge for the District of Wyoming, Respondent*. With its numerous exhibits, the petition consumed two hundred pages, enumerated the petitioners' grievance against Judge Brimmer in fifty-seven numbered paragraphs.

"This application is not a 'sour grapes' response by disgruntled lawyers or litigants who have disagreed with the Court," Grutman asserted. "The amazing hostility directed toward the defense of this case cannot logically be attributed to anything other than his disavowed—but nonetheless deep-seated and very real—antagonism toward *Penthouse* magazine on account of its sexual orientation and explicitness." After many pages he came to what I thought to be the heart of his complaint—Judge Brimmer had set the trial to begin on February 9, 1981. With sounds of panic now clearly discernible, Grutman argued that Judge Brimmer had set the trial of this case at a time when he, Grutman, had been previously ordered to try another case in the Supreme Court of Nassau County, New York. But that was only a state court case. Judge Brimmer presided over a more prestigious federal court, which the judge believed had the right to preempt the calender of state courts, leaving Grutman to complain, "Judge Brimmer, nevertheless, remains adamant that this trial must go forward on the day he has arbitrarily selected, even though he is aware that by so ruling, he has stripped the defendants of counsel."

Shortly before Grutman had filed his petition in the Circuit against Judge Brimmer, Grutman called asking that I agree to a continuance. For a man who could cover you with mucilaginous charm the way a French chef spreads his irresistible sauces, Grutman's phone call was demanding, short, mean. It was obvious that he didn't want a favor at all, and as soon as I read his petition to the Circuit Court, the nature of his new strategy became immediately clear.

He complained to the Circuit: "Upon hearing this [that the trial was set on February 9], Mr. Grutman immediately telephoned Mr. Gerry Spence, plaintiff's counsel, on January 19, 1981, to request him to consent to a modest continuance. Riding on the back of Judge Brimmer's rage, however, Mr. Spence obviously finds it preferable to go forward on February 9." Grutman needed to prove to the court, as a condition to his argument, that he had requested a continuance from me and had been refused.

"I misjudged Grutman's game," I said to my men. "He's dug himself in for one last-ditch stand—either Brimmer goes or he goes. He's shooting everything he's got right now. If he wins in the Circuit, we'll have to reargue three fourths of what Brimmer has already ruled on to a new judge, and it'll be this time next year before things get in shape again for another trial date. Then Grutman will have a whole new set of moves—and that's all assuming he hasn't talked the new judge into throwing us out of court. But if Grutman loses in the Circuit, that means the case goes to trial on February 9, and our friend Grutman will never try this case. He can't. Not now. He's filed his affidavit swearing to the Circuit he has to try that other case in New York and can't get out of it. He's locked himself in. If he loses in the Circuit, he's out of the case for good."

"He's afraid of it," Schuster said, sitting there on the table looking like a Yale professor about to address his class. "He's representing a smut peddler in front of a conservative Wyoming jury that won't like any part of Guccione or *Penthouse*." Schuster had it figured out right.

"Yeah," Eddie said, "but you forgot his biggest problem. He's afraid of you, Gerry. He doesn't think he can beat you."

"I'll tell you something, Eddie," I said. "I don't think Grutman's afraid of anybody. If anybody's afraid of anybody, it's the other way around."

"I disagree," Eddie said. But I'd looked at myself a lot—made a lifetime study of myself. I didn't know how I looked on the outside to others, but I knew how I was on the inside where people on the outside couldn't see. I didn't look fierce in there. I felt my own fear. I never walk into a courtroom without feeling it, no matter who is on the other side.

"The thing you forget is that Grutman isn't any different than anybody else," Eddie said. "He's got his feelings too. He may never admit it—probably not even to himself—but I say he's afraid of you, and that's why he's getting out."

"No," I said. "He wouldn't say that case was set in New York if it weren't true."

"Well, come on, Gerry," Eddie said. "You know as well as I do that *he* has the choice of which case he's gonna try. It's *his* choice. I say he's scared a ya, because if he loses this case to you, he could also lose his biggest client—*Penthouse*. Why should he take that chance? He's taking care of himself. He's got himself in another one of his no-lose positions. If he can't get Judge Brimmer off the case and get the trial postponed, then somebody else will have to try this case and somebody else will have to lose it and take the blame. He's got himself a built-in excuse."

"And he's got a built-in appeal if we win at trial," Schuster said. "He'll claim that some unprepared lawyer had to come in at the last minute, and that's why *Penthouse* lost—Judge Brimmer made them lose. Maybe the Circuit will agree with him."

"Nah," Eddie said. "Those judges ain't gonna agree with *Penthouse* on anything." He laughed his high laugh. "I can smell a big kill comin' a mile off. Grutman finally outsmarted himself."

In his suit in the Circuit against Judge Brimmer, the thing that stuck in Grutman's craw the worst was that Judge Brimmer had taken Kim Pring down from the rack. Grutman complained bitterly that Kim had willfully disobeyed the magistrate's order and would not accept Judge Brimmer's explanation that he'd relieved *both* Kim and Guccione from answering questions about their private lives. Grutman said such "limp reasoning" was preposterous—shocking. "Mr. Guccione's sexual experiences have nothing at all to do with this case—plaintiff's sexual experiences are what this case is all about!"

Grutman spoke the truth. Men have always been able to stash away their little obscenities in secret places, but it had always been their right, their dear, clear right to strip women naked, to invade their privacy in the public courtroom. Grutman pleaded that the Circuit Court must stop Judge Brimmer from making a mockery of justice and abandoning longstanding articles of faith in the law.

"Without the aid of this court, a grave miscarriage of justice will surely result."

Grutman argued that the judge's position on the law was false and rose out of his own deep-seated prejudice over *Penthouse*'s explicit treatment of sex. That, according to Grutman, was what caused the judge to stray from the true doctrine with his unprecedented ruling that *those questions* need not be answered by Kimerli Jayne Pring. That was heresy, was it not? The *Malleus* defined it in the language of Augustine: "A heretic is one who either initiates or follows new and false opinions. Heresy is a form of infidelity, and infidelity exists subjectively in the intellect, in such a way that a man believes something which is quite contrary to the true faith."[1]

Grutman argued: "The plaintiff in truth could be as wanton and promiscuous as the 'whore of Babylon,' yet the effect of Judge Brimmer's decision is to declare by judicial fiat that her reputation is impeccable and unassailable. Plaintiff has voluntarily placed her reputation at the very forefront of this lawsuit, yet the Court has bizarrely foreclosed defendants from even discovering from her the crucial facts about her reputation for which she demands $100 million dollars."

Schuster researched the law, and our young associates made certain discreet inquiries here and there and checked the records, and we filed affidavits setting out the facts they discovered. We showed that Grutman had known of the trial setting in this case at least since December 4, 1980, and that just a few days before, on December 1, 1980, Grutman had told the opposing counsel in the New York case that he couldn't try that New York case in February because he had an "absolutely irrevocable engagement" in California in another libel case, which turned out to be a suit brought by Louis Nizer and other lawyers for Rancho La Costa against *Penthouse* for having reported in one of its pieces of so-called "investigative journalism" that Rancho La Costa was a watering hole for the Mafia. The trial in our case was set to begin on February 9, and the La Costa trial was set for February 10 and had been for several months, and the case was expected to last for many weeks. In Grutman's motion to postpone our trial, filed December 30, there wasn't the vaguest hint that the La Costa case even existed. At the same time, the New York case was to begin on January 26 and was to last a number of weeks as well. It now seemed apparent that Grutman was juggling three trials scheduled during the same period and had apparently made no effort to set either of the other two trial dates aside. It also seemed clear enough that Norman Roy Grutman was making his choices.

Now Schuster came bursting into my office. "He's made a fatal error! He has to include Guccione's affidavit in his papers to the Circuit. It's absolutely required," he hollered pointing to a large book in his hand, "and he left it out! He loses!" Surely Grutman hadn't overlooked filing the one paper that was absolutely essential to his case. Perhaps he was playing a game too subtle for me to understand.

Schuster filed our brief, arguing: "The tactic of *Penthouse* has not been to lodge a good faith defense in this case, but to attack all parties concerned instead. . . . It becomes apparent that one of the devices of *Penthouse* has been to seek the intimidation of all who are involved in the litigation—plaintiff, counsel, *and even the Court itself.*"

We discovered that Grutman had also attacked the trial judge in the La Costa case. He took Judge Kenneth W. Gale to the California Court of Appeals, claiming "hostility" and "bias" and "corruption." The La Costa lawyers charged in their opposition brief that *Penthouse* had hired sixteen or seventeen full-time "investigators" and "agents" to "investigate" all aspects of Judge Gale's personal life. They argued to the Court of Appeals, "We submit that such a tactic is unconscionable, reprehensible, and does not comport with ethical legal practice. To attempt to intimidate a judge by so gross an invasion of privacy should, we submit, be sternly reprimanded by this court."

The La Costa attorneys accused *Penthouse* with repeatedly demonstrating its contempt for the judicial process, claiming that in a libel action brought by *Penthouse* in New York, the United States District Court found, after a full hearing, "that *Penthouse* had made a mockery of discovery, that its chairman, Robert Guccione, and its counsel, Norman Grutman, had testified falsely under oath, and the court dismissed the case." They cited the case of *Penthouse International, Ltd.* v. *Playboy Enterprises, Inc.*, in which *Penthouse* sued *Playboy*, claiming *Playboy* had misinformed *Penthouse*'s advertisers and potential advertisers concerning *Penthouse*'s circulation figures. Judge Thomas Griesa had granted *Playboy*'s motion for dismissal of *Penthouse*'s complaint on the ground of "willful misconduct on the part of *Penthouse* and its attorneys." Judge Griesa wrote in his opinion: "*Penthouse* and its attorney flagrantly and willfully violated the rules of the discovery process over almost the entire course of [the] litigation. This was accompanied by subterfuge, misrepresentation and false testimony. *Penthouse* made a total mockery of the discovery process in this case."

Near the end of their brief, the La Costa lawyers summarized: "If we permit unscrupulous attorneys to rip and tear at the very fabric of justice, we will soon find that no man will be willing to become a judge, and that the judicial process itself will wither into disrepute."

My duty has never been to defend Norman Roy Grutman, but fairness demands I acknowledge he has never lied to me. It's easy to call a man a liar when you have the protection of the law to do so. Lawyers can't be sued for libel for what they say about each other in court. It's true that Grutman sometimes said poignant, even outrageous things and took hard, even hostile stands. He might even be mean at times, surly, disrespectful. But there were those who would point their fingers and say the same of me.

Grutman could take an innocuous little sliver and, with the magic of his words, turn it into a hefty legal lance and run it through his opponent. That is the art of advocacy possessed by few who claim it. That his opponents felt the pain of being outmaneuvered, outlawyered, of being run through by him, was understandable. That his opponents were often able only to stand there helplessly watching him slice their cases into neat pieces and serve them back as hors d'oeuvres on the judicial platter must be frustrating to them, even humiliating, especially when he often did so with that awful arrogance. Worse, his arrogance was well-founded. His verbal swordsmanship was devastating, he was a master strategist, and he refused to be intimidated by the judges. Instead he liked to stick his thumb between the judicial ribs, and the judges weren't used to that either. Grutman could stir up more trouble than a hound dog in the henhouse, and he knew how to turn the trouble to his advantage. But Guccione hadn't hired him to coddle the sweethearts of the bar. Grutman represented his client, and that, in the end, is the highest calling of any lawyer.

It is easy for judges sitting above the mess and muck with all their power and untouchableness to make their searing, hurtful comments that cut to the heart of an attorney. What Judge Griesa had said against Grutman, true or not, overstated or not, hurled out at him in a fit of judicial rage or not, whatever it was he and other judges had dumped down on Grutman, deserved or not, would be quoted against him forever, even as I have quoted it here. Judges, too, are protected from libel suits. I thought that in some of his deepest parts Roy Grutman must have known the pain and feeling of helplessness that comes from being the victim of a defamation. Every time a lawyer takes a case and must confront a snarling judge or an adversary brimming with hatred, he must bear the ugly brunt of it. It is a big price to pay for the privilege of representing a client.

Later Judge Walter Mansfield of the Second Circuit Court of Appeals stated, "On this record we cannot say that Attorney Grutman made any willful misrepresentation. Conceivably he was misled by this client."

A sadness came over me as I read this terrible despoiling of men. I thought of the energy wasted, as in war, and of how good lawyers and sincere judges were often so frustrated. But, most of all, I thought of all the ordinary people in this country where justice is supposed to be available equally, who could never purchase for themselves a lawyer like Roy Grutman, even if their very lives were at stake.

The La Costa lawyers claimed their case had taken seven years to bring to trial, "as a result of petitioners' success in delaying the day of reckoning." Now Schuster told the judges in his brief to the Circuit that what the defendants had been unsuccessful in accomplishing directly by their attempt to postpone the trial, they were attempting to accomplish indirectly by this suit against Judge Brimmer. Delay was the tactic. Schuster wrote, "The real motive behind the recusal procedure [the procedure to remove Judge Brimmer] was not for relief from alleged prejudice, but because the defendants *seek a continuance of the trial set for February 9, 1981.*" My bet was that the trial would start on that date, exactly on time, whether Norman Roy Grutman chose to come or not.

It was also a good time to see if there was the slightest sentiment developing for settlement talks. It's the duty of a lawyer to settle his case if he can. Most cases never get to trial—if they did, the courts would be fifty years behind. As the plaintiff's attorney faces the day of trial, he begins to see in his case the defects that his zeal has previously glossed over, and as the defense attorney faces the same day of reckoning, he begins to realize that the plaintiff's case may sit better with the jury, that a jury could hit 'em big, and that there are always the costs of trial for the client. But most lawyers never settle cases until they have to. By setting a case for a prompt trial, the judge settles more cases than all the puffing and positioning and clever moves of any lawyer.

I called Grutman to test the water. Maybe now that the trial date was set, if Grutman was really caught in a bind between New York and Wyoming, well, maybe he'd see the wisdom of recommending that *Penthouse* plunk down a million dollars or so, instead of ending up with a jury's verdict that could be five times larger. Besides, he could avoid setting new and dangerous precedents. I thought a million dollars might discourage the likes of *Penthouse* from publishing scurrilous things about innocent people in the future and a million dollars might do justice for Kim—clear her name, and the press could make quite a thing of it, and when the smoke cleared she'd be proud again. My part of a million would make me feel a little better too— pay off some of the husky six-figure bills that were mounting in the case. I didn't even want to know how much time and money we had in it. To think of it caused me to moan in the night.

But Grutman wasn't interested. *Penthouse* never settled cases, and furthermore, he said, "I wouldn't be a party to making *Penthouse* the victim of Miss Pring's insatiable greed. So far as I am concerned, I will never recommend a penny to appease such frivolous litigation as she brings. I will never be a party to such extortion."

"Well, Norman," I said. "That's pretty strong language."

"You do that maliciously," he said. "You know I am offended at being called Norman. That's part of your style, Mr. Spence, which I find most abhorrent and indecent. You are an uncouth country cad."

"Well, Norman, I hear you're not coming to our trial," I said. "You afraid to meet me at the O.K. Corral at high noon for a little shoot-out?"

"I don't find your dreary metaphors in the least humorous, Mr. Spence, but if you persist in those delusions—of seeing yourself as Wyatt Earp or the Lone Ranger or some such equally ludicrous ruffian, I would suggest you seek psychiatric aid. So far as the trial in Wyoming is concerned, where your avaricious little strumpet is attempting her rather maudlin shakedown of *Penthouse*, too ordinary a shakedown for you to be involved in, Mr. Spence, I might say—yes, I will be only too happy to meet you at the O.K. Corral, as you so banally put it, if you have the courage to grant me a continuance of a very reasonable time. Otherwise, I can only conclude that you are afraid to meet *me*, when, Mr. Spence, your offensive bragging and bellowing and bullying would be terminated, once and for all."

14

Grutman lost his case against Judge Brimmer in the Circuit Court of Appeals. The judges there turned him down cold, which left him to face a judge whose tail he'd twisted damn near off. He had no other moves. He steadfastly maintained that his presence was required in New York, and now a Mr. David Carmichael rose to address the Court and said, "Your Honor, as local counsel for *Penthouse*, I would like to make an introduction. As you know, Mr. Grutman is detained elsewhere, and to represent *Penthouse* for the trial of this case is Mr. Tom Kelley, seated at the end of the table, and next to him, Mr. Paul Cooper, both of Denver, Colorado." Carmichael smiled at the judge. "You might know Mr. Cooper. He was in the U.S. Attorney's Office at the same time that you were Wyoming's attorney general, Your Honor, and it might be that your paths have crossed." If they had, the judge gave no indication. "These attorneys are members in good standing of the Supreme Court of Colorado, the Tenth Circuit and the United States Supreme Court, as well as the District Court in the District of Colorado."

"All right. Gentlemen, we are glad to have you with us," Judge Brimmer said. "I want the record to show here and now that I do *not* grant the withdrawal of Messrs. Grutman and Daichman, who have heretofore represented the defendants *Penthouse* and Cioffari in this case." The judge was frowning and sounding very angry. I gave Eddie a quick glance and raised my left eyebrow slightly. He knew what I meant. "I want the record to further show that from my own observation of CBS television on Monday, February 2, 1981, I saw Mr. Grutman in Lynchburg, Virginia, speaking on national television, where he had been appearing that day in connection with a hearing of a case of Mr.—"

"Falwell, Reverend Falwell, Your Honor," I said.

170

"Yes, Falwell, who also has a matter against *Penthouse.*"

It seems the Reverend Jerry Falwell had given an interview to a couple of free-lance writers and was furious when it appeared in the March issue of *Penthouse.* Falwell claimed the interview was stolen. It was the work of the devil, a vicious conspiracy. He assured his flock that the writers had promised him the story would not be published in any pornographic magazine, and he hollered to high heaven that "that magazine," he didn't even want to say its name, "is exploiting me financially and hurting me spiritually." Guccione gleefully called Falwell "a liar" and a "hypocrite," and the press was having a field day and everybody was just happy as hell about the whole affair, maybe even, secretly, Jerry Falwell, who had never had so much national attention. He sued for a temporary restraining order, asking federal judge James C. Turk to prohibit the distribution of the magazine's March 1981 issue. He hit at *Penthouse* on his television show; he raged in the press—he was, to say the least, shocked to his very marrow.

Imagine! Guccione publishing an interview with Jerry Falwell, this man who was America's principal spokesman against the evils of sex and pornography, this man who would repress sex like a two-ton setting hen on a bunch of eggs. There he was, the Very Right Reverend Jerry Falwell, smiling out at the *Penthouse* readers, only a thin page separating him from those naked women, and when you closed the magazine their unspeakable parts were stacked atop his pious face! Some claimed he must have died and gone to heaven. Others contended Satan and Falwell had come to a meeting of the minds, that probably the devil would be making a guest appearance on Jerry Falwell's television show.

Grutman was at it again on behalf of his clients Guccione and *Penthouse.* At a hearing to lift the temporary restraining order against *Penthouse,* Grutman told Judge Turk: "This is a media event contrived by the Reverend Mr. Falwell," whom Grutman described as "an admitted public figure who craves the limelight," the same stale ammunition he'd fired against Kim only a short time before when he told the press, "this is a contrivance dreamed up by plaintiff apparently as a publicity stunt."

At the hearing Grutman attacked Falwell with a fury. Falwell had suffered no injury. Hadn't *Penthouse* described Falwell as "one of the most important men in America today?" To which Falwell had answered that the praise "was not cast in a light I appreciate." Grutman pressed him to answer his questions precisely, "so you won't have to talk about it as an anecdote"—Grutman's way of reminding Falwell that the year before a spokesman for the White House had accused Falwell of lying about a supposed conversation between him and President Carter on the subject of alleged homosexuals on the president's staff. Later Falwell confessed the conversation hadn't taken place at all. Falwell tried to say he'd told the story as "an anecdote"—that he hadn't really lied.

Grutman prevailed. Judge Turk lifted the stay order and the March issue of *Penthouse* marched out to millions with Falwell's interview intact, the newspapers screaming their headline: FALWELL FAILS TO STOP *PENTHOUSE*. But Grutman's victory wasn't enough. After the hearing he took after Falwell again on the courthouse steps, telling the press that *Penthouse* was considering a countersuit against Falwell. "He has made some awful remarks about the magazine that went across the country. We've taken a lot of lumps on this," Grutman said, looking very solemn. "After having called the magazine a lot of things, they expect to walk away unbloodied."

The Reverend Jerry Falwell, looking even more solemn, replied, "That magazine has succeeded in damaging my reputation, and now begins the mammoth job of going out and repairing the damage that *Penthouse* has done to our ministry." He also threatened suit. Then Grutman had turned to Falwell and pointed his finger at him in front of an excited gallery of press and said in his Moses voice, "Ye shall know the truth and the truth shall make you free," and when the pressmen had stopped laughing, Falwell said, "God will get the last laugh."

I could never understand why these two, Guccione and Falwell, should torment each other so. They were brothers under the hide. Their views on women were identical. In *Penthouse*, women were naked, dissected by the camera into parts, and were merely sex things. Falwell's Moral Majority, from its opposite stance, also saw women as things to be put in places—not in Guccione's places, but in *some* place, trapped with the kids at home, house objects first, objects to be manipulated by the church, to bear offspring like broodmares, not persons but objects. One could not join the Moral Majority if one didn't put women in their fifteenth-century role, in those morally and spiritually quarantined quarters that made it plain that sex was dirty, the stuff of the devil, and that women were, in the words of Napoleon, "nothing but machines for producing children." Falwell

and Guccione needed each other. Falwell's Dark Age morality of re-
pression was the sire of pornography, and without *Penthouse* and its
ilk, the Moral Majority would lose its most convenient and conspicu-
ous enemy—pornography. God and the devil are at each other's service.

On NBC's early morning show, *Tomorrow Coast to Coast*, Guccione turned to the Right Reverend and said, "I'm telling you now
that you are a liar! You have a chance to go to court and disprove
that or sue me for calling you a liar. I will prove before the entire
world that you are. I challenge you to take me to court." Then Falwell said Guccione was a liar, too, because Guccione accused Falwell
of saying at a recent rally in Florida for Anita Bryant that all homosexuals should be shot. "I never said that," Falwell hollered at Guccione, "and that makes you a liar!" Despite the ragings Guccione and
Falwell used each other—Falwell got his publicity and Guccione his
record-breaking sales. At Peter's News Stand on Main Street in
Lynchburg, the owner said, "It's unbelievable. We sold out of *Penthouse* very shortly after it went on sale Monday morning."

The Wall Street Journal wrote, "Everyone's atwitter this week
over the fact that an interview with Reverend Jerry Falwell, head of
Moral Majority, is appearing in *Penthouse*, the lurid girlie magazine.
This is the interview in which the fundamentalist preacher de-
nounces Jimmy Carter for having granted an interview four years
ago to the slightly less lurid *Playboy*."

Falwell got many miles out of the *Penthouse* interview. He did sue
Penthouse—for $10 million—and the press carried many stories
about the case. Then Falwell boosted his claim against *Penthouse* to
$40 million and there were more stories.

The Wall Street Journal came to his support. The nation was a better place because of Jerry Falwell, "and although we don't agree
with Rev. Falwell on everything, we do believe it's not a sin to believe in sin." Falwell's adoring flock also rushed to his side. They
made a blessed martyr of the Reverend and wrote scathing letters to
Judge Turk, who, they said, would "perish in hell" unless he sought
God's forgiveness for his decison to permit the distribution of the
March issue of *Penthouse*. One writer from St. Paul said he was
proud he had encouraged his six children not to seek careers as
judges, but instead to do something people would respect. A Michigan writer said Turk was adding respect to "the filth and mind-con-
trolling tactics" of pornographers. "You earn and deserve no respect.

Judges are to be feared as much as Satan because you allow him to control you. You are making a mockery of God's servant and God's word." The letter said the judge was "a murderer of men's souls when you give license to pornographers. If you were a man of intelligence, you would go to Falwell . . . and let him tell you how to be a true child of God."

Grutman, too, got his share of the ink. On national television he wore one of the 150 black silk ties he said he purchased in Paris, and he had his red bandana handkerchief, his trademark, tucked jauntily into his black deacon's jacket and he called Falwell "Foulwell," and he was, to be sure, dandy as the devil and in rare form when the cameras zoomed in on him for the nation to see. Judge Brimmer had caught the act and wasn't amused, not one little bit.

Judge Brimmer set his jaws and scowled first at Kelley and then at Cooper. "Grutman's being in Lynchburg on February second could be contrary to his affidavit that is on file in this case, in which he said he had a case starting in Nassau County, New York, on January twenty-seventh that would last four weeks. Obviously that is not true from my own observation."

I looked at Eddie again. He knew what I meant, which was to say nothing, do nothing, don't even blink when things are going that good for you. The judge continued. "The affidavit filed by the plaintiff would indicate that there has been no effort on behalf of Mr. Grutman to have the case in Nassau County, New York—*Cardona* versus *The University Hospital*—postponed, or his own schedule changed in any way." He scowled at Kelley, then at Cooper. Silence. "It further appears to this Court that even if Mr. Grutman were required to be in Nassau County, his associate, Mr. Daichman, who has appeared at every hearing in this case from the very first, could be here."

He turned to Kelley and Cooper. "I appreciate the fact that Messrs. Kelley and Cooper were hired by *Penthouse* last week, as I understand it, and while I presume that that places you under a duty of Herculean labor in a short period of time, nonetheless I am sure that you are equal to the task. This case has been set since December fourth and it will remain set! Your motion for continuance will be denied."

Cooper moved back from his chair to get up. He was a tall man around forty who looked like he'd spent a lot of time in the gym keeping trim. He wore a finely tailored chocolate-brown suit and his hair was lighter brown, the color of prime otter. He touched his hair lightly in the back at the cowlick to see that all was in place. He had a deep dimple in his chin and glasses and all—I thought he'd make a good-looking Clark Kent.

"You don't need to stand; you can sit. We are informal." The judge smiled at Cooper.

"With regard to our continuance request," Cooper began, and he ran his forefingers across both eyebrows to test for hairs out of place, "I think, in fairness to the Court and opposing counsel, I should explain further a couple of items as to the reason and the scope of our request." Cooper kept his eyes fixed on the papers before him and didn't look at the judge. He was requesting only a very short continuance, and he assured the judge he was not trying to postpone the trial in order to give Grutman time to get back into the case at a later date. "We are in the case for the duration," Cooper said.

Judge Brimmer wasn't satisfied, pointing out that even opposing counsel in Grutman's New York case thought there was some flexibility in the trial setting of that case. "In other words, it looks to me like that is undoubtedly an excuse of Grutman's. I think that he fears the case, or maybe he thinks he has made me mad and wants to get out. I think he has left his client. Well, as far as I am concerned, that is a problem between him and his client."

Cooper tried to appease the judge. Grutman was on television in Virginia while his case was supposed to be going on in New York because Cooper was led to believe "the trial has started, and other counsel are picking the jury for Grutman, and that is the explanation for his appearance on TV." The judge reminded Cooper that there was no sworn statement in the file setting forth such facts. As I found out later, Grutman's trial in New York didn't start on January 27 but instead never got under way until February 13, and before the case was over, he settled it out of court.

"What is your defense to this case, Mr. Cooper?" the judge asked.

"The privilege of freedom of speech," Cooper replied. But *privilege* is a word with a special meaning in the law, and Cooper talked of it as if it were some new, vague, and mysterious idea. It applied to the Miss America Pageant because it was a "public occurrence," he said, and he spoke with great authority, and once he even looked at the judge as if it was slightly mortifying that the judge had never heard of his theory of "privilege."

Judge Brimmer didn't understand. "Are you contending that this article has a social value that entitles it to be considered newsworthy?" the judge asked.

"No," Cooper said. "We are alleging that the article is fiction and as such is protected under the First Amendment, whether or not she is a 'public figure' in the classical sense." He talked on, conceding that Kim was not a public figure in the same way as the President of the United States, but the question of her being a public figure should be submitted to the jury, he argued. If the jury found she was a public figure then, of course, we'd have to prove *Penthouse* published the story with actual malice—first-grade libel law under *New York Times* v. *Sullivan.*

Finally I spoke up. "Judge—I've had a hard time from the very beginning understanding how these people can say Kim is a public figure and at the same time say, 'But this is all fiction and therefore she doesn't really exist.' It must be clear that by definition a public figure is a *real* person, and can't be a fictional person. How can they go both ways? I don't think it's right that they should be able to walk up in front of a jury and confuse them by saying, 'Look, she is a public figure so they have to prove malice, but remember—this is fiction, she doesn't exist.'

"The Supreme Court says we ought to be able to talk about our leaders and politicians in a free country. But these people agree there isn't any social issue in the article, so there couldn't possibly be a public figure issue in this case." I gave a little flip of my thumb in the direction of Cooper and Kelley. "And if there were, then there can't possibly be any suggestion that this thing is fiction."

The judge didn't even look up. "I'm going to submit to the jury whether she is or is not a public figure." Eddie could tell I was about to get up and start a war.

"That's all right, Gerry," he whispered. "They'll look silly arguing to the jury that she's a public figure. The judge is gonna let 'em look silly." I stayed in my chair. The judge went on.

"And then I will secondly ask the jury whether or not they believe that this article, that you call fiction, really refers to Miss Pring," the judge said, still not looking up. "And then, if so, was it false? And then we will get into the damage issues later."

We had also included in our complaint against *Penthouse* a cause of action for invasion of privacy and one called "outrage," which is defined as conduct by the defendant so extreme in nature, so outrageous that the same cannot be tolerated in a civilized society, but Cooper argued that the public figure doctrine had something to do with this theory too. "Mr. Cooper," I said, "don't you recognize that even a public figure can be dealt with by the media in such an outrageous way that a tort is created? That's the essence of outrage."

But Cooper launched into the vague and mysterious again. You could hear it in his voice, like a father telling his children ghost stories. "I don't think," he began in a low, almost breathless voice, "that in certain cases such as the physician rendering medical services"—we all waited with growing anticipation as to how the rendering of services by physicians had anything to do with a case of libel—"where there are certain elements"—they were apparently secret elements—"and certainly in a First Amendment case, when"—more mystery in his voice—"there are certain required elements, that you can avoid having to avoid those elements by calling it an outrage. That's my point." He quickly glanced from lawyer to lawyer with a look that told us he hadn't expected us to understand his point in the first place. The judge shrugged his shoulders and said he would also submit the issue of "outrage" to the jury.

Then the judge wanted to talk about punitive damages. I thought that was what the case was really about—damages to be awarded against *Penthouse* if there was "actual malice." There were long arguments about what 'actual malice' meant, the standard definition being "publishing with knowledge of the publication's falsity or with a reckless disregard as to whether it was false or not." The judge asked Cooper and Kelley if they agreed with such a definition or whether they would insist that "actual malice" must be proved by "ill will, hostility, or deliberate intention to harm."

Kelley, a smallish, pleasant-looking man of indistinguishable age in a gray suit, spoke in a gray tone, as though nothing he said would be understood by those present anyway. His face reflected great profundity. "We think the standard has to be worked in such cases," he said, "so as to apply the Supreme Court's test of recklessness to the author's state of mind, as to the propensity for the story of applying to a real person or a real set of facts."

"Whatever the hell that's supposed to mean," I whispered to Eddie.

"Beats me," Eddie whispered back. Then the judge said if we proved *Penthouse* was guilty of actual malice, he'd let us reopen our case on the question of how much the jury should award to justly punish *Penthouse.* "Bear in mind," the judge said, "I have given a punitive damage instruction four times in five years, and have been reversed twice by the Circuit. I am skittish on that subject."

With the circuit judges looking down his neck, Judge Brimmer wasn't going to let me start right off talking to the jury about a lot of money to punish *Penthouse* until I'd at least proved malice, although once he turned to the *Penthouse* lawyers and said, "You know, off the record, I can't understand how there would be too much dispute about 'malice' in this case and why there is all this haranguing about it. When you call a person a coc—" he started to say the word in its commonest street vernacular because, after all, he was a man who'd been raised in a tough Wyoming town and he knew the language of the people. But now out of respect for his office he thought better of it. Instead he said, "When you call a person *that* in Wyoming I think you can almost presume 'malice' in the law, because that's about as bad as you can call a person around here, and you have to know that it will cause injury if you publish it."

Next, Cooper wanted the judge to rule out all the pages of the August issue of *Penthouse* except the article itself. He didn't want a Wyoming jury to see all of Guccione's artistry, his proud and courageous firsts, I thought. Cooper argued on behalf of *Penthouse* that the probative value of the whole magazine before the jury was outweighed by the prejudice it would cause. Prejudice! Hadn't *Penthouse* always been perfectly proud to present itself to millions of American men to slaver and slobber and erectify over? Why shouldn't the total magazine now be seen by the six persons who would compose the federal jury? Why shouldn't the jury see those pages between which *Penthouse* had inserted this Wyoming woman, between closeups of fornicating lesbians and women masturbating themselves, and the condom and dildo ads?

"I think the rest of the magazine is part of the *res* [the substance of the case]," the judge said. "You will have the appropriate objection and you may test me out." It was His Honor's way of saying, "We'll see whether the Circuit Court of Appeals will reverse me on this ruling or not." I thought the judge felt pretty sure of himself.

Judge Brimmer wanted to know which of over a hundred witnesses we'd actually bring to the trial. Even the *Malleus* held that in the trial of a witch "it is necessary to know how many witnesses there should be, and of what condition."[1] Under the name of each, we'd dutifully set forth a summary of the witness's testimony, as required by *Smith* v. *Ford*. The judge read through the pages like an expurgatory dose of salts.

How many witnesses should be permitted? There again the *Malleus* had given guidance: "When a person is duly found to be publicly defamed of some heresy, and nothing is proved against him except that defamation, a canonical purgation shall be imposed upon him. That is, he must produce some seven, ten, twenty, or thirty men, according to the extent to which he has been defamed and the size and importance of the place concerned, and these must be men of his own station and condition. For example, if he is a secular, they must be seculars; if he be a soldier, they must be soldiers who purge him from the crime for which he is defamed . . . men professing the Catholic faith and of good life, who have known his habits and life both recently and for a long time . . . and if he cannot find sponsors he shall be considered as convicted, and is to be condemned as a heretic."[2]

The judge started down our list of witnesses.

"Gus Fleischli's testimony about how proud Miss Pring was to be a representative of Wyoming is irrelevant—looks to me like hearsay anyway," the judge said.

I fought for each witness. "Are you saying that a young woman who is proud of being Miss Wyoming, who is proud to represent her state and who is devastated by what *Penthouse* did to her can't show all of this by independent evidence?" I sounded incredulous.

"It's wasting the Court's and jury's time," the judge said. "It's a great argument to the jury. Make it to the jury." He struck several other witnesses including Dr. Carlson, the president of the University of Wyoming, who would testify the whole state was defamed by the article, causing Kim further embarrassment and hurt feelings.

"Governor Herschler doesn't know anything about this case," the judge said. I thought he'd know how this vicious story spread through the state like an evil disease. The judge wouldn't hear of it. The governor was an old friend of mine, and the judge's as well. The judge said, "The governor wrote me a very funny little note—said he would testify almost to anything as long as they told him what to say and paid him properly," and everybody laughed, but no, the governor wouldn't be permitted to testify.

Nor could we call Miss Idaho. *Penthouse* had offered her $10,000 to pose nude—about "twenty times what *Penthouse* usually pays those poor girls," I said, "which is five hundred dollars apiece." The $10,000 offer was a clear attempt to undermine the pageant, proper evidence of *Penthouse* malice, "and when she refused to pose, they dispatched Mr. Cioffari to Atlantic City." But the judge said no to Miss Idaho and hurried down through the list of witnesses that had taken us the best part of a year to find and interview and prepare for trial. Now, in the flick of the judge's thumb, most of them were thrown out on one ground or another before they even got into the courtroom.

"Jesus Christ," Eddie whispered. "He's guttin' our case."

Then the judge ruled Guccione's photography irrelevant, and whether it had any artistic value likewise irrelevant. This wasn't an obscenity trial, and moreover, the stories written by Cioffari for *Penthouse* and other girlie magazines were irrelevant, and before I could protest the judge's ruling, out of the blue he poked his finger into that most tender place in the case. He spoke to Cooper. "There has been an attempt to interrogate Miss Pring as to whether or not she is a virgin, whether or not she has had sexual intercourse."

"We don't plan to go into that stuff at all, Your Honor," Cooper said.

"That's all irrelevant," the judge said. "I believe the law is pretty clear on those specific issues, but if you—"

"We understand Your Honor ruled that out. And since there has been no discovery on the matter we don't plan on asking those questions."

"Bullshit," Eddie whispered loud enough for the judge to hear, and when the judge turned to stare, Eddie looked innocently back at his pad and continued his complicated doodles that resembled webs created by a schizophrenic spider.

"The basis of my ruling in this statement in Louisell and Mueller's *Federal Evidence,* page one sixty-one of Volume Two, which says, 'It seems that evidence of particular instances of conduct should be received only with caution or not at all, regardless of the nature of the statements complained of, for such evidence shows not that the plaintiff's reputation is bad, but that it ought to be bad.'"

Judge Brimmer said, "Now I think that your interrogation of her on this point would be wrong," but he quickly amended his ruling. "Now let me be sure that you don't misunderstand me. I'm inclined to think that on your part of the case, if you come back with seventeen members of the football team who each say that they slept with her three times a week for four years—I think that probably would be relevant." He laughed.

"Why?" I asked, without laughter.

"It goes to the mitigation of damages," the judge said. He strained for more exact words, shrugged his shoulders, and said, "Well, what I'm saying is, they don't have the right to embarrass the plaintiff by those things, and I don't believe these gentlemen now have intended to ever do that." The judge turned to Cooper for confirmation. Cooper said nothing more.

The judge looked at Kelley.

Kelley said nothing.

I argued back. "Supposing the evidence is that her reputation is spotless—that everybody up and down the street believes she is a virgin, but that unbeknownst to the public at large she has had a sexual relationship with A, B, C, and D, none of these escapades having affected her reputation. She seeks damage to her reputation which is unsoiled. Specific contrary acts have been held not to be admissible." I relied on Louisell and Mueller, not the *Malleus*'s Kramer and Sprenger. "That's like *Penthouse* saying, 'Well, if she had a good reputation before, wait till we get done with her in this trial. She won't have any reputation at all. And if we ruin her reputation in the trial, we won't have to pay her any damages.' "

The judge said, "So that goes back to this idea of saying that if her reputation isn't bad, it ought to be?"

"That's right," I said.

That's right. What are this witch's deeds? What is her reputation? If it isn't bad, it ought to be.

That's right.

That's right.

Just before the recess, Judge Brimmer ruled that Dr. Victor Cline wasn't going to testify. "Not in my courtroom," he said. The judge was wiping us out. I looked under the stalls for feet in the men's room to make sure we were alone. "Christ, we can't lose Cline," I said. "We've got to have him to prove malice."

Eddie nodded. "Yeah, but be careful with the judge." He looked worried and sounded worried too. He changed the subject. "What do you think of Cooper and Kelley?"

"Cooper's pretty. Kelley's smart." I said. "Cooper'll want to fill up the jury box with young women. I used to do that—thought they'd fall in love with me. We'll let Cooper have the young women. They'll listen to their daddy."

"You better get the judge to listen to us about Cline," Eddie said, "or school's out." Victor Cline was a psychologist who taught at the University of Utah and once served on the President's Commission on Pornography. After reviewing the numerous *Penthouse* publications, he concluded that "pervasive maliciousness" was a part of *Penthouse's* editorial policy itself. His position was that *Penthouse* purposely attacked everything dear to Americans, every institution, every sacred ideal, not for any justifiable, constitutionally protected reason, but to shock its readers and to milk them for the profits—like they milked prize bulls of their semen, I thought—shocked it out of them. I'd seen it many times. They stuck an electric prod about the size of a shock absorber on a Ford truck up the bull's rectum, gave him a hell of a jolt—I don't know how many volts, but it knocked a bull weighing over a ton to his knees, and he'd let out a pitiful squall, and the semen came spurting out. They collected it—every last precious drop—froze it and sold it—terrible thing to do to a dumb animal, but the profits could be immense. It seemed to me that *Pent-*

house treated its readers a lot like that—shocked them to their knees—showing the President consorting with whores and lesbians or portraying Christ as some simple-minded bum stumbling across the street dragging his cross. There were few values, few limits, little was decent, little sacred—whatever would shock the last penny in sales out of the reader had become the principal test.

"*Penthouse* has the absolute right to do so," Schuster had argued. "That's the one thing that *is* sacred—its right to do so. That's what freedom of speech is all about—as long as it doesn't libel somebody," he added.

I argued back. "Can I show the President of the United States servicing a pig and claim constitutional protection? That isn't freedom of speech—that's milking the bull." *Penthouse* had the formula all right and shock was an important part of the formula. Shock was money—shock and trouble.

"Because *Penthouse* shocks to make money rather than to preserve democracy makes it no less constitutionally protected," Schuster said, and I agreed with Schuster. *Penthouse* did have the *absolute right* under the First Amendment to publish anything it chose and that right should be zealously guarded, never censored, never chilled, even if there was a pernicious intent to destroy every American institution right down to the Easter Bunny and motherhood—even if the attacks sprang from an insatiably malignant heart, the right to publish what it pleased about America, or anything else for that matter, should be protected, and was. *Penthouse* was even free to libel innocent public persons so long as it didn't do it maliciously. This *is* America.

But an American citizen has a right to be protected against libels—that is an important right, as important to Kim Pring as Guccione's right to attack and degrade and shock his readers for profit. If *Penthouse* had libeled Kim Pring in the process, and if we were required to prove malice before we were entitled to recover our damages, then I argued proof of a malicious *Penthouse* editorial policy would be relevant, and I needed Dr. Cline to prove it. Why couldn't I jump over the protective "malice fence" that was thrown up around the media in *New York Times* v. *Sullivan* by showing that the editorial policy of *Penthouse* was, as Cline argued, "pervasively malicious"? Hard rules demand inventive minds.

We took our places again in the courtroom. The judge sat back for a minute, looked down at his file, rubbed his chin, and thumbed absently at the pages. I began to speak. Eddie nudged me. I waited.

"Now I guess I was maybe a little too sweeping in my statement that Dr. Cline wasn't going to testify *at all,*" the judge said. "I think there is an area that he might possibly be able to testify to." He picked up his rule book. "Rule 404(b) says, 'Evidence of other crimes, wrongs or acts is not admissible to prove the character of a person in order to show that he acted in conformity therewith. It may, however, be admissible for other purposes, such as proof of motive, opportunity, intention, preparation, plan, knowledge, identity or absence of mistake or accident." The judge turned to me. "You see, basically what you are talking about is *other* acts."

"That's correct," I hurriedly agreed.

"Your Honor?" Cooper said almost timidly. "I don't want my silence to be thought to be agreeing with the—"

"You are not thought to be," the judge said, returning to the file.

"My problem with Falwell is that that is something that occurred this month and it is a due-process matter." Cooper looked very discerning, one corner of his mouth flicked into half a smile and back again. "I don't know that the true facts of that could be known at this time, and for us to try and defend against an act that is just occurring at the present time, there are proceedings going concerning Falwell, and I—"

"Counsel for the defendants in this case is *still* Mr. Grutman," the judge said, "and Mr. Grutman is counsel for *Penthouse* in that case as well. You surely have knowledge of both."

"I don't," Cooper said. "Now, you know, I—"

"His knowledge is your knowledge, because he is not out of this case!"

Cooper capitulated. "I understand that. And as I understand it, he hasn't even filed a motion to withdraw."

"If he chooses to not appear next Monday, that's his worry."

"I understand that," Cooper said again.

"He can tell *Penthouse* his reasons for not appearing when he defends their malpractice suit, but I haven't released him and I shall not release him!" I looked out of the corner of my eye at Eddie.

When it came to the *Penthouse* witnesses, I objected to their witnesses testifying at all. Cooper had not complied with *Smith* v. *Ford,* which required that he not only name all witnesses but also set forth a complete statement of what their testimony would be. I knew the *Smith* case. I'd represented Jack Smith against Ford Motor Company—a case in which two couples, on the first morning of their vacation trip, the women in the backseat, the men in the front, everybody's seat belts fastened like careful citizens, were struck head on by a drunken Indian who had crossed over. Both women in the backseat were nearly disemboweled. Both died. It was strange that the men in the front nearest the forces of the impact should both have survived.

We investigated. The seat-belt brackets in the backseat had been installed upside down so that the forces of the collision, contrary to design, were on the soft stomach instead of against the strong pelvic bone. First I sued Ford Motor Company for the men's loss of their wives, and the jury awarded a total of $600,000 damages for two dead women. But later I also sued for the injuries to Jack Smith, the passenger in the right front. I'd also discovered that the front seats were defectively designed and also improperly tested. In the later case, the jury had awarded $800,000 for Jack's injuries alone, but the Tenth Circuit had set the jury's verdict aside and sent the case back for a new trial. I thought the real reason for the Circuit's decision was that the judges couldn't bear it that Jack Smith got $800,000 for his injuries, then a record verdict in the state. After all, Jack was an ordinary fellow from the little cowtown of Dubois, Wyoming—wasn't even a cowboy. He did odd jobs with his bulldozer during the short summer season, ate the fish and wild game he took from the mountains, and eked out a pretty simple life that most of the Circuit judges couldn't know much about. It was immaterial anyway. They were interested only in the law. But one thing they did know, and that was that $800,000 was too much money for Jack Smith. They never said so. Instead, they said Judge Brimmer had erred for letting our doctor testify without our having advised Ford in advance of trial that the doctor would also state that the cause of Jack's injuries was the manner in which the seat had been designed. It wasn't fair to surprise Ford Motor Company like that, not Ford, with its fourteen thousand engineers. We'd have to try the case over. Judge Brimmer had been more than a little irritated when the court reversed on such flimsy grounds. But appellate judges do as they please.

Jack was never the same again after the accident and later died of his injuries. Ford offered him a little more than $300,000 if he'd settle without another trial and he took it. He said he couldn't endure another trial, couldn't bear reliving his hundred-mile ride in the ambulance to the hospital at Riverton, couldn't bear the memory of lying next to his wife, begging her not to die. And all the pleading didn't make any difference because she died anyway. Eight hundred thousand dollars wasn't enough. Ford was stealing the case.

Cooper and Kelley's pretrial memorandum didn't comply with *Smith* v. *Ford* because it was silent as to the specific testimony their witnesses would give; and the judge, remembering his reversal, was critical. "This is a pretty good example of statements that don't meet the standard for a pretrial memorandum, because they are conclusory. The *Smith* versus *Ford* rule is that you must state what they are going to say, and if you don't, they are not going to testify."

The judge turned to Eddie. "As Mr. Moriarity remembers, last year, in another case, he tried to show that the pilot of a helicopter was drunk the night before the accident, but when we reviewed what he had said in his pretrial, by gosh, it wasn't there, and he didn't get it in." The judge chuckled. He was trying to be nice, trying to follow the law. "You can have till tomorrow to file your full statement of what your witnesses will say."

"But judge, that isn't fair," I said. "We are going to receive notice of these for the first time tomorrow." The judge looked trapped.

"I know that, Gerry, but I have no other way of doing it."

"But *they* are in violation of *your* rules. They have to file the memorandum six days before the pretrial. If we have to comply, why don't they?"

"I agree with you, but the—" I could feel the kill at hand. I pressed. Very hard. If I could get the judge to rule out their witnesses, we'd never have to try the case. *Penthouse* would pay off like the lottery.

"We've complied. They haven't."

"That's right. But they are going to have to be able to have some witnesses here. You can't have a trial without witnesses, can you?" The judge looked at me, asking me to agree—to show a little mercy for the opposing lawyers, for him and his problem in administering justice. But it was time to kill.

"They have had the same amount of time under the same rules as we have," I said, hitting my fist on the table.

"I agree," the judge said. "I will give them until tomorrow, as I said, to file a proper statement."

"We won't get it until Monday." That was the first day of the trial—a lot of good that information would do us on that late date. "That isn't fair, Judge. You've always been fair."

"Yes, but—"

"You have always treated us the same." The road runs both ways.

"All right. You better have Eddie stay here until tomorrow to receive it." That still gave only the weekend before trial.

"But they are in violation of the rule *today!* They should have filed this six days ago!"

"Are you saying they can't have anybody testify then?"

"These are *new* witnesses we've never heard of before this minute, and they're six days late in filing them according to your rules. Those rules either apply or they don't. They haven't complied with *Smith* versus *Ford*. We are entitled to be fairly treated, Judge." Finally the judge balked and did what judges do when they get cornered—he'd decide the matter later, "take it under advisement," as they say.

"Don't let him off the hook," Eddie whispered.

Cooper said, "The remedy for late endorsement of witnesses is a continuance, and if Mr. Spence wants one, I think he is entitled to it, and I will not object," and by that little aside Cooper divulged his game. The judge didn't need me to spell it out for him, but I did.

"Well, Your Honor, he's put you in a box where you look pretty bad. You have to say, 'You endorsed ten witnesses late—not only late—but six days late, and you didn't comply with *Smith* versus *Ford*, so you can't call any of them.' Then he's going to say, 'Well, I guess we can't get a fair trial and we want a continuance.' And that forces you to—"

"All right," the judge said. He knew. The judge looked at his file again and began thumbing, the blasted thumbing that always seemed to silence me, because who can speak to thumbs flying after pages? The judge would hear nothing more on the matter, that was plain, and so the arguments drifted, whether Cioffari's previous articles could be shown to the jury being one of the matters considered. "Every one of his articles deals with either fellatio and voyeurism, or unnatural sex," I said.

"It sounds like he's interested in that, but that isn't an issue in the case," the judge said.

"But it is," I argued back. "*Penthouse,* you see, has published his stories previously, knowing that he publishes thinly disguised articles, and knowing that—"

"All right," the judge said. He decided to let one of the articles go to the jury, the least offensive, but not the others.

"I am about to have a heart attack," I said, which got the judge's attention. He looked up to see if it was true. "I cannot believe you can rule correctly on these matters not having fully heard our opening statement and our theories on these exhibits."

"I'm not going to rule on them. I am just giving you a little preview of the coming attractions," the judge said. "And you are going to submit to me a written offer of proof"—a statement of which each exhibit will prove—"and I am going to rule on that, and you are going to have everything in it that I need to know," he said. I edged out a little closer to the precipice. We had hundreds of exhibits listed.

"I am going to do that by Monday morning?"

"Yes." That would be impossible. "Get your secretary here from Jackson." I said I couldn't get it done if I brought all five of our secretaries from Jackson.

Then the judge exploded. "The one thing that I am here to tell everybody in this case—and I am going to state it right now! This trial is not going to be a circus!" But under the explosion, I could hear the judge's anxiety seeping out. It's hard on a trial judge to have nine other judges peering down the back of his neck from those high, safe, antiseptic places, judges who, like generals a hundred miles behind the lines, tell the soldiers up front with their guts exposed to the flak how they should have fought the war, appellate judges who write their opinions with that sometimes biting verbiage, sometimes plain nasty words that can embarrass the judge and that lie in the books forever. A trial judge is as sensitive as a maiden, but he covers it with power, sometimes with anger, which is all he has to cover it with. He says he doesn't care if he's reversed, that he's satisfied if he does the best job he can, but it hurts him to be reversed—hurts him very much—and he's also afraid that someday he'll lose control of his case. That's the nightmare of the trial judge—that with all that power over every lawyer in the case, he still won't be able to keep control and it'll get away from him. When I was a kid I was always afraid that the old team of horses I drove on the buck rake, the gentlest old nags on the ranch, would someday run away with me, and sure enough one day they did—tore the rake all to hell—scattered pieces of the rake across a forty-acre field.

The trial of a case is a dirty, brutish business, and the judge as well as the lawyers, not to mention the parties, all are victims of the process, pitting humans against each other in the crunch and grind of this so-called "search for truth," if truth can be found in war, because it is war. But one thing that can always be found in any war is the bleeding and the dead. Fighters grow tough from it. Yet in a trial we are all still afraid and we all still get hurt.

I launched a new attack.

"Your Honor," I began. "I told Mr. Cooper when he called to ask for a continuance of this pretrial conference that we would be happy to help him, give him any information on any of the witnesses or exhibits that we had. I was told by Mr. Chad Milton of C.N.A., the insurance company who hired Kelley and Cooper—I was told by Mr. Milton that C.N.A. hired these lawyers on January nineteenth. On the twenty-first of January, I met with Mr. Milton, and Mr. Larry Worell of C.N.A." The judge was peering at me, waiting to see what my new move was. "We had met in a settlement conference in our office in Jackson, which got nowhere." The insurance men had come just to size me up I thought and offered piddling little—as if the case were only of "nuisance value," as worthless cases are referred to in the industry—a case worth far less than what it would cost the company to defend it. The insurance people had left us no choice but to go to court.

The judge listened. "And Milton told me at that time that Mr. Kelley would be totally prepared to defend this trial. On the twenty-sixth of January, I received a call from Mr. Kelley telling me that he was in the process of preparing for the trial, among other things." Then I dumped a big rock into the boiling soup. "Mr. Worell of C.N.A. tells me that Mr. Grutman is in charge of the defense of the case and will control it from New York."

The judge looked over at Cooper, oblivious of the fallen mask now revealing the angry man. "Is this true?" The judge's mouth was tight, one eyebrow raised very high.

"He has not withdrawn," Cooper began. He groped for the right words. "He is not controlling our—we are trial counsel and we are going to be trial counsel." The judge was not convinced.

"Are you still consulting with him?"

"Your Honor, I would be happy to explain to Your Honor the relationship. It is somewhat complicated." The judge didn't answer. "Mr. Milton, Mr. Worell are not with C.N.A., but I would not—I don't feel at liberty to explain it in open court with opposing counsel. These involve privileged matters. I have no objection to—"

Eddie whispered. "You got 'em now. Look at him twistin'."

"Don't grin," I whispered back with a very serious face, and Eddie looked down again like a sleepy Irish monk and continued drawing his crazy doodles on his yellow pad.

"I want to know right *now!*"—the judge held back short of a shout—"Is Grutman directing any of your activities? Is he by long distance directing anything to do with this case?"

"Well, he has control over the settlement. We cannot settle the case without him," Cooper said.

"You call him tonight, and you tell him he better be here Monday morning. If he is taking any active part in this case, his absence is contemptuous."

"Well, I will pass the word on to him," Cooper said.

"You pass the word on to him!" the judge said.

Grutman practiced in Judge Brimmer's court at the will of the judge—so it has always been, even in the days of the *Malleus*, the lawyer was admonished: "His behavior must be modest and free from prolixity or pretentious oratory. Secondly, he must abide by the truth, not bringing forward any fallacious arguments or reasoning, or calling false witnesses, or introducing legal quirks and quibbles if he be a skilled lawyer, or bringing counter accusations; especially in cases of this sort, which must be conducted as simply and summarily as possible. Thirdly his fee must be regulated by the usual practice of the district."[1]

The *Malleus* cautioned the judges further about certain lawyers who are thorns on the rose of justice, that such a lawyer "must not by any means so conduct his defense as to prevent the case from being conducted in a plain and summary manner, and he would be doing so if he introduced any complications or appeals into it; all which things are disallowed altogether. For it is granted that he does not defend the error; for in that case he would be more damnably guilty than the witches themselves, and rather a heresiarch than a heretical wizard."[2] The *Malleus* had spoken.

Judge Brimmer had also spoken.

Cooper tried to reassure His Honor about Grutman's participation in the case. "But he is not controlling my actions, and I think the court should be aware of that. He is not controlling our firm's actions. We are retained by separate clients."

"You are retained by *separate* clients?" the judge asked.

"We are retained by the insurance company to represent *Penthouse*. Mr. Grutman was retained by *Penthouse* direct."

Now Judge Brimmer was staring at Cooper, waiting for a better explanation. I intervened. "Let me lay it out for you, Judge. It is very simple." But the judge already understood.

"There is a large deductible. I conclude that," the judge said, referring to the amount *Penthouse* would have to pay before the insurance company paid anything.

"Now under that policy Grutman is hired by *Penthouse*," I said, "but C.N.A. has the right to approve or disapprove of him. They have approved of Grutman up until this time. When Grutman stepped out, they hired Kelley and Cooper, but the gentlemen from C.N.A. tell me that Mr. Grutman insists on calling the shots in this defense, and that he is calling the shots from New York." I wasn't done with Cooper yet. I still had him on the ropes.

"Mr. Cooper tells me that he went back to New York to deal with Mr. Grutman." Cooper had told me so over the phone one day sometime earlier, and now I continued the pounding. "And I believe if you ask counsel, as an officer of this court, whether he doesn't report to Mr. Grutman, and whether Mr. Grutman doesn't tell him how this case is to be tried, you will find that that is exactly the fact."

"All right," the judge said. He looked at Cooper for the answer.

"It is not C.N.A., but the broker company," Cooper said. "And through the C.N.A. policy it is—"

"It says C.N.A.," I said. The policy had been provided us in answer to some of our earlier interrogatories and was in the file.

"It is a C.N.A. policy but—"

"The C.N.A. policy says they have a right to approve or disapprove the attorney for *Penthouse*, black-and-white," I said. Cooper said he could assure the court that the trial decisions would be theirs, "but I cannot tell you that Grutman has no control over the case, because it is—"

"Well, at this point—"

I interrupted the judge. "Mr. Grutman has simply outmaneuvered us again, Your Honor. Either we are prejudiced by a continuance, which has been their whole game from the time Grutman took you to the Circuit Court of Appeals—it's either get a continuance or, ha-ha, Mr. Spence, if we don't get a continuance you have to face a whole series of witnesses that you have never seen or heard of before in violation of the Circuit Court's requirement under *Smith* versus *Ford*."

"All right," the judge said with a hollow, hopeless sound in his voice, thumbing through the file again, thick as a set of encyclopedias. Suddenly he reached out and "took the bull by the horns," as

Eddie liked to say. He ordered that Cooper and Kelley phone me the next day as to what their witnesses would testify to, and being fair, and the road running both ways, the judge found that certain of their exhibits would not be allowed in the case either.

"Your Exhibit C is the contestant's contract with the Miss Wyoming Scholarship Pageant. How is that relevant?" the judge asked Cooper.

"I am unable to state at this time," Cooper said, and there were other exhibits the relevance of which Cooper could not explain and which the judge therefore disallowed. Then Mr. David Carmichael, the Cheyenne attorney for *Penthouse* who had been in and out of the courtroom but who had remained silent throughout the proceeding, walked over to our table. "Your Honor," he said, "I want to hand Mr. Spence the report which was furnished by the private investigator concerning interviews."

"That has already been ruled upon," I said, trying to shut the gate again, to get the court to say that none of these new witnesses would be permitted to testify under *Smith* v. *Ford* and the court's own six-day notice rule.

"No," the judge said. I looked quickly at the list. It contained the names of men I knew Kim Pring knew.

I whispered to Eddie to hand me the subpoenas in his file. Then I said to Carmichael, "While you are standing, come here a minute, please, Counsel. I want to give you four subpoenas—for Cioffari, Hofler, Goode, and for Mr. Guccione."

"Your Honor, you previously mentioned that Guccione was not a managing partner and, therefore—" Cooper began to protest.

"Not a what?" the judge asked Cooper.

"Not a managing partner or a party," Cooper repeated.

"He is the publisher, the sole owner of the magazine. If they have subpoenaed him, he is a party in interest and he will be here!" the judge said.

"He gave you one more shot at the king," Eddie whispered.

I nodded. One more shot at the king.

16

On February 9, 1981, at 9:30 sharp, Judge Brimmer gave the prospective jurors his friendliest Wyoming smile. After all, they were captives, snatched from their homes and work, from their ranches, like God calls his children, and God, a computer located in the General Services Administration in Denver, had summoned these twenty-eight good citizens from Laramie, Albany, Platte, and Goshen counties to appear. Nobody quite knew for sure what the penalty might be for one's failure to show, but everybody knew it was one's duty as an American citizen—that one must—and this morning all twenty-eight who had been summoned out of the heart of Wyoming answered, "Present," when their names were called.

"Ready for the plaintiff?" the judge asked.

"Ready for the plaintiff," I said, trying to sound solid, confident.

"Ready for the defendant?"

"We are *present*," Cooper said. "We still maintain our motion of last week that was denied." Cooper didn't want to admit on the record he was ready—didn't even want to speak the word "ready," lest later, on appeal, it might be argued he had confessed his readiness at the time of trial, leaving no substance to his motion for a continuance.

"But you are *ready*?" the judge persisted, trying to protect his record.

"*Present*," Cooper said, as he sat down again.

"I will take it that 'present,' means ready, so we will proceed."

The clerk called the names of the first twelve persons drawn, and as each was called, each walked to the jury box and took the seat assigned by the bailiff. They were men with red faces and white foreheads, sprightly housewives stamping with small quick steps, lumbering laborers, a schoolteacher—they came, some self-consciously, some very seriously, some smirking in embarrassment from being watched by a whole courtroom as they paraded up to the jury box like contestants at the Miss America Pageant. Some loped to the jury box, some labored to it like men struggling up a mountainside, and one woman walked with her thighs pressed tightly together. I watched their faces. One man with a sardonic grin winked at another juror as he swaggered up, and one woman with the face of a ferret walked slowly, one measured step at a time, as if she were stalking something, and another had the calm, sweet look of the Virgin herself.

I observed their dress. I saw the rancher in his church and funeral suit, the lapels the wrong width, the knees bagging slightly, and the old wool shining from too many pressings at home, and I knew the man took his duty seriously. Several of the younger men wore blue jeans. There were no more than a couple of ties in the bunch. Some of the men wore boots, but the older rancher had on round-toed, black shoes. They were freshly shined.

"Do we have a representative of *Penthouse?*"

"Yes, Your Honor," Cooper answered. "We have present Mr. Robert Guccione, but Mr. Daichman will be the designated representative of *Penthouse,* with Your Honor's permission."

"All right," the judge said, sounding polite, looking pleasant. Now the judge told the jury our contentions of libel and that the defendants claimed it was fiction, privileged under the First Amendment. My eyes never left the jurors' faces. They told me nothing. One man frowned, but I didn't know why. The defendants contended that the plaintiff was a public figure, the judge said, and that therefore "she must demonstrate that the defendants acted with actual malice. . . . Well, that gives you a brief thumbnail sketch of the nature of the case." The judge's voice was very friendly. "Have any of you formed an opinion about the case in any way?" No one answered. No one raised a hand.

I needed to talk to these jurors the way two men sit down on a log in the woods on a nice fall day and talk things out, and begin to trust each other. They would be my jury, not the judge's. I needed to know these folks who would try my case, get a good feel for each of the jurors in my deep belly, that magic place from which I would try my case. I wanted to holler to the judge, "Your Honor, please, sir, if it were your daughter whose life was at stake, you wouldn't want me to entrust her case into the hands of strangers. Let me talk to these jurors. Let them talk to me." But Judge Brimmer did the *voir dire,* the questioning of the jury, himself. It was otherwise in the state courts, but in the federal court before Judge Brimmer, the attorneys must remain silent.

I wanted to argue to the judge, "Judge, you locked up your car against petty theft when you came to work this morning. We are so careful with *things*. But my case can be taken from me by the prejudices of these utter strangers, by prejudices your questions can never reveal. How can that be justice? Must my client stand for judgment before her enemies? How can I choose fair people to try my case if I cannot talk to them?" I sat mute, listening to the judge, feeling helpless.

"Is there anyone here who has never seen the inside of a *Penthouse* magazine? Okay, a few of the ladies." Eddie and I made notes. None had read the November issue of *Rocky Mountain Magazine*. Only one had seen my picture on the cover. The judge did read certain questions to the jury that both sides had submitted to him, but he read them as if it were his duty to do so, to get it over with, and read in that manner, not a juror responded to them. One of our questions was "Does anybody have any prejudice against large sums of money being sought in a suit of this nature?" Of course, no one raised a hand.

A few of the jurors knew who Kim Pring was. One man said, "Eight years ago Miss Pring and my daughter was in direct competition in baton twirling. It didn't involve me none. I couldn't stand the hair spray," and everybody in the courtroom laughed.

"Well, Miss Pring won," the judge said. "Are you sorry about it?"

"Nah. It didn't make no difference, as long as I didn't have to go." Everybody laughed again. Eddie gave me a nudge under the table and put an X through the man's name. I nodded. Then the man said, "I think Kim Pring practiced a little more."

"So you are quite objective about that?" the judge asked.

"Yeah. With seven of them you have got to have a lot of that objective." More laughter. Eddie put another X by the man's name.

The judge read some of Cooper's questions. "Do any of you object to constitutional protections for literature, even though you may personally find it tasteless or pointless or object to photography that explicitly depicts the human body?" Nobody raised a hand. Not a face flickered.

The judge droned on, reading the lawyers' questions. I watched the jurors for signs. Some of the men slouched down in their chairs.

The women sat passively, their legs crossed, their arms folded, protecting them from whatever assaults their psyches foresaw. How could I root out those who hid their prejudices behind those wooden masks, who were against all lawsuits in general, or were repulsed by baton twirlers, or hated these so-called flamboyant lawyers who showed themselves on the covers of magazines in buckskins and came to court with big hats flopped down on the tables? There was no way for me to indentify a closet porno-freak or a rabid First Amendment absolutist. The judge's questioning was like the preacher reading vacantly from Scriptures to the first row in the congregation while we stood at the door and watched. Then we would choose six of them as our jury.

"Does it offend you that the law gives different treatment to a person who might be called, in the eyes of the law, a 'public figure'?" One of the women with her arms tightly wrapped around herself began to rock.

"Does anyone here object to humor or satire about beauty pageants, or baton twirling as a talent, or the Miss America Pageant, or the office of a state beauty queen?" It was another question submitted by Cooper and Kelley. Maybe Grutman composed it. A tired, thin-faced man looked patiently up at the ceiling. Who were these people? Who could possibly know? And in a few minutes we would be asked to make choices among them—to exercise our peremptory challenges, as they are called. "Any further questions?" the judge asked the lawyers.

"Yes, Your Honor," I said. "Could you have the jurors tell us what organizations they belong to?"

"Yes," the judge said, and now the jurors themselves began to speak. One belonged to Frontier Lions Club and worked with the Boy Scouts of America. "My wife, she don't belong to any organizations, except just going to church like the rest of us," another juror said.

"We go to the base chapel," still another juror said. He'd been stationed at Fort Francis E. Warren in Cheyenne, but now he was retired from the air force and worked as a maintenance man for the Wyoming Highway Department.

A very pious-sounding, paunchy man said, "I'm Presbyterian, and I belong to the Masonic Order and the Shrine, retired from the telephone company, and I belong to the Pioneers and the AARP organization." Too tight with money—indoctrinated by a work life harassed by telephone-company budgets, likely prejudiced against the nameless masses from which Kim Pring was spawned, and toughened against people from years of dealing with complaining, bickering, trouble-making customers. I put an X by his name and smiled back.

"We belong to the Baptist church and my wife is a P.E.O. She is also very active in church work," another juror said, and yet another belonged to the VFW and the American Quarterhorse Association.

"I belong to a pinochle club and my husband is a Mason. That's about it," a secretary to the school district said.

"I belong to the Moose Club," the classroom teacher said. "I am also a member of the Plumbers and Pipefitters Local No. 192. And I am also on the board of directors of the Grace United Methodist Church." Each juror spoke up in turn.

"Ya gotta be a member of a church and a Mason to be called on this jury," Eddie whispered.

"That isn't all bad, in this case," I whispered back.

Each side struck three names. I took off the country comedian whose daughter had competed with Kim, and the retired telephone man and the rancher, a man like my grandfather Pfleeger, hardbitten from a hard life, a fellow who thought tithing was putting a dime in the collection plate at Easter.

Cooper and Kelley took off those who appeared to be the most avid church members, but they had only three challenges. The six remaining of the first twelve called, with an alternate, was the jury—chosen just like that. In choosing the alternate, I struck the woman with the countenance of the Virgin.

"How come ya want to take her off?" Eddie asked. "She's a nice-lookin' woman."

"Yeah, I know," I said. "Nobody with a face like that has experienced very much about anything" was all I had time to say. I wanted jurors who could get angry.

"Mr. Spence, you may make your opening statement."

"Thank you, Your Honor."

I walked slowly toward the jury. The jurors sat up stiffly as I approached, watching me, wary of this big man they had all heard of, this so-called famous lawyer who had tried the Karen Silkwood case and who had been in the papers and on television—a man who had raised hell around the country for a long time. The bastard wasn't going to pull the wool over their eyes. Big-shot. Gotta watch those big-shot lawyers.

I didn't invade the jurors' territory. I could feel their fierce energy, and it held me back. Their arms and legs were crossed as if my words, my simple presence, would penetrate them. I began speaking to them in a quiet voice.

"Ladies and gentlemen: I never start a case without feeling a little anxious. You'd think after all these years I'd get over being so anxious, wondering, worrying whether or not I am going to be able to do what I set out to do here—to represent my client the way I think she needs to be represented in a very important case. I just needed to share that with you." The jurors stared back.

"I suspect that some of you maybe feel a little anxious, too. None of you probably hold yourself out as experienced jurors, and I suspect that in your minds you wonder, 'Am I going to be able to do my job right? It's an important case and I need to be a good juror.'" The jurors stared back.

"And the surroundings are strange here, this courtroom full of people most of us don't know, and usually we're doing something else.

"It's a big thing we are setting out to do here together." Several of the jurors' faces were beginning to relax slightly. I stepped forward slowly, but only a single step so as not to frighten them away from me, like a man trying to creep up on a herd of skittish horses. "And you ought to know that what we are setting out to do together is done by human beings—that I am one of those, too, just like you, and you are like me, and like the judge—although some of us lawyers, when he comes down on us, don't think so. But he is human too." I looked up at the judge and gave him a big smile and he smiled back, and now, with the judge smiling at me, I took one more step toward the jury.

"We have some friends here," I said. Then I introduced the clerk and the court reporter and the bailiff and the judge's clerks as if they were all my best friends. The court people nodded to the jury and smiled, and things began to loosen up a little. I came one step closer. The maintenance man in the back row uncrossed his arms. I spoke to him.

"An old friend of mine, Judge Theis, the federal judge at Wichita—Judge Brimmer knows Judge Theis very well"—I smiled again at the judge, and he stayed friendly—"and Judge Theis used to say, 'You know, folks, if you want to get the water cleared up, you better get the hogs out of the spring,' and I hope to clear the water up a little bit this morning, because I know that as you sit here, you are saying to yourselves, 'Well, what's this important case all about? Why does Mr. Spence on behalf of his client, Kim Pring, believe this is an important case? Why does he contend that it is a case that may even have historical and—"

"Your Honor," Cooper jumped to his feet. "I object to counsel inserting his personal beliefs in opening statement." That's how I wanted the jury to first see Cooper—on his feet, objecting.

"Basically, the objection is sustainable. However, it is in the nature of a preliminary remark and I don't regard it as prejudicial," the judge said. And that's how I wanted the first ruling from the judge—in my favor. I glanced at Eddie. You can always tell when an Irishman is happy.

"Thank you, Your Honor," I said. "*Penthouse* is a corporation. It is entitled to have representation here, and it has Mr. Guccione. He is the gentleman sitting over there in the *brown velvet pants*." I walked away from the jury now toward Guccione. The jury watched me go. Guccione saw me coming. He jerked up from his slouch on the front pew in the spectators' section and glowered back at me. The jurors stared at him. I kept walking toward him, faster, as if mounting an attack. Guccione began to get his legs under him, ready. Then almost on top of the man I stopped. I pointed to Guccione the way one points at the accused. "He is also the founder, the publisher, owns all the stock—he is the sole shareholder of *Penthouse*."

"Your Honor, I object as to the relevancy of this."

"Overruled," the judge said.

I started back toward the jury now, slowly, with a respectful sound back in my voice. "Now the evidence is going to show you the kind of magazine this really is, and what kind of—"

"That's irrelevant and beyond the pretrial order, Your Honor. It is not an issue." Cooper's face was red. He stood waiting for the judge's ruling like a man braced for my next assault.

"Well, I take it you are referring to the August 1979 issue. It is relevant to that extent—continue, Mr. Spence."

I looked at Cooper and said very quietly, "I would say, ladies and gentlemen of the jury, that the gentleman for the defense will have an opportunity as soon as I sit down to answer me fully without me interrupting him, because I don't do that to attorneys." Cooper sat down.

I told the jury that in a free society there are many important issues and we must be free to talk about them. "If a publishing company like *Time* magazine, for example, has to be absolutely certain that every single little thing that they put down about a president or a vice-president or a public figure or a senator is absolutely correct or else be sued for millions, they couldn't afford to take the chance of publishing. You can see that."

The secretary for the school district nodded up front. I spoke to her.

"So the Supreme Court says, 'If someone is a public figure you can say anything you want about them so long as you don't say it with reckless disregard for the truth, but if you are reckless in what you say, then Katie-bar-the-door,' and *Penthouse* contends in this case that little Miss Pring, from Cheyenne, Wyoming, was a public figure, and therefore they can defame her, and say anything they want to about her. Well, whether she is the kind of a public figure we've been talking about is going to be up to you to decide. Whether or not the Constitution ought to permit a publisher like *Penthouse* to say whatever they want to about somebody like Miss Pring, under the guise of 'public figure,' is going to be for you to decide." I waited.

Then I told the jury there was nothing political about Kim Pring. She had nothing to do with government or public issues or policies. She was just a baton twirler, "like somebody gets to become the Job's Daughters' Queen." I looked at the Masons on the jury. "This case, ladies and gentlemen, deals with the abuse, the absolute abuse of the First Amendment of our Constitution by Mr. Guccione and his people in order to sell their magazines."

I moved up almost to the rail of the jury box. I touched my hand to it, and I spoke very softly to the women in the front row. "*Penthouse* claims their Miss Wyoming is a fictional character. But the evidence is going to show that they, on the one hand, are saying, 'She is a public figure,' so they can say anything they want to about her—'We can defame her and libel her with impunity and nobody can do anything about it'—and they can walk out of the courtroom laughing. But on the other side of the case they will say, 'But she doesn't even really exist. We weren't even talking about anybody who was real." My eyes met with the personnel officer of the Wyoming Air Guard who sat in the back row of the jury on my left.

"You are going to hear Mr. Guccione say to you when I cross-examine him in a little while that 'Every time somebody files a lawsuit against us, we just make more money.' " Then I told the jury that at the right time I was going to give them some facts and figures "that will stop this practice." That little hint was as close as I could come to telling them about punitive damages. "And I think, Your Honor"—and I gave a slight bow to Judge Brimmer—"and ladies and gentlemen"—and I smiled at them—"that's why I have said to you that this case is such an important one."

I told the jury Kim Pring's story, of how she had been born crippled and of her long years of struggle. "She has what all champions have, and she brings it into this case, and you will see it in the course of this trial. She has courage and she is here because she has courage. One day she became the greatest baton twirler in the United States.

"It took a lot of time and a lot of money, and her mother and daddy worked hard. Her mother sold Avon products door to door to get enough money to buy the lessons and to make her little dresses and costumes." I told how she had won the Miss Wyoming contest, and then I said to the women in the front row, "She doesn't hold herself out to be a beautiful woman, although I would be proud to have daughters as attractive as she, and she doesn't hold herself out to be a sexual being. She holds herself out to be a decent, comely, ordinary woman."

Kim had received her degree from the University of Wyoming in business administration and she hoped to be a businesswoman. "That's my client. That's Kimerli Pring. Folks, she is a proud woman, and lots of people looked up to her—little boys and girls—she's been a heroine to them. And one of the things you will see as a part of the damage—that has just broken her into bits—is that little children who have loved and respected her now wonder about her, because the evidence in the case is going to show"—and I began backing away from the jury so I could speak louder, so that I could let the feelings roll—"that this is the most filthy, degrading, degenerate article—"

"Your Honor, I will object," Cooper shouted.

"That's my proof!" I shouted back.

"Excuse me, he said 'article'!" Cooper shouted again.

"Proceed," the judge said quietly.

"—that man's mind can concoct." I finished the sentence. Then I told the jury how *Penthouse* claimed that all the numerous similarities to Kim Pring in the story were now mere coincidences, and how twenty million people read this magazine coast to coast and in a dozen countries across the world, and how people thought that Kim must have agreed to such an article.

"You know, part of the formula, as will be shown in the August 1979 *Penthouse*, is to shock. That's how they sell magazines—by shocking people. The word is *shock!* And when they run out of things to shock people about they find new things." I said that the article in *Penthouse* about Kim was one of the most *shocking* stories that they would ever read. I said I was going to have trouble reading it to them, but that I wanted them to hear every word of it because they needed to hear every word. "They take people that we all know, real people, with real names, who they think are public figures so they can hide behind the 'public figure' provision of the Constitution, and then they say the most shocking, degenerate things about those people." I was coming up on a good crescendo. "And the public out there, the evidence will show—"

"Your Honor, I will object. This is clearly argument, not opening statement."

"Appears to be argument," the judge said.

I went right on. "The public that reads those shocking things thinks it must be true or they couldn't publish it.

"We are going to show you that part of their formula for success has been to put a sugarcoating over—"

Cooper jumped up again, anticipating what I was going to say. "Your Honor, I must object. This is irrelevant."

"This may go to the editorial policy of the magazine, which is relevant. Objection overruled." The judge looked unperturbed, fully in control, relaxed.

I took the judge's lead. "Yes, I should have used the words 'editorial policy.' The editorial policy conducted by Mr. Guccione, masterminded by Mr. Guccione, who sits within the sound of my voice, was to fill that magazine with articles by great writers, by leading statesmen, by important people, which became the sugarcoating over the pill that he really sells. The pill, the evidence will show, is pornography—and obscenity is the center of that pill."

"Your Honor, that is not the issue in the case."

"Yes, pornography or obscenity is not an issue. Sustained."

"Let me put it another way," I said. "The outrageousness in the center of this sugarcoated pill was evidenced by things in the magazine which you will see and read—the deviate pictures—the degenerate language in that magazine—"

"Just a minute," Cooper shouted. "I would ask counsel to abide by the Court's rulings."

"I have ruled that obscenity and pornography is not an issue. The issue is a libel issue."

"I understand that." I went back to the safe words of the judge: "editorial policy." "My point is the *editorial policy,* as it relates to the article in question; and the evidence is going to be that part of Mr. Guccione's formula is to undermine every decent American tradition—and he laughs because it creates *shock.*

"And when you create shock, you create readership, and when you create readership, you create money. And so the Miss America Pageant was the victim of that attack . . . and I am going to show you that they intended to attack Kimerli Jayne Pring, and I want you to remember that at twelve o'clock noon on this day I told you that the evidence in the case was going to show you that they set out *intentionally* to do this . . . and I want you to listen as the evidence is unfolding and see if you don't agree with me that there was an intentional undertaking on the part of that magazine directed by *those people*"—I hurled my arm in the direction of Guccione—"to undermine, ridicule, and destroy the Miss America Pageant, believing as they did that everybody involved was a public figure, and that they therefore had a *license to defame.*" The jurors leaned forward in their seats.

I gave the jurors the details of the story, about Miss Wyoming committing fellatio on her boyfriend and how she discovered this supposedly "unique talent" by which she could even make men levitate, and how everybody from *Penthouse* thought that was hilarious. Then I looked at Cioffari, who was seated next to Kelley. Cioffari wore a sharp, dour look on his face and on his back an old sports jacket.

"And Cioffari wrote about how she was poor and came from a poor state. The evidence will be that he held Wyoming up as some kind of mangy little poverty-stricken state that couldn't afford to put Miss Wyoming in a first-class hotel—he had her staying at the Beach Queen Motel with her coach upon whom she performs fellatio in front of a national TV audience. She says to her coach in the article, 'I want to show them my real talent.' Her *real* talent in that story is to commit fellatio on her drunken forty-year-old coach—they have her taking his penis in her mouth in front of that audience and levitating him, and the people are shocked in the story as Mr. Cioffari knew that they would be shocked." Cioffari stared.

I told the jury about our causes of action for invasion of Kim's privacy. "It is a cause of action where somebody is held up in a false light, even as a monstrous joke. I think you will finally conclude that they can't get away with saying 'This is just a joke,' that 'Everybody knew it wasn't true,' because it invaded her privacy."

"You have got six minutes," the judge said to me, smiling his unwelcome words.

"The amount of damages in this case must be appropriate for the case. It has to do justice. It has to have some social meaning. Whether the damages should be seven million or a hundred million is up to you. I am not presumptuous enough to tell you what you should do."

Then I explained that if one person told another that Kim Pring did fellatio in public that it wouldn't be unreasonable to ask for two dollars for that insult. But in this case the insult was spread out to twenty million readers of *Penthouse* and it was therefore up to them to determine whether $40 million would be justice. Would $40 million be justice? Would it be enough?

I spoke about how the article had hurt Kim, caused her to lose her confidence. We would have psychiatrists who would speak of the scars that were left. "And based on this evidence, based upon this abuse of that sacred document we all love so much, our Constitution, we are going to ask you to do complete justice in this case, and, at its conclusion, I will give you my client, Kim Pring."

Kim was happy at lunch. Eddie said I did great; he said I had the case won. I couldn't eat.

At 1:30 sharp we reconvened, absent the jury, in the judge's chambers. Cooper looked very serious. He said he had an important motion. I knew what it would be.

"Your Honor," Cooper began with one slight caress of his eyebrow. "I would move the Court at this time to grant a mistrial on this matter based on the opening statement of opposing counsel. The entire tone of the opening statement was to inflame, impassion, and prejudice the jury."

The judge looked very gravely at me and said nothing. If the motion were sustained, the judge would dismiss the jury and we'd have to start the trial over at some later date. The judge leaned back in his chair to listen to Cooper. Eddie, who was also watching the judge, whispered, "We're okay."

When Cooper had finished, the judge said, "The Court doesn't feel that there has been any prejudice committed. While the pretrial order made clear some areas that were not to be invaded, Mr. Spence may have teetered on the brink of them, yet I don't think he fell into the forbidden subjects of punitive damages and obscenity."

Then we went back into the courtroom to the waiting jury. "We will be favored by the opening statement of the defendants," the judge told the jury.

"Thank you, Your Honor. Mr. Spence has referred to it as an important case with all the skill and drama that he possesses. The case should not turn on the skill or the entertainment value, or the dramatic presentation by the attorneys." He stopped and gave a long accusing look at me. I looked back hard at him.

Suddenly Cooper turned to the jury and said angrily, "Mr. Spence can talk forever about how he doesn't like me to object, and I am going to keep right on objecting and trying to keep the case on its issues. Whether you like what I do or don't, or whether you like what Mr. Spence does or don't like what he does, I implore you to decide this case based on the evidence—the facts and the law as Judge Brimmer instructs you at the end of the case—not the law as given by Mr. Spence on opening statement." Cooper turned and looked at me again and his face was tight and red. Some jurors had hard eyes.

"Now basically this case involves a suit for large sums of money by a former Miss Wyoming contestant for Miss America, who is claiming that there were similarities to a fictional character named Charlene in a humorous fantasy about a girl ..." He admitted that Cioffari was at the Miss America Pageant for *two days* in the finals, and then corrected himself, saying, "For two and a half *hours* of the finals ... he sat in the very back, could hardly see the contestants on stage; he had to look at the TV monitor, didn't read the newspaper, never saw anything about Kim Pring because she was not a finalist. He didn't know Kim Pring; he didn't know Miss Wyoming, and the evidence will show that he was not consciously aware of any of the similarities which counsel claims tie this to Kim Pring." Cooper paused, then forged ahead. "The evidence will show that there was no malice by either Mr. Cioffari or by *Penthouse.* Even the plaintiff herself knew it was unbelievable."

Cooper told the jury that Kim Pring was only making about $3,000 a year. "She took her baton twirling very seriously, and she objects to having fun poked at it and fun poked at what is important to her, the beauty pageant, the work she did. And I think it is easy to understand

and sympathize. None of us like to have things we feel are important poked fun at." Cooper didn't sound sympathetic.

"On the other hand, we all know that sometimes it is a good thing to have that occur in our society, and that the alternatives to a society which permits the free expression of opinion, history has shown to be much worse. . . . The evidence will indicate that from the time she was a young girl, her mother pushed her into the public limelight. Such mothers are sometimes referred to as 'stage mothers'— they get their daughters into things."

Cooper reviewed all the appearances Kim had made—her picture on the covers of magazines, her entry into beauty contests. "She voluntarily appeared on the cover of a magazine in Peru known as *Gente* in 1975, before this article was ever written. You will see a copy of that magazine," Cooper said with a taint of disdain creeping into his voice, "an article in which her agent's telephone number was listed to be called by her Peruvian sweethearts. The evidence will indicate that this magazine has much of the same type of material which Mr. Spence finds so objectionable in *Penthouse* magazine."

The similarities between the real Kim Pring and the Charlene in the *Penthouse* story were mere coincidences, Cooper said, and then he recited a long list of differences: her name wasn't Charlene and she didn't wear orange and black jersey shorts and she never had a male coach (which wasn't true). He enumerated other "differences" and ended up saying, "And the evidence will show that the twenty million who supposedly read the article, if such is proven by the evidence, would have no way of connecting this to Miss Pring." He spoke of the experts they would call to explain about the workings of fiction. "The nature of fiction is to utilize true events and sometimes thinly disguised real people," he said, "but this was clearly recognizable as a fantasy and even beyond fiction."

Now Cooper studied the jury very seriously. They stared blankly back.

"Your individual feelings about your state, about other things you may firmly believe in, may be severely brought into question. And you may not want to decide this case on the evidence. It is very easy to get picked up with Mr. Spence's emotion, and to nail somebody from out of state, if that is the way you are so inclined." I couldn't tell if Cooper was angry at me or Kim Pring or the jury. I doubted that they could tell. "But the evidence will indicate that this was a story, in the genre or type of humor or satire; that, like it or not, is a legitimate literary device. It may sometimes cause people discomfort, harm, upset. Yet it is still a legitimate literary device.

"Now Mr. Spence very carefully in his opening indicated this was sort of a team, you and he together, going out to get the big corporation from the East, and maybe to take out your frustration on a lot of things we don't like about our society today. Well, I would suggest that you will be instructed, and you already have been instructed as to your role in this case, and that is to decide the facts and apply the law as given by Judge Brimmer."

Eddie whispered, "He put the jury on our team, and he ain't bein' very nice to our team."

Cooper said, "As I indicated, when the evidence is analyzed, I think that you will find the article to be—" he caught himself. Now even he was calling it an article—"the *story* to be a nonmalicious fantasy about public events, about public sacred cows, if you will—"

"He shouldn't call the Miss America Pageant a sacred cow," Eddie mumbled out loud and the secretary on the jury in the front row looked at Eddie as if she had heard him, and then Cooper said that it was a story published just to entertain and wasn't about real people or events, "and for that reason, you should return a verdict in favor of the defendants. Thank you."

I stood up, letting the dust of the dialogue settle. The jury waited.

17

"Call Bill Storms," I said.

The jurors watched a man in his late forties walk down the aisle to the witness stand, a man without pretensions wearing his Sunday suit and a pleasant, self-conscious face. I wanted a good-first-impression, down-home witness the jury would like, one who, knowing Kim and her family, could bring the jury and the family together at the beginning of the case.

Storms was retired from the air force and ran his own small business, the B&B Sewer Service. He was a gentleman—anybody could tell that the minute he began to speak. He said the two families had been in the air force at Cheyenne together and he'd known the Prings since Kim was a baby. "We didn't have much rank, and we didn't have much money, so the Prings and us spent a lot of time at each other's house playing cards and discussing our families." As for Norman Pring: "Well, I'd trust the man with anything. They was good people," he said, and "Kim was raised decent." I liked the man. I glanced at the jury. They liked the man. He was one of them.

He talked about Kim as a small girl, "chunky, not your typical cute little girl, pretty chunky and she had that clubfoot. She was still shy, though her baton twirling brought her out of it, and she developed into a person that just exemplifies what Will Rogers said—she never met a stranger, and she just loved the whole world and loved life and was just a real nice person—a nice person for anyone to know." Bill Storms's eyes got wet.

Yes, he'd read the Miss Wyoming article and it made him mad: "Because in reading the article they had really invaded somebody's privacy. They put somebody on display."

Cooper jumped to his feet. "I object. That should be stricken."

"Yes, the conclusion of the witness is stricken," the judge ruled.

One Sunday morning Storms said he had coffee with the Prings. Something was bothering Mary Jayne, Kim's mother, and later that morning she had handed him the magazine. Right off he knew who the article was about, Miss Wyoming being a baton twirler and all, and her blue warm-up suit and her blue chiffon gown that Kim and her mother had gone to Amarillo, Texas, after, and there was even a similarity in the illustration—that blond hair she often wore in the same style as in the drawing.

"Did calling her Charlene instead of Kim disguise her?" No. It was Kim, all right. Didn't make any difference because there wasn't any other baton twirler at the Miss America Pageant except Miss Wyoming, and Miss Wyoming, the baton twirler, was Kim Pring.

"Were you angry when you read the article?"

"I was very angry."

"Why were you angry?"

"Because in reading the article they had really invaded somebody's privacy. They put somebody on display."

"That should be stricken," Cooper said.

"Yes, the conclusion of the witness is stricken."

"Without using the words 'invasion of privacy,' tell me why you were mad."

"Well, there was no doubt in my mind they were talking about Miss Wyoming, about Kim Pring, which to me is not right for them—for somebody to ridicule somebody like this. I see it every day in those sewer lines and that's exactly what they were doing to her—dragging her through it."

Bill Storms said he'd seen the pictures of the nude women in the magazine, and that to him it was pure smut, and Cooper objected again, and the judge sustained the objection. Then he said, "They can do with the magazine what they want to, the pictures or anything else, as long as it doesn't get into the personal lives of a person in the detail that they have gone to in this article."

"Do you know how Kim Pring reacted to that article?"

"Very hurt." Bill Storms looked sad. "And disturbed," he added for good measure. She stopped practicing the baton and didn't seem to care anymore after that. She'd dropped out of the university and came back home to the community college in Cheyenne. After that she wasn't as friendly and outgoing. "I asked her why she didn't go back to the university and she said, 'Because I don't know how people will accept me.' And she said, 'The talk—I don't know really whether I am up to it.' "

Storms said he heard people joking about the article, comments like " 'If she has got that kind of talents, well, boy, I would sure like to spend a night with her.' "

Cooper asked a hundred or more questions before he finally got to what his cross-examination was about. "Now she told you that she didn't know how people would accept her and that's why she didn't go back to school at Laramie, is that right?"

"She was afraid of the adverse reaction," Bill Storms said.

"Now was this consistent with the kind of toughness that you knew of her when she was going towards a goal?"

"No, it wasn't."

"If you didn't see the pageant, why did you connect a blue warm-up suit and blue gown with Kim Pring?" Never ask "why" on cross-examination. The witness will tell you.

"I had seen the gown. I had seen pictures of her . . . blue stuck in my mind. I think that's because blue was something to her."

"And you thought the article was about Kim Pring?"

"I *knew* the article was about Kim Pring."

"How did you know?" Never ask "how" on cross-examination. The witness will tell you.

"You can't refer to Miss Wyoming of 1978 and baton twirling without it being associated to Kim Pring."

At the recess Eddie and I went out to the big marble hall, and Kim went to find her mother who wasn't permitted in the courtroom because of the rule that no witness is permitted to hear the others' testimony. Mary Jayne Pring was left alone in a witness room a short distance down the hall to wonder what was happening to her daughter in that courtroom, and Kim also had to face her trial alone. The woman was pacing back and forth. I walked in and put my arm around her. "It's okay, Mama. Everything's going good in there."

"Yeah," Eddie said. "We're way ahead." He talked nice and gentle to Mrs. Pring. "An' the jury doesn't like Cooper." He gave her a kind smile.

"I don't know, Eddie. He's awful pretty," I said, "and we got three women on the jury."

Kim laughed and her mother heard that good sound and the worried lines around the mother's eyes began to dissolve.

Mary Jayne Pring handed Kim a sandwich. "You have to keep your strength up in there. You have to be strong."

After the recess Eddie brought a blowup of the article into the courtroom. Each page stood over seven feet tall. I used a pointer and read it to the jury word for word, the jurors reading the article along with me—about how Miss Wyoming had discovered her special talent at Colter Bay with the Tetons looking down on her, about how her boyfriend began " 'to pour into her' " and about everything rising—" 'not only his soul but his body too, a good inch or inch and a half off the ground, [until] he hung suspended from her mouth.' "

I read every word slowly, like a father reading to his children at bedtime. I read about her being in her "baby-blue chiffon" at the Miss America Pageant and about the fight that took place between the contestants backstage, how Corky, her coach, was drunk and hiccuped and leaned over and put his hand on her knees and how she cried " 'in loud, breathless sobs, leaning against him.' "

I read on. The jury saw each word and listened. " 'Holding her tight, he [Corky] closed his eyes and patted her. All summer he had dreamed of holding her, but his gesture now was without lust. . . .' " Eddie held the blowup of the article in front of him. I read a little while to one juror, then to the next, and I read to each in turn. " ' "I have real talent," she sobbed. "I have real talent." ' "

" ' "I know darlin," [Corky said], "I think what it was, honey, is that you're just too damn sexy. I mean, you don't even have to do anything; it just oozes out of you as natural as . . . sweat. . . ." " He hurried to finish before it went dark altogether. "And anything too real scares the shit out of people, I guess." ' " I glanced at the judge. He was listening carefully.

And then she was on her feet, wiping the tears from her face. "Help me, Corky. Help me show them . . ."

"What are you doing?" he wanted to know, feeling the stage careening around him and trying to regain his balance.

"Shhhh!" She knelt down and unzipped his fly. She wanted to show them that her talent was nothing to be feared, not dangerous, but beautiful and necessary.

"Not here," he pleaded, and dreaming of the long night's privacy at the Beach Queen as she dipped inside his pants with one hand and steadied him with the other.

"Trust me," she whispered, and she slipped him into her mouth just as Emory Dukes announced the fourth runner-up. . . .

As Emory Dukes called out the third and second runners-up, she imagined the questions that the judge would ask her when they realized their mistake, when they saw to what uses her talent could be put.

"Why do you want to be Miss America?" "Because I want to help the people of the world; I want to be the special ambassador of love and peace."

"Would you blow the entire Soviet Central Committee to prevent a Third World War? Marshal Tito? Fidel Castro?" "I would, I would." And in her mind she saw rising above the towering Tetons, like movie credits, the words: MISS WYOMING SAVES THE WORLD! ...

The audience was whistling and clapping for the new Miss America as Miss Wyoming took another deep breath and drew on Corky with all of the energy she had left. An inch off the ground now and rising, Corky forgot himself completely and began to make low, gurgling noises. ...

Emory Dukes launched into "There She Goes" as Miss Alaska, flowers in hand, innocent smile flashed to the world, started down the runway. But the television cameras did not follow her. They remained stationary, trained down the alley where they had a head-on view of Miss Wyoming. Dreaming not of USO shows and appearances at 4-H clubs but of *what a Miss America should be* [I emphasized the words], she knelt in service to her country with her eyes raised to Corky, his head and arms flung back in unimaginable delight, having just passed the three-inch mark and still ascending.

That was the end of the story. I looked at the jury. There were no snickers, no smiles. I said, "Thank you, Your Honor."

I continued questioning Bill Storms. "Now Mr. Cooper asked you about the jokes you heard about Kim Pring in the locker room among men, and he wanted to know if they weren't like ordinary filthy jokes men tell. Was there a difference?"

"Yes, there was. A joke is something you laugh at and I didn't find these very funny. They were just comments about her—the talent they claim in this." Bill Storms pointed at the blowup of the *Penthouse* article now standing against the wall. " 'Boy,' they said, they 'would sure like to get a blowjob like that.' "

Then Cooper asked him on recross-examination, "You know that those things didn't really happen?"

"That's correct."

"That's all I have," Cooper said.

I called Flo Armstrong. The jury watched this stately older woman walk in small, hesitant steps toward the bar of the court. She looked up at the judge for his permission to enter such an important arena, and the judge smiled and motioned her forward to the stand. She sat down and adjusted her glasses slightly.

"Are you a little nervous, Mrs. Armstrong?" I asked with a reassuring smile.

"Oh, sort of." Then she thought she ought to explain her shivers. "It was cold in that room," she said, meaning the witness room where she'd been waiting. She said she'd been in the Pring home many times, and that the Prings, and Kim too, were "very dear friends." Her voice sounded sweet and grandmotherly. The jurors had pleasant looks on their faces.

Mrs. Armstrong had grown to know Kim at the time she'd broken her back in an automobile accident. "Little Kim was only in high school at the time and came over and cleaned my entire house, including my bathtub, everything, and I offered to pay her and she wouldn't take a dime." Kim came back several times and did up her dishes too. "She is a very beautiful, talented, compassionate, lovely girl."

"Thank you," I said. "Can you state whether or not there was any feeling locally about a Cheyenne girl going to the Miss Wyoming contest?" Cooper didn't object.

"Oh, of course. Everybody was talking about how proud we were of having Kim win Miss Wyoming." Then Flo Armstrong said she'd read the article but she truly didn't know what some of the words meant until she asked her son. "He is a paramedic so he explained it to me," she said, as if it took special training to understand what the article was about. "It was a very degrading article."

"If I used just a word, one word—'outrageous'—would you agree with that?" I led.

"Yes," she said before Cooper could get his objection out.

"Objection. Leading."

"Sustained. The answer of the witness is stricken, and you are instructed to disregard it," the judge said to the jury, sounding a little testy. I gave the judge an apologetic smile.

"Now, after your son explained it to you, did you find anything humorous about it?"

"No, not at all."

"Did you laugh?"

"No . . . in fact I cried."

"Do you know anybody who read the article who laughed?"

"No, none whatsoever."

She said she had talked to Kim on the phone, and Kim was crying—said she was so embarrassed. "I said, 'Well, let's go out and have a cup of coffee or something,' and she said, 'No, I just don't want to go anywhere.' "

She'd seen quite a change in Kim. The girl had put on a lot of weight—didn't seem to care anymore—she'd lost interest in everything, whereas before she'd been a very vivacious person. "She doesn't laugh. She doesn't joke. Kim was the type of a girl that if you walked in the house, Kim would throw her arms around you and kiss you. Now if you walk in the house, Kim would probably go upstairs."

On cross-examination Cooper asked, "The Kim Pring that you described and knew was a very unique person, wasn't she?"

"Yes, she was."

"She was unique in the way she served her community?"

"That's right. She has gone to the VA Hospital with her little students time and time again, and gave performances there. If she was ever called on to do anything, she did."

"And there were none of *these* activities that you have described mentioned in this story? You didn't really believe that the things talked about in that story happened, did you?"

"I didn't think that Kim would ever do anything like that, no."

"Call your next witness, Mr. Spence," the judge said. He moved his cases right along, no dillydallying. "Try your cases, gentlemen," he would say. "Try your cases."

I called Robert Hofler, the senior editor at *Penthouse*, who still looked like the same twenty-five-year-old I'd seen in front of the magistrate. I picked up a copy of his deposition and set it down on the podium. I would hold him to his prior answers.

Again he admitted *Penthouse* had the right under their contract with Cioffari to change the article as they wished. "Now that means, doesn't it, Mr. Hofler, that had you wanted to, you could have cut out that whole section about oral sex?" Yes, and he admitted he could have changed the article from a story about Miss Wyoming to one about Miss New York. "But you know that you have a lot more customers for your magazine in New York than you do in Wyoming, isn't that true?" He admitted it. "And you don't want to offend your customers, do you?" He admitted that too.

The next morning Cooper called a meeting of all the attorneys with the judge in chambers. "To what do I owe the honor of this visit?" Judge Brimmer asked.

"The next witness is going to be Mr. Guccione," Cooper said. He was tense and pacing, and soon began to argue that the Court should prohibit me from cross-examining Guccione about any articles in *Penthouse* except the one in question. He was trying to put a protective judicial cloak around his client before he took the stand. Perhaps he was worried I would torment the man in front of the jury and cause him to become so riled he'd turn the jury against his case. My plan exactly.

"Your Honor," Cooper said, "we would ask the Court to instruct opposing counsel, based on his histrionics and movements around the courtroom yesterday and his apparent hatred of Mr. Guccione in front of the jury . . . as Your Honor will recall, he would approach him and be almost screaming at the top of his lungs—"

"I noticed Mr. Spence going over and standing by Mr. Guccione and pointing to him and what not, and I was inclined to think that was improper, but no objection was made at the time." Then the judge said to me, "Let's not do it again—going clear across to the north side of the courtroom where Mr. Guccione was, was a little extreme."

Cooper pressed further. "I'm afraid that in cross-examining Guccione about his policies that we're going to have *other* issues shoved in—"

"No. No, we are not," the judge said.

"Well," I said to the judge, "I told the jury, and I think I have told you and everybody, that Guccione takes people and then says anything he wants to about them because he can't be sued since they're public figures." That was the *Penthouse* scheme that evidenced malice across the board, I argued.

After a moment Judge Brimmer began to speak to us in a very patient way. He said he thought that in the Falwell matter there were enough similarities that questions on that matter might be relevant. "I assume Guccione is going to deny that that's his policy and call his editors to support him, and then it's an issue of fact for the jury to decide," the judge said.

"Well, Mr. Spence told the jury that there is a goal to shock, and somehow that makes anything that Mr. Spence finds 'shocking' admissible in evidence, and we have lost control over the focus of this case," Cooper argued.

Finally the judge turned to me and said, "Well, I suppose you could ask Guccione 'Isn't that what you did in the current issue about Reverend Falwell?' and he could say yes or no." Then Judge Brimmer turned to Kelley and referred to a quote Kelley said was on a certain page of some case and the judge said, "I cannot find those phrases on that page."

"Well, I apologize if the page is incorrect, but I guarantee you that the phrase is in there," Kelly said, and after that we went back to the courtroom and Hofler took the stand once more, looking like a young man who hadn't slept all night worrying about what the boss would think of his testimony. Guccione still sat in the front pew waiting to take the stand and then to get the hell out of Wyoming. I could hear him grumbling in his gravelly voice to a small pasty-faced man sitting next to him. Someone said the man was Guccione's bodyguard.

"How come Mr. Guccione can sit in here and listen to these witnesses and my mother can't?" Kim whispered to me.

"They say he is the corporation's representative, so he can stay. Corporations aren't alive. They have to have somebody alive to stand in for them," I said.

I gave Hofler a good-morning smile and a nod and then began a new attack. The in-text headlines on each page of the story were called "blowup quotes." "What you wanted to do with these 'blowup quotes' was interest the reader, isn't that true?" Yes, he admitted, and he said he had picked the words " 'Would you blow the entire Soviet Central Committee to prevent a Third World War?' 'I would, I would,' she thought."

I read, " 'With the baton in her mouth, Miss Wyoming stroked outward along the polished chrome in the direction of the judges.' " There was a small replica of the front-page illustration of the half-naked Miss Wyoming with the baton to her lips. "Those two [the quote and the picture] kind of go together, don't they?" I pointed to the large blowup of the page in question that the jury was watching.

"Yes."

"And so the reader would look at the baton in her mouth, and read the language 'With the baton in her mouth, Miss Wyoming stroked

outward along the polished chrome in the direction of the judges.'
That's a shocking statement that would catch the eye of a reader,
isn't that true?"

"Well, it would catch the eye of the reader, but I don't think it
would shock them."

I looked over at the women in the front row of the jury, and raised
my eyebrows. Then, like a matador to a bull he now dominated, I
turned my back to Hofler and, facing the jurors instead, I continued
to question him. "It implies that Miss Wyoming committed fellatio
on the baton, isn't that true?"

"Well, I don't think you can perform fellatio on a baton. ... I
don't think I understand."

"Don't you think that was meant to depict some kind of oral sex on
the baton?"

"It was symbolic of that."

"And you don't think that the symbol of oral sex on the baton is
shocking, isn't that true?" I still faced the jurors while asking the
questions of the witness behind me.

"No, I don't think it was shocking."

Now, my eyes fixed on the secretary in the front row of the jury
box, I said to Hofler, "It seemed kind of like old stuff at *Penthouse* for
people to do that sort of thing, symbolically, real or otherwise, isn't
that true?"

"Yes."

"Thank you," I said. Hofler was looking at his hands. He admitted
now there was nothing on the title page of the article to let the
reader know it was fiction and he admitted that nowhere in the article was the word "levitation" used by the author. "That word was
first used by his attorneys," I argued. He admitted that despite the
fact that *Penthouse* had a staff of available researchers, neither he nor
anyone else at *Penthouse* had made any survey to determine how the
average person who read the article would take it. I watched the
jury. Later I said, "Do you recognize the fact that some people might
read the article and not understand the idea of levitation?"

"No one that I know would not know the idea of levitation."

"You don't know any nice old ladies?"

"Objection. It is totally irrelevant."

"Sustained."

"And your researchers could have discovered, as they scanned the
article, where Kim Pring was from—they could have discovered if

she ever performed in Laramie—they could have discovered it all with a thirty-five-cent telephone call, isn't that all true?" Yes, and he also admitted his researchers could have asked Kim questions like "Did you perform at Laramie? Did you practice at the gym? Did you have a male coach? Did you wear a baby-blue warm-up suit? Did you wear a blue chiffon dress?"—all those questions could have been asked had somebody at *Penthouse* wanted them asked.

"You know the Miss America Pageant is quite a proper pageant, isn't it?" Sometime I would have to argue for the virtues of the Miss America Pageant despite my own view it was purely a commercial extravaganza presenting women as things—walking mannequins, more or less—along with the other objects sold, the hair spray, the shampoo, the soup. For me, these young women were reduced to pretty painted puppets with wet enameled smiles and flashing teeth.

The pageant could be defended as a throwback to ancient ceremonies where virgins were sacrificed to the gods. These young women of America were offered to the new gods of commerce—perfectly normal young women transformed into wiggly, sweet, smiley, nearly, but not quite, sexy thingamadoodles by which Kellogg's cereal and Stayfree maxi-pads would be sold to the housewives of America. I could make no such argument to this jury. The politics of a trial demand a consistency of position in a world where all truth and all ethics are situational and therefore often inconsistent.

"If you had little children, you wouldn't be ashamed to take them to the Miss America Pageant, isn't that true?" I asked Hofler.

"No."

"You know, Mr. Hofler, that the Miss America Pageant doesn't have very much to do with beauty. It has mostly to do with poise and talent and graciousness, and things that we like to see in our young women, isn't that true?"

"I don't agree with that," Hofler said. "I think that beauty is a major part of it. I remember when I was in grade school and went to the Catholic church, the bishop in the archdiocese said no Catholic women in the state of Iowa should be in the beauty pageant and he called it a 'cattle show.' "

I turned to the jury again. "Well, if the Miss America Pageant is a 'cattle show,' what do you think your priest would think of this article?" I gestured with a disgusted look in the direction of the seven-foot blowup of Miss Wyoming staring lustfully from the title page of the story at her phallic baton, her lips parted and waiting, her exposed breast nearly in everybody's face. I caught the eye of the two Masons on the jury.

"I have no idea what he would think," Hofler said. "At my tenth reunion I met my guidance counselor, who is a priest, and he seemed to be very proud of the idea that I was working for *Penthouse.*"

"I see," I said. "Did you ever send him copies of things like this that you were working on?" I pointed again to the blowup.

"Objection!"

"Sustained."

"Don't you recognize that the young women in the Miss America Pageant are tested severely for their poise and their grace?"

"All right."

"And wouldn't you admit that their talent is also an important part of it?"

"Yes."

"You have seen women with beautiful, wonderful talents on that show, haven't you?"

"Sure."

"Women who sing beautifully, dance, do acrobatics?"

"Yes."

"Do you think that's right and good and decent?" I sounded like the priest myself. I hated it. But it was war.

"The talents, yes."

"And so, isn't it true, Mr. Hofler, that what you and *Penthouse* have done in this case is to take an institution, an *American* institution, that deals with sex and womanhood in a proper and acceptable way, and you have undermined it with that article so as to show it as ugly, ludicrous, and obscene—isn't that true?"

"Objection. Calls for a conclusion of the witness he cannot make," Cooper said.

"Sustained."

"Assuming that people who read this article believed that it was about a *real* Miss Wyoming, the article would hold the *real* Miss Wyoming up in a false light, isn't that true?"

"Yes." With that admission I began prying the wound open wider.

"Now tell the ladies and gentlemen of the jury if it isn't true that the ways she would be held up in a false light are as follows: One, that she performed symbolic oral sex on a baton? That would be a false light, wouldn't it, under that assumption?"

"Yes."

"And that she performed fellatio on a boy named Monte on the shores of Jackson Lake—that would be a false light, wouldn't it?"

"Yes."

"And that she performed fellatio on her drunken coach, in the presence of sixty million television viewers, that would be a false light, would it not?"

"Yes."

"And that she would be willing to, using the language of the article, 'blow the entire Soviet Central Committee'—that would be a false light too, wouldn't it?"

"Yes."

"Now you had an *in-house attorney* at the time, who was an employee just like you?"

"Yes."

"By the way, how many employees work for *Penthouse?*"

"Oh, I don't really know. Maybe two hundred."

"But you also had an *out-house counsel,* didn't you, by the name of Grutman?" There was laughter in the courtroom. I didn't smile—not even a faint hint of one—one dare not with the jury watching.

"Mr. Grutman, yes."

"Counsel, I think the term is '*retained counsel,*' " the judge said. The judge didn't smile either.

"*Penthouse* had all the experience, all the manpower, all the attorneys, all the researchers—you had everything you needed to prevent this sort of thing from happening, didn't you?"

"Yes."

"Now the reason *Penthouse* didn't prevent this from happening is because it didn't mind at all if it got sued, because when it gets sued, it gets publicity, and that creates a greater readership and sale and revenue—isn't all of that true?"

"Object to the compound question," Cooper was on his feet again.

"Overruled."

"No, that is not the policy, the reason."

"Haven't you seen Mr. Guccione say on television or otherwise in the newspapers that the suit or complaints of Reverend Falwell simply increased his readership or his subscriptions by half a million readers?"

"Objection. That is not a statement of policy. There is no factual foundation for it at this time."

"Overruled."

"I haven't—"

I took a step or two toward the witness to break the subconscious protective barrier of the podium. The sound in my voice was accusatory, but I asked quietly: "Haven't you heard Mr. Guccione state that he couldn't afford a public-relations man with the genius of Reverend Falwell for increasing *Penthouse*'s circulation? Didn't you hear that?"

Hofler answered that he hadn't been up at one o'clock in the morning when Guccione had been on television, and no, he hadn't heard. But now the jury knew by his equivocal answer the statements had probably been made. They peered over at Guccione, looking for some sign of denial from him. Guccione only scowled back like an imperious gibbon caught in the monkey house.

Hofler claimed that *Penthouse*'s in-house counsel, one Joseph Kraft, had read the article and thereafter had asked some questions about it.

"Would you say that Mr. Kraft was intelligent, sophisticated?"
"Yes."

"He is a lawyer—well educated, well trained?"
"Yes."

"And after he read the article, he came to you and asked you if the article was 'made up,' didn't he?"
"Yes."

"And he not only asked you if the article was 'made up' but he asked you, 'Is it fiction?' Isn't that true?"

"Yes." But Hofler denied knowing of any deal made with Cioffari to write a series of articles about contemporary American life springing from *actual* events. I handed Hofler an editor's page from the preceding December issue of *Penthouse*, marked Exhibit 370A. "What does your magazine itself say?"

" 'This story is one in a forthcoming collection by—' "

"Please don't mumble. Read it clearly."

" 'This story is one in a forthcoming collection by Cioffari in which all the stories spring from actual events in contemporary American life.' "

"Are you saying to the ladies and gentlemen of the jury that you didn't know that there had been some kind of an arrangement between *Penthouse* and Mr. Cioffari as early as 1978 to write such articles?"

"I didn't know about this collection of articles."

I contended that the original uncut version of the Miss Wyoming story showed that Cioffari actually intended to write about a real, not a fictional, person. For example, Hofler had cut parts of the story that further identified the real Miss Wyoming—that she was "blonde and blue-eyed," and had been accompanied to the pageant by an elderly woman in a wheelchair. In the story Cioffari had made reference to a sickly old aunt, and Hofler had cut that too. Hofler cut Cioffari's statement that his heroine had been the majorette in the school marching band for four years, Kim's exact history as well. Yet throughout his testimony, Hofler steadfastly insisted he did not know of the existence of the real Miss Wyoming, Kimerli Jayne Pring.

In front of the jury and the glowering Guccione, Hofler wouldn't admit—perhaps couldn't—that ordinary people might conclude Kim Pring had consented to the article. I pulled out Hofler's deposition and turned quickly to his previous testimony, which I now read to the jury and to Hofler. I had previously asked in his deposition if he left room for the possibility that some people might believe the article was published with Kim's permission. He admitted that some people might.

"I will object to questions about *possibilities*, Your Honor." Cooper was speaking as much to coach Hofler as he was to lodge an objection with the judge.

"Overruled," Judge Brimmer said quietly.

"Do you remember stating that?"

"Yes."

"Is that your answer today?"

Trapped, Hofler took the lead from Cooper's objection. "That is a *possibility*," he said.

On cross-examination Cooper tried to transform his witness into just an ordinary boy raised on a small farm in Norris Springs, Iowa. But the sound of Hofler's voice wasn't a farm boy hollering at the cows or slopping the hogs, and he didn't walk like a farm boy who'd spent a lifetime sloughing through the mud and plowed fields, nor did he sit up there on the witness stand like a farm boy who'd spent a thousand dreary days and half that many nights on a bucking old tractor out in the fields. He seemed proper, even, prissy, and his voice was sweet and high.

"It ain't comin' off," Eddie whispered.

Cooper hauled his witness through the endless details of the editorial process at *Penthouse*, and his testimony dragged on as if Cooper were punishing us for having called the witness in the first place. It was a "*story*," not an "article"! Cioffari was paid $1,500 for the piece, which Cooper was now calling "the writing." He went into endless explanations with Hofler as to how the form-contract that *Penthouse* used for its writers operated in practice—they wouldn't change a story without consulting the author even though they had the right to do so, and he had the witness explain how the researchers worked. This was fiction, so there wasn't anything for them to inquire into, and that's why Kraft, the attorney, had done nothing about it.

Cooper spoke of satire. "And all satire makes fun of something or someone?"

"That's true."

"And the fact that *Penthouse* utilizes satire in its magazine, is that, in your knowledge, any indication that *Penthouse* is doing anything other than stating opinions in the form of satire?"

"That's argumentative and conclusory and leading," I said, standing up from my chair next to Kim at plaintiff's table. We were closest to the jury.

"Overruled."

"And is it your understanding that the statement of opinion by a publication is a constitutionally protected freedom of the press?"

"Yes."

"And, therefore, did you do any research or checking on that type of statement of opinion?"

"Only on the advice of counsel."

"And did you receive any such advice as to the article about Miss Wyoming?"

"No."

"The *story*. Excuse me," Cooper corrected himself.

"No."

"That's all I have," Cooper said, pressing down his cowlick with a quick gesture of triumph.

The judge turned to me. "Any redirect?"

"You bet," I said. I jumped up. I began my first question before I got to the podium. "About your *understanding* of First Amendment protection—isn't it also your understanding that there is no First Amendment protection for obscenity?"

"Objection and ask that it be stricken," Cooper hollered.

"Objection sustained. The witness won't answer."

"Do you have some kind of constitutional protection for a statement in the article about Miss Wyoming committing oral sex? Do you think that's constitutionally protected?"

"Yes." I looked at each member of the jury quickly as if to say, did you hear that?—and the jurors looked back saying, yes, they had heard, and then I came upon my last series of questions to Hofler.

"Well, Mr. Hofler, when you talk about 'opinion' that the Constitution protects, you want to have the right to criticize political acts, don't you?"

"Yes."

"You want to have the right to object to wars?"

"Yes."

"To laws?"

"Yes."

"To social programs?"

"Yes."

"To matters of public interest?"

"Yes."

"And those are the items to which you believe that constitutional protection applies, isn't that true?"

"Yes."

"Do you think you have the constitutional right to libel someone?"

"No."

"Thank you." I said and sat down.

In the judge's chambers after the noon recess, I said to Eddie in front of the judge, "Eddie you talk to the judge. He listens to you better than he does to me." I wanted to stop Cooper from cross-examining his own witnesses after I had finished with them—like he'd done with Hofler. I wanted the leading stopped.

The judge listened to Eddie's argument and then he said, "I'll tell you what I'll do. I will enforce that part, if you gentlemen will agree that you will not ask any more leading questions yourself on direct." The judge looked at me with a knowing smile. "Now I suggest that with Mr. Spence that may be an impossibility. In fact the usual Spencerian technique is to ask the leading question, and then to rephrase it properly when objection is made. That's something I have observed for years. If we are going to start quibbling about leading questions, let's be sure our own house is clean."

"Well, I'm getting better." I smiled at the judge.

"You really are," the judge said.

"I have a right to lead an adverse witness," I said, and everybody knew that it was all right between the judge and me, and that the judge had heard Eddie, and that when we objected again to Cooper's leading of his own witnesses the judge would remember.

Then I couldn't eat my lunch again, and perhaps for good reason. The next witness right after the noon recess would be, of course, Robert C. Guccione.

18

Before Guccione took the stand, of course, he met the press—
Time, Newsweek, the Associated Press, the Denver *Post,* the local
Cheyenne paper—press persons pressing Guccione for answers to
their vacuous questions, for as hard as the press fights for its rights,
the right it most often exercises is to be dreary. I listened from a distance.

"What do you have to say about the lawsuit?"

"It is a spectacle brought by an opportunistic publicity seeker."

"How do you think you'll do up against Spence?"

"Who is Spence?"

"Do you think your brown velvet pants and your traditional gold
chains will go over with a Wyoming jury?"

"If the jury has ordinary intelligence they should be capable of
perceiving that a man's taste in dress is hardly the issue in this case.
What about what's his name?" He pointed at me.

"Spence?"

"Yeah, Spence. What about that silly twenty-gallon Wyatt Earp
hat he wears and those shit-kicker boots—ask him about his dress."

I reached into my briefcase, pulled out a baby-blue T-shirt, and
approached Guccione. As I did, I grabbed Cooper by the arm. He
jumped, taken aback that I should have touched him. "Come on," I
said. "I got something for your client."

"What?" Cooper said, pulling away from me.

"Come on," I said, grabbing him by the arm again and shaming
him with the sound of my voice when he jerked back a second time. I
walked on toward Guccione where he was holding forth to the reporters, his back to me. Cooper followed. I tapped Guccione on the
shoulder, then I tapped again. The reporters facing Guccione saw me
and began to smile, and one nodded to me. It was only when the man

realized he'd lost his audience that he turned quickly to see who was at his back.

"How ya doin' there, Bobby?" I said.

Guccione's face fell. His bodyguard moved quickly in front of him. Cooper crowded up. The reporters pushed in closer. The courtroom crowd stopped their incessant quacking and the place was suddenly silent.

"I brought you a present," I said. "Here." I held up the baby-blue T-shirt for everybody to see. It had my picture on the front. I turned the shirt around. On the back in large block letters were the words: GERRY SPENCE IS A NICE GUY. The audience laughed. Guccione glowered and his dark face reddened. "With my best compliments," I said, handing him the shirt. "Gerry Spence *is* a nice guy. You'll see." I smiled a long smile and raised my eyebrows, and the crowd laughed again.

"Still a wise guy, huh?" Guccione retorted. The crowd, either fickle or fair, laughed for him now. Guccione grabbed the shirt and threw it in my direction, and then I picked it off the floor and gave Guccione a small bow and walked back to my table just before the jury came in.

"What the hell was that all about?" Eddie asked.

"Just gettin' the bull ready for the fight," I said.

"Yeah?" Eddie said. "I don't think that bull needs it. Look at him!"

The bailiff hit his gavel, Judge Brimmer took the bench, and everybody fell into silence. I looked up at the judge as innocent as a sinner can look.

"Call your next witness," the judge said.

"Plaintiff calls Robert C. Guccione," I said.

Guccione sprung from his seat. He marched toward the witness stand with a steady, rapid gait—the striking of his heels on the carpet, as if he were stomping over the enemy, distracted from the natural grace of his stride. Every eye in the courtroom appraised him, this man in the brown velvet pants and pointed high-heeled French boots. He raised his hand, the clerk administered the oath; and Guccione took the stand, scowling out over the courtroom and at me. His bodyguard moved nearer to him, just outside the bar. Guccione was alone in the pit.

I kept him sitting there silently until the loud edge of uneasiness began to emerge from the silence. Never once did the man look at the jury, even ignoring them, I thought, as if they were a distasteful part of the courtroom furnishings. Finally I stood up to examine, and Guccione quickly refocused on me with a perceptible sneer on his face. As I stared back, his expression remained frozen as though what I saw was what I got, was who he was, as if those were the base lines of both face and heart. He was a man steeled and ready. I approached the bull.

Ha, Toro.

"Good afternoon, Mr. Guccione," I said. My guts churned, the adrenaline running free.

"Good afternoon," he growled back reluctantly.

"How are you today?" I smiled.

"Very well, thank you." He glared down at me from the witness stand, waiting for my first thrusts—for this fight to which he was now fully committed to begin—a fight, I thought, he was eager for. He really had nothing to lose except the deductible on his insurance policy, a trifling sum compared to the money that trouble had always generated for him. The insurance companies were at risk, not Guccione—ten million out front—and Cooper and Kelley were hired to protect the companies, not him. Grutman was his personal lawyer, and Grutman had manipulated things so that by his not being here, Guccione had been provided better protection in the record than if Grutman were here in the pit facing these uncouth rowdies from Wyoming. He was not uneasy in the slightest; that was obvious, but irritated and impatient to dispose of me.

"You are the founder of *Penthouse* magazine, and its sole shareholder, are you not?"

"That's correct."

"The publisher?" Feel him out.

"Yes."

"The editor in chief?" See if he charges cleanly.

"That's correct."

"The chairman of the board?"

"Yes." He was waiting for an opening.

"And one of the things you try to do is to keep your readers satisfied, isn't that true?"

"Yes, of course."

"You want them to buy your magazine."

"Very much so." The expression never changed on his face. His mouth moved mechanically. But his eyes were alive. He was a dangerous witness. I could not turn my back on him.

"Your magazine is sold in Germany?"

"Yes."

"How about Japan?"

"It is sold in Japan."

"The Netherlands?"

"Yes."

"Belgium?" He was waiting.

"Yes."

"France?"

"Yes. I would say at least a dozen countries."

"Maybe twenty?"

You could hear his impatience growing. "I have no idea."

"How would you, as president of *Penthouse*, find out in how many countries your magazine sells if you wanted to know?"

"I would ask our national distributor."

"You have never done that in all of these years?"

"No, because it is unnecessary to know that. You may sell three hundred fifty copies in Swaziland."

"Do you sell three hundred fifty copies in Swaziland?"

"I have no idea."

"You haven't checked that out?"

"How many copies do you think are sold outside the United States?"

He grimaced impatiently. "For the third time—an additional five hundred thousand copies."

"Well, please don't get too impatient with me." I smiled at the man again. He didn't return the smile. The duel was under way. He was a quick, extremely intelligent man with great experience in the courtroom. He would give me no answers that would hurt his legal cause, no admissions, that much I knew. All I could hope to do was to unpeel one side of the man for the jury to see—to reveal for them his hostility, his arrogance—to present a man to the jurors whose power and native ability to dominate would cause them to fear him, as a deer instinctively runs in panic at the first scent of the wolf.

We hate what we fear and will try to destroy it.

For the jury, for me, the struggle must become one between the forces of good and evil, finally the drama of every trial. There sat the glaring Guccione—the words he chose to answer my questions, their very sounds, creating the tensions, the images in the minds of the jury that would frighten and thus repel.

I cared little about the content of his arguments. I was bent on how I might display him, or better, how, in the turmoil of battle, he would display himself—as dangerous, perhaps wicked—because in the end, the logic of the word never prevails, not with the jury, not with the judge, not with anyone. The jury would not decide the case on Guccione's arguments. Never. But on Guccione himself. Logic is only a tool to accomplish what the emotions already desire.

Now, before the jury, Guccione was contained, deliberate. Already he had toned down the caustic, hostile behavior he had displayed at his pleasure during his deposition. He was seeking to portray himself as a respectable, intelligent, quite innocent man, minding his own business, who had been rudely interrupted in his work by these greedy, groundless claims made against him. There was a perceptibly self-righteous air in the way he presented himself, yes, even in the way he sat so straight in the witness chair, as if the effrontery of it all were barely tolerable. He, too, was fighting for the role of the just and the good.

I knew Guccione would wish to win the polemic, to capture the most points in the debate that was about to take place. He had prevailed in such engagements, perhaps hundreds of times before, and with the same arguments. As I sized him up, he would perceive that winning the debate would make him right and therefore good.

But no. Even *novilleros* never try to outcharge the bull. I had learned that painful lesson long ago—never engage your opponent where he wishes to fight—in the arena of his own arguments. Besides, in the courtroom one can win many an argument and lose the jury. In a trial one does not win arguments. One wins jurors.

Guccione was impatient to get on with it. I let him stew. I made him answer more barely relevant questions. He hated it.

"How many languages is *Penthouse* carried in?"

"It is published in Italian, German, Spanish, and there is an Australian edition, published in English; however, it is an edition exclusive to Australia. And there is an English edition exclusive to England."

"Of course you don't have to change the pictures, do you?"

"Yes."

"Would it be fair to say that some of the countries won't permit the pictures that are published in your American edition?"

"No."

"Object. This doesn't relate to the editorial policy of this article. Your Honor; it is required—"

"Sustained." I must handle Cooper, who came at me now like another bull from another direction. If his objections caused me to lose my concentration, which would be his tactic, I could stumble and be trampled. I must anticipate his objections and the judge's rulings too, for the judge could turn the jury if I were careless, if the jury perceived me as being unfair, for a jury will not permit a lawyer to win by violating the rules.

"Now, as your circulation increases, in a general way your advertising rates go up, isn't that true?"

"That is correct."

"And to give us an example of that, about how much would one color page in *Penthouse* magazine go for?"

"Approximately thirty-five thousand dollars."

"For just one page?" I sounded incredulous.

"Yes," Guccione said as if he were answering some pest. I looked at the jurors and raised my eyebrows. The men leaned away from the witness, pulled back, their arms folded tightly across their chests. The men stared. I glanced at the judge. He was also staring with uncommon concentration, the dispassionate look faded, the cheek muscles tensed, the jaw set, the forehead no longer with a frown but the skin pulled drum tight across the skull—a man committed to hear clearly, accurately, this witness before him.

"How many pages of advertising do you sell in *Penthouse* a year?" I continued.

Cooper objected, "This is irrelevant at this stage, Your Honor."

"Yes, I think it is. Sustained," the judge ruled very quietly. I could remember times as a young lawyer when, faced with a hostile witness and a lawyer on the other side who stood objecting to my every question, and with a judge who sustained them, I became frozen, catatonic almost, unable to speak a word or form a question. I could only stand there in front of the jury, my face reddening, knowing I was a fool, knowing that everyone else knew it also. Then the judge would bark down from the bench, "Ask your next question, Mr. Spence," knowing I couldn't ask one—not even one—and I knew that if I could, he would only sustain another objection to it. I wanted to hide someplace, but there is no place in the courtroom to hide. It is an arena in which one survives or not in the open, in which one is gored and trampled or not, where there is no cover.

I could feel old fears. I kept my eyes on Guccione. I asked the next question as if there had been no interruption. "You heard me tell the ladies and gentlemen of the jury that one of the secrets you use is to create a shock for the reader."

"Yes."

"You, of course, don't agree with that, do you?"

"Absolutely not."

"Do you like to surprise the reader?"

"How does one surprise the reader—by putting something inside the magazine which is billed as something else on the cover?" He was trying to engage me in his arguments. I ignored his question.

"Did you think that the article, 'Miss Wyoming Saves the World' was a shocking or surprising article?"

"Not in the least." I gave the jury a quick look.

"You laughed when you read it?"

"No, I didn't laugh. One can enjoy something funny without laughing at it."

"Did you laugh inside?"

"I found it amusing." Guccione didn't sound amused.

"Make you feel good?"

"Anything that I find amusing makes me feel good, yes." They were words in a crowded courtroom that were heard not just as words now but as the sounds of the struggle between that one witness and the lawyer that had become the case. I held the witness tight to the questions, gave him no chance to break loose where he could do damage with his own arguments. His attempt to appear civil did him no good. I stirred at Guccione's pot, kept it boiling so that the angry sounds and signs seeped out in his answers. He would antagonize the men. I watched the women.

There would be those quiet questions that pass in the mind of a woman as unannounced as a soft wind in the night. Could there be gentleness in such a man? Could such a man possess her by some irresistible power, press her into whatever fetters, fill her life with the tyranny a woman feared? He was close enough to the women on the jury that they could see him breathe—perhaps catch a faint trace of him in the languid rolling of the courtroom air. They could feel his presence, his dark aura. He was intriguing, mystifying, compelling as a devil, exciting as dark dreams. The women also folded their arms across their breasts and crossed their legs tightly. I could see their open nostrils, their open eyes, their tight mouths. They sat still as frozen sculptures dreading the sorcerer's touch, yet yearning for it, fearing bargains that can transform a woman and send her wandering into the night mumbling her own black incantations. Suddenly I realized all the women on the jury were beautiful.

"You say you try to produce the best possible magazine?"

"That's correct."

"I counted forty pages of full-color pictures of nude women including women in lesbian relationships with each other. Were you talking about all other editions of *Penthouse except* the August 1979 edition?"

"Your Honor, I object. Irrelevant—beyond your orders and I reserve the matter for later consideration," Cooper said, warning the Court and me he would move for another mistrial at the first opportunity.

"Yes," the judge said. "The other content of the other magazines is irrelevant here today." But the judge's voice was flat and passionless. I was all right.

I said, "I want to talk to you about the August issue now. Hear me. I am only going to talk about the August 1979 issue."

"Yes."

"You have it in front of you. Have you seen the issue?"

"Of course."

"Have you thumbed through it recently?"

"No."

"Just take a minute and do that—just rather quickly." Guccione reluctantly took the magazine in his hand. The women watched his fingers move through the pages, as if he were able to capture the women within between his deft right thumb and forefinger while he held them down with his heavy other hand.

"I noticed you didn't read the index. Take a look at the index very quickly, too, if you would, please." He was not a man who took commands easily. I walked up beside him to view the exhibit. I put on my reading glasses.

"May I have my glasses, too?"

"You can use mine if you like."

"I don't know that they would be the same as mine." One does not take gratuities from the enemy. Daichman fetched his glasses.

"Now, would you say that that issue is up to standard for you?"

"Yes," he said stewing, impatient. "This issue is in my opinion an excellent issue of *Penthouse.*"

"All right. Are you proud of it?"

"Yes, of course." I gave the jury another quick look. I thought they knew what I meant.

"And you wouldn't mind if the ladies and gentlemen of the jury took it in their hands and looked at it?" I handed the magazine to the woman on the end. She hesitated as if I were handing her something nasty. I gave her a reassuring smile and held it out again for her. Then she took it quickly and looked down without opening it.

"Who is Xaviera Hollander?"

"Your Honor, I must object. This is irrelevant."

"Sustained."

"You have a column that deals with deviate sex that's handled by Xaviera Hollander?"

"Same objection."

"Sustained."

"Are there contained in that issue certain letters which have been written to what is called 'Penthouse Forum'?"

Cooper hollered: "I would ask the Court to instruct counsel not to ask further questions along these lines."

"That's right, and you are so instructed," Judge Brimmer said. Careful. I would still be all right if the jury saw my questions as proper and the judge's rulings as overly technical, perhaps even protective. But Guccione needed no protection.

I looked up at His Honor and asked in dismay, "I can't ask about the contents of the '79 magazine in question?"

"The other contents of the magazine speak for themselves. The jury may consider this article in relation to those. They can read it and see it for themselves. There is no need for questions about it," the judge said. The woman with the magazine now opened it cautiously.

"Relative to that magazine, do you try to let your readers believe that your magazine has some socially useful function?"

"I don't ask my readers to believe anything."

"Do you ask your readers to believe that you are courageous in exposing the truth?"

"I don't ask my readers to believe"—Cooper tried to object, but Guccione shouted through—"anything! Then I don't—don't get me wrong—"

I interrupted him, pushed him now. "Do you have a current advertisement going on national television in which you appear and say to the people, 'It's what you don't know that can hurt you'? Do you say that?"

"No."

"And do you have writers who investigate?"

"We do."

"Isn't it true, Mr. Guccione, that all of those articles are nothing more than sugarcoating to cover the real thing that you are selling, which is, indeed, sex?"

"Absolutely not!" Guccione shouted again.

"Haven't you said that, in effect, a number of times—the latest of which was an interview you had with Morley Safer of CBS's *Sixty Minutes?*"

"No."

"Do you know Morley Safer?"

"Yes."

"Were you interviewed by *Sixty Minutes?*"

"Yes."

"Didn't Mr. Safer ask you this question: 'What you are doing is hiding the most obscene smut behind the skirts of the First Amendment.' Didn't he ask you that?"

"I don't recall."

"It is irrelevant," Cooper said.

Judge Brimmer advised, "At this point it becomes relevant because the witness denied that he was 'sugarcoating sex.' He may be asked about the truth of that statement. It goes to credibility."

"The answer is that I don't recall ever using the expression 'sugarcoating.' I don't remember Safer making those remarks to me. And if you have the transcript of our interview, I would like to see it to refresh my memory." Guccione was court-wise. He would get no deeper into the trap.

"Yes, I will show it to you in just a moment. I want to ask you one question first because, indeed, one of my purposes in cross-examination is to determine whether or not your memory serves you well."

"You are not cross-examining me! I am your witness," he said, sounding more like a raging lawyer than a witness as he attempted to find refuge in the rule that holds one may not cross-examine his own witness, a rule Guccione must have heard in his countless appearances in court proceedings.

"I don't claim you, Mr. Guccione," I said. There was laughter from the audience.

The judge struck his gavel. "You are called as an adverse witness," the judge said to Guccione. "Under the rules one may call his opponent and cross-examine him."

"Now, Mr. Guccione, didn't you tell Mr. Safer that it was necessary for the sale of your magazine to have both articles and pictures of naked women?"

"I don't recall what I said."

"I am going to ask you, Mr. Guccione, if this refreshes your recollection." I read out loud to Guccione from the 60 *Minutes* interview by Morley Safer. "Mr. Safer is saying to you, 'You also publish articles by well-known writers who no doubt you pay a lot of money to, but you say that the pictures are what sell *Penthouse.* Why bother with the articles?' And do you remember, Mr. Guccione, answering, 'Well, for a very simple reason, Morley. If we were to publish only pictures in *Penthouse,* we wouldn't have anything like the sale that we now have. And by the same token, if we were to publish the good editorials that we publish in *Penthouse* only, exclusively, we wouldn't have the sale. It requires a combination of both.' Didn't you tell him that?"

"Your Honor, I object. This is not a statement under oath and it is improper impeachment because the witness hasn't denied it. He doesn't remember the interview."

"I am asking him if this refreshes his memory," I said.

"All right. He may answer," the judge ruled.

"It doesn't refresh my recollection as to that particular interview because, as I say, that happened some years ago. And I have since given perhaps hundreds of interviews. . . ."

"Didn't you also tell Mr. Safer that one of the reasons that you put those articles in there is so that there will be some redeeming social value in the event you are charged with obscenity?"

"Certainly not," he said. But I had Guccione's interview with Safer in front of me. Safer had pointed out that one of the reasons for publishing articles by well-known writers was the "calculated decision," as Safer called it, that "if you are hauled into court, there is the redeeming social value," to which Guccione had answered, "Oh, yes. No question about it. No question . . . a lot of magazines would have a hard time defending themselves, because they don't have that sort of redeeming social, political, artistic and whatever matter in their pages. But we do, very much so. We always have had, long before it became a decision that to contain this kind of material would help us in any defense when we go to court."

Now Guccione had said, no, certainly he had not told Safer any such thing, and Cooper, of course, objected, and the court sustained. No matter—the jury had heard my question. I forged ahead, next pointing out to Guccione that there were forty pages of naked women in the August issue and the longest article was only eight pages. Cooper objected again. The judge sustained again. I thought the questions proper, and Cooper's continuous objections were beginning to tire the jury. I thought they perceived him as obstructing the flow of testimony, as preventing them from hearing what they wished to hear, and anyway, perhaps the information I wanted to convey to the jury was sometimes better contained in my questions than any answers I might hope to get from Guccione. Moreover, there was no way to predict the Court's ruling in advance, the legal questions being very close. A question might be permitted one moment and a like question rejected the next. I could not assume the judge would rule against me until each question was tested, and in the testing I was winning even though the judge often ruled against me—cautious rulings I thought, made by a judge who knew how to keep a safe record.

I showed Guccione a cartoon of Christ bearing His cross through an intersection marked CROSS CROSSING.

"Do you consider Christ carrying the cross as one of the basic Christian traditions and one of the basic Christian values that we hold dear?" I asked, joining up with the Church in the battle.

"In a free society such as ours, there is no such thing as a sacred cow. Anything is susceptible of satire. Whether it is Jesus Christ, or whether it is Miss Wyoming. According to our Constitution, there are many people in our country, equally American, who don't accept the crucifixion, don't accept Jesus Christ. What about them?" I agreed, but this was war. I gave the jury another look. They did not agree.

Then I questioned Guccione on other cartoons, one attacking the Metropolitan Museum of Art, called in the cartoon "The Metropolitan Museum of Feces," showing a pile of steaming dung, and one showing a woman, with her legs cut off, soliciting on a street corner. She held a sign reading REDUCED, HALF PRICE.

"Do you think crippled people should be laughed at?"

"No, but I don't think that because they are crippled they ought to be beyond comment, beyond humor, beyond satire." I looked at the woman in the front. She looked down as if she were ashamed for him.

"Do you think the article in question is embarrassing to anybody?"

"Sorry, which *article?* The *short story* here, do I think it is embarrassing to people?"

"Yes."

"I cannot imagine how anybody could be embarrassed by it."

"You do have daughters, don't you?"

"Yes, and they both work for the company."

"You have some sons, don't you?"

"Yes, I do."

"Now nothing embarrasses you very much, isn't that true?"

"It is not true."

"All right, I'm going to ask you if you haven't even made a statement in a public interview about the quality of your own sexual organ?" It was war. Cooper objected and the court sustained.

"My question then is: Do you think your threshold for being embarrassed is a little higher than, say, the ladies and gentlemen of the jury, or Miss Pring?"

"Are you saying that with respect to this article?"

"I am."

"I don't understand the connection. In what way would I be embarrassed?"

"You don't understand the question?"

"Certainly not in that context." But the jury understood. I let it go.

"Even your own investigators found that this article embarrassed Miss Pring, isn't that true?"

"That, absolutely, I have no knowledge of," Guccione said.

"Didn't you say that the ruckus that Reverend Falwell was raising about having been published in your magazine just increased your sales—didn't you say that?"

"That is absolutely correct."

"Didn't you say that you couldn't afford a genius like Reverend Falwell for publicity?"

"Absolutely right. I couldn't."

"And isn't it true that the more you get sued, the more publicity you get, and the more magazines you sell?"

"As far as lawsuits, no. No correlation." I looked at the jury. I let his answer go.

"Mr. Grutman is your attorney?"

"Yes."

"Mr. Grutman was with you when you made the attack on Reverend Falwell, isn't that true?"

"I did not make an attack on the Reverend Falwell."

"Didn't you call him a liar?"

"I called him a liar on television after his attack on me."

"Didn't you say that he was worse than Khomeini?" Cooper objected and the judge sustained. It made no difference. I was all right with the jury. Then the judge gave them a cautionary instruction to protect the record.

"Evidence of other acts," he began reading from the rule, "while not admissible to prove character may be admissible to prove motive, opportunity, intent, preparation, knowledge, plan, identity, or absence of mistake or accident." He explained to the jury that such evidence about the cartoons and Reverend Falwell was admissible only for such purposes. He was a cautious judge.

I nodded to the judge in agreement, then turned to Guccione with my next question. "What I'm trying to point out is that after Reverend Falwell tried to stop the publication of your magazine for the month of March, this year, you, with Mr. Grutman, attacked him personally, did you not?"

"No."

I pushed it further. "Isn't it true that you called Reverend Falwell a 'very narrow-minded, a very bigoted man, oppressively opinionated, and a hypocrite'—didn't you say that?"

"Yes."

"Now in the same way, after Kim Pring filed this action, didn't your attorney publicly and in the press also attack her by saying, 'This case is a contrivance dreamed up by the plaintiff, namely, Kim Pring, apparently as a publicity stunt?' Didn't your attorney make that statement?"

"I have no idea."

"And to the same extent that your attack on Reverend Falwell increases your sales by a million, don't you believe that your attorney's attack on Kim Pring would likewise increase the sales here?"

"Objection," Cooper said.

"Sustained."

"As a matter of fact, it is part of your policy to tear down institutions like the Miss America Pageant, isn't that true?"

"That is absolutely incorrect."

"And it is part of your policy to create shock in order to sell magazines, isn't that true?"

"That is wrong." His denials made no difference. It was my questions that carried the facts and tested his credibility.

"And haven't you said publicly that the shock helps sell your magazines?"

"No . . . I would be demeaning my magazine if I said that."

"Have you ever heard Kim Pring make any public statements about public issues?"

"I have no knowledge of Miss Pring; I have never known of Miss Pring. To me Miss Pring is not an issue in this case."

"Yes, I understand."

"We have a purely fictional character here which you, and you alone, are attempting to imbue with a character of a real live person." Guccione was trying to make his own arguments. I held him back.

"May we have the speech stricken again, Your Honor?" I asked.

"Yes, the answer is stricken as nonresponsive."

"You had never heard of Kim Pring before the filing of this lawsuit, isn't that right?"

"That is absolutely right."

"Then she must not be much of a public figure, if you haven't heard of her."

"There are public figures I have not heard of—athletes, baseball players whose names mean something to practically every young man in the United States and they mean nothing to me."

"Let's see. Do you claim the right to publish an article about O. J. Simpson giving public cunnilingus because he is a public figure?"

"Objection, irrelevant."

"Sustained."

"You have had a long-standing desire to undermine the Miss America Pageant, isn't that true?"

Now Guccione got in bed with the Miss America Pageant. It was war. He said, "I think it is a grand old institution and it makes a lot of people happy, and, therefore, it is good." He admitted that Kim Pring should be proud about being Miss Wyoming and about being in the Miss America Pageant, but he didn't think she could possibly be embarrassed because the story was not about her.

"Do you think that if people saw the story as being about her that it would humiliate her?"

"I don't understand the question." His tone was angry.

"Yes," I said in a kind way.

"What does 'yes' mean?" Guccione screamed. "I did not understand the question! I would like to reply to it!" I ignored him and went on to the next question.

"You recognize that people can be hurt by libel?"

"Oh, yes."

"You know that yourself, personally," I said, referring obliquely to his suit against *Hustler.*

"Objection, it is irrelevant," Cooper said, and the judge sustained him.

"You recognize that people can be hurt by ugly jokes about them, don't you?"

"Yes, of course."

"Do you recognize, Mr. Guccione, that a libel which holds a person up to ridicule may be hurtful to such person?"

"Absolutely."

"Do you recognize that a story about a person who is recognizable in the story, which holds that person up to a false light, can be hurtful to that person?" My questions were coming fast. I was pressing for quick answers.

"If it is about a true person, and that person is perceived to be true by the rest of the world, I agree with you, absolutely." It was a sudden, unexpected and damning admission. I left the matter quickly before the witness could alter his answer. I had the admission I needed from him.

Eddie was grinning.

I felt damn good.

Now it would be up to the jury to decide whether the rest of the world would read the article as being about a real, live Miss Wyoming named Kim Pring, and if they did, well, by God, this could be a hell of a case after all.

19

"May I have a moment, Your Honor?" I left Guccione sitting there waiting and walked over to Kim, gave her a small pat on the hand, and sat down beside her. The jury was watching.

"What do you think?" I whispered.

"I don't think that jury likes Guccione at all," she whispered back. "How could they?"

Then I whispered in Eddie's ear, "What's going on?" It was a question I ask a hundred times during every trial. "What's going on?"—a question no lawyer standing before the jury can answer for sure. It's hard to have a vision of yourself. Under fire, one's view of one's self gets twisted with fear and clouded with hope. There's precious little feedback. Your side loves you and their own judgment is blemished. But I always asked the question anyway. I had to know.

"Well," Eddie whispered in quick words, "You gotta be careful that you don't get too mean with 'em. You could neutralize what ya got goin'. The jury's for us right now, but you're gettin' pretty close to bein' as mean soundin' as he is. We could lose the advantage real easy." The jury was watching us. The judge was waiting patiently. Guccione looked angry, wanting to finish the fight.

"Is the judge hurting us?" I whispered.

"Well, I don't know," Eddie said, looking very serious, "You gotta be careful of him. He could blow up on ya any minute."

One cannot, because of his fear of the judge, run from the ring. One must stand and fight or lose the fight, and if the judge blows, well, he blows.

"I mean, you got the advantage now," Eddie said. Guccione's comin' off like some eastern smart guy. But he's tough. You could lose the advantage real quick if the judge turns on ya. It's real close right now."

"Okay," I said.

"And don't jump at Cooper or anything."

I kept my eye on the judge. He was fussing at the bench, impatient with this impromptu conference while the whole courtroom waited for us.

"You better get out there. Look at the judge, Gerry. He's ready! Play for the breaks. Be nice. Real fucking nice."

"Okay," I whispered back. I started toward the podium to calm the judge.

"You're winning, Mr. Spence," Kim said as I left the table.

"Thanks," I said out loud. I gave her another pat on the hand while the jury watched, and I saw a small kind smile on the face of one of the women.

I began another attack. But I was nicer and I smiled at Eddie and he smiled back and I smiled at Guccione.

"On the front of the article do you see the word 'fiction' any-where?"

"No," he snorted, "anymore than you may read the labeling on a piece of corn that says 'corn.' It is obviously fiction."

"Well, I would admit that it would be rotten corn, but not porn." I couldn't help it, the fucking words just slipped out. There was laughter from the audience. I glanced at Eddie. He wasn't smiling. The courtroom is no place for smartasses. I didn't smile. I hurried on to the next question—any question. "Do you think that all people who read the article in question would find it humorous?"

"I don't think it is possible—"

"I really don't need a speech," I interrupted. I was in the fight again up to my ass. "Just—"

He interrupted me. He was shouting to be heard. "I would like to finish—"

I interrupted Guccione. "Just say—"

He interrupted me. "I said, I did not—I said I don't think it is pos-sible"—Guccione screamed his answer through—"I didn't finish—I don't think it is possible for anybody to produce anything, a great work of art by Michelangelo is not going to be appreciated by every single human being. There are going to be people who don't like it; there are people who don't like the *Mona Lisa*. There are art stu-dents—"

"Yes." I tried to stop him.

"—that hate the *Mona Lisa* and everything it stands for. And there are others who love it."

"Isn't that in—"

He interrupted me again. I couldn't control the bastard. He'd gotten loose and now he was spewing his argument all over the place. It wasn't what he said. Right now I didn't care what he said. I just didn't want the witness running loose, out of control. If he broke loose once, he'd try it again, and if I finally lost all control, I'd lose the fight.

"I think it is the best single work of art ever done," Guccione said. Finally he stopped. I let a lot of silence fill in.

The jury was waiting. Then I said, "I guess you would really like the jury to think this article is something like the *Mona Lisa* or a Michelangelo?"

Guccione snorted again in disgust. "I didn't suggest that. I gave you an example."

I looked on the far left. The coach on the end had his head laid back and was looking up at the ceiling. God! Maybe he was tired of me, disgusted with this incessant bickering, the endless interruptions and arguments. Maybe I had pressed too hard and it was all backfiring like Eddie said. I pressed on anyway. At least there would be a fight.

"So my question is, do you think, yes or no, that some people might believe this article to be absolutely *revolting*?"

"No, I cannot understand anybody thinking it is absolutely revolting."

"Thank you," I said. Guccione threw his head back. What had he said for which he should be thanked? Then he added the words to make certain I had wrested nothing from him.

"—unless their brain is *tainted* in some way!"

The man in the back row on the far left suddenly stared down at Guccione, and I knew we were all right again. The mood of the interrogation had broken.

"Unless their brain is tainted?" I looked at Guccione, and said nothing. I smiled at him. I let another long silence underline his answer, let it echo in the mind's ear, stood there just smiling at the man, the jury watching, hearing the words—unless their brain is tainted—which told the jury, clearly, that if there was one among them who felt the article was "absolutely revolting" he had now been adjudged by Guccione as one with a "tainted brain."

I looked from juror to juror, looked each one in the eyes, and in the looking I asked, "Is your brain tainted?" I looked long enough for each to give an answering look. Their brains were *not*, and the man on the far left in the back row gave me the smallest acknowledgment.

"Well, I have no further questions," I said.

"Let's take a ten-minute recess," the judge said, and the bailiff hit his gavel and the lawyers jumped up and so did the audience, and suddenly the room was like the Chicago Board of Trade on Friday, and people were laughing and hollering and running everywhere.

"You got his ass now," Eddie said.

"He got himself," I answered.

"He's finished. Look at Cooper!" Eddie laughed. Guccione was stomping down off the stand. Daichman and Cooper pulled Guccione over to their table. His bodyguard crowded up. "Look at him! He's got ten minutes to get him shaped up again before he puts him back on the stand, and ol' Guccione ain't gonna listen to Cooper or anybody else. You got him crazy. He ain't ever gonna be nothin' but crazy now!"

"What do you think, Kim?" I said. She just smiled and shrugged her shoulders like she was happy. The ten minutes passed like a single gasp for breath, and the bailiff hit his gavel again and the court came to order. Guccione stomped up to the witness stand once more and Cooper began.

"I would like to give you a chance to explain your last answer," Cooper said to Guccione, and then Cooper asked the reporter to read Guccione's "tainted brain" answer so everybody could hear it again. Eddie looked at me like he couldn't believe it. "What did you mean by that statement?" Cooper asked.

"I believe that vulgarity and ugliness is as much in the eye of the beholder as beauty. If someone has a vulgar mind, salacious mind, they will see vulgarity and salaciousness everywhere; just as if you have a beautiful mind, then you will see beauty everywhere. That is what I meant by that expression."

Eddie leaned over and whispered, "Yeah, and now he's telling the jury if they think the article is revolting they got an ugly mind. Jesus Christ!"

Cooper flailed on. "Did the word 'absolutely' play a role in your answer to Mr. Spence's question? He used the word 'absolutely.'"

"Yes, for anybody to find that short story *absolutely revolting* they have to already have it in their minds."

Eddie whispered, "He's doin' it again!"

Cooper tried once more; I'll give him credit for that. "Did you mean to indicate that there were certain portions of the story that, if they were about a real person, some people might find offensive?"

"If it was about a real person, yes, it could easily be offensive."

Christ! They were giving the case to us! Cooper gave up. He launched into long, safe questions about the different kinds of fiction, and Guccione talked on about the very thinly disguised characters he knew about in fiction, stories about Howard Hughes and Onassis. He said there was fiction such as this, "in which the events and characters depicted are in and of themselves so absurd as to eliminate any possibility of a normal, reasonable person interpreting them as fact or as reality."

Then Guccione got loose again, this time from his own attorney. He ran wild, like a charging beast, his eyes fierce with anger, his voice uncontained. "Anyone who could read this particular piece of fiction and say that the events are such 'that they are acceptable to me as fact' would have to be someone *with the educational level of a flatworm!*" Cooper stopped caressing his cowlick, his hand frozen in midair.

Now we're all flatworms! Eddie shut his notebook as if to say the trial was over.

Guccione raged on. "Because I think every man, woman and child, perhaps not child, but I think perhaps every man and woman in the United States appreciates that you cannot levitate, not only a person, but you cannot levitate anything!"

Cooper changed the subject again. Finally he got to the Falwell matter. Guccione insisted that he had not commissioned the interviews; they had been purchased from two independent reporters and not a single word had been changed. Then the bull was loose in the ring again, out of Cooper's control. Guccione struck in every direction. "All this business in the press was created by Falwell, not by us, by Falwell saying that those interviews were obtained by deceit and trickery. We were able to prove that they were not!" he said, his upper lip curling with the words. "Hence, my calling Falwell a liar! Nor was I the only person who called him a liar. He was also called a liar by President Carter. He was called a liar by *Newsweek!*" He didn't stop for a breath. "His mixing of church and state, his political position, has been criticized by Billy Graham, among others."

He had put himself in the correct company, all right, with President Carter and *Newsweek* and Billy Graham. Guccione glared over at me and told about the investigative reporting his magazine had done. He talked about the La Costa case, how *Penthouse* had been sued for having called La Costa, a $250 million resort near San Diego, "a watering hole for organized crime."

Guccione went on explaining how "investigative reporting was a very important part of the editorial format," and, like a man of great consequence, he spoke of investigating the government, the Office of the President, the American Cancer Society, organized crime, German testing crews and missiles in Zaire. Very solemnly Guccione said, "It must be something that dramatically affects or is potentially capable of affecting the lives, the well-being, et cetera, et cetera, of the American public." He claimed the Miss Wyoming article was as different from investigative reporting as "chalk and cheese."

"We check everything in finite detail," he said. Then he volunteered again, "We have never suffered any successful libel action against us as a result of our investigative reporting."

"I ask that that be stricken," I said.

"It is nonresponsive." The judge looked down on Guccione. "The question was 'Do you check in detail'?"

"Yes," Guccione said, looking up at the judge. Guccione said the story was not turned over to their in-house counsel because "the story is fiction in law, and we must look at it *in law* because this is a part of the editorial process."

"I object, Your Honor, to counsel and this witness continually suggesting to the jury what the law is. That's for the court to decide."

"All right. That's correct," the judge said.

But Guccione wouldn't stop. "It being fiction, and being obviously fiction to us, we would simply turn it over to in-house counsel, but it would not go beyond that because there is no possibility of libel in law if it is *fiction.*"

"Just a minute!" I jumped to my feet.

"Gentlemen!" the judge shouted.

"You can't reach a legal conclusion!" I said.

"The last part is stricken!" the judge said, turning to the jury. "You are instructed to disregard Mr. Guccione's opinion as to whether it is or is not libel."

Maybe we had lost the fight by such an inglorious deed as a low blow. No judge, no referee, could order that the pain from that blow to the groin must not be felt. Maybe the jury believed that if it was fiction, it wasn't libel. That wasn't the law. But how can one know what the jury believed by now?

Then Guccione insisted that in fiction it was impossible to check whether some person existed somewhere who met the descriptions of the character in the fiction. "Maybe the character in the book has flaming red hair, a red beard, one arm and six toes on each foot. The likelihood is that there is someone in the world precisely like that—you cannot check out all those details."

He hadn't commissioned Cioffari in advance to do any stories, and only 4 percent of the total number of the copies of *Penthouse* sold were by advance subscriptions. The rest were sold on the newsstands, he said, for whatever that testimony was worth. Then Cooper swaggered back to counsel table where Kelley was grinning.

"That's all the questions I have," Cooper said.

"Get his ass," Eddie whispered and gave me a little shove toward the podium.

"Mr. Guccione, we all know that there may be people in this world with six toes, don't we?" I was very quiet.

"Yes." He waited for the nature of the attack to unfold.

"When you publish a writing about a Miss America contest, you would admit, would you not, that there is, in reality, such a contest?"

"Yes."

"You would admit, would you not, in reality, that there was a Miss Wyoming at that contest?"

"Yes."

"You would admit, would you not now, that there was a Miss Wyoming at that contest who used a baton? You now know that, don't you?"

"I accept that Miss Pring is a baton twirler, yes. And I say that is one of the coincidences."

"You will admit that there are a real set of mountains called the Tetons?"

"That I don't know."

"You don't know?" I looked over at the jury. "Would you know if there is a Laramie, Wyoming?"

"Yes."

"Would you admit that there is a Jackson Lake."

"I don't know." The jury knew.

"Would you admit that there is a boardwalk in Atlantic City?"

"Yes."

"Would you admit that there are judges at the contest?"

"Yes. I also admit that there was an audience at the contest."

"Thank you. Would you admit that there were other contestants by the name of Miss Wisconsin, Miss Vermont, Miss Massachusetts, and the like?"

"I admit there were other contestants carrying the titles of Miss Wisconsin, Miss Alaska, and so on. But that doesn't make them real people."

"Would you admit that Miss Wyoming wore a blue gown as in your story?"

"In the story she wore a blue warm-up suit, I think. . . . I also believe there must be a million blue warm-up suits in the world."

"Would you admit that she was the only baton twirler there?"

"I really don't know. I have no knowledge of that particular pageant."

"Would you admit that she did what is known as a 'mouth roll' with her baton?"

"I have no idea."

"You don't know?" I asked incredulously.

"I don't know."

"You didn't inquire?"

"Why should I inquire?" Guccione shouted.

"You didn't inquire?" I asked again, quietly.

"I have not inquired."

"And you talk about the people having to be as dumb or as uneducated as a flatworm if somehow they believed that article, isn't that true?"

"If they believed that article"—then he corrected himself—"this *short story* to be true?" he asked.

"Yes," I said.

"They would have to have extremely limited intelligence, yes." I looked up at the coach in the right back row. He was not looking at the ceiling.

"They would be stupid people?" I pressed him, still looking at the juror.

Suddenly Guccione yelled at me. "Do you believe that it was a true—you, Mr. Spence, did you believe that that was a true story?"

"Mr. Spence is asking the questions, Mr. Guccione," the judge said. "Go ahead."

"Well, Mr. Guccione, I would like to answer your question," I said.

The judge interceded. "You don't need to, Mr. Spence. Ask your next question."

"I think you also told the ladies and gentlemen of the jury that if people find the article to be ugly, it must be because they have an ugly mind, isn't that right?"

"No, that is not what I said."

"Didn't I hear you say that if people have ugly minds they see everything ugly, if they have beautiful minds they see everything beautiful, isn't that right?"

"Yes, I said ugliness is in the mind, in the eye of the beholder as beauty is in the eye of the beholder."

"Mr. Guccione, if the jury found this article to be ugly, and deviate, and degenerate, and outrageous, would you say that that's because they have ugly minds?"

"Objection, Your Honor!" Cooper hollered.

"No, because you persuaded—" Guccione charged ahead of the Court's ruling.

"Just a minute." The judge stopped the witness. "Let your counsel make your objections."

Cooper shouted: "It is irrelevant and assumes matters not in evidence, and involves speculation and is argumentative!" He stopped when he ran out of grounds.

"Sustained."

I left it. They could try to un-ring that bell.

Toward evening and without time to call another witness, the court permitted us to show the video of the Miss America Pageant to the jury. We gathered around with the jury like friends at home in front of the TV set, the judge himself having come down from the bench to take a seat at the east end of the jury box. Cooper and Kelley crowded in. Kim pulled up a chair. I don't know what happened to Guccione. Then I said to Eddie, "Let 'er roll," and she rolled. It made me cringe to watch it like hearing the town soprano in front of a whole room of people singing slightly off key, ever so passionately, her head shaking at her own terrible vibrations like an old truck with a bad clutch.

Bert Parks, plump as a little hen and long past fifty, couldn't sing and couldn't dance, but for over an hour he bravely tried both. I was enthralled by the phenomenon of that great gaping mouth stretched so wide one could see his second molars, maybe his wisdoms, and "the girls" as they were called (Oh, aren't they beautiful!) tried to emulate him, because if a contestant stopped smiling, even for a second, if just once *both* the uppers and the lowers weren't visible simultaneously, then she lost.

Each of the fifty "girls" came forward alphabetically by state as Bert Parks hollered out their names with the grace and gusto of a circus master, and between the Campbell's soup commercials and those for Kellogg's and Dry Idea ("the deodorant without much water"), "the girls" tried to tell who they were and where their state pageant was held, and all the time they tried to speak, they were required to hold their mouths open in those horridly grotesque smiles that revealed a staggering fortune in orthodonture. Kim was the last, because alphabetically Wyoming is last, and I thought she was the blondest and the prettiest, and I was proud. I watched the jury. I couldn't tell how they felt.

Then Miss America of 1978 was displayed like last year's car, and Bert Parks sang, "Oh, look at her! Look at her—a miracle, a miracle!" and my stomach muscles cramped up again. "She walks in radiant beauty," he sang and pretty soon he got the words slurred and you couldn't hear them at all—thank God for small favors. Jesus Christ, I thought, this will never be over. We could lose the case right here.

Bert Parks scratched the tip of his nose with a well-groomed finger and announced the top ten. "Always a picture to behold," he said. I stole a glance at the jury. One of the women had a soft, sweet look on her face, like mothers have when they watch their children perform at the Christmas program at school. When the ten finalists were announced, each in turn cried, her mouth frozen open in that insipid smile. One, as tall as Wilt Chamberlain's mother, had her hair done up so she was even taller, and one was hugged by Miss Texas who was also tall, and Miss Kansas looked the healthiest, with broad strong shoulders and the arms of a hefty farm girl. They all walked in the same dainty steps—long-legged or short-legged, it made no difference. Kim wasn't one of the ten finalists. This was too sophisticated a business for a little baton twirler from Wyoming. Besides, you can't have a Miss America who runs around throwing a baton up in the air, for Christ's sakes.

The judges were introduced, mostly post-menopausal women and men, an old fashion designer, an old singer, an old actress, an old bandleader, an old producer, and one barely known, rather young, very obviously black TV hostess (which took care of that problem), and then we saw Mini-Wheats from Kellogg's and Manhandlers soups from Campbell's, and Bert Parks came back and tried to sing a medley with his co-hostesses, a couple of older-model Miss Americas.

The "girls" on the TV commercials were also smiling because they'd discovered that Dry Idea "doesn't make you wet so it doesn't make you wait."

Miss Ohio was a belly dancer whom I liked a lot because she was good at it and did it. By God, she did it! She hit with her hips—hit, hit, hit, hit with her hips, and then she sucked it all back again with her belly and smiled, never stopped smiling once through it all. But we can't have a Miss America belly dancing around the country either. She was out.

A couple of "the girls" played the piano, one pounded hell out of it and ran the notes together, but nobody gave a damn, and everybody applauded because it was wonderful to see this "girl" about six feet tall kicking the hell out of things, out of the piano, out of the classical strain nobody had ever heard before and never wanted to hear again.

Some of "the girls" sang—beat it out louder, and with more pain while still smiling than I thought possible. I actually feared for one of them. Miss Kansas, dressed like a gypsy, fiddled. Her face never changed expression once—she never blinked once, never even raised her eyebrows once like Bert Parks always did. She just smiled that smile and fiddled. Then the proceedings were interrupted by this perfectly smiling housewife who confessed she used to be a "three-soup wife," but now she was a "twelve-soup wife," and her husband looked at her with his own great prideful smile.

Miss Florida played and sang her own arrangement of "Love Story" and I liked her because she didn't seem so serious. She seemed to be having fun, and Miss Alabama, with a white flower in her hair, sang "This Is My Beloved," and her smile never faltered one little bit through all the pain of the lyrics, and we got Rice Krispies and the little elves, Snap, Crackle, and Pop, before Miss Louisiana, with a red flower in her hair, sang "Italian Street Song." I also liked Miss Louisiana. I would have picked her because she seemed so genuinely, deliriously struck with joy and was so full of spunk and all, and she made me happy as hell. "Zing! Zing! Zing!" she sang. Besides, I like black-haired women. God Almighty, I felt happy. I looked at the jurors and they all seemed very happy too.

Miss Virginia did a pretty damn good acrobatic dance—no pad or anything to land on, just the hard stage, and no mistakes that I could see, and right after that came Toni Silk Wave and Soft and Dry, followed by the "cattle show," as Hofler's priest had called it—the swimsuit competition—the dairy breeds ranging in size and shape from petite little Jerseys to long-legged Holsteins, and there were quite a few Guernseys and a couple of big Swiss breeds. They were a comely lot of heifers all right, parading around in high heels on the ramp, waving at the crowd, some walking stiff as goats, but all of them too white, too soft and tender. Except for Miss Kansas, I thought they should get out in the sun and do a little hard work.

Miss Louisiana, my favorite, lost it in the swimsuit competition. There was something too ferocious about her walk, the way she pounded the air with her fists in cadence with that running gait—too aggressive for Miss America—can't have such fast hard-steppers. Gotta have medium-steppers, easy-steppers, and then came Ultra Max shampoo and Adorn hair spray, and the "fifty girls" sang something about a band that plays for you and that they were going to "do it, do it, do it, one more time," and they all leaned over in unison and shook their shoulders and everything young and firm shook too, and everybody clapped, after which a smiling antiseptic-looking blonde interrupted to tell us that she liked her hair to be naturally clean and that's why she used Earth Born.

Kim was one of eight who got a special $2,000 scholarship for her talent. Nobody told us what their talents were, but when they announced Kim's name everybody clapped the loudest like they loved her the best. There she was, more beautiful than I could have imagined, shapely, graceful as any princess in her baby-blue chiffon gown that her mother paid $900 for in Amarillo in '79 before things got expensive.

Then Bert Parks came on one more time. He sang "Miss Amer-e-ka, you're beautiful," with his quavery voice sliding up and down like a dilapidated, rattling old roller coaster, during which we were supposed to get teary, because this was the last moment for the reigning Miss America of 1978, and she sang, too, and we were saying good-bye to her forever, and I just got plain sick, a condition not much improved when they mixed in some Campbell's Manhandlers split-pea soup.

But they did stop. Now Bert Parks and one of the vintage Miss America co-hostesses sang "Who's It Gonna Be?" and Parks ended the song saying, "Beats me!" and then he hollered that the ballots were in!

"Have you picked her?" he asked us all. "Oh, who would it be? Who? Who?"

We were shown all ten smiling mouths again which, by this time, we had come to recognize by the bicuspids. I liked Miss Nebraska. She looked straight ahead and didn't move her eyes back and forth in little shivers to make them sparkle, and I was still pretty high on Miss Louisiana. She sang the national anthem at Super Bowl XII, they said. And then we had Dry Idea again.

"O.K.," Parks said. "This is it!" He walked over and picked up the judges' decisions. He announced Miss Washington as the fourth runner-up. She got $5,000. She smiled excitedly. The third runner-up was Miss Ohio, and she seemed happy, and Miss Florida got $10,000 in scholarships for being the second runner-up and she rolled her eyes and seemed almost insane with joy, and then Miss Alabama got $15,000 in scholarships for being the first runner-up, and I thought they all wished to Christ they could get back in the lineup again because they would have a chance at being her, Miss America, like they had always dreamed of. One thing. None of them cried. I was glad of that. I would have probably cried, too. They took it like sports. It was against the rules to cry. You can't have a bunch of disappointed "girls" up their crying like spoilsports. Can't spoil it for the television viewers. They are the customers. Then they called out her name.

"Miss Virginia!" Miss Virginia, very blond, very, very blond Miss Virginia, who would get $20,000 in scholarships, was Miss Amer-e-ka, Parks announced, and she was crowned immediately before the judges changed their minds, or before she did. And she really did cry—real tears, joyous tears. Oh, God, it was for real! She waved to the crowd and she did have a pretty face and the prettiest blue eyes. I just hadn't noticed. I was looking at the black-headed ones.

She walked the ramp to the music, "There she is, Miss America," and she was happy, truly happy-happy, waving at the cheering, clapping crowd, and I was happy, too. God, I was happy, and Bert Parks said, "Thank you, and good night," and the announcer reminded us that the Miss America Pageant was brought to us by Kellogg's, Campbell's soups and Gillette's Dry Idea, and that was it. The bailiff turned on the lights in the courtroom, and there we were back in the pit again, in Cheyenne, Wyoming, and the dream was over and the nightmare about to begin.

20

Wyoming has always been a man's place, a place for toughs, for hard-bitten, brawling cattlemen who love bawling herds, for mountain men who bred with the Indian women in the summer like bears in heat. Wyoming has always been a frontier place of dust and booze and sweat, and vulgar laughter, and bucking horses and six guns and honky-tonks, and blood and wide-open spaces for men to run to, for men to get lost in, of mountains and glaciers and endless forests, and rushing crystal rivers, and skies that connected directly with eternity. As late as 1870 there were six men for every woman in the state. George B. McClellan, a pioneer cattleman from Big Trails, Washakie County, said that from 1877 to 1883 he never saw a white woman. He said, "Barbed wire and women are the two greatest civilizing agents in the world."[1]

But finally the Union Pacific reached Cheyenne, the capital city, as it was called, and it grew overnight into a town of six thousand wretched souls, most of whom lived in makeshift shelters, in tents and under wagons. Among them were four hundred women and two hundred children. By April of the year 1868, a 40-by-100-foot walled tent had been pitched for use as a combination saloon and gambling house, and within a short time a man could buy himself a drink in any one of seventy saloons, which varied from mere holes in the wall to the Greenback Rooms, a 100-by-112 foot building sporting two bars and billed as "the largest saloon in the western country."[2]

The citizens of Cheyenne had their various complaints: The water was foul, and the hogs ran loose, and nobody picked up the dead animals that lay in the muddy streets for days. There were no sidewalks, and fast women were said to abound in the upper rooms above the saloons like rats in the attic.

James Chisholm described the bawdy houses: "They are generally crowded to the door all night long, and the sound of fiddles and banjos mingle with the voice of the master of ceremonies. 'Only two more gentlemen wanted for the next dance,' as you hear it from the various halls, conveys the idea of a whole city being one huge rustic festival—an impression which is by no means sustained on entering these halls of mirth. A space in the center is devoted to the terpsichorean art, where females of the lowest type may be secured as partners in the dance, while Faro tables, Keno and all imaginable games constitute the side dishes. The town needed law and order. Having neither the time nor the talent to author their own, the city fathers adopted the ordinances of Denver, Colorado.[3]

By 1870 there were those who mourned that Cheyenne grew no faster. "What is there to bring people here or to keep them after they are here—a bare, brown sore, a desolate town with hardly any beauty in it . . . a cemetery which is the picture of the abomination of desolation standing where it ought not, all the dirt and garbage of the city hauled out on the windward side, and left in ugly heaps to be blown back in our faces." There were no trees. One man wrote, "I found in my recent visit to the East that no music in the world had ever been so sweet to my ear as the music of the wind rustling again in the leaves above me."[4]

Cheyenne had its Chinatown, shacks of old boards and boxes and smashed tin cans as roofing, and the Union Pacific had built rows of small yellow company houses that all looked alike. One woman wrote in the Cheyenne *Leader* in 1872 that every family had three to five dogs, "that the place looked like an Indian village with the beasts yapping and tearing at her clothes and tin cans rusting everywhere and empty bottles littering the vacant lots and the alleys and the streets."[5]

Later the cattlemen came, established their headquarters in the town, and visited their ranch holdings in the summer. The businessmen and merchants who had prospered built about forty mansions along Carey Avenue of the heavy Romanesque style—with an occasional Gothic among them—all irrelevant to the landscape. The owners planted cottonwood trees and lilac bushes, and built churches on lots donated by the Union Pacific so that God, too, could get a toehold.

Finally the capital was established in Cheyenne, a place in Wyoming as far as man could get from the empty center of the state, a place nearest the East, nearest civilization, because what was west and north of Cheyenne, what was behind it, was wild and dangerous and Indian, and uncouth, and no place for women.

Cheyenne didn't look like a frontier town anymore. It had long shaded streets and small solid houses with pretty lawns that had been in place for half a century. There were brick schoolhouses and the largest depot in the state and a capitol building with a gold dome and other modest government buildings of eclectic architecture, none especially noteworthy. Downtown there were the garish, multicolored neon signs, and new fronts on old buildings, and a strip of used-car lots and motels, one of which was the Hitching Post where I stayed because the people knew me there and were kind, and I get lonesome easy.

One had to admit that by now Cheyenne looked a little seedy, like a potbellied middle-aged dandy who tries to cover his condition with a styled haircut and a loud sports jacket. The Federal Building, including post office and courthouse, had been recently erected on the edge of downtown. Inside this plain structure was located the federal courtroom, a dignified place—I mean, one where rules keep people from being themselves, like in church. But on the eleventh day of February 1981, before Judge Brimmer had ascended the bench and called the court to order, the courtroom was loud and rowdy.

In his chambers safe from the commotion, Judge Brimmer conducted the usual morning pretrial session. "This Miss America Pageant film was pretty tedious. I noted that one of the jurors was fast asleep, and a couple of others nearly," he said, and then he overruled Cooper's regular morning motion for a mistrial based on my alleged misconduct of the previous day, and we all went into the courtroom, which, when the judge took the bench and the rest of us our seats, fell immediately still, the way the chatter in a town of prairie dogs pales to silence when a pack of coyotes makes its appearance. I broke the silence. I called James Goode, the editorial director of *Penthouse*, the next witness.

James Goode wore no tie and, as far as I could tell, the same old rumpled suit coat I'd last seen him wearing in New York seven months earlier. He looked like a man who'd been breathing cigarette smoke and the fumes of printer's ink until his hide was thoroughly embalmed. He looked like an editor.

After a few preliminary questions I suddenly asked, "Will the magazine appear in Sicily?"

Cooper jumped to his feet to object. But he couldn't think of what to say in front of the jury. He stood there for a moment without saying anything, and then slowly wilted back into his chair. Goode didn't answer the question. I left well enough alone.

"You think that what is shown to the public ought *not* shock and destroy and undermine basic American traditions, isn't that true?"

"Yes."

His admission surprised me. I didn't agree with him. If someone believed American traditions were false, or wrong, or evil, well, the public should be apprised of those ideas. He admitted this lawsuit had a certain publicity value for *Penthouse.* I looked at Eddie. He flicked his fingers at me to say, "Get him. He's gettable."

"And no matter what happens you always win, even if you are sued, isn't that true?" I asked.

"No."

"The net result of the attempt of Jerry Falwell to stop the publication of your magazine was just the opposite—it just sold more, isn't that true?"

"I believe it did."

"Yes, and you and Mr. Guccione sort of laughed about that, didn't you?"

"No."

I laid out a hypothetical question: Goode was to assume that his researcher reported to him all the facts about the real Miss Wyoming at the pageant. She'd done a "mouth roll" and worn the baby-blue warm-up suit and evening gown of baby-blue chiffon. There actually was a mountain range called the Tetons and a Colter Bay on Jackson Lake. Wyoming was a poor state without a large-enough budget for Miss Wyoming to stay in one of the big hotels surrounded by stately people. The researcher found that there was an old lady who had actually gone with Miss Wyoming to the pageant because of her affection for her, and that the real Miss Wyoming did, in fact, have a male baton-twirling coach.

Goode was to also assume that his own researcher called his attention to the fact that Bert Parks, just like Emory Dukes, the emcee in the article, was a veteran of twenty-four years at the Miss America Pageant, that Cioffari had actually attended the pageant, and that there were other facts from which the researcher could conclude that the story was about a thinly disguised Kim Pring.

I took one step toward Goode.

"Now, Mr. Goode, assuming that your researcher gave you that information, would you have published that article?"

Cooper jumped to his feet. "I object. The question assumes facts not in evidence." But after I assured the judge that Kim Pring did, in fact, have a male coach, and that I would produce evidence of the same during the trial, he overruled the objection.

"Would you have published the writing without doing anything more?" I asked Goode again.

"No," Goode said.

"At the time the check was handed to Mr. Cioffari in payment for his article, this young lady, right here"—I stepped back a couple of steps and put both hands on Kim's shoulders—"was still the reigning Miss Wyoming. Did you know that?"

"No, I did not."

Then I went through Cioffari's Elvis Presley story with Goode, and he admitted it was, indeed, a thinly disguised story about Elvis Presley, one of those stories "that springs from a contemporary American event."

"Anybody with the intelligence of a flatworm who reads it would understand that, would he not?" Cooper objected, of course.

"Do you think the Miss Wyoming article has to do with any social issue?"

"It does not."

"You are in the hub of things back there in New York?"

"In a certain sense."

"You worked for *Life* magazine?"

"Yes. I was also the executive editor of *Viva* while I was also the editor of *Penthouse.*

"Now with all of the knowledge you had, whatever that may be in New York, you had never heard of Miss Wyoming before, had you?"

"I had heard of the title, but not the person."

"So as far as you were concerned, she wasn't a public figure to you, was she?"

"Objection, Your Honor. Calls for a conclusion."

"He may answer."

"Personally and professionally, she was not a public figure to me," Goode said.

"Thank you," I said. I exchanged looks with the jurors for a moment.

Goode's testimony went on for hours. He admitted that a fictional as well as a nonfictional article may hurt a real live person. "Writings do have that ability, yes," he said. I thought that was a key admission, and Goode admitted such a writing could invade a person's privacy.

"Do you believe that a writing can evoke such an outrage of anger—that it can be deemed outrageous?"

"Objection, calls for a legal conclusion."

"He may answer," the judge said.

"Yes," Goode said. When I was through with Goode, I asked the judge for a moment to consult with Eddie, and Eddie handed me a slip of paper with a question on it.

"Mr. Goode, do you agree that a real person would be hurt by the following language: 'She drew his flesh into her, not with her mouth alone, but with her entire body, the deepest most remote parts of her uniting in common effort, calling to him, worshiping side by side with her lips and tongue, and the warm tube of her throat, all of her, body and soul, crying in harmony for nourishment'?"

Cooper's objection was overruled.

"It is possible that a real person might be injured by that writing," Goode admitted, and that was where I left him, that admission reverberating in the jurors' ears, while Cooper hurried to the podium to examine this witness, his witness. Outwardly Cooper seemed calm enough, but I could see the fire in his eyes. He asked his own hypothetical question about a piece of fiction depicting the mayor of New York who "did something in the middle of New York City in a parade," and would he have any concern about the privacy or the truthfulness of the article, to which Goode replied that he would, indeed, be concerned about the truthfulness of the fact. Cooper quickly let the matter drop and moved on to other questions.

Goode fought against the idea of malice. He had purchased the story to amuse his readers, and the fact that a magazine decides to publish fiction that might upset someone who likes baton twirling did not, Goode said, mean the magazine had ill will toward baton twirlers. He liked Cioffari's stories. "I would like to buy more stories from Mr. Cioffari and publish them."

When Cooper sat down, Eddie said, "Go get that guy. You ain't got him half squeezed dry yet."

I held Goode's eyes for a long time before I spoke. The jury waited, wondering. Suddenly I said, "You want to buy some *more* stories from Mr. Cioffari?" like I couldn't believe what I had heard with these ears.

"Yes."

"You thought that was a *good* story?" Same sound.

"Yes, I do." I looked at the jury, my mouth open.

"You *liked it a lot*?" Same sound.

"Yes."

I shook my head sadly. "Do you care if your readers are outraged?"

"No."

"Do you care if the readers of your magazine can identify a live human being in this so-called fiction and are thereby angered? Does that bother you?"

"Could you rephrase the question?"

"No, I think it is a fair question." I picked up his deposition and began thumbing through the pages as if to find the place where he had previously said such a thing. Goode was watching intently. I stopped thumbing as if I had found the place and looked at him for the answer.

"It would bother me in a moderate way, yes." Goode said.

"Do you believe that free speech is a very dear and sacred right of Americans?"

"Yes, I do."

"Do you believe that like other rights of Americans it can be abused and lost?"

"I believe that the right of free speech can be abused by the misuse of free speech."

"Yes," I underlined his answer. "Do you think that free speech should include the right of publishers like yourself to libel other people?"

"I do not believe we should libel anyone."

"You think the article was funny, too?"

"Yes."

"Thank you."

Cooper jumped up. "Your Honor, I am going to ask if counsel could be instructed not to say 'Thank you' until he finishes his questioning. If he wants to say 'Thank you' then, that's fine. But his attempt to make a point in that manner is improper, and I would ask that he be instructed not to do it. It happens numerous times."

I looked sadly, patiently, up at the judge.

"Well, I don't think it ever hurts to say 'Thank you.' Go ahead." The audience laughed. So did the jury.

"Thank you, Your Honor," I said. The audience laughed again. One of the ladies on the jury smiled.

I next referred to the forty pages of color photos of nude women and parts of women. I picked up the magazine and thumbed through the pages. "Do these meet the standard and policy for such graphics?"

"I have nothing to do with the graphics of *Penthouse* magazine," Goode said.

"All right, thank you. Does Mr. Guccione have something to do with those?"

"Objection."

"He may answer."

"Yes, he does."

"Levitation in the context of fellatio is absurd, isn't that true?"

"Yes."

"So if Miss Pring were to accuse *Penthouse* of having held her up in a false light, of absurdity, of having held her up in such a way that she was seen to be ridiculous, and laughable, wouldn't you agree that her complaint is true?"

"Objection, Your Honor. It calls for a legal conclusion."

"The rules permit an expert—and Mr. Goode is an expert editor—to give an opinion on the ultimate issue, and this is the ultimate issue. So I will let him give his opinion."

But this time Goode denied that her complaint was true. He spoke of "verisimilitude," saying it meant "like reality or the semblance of reality," and that verisimilitude played an important part in most fiction.

"One last question," I said. I picked up a dictionary lying on our table. A lawyer ought not go to court without one. "Verisimilitude—" I began to turn the pages looking for the word. The jury watched. "Verisimilitude. This isn't a very big dictionary—just a little one. It cost two and a quarter. It's a Random House dictionary."

"Your Honor, I would ask that counsel's introductory statements be stricken and the jury instructed to disregard them."

"Sustained. So ordered." The judge sounded as if he were tired of the objections. But he had to rule when they were made. It was his job.

I handed Goode the dictionary opened to the word. "Can you take a peek at that word there for me? What does it say?"

"Well, in this dictionary it says, its first definition is 'The appearance of truth,' and its second definition is 'Something having the appearance of truth.'"

"Do you agree with that definition?"

"No, I don't think it is an adequate definition."

"All right," I said. "Thank you. I don't have any more questions." I sat down.

Cooper was up in a flash. "I noticed Mr. Spence had a dictionary yesterday. If I could refer to it, I might have a few more questions." He thought I'd gone definition hunting in dictionaries.

I resisted a little. "It belongs to the judge," I said.

"Could I borrow that one, Your Honor?" Cooper asked. What he was about to do could be dangerous. Had he looked up the word in the judge's dictionary? Was the definition different than in my $2.25 paperback?

"Referring to the Second Collegiate Edition, does that appear to be substantially similiar to—"

"If I can find it," Goode said, flipping through the pages with the deftness of a dealer handling a deck of cards. I waited. If the definition was much different, the jury would think I had tried to trick them with a cheap dictionary, and that would be devastating to my credibility. A little drama like this could stick in the jurors' minds for the remainder of the case, and Cooper would remind them of it every chance he got. I couldn't stand it. I walked up to the witness stand and read over Goode's shoulder.

"In the second dictionary, the first definition is 'the appearance of being true or real.' And the second definition, 'Something having the mere appearance of being true or real.'"

"Does that definition seem to you to more accurately portray the way it is utilized in literary circles?" Cooper asked. He sounded as though he had just made a very large point.

"Yes, it is a more adequate definition," Goode said, sounding as if he had just confirmed a very large point.

"Thank you."

I hurried to the podium. "Are you really telling the ladies and gentlemen of the jury that there is any difference between those two definitions? Let me read them both. One says 'The appearance of being true or real, something having the mere appearance of being true and real,' and the other one says 'The appearance of truth, something having the appearance of truth.' You think that's substantially different?"

"Were you asking my opinion?" Goode said.

"Yes, sir."

"I couldn't tell." There was uproarious laughter from the gallery. The jury laughed. I laughed. The judge laughed. Cooper tried to laugh too.

"I couldn't tell either. Thank you, Mr. Goode."

"Thank you," Goode said and stepped down from the stand.

I called Bob Brenner—I watched him walk to the stand—a member of the Cheyenne Kiwanis Club, that organization of benevolents who gather together in order to do good and to do business with each other and to sing songs of brotherhood—and when the luncheon is over, the brotherhood disperses and they return to hard places: Mr. James P. Digby to the Credit Bureau to twist out the $26 payment Sally Mae Parsons missed to Dr. Howard R. Roth for her hysterectomy, and as Dr. Roth pushed back from his plate where the chicken bones were scattered like some minor archeological dig, Percy P. Spellman, the undertaker, shook the doctor's smooth hand because they said they were friends, and then the doctor scurried back to his office where the people were packed shoulder to shoulder, holding their breaths from each other, reading magazines soft from much kneading. The doctor kept a daily quota of patients, religiously— drop one or two a week here and there, let up just a little, and you can see it plain as day on the yearly totals—"The figures don't lie, but the patients do," he told the undertaker, and they both laughed and patted each other on the back, and then after releasing the undertaker's cool hand, he laid his own on his first patient for the afternoon, Minnie Mulhaver, a nice old girl who worked at the K Mart, who said she had a lump on her breast but she didn't think it amounted to much—just wanted to be sure is all. The store manager, a fellow Kiwanian, sent her to the doctor, told her the doctor would treat her right, all right.

Bob Brenner said he had seen Kim come up through the Kiwanis Club's youth program called Stars of Tomorrow, starting when Kim was in grade school, and he said she was a very dedicated little girl whom people referred to as "the baton twirler." He said the public as a whole didn't know her personally by name, and he did not consider her as a public figure. He'd never heard her referred to in connection with any public issue, nor had she injected herself into any, but he'd heard derogatory remarks about her since the article. It was

embarrassing, he said. Now she was referred to as "the blowjob artist," and he'd say, "Wait. You have the wrong person," and they'd
say, "Yes, but she *is* Miss Wyoming. She is the baton twirler and
that's a cheap way of getting publicity." People who didn't even
know her would ask, "What's she trying to do?"

"What did you think of the article?" I asked.

"My initial reaction was shock. I was hurt. I did have a personal
involvement with Kim and any other child who came up through the
ranks of Stars of Tomorrow and the Junior Miss Pageant that I
worked on as a volunteer. I put a lot of hours in. I felt very hurt about
it. I felt a great deal of sympathy for Kim, because I again related this
article to our Miss Wyoming, Kim Pring."

"Thank you, Mr. Brenner," I said.

On cross, Cooper had him admit there wasn't a better-known
baton twirler in Wyoming than Kim Pring. He couldn't remember
with whom, exactly, he'd had those conversations about the "blowjob artist." There had been hundreds of them in the community—at
work, the warehousemen and such. But he admitted that he himself
didn't think any less of Kim Pring today than he did before he'd read
the article.

"You don't think that Kim Pring did any of those things, do you?"
Cooper asked.

"I don't believe that she did, no."

"You don't believe anybody could do some of the things that were
in this story, do you?"

"Absolutely not," he said.

"Thank you, Mr. Brenner. That's all I have," Cooper said.

I stood at counsel table and asked one more question: "Do you believe that other people believed that?"

"Yes, I do."

"Why?" I asked only because I knew what his answer would
be. He said he had to defend Kim against what people were saying,
hundreds of them, and then Cooper jumped to his feet. He wouldn't
give up.

"And those hundreds didn't mention her by name, did they?"

"No, they didn't."

"Thank you," Cooper said. And I wouldn't give up. I stood once
more.

"So she wasn't a public figure, was she?"

"I guess not, no," Brenner said.

"Thank you," I said. "That's all."

"Call your next witness," Judge Brimmer said.

"Call Cioffari."

"Dr. Cioffari will please come forward," the judge said.

Cioffari trudged to the witness stand. He sat stiff as a witch's stick. It would be the third time for Cioffari and me. Third time.

Third time is the charm.

21

From the first day, Philip Cioffari sat next to his lawyers at the defense table, doing nothing, not even making a face, sitting silent, still, like some small animal trapped in a bad place. As I watched him during the ensuing days of the trial, I witnessed a gradual shrinking up, an imperceptible withering. On the first morning his face looked puffy to me, but by the time I called him to the stand the man's cheeks seemed sunken and his eyes had retreated, and his face looked like a paper bag with the air popped out of it. He walked to the stand, his head bobbing in cadence with each step like a long-suffering beast of burden. Dead eyes. I felt a tinge of sadness.

Each of us has our trap with our name engraved on it, small metal signs sitting on small metal desks or screwed to the doors of dinky offices, or our name contained in a distant computer on the payroll or on the mortgage of the family farm or home or car, or our names changed to Mrs. or Mom—it makes no difference. When we die, our names are engraved on cheap headstones or great monuments set above our final trap from which, in relative equality, we patiently rot and ooze our way to freedom.

Philip Cioffari was trapped in this job at slave's pay—a nation of churls and oafs, blockheads and the sons of blockheads having ordered the starving of all professors of literature as punishment that they should have pursued their passion—to teach, thereby to write. It was, perhaps, his wish to write like D. H. Lawrence or Henry Miller. Under the shelter of the Constitution even Nabokov had written as he damned well chose, about the sexuality of an older man with a young girl, and he had been acclaimed for it, loved. He got rich, and he was a Russian, for Christ's sakes. Half the college professors in the country yearned to be published, thousands of them pounding away at old tinny typewriters in repulsive places, year after year pitifully posting their work to the few markets for short fiction that still remained. But most markets had disappeared along with the readers, the way the buffalo bird died out when the herds were slaughtered.

Cioffari had written his story, fussed over the words, written and rewritten. That is the tedious lonely work of every writer. He sought to create a story that pleased him. But the editors at *Penthouse,* none of whom could probably write a decent line themselves, sat like judges eager to render the death penalty to the child of his labors unless what he submitted tickled their coprophilic whims.

He had finally finished his story and submitted it, as usual, through his agent, who cut out his percentage first, and he had signed the contract required by *Penthouse* that gave editors the right to alter his work, a foul and unspeakable evil, like Picasso being required to give his dealer the right to color in the spaces on his paintings to match the customer's decor. He was paid $1,500 for his story, a little less than $400 per printed page, and after the commission was deducted, he probably hadn't received five dollars an hour for his labor.

Penthouse, of course, used his work to create the so-called "book," as each month's magazine was designated, into which numerous slick advertisements were inserted, and from which Guccione's coffers would bulge like a woman swelling with a perpetual pregnancy. Advertising is like rat dung in the pantry. It stinks things up so badly a person is tempted to throw everything out. But rat turds command a high price, a single page of advertising in *Penthouse* fetching from Seagram's Distillers or Reynolds Tobacco some twenty times or more what *Penthouse* paid Cioffari for a page of his writing. Yet Cioffari was grateful.

As he typed away in the night, never once had Cioffari envisioned he might end up in such an appalling place. A courtroom, where others fight over what he has created like hyenas over a dead calf, is no place for a poor professor. He was still trapped. He could not run. He could not jump up in the middle of this awful brawl and holler, "Stop it, for Christ's sakes, please stop it!" He couldn't even make a bad face for fear some juror would see him. And who would speak for him?

Who would tell the jury how it was to be a victim of *Penthouse?* In that I thought he and Kim were kin. And his lawyers—well, he had not chosen them. What did they know of him? They appeared as fastidious as old maids about rules and ethics, but these lawyers who represented him and *Penthouse* at the same time would never permit him to tell the jury that he, too, was trapped by the magazine.

He had relied on *Penthouse* and their lawyers with their worldly knowledge and their legal power to protect *him*. He needed the money. What did he know about the law? And if, indeed, he committed those libels, then he had a right to expect, and did expect, that *Penthouse* would protect not just his money interests—what can they take from a poor professor, his books?—but save his personhood, his pride. His name, too, his reputation too, was at stake. Didn't he have a just claim against them for permitting him to be dragged into this mess, and for the paltry sum of $1,500? Who would fight for him? He could lose his job if he didn't get back to his teaching.

But the lawyers had called his attention to the fine print in the contract he had signed that provided he would protect *Penthouse* and pay *them* back "any loss, damage and expense (including reasonable attorney's fees) that we [*Penthouse*] may suffer or incur . . ." as a result of publishing the story—a poor professor on the stick for *Penthouse!* That is justice?

Now who would speak to the jury for Philip Cioffari? He himself could never speak against *Penthouse*. He had sold them stories, and he had heard Goode say that he, Goode, would like to buy more stories from him. Only a fool bites the hand that feeds him. One does not speak out. One is not free to speak despite the Constitution. He was only a professor trapped in *Penthouse*'s fight, silenced by lawyers the insurance company had selected and paid. Under his contract with *Penthouse* they owed him nothing, not even his legal defense. He owed *them*. He must cooperate. He must sit in the chair and say nothing and look nowhere.

When Cioffari took his seat on the witness stand, he looked at me as if he did not see me and I felt pity. I thought of the small boy trapped in the Bronx, killing the swamp rats, the arrows bursting their guts. I thought of a small round-eared pack rat I had found in the granary of the horse barn at my grandfather's when I, too, was a boy. Somehow a board stored on the rafters had fallen on the rat and pinned the poor creature to the concrete floor. How long he'd been there in the dark under that board I couldn't guess. There had been a scattering of grain on the floor within the radius of his entrapment that he'd eaten. When I found him, his hind quarters pinned under the board were shrunken away and his feet were pink and hairless and his toes curled inward as if desperately clutching at something. All the hair was gone from the back half of his body.His tail had rotted off, and an offensive odor was emitted when I lifted the board off him. The side of his head that had lain next to the hard concrete had grown flat. I watched in horror as the rat dragged himself along by his front legs, a fraction of an inch at a time. Finally I put the board back on top of him so I couldn't see him, and I jumped on the board as hard as I could to spare both him and me the misery. Then I jumped one more time, and I never lifted up the board again.

"Dr. Cioffari, where do you live?"

"I live in New Jersey."

"How long have you lived in New Jersey?"

"About sixteen years."

"You have a doctorate in English literature?"

"Oh, yes." He said it was from New York University, and that he taught creative writing, poetry, and fiction, among other things.

"What is 'semi-fiction'?"

"I don't know what semi-fiction is."

"You never heard that term before?"

"Not before the lawsuit, no." The witness reached for a glass of water.

"Yes, have a drink," I said.

"I can?"

"Oh, it's perfectly all right," I said. I watched the man take a swift quaff with a shaking hand. Something was wrong with the witness. I concentrated for a moment, but nothing came to me. I asked the next question. "Do you think young people need role models to follow?"

"Possibly at times."

"Now in your fifteen years of teaching have you ever brought one of your writings to the class and used it as a teaching vehicle?"

"No, I have not." He looked sick. Something was bothering him—something beyond my questions. I opened up my mind again. No special light came in.

"Now *Penthouse* magazine is undertaking your defense here for you, isn't it?"

"Yes, it is." He took another drink of water. His hand still shook.

"And paying your attorney's fees?"

"Yes, they are."

"How many articles have you sold?"

"Roughly, approximately fifteen." Fifteen!

"I thought I asked you that question before and you provided us with all of the copies of your articles. I only had eight or nine. Are there others that you have sold that we aren't aware of?"

"I had overlooked the fact that I had written several stories under a pseudonym."

"Well, I asked you that question! I asked you under oath, you remember, if you had ever written any articles under a pseudonym and you denied it. Do you remember that?"

Cooper objected and the judge asked me to refer to the exact page in Cioffari's deposition. "I am surprised by the witness," I said to the judge. "I don't have the page. I will find the page with the help of counsel." I gave Eddie the nod, but he was already furiously turning the pages of Cioffari's deposition looking for the prior testimony. I stalled.

"How many articles have you written under a pseudonym?"

"I believe three or four that I can recall."

"What pseudonym did you use?"

"I believe the name I used was Rivers."

"What was the first name?"

"I don't recall." He looked terrified.

"Where did you write the articles?"

"They were written for *Hustler* magazine." *Hustler?* I looked over at the jury. *"Hustler?"*

"Yes."

Eddie was still madly flipping the pages. The jury was watching him.

"You wrote four articles for *Hustler* magazine! Can you give me the times when those articles were written?" Eddie was speed-reading.

"No, I cannot. They were roughly—it was around the years 1975, '76, I believe."

"And when did you first remember after your deposition was over that you had written those articles for *Hustler* magazine?"

"I don't know exactly when I remembered."

"Your last deposition was taken here on September sixteenth, 1980. Do you remember that?"

"Yes, I do." Eddie was still wildly flipping the pages, reading full pages at a time. The jury was watching. Cooper was nervous. He got up once to object, thought better of it, and sat down again. The stall was only underlining that Cioffari had, in fact, testified differently at least once before. What exactly had he said in his prior deposition about writing under a pseudonym? The jury wanted to know. So did I.

"Did you remember those four articles in *Hustler* magazine after that date?"

"Yes."

"How much after the September date?"

"I don't recall."

"Did you give that information to your attorney?"

"It didn't even occur to me, no." He grabbed for the water glass.

"Does he know that now, as you sit here?"

"Yes."

"He knew it *before* you took the stand?"

"I guess, yes."

"Your Honor, he can't ask what I discussed with my client. I ask that he be directed not to do that again," Cooper shouted.

"Go ahead with something else, Mr. Spence," the judge said. Cooper knew the page in the deposition. I could see he had the deposition open. But he was losing the game.

"I would also point out to counsel that the phrase he is looking for is on page thirty-four," Cooper finally said.

"Thank you," I said. Eddie handed me the deposition.

"Let's see," I began reading down the page quickly to myself. "Let's see if you recall this testimony. Were you under oath then?"

"Yes, I was."

"And you swore to tell the truth?"

"Yes, I did."

"And you were sworn just like you were here?"

"Yes."

"There was a reporter who took down your testimony then?"

"Yes."

"And at that time were these sets of questions asked of you by me: 'Have you written any other articles for any other magazines or periodicals or books or other matters that we have not mentioned now?' And your answer was 'No.' Do you remember that?" The man nodded. Now Cooper tried to mitigate the damage.

"I'll stipulate the pseudonym articles were not mentioned, Your Honor."

"All right, thank you," I said. But I went right ahead with my proof. Cooper's stipulation couldn't stop me from showing Cioffari's prior testimony to the jury. "The next question: 'This is your *total* repertoire of writings, is that right?' And did you answer 'That's right'?"

"I believe I did, yes." He couldn't deny it. It was in black-and-white in front of me.

"Were you under oath when you made that answer?"

"Yes."

"And then the next question: '*Have you written under any pseudonym or pen name?*' And was your answer '*No*'?"

"I believe it was, yes." He grabbed for the water again.

"And were you under oath then the same as you are now?"

"Yes."

"And, Mr. Cioffari, your statement now is that you just *forgot* four articles that you wrote for *Hustler* magazine, isn't that correct?"

"Yes, it is."

"And you are saying to the ladies and gentlemen of the jury that you didn't intend to lie under oath when you gave those answers?" I looked sternly at the witness, then at the jury.

"Yes."

"Object to the form of that question, Your Honor. He has testified as to what occurred."

"Overruled. His answer may stand."

"And your testimony is that you forgot not only one but *four* of those articles, is that right?"

"Yes."

"Isn't it true that you didn't really want me to know that you had written articles for *Hustler* magazine?"

"No. I am not concerned whether you know that or not." Now he was sounding testy, and it would be all right for me to be a little mean in return.

"Didn't you feel that you should let me know that you had made a *misrepresentation* so that I could properly prepare my case for my client?"

"No, I did not consider that."

"Did you ever request your attorney to straighten that matter out?"

"Your Honor—" Cooper jumped to his feet again.

"I will withdraw the question," I said. But I wondered if an attorney had an ethical duty to tell the court that his client had falsely stated a material fact under oath, especially if the lawyer and his client contended it was all an innocent mistake. May the lawyer, an officer of the court, remain silent, hoping that his opponent will never ask the right question and the past false testimony is never revealed, thereby leaving the court and his opponent hooked on the falsehood; but if the truth is discovered, may he then, without having previously disclosed it, shrug his shoulders and say "Well, it was all just a mistake," even if it was?

Cooper was on his feet again. "I object to this line of questioning and I object—"

"Sustained," the judge ruled. Was I the only one who had been shocked by what ordinary persons, these jurors, might see as perjury? Jurors do not understand the niceties of the law. Perhaps I was equally ignorant. I should deliver the presumption of innocence to Cioffari. I looked at Judge Brimmer for a sign. His face was a mask. Cooper's face revealed only his obvious sense of disdain, a disgust that pained him to the very borders of endurance that I should make so much of this simple matter. I looked at Eddie. He was looking down as if he were too embarrassed to watch the witness. I left the podium and walked quietly over to counsel table and leaned down to whisper.

"Jesus Christ, Eddie, what do you think of that?"

Eddie whispered back. "Take it easy," he said. "Don't go too far. It can backfire." I looked at Eddie with dismay. He saw the look. Then he motioned me back. "The jury knows," he whispered. "You don't have to tell them another thing."

"Now you have written articles for *Chic* magazine, have you not?" I began again, easier this time. Cioffari's sallow face had darkened. There was a purplish tint along the edges of his ears and at his temples. His mouth hung slack. My pity vanished.

"Yes."

"And you have written for a magazine called *Gallery*?"

"Yes."

"And those are generally cheaper imitations of *Penthouse*, the same type of format?"

Cooper jumped up again. "Objection, irrelevant!" he shouted.

"Overruled." Judge Brimmer would never try to limit me now. The judge spoke quietly. He gave no hint to his own emotions. Yet I heard his invitation to continue the attack.

"And *Chic* magazine is a magazine that has numerous pictures, color pictures of naked women in various poses and various configurations, isn't that true?"

"Among other things, yes," he said.

"And so is *Gallery* such a magazine, isn't that true?"

"Yes."

"And both of those magazines have pictures of women with exposed genitals, isn't that true?"

"Yes."

"This is irrelevant, Your Honor."

"I said that he could go into it generally. But we have covered the general subject now, Mr. Spence."

"All right. Now does it make much difference to you, Dr. Cioffari, where you publish your article?"

"Yes."

"Were you ashamed of the fact that you had published four articles in *Hustler* magazine?"

"Sir!" Cooper shouted at the judge as if my question had been a blow to the testicles. He leaped to the bench. "Your Honor! Objection!"

"Overruled!" the judge said. The jury looked very sternly at Cooper.

"Just a minute!" Cooper yelled again. "He has to answer the question whether he was *ashamed* of the fact that something was published in a magazine in a civil case." What did Cooper mean by that?

The judge said, "The point is, it goes to the credibility, whether or not he concealed it under oath at the time of his deposition." Cooper had finally forced those words from Judge Brimmer's mouth. Now the jury heard the judge speaking from that high place about Cioffari and whether he had hidden the truth, under oath.

"There is no claim he concealed this under oath!" Cooper said. The lady in the front row suddenly crossed her arms and shook her head in short, violent staccatos.

"There certainly is, Your Honor," I said.

"I am sorry," Cooper said as if waking from a dream. "This is *Hustler*, excuse me, Your Honor." He sat down slowly, stunned. I stood silently watching him so that the jury would turn to see him too. What they saw was a man fading. Kelley tried to whisper something to him, but he stared straight ahead, silently. I pressed on. It was time for the kill. It must be clean. There must be grace, even compassion.

"Were you ashamed of publishing four articles in *Hustler* magazine?" I said kindly.

"I wasn't—well, let me put it this way: The stories in *Hustler* were what are called formula fiction, and formula fiction is when you are asked—or there are certain requirements that the magazine stipulates in order for it to publish your fiction." The man spoke in plain flat sounds, as flat as a stack of lumber, but I could hear a faint sadness. "And to the degree that that interferes with the general creative process, and that, therefore, the stories were not, you know—" he hesitated. He looked down at his hands. "I wasn't given free rein in the creativity of the story."

I gave him plenty of time. I waited to let him say anything more that he might want to say in his own defense. Then he added, "To that degree, I feel it does not represent my best work and it does not represent the full range of my creativity."

"Is that why you didn't tell me about those four articles—because it didn't represent what you considered to be your best work?" I asked the question very gently.

"No," he said. I looked over at the jury. Several of the jurors were staring at the floor.

"Isn't it true that that's why you used the pseudonym, Rivers, for those articles?" I said, trying to tell him I understood, but he would only repeat the stance he had already taken—this didn't represent his best work. Then I said, "And you are still telling the ladies and gentlemen of the jury that you can't remember a single title of those four?"

"Yes, I am."

"You can't remember any of the words in any of the titles?"

"I cannot."

"Not one word out of *four titles*?"

Cioffari shook his head. "I cannot remember," he said. The woman in the front row began shaking her head again.

Then he said the *Hustler* formula fiction required at least one explicit sex scene.

"There were explicit sex scenes in 'Miss Wyoming,' weren't there?"

"I don't consider that explicit sex." Now another woman in the front row crossed her arms.

"Oh, well!" I said. "Then the ones in *Hustler* were even worse than the ones here, is that correct?"

"Objection. That's argumentative," Cooper said, coming alive once more.

"Overruled."

"Let me ask you in a general way. When you say 'explicit' you mean something that was more explicit than the Miss Wyoming article, isn't that true?"

"Yes."

"And that's what *Hustler* wanted, and that's what you gave them, isn't that true?"

"Yes."

"On four separate occasions?"

"Yes."

There were other questions, but as Eddie had later whispered, "He's dead in the water. You don't need to chop him up anymore. The jury won't believe anything more that he says. If you beat him up too bad now, they might even start feelin' sorry for him. I doubt it," Eddie said, "but he's had it."

I questioned him about having actually been at the pageant and whether he'd seen the newspaper story that called Kim "a crowd-pleaser," and told how she "balanced a spinning baton on her back, neck, shoulders and even in her mouth." He still insisted he'd never seen Kim or the news story before he wrote his own story for *Penthouse*. It was just an unexplainable coincidence that his story was about a Miss Wyoming who was doing the same thing in the same place dressed the same way.

Then I asked him if, when he wrote about Miss Wyoming doing oral sex, he didn't realize that in doing so he would hurt not only the woman whose name he selected, but her friends, her relatives, her state, the people, the little children who looked up to her. "Didn't any of that occur to you?" I asked.

Cooper objected and demanded a bench conference. Then Cooper's voice began to rise above the whisper required at the bench. "It is highly, highly, highly prejudicial; it is coming on top of a complete circus of facial—"

"He is talking so loud the jury can hear," Eddie whispered up to the judge. Nothing would stop Cooper.

"—facial gestures, of acting, of discussions at the counsel table that are being listened to by the jury regularly—"

"Oh, come on," I said.

The man wouldn't stop. "And they are totally outrageous and I move for a mistrial! I am—"

"Just a minute!" the judge finally stopped him. "I know of no actions or statements at counsel table that have been heard by the jury. I heard none and I have observed none."

"For the record," Cooper said, his voice still heard above the whispers of the judge, "I have called this to the court's attention once before when this occurred."

"I don't think you have mentioned it before." I hadn't heard any such thing. But Cooper insisted. Finally the judge ruled there had been nothing said by Eddie or by me that the jury could hear, nor had there been any "facial gestures" that had influenced the jury. "That's what you're implying now," the judge said, "and I have seen none of it."

But Cooper raged on about "hundreds of other prejudicial items of evidence and statements of counsel," referring to me, and he tried to convince the judge that I was making the jury believe that "somebody who writes about sex has malice."

The judge didn't budge, not an inch. "I don't think that the jury has that idea at all. Your motion is denied," the judge ruled.

Before the jurors had gone home for the day, the judge, as usual, fully admonished them. They must not talk about the case—not to each other—not to their spouses—not to anyone, and they must not make up their minds, not yet, not until they had heard all of the evidence—and the jury had filed out and left us there alone in the courtroom. I felt like an old car alongside the road run out of gas. I sat back in my chair at counsel table. Eddie and Kim sat there too without words, too worn out to get up and leave.

"We got 'em," Eddie finally said. "Cooper's comin' apart at the seams."

"Yeah," I said. I watched Cooper and Kelley leave. Cooper almost bolted for the door. Kelley walked out behind him like a smart little monk, still cocky, still looking pious and uppity, carrying his briefcase like a bag full of Bibles.

"It's all over for 'em," Eddie said, "if we don't blow it."

"Yeah," I said. "But they'll come up with something."

"I don't know. All they can do now is play for the record—for the appeal."

"They've got to do something more than that," I said. "They'll come up with some surprise witness at the last minute—something. Somebody. They'll pull something," I said. "We gotta be careful. They're not going to go down this easy."

"It wasn't *that* easy," Eddie said. "I don't think they even know how much trouble their case is in. They act so goddamned pure. And when the jury finds for us, they'll go hollerin' up to the Court of Appeals about our ethics—you wait and see. That kind always does."

But I knew the fight wasn't over yet. "Can they get anything on you, Kim?" I asked.

"Nope," she said. I looked at her carefully. I could see she was telling the truth, the unvarnished truth—either that, or I was the biggest fool who ever drew breath in a courtroom.

22

A waitress with eyes half open brought Eddie his bacon and wide-awake eggs in the predawn of an empty restaurant.

"Where's all the customers?" I asked.

"All but the stupid is in bed," she said.

"The early bird gets the worm," Eddie said, smiling.

"The early worm gets ate," she answered. She poured my coffee.

"We need to take the offense today," I told Eddie. "I'm getting tired of Cooper's every-morning motion for mistrial." Eddie nodded. The judge always overruled him, but his relentless accusations of my misconduct each day before the trial got under way caused the judge to scrutinize me the way a storekeeper watches a customer who is called a thief every morning just before the store opens.

The waitress filled the coffee cups again. Eddie stabbed his egg and wiped it up with the bacon.

"You sure got Cioffari good yesterday," Eddie said, chewing hard, "and *Penthouse*'ll go down with him. That's what they get for puttin' all their eggs in one basket." He took a sip of coffee to wash down the toast.

"I felt sorry for him," I said. "Couldn't help it."

"The jury doesn't feel a bit sorry for him."

"Well, I don't know. Just think about it, Eddie. *Penthouse* is hollering about its freedom of speech—they want the world to know they're engaged in this holy war for freedom—not for the love of pornography, or money, but for freedom! Right?"

"Right," Eddie said, looking up at me now for the first time.

"But who's free?"

Eddie sponged up more egg with another piece of toast and stuffed it in his mouth and shrugged his shoulders.

I said, "Cioffari's real freedom is the freedom to starve if he doesn't write what the pornographers want." I took a swig of my own black coffee. "It must have devastated him to admit in a public courtroom that he'd written for *Hustler.*"

"Yeah," Eddie said.

"And he had to sign that contract with *Penthouse* or he didn't get published—Write your heart out, boy. Pay is five bucks an hour and we'll rewrite what you wrote as we please. And, boy, if we get sued for what you wrote, you'll pay all our attorney's fees, and if we lose, you also pay the bill." I was arguing to the top of Eddie's head, which was still being fed near the plate. "That's real freedom of speech, isn't it?" I hollered.

The waitress came over. "Ya want somethin'?" she asked.

"No," Eddie said. "He's just gettin' tuned up for the day."

"And when Cioffari gets sued, he doesn't even have his own lawyer—has to take the lawyer the insurance company gives him."

"He's got the right to get his own lawyer," Eddie said, looking up between bites.

"Not unless he can dig up fifty thousand, maybe a hundred, if he wants lawyers like Cooper and Kelley." I waited for Eddie to say something more. He kept on feeding. "So poor old Cioffari has to sit there and keep his mouth shut or he's had it. There's your freedom! Right?"

"Right," Eddie said. "You're really on one."

"So what we're talking about is the freedom of *Penthouse* and *Hustler* to sell their obscenities—not Cioffari's freedom to write—not even his freedom to defend himself!" Eddie looked a little embarrassed, but I needed to holler about it, goddamn it. "Do you hear me?"

"Christ, everybody in here hears you, Gerry." He laughed a little and looked around. The waitress was staring, looking scared now, and a couple of customers who'd sat down in the meantime glanced over in our direction wary, worried. "They might call the cops," Eddie said.

"Jesus Christ, I'm not even free to talk about freedom," I hollered, and Eddie was laughing now.

"You're free to talk. But there's a law against hollerin' called disturbin' the peace," he hollered back louder than I was hollering. And now a big old fat chef with a greasy apron came walking over toward our table with a mean look on his face.

"What a fuck's a matter, boys?" He had a frying fork in his hand.

"Damn good eggs," Eddie said. "And ya cook 'em just the way I like 'em," he said. I nodded, and gave the man a big smile.

"Try an' hold 'er down a little, boys," he said.

"You bet," I said, and when the chef had left I said, "Now that's freedom for you. If an ordinary citizen opens up his mouth, he'll get a fuckin' fork shoved up his ass."

"You're gonna get us kicked out of here yet." Eddie started laughing again.

"No wonder all we've got in Washington is a bunch of little, crooked, two-bit, pip-squeak, mealymouth, milk-toast, politician, sons a bitches! An honest person wouldn't get near the place!" I hollered. "Wouldn't dare."

"Yeah," Eddie said, finally getting with it. "You couldn't hurt the reputation of those guys we got in Washington if you dumped a bucket of shit on 'em every day. The smart ones—the good ones—stay outta politics, make all the money, and buy the politicians."

"Yeah," I said. "But it pisses me off. What is all this about 'robust debate' on public issues the Supreme Court talks about and says it protects? The most important of all rights under the Constitution is the right of the ordinary citizen to engage in robust debate. But if a person speaks out publicly, the Supreme Court says he has injected himself into the affray, and now he's fair game for any crackpot of the press, any witch hunter, any mean-minded member of the media to libel because he's a public figure. So the citizen in a democracy, if he knows what's good for him, better keep his mouth shut. Some First Amendment rights citizens have! The big corporate press has them. The pornographers have them. *Penthouse* and *Hustler* have them. But the ordinary citizen does not have them! What decent, intelligent citizen would ever breathe a word? The First Amendment rights of the media aren't chilled by libel suits—the First Amendment rights of citizens to exercise their freedom of speech are chilled by the press," I said, "and the Supreme Court encourages *Penthouse* and *Hustler* to sell their slime." I was on one, all right.

Eddie wiped up the last of his eggs with the last of the toast, made it all come out even, which is a talent in itself. Then he stuffed it. "You better save a little for court. This is gonna be a long day," he said.

"I'm not talking about censorship," I hollered. "I'm talking about libel! You can't censor! A reasonably intelligent man doesn't cure the boil on his nose by chopping off his head," I said. "You can't even try to censor—the boils of *Penthouse* and *Hustler* are the price we pay for free speech." I left the waitress a big tip for the big trouble we'd caused. "And the porno boys are big boys playing hardball, so if we can prove they maliciously libeled Kim—then they lose, and by God they ought to lose! That's the price *they* have to pay!" I slammed my fist down on the table one last time, and the silverware and plates jumped and rattled. "And we'll make 'em pay, by God!" and then we did get the hell out of there. When Eddie was a kid they called him and his pals the "Butte Rats," and one thing a Butte Rat knows is when to fight and when to run. Eddie threw the chef a friendly wave good-bye.

When we got to court Cooper was waiting for us with his latest attack, claiming that the newspaper story the morning before about my little exchange with Guccione over my SPENCE IS A NICE GUY T-shirt had prejudiced against *Penthouse*. He thought the jury had read it and, Cooper argued, I had *not* been *free* to speak to Guccione, even though Cooper had been present, and certainly I was *not free* to speak to him in front of the press, *nor free* to ever speak to the press about what I thought about the case. Lawyers, being somewhat less than ordinary citizens, have fewer freedoms themselves.

Cooper also demanded a mistrial. What really riled Cooper this morning was my alleged continuous mispronunciation of the Italian names in the case—I *wasn't* even *free* to pronounce the names of the people in the case using the correct Italian pronunciation—like the multisyllable accent to the name Guch *own*-ee—and he argued that I certainly shouldn't have asked that question about the sale of *Penthouse* in Sicily.

Although I agree the press must never be censored, trial lawyers are censored in every case. We are criticized for being such liars, but if we were always to tell the truth we'd never again see the light of day. Sometimes it is contempt of court to tell the truth—to tell the jury, for instance, the defendant has insurance, or to inform them of the arguments at the bench—countless truths are always withheld from the jury. And what a lawyer thinks, he most often can never say—that he thinks some judge is a sanctimonious, bullying old bigot who's sold out to Corporate America and hates people or that his opponent is a crook. The law has no tolerance for truth.

"I never noticed Mr. Spence's mispronunciation of Mr. Guccione's name," Judge Brimmer said for the record.

"There wasn't any," Eddie said for the record.

"I'm inclined to think that hasn't happened," the judge said to Cooper. "I think you're overly sensitive on the issue. I did notice the Sicily reference, of course, and wondered about it at the time, but you made no objection. I suggest to counsel that that shan't be done again." The trouble with good judges like Judge Brimmer is that they're held up as examples to prove that the judiciary as a whole is solid and fair and functioning rather than as examples of the exceptional judge who proves just the opposite condition of the judiciary.

Now Eddie got his chance. He moved for default judgment against both *Penthouse* and Cioffari because of their failure to produce Cioffari's *Hustler* stories. Their failure to do so was "absolute blatant bad faith and a willful and intentional disregard of this Court's orders," Eddie argued. "Your Honor," Eddie said, "I'll tell ya somethin'." The judge waited to hear what the "somethin'" was. "If we did this—well, we know the Court, and we know what would happen to us if we blatantly violated this Court's order."

"I'm going to require Mr. Cioffari to produce the articles for examination and he will not be excused from court until he does—I don't think that the defendant's default is willful in this instance because I can't imagine competent trial lawyers for the defendants putting themselves in such an awkward position as having it appear that their principal defendant is a liar."

Back in the courtroom I continued my cross-examination of Cioffari. I could see Eddie furiously rummaging around in our file boxes. Suddenly he rushed up to the podium and handed me an issue of *Hustler* with two places in the magazine marked with paper clips. I flipped to the pages quickly while the jury watched. There it was!—the cartoon in *Hustler* that Guccione himself had sued on—and in the *same issue* a story by one J. R. Rivers!

I turned to Cioffari who had been watching me anxiously. "By the way, Dr. Cioffari, was the pseudonym you used in *Hustler* J. R. Rivers?"

"It may have been, yes."

"One of the articles that you published there—was it entitled 'Vegas Dreams'?"

"That sounds vaguely familiar."

"Published in May of 1976 in *Hustler*?"

"That's possible."

"May we approach the bench?" I asked the judge. I motioned

Eddie up to talk to the judge again. Cooper stood there, his face reddening. "May it please the Court," Eddie began, "Your Honor. After our conference we went back and checked the *Hustler* articles we had and our exhibit marked—"

"You say you did this in the last few minutes?"

"Yes, Your Honor," Eddie said. He had discovered in our Exhibit 347A the article "Vegas Dreams," with the subtitle "Getting Fucked by Lady Luck," by J. R. Rivers. Eddie told me later he'd gone up to Kelley and asked him if J. R. Rivers was Cioffari's pseudonym and Kelley had told him he didn't know. "Mr. Spence has just now proved that that was the name he used and we respectfully submit that is absolute evidence of the intent of *Penthouse* to disobey this Court's orders in the discovery." Eddie was shouting as loud as a man can shout in a whisper.

"I'm worried about the jury hearing this, Your Honor," Cooper said.

"Where is the article?" the judge asked me.

I held the *Hustler* up for the judge to see, and now Cooper whispered, "The jury can see the magazine."

Judge Brimmer ruled quickly to bring it to an end. "It may be relevant to another libel suit, but not this one. If I were to let this in, I think that would be sure and certain grounds for reversal and probably definite grounds for a mistrial." Perhaps the truth does not always lead to justice.

Then I put one last question to Cioffari: "I want to know if you have an explanation to the ladies and gentlemen of the jury why the following total likenesses to Kim Pring appear in your story:

"One, that Wyoming had never had a winner at Atlantic City before.

"Two, that you were only there on the particular year and night when Miss Pring appeared, and that *Penthouse* was advertising in its magazine your forthcoming series of stories related to 'contemporary American activities.'

"That Miss Wyoming was picked for your story out of fifty other contestants.

"That you selected the talent of baton twirling for your character.

"That Miss Wyoming did a routine with her mouth, as also did the character in your story.

"Both the woman in your story and the woman in actuality had a blue warm-up suit.

"That it wasn't only blue, that it was a special kind of blue—baby blue.

"Ten, both women had a blue dress, not just one of many colors of blue, but a *baby*-blue dress.

"Eleven, that of all the available materials in the world, the dress was made of chiffon, both in your story and in actuality.

"Twelve, that both women had been at Laramie, Wyoming, some four years.

"Thirteen, that in the story, as you wrote it, and in actuality, both women had been half-time favorites at the games.

"Fifteen, that Miss Wyoming in actuality and in your story had a male coach.

"Sixteen, that she was from a small contingency, did not have large numbers of people around her, and did not stay in ritzy places—

"Now maybe you will be able to explain to us how all of these likenesses came about—"

"Objection," Cooper shouted, interrupting my question.

I tried to continue. "There were fifteen or more—"

"Objection," Cooper interrupted again.

I continued on. "—in fact there were fifteen or more actual identical similarities between the woman you call Miss Wyoming at the Miss America Pageant and the woman who, indeed, was Miss Wyoming at the Miss America Pageant?"

"I object," Cooper said. "It assumes multiple matters that are not in evidence."

"He may answer," the judge ruled.

"First of all, I don't accept any of the statements that you made in the question so I can't answer your question as you've stated it," Cioffari said.

"Thank you," I said. I looked over at the jury, and with a shrug of the shoulders I let it go at that. The jury knew. Cioffari stared back at me. In fact, he was willing to stare me down. I turned away.

"Do you agree that if people say this article is about Kim Pring that the article would invade her privacy?"

"Objection."

"Overruled."

"I have no idea."

"Do you think you knew how Kim Pring herself felt when she read this story?"

"I have no idea how she felt."

"Did you care?"

"I didn't know the woman."

"Are you proud of this story?"

"Yes, I am."

I had Cioffari's prior affidavit previously presented by Grutman in support of his motion for summary judgment. I thought Cooper had probably overlooked preparing Cioffari for questioning on it. The affidavit said, among other things, that the Charlene in the story was an "outrageous character."

I paused a moment to gather the jury's attention. "Do you believe that the character Charlene in this story was an "outrageous character."

I paused a moment to gather the jury's attention. "Do you believe that the character Charlene in this story was an *outrageous character?*"

"No. I don't understand the term as it applies to Charlene."

"You don't *understand* the term as it applies to Charlene?"

"And to this particular story, which is phantasmal," Cioffari said.

"Well, let's see if you don't understand the term," I said. I picked up the affidavit from the podium where I'd laid it.

"Now, I'm going to ask you if, under oath, you didn't make this statement: 'There is no way that any sensible individual could possibly identify the *outrageous* fictional character, Charlene, with plaintiff's Miss Wyoming contestant of '78, with any other person, or with the actual Miss Wyoming Pageant of 1978, or any year.' Did you make such statement under oath?"

"Yes, I did."

"Did you, therefore, refer to the character in your story, Charlene, as *outrageous?*"

"Yes, in the sense of 'preposterous.' "

"Would you like to correct your prior statement in which you denied having referred to the character Charlene as *outrageous?*"

"I guess I would like to correct it to clarify it in the sense of 'preposterous' rather than—"

"Would you like to correct anything in the record that suggests that you actually *knew* Miss Wyoming was a baton twirler?"

"No."

"That's all," I said. "Thank you."

When Cooper asked his questions, Cioffari had no trouble either understanding or answering them.

"Mr. Spence has been very critical of you for forgetting about the pseudonym articles or stories that you did."

"No," I said from the table, "not critical of *forgetting*, Your Honor, but critical of having stated under oath *contrary* to his deposition." Cooper ignored my aside.

"Do you today have available copies of those?"

"No, I don't." He explained that those stories didn't please him and weren't representative of his writing, and so he hadn't kept copies and that he had written them when he was in financial difficulty. He had a serious intestinal problem, adhesions from a former operation, and he had been hospitalized four weeks and the lingering effects of the illness went on for months afterward, and, he said, "I had continuous doctor bills for up to six or seven months after the operation."

"How long have you been writing?"

"About twenty years."

"How much money have you made from writing over that twenty years?"

"About sixteen thousand dollars." He said his take-home pay as a professor was $700 every two weeks.

"Now, how do your expenses compare to your take-home pay?"

I objected, and the court sustained.

Cioffari told the jury he'd been the youngest full professor in the college's history, and that he was in charge of bringing outstanding literary figures like Edward Albee to the campus, and he'd published in the *Michigan Quarterly* and the *Northwest Review*. He, too, defined *verisimilitude* and explained he'd gone to Atlantic City in order to get a feeling for the actual physical conditions of Convention Hall—the high ceilings, "the sense of smallness that a person might have in this huge vast land." He was sounding better, even poetic I thought—just a poor professor trying to make an honest buck the best way he could.

He'd watched the pageant a couple of hours—watched the belly dancer and thought she couldn't win because she was too obviously sexual, which, he pointed out, was Corky's opinion of Miss Wyoming in the story, and he had left before it was over in order to catch the last bus home that same night.

No, he hadn't intended to attack Kim Pring or make fun of her, he said. He'd been in Wyoming, and the most impressive thing he'd remembered were the Tetons. So in his story his character had been

inspired by the landscape, and the idea of the mountains were symbolically related to uplifting because, he said, they do uplift. "They
do rise above and, of course, that in itself connects to a number of
motifs in the story including levitation."

Eddie looked worried.

The color blue—well, there was a whole motif of blue working in-
ternally in the story to unify it, he said. It grew out of the Tetons, the
blue gray, and the light-blue warm-up suit was probably the most
popular color warm-up suits came in, and also the significance of
baby-blue relates to "character development," he said. The character, Charlene, is just out of high school. She is very young. In essence
she's babyish.

He said he'd used the baton because it could tie in with the image
of oral sex. He had a friend named Marilyn who was a high-school
baton twirler, and he'd read a novel by Harry Bruce called *The Feast
of Snakes,* which opened with a description of a baton twirler at a
football game.

At the bench Cooper said to the judge, "They [meaning me] have
left the impression with the jury that whatever happens in this case is
going to be paid for by *Penthouse.* It is *not* the case. Cioffari has no
insurance policy. He is *personally* liable, and to leave the jury with
the impression that he's being indemnified by *Penthouse* is totally
false. This is not governed by the normal rules about insurance or in-
demnification."

"It is governed by the normal rules of ethics," I said.

"It's great to hear you talk about ethics!" Cooper retorted. We
were crowded up there whispering, pushing for position so the judge
could see us, hear us, like little chicks in a nest vying wildly for the
worm, all mouths wide open. There was a subtle shoving from Cooper and I shoved back, a long, hard, slow, powerful force that pushed
him from his position gradually, and then steadily I let my elbow
move out as an obstacle that preserved my space immediately in
front of His Honor.

"Evidence of no insurance is equivalent to evidence of poverty,
which is an inadmissible plea," the judge said. "I recognize the fact
that there was testimony elicited by the plaintiff yesterday that *Penthouse* was defending the suit—to which no objection was made. I
was surprised there was none."

"I was in shock," Cooper said.

"And had you objected, I would have sustained it. However, there being none, I think now to go further would exacerbate the situation—it would be a forbidden poverty plea," His Honor said. Justice works in wonderful ways relying as it does on both sides *not telling the truth.* "And you're making an assumption that I don't make," the judge said. "The fact that *Penthouse* is providing the author with an attorney doesn't necessarily imply that they will pay the judgment."

Next Cooper had Cioffari explain to the jury why he had chosen Laramie—he wanted a large city in Wyoming, and there was the alliteration in the words Laramie Lizards, which he liked. "It is a device used very often in poetry and sometimes fiction writing as well to produce a certain effect," he said, as if the jury wouldn't otherwise know.

I slipped a note to Eddie. "How's he coming off?"

"The jury's checking him out," Eddie wrote back.

Cioffari said he'd constructed the story out of his imagination, out of his sense of symbol and form. He lectured to the jury about contemporary American literature, which he said had emerged in this country in about 1945. One of the editors at *Penthouse* had called him and asked about what he was working on and that is when Cioffari told about his planned collection of stories based on contemporary American events. He said he told the editor that he would appreciate it if *Penthouse* made mention of his work so that any publisher who read the Miss Wyoming story and liked it might consider his upcoming stories for future publication.

"Did *Penthouse* exercise any control over the topics you covered or wrote about?"

"Absolutely not."

"Thank you, Mr. Cioffari. That's all the questions I have."

"Any redirect, Mr. Spence?" the judge asked me.

"You either gotta kill him or let him go," Eddie whispered to me as I got up.

"Should I let him go?" I whispered back.

"Well, he ain't exactly dead in the water anymore," Eddie said. He grabbed my sleeve as I got up to examine and whispered, "Right now he's just sort of a poor innocent professor again."

I began with a sound to my questions that immediately made the man defensive once more. Since he had testified that in many ways the Charlene in the story was a baby, I now asked him if he hadn't chosen to have this babyish young woman commit oral sex—and was that funny? His response came back as arguments instead of answers, and his voice sounded harsh.

"I wrote the kind of story that I wanted to write," Cioffari said.

"Thank you very much," I said in a very nice voice.

Cooper jumped up. "Does Your Honor still think his 'thank you's are harmless?" A lady on the jury snickered. Cooper saw her and reddened again.

"As I've said before, it never hurts to be polite," the judge said. "Counsel will refrain from any inflection in saying it, though."

"You have told us repeatedly that the night you were there the Convention Hall was not clear full," I said. Cioffari nodded. "Now if the unrefuted evidence in this case becomes that on the night of the finals the Convention Hall was packed—standing room only—would it then be your testimony that you were there on the night of the *talent show—the night before?*"

"No, I was not!"

"Well, on the night you were there it was partially empty. We can rely on that, can't we?"

"Well, it's my recollection it was partially empty," he said.

"Thank you," I said again.

Cioffari had told the jury that his publications in the literary journals did not have explicit sex scenes in them. On cross-examination I handed him his rat-killing story published in the *Michigan Quarterly*. To this point the judge had ruled it out. But now Judge Brimmer said the story was material to show any contradiction in Cioffari's prior testimony. I walked over to Cioffari. I could see him brace against me.

"I would like you to read with me from your article in which you say there were no explicit sex scenes and ask you to see if I read it correctly." I put the article in front of him, and began to read aloud, and when I'd read the part about the woman's legs being spread apart and the sore in between I stopped and looked at Cioffari. He glared back. "Do you consider that explicit?"

"I don't consider that an explicit sex scene, no. The boys are looking at a magazine."

He told Cooper he had submitted his writings to the Bread Loaf Writers Conference, founded by Robert Frost. He claimed it was the most prestigious conference in the country. He'd received a scholarship to the conference.

"Did you submit your writings from *Hustler?*" I asked. It was a mean question.

"No, I did not," Cioffari said.

*　*　*

I snapped off the light between Eddie's bed and mine.

"You did good today," Eddie said.

I stared up at the ceiling in the dark and I could see that one juror in the back on the end also staring up at the high vaulted ceiling in the courtroom. I couldn't get him to look at me. Maybe the man couldn't bear the sight of me: a man can look at whomever he pleases, but when Cooper spoke he followed everything Cooper did and said—even had a friendly smile for him now and then. I was in trouble with that juror, and then I drifted off to sleep, making my arguments to that one juror, and to him alone, and no matter what I said or did, no matter how I bellowed or begged, I still couldn't get the man to look at me. Not even once.

23

The jury watched curiously as this tall black man approached the witness stand, carrying muscle on tendon and bone in graceful ways. I called him "Dr. Wideman." Where the hell did this guy come from anyway, all dressed up in his dark-blue Sunday-go-to-meeting suit and freshly starched collar, and walking down the aisle of the courtroom with such pride in his stride?

This Dr. John Edgar Wideman was past forty and had a face you liked to look at and those wondrous large hands, one of which he held up to take the oath displaying long fingers that curled slightly outward, fingers a piano player would cherish. He took his seat and looked quickly at the jury and gave them a shy smile, displaying strong teeth. When I was a kid in Sheridan, Wyoming, we didn't have any "Negroes." There was a black porter on the train my mother and I took to Grandpa's in the summer, I remember that, and I remember his hands were light-colored on the palms. I gawked at him. And then my mother shook my wrist lightly and whispered in my ear, "Staring isn't nice, Gerry. He has feelings too, you know, just like you and me."

Watching Dr. John Wideman take the stand made me feel good, perhaps because I felt like a black man myself, which is hard to explain. I think I felt black because I had been poor, and poor is bad, and being black was both poor and bad, and nobody likes poor people, not even the poor, not even the blacks, and I wanted to be somebody, but poor people and blacks, although they had the legal right, weren't supposed to be somebody. Not really.

On the stand Dr. John Edgar Wideman's face soaked up the light and his features seemed to blend into themselves, but I could see his eyes, and they seemed patient, maybe sad. He sat relaxed, waiting for my first question. I'd called him as an expert on literature

293

and writing. There was something inherently ludicrous about that, I admit, although no one would dare mention it—but experts are white, usually with gray hair, a condescending air, a massive *curriculum vitae*, and they charge a thousand a day to testify in court, whether they know a damn thing or not. I looked over at Cooper. He was grinning, whispering something into Kelley's ear, and Kelley was nodding.

Wideman spoke to the jury in a quiet voice. He had grown up in Pittsburgh and played basketball, of course. Then he had gone to the University of Pennsylvania and won a Rhodes scholarship and attended Oxford University in England. The man was talking to the jurors like a neighbor over the fence. He had become a tenured professor at the University of Pennsylvania and was director of Afro-American studies. He was married, had a couple of kids, had taken a position at the University of Wyoming to give his children an exposure to a different part of the country, and he had stayed. He taught creative writing, poetry, and American literature. He'd written three novels—two more would be released in October—besides having published in *The New York Times Book Review*, *American Scholar*, and numerous other scholarly periodicals. He was a member of Phi Beta Kappa, and, he added, he played semi-pro basketball—don't forget that.

Dr. Wideman told the jury he had read Cioffari's stories, and incidentally, he'd seen Kim Pring perform with her baton at the halftime ceremonies at the university. He said when real persons are used in fiction, it gives the reader a double thrill—but there are dangers—the writer is trying to have it both ways. A story about a black civil-rights leader born in Atlanta, who fights an evil sheriff and who stages a march across a bridge in a southern town, is not fiction about Reverend Smith but fact about Martin Luther King, and if the man is portrayed as dishonest, a womanizer, and someone who has sold out to the white power structure for his own benefit—well, there is a danger in this.

"It's a way of saying things about people that can distort the truth—you could endanger the reputation of a well-known figure. You could distort history. Actually, placed in your hands is a certain power—you are sitting at the controls of the media and can allow pictures that are half truth and half not to be hoisted into the public view. I don't know if there is any writer who would say that the ability to write gives you the right to inflict gratuitous harm on people."

Great power imposes great responsibility. I spoke respectfully to this man. He said, "This story presents a classic case of how a writer can manipulate fact and fiction to get the reader's attention. Let's begin with the cover. In very bold letters, MISS WYOMING'S UNIQUE TALENT is trumpeted across the stage. If I pick that magazine up, I'm going to immediately think of an actual person, and I'm going to ask myself, well, what is this talent? I won't see it as the latest fiction by James Baldwin. It just says "Miss Wyoming's Unique Talent," so that when I open up that magazine, I'm already predisposed to look at the real world, to look at the factual world. I read the story not just as a figment of someone's imagination, but I'm beginning to make connections between the world as I know it and the world as it exists in this story."

I asked Wideman, "What is the ultimate effect of the use of this technique?"

"That somebody was hurt, an actual person—a *living, breathing person* suffered some harm and damage that followed directly from the publication of this story." I heard this man. He was also a living, breathing person who knew about pain. And there was a book festering in him then, a book he has written since, *Brothers and Keepers,* about his own brother who was in the penitentiary for life for murder. He had asked, "For every black man who becomes a Rhodes scholar, how many get wasted? Is my brother the price for everything I gained? Have I ransomed him for whatever success I've had?" Robbie Wideman and two buddies, Dukes and Rice, all from Pittsburgh, had stuck up a man, a fence, and Dukes had lost it and shot the man, and John Wideman's brother was in prison for life. John could still hear a line from Robbie's poetry:

> *My mother had five nigger babies*
> *And America couldn't give us all a piece of pie.*

I thought the heat and pressure of his torment had changed John Wideman the way gold is extracted from the harder rock. I knew something of the guilt of the man, the scholar, the author, this black who had made good and moved away from his people to the great plains, the white plains of Wyoming. But guilt creates strong ears for hearing other humans.

I asked him, "What in your opinion could have been done to prevent the hurt to Kim Pring you have testified to?"

"The simplest thing in the world would have been to call this pageant something other than Miss America, leave Wyoming out of it, leave the baton twirling out of it, and still you would have the roots of a story. You wouldn't damage anything substantial in the story by removing that factual material. It would take any of us ten minutes to remove the material that's hurtful." He looked at the jury and smiled sadly. "I was just astounded there was such a flagrant disregard for that kind of simple basic human responsibility," he said.

"Can fiction libel people?"

"Yes, it can."

"Explain why and how," I asked.

"I'm the only black professor at the University of Wyoming. If someone wrote a story about a black professor who was a homosexual and giving out grades for sexual favors to his students, that would be a fiction. I promise that would be a fiction!" He raised his eyebrows and burst into laughter and the jury laughed with him, all except the man in the back row on the end who was still watching the ceiling. "But I can just see myself going back to work and trying to address classes and my colleagues if someone wrote that story. It would be fiction, but it would be libelous, and I would hope that the law would offer me some redress if someone did that to me."

Cooper objected, and Judge Brimmer overruled.

"Mr. Guccione, under oath the other day, said that if the publishing industry was required to check out articles like this, it would put the industry out of business. What do you say about that?"

"I don't think that an added expense justifies the human misery and difficulty and pain. . . . The power that's invested in a publishing house that has millions and millions of readers—that's a power that corrupts and you can't give anyone that kind of power. You'd hope that with that power comes some sense of moral and ethical responsibility."

"What do you have to say about the failure of *Penthouse* to investigate in this case?"

"I was surprised that such a transparent, flagrant, obvious use of an actual person would occur in a nationwide magazine," and he thought that the failure of the *Penthouse* editors to make any further inquiry when they knew there was a real Miss Wyoming, was a "very disturbing kind of arrogance—I say arrogance because there *was* a Miss Wyoming, and there *was* a beauty pageant, and any story about a Miss Wyoming would involve actual living human beings and should connect in anybody's mind with the potential of the story to hurt a person."

And what about the fact that the story involved levitation—that we all knew to be impossible? "Well, unfortunately," Dr. Wideman said, "the next time I see Miss Wyoming walking across the screen, if I happen to be watching the Miss America Pageant, it's going to be hard to get that out of my mind. I'm going to remember this whole scene. I'm going to have a lot of unpleasant associations. . . . No matter how ridiculous the details are, if the events in the story are striking or unusual or absurd, the unusual stays with you, and then the obscene or the libelous parts would also stay." The jury held to this man who spoke to them in an easy voice, and looked them directly, kindly in the eyes.

"How did it make you feel as you read this story?"

"I read it as a professional and I've already expressed my shock at what I see as a rather ridiculous negligence in the piece. Why didn't you as a writer or as a publisher give the person inside of the story the benefit of the doubt? Why didn't you make any attempt to disguise the actual person?

"As a critic, as a fellow writer, I found the story not very well written, not very exciting; as a piece of literature, I think it's negligible and it's not really worth talking about very much." Sorry that he felt compelled to say that, Dr. Wideman looked down at his hands. The jury looked at Cioffari.

"And I think that if people knew what I knew about the story, that there was an actual living, breathing person who was being very savagely, flagrantly abused in the story, it would cause outrage."

"Now Mr. Guccione said that anybody who had an opinion that this article was absolutely revolting would have to have a 'tainted brain.' Do you agree with that?"

"Absolutely not. There is a whole range of moral and ethical values in this country, and plenty of people who, just on the basis of the subject matter alone, would be quite upset."

"And Mr. Guccione said that if any person believes this article was about Kim Pring he would have to have the 'intellect of a flatworm.' Do you agree with that, Dr. Wideman?" I asked.

Cooper laid out a series of objections claiming I was quoting Guccione incorrectly. I rephrased the question.

"Do you believe that those who might think this article was about Kim Pring would have the intellect of a flatworm?"

Cooper would object again, but by now who gave a damn?

Finally I said, "Do you believe that anybody who thought this was a story about Kim Pring would be stupid?" The jury laughed.

Dr. Wideman laughed, too. Then very seriously Dr. Wideman said, "Well, giving the comment the benefit of the doubt, there is a little germ of truth there in the sense that none of us believe that somebody committing fellatio on another person has the power to make them levitate—but that's really not what we're talking about. What we're talking about is whether or not this story caused tremendous pain and trouble for a human being because it didn't make a decent attempt to disassociate her from this fictionalized framework. So, no. I don't know of any action you can perform on another human being to levitate them, but I do know"—and the man spoke very quietly—"I do know you can hurt people by saying evil things about them whether they are true or not, and in that sense, obviously damage was done."

I sat down.

Then the attack came. Cooper's voice sounded angry. I didn't want to look.

"Did you ever read *Peter Pan?*"

"Yes," Wideman said.

"Did you check out to see whether there was a little funny person with a green suit, toes, et cetera, before you would publish that?"

Dr. Wideman smiled. "I probably at that time *believed* there were those kinds of people." The jury laughed with him. Now Cooper asked a long series of questions about the professor's previous novels, about the meaning of the characters, the symbols, their likenesses to specific people, genre—the sounds of the questioning took on long monotonous rhythms and Wideman's answers sounded the same. The jury was restless.

Finally I stood up. "Your Honor, if we're just going to stall till five o'clock, couldn't we call it quits now?" which brought laughter from the jury and the audience.

Cooper shouted, "I'm not stalling, Counsel!"

The judge pounded his gavel. "Please sit down, Mr. Spence." More laughter.

"Could he tell his gallery to *shut up?*" Cooper suddenly screamed, pointing to the laughing audience. I looked at Cooper. The man was standing there, shaking, red-faced, stunned at his own outburst. I said nothing. Then I slowly sat down. In a moment Cooper collected himself and began anew, and droned on until 5:00 P.M. Lawyers don't win cases. Their opponents lose them.

The next morning Jeffrey Daichman asked the judge to let him go back to New York. "I would like to say that it's been certainly a pleasure and a privilege to be here," Daichman said.

"Well, Mr. Daichman, you didn't start out on the best of terms." The judge was smiling.

"I understand that," Daichman said.

"But you have been a gentleman here. So no hard feelings." The judge offered Daichman his hand and Daichman took it and then walked on past Eddie and me without a word, and we shrugged our shoulders and went back in the courtroom. Cooper had dug up some interview Dr. Wideman had given years before and was beating him over the head with it, and arguing about the explicit sex in the writings of Joyce and Baldwin, and I was impressed with Cooper's intimacy with American literature and his ability to wrestle with a Rhodes scholar on these various subjects. Then Cooper began questioning Wideman about Swift's satire, about the rich English eating poor Irish babies as a solution to the control of the population, and at the last, he wanted to know how well Wideman knew Kim Pring.

"You said you saw her at half time. Do you know her any better than that?"

"No. After my testimony yesterday she came up and said, 'Thank you,' and gave me a hug. That's all."

"She was in tears and you hugged her back?" Cooper accused.

"Yes," Dr. Wideman said. I looked over at the jury. One of the older women looked at Kim and gave her a kind smile, and then Cooper tried to show that Wideman and I had also been talking since the doctor's testimony of the evening before.

"Now I did talk to you this morning. Do you recall?" I asked Dr. Wideman on redirect. "I was standing over there and congratulated you on your clear explanations to the jury yesterday."

Cooper hollered, "Object, and ask that that comment be stricken!" and the Court ordered it stricken. Maybe Cooper wouldn't ask the next witness about my conversations with him.

Dr. Wideman told the jury that Joyce and Baldwin had been very careful to protect innocent people, that he'd never heard of them being sued, and finally I looked right at the judge and asked, "Is that one of the standards that you were mentioning yesterday that you felt had been *recklessly disregarded?*"

"Yes," Dr. Wideman said. There was the necessary proof to go to the jury on punitive damages. Wideman said, "When you write something, to the best of your ability you try not to harm innocent people—that's what bothered me about the story—harm for no good purpose. There is no reason to go after Kim Pring," he said. "What evil is she bringing into the world? What has she done to the author? What is he trying to change about the world that he needs to involve a young woman from Wyoming?" I couldn't have said it better. I thought John Edgar Wideman and I were brothers stuck out on the plains of Wyoming alone.

We found this nice kid named Tracy Wilson, a student at the University of Wyoming, who had known Kim since they were sixth graders—pals, nothing more. As he walked to the stand I could see them, fuzzy and white as pink-eyed rabbit children hopping in the halls among the other children, and what they knew of themselves or each other was nothing.

He said Kim usually missed the punch lines of dirty jokes, and that when he'd come across the magazine and read the story, it made him really mad because it was about Kim. "And I thought, how could they do that?" He'd heard a lot of comments from people wondering if Kim was really like that. People would nudge him in the ribs and ask, "Is there anything to that?"

After the article, Kim became depressed, he said, and lost her bubbliness. "Everybody knows you can't levitate somebody, but as far as the sexual connotation is concerned, it tainted her reputation. Even today in the office where I work they still ask me, you know, what is she really like and that's something that she's going to bear with her for the rest of her life." He looked very sad, this kid.

Then Cooper attacked on cross-examination. He wanted the names of all the people who had told him those things, and Tracy gave him a couple of names, but that wasn't enough. He wanted to know exactly what each person said, and the kid couldn't remember exactly, and then Cooper said that was all.

"Thank you," Tracy Wilson said. "Do I get to watch the rest of the trial?"

"Yes, you may stay in the courtroom now," the judge said and the kid hopped down off the stand, and Kim reached out for his hand and gave it a little squeeze and said, "Thank you, Tracy."

Cooper rushed to the bench hollering in a loud whisper to the judge, "Could we get an instruction that Miss Pring should not talk to the witnesses after they leave the scene, which just occurred with Mr. Wilson?"

"Yes, tell her not to be demonstrative," the judge said to me, and then he yawned and looked at his watch.

"I didn't notice that she was demonstrative," I said.

"I didn't notice it either," the judge said, and yawned again, and then he looked down at Kim and gave her a small judicious smile.

When I assured the Court that Dr. Victor Cline had written over a hundred articles on the effects of explicit sex on readers and would testify only on how the article would affect the public's viewpoint of Kim, the judge finally agreed that I might call him. He was a Salt Lake psychologist and professor of psychology at the University of Utah. He'd written a book entitled *Where Do You Draw the Line? An Exploration into Media Violence, Pornography, and Censorship*, and he'd written a chapter for the minority report in the *Presidential Commission Report on Pornography*.

He had nine children.

He said the purpose of *Penthouse* was to turn people on sexually. The technique of mixing legitimate articles with highly graphic, very explicit visual materials, and very sexually arousing materials, is a way of legitimizing the magazine, that is, he said, giving it the appearance of being a serious magazine concerned with serious topics.

"I see," I said. "So the reader has an excuse for buying it?"

"He has an excuse for buying it, and I think that is just a marketing technique."

"I was depressed and angry when I read this article because I knew pretty much what the effect of such an article would be—I see it as a form of sexual molestation, not physical but psychological," the doctor said.

"Molestation?"

"Yes, absolutely. I have treated many women who have been molested sexually, and I see this article as an intrusion into a very personal privacy by linking her with explicit sex in such a way that she can never erase it from her mind." He spoke in whispered words. "It is an assault upon her self-respect."

"Well, but Doctor, it's claimed here that the article on its face is absurd—fellatio causing levitation. What do you say about that?"

"Well," he said, in a very slow and authoritative way, "I think that it makes it *even worse* for this reason—this is a highly unusual kind of association. The very fact that it's unusual means that the linkage will never get lost. There is not a single person in this room"—he stopped to look at the full gallery of spectators, motioning to them as if they were his witnesses to the truth—"not a *single person* who, as long as he or she lives, will ever forget this *or her* wherever they see her or hear her name. There is no way any of us can ever forget it, nor"—he looked sadly at Kim—"will she ever forget it." I looked at Kim. She was quietly weeping.

"Well, Doctor, the readership of the magazine is shown to be as many as twenty to twenty-five million men all over the world. What do you think that widespread kind of recognition in this country and the world would have on a Wyoming girl?"

"Well, in a word, I think it will be castastrophic," the doctor said. I quietly sat down by Kim.

Cooper attacked.

There were eighteen people on the President's Commission on Pornography, and he, the good doctor, was one of only three who had filed a minority report. Cooper had the doctor admit he'd never tested Kim with a single one of the battery of psychological tests, his standard tools, and then Cooper, with uncustomary brevity, sat down.

I then asked, "Dr. Cline, do you feel you needed to interview Kim Pring or the readers of the article in order to come to your opinions?"

"No. I can still draw certain conclusions from having worked with people who have been victims of this kind of an attack—even though I've never interviewed or tested the client."

"Thank you, Dr. Cline," I said.

"Call your next witness," the judge ordered.

"Call Kimerli Jayne Pring," I said.

24

Kim Pring wore a clean, starched blouse and tried to smile. Her hair, done up loosely on her head, was blond as morning prairie grass. She would never be ready—not for such an ordeal as this. She had become the "Once Accused."

She moved across the courtroom toward that same chair. By now she had come to believe the ugly defamation because the lie itself had changed her. She was this different person who must forever wear the cloak of the Once Accused like a new but filthy hide and, now clothed in it, she must convince these strangers staring, these six, that she was not the person she had, in fact, become—that woman, that *Penthouse* girl. Even as she walked to the witness chair, the jurors had already judged her—their decisions against her having been rendered long ago in the dark corners of their beings where the secret mind reached out its long and loathsome fingers of judgment and found that the Once Accused, indeed, had always been guilty.

Even the *Malleus* cautioned: "Let care be taken not to put anywhere in the sentence that the accused is innocent or immune, but that it was not legally proved against the accused; for if after a little time [she] should again be brought to trial, and it should be legally proved, [she] can, notwithstanding the previous sentence of absolution, then be condemned."[1] The State never releases its hope that some day the accused may be found guilty. No jury is permitted to find the accused innocent, as, indeed, we are all presumed to be, for the State will only admit its charge was never proven, hence the finding of not guilty—only that much will the State admit. But never, no, never will the State consent to a finding of innocent—for the defendant, by the charge, has become the Once Accused and can never again be innocent.

I watched the men watch Kim walk to the stand, their faces

trained blank as pulpwood. I saw a finger twitch on the man in the back on the end. That's all. He must have seen her mouth as I had seen it, the extra-full lips, and he must have, at no more than a glance, seen her young body—but his face remained like a mask. There would have been scenes in his mind's eye, secret scenes. If one were to ask the man, "What were you thinking just then as she walked to the stand?" perhaps he would say, "Why, nothing. Nothing at all." Or perhaps, because what he saw seemed harmless enough and being slightly sentimental, he might have said, "To tell you the truth, I was thinking about my Aunt Dorothy. Don't know why [nervous laugh, perhaps]. She used to let us kids lick the fudge kettle at Christmas time."

Kim stepped up to the stand, took the chair, and crossed her ankles.

I took her through the preliminaries, her history about the club-foot, the operations and all, her twirling lessons beginning at five, the competition since she was nine—and slow down just a minute, Kim. You're nervous, aren't you? You've been worrying about this for a long time, haven't you?

She told how she had gone to the nationals every year since she was fourteen, and was runner-up to Miss Wyoming in 1976, and Kim, please, just slow down a little. We've got plenty of time. She gave a little nervous giggle. "I've got a gift of gab sometimes," she said.

We showed the jury her scrapbook. She practiced four, five hours a day, every day. "All I'd worked for came true in 1978. I won Miss Wyoming and I won the United States Grand National Twirling Championship. It couldn't have been a better year for me, and I felt so confident—been trying for fourteen years." She began to forget the Miss Wyoming smile as she sat there remembering. I was glad.

"My father was a maintenance sergeant in the air force so we weren't the old traditional type people here in Wyoming, but once I became Miss Wyoming, we were here to stay." Little children looked up to her too. "I just hope that they see me as a good image and that they respect me, and I hope that through my teaching them I can help them achieve as much happiness as I have had through my twirling."

Then I thought I'd better get this goddamned *Gente* magazine thing out in front of the jury. Yes, she'd gone to Peru to perform at their Internacional de Primavera, comparable to our Frontier Days, our rodeo—with seven of the nation's best baton twirlers. She had never seen or heard of that magazine and had no knowledge her picture would appear in such a publication. The telephone number in the magazine was her chaperone's, not hers. She was fully clothed, in the cowboy twirling outfit she wore at the Wyoming football games—and so that was that.

I handed her a baton and had her demonstrate to the jury how she did the mouth roll—teaches the exercise to little girls, a decent exercise—see, it's part of a hand roll and it goes through your mouth—see, in slow motion like this, and it turns in the mouth just right here, like this. You can do it one-handed like this or you can do it with both hands coming off of these elbow rolls. This is an elbow roll. You can come off of it with two elbows, see, and it comes over here up into the mouth, up, one-handed, and no hands, like that.

The night she had performed her twirling, the house was about half full—never is completely full on those preliminary nights. She started off her routine with two batons, and then she set one baton down and went through a one-baton routine, balancing the spinning baton on her back, her neck, her shoulders, then in her mouth, and after that, she threw one baton in the air and bent over and picked up her two other batons and started juggling all three of them for the finale. She got a standing ovation from the crowd that night, and it was so overwhelming to her—everybody standing, clapping for her.

But on the final night, the night Cioffari was allegedly there, she said the house was packed. They had to bring in extra folding chairs for the overflow.

"Kim, when did you learn about this article?"

"I learned about it in July on Friday the thirteenth."

"And what is today?"

"Ironically, it's Friday the thirteenth. I learned about the article from a man who called." She gave his name. He told her, "This article is about you. I think you ought to try to find a lawyer to help clear your name." She asked the man, "Is my name mentioned?" and he said, "No," and then she said, "He went into the depth of what the article was about, and he said he identified me readily."

"What did you do, Kim?"

"I started crying. I was very hurt. I felt helpless. I was crushed. I took what he had to say as being true and that's why I think my feelings were so hurt. So my mom got out of bed and we got dressed and we went down to the newsstand and we bought a *Penthouse* magazine and read it."

"Would you share with the ladies and gentlemen of the jury your feelings as best you can?"

"I could not believe it. I was crying. I felt like everything that I had done in a matter of twenty-three years had been crushed in a thirty-five-hundred-word article." She was holding the tears back. "Everything I stood for. Everything I represented. Everything I worked for. Everything I've dedicated my entire life to was ruined. That's exactly how I felt. I was hurt, and I was angry, and that's why I sought your help." She began to cry softly, and there were tears forming in the eyes of some of the jurors and in my eyes, too.

"What experience did you have, Kim, after this article was pretty well distributed within the state?"

"Since that Friday the thirteenth I have not had one free day, and what has hurt me the most, I think, is that friends or not friends, anybody that talks to me about this cannot talk to Kim Pring anymore. They are talking to Miss Penthouse or something that has to do with the article. Nobody even knows me for what I stand for anymore, and that is the hardest thing I have had to contend with." She began to openly weep, and I thought she was weeping not for herself but for the woman who had been lost that Friday the thirteenth, that Kim Pring who was a happy champion with a big Wyoming smile and three batons in the air all at once. I looked up at the judge.

He said quietly, "I think it would be a good time to take a recess, Counsel, even if it is a little early. We'll stand in recess for ten minutes." I didn't talk to Kim during the recess. Emotionally she was where I wanted her—in it, feeling it, talking to the jury. I gave her a big hug when she came off the stand and sent her to her mother who was still waiting in the witness room after all these days.

After the recess she told it without the tears, about guys who would call her up and ask her to perform "certain favors," as she called them, "and they asked me if I was that good to get into *Penthouse* magazine, would I do it on them?" The calls were coming quite regularly—sometimes they would ring every hour, three o'clock, four—five in the morning, all through the night. "I couldn't go out anymore. This year at Homecoming was the first time I got to go and just enjoy myself and watch, and as I was walking down the street two boys in a pickup went by yelling, 'Hey, Penthouse!' and 'Come on, Penthouse!' I've heard people just in a social atmosphere say, 'Hey, there is that girl in *Penthouse* magazine, and make just crude and rude remarks. *Penthouse* has taken the skeleton of me, everything that is good and decent in America as far as the Miss America Pageant is concerned, everything I have done in my life that has been good and decent and has turned it into this. I mean, I went from the most decent person to the most indecent person in a matter of, like I said, thirty-five hundred words—people wondering was I like that girl in the article. Is this a publicity stunt? Do I want more than being Miss Wyoming? Do I want to further my career? Is it a joke, Kim? Are you doing this on purpose? These are the kind of things I've had to deal with ever since this article came out."

She left the university and came home to live with her parents—went to the community college in Cheyenne. Then in October it snowed, and she said, "When I came out to get into my Volkswagen there it was, written in the snow across the windshield 'Give me head,'" and she looked at the women on the jury like they wouldn't, of course, know what that meant and so she said it plainly, "Which means in our young terms, give me a blowjob. I had that written on my windshield! Also I've had broken beer bottles placed underneath my tires, and I've had notes slipped under my door and—"

I interrupted her to slow her down. "Did you receive any calls from professional people like reporters?"

"Yes, I did, and *The Washington Post* called me. They wanted an interview. I refused. They accused me of doing this strictly as a publicity stunt. Girls would give their eyeteeth to get into *Penthouse* magazine was what she was accusing me of. This was all a lowly Wyoming girl could do was to get something like this done."

"How has this affected your social life, Kim?"

"What social life? One night I recall this guy coming over to my boyfriend and saying, 'Yep, that's that majorette. She's a hell of a majorette, but I bet she can give a better blowjob.' My boyfriend didn't hit him, but he had good words with him and we left immediately. I don't go out to the bars and lounges anymore."

Then she told the jury that only three of the twenty students she had been teaching when the article came out reenrolled in her classes, and one of her students, whom she'd taken to nationals, who'd even won a national title that year, dropped her for "certain circumstances."

"They say I have a low moral character and the parents say that they don't want their daughters to take from me anymore."

"How does that make you feel?" She was ready to cry again.

"All I can do is just try to keep fighting."

"Is that why you're here—to continue your fight?"

"You bet."

Then she stopped. She looked at the jury a long time, and I let her have her head, let her go where she wanted to go. "I want to make another point, too," she began. "No amount of money will ever repay me for what they have done to me. No amount. And you know what? I don't care if it was one hundred million dollars, two hundred million, three hundred million. It doesn't matter. If you awarded me that and if I could give it back for the same life that I had, I would. Because I will never have a normal life again." She was fighting against the threatening sobs. We fought for her also. "I am not a normal person anymore." Then she spoke almost to herself, "I am a good, clean, wholesome person, but the way people make me think, they make me feel dirty, and cheap and low, and—immoral."

Very quietly I said to Cooper, "You may examine."

Cooper was interested in her, but only like an accountant—in her earnings, her work history, beginning from age fifteen, her charges for baton lessons—used to be $7.50 and now it's $10 an hour. She had made $1,874 the year she was Miss Wyoming, and in 1977 only $794.06. Nothing suggested he acknowledged her membership in the human race. She was merely the source of certain statistics, numbers, facts.

She admitted she didn't have a phone tap put on to catch the callers. She had called the campus police. Hadn't she lied? Because in her deposition, hadn't she denied ever calling the police? But she said she'd called the police *since* she gave her deposition. Cooper tried to make a public figure of her. She and some other kids, twirlers, had appeared a couple of times with the Frank Zappa band. She had been in the Miss USA contest. Her picture had been on the program of the Brigham Young–Wyoming football schedule. When she was ten and won the state twirling championship, her picture had been in the *Wyoming State Tribune*. She had her picture on the cover of *Twirl* magazine, a magazine of the sport, and in *Drum Majors* magazine, and that was as early as 1975, and her picture in *Twirl* showed her with a six-shooter and a cowboy hat.

"Isn't that a *promotional* type photograph you chose?" Cooper asked.

"No. It's just that I've always felt somewhat like an underdog, I suppose you could say, because nobody from Wyoming has ever won anything nationally in baton twirling. I was the very first, and I show a lot of respect, a lot of love for the state of Wyoming, and I dressed up in my Wyoming attire, the cowboy hat, the fringe on the costume, the boots. This is why I chose this picture."

"It doesn't mean to indicate that you were a pistol shooter or worked on target shooting or anything of that type?" Cooper asked, feigning ignorance, mocking. A couple of jurors in the front looked at each other.

She had been nominated for Outstanding Young Woman in America for 1979, and she'd been in parades, and she had appeared in *Gente* magazine, he mentioned again, and gone to Peru, he also mentioned again, and in the *Miss America Manual* there were instructions on "Meeting the Press," and yes, she'd won over five hundred first-place trophies in twirling. Five hundred!

Then Cooper started on the color of her warm-up suits, and Lord knows what else—on and on. Perhaps he was trying to destroy the witness by making it appear it was she who was boring the jury. Finally Cooper went to the bench asking permission of Judge Brimmer to use the remainder of the afternoon to show the jury the rest of tape on the Miss America Pageant.

"What he's trying to do is stall. Your Honor, I want him to finish," I said. The judge didn't pay the slightest attention to me, and he and Cooper went on talking at the bench. I repeated, "I want him to finish up with her."

Cooper went on as if I weren't there, the judge listening, nodding.

"I would like him to finish his examination so she doesn't have to go through a weekend of further misery worrying about this. I want it done with! We gave him plenty of time. He's still got a half an hour."

"I can take as long as I want," Cooper said, "I'm not going to finish today."

The judge, as if he hadn't heard a word I said, went on talking to Cooper.

Finally I exploded. I slammed my open palm against the side of the bench. Slap! The judge jumped. Cooper stopped talking. "Judge, I know you're trying to be fair, but I want to know why my requests are falling on deaf ears?"

"What requests?"

"I want him to complete! This woman has been through hell.

She is entitled to have him complete his cross-examination and not stall!"

"Well, that's what I'm saying. I have said that he's going to and he has said that he will. I don't say that it has to be done by five tonight, but we're going to keep going until about then and we'll quit." It was only the smallest victory, not worth the breath.

"This guy is not going to cross-examine her. He's going to wear her away," I said to Eddie.

Cooper continued the stall—there was nothing I could do to stop it. The dress had a white stripe on it and was not, therefore, *all* baby-blue. Yes, and at the time the magazine hit the stands she was no longer Miss Wyoming. Yes, the Charlene in the story called baton twirling "stupid," and Kim Pring didn't feel that way about baton twirling; therefore the story was not about her. There was no Beach Queen Hotel. She never had a coach called Corky. Kim didn't drink, while Charlene did, and she was never at Colter Bay with Monte Applewhite. Therefore the story was not about her but about the fictional Charlene. Cooper went on. And on. Her routine with the baton was different from Charlene's, and the actual winner was Miss Virginia—different from in the story, and the first runner-up was Miss Alabama, and that was different too, and the second runner-up, and on through the fourth runner-up, for Christ's sakes, and the fifth. Kim knew them all, and they were all different and there was no fight between Kim and Miss Alaska, and Kim never wore her hair over her eye like in the drawing, so obviously the story wasn't about her.

No, she had never bragged to anybody about being in *Penthouse*. She'd shown the article to the Cenedeses, parents of one of her students—they were her friends and she wanted their reaction, but that's all, and yes, she could see the whole audience on the final night, not from the stage on account of the lights, but you get a good view from the ramp. No, she didn't have a newspaper-clipping service, and—the stall had prevailed. The magic hour of five having arrived, the court called a recess until Monday morning.

At dinner Eddie sat silently messing with his peas, as if he didn't have the heart to stab them or the energy to chase them around the plate, and Kim seemed too depressed to speak. It was a nice little room in the Hitching Post, and people were laughing and the waitresses were bouncing by and smiling, but at our table we were soaked in a heavy gravy of gloom.

"Why all this?" I finally said. "We're ahead, way ahead."

Eddie looked up, said nothing.

"Eat your food, Kim," I said like a father to his child. She took a nibble at the rice.

"What's the matter? He killed himself. What's the matter?" I asked. I stabbed a piece of steak.

"He's gonna come up with somethin'," Eddie said. "That's what the stall was all about. He needs the weekend to get whatever he thinks he's got."

Finally I said, "I know. That's what I want to talk to you about, Kim. What's out there? What stumps can he kick over? What bugs can he find underneath? Who's it gonna be?"

"Nothing, Mr. Spence. Nobody." She kept looking at the rice on her plate.

"Something wrong with your food?"

"No."

"What is it?"

"Absolutely nothing," she said. Then she laughed and took a big mouthful, and chewed it with huge bites like some ferocious beast masticating through an evil grin, and she made her eyes big as silver dollars and said, "Ummm, it is goo-ood!" And then she laughed again and we all laughed.

"You were perfect today," I said.

"You gotta watch 'em, Gerry," Eddie said. "Watch 'em like a hawk. They're desperate. They're gonna pull somethin'."

Goddamn the worry. It covers everything, stinks up everything. What will he come up with? What will we do? We had this thing stopped once. Now it had all been opened up again, because if a woman dares declare herself a woman of good repute, and Kim had, the law invites them to bring in their miserable witnesses who will say the opposite. The directions of the *Malleus* are clear. "If they [the witnesses] give evidence of fact, so much the better. But if they only give evidence as to her general character, and the matter stands so . . . he [the judge] shall take the evidence of the fact and of her bad reputation given by other witnesses as proof that the accused must be strongly suspect and on these grounds he can sentence her to a threefold punishment . . ."[2]

We worried on.

Reputation testimony in the eyes of the law is hearsay. But it's "okay hearsay." In any witch trial reputation testimony was vital. "It is asked," the *Malleus* says, "what is to be done when, as often happens, the accused denies everything. We answer that the Judge has three points to consider, namely, her bad reputation, the evidence of fact and the words of the witnesses; and he must see whether all these agree together."[3]

We were early to court Monday morning. So were Cooper and Kelley. So was the judge. We came together in chambers like air rushing into a vacuum, no preliminary pleasantries, Cooper starting right off, sweetening up His Honor by delivering the three stories Cioffari had published in *Hustler*. Now he claimed there were only three, not four, and Judge Brimmer, smiling and businesslike, ruled they could *not* be shown to the jury, or even mentioned—irrelevant, he said.

Cooper moved for a continuance of the trial or a mistrial. He had new information on Kim Pring.

"Let me ask, is Mr. Grutman still pulling the strings from New York on this trial?" the judge said.

"Mr. Grutman is still whatever the relationship has been in the past—yes."

Judge Brimmer looked hard at Cooper now. "We discussed this matter at the pretrial and you *specifically* said you had no intent or interest in going into these things! Now you're bringing it up again," he said. Then the judge pointed at Cooper. "And what I'm wondering is, is Mr. Grutman still directing the course of the trial and if so, why isn't he here?"

Cooper shrugged his shoulders. His answer was terse. "Yes, and I don't know."

"So he's the one who suggested this course of action to you?"

Cooper now claimed a certain unnamed person, a mystery witness, had called Grutman in New York to announce that Kim Pring had performed fellatio on him—not only on him but on one other man as well.

I had always known it would come to this. It always does. Instantly I felt a nearly uncontrollable urge to smash faces and lay bodies to the ground. I started to get up. And the act of getting up brought me to my senses. I sat back down. Then I thought I'd better leave. I got up to go. I couldn't. I could do nothing. I was trapped in the sewer. I slumped down into my chair and let the mind take over, the blessed mind that countermands the vicious voices in the belly. What man would call Grutman in New York and tell him Kim had performed fellatio on him? For what earthly gain? For what purpose? I mean was it "Miss Wyoming gave me a blowjob and I just called up to let you fellas know—thought you might be interested? And she blew my buddy, too." Right? Christ!

Grutman was safe enough in New York, free to communicate these malodorous messages across a continent by sterile wires. He was beyond the court—beyond me. Yet he was with us as surely as if he sat there in his pious black coat next to Cooper and spewed out these dregs. Where was Grutman, goddamn it—this foe we could not see, this enemy we could not even touch, but who could decimate us by such as this?

"At the pretrial I indicated we had no evidence to offer that would go to this issue, and that is still the case," Cooper said. "However, during the course of the trial, I have had attorneys approach me who have read about the case, or who have been watching the case, and who have said that either they or someone they know went to school with Kim Pring, and they don't understand how she can be testifying as to this *great reputation* because they have information to the contrary. She put on evidence Friday of her absolutely pure reputation, untarnished in any way, and we are unable to meet that. For that reason, we would ask the Court to either continue the matter or declare a mistrial to permit time for us to go into that."

Cooper and Kelley no longer chose to defend *Penthouse*. Why defend *Penthouse*? They had finally reverted to the traditional attack made against all women who claim they have been beaten or raped or maimed—that whoever she be—no matter—she is a woman, less-than-no-one. How could a "less-than-no-one" have substantial rights? How could a "less-than-no-one" be hurt? It must be clear, therefore, that the said "less-than-no-one" is entitled to less than nothing. I looked at Cooper and Kelley sitting calmly across from me, and I thought of the pope's dear sons of five hundred years ago, Kramer and Sprenger—saw their faces illuminated by a heavenly glow, and I heard the righteous timber of their voices filling the judge's chambers with sounds of virtue, fortified with a fresh decree from His Holiness Innocent XIII, reaffirming the natural right of all men to lay waste to women in accordance with the procedures commanded by the sacred *Malleus Maleficarum*.

Judge Brimmer broke the spell. "As I remember, you had two detective services who made investigations—"

But Cooper said that none of the detectives could locate this mystery witness, a man who knew Kim Pring, perhaps in the biblical sense, and a man who had made himself known to Norman Roy Grutman in New York. "He has communicated, supposedly, by telephone with New York counsel," Cooper said again.

I tried to speak rationally. "This is nothing more than rank hearsay," I began. Perhaps if I spoke in legal terms like a lawyer the judge could hear me. "Specific acts," I said quietly, "would be totally immaterial on the issue of reputation, the reason being that if she had committed fellatio a hundred times on a hundred different people, if her *reputation* has not been affected, the specific acts themselves are inadmissible. Specific acts are not an issue in this case, *and have been ruled not an issue!*"

The judge made no response. He turned to Cooper. "Do you have any witnesses?"

"They've just made the comments and obviously I've had other things to worry about," Cooper replied.

I had no doubt the bastards had made comments to Cooper. They'd made them to me, too, the sniveling fools with their stupid, leering faces, jabbing me in the ribs, blurting it out: "Man, the way I hear it she'll blow anybody who's got one. Ha. Ha. I talked to a friend of mine who knows her personally, and—"

After the *Penthouse* article, the stench of the libel had spread everywhere, and since the trial it had grown worse. Even a loyal secretary came up to me one day and painfully reported she had heard from several sources she considered reliable that Kim was well known for giving the boys on the football team whatever they wanted, whenever they wanted it. Nobody was willing to give this woman the benefit of the doubt—to remember, honestly, carefully, that none of these stories had been heard by a living soul until *after* that vile writing. Her reputation was the product of the libel. She was being convicted by the very defamation of which she complained.

The judge pressed on. "Well, what I'm trying to get at is this: Was it some local attorneys? Is there more than one? It may be two—three?"

"Two or three," Cooper said.

"Have they said that they understand her reputation to be bad, or is this the product of a rumor mill?"

"They are not claiming to have had any personal sexual contact with her, but they are claiming to know her reputation from either high school or college and her reputation is not as it is being portrayed in the court," Cooper said.

What should His Honor do? These lawyers were officers of his court. Now he was informed his very officers had knowledge of the plaintiff's bad reputation. Follow the *Malleus*. Its eternal voice carried through the centuries: "When the accused does not stand convicted either by her own confession, or by the evidence of the facts, or by the legitimate production of witnesses, nor has there been anything proved against her except that she is the subject of common aspersion . . . by both good and bad in such a village, town or Diocese," then "a canonical purgation shall be imposed upon [her]."[4]

I said, "I don't understand how counsel can come to this court after having two detective agencies investigate for months, who found she had a good and decent reputation, and now say what they are saying."

The judge put Cooper to the test. "Do you want to endorse these two or three attorneys as additional witnesses?"

"I might if I can have that possibility. I would have to interview them and make sure exactly what they know."

"Well, I'll give you that possibility," the judge said.

But that didn't satisfy Cooper. That wasn't what he wanted at all. "Our main problem is that I think we might have discovered a lot more evidence had we been able to ask her *who* she dated and *who* she might have done these acts *with* and then talked to those people and find out from *them* what her reputation is."

"Well, my ruling on that matter was that specific acts of moral misconduct of the type Mr. Grutman tried to go into on the discovery deposition were not admissible, and I take my stand on that, and *they are still not admissible!*" His memory would be blessed among judges. "As far as your present information goes, it would look to me that you have investigated this subject. Now maybe Mr. Grutman didn't do a thorough job of it. Obviously, from what you say, his detectives didn't talk to the right people—but that's Mr. Grutman's fault, not yours certainly. I'm going to deny the motion for continuance."

Then the judge paused a moment as if he were still receiving the ancient edict of the *Malleus*. "I'll leave the door open to additional witnesses if you find somebody who knows her reputation, and will say to the contrary." It *was* the law. Should a woman dare claim she is a woman of good repute, well then, is it not fair that those she sues be permitted to prove the opposite? My God, we would never be shed of it! Never.

I asked Cooper to give me the names of these attorneys, these supposed new witnesses but he refused. "As soon as I talk to them, yes," he said. "I don't even know one of them. One of them just talked to me out here." I turned to the judge and asked him to order Cooper to give me the names of these lawyers, but the judge said he would issue no such order until Cooper had first spoken with them himself.

Now Kelley raised the whole seamy issue yet one more time. "Our problem," Kelley said, "is that we think, on the issues both of reputation and truth, we should be entitled to cross-examine her about *specific acts* and about her reputation—" That's what they wanted now, for Christ's sakes, to ask her *those questions* in front of the jury! They would gladly, shamelessly stretch her on the rack before this very jury, and if she refused to answer, what would the jury say? And she would refuse to answer! I would never let her answer, and that would be the end of her case.

The judge said nothing for a long time. Once he mumbled something under his breath, and for the moment he seemed unsure. Then he wanted to know: were Cooper and Kelley going to have that mystery witness in court, the one who had allegedly called Grutman?

Eddie whispered, "He just ruled that out!"

Kelley said, "He's avoiding service."

Then the judge said, "I feel that to permit cross-examination of Miss Pring on specific acts is something we already ruled on in the pretrial conference, and I see no reason to change my ruling at this time."

"I understand your ruling, and I just wanted to complete our record," Kelly said.

Now Cooper wanted to separate Cioffari out of the case for a later trial, because he said that evidence admissible against Cioffari might not be admissible against *Penthouse,* and vice versa. It was a little late for them to recognize those conflicting interests. Even now they did not offer to withdraw from representing either Cioffari or *Penthouse.* The judge said their motion was untimely, and overruled.

The jury had been waiting for twenty minutes, but Cooper wasn't finished. "I think Dr. Cline's testimony about psychological rape was fantastic, highly prejudicial, and extremely appealing to passion and prejudice. I would note, in passing, after Miss Pring's testimony, where she broke up on the stand and we had a recess, that the two women jurors in the front row appeared to have been crying during the recess." He curled his lips around his words.

Dr. Wideman's testimony also appealed to passion and prejudice because he used such words as "arrogance" and "exploitation" and "reckless disregard," and Cooper argued, "There was the statement by Miss Pring just before the afternoon recess that two or three hundred million would not be sufficient to compensate her for this injury, and that if she could get her good name back she would gladly give the money back. I think that is the most inflammatory and prejudicial thing I've ever seen. As I say, two jurors returned from the recess and had obviously been crying. I don't see any way to cure that but by granting a mistrial."

Then the judge overruled that motion too. But it was what the judge added to his ruling that frightened me—foreboding words he spoke with a tired resignation in his voice, "I'm just at this point loath to scuttle these weeks of work with the granting of a mistrial." He sounded doubtful about the correctness of his past rulings—as if he might have committed serious error somewhere, and his words implied that if we won, maybe he'd have to set the jury's verdict aside.

The judge got up from his chair. The conference was over. "I'd like to make a record as far as we're concerned," I said. The judge stood there impatient to go. "First, I didn't see anybody crying. Second, even if there was a juror crying, it is no grounds for a mistrial."

"You've already won the motion. Why are you making a speech?" the judge said, walking toward the door. "All right, we'll go to court now. Thank you, gentlemen."

"We're in trouble, Eddie," I said as we walked into the courtroom. "The judge can't unload on them or he'll get more error in his record. We've got to be careful or he'll dump this case. We've got to be sweet, got to be perfect. Just perfect."

"Yeah, but we gotta win with the jury," Eddie said.

"Yeah, we got to win with everybody," I said.

Then the judge came in and smiled good morning, as if not a goddamned thing had happened, and I smiled up at him, looking as darling, as innocent as a choirboy, and Cooper and Kelley looked as pious as monks. Cooper smoothed down his eyebrows, first the right one and then the left, and he reached back to see that his cowlick was still in place, and then the judge nodded to me to send Kim back to the stand.

"Good morning, Miss Pring," Cooper began.

"Good morning," she said, trying to sound cheerful. She wore a clean, starched, pale-pink cotton dress with a little ruffle around the neck.

"Did you ever date a person named John Hull?"

Jesus God, who is he?

"We were very close friends," she said. "We worked together with Gus Fleischli, the year Mr. Fleischli ran for governor. We did more business things together."

"You saw Dr. Wahl twice?"

"Yes."

"And at that time you were complaining of weight gain, headaches, nausea?"

"Yes, and I couldn't sleep."

"And did you tell the nurse that you were having problems because of this case?"

"No—it was because of the article."

"At that time you were taking *birth-control pills,* is that correct?"

Goddamn it. There it was!

You'd just as well have asked those questions the court ruled out. Are you a virgin, Miss Pring? Who really cares anymore if a woman is or is not? The hymen is one of the most useless parts of the human anatomy. Are you a virgin, Miss Pring? It is not the answer that is damaging. It is the question—the attack the question makes on the privacy of a person. Whose business? By what right is such a question asked? He could just as well have asked "You were, were you not, Miss Pring, having regular intercourse with somebody, which required you to take birth-control pills?" What good did it do to object? The jury had heard it. The bell had been rung, and you can't unring it.

I didn't move. I didn't say a word.

"Did the doctor tell you to get an unlisted telephone?"

"I don't recall if he did or not."

"Did he give you a prescription for Tagamet?"

"Yes, he did."

"And you went back to him a second time, and you were feeling much better, isn't that correct?"

"Yes."

"And you had gotten off the *birth-control pills* because they had led to high blood pressure up at Laramie—you'd gotten off of them, isn't that correct?" It must be the birth-control pills that made her feel so bad, not the *Penthouse* article. She nodded. I said nothing.

"And you didn't feel any need for psychotherapy?"

"Not at that time."

"And you indicated to him that you had never filled the prescription for Tagamet?"

"I never had it refilled. He gave me several bottles in his office and that's what I took."

"How many in a bottle?"

"He gave me Mylanta. I did not refill the Tagamet prescription."

"Now none of your friends who knew you would think that this story truly and accurately portrayed real events in your life?"

"I believe all my friends thought that the article took the entire skeleton of everything I stood for and made me the blowjob artist of the whole world."

Then he asked her if she didn't know that anybody who read this article would recognize it as fiction and she said, no, not *everybody*, and he pulled out her deposition.

"Could you refer to page one fifty-eight." Then he read to her from Grutman's questions of months ago.

"Question: 'Would you not have expected that anybody reading it would recognize it was fictional?' Answer: 'I agree.' Question: 'And anybody in their right mind would know that that was pure imagination, correct?' Answer: 'I agree.' You said that?"

"I agree," she said.

He wanted to know if Kim didn't know another phrase other than the one she'd been using which meant "to perform fellatio."

"What?"

He didn't want to say it. "One known to young people, am I correct?"

Kim made Cooper say it. "What is it?"

" 'Go down on,' " he finally said like he was ashamed to have spoken the words in the jury's presence.

"Yes," she said. And now Cooper had proved she knew those dirty words, that she wasn't lily-clean, that she used birth-control pills, and therefore, what was such a woman complaining of?

Still he wasn't through with her. He asked her questions on every small point imaginable—a half-dozen questions on when people retire from twirling—another dozen, twenty even, about whom she had showed the story to—and why, and back to her weight problem, clear back to the time she was a little girl, and on and on, like some pathologist examining the corpse, beginning with the thumbnail on the right hand.

"Is your hair the same color now as it was at the time?"

"Yes."

"Is that the color it normally is?"

"Yes."

"Thank you. That's all I have, Your Honor."

I walked to the podium. I needed to bring this whole woman back to the jury. The sense of the woman's soul had been lost in the hours of monotonous cross-examination. This was a woman who had been maimed and raped. Who could remember that any longer? I wanted the jury to feel her pain once more. It is possible to hear the dull thud of fist against flesh until the sounds themselves become only a humdrum beat, as the agony of Christ has now become only the chanting of a priest moving the congregation to slumber.

Start easy. Take it slow. Resurrect her. Let her resurrect herself.

"Kim," I began, "I take it that some time during your life you had a boyfriend, a betrothed, perhaps, whom you were in love with?"

Did love make sex for a single woman all right with the jury? It was all right for the *sons* of the churchwomen. It's all right for the *sons* of Masons.

"Yes."

"Why didn't you unlist your telephone?"

"I thought I'd be going back home. As long as I was leaving, I didn't see any use in calling the telephone company and bugging them about it."

"Now counsel wanted to know why you showed the article to so many people, and I think you explained it several times."

"Yes. The article made me feel very bad."

I led her. "Would you tell the jury whether or not you were needing any comfort and concern from your friends?"

"I needed a lot of comfort and concern from my friends. Everything I had ever worked for was ruined and I needed their help. I needed them to talk to me. I needed them to especially be my friends."

"Kim, slow down a little bit. Now Mr. Cooper wants to know about whether there was publicity about the litigation, and I think you've said there was. Did you ask for any of that publicity?"

"No, I didn't ask for it."

I tried to find out whether writers had access to her during the Miss America Pageant. Yes, they had special access, she said. One morning was totally dedicated to writers.

"What kind of writers? Would you be able to identify them now as to who they were?"

"No, I wouldn't."

"Did you make any attempt to keep track of who they were?"

"No, I didn't."

"Counsel asked you something last Friday about calling baton twirling stupid. Do you remember that?"

"Yes."

I wanted her deep feelings to surface once more. Maybe those feelings had become entangled and lost in Cooper's cross-examination in which he had displayed Kim's life as mere data—long, deadly boring, unemotional paper tapes that had wrapped the memory of the jurors like mummies. Perhaps that had been the shrouded genius of Cooper's cross-examination after all.

"How did it make you feel, after having spent a lifetime becoming the national baton-twirling champion, to read an article having Miss Wyoming say that the baton was stupid?"

"I think that that was very degrading as far as my whole career is concerned from when I was five till I was twenty-two—how important my baton twirling was to me—it's just stupid—and it hurt me very much." It wasn't working.

"Did it, in your judgment, affect the attitude of little children toward you?"

"What am I going to do with all these little kids? I feel hypocritical teaching them toward such a career. Is that going to make them end up in the center of *Penthouse* magazine?" She was exhausted. Now nothing came but jumbles of thoughts and fragments of feeling. I couldn't get Kim Pring back. I couldn't appear maudlin either. It was gone. I had her simply tell the jury she'd never made the statements contained in the story—about calling other contestants bitches, about suggesting the baton is a penis—that she didn't see twirling as something sexual nor did she teach little girls that it was, that she wouldn't do what the article suggested to the Soviet Central Committee. No, she wouldn't do that. Then I quit.

"That's all, Kim," I said quietly. I left her there. "I can't get it back, Eddie," I whispered.

"I know. A guy never can," he said.

"I hope the jury remembers what this case is about," I said.

On his first question on recross-examination, Cooper was at it again. "Do you know where John Hull is now?"

"No. He lives in Cheyenne. I know that much." There was nothing. I was convinced of that. But if he kept asking about this John Hull often enough he'd convince the jury there was something being kept from them.

"Do you know what kind of work he does?"

"I believe he's a radio disc jockey for KRAE radio station." He wanted to know if she had pledged a sorority. She said no. She'd gotten offers, but she'd refused them when she realized how they would interfere with her practice, the evening meetings, the sings, and the like. After that Cooper asked a long series of questions that had no purpose except to put more distance yet between Kim's answers to me and where Cooper would eventually dump her. When he had taken her far enough down the road and the jury was satiated, when Kim seemed boring too, Cooper dropped her.

"That's all I have, Your Honor," Cooper said.

I watched her get down from the stand. She gave a little smile to the jury, and they gave her a polite glance and she headed back to our table. I got up to help her into her chair. Maybe we had all grown used to the misery. Maybe misery was the status quo. I only knew I could never get her back again. In the eyes of the jurors, the tears would never flow again for Kim Pring.

25

Rick Duff said, "I was mad as hell when I read the article." He'd called *Penthouse*. Duff, executive director of the 1979 Miss Wyoming Pageant, told how, when he'd called the magazine's home office he was transferred to the legal department and spoke to one Joe Kraft, the elusive Joe Kraft we'd been trying to subpoena for months—*Penthouse's* in-house lawyer who supposedly gave the Miss Wyoming story a legal reading.

"What did you say to Kraft?"

"I told him I was angered at the article for taking a potshot at Kim. Kraft said he was not aware of the article. He said he would have to get back to me with more details."

"Did he say why?"

"Because he hadn't read it. That's what he said." Later Kraft did call Duff back. "At this time he told me that the writer of the article had been to the Miss Wyoming Pageant the year before—we were in July of '79, so he must have been there in September when the pageant was held, and that the article was purely fiction derived simply from the memory of the writer—what his thoughts were at the time of the pageant."

I looked at the jury. They stared blankly back.

Did you hear that? He didn't read the goddamned thing! And the writer had been *at the Miss Wyoming Pageant?* No wonder we couldn't get him served. No wonder.

I looked at the jury again. Everybody is so fucking cool nowadays! Trust the jury—that's what I always tell young attorneys. Now trust them.

I called Dr. Angela Howdeshell. She was a small, dark woman from the Philippines, with a mystical air about her. The mind drifts, like unruly waves in an eternal ocean, and time dangles so that years pass in a fleeting second, and as the woman walked in busy steps to the witness stand, I saw wet jungles and deep enchanted forests, and I could hear my mother telling me there had been headhunters in the Philippines. My father used to tease her. "You almost had a head-hunter for a daddy," he'd say to me.

"Oh, Daddy!" I'd say back. I was only a small boy. It was a stan-dard family story told dozens of times.

"No. No," my mother would try to explain again, as if all her prior explanations had gone unheard. "No, I was just nice to this young man at college." That's what my mother got for being nice to every-body. "I never even had a date with him. He was so lonely, and I felt sorry for him, and I would talk to him a lot. He misunderstood me. In the Philippine tribes a woman was not friendly to a man unless she wished to marry," she said, "and I didn't know that." My mother looked so sad and kind. "And one day he asked me to marry him. His father was a chief. Very big man in the Philippines. I loved his name. It was Pallegio Palankio. His grandfather was a real head-hunter."

"And your grandfather is just a farmer," my father said to me. "It would have been a lot more fun to have had a headhunter for a grandfather. You would have been 'Little Pallegio Palankio,'" my fa-ther laughed, and I said I would never be a little Pallegio Palankio. I liked it that my grandpa was a farmer, and I liked the farm, and I was glad that my father had come along and saved my mother and me from being half headhunter. Fathers are wonderful.

Now out of the forest tribes came this headshrinker, this tiny, mod-ern shaman. She called herself a psychiatrist. She sat down in the witness chair and raised her head slightly, waiting for my first ques-tion—her eyes seeing everything like the eyes of a small forest ani-mal.

Dr. Howdeshell had examined Kim. She'd had done a standard psychiatric workup, and like most psychiatrists, she put a label on her patient—chose the label out of a book of labels called *Diagnostic and Statistical Manual of Mental Disorders*, and the labels had num-bers. The psychiatrists pin the labels on their patients the way col-lectors pin labels on butterflies. But a label has never helped a butterfly understand itself. Labels are for labelers.

Dr. Howdeshell used long, heavy words: "Adjustment reaction of adult life secondary to stress reaction—a maladapted reaction to a psychosocial distress manifested by impairment and situational and occupational functioning of the individual," a very intimidating way to talk about a human being, as demonic sounding as the evil chant of any witch. The woman's accent lent a mysterious aura and seemed to enhance her power, but the words did not come easily for her, all of which was clearly predicted in the *Malleus*: "A witch loses all her power when she falls into the hands of public justice."[1]

I was able to get her to say that Kim had been injured, her self-image shaken. She was easily hurt by people, the doctor said, because she depended on the affirmative things people said about her for her self-esteem, and she worked hard to achieve it. That's why she had become a champion—to earn the approval of others. She was outgoing and warm, but a very vulnerable person.

"And what effect did this story have on her?" I asked.

"Well, there were insinuations, the phone calls, the remarks made about her which disintegrated the very ideals that she stands for." Dr. Howdeshell had abandoned beauty as a principal issue of her life, if, indeed, it had ever been one. But I could see it there at forty-one, that strange primitive loveliness the Philippines put on their women. She spoke in a flat narrow range, devoid of emotion, as a scientist who sees emotion as something to be examined, not to be experienced. She said Kim Pring's emotional well-being had been traumatized.

"In what way?"

"The only similarity I can say is that there was an emotional rape."

"I don't understand. How do you make the comparison?"

"Because it *is* a rape." It was rape. I could see that. One was physical. One was emotional. But both were rapes, the taking, the wresting away of what one does not wish to give to another, and from both there was a special kind of bleeding and both left scars.

Kim needed therapy, she said, and even if it was successful, she would carry the scars for the rest of her life. "Twenty years from now she'll walk into a restaurant and the people at the next table will be looking at her and she will start thinking, 'I wonder whether they read the article in *Penthouse*. I wonder what they think of me.'"

Cooper seemed more eager than usual to launch his attack. Where were her records? Had she brought them? No, she said. I was glad of that. Records, the written reports, the psychological tests—they can be picked apart, the way you pick the butterfly apart, the leg, look at it, the little hooks on the leg, see them, hideous, menacing little hooks, the face of the butterfly—ghastly!—like a monster's out of some horror film, the eyes like evil globes, the mouth built like some grinding machine, its shafts and flanges pursed to do its pernicious deeds, as if it could consume an arm in a single snapping of its horrid lips—and the wings—covered with disgusting hair that emerges in helter-skelter patterns like the hair on the back of a mangy bitch.

"Isn't it normal for doctors to bring their medical records when they come to court?" Cooper asked.

"Some do and some don't."

"You don't have anything about psychological rape in your report, do you?"

"No. It was not there."

"You don't have anything about her having a personality that's dependent on others in your report, do you?"

She was not used to such attacks, not quick on her feet in this pit. Cooper bore down now, his head and jaw thrust out in a fighting mode, his stance forward, his eyes squinting at her. She barely squirmed in her chair, but Cooper caught that slight signal of distress and moved in for the kill. Sensing it, the doctor suddenly panicked and blurted out, as if by so doing she would be saved, "I sent *two* reports to the lawyer. One is a psychological testing."

"Your Honor, I would ask that they be ordered to give me the *other* report," Cooper demanded.

I said, quietly, "This *is* her *only* report."

The judge sensed something was amiss. "Do you have another report on psychological testing?"

Eddie jumped in, exuding honesty like an Irish boy at confession. The doctor had been his responsibility, and as Eddie saw it (and he was correct), if the jury thought we were intentionally holding back, we could lose our credibility and the case would go down with us. "We would be more than happy to provide it," Eddie said.

"Produce it if you have it. You were ordered to produce *all* reports that this witness gave," Judge Brimmer said.

"It's not *her* report," Eddie corrected the judge.

"She only gave *one* report," I said, which was true. I said it almost on the brink of a yawn, but my belly was churning and my heart was beating in my ears. "The other report was the psychologist's report, not Dr. Howdeshell's." I knew what was in that damnable report.

The judge turned to the doctor. "You gave the report of the psychologist to Mr. Moriarity?"

"I remember mailing it to Mr. Moriarity."

"Very well, gentlemen, produce it," the judge said, sounding as if we had been caught withholding material evidence. The jury watched. The jury stared.

I said in an almost lazy way, "We only understood we were to produce the reports Dr. Howdeshell made. But we have no objection." What else could I say?

"There could have been no mistake about it, Counsel," the judge said, shaking us, dangling us like larcenists caught in thievery. Suddenly the jurors looked hard.

"We have no objection to providing the report, Your Honor," I said again. Then Cooper was on her, a praying mantis on a ladybug. I knew what was coming. I tried to look unconcerned. I leaned back in my chair and gazed at the ceiling. Eddie handed Cooper the report.

"Did she tell you about an incident with a boyfriend she had before she went to college—a boyfriend in Chicago who *committed suicide*?" Cooper asked.

There it was. I rocked quietly in my chair, closed my eyes, and let my mouth drop open slightly. I yawned again.

"Well, in your experience as a psychiatrist, isn't that more likely to cause psychological trauma than someone who was written about in a story?"

I glanced at the doctor, who appeared to be breaking into a cold sweat. Her upper lip trembled. "The article—" she paused, looking over to me for help. I rocked. I couldn't help her. It had to come and it had to pass without my interference—"she is much more vulnerable to other people's reaction," she said.

"You mean it wouldn't bother her if her boyfriend committed suicide like it would if somebody said something bad about her?" The sound of Cooper's voice was mocking. I glanced at the jury again. They saw this little woman struggling for her life, this small woman with her foreign accent, fighting, as Kim Pring had fought. Perhaps the jury wanted her to win, at least to survive.

"It would bother her, but not to the extent as to what—"

"Not to the same extent?"

"Yes." She seemed frightened.

Suddenly Cooper asked, "She indicated she was hoping to get a lot of money out of this?" He had no basis for that question. No such statement was in the report he held in his hand. It was clearly a prejudicial question against which I had no protection. Cooper could ask for his mistrials. I couldn't, but the judge might grant one for me, and Cooper knew it, hoped for it. I rocked in my chair. And rocked.

"No," she answered.

"She didn't say so?" Cooper acted surprised.

"No." Then she said, "When I was seeing her last fall, she stayed in her apartment, stared into space, crying—if she wanted something from the department store she would ask her mother to go get it because she didn't want to go out there in the public."

"Your Honor, could I have a couple of minutes to review this report?" Cooper asked. Now it would surely all come out.

"Do you want more time than that?" the judge asked.

"It's four pages," Cooper said, frowning and flipping at the pages.

Then it was the judge's own idea that the doctor also fetch the rest of her file and have it back from Laramie before the session began— that is, the judge said, if Cooper wanted the file.

Cooper came over. "I want her records," he said, with Kelley standing as witness.

"Come on," I hollered over my shoulder to the doctor as I hurried out of the courtroom, the doctor running behind me with dainty steps. In the witness room I asked, "What the hell's in those notes, Doctor?"

"I don't know," she said, pale as paper. "I can't remember—it's just whatever Kim told me."

"Call somebody. Get them over here. I want to see them before Cooper does." Then the little psychiatrist disappeared from the room like a shadow dissolving into the forest. "Jesus Christ, Eddie. Why the hell doesn't the judge stay out of this?"

"Thinks we held back on him," Eddie said.

Kim was standing there looking scared.

"What the hell did you tell her?"

"I just answered her questions. I don't know."

"Did you talk about your sex life?"

"I don't know." She looked like she was about to cry. "Goddamn it," I said. "I'm sorry." I grabbed her and gave her a hug. Mrs. Pring was standing there too, like a mother robin with a baby out of the nest. "Don't worry, Mama. It's going to be okay. You and Kim go get something to eat." I couldn't eat.

At 1:10 P.M. Dr. Howdeshell's records were delivered from Laramie—just fifty miles away. I read them quickly. It was worse than I had feared.

"All we can do is play the breaks now," I said to Eddie, and when the judge called the court to order, I sat back in my chair again and began to rock and look lazy. Eddie started another crazy web of doodles, waiting for the slaughter to start. Cooper had her file in his hand. The little doctor held on to the witness chair, braced against his first question. Cooper knew what to do with the records all right.

"Dr. Howdeshell, this is your original file in this matter?" he began, holding up her folder for all to see.

"Yes."

"Where is the part about her boyfriend who committed suicide?"

"The man's name was Bob," she said. The jury leaned forward, sensing something startling was about to happen. "He committed suicide in March of 1976."

"All right. Did she feel at all responsible for that?"

"She felt bad, but I did not perceive any feelings of responsibility. It was a hurtful situation for her that occurred in 1976." Then it came. There was nothing I could do to stop it. I couldn't have even asked the judge to order that part of the doctor's report out—not with the judge feeling that we'd held back on him.

"And she had her *first sexual* relationship with a man at age nineteen?"

"At age nineteen, yes."

"And with *only* four men totally?"

Goddamn it!

Four men?

Four men.

Tell it to the jury.

What could I do?

The doctor looked confused. She started to say something, but the few words that came out made no sense. She stopped and started again. "Sex has to be in a very involved, close relationship, not just a matter of fact," she finally said.

Cooper ignored her answer. "All right. And Bob was *one* of those *four*, is that correct?"

"Yes." Finally he had done it. Are you a virgin, Miss Pring?

Who?

Bob?

Who else?

"Now you had no testing of her before Bob committed *suicide*?" He had to keep saying the word. Suicide. Suicide. Four men. Four. He kept emphasizing it. I looked up at the ceiling again, and rocked slowly in my chair. I watched the jury between the slits in my eyes. Occasionally they would look at me to see my reaction, but I kept on rocking, and then they'd look at Kim. She had her head bowed beside me. Cooper was doing it to us. He made his points precisely, skillfully and, goddamn it, he'd done it, and I knew it, and the jury knew it. He sat down. I wished to God I'd never brought Kim here.

There is no justice in seeking justice. It was a trial by fire.

I approached the podium very slowly. The jury waited. What would I do? I could feel the juices flowing and I thought, well, the worst is out, so whatever else there is can only help.

"Now this report, Your Honor, was marked and identified in the Pretrial Order as Exhibit 420." I held up the psychologist's report Cooper had been reading from. "We offer into evidence the entire report."

"Any objections?" the judge asked Cooper.

"Yes," Cooper said.

"Well," I said very slowly, very seriously to Cooper. "You objected because we *didn't* produce it. Now we're offering it and you still object?" The judge ruled the report in. I began to read what the doctor had written: "The information she provided seemed quite *honest*—" and Cooper screamed an objection again, interrupting me, and the judge sustained him, admonishing the jury that the report was not to be regarded as true but was merely to be considered as the basis for Dr. Howdeshell's conclusions. The judge was getting gun-shy as hell about his record. The report was hearsay. Well, if I couldn't shove it up all at once, I'd shove it a sentence at a time.

"The report says: 'In describing and discussing changes that had happened in her life, following the publication of the *Penthouse* article, Kim became very agitated, both physically and emotionally.' Did you find that to be the truth when you went through this with her?"

"That is the truth."

"Have you brought *all* your notes to the court as you were directed by the judge during the noon hour?"

"Yes."

"Does it even include correspondence from us?"

"Yes."

"And so is Exhibit 420-A the *complete* raw data upon which you made your determination?" I was shoving it.

"Yes."

"We offer into evidence Exhibit 420-A." Now object again. Object, please!

"Objection!" Cooper hollered. "Self-serving, Your Honor. We pointed out the pertinent portions."

"Overruled," the judge said. The road runs both ways.

I began reading paragraphs aloud to the doctor. With the aid of her written records, the doctor and I began singing beautiful songs together. The report said that when Kim started to talk about the *Penthouse* article she talked very fast, and got very excited. Surely the jury remembered me saying, "Take it easy, Kim. Slow down."

I read another paragraph—read it slowly, emphasizing the important words: " 'Kim's attitudes toward sex and marriage reflect traditional social values, where casual sex, without a close, loving relationship, is condemned, as are the people who engage in it.' What does that mean, Doctor?"

"That means that Kim approves of sex only when there is a close relationship, where there is emotional investment, that casual sex is taboo as far as she is concerned."

I gave her answer plenty of time to soak in. Even the jury looked relieved. I turned away from the jury, glanced at Cooper, and gave him a wink the jury couldn't see. Cooper glared back.

"What is casual sex? Just sex for sex's sake?"

"Yes. No love—just sex for sex's sake." I kept at it.

"Was she against that?"

"She *is* against that."

"Does that have something to do with your conclusion about her being an all-American-girl type?"

"Yes. She is down-to-earth."

"Now, Dr. Howdeshell—counsel, out of the entire file—out of your *en-tire file*—asked you only about *one* page." I motioned to Cooper and turned to him and gave him a very long look, "And that, interestingly enough, had to do with *sex*. I want to ask you ... " I waited until the doctor was concentrating hard on my question. "Is there anything *here at all* that says that she actually had her first sex *relationship* at nineteen or does it say something *quite different* from that?"

"It says, '1975, nineteen, first sex.' "

"And what did that mean to you when you wrote it down?"

"That she had first *become aware* of sex at nineteen."

"Is there any indication in your notes at all that she had *sexual relationships* as suggested by counsel with *four men*?"

"No. I did not ask her. What I asked her is what is her attitude about sex."

"What did she tell you?"

"That sex is something that one has to feel good about and that sex is something that occurs in a very involved relationship—and that is this four men that is stated in my report." Her heavy accent was taking over now. She tried to explain. "I explored as to how involved she was. Of the four relationships, the minimum was one year, and the longest was three years. So they are all involved, continuing relationships."

I kept at it. "Would you say that your own investigation supported that of the psychologist, that she was against sex for sex's sake and casual sex?"

"Yes."

Cooper jumped up. "Just a minute! I'll object. Oh, never mind." He sunk down into his chair again. "Never mind." He faded off. "Excuse me."

But I wasn't through. "And on the very next page is there a notation there about her feeling a close relationship with Charlie?"

"They play racquetball together. They go to the health club. They did not live together."

"They did not live together?"

"No," she emphasized that. "They watched TV together. They see each other during lunch hour—eat at McDonald's."

"And did you come to a conclusion she was a decent girl?" Come on, object to that. Cooper was too smart for that. He sat there fussing in some papers. The arrogant look was also gone from Kelley's face.

"I believe that she *is* a decent girl."

Now I pushed it one more time. "She was a girl who shared with you her intimate life as well as she could, is that correct?"

"She did. She was open."

"Did you feel she was honest with you?"

"I felt that she was honest. She *is* honest." Dr. Howdeshell said Kim felt hopeless because she could not stop any of the insinuations, the rumors, the continuous remarks made against her. She began to question her own attractiveness, and kept wondering what she did wrong to make somebody write something like that about her. She had become plagued with self-doubt, and that was painful, very painful, the doctor said. "She withdraws to protect herself from all of these remarks and insinuations," she said. "She had not even interviewed for a job."

The suicide had occurred five years earlier and had nothing whatever to do with her current symptoms, the doctor said. The jurors looked over to see what Cooper's reaction was. He was touching his cowlick, lightly.

We rested our case after Dr. Angela Howdeshell. A hundred more witnesses wouldn't make it better, and there's a time to stop, a time when one more question topples your argument. Now that our case was all in, Cooper moved the court to dismiss it and to enter judgment against us. We'd proved nothing, he contended. He was entitled to a directed verdict, but Judge Brimmer overruled him.

"Call your first witness, Mr. Cooper," Judge Brimmer ordered from the bench. Cooper called a man named Frank Pierson.

Pierson was famous in the movie world as a writer, director, and producer: he'd produced such shows as *Have Gun, Will Travel,* and *Naked City* and he'd written *Cat Ballou, Cool Hand Luke* and *Dog Day Afternoon* and had been nominated twice for Academy Awards and won one for *Dog Day Afternoon.* He was the vice-president of the Writer's Guild of America West. Frank Pierson had one serious flaw as an expert witness. He was an honest man, and that caused him some problems.

He testified that he had read the Miss Wyoming story and didn't think a writer would be required to investigate, given the fact that the story was obviously a fantasy, and was about a stereotype, a baton twirler. Besides, the chances were that any given Miss Wyoming or Miss Any State of the Great Plains or Midwest would end up being a baton twirler, they are so common, and blue is such a common color, so, no, who would investigate? Anyway, there was nothing you could do to prevent someone coming forward to claim she was the person in the story. Cooper turned the witness over to me for cross-examination.

"Mr. Pierson," I said, smiling, "I take it that you're here to protect the interests of writers from any unreasonable restriction of their constitutional privilege, would that be fair?"

"Yes, sir. That's the reason I'm here."

"And you feel very strongly about that?"

"Very strongly."

He was worried about the recent *Bindrim* case in California, a case of supposed fiction in which the author had disguised Bindrim in the writing, but the jury found against the writer anyway.

"Now, Mr. Pierson, I think everybody agrees with you that writers do have constitutional rights and that those are important rights and ought to be protected. You take that position, don't you?"

"Yes."

"On the other hand, for every right that we have there is a responsibility, isn't there?"

"I believe that as well."

"Writers have responsibilities to innocent people who might be hurt, as a result of the carelessness or recklessness of the writer. Would you agree?"

"I believe that, yes."

"Now I think an analogy might be in order: You have a right to drive an automobile, but you have a duty not to run over people carelessly or recklessly. Would you agree with that?"

"Certainly."

"And wouldn't that, in a nutshell, sum up your own basic philosophy about the rights and duties and responsibilities of writers?"

"I believe so, yes," he said.

"And I take it that you also agree that this precious right of ours to freely speak and write can be lost if it's abused?"

"Most certainly."

"And so there is a responsibility to not only *protect* those rights, but to also *save* them from abuse?"

"Yes."

"And so if this is a case that seeks to stop the abuse of the First Amendment, you would support such a case, wouldn't you?"

Cooper was up on his feet. "Your Honor, I'm going to object—"

"Sustained."

"You agree that writers aren't a special group with special consideration. They should be treated like everybody else with respect to their moral obligations, isn't that true?"

"Yes."

"Don't you think, therefore, that they have the duty to use reasonable care not to injure innocent people by their writing?"

"Yes."

Frank Pierson agreed that if a writer went to the Miss America Pageant to write about a particular participant whom he saw and knew to be a baton twirler, he had some responsibility to disguise her. He said that *Dog Day Afternoon* was based on a real person, and he admitted that legal waivers were obtained from everyone concerned, that he had changed the names, and that they had been changed again by the studio.

"Are you aware of the movie *The China Syndrome?*"

"Yes."

"Were you able to recognize the events there as being awfully close to the events that took place in the Silkwood case?" I had tried the Silkwood case.

"They were parallel, yes."

"But whoever wrote *The China Syndrome* changed Karen Silkwood from a woman to a man—it was a man who was killed in the car, not Karen Silkwood, isn't that true?"

"I believe that's true, as far as I can recall."

I paused long enough for all the echoes to quiet. I waited until I had gathered up the full attention of the jury—let them wait an extra moment for what I considered the quintessential question.

"The bottom line on this whole business is, is it not, that it doesn't make any difference if it's fantasy or real, you can get hurt from something that's obviously and clearly fantasy, isn't that true?"

"If the identification is made," Frank Pierson said.

"Exactly! The monstrous joke, for example, if written about, could hurt the person who's identified, isn't that true?"

"In a hypothetical case, certainly."

Then Frank Pierson admitted freely that if the writer writes a piece of fiction about an identifiable person and tells the publisher it is fiction, the publisher also has a duty to reveal to the public that it is fiction and not to hide the fact that it is fiction. He admitted that. I looked at the jury to emphasize my point, and hypothetically I asked Pierson whether, if the writer knew he was writing about a real person and he knew this person was easily identifiable and he knew that what the writer wrote would hurt this person, did he think that set of facts would indicate he might have been guilty of recklessness?

"That certainly seems possible, yes."

I read a carefully phrased question to Pierson. Would he, as a writer, be willing to live by the following test for responsibility in fiction: "Whether a reasonable reader would understand that the fictional character therein portrayed was in fact the actual person described." Cooper was objecting again all over the place, but finally the judge let Pierson answer, and Pierson said yes, he agreed with that.

"Now would you be surprised to learn that that is the test set out in the *Bindrim* case?" I asked.

Cooper objected, and the judge said the question was improper, and I let it go. The jury knew. That was my case, pure and simple, proved best by the cross-examination of *Penthouse*'s first witness.

"Thank you, Mr. Pierson. That's all I have," I said.

"I wish we could stop now, Eddie," I whispered. He paid no attention to me. He was staring at the woman walking down the aisle toward the witness stand.

"Christ, look who they're bringing in!"

"Who's that, Eddie?"

"That's Barbara Cenedese."

"What the hell can she say?" I whispered. Eddie looked worried. We both turned to Kim.

"I don't know. She's probably mad at me," Kim said.

"Why?" I asked, but before she could answer, the woman took the stand.

Oh, God, I thought. Now we'll lose our case on one mad mother's testimony. How can you ever win? There's always somebody lying in the weeds. Even Christ had problems with one of his closest friends.

Then Barbara J. Cenedese took the stand like a woman with work to do.

26

The woman was already leaning forward in her chair, ready, perfectly ready. She looked slightly hungry, her deep-set eyes and pallor suggesting a long leave from the sun. "Are you appearing pursuant to subpoena, Mrs. Cenedese?" Cooper asked.

"Yes, I am," she said, a message to me the woman was about to do her dirty work, that she and the lawyers had struck a bargain—we'll protect you with a subpoena. If anybody criticizes you, well, you can say, "I had no choice. I was subpoenaed and I had to testify to the truth, you know."

Cooper made it even clearer. "Have you indicated you didn't want to testify?"

"Yes, I did," she said, as a matter of course, a woman only doing her duty. I could feel it coming.

"Do you know the plaintiff, Kim Pring?"

"Yes. I've known her a long time, six or seven years."

"Were you involved with her in a conversation about a story in *Penthouse* magazine?"

"Yes." I made no objections—did nothing, said nothing—made as little as possible of whatever trouble was about to come. I wanted to disappear and have Eddie call me when it was over. "She'd come for my oldest daughter, Tammy, and was getting ready to leave and she hollered at me and she says, 'Hey, look,' I think this is what she said, 'I made *Penthouse.*' " She said it as if Kim was elated about it, celebrating.

"Did she show you the story?"

"Yes. We stopped and we read the story."

"Had you known anything about the story before then?"

"No."

"That's all I have," Cooper said.

337

I started for the podium. A lawyer ought not cross-examine every witness—in fact, I looked for witnesses to whom I might just say, "No questions." But the jury would wonder about no cross-examination of this witness—what she said must be true. Kim must have been happy to be in *Penthouse*. I could at least attack her—show that she and Kim had had their problems. I got to the podium and looked her over, a little thing waiting for the onslaught. The jury would hate me. But one thing I knew—whatever her relationship with Kim had been in the past, it was still a part of her, even now. Friendship is an incurable disease and they had been friends.

"Mrs. Cenedese, I'm sorry you have to be here. Kim was your friend, wasn't she?" I sounded gentle, sad. I looked sad. I was.

"Yes, and she still is." And that made it worse, because here was this woman finding herself helpless to do anything but tell the truth against her friend—subpoena, you know. I gave Mrs. Cenedese a warm smile, and spoke to her like a friend myself.

"And, Mrs. Cenedese, I guess you know that friends from time to time *need* each other, don't they."

"They certainly do," she said. Cooper and Kelley had undoubtedly prepared her and now she seemed relieved I hadn't attacked flat out.

"And sometimes when a friend suffers"—I turned and looked at Kim—she looked devastated, and Mrs. Cenedese looked at Kim, too—"sometimes she'll go to her friend to talk about it?"

"Yes."

"I take it that you make room for the possibility that Kim certainly saw you as a friend then?"

"Yes, she did."

Build it. "And you were glad to have her as a friend, weren't you?" Kindly, friendly.

"Yes."

"And glad to have her now?"

"I am."

"And she is a decent young woman, isn't she?" Get that much from her.

"Yes, she's very decent."

Get a little more. "And you're proud you know her?"

"Yes, I am."

You ought to quit. But something in the belly says, try it—listen to the belly. Careful. I gave Mrs. Cenedese a nice smile and asked the next question almost with a shrug. "And I guess you make room for the possibility that when she came to you as a friend that she wanted to share some concern she had about that article?"

"I think Kim thought she could come to me and talk to me about it, yes." God bless her. God bless friends.

"And that it would help her?"

"Yes."

Now having painted the picture, put the magnificent frame around it. "And that she expected and *got* comfort and solace from you, isn't that right?"

"Yes, I think she did." She gave me a friendly smile back.

"Thank you. And you were kind to her, weren't you?"

"Yes."

"Thank you, Mrs. Cenedese. I have no further questions." The human being in the witness had been spoken to, and the human being had spoken back.

Cooper shrugged his shoulders. "No questions," Cooper said, like nothing had happened, nothing at all.

Now at the bench Cooper claimed he had a certain witness whom, because of time restraints, he had to put on first thing in the morning, and therefore couldn't we recess for the day because he couldn't finish up with Dr. Clark before five, but when the judge said, no, we'd take the witnesses as they came, Cooper began his questioning of Dr. Herbert Clark, a professor and psychologist at Stanford University, who explained to the jury that he was really just a small-town boy from Deadwood, South Dakota, who had made good, who graduated "with distinction" from Stanford, had received various awards including a National Science Foundation award and a Guggenheim Fellowship, and who, by the age of thirty-five, had become a full professor.

"Is that pretty young to make full professsor?" Cooper asked.

"It's not bad," Professor Clark said. He smiled at the jury. His interest was language, that is, how people understand and use language, the mental processes people go through as they speak and listen. He told the jury his field was called "psycholinguistics," and since he was just a small-town boy, he smiled at the jury again. "This is just to make things difficult for people." He'd authored a couple of books on the subject, including a textbook. He'd read the Miss Wyoming story and he had opinions about it, but they'd have to wait until the morning. Judge Brimmer recessed at five sharp.

"Who's going to be the secret witness in the morning?" I asked

Eddie as we walked out the courtroom door, and, of course, Eddie didn't know. "Who's it gonna be?" I asked Kim trying to sound like Bert Parks.

"Not me," Kim said, catching on. "Thank God, it's over for me."

We got into the elevator. The door shut. "They're getting desperate." The door opened and outside the omnipresent Cheyenne wind was blowing, and the chill factor was sub-zero, and I was aching and weary. "They've got nothing to lose by dumping in anything or anybody. Who's it really gonna be?" Surely she knew.

Ordinarily, we would have known who or what, but not in this case. The *Malleus* explained: "For although different Popes have had different opinions on this matter, none of them has ever said that in such a case [in the trial of a witch] the judge is bound to make known to the accused the names of the informers or accusers. . . . On the contrary, some have thought that in no case ought he to do so. . . ."[1]

Later I said to Eddie, "Well, they've probably hired an army to serve a subpoena on that secret witness out there who was supposed to have called Grutman to tell him Kim gave him and his buddy a blowjob," and the last thing Eddie said that night was "It's all a lotta bullshit, Gerry. Don't worry about that." But I knew they'd call someone, and the *Malleus* had instructions: "When the Advocate for the accused is not open to any objection, but is a zealous man and a lover of justice, the Judge may reveal to him the names of the witnesses, under an oath of secrecy."[2] But we were the witch lawyers. We were the heretics ourselves, and we would get nothing.

I dreamed all night like I did as a kid when I had a high fever, jumbled dreams that echoed in senseless fragments across my mind, dreams of arguments I made over and over, endless arguments that I screamed at the judge—tell me the witness's name—the name— order Cooper to tell us the name! But I couldn't make the judge hear! I beseeched him. Begged. Justice was blind and justice was deaf.

The desk rang our wake-up call at 5:30 A.M., and the first thing I said was "I don't care who it is. I'll cut his fuckin' head off and shove it up his ass." I was afraid and anger feels better in the belly than fear. I thought we had our case won. It was a case sitting there as pretty as I could ever get it, and they were going to blow it all to hell if they could—somehow, with someone, with something. For sure.

I couldn't eat breakfast. I was actually relieved to meet Cooper for the morning session in the judge's chambers.

Cooper began: "In terms of our development of character witnesses"—why didn't he say it like it was?—as to witnesses they were going to call to trash Kim Pring—"we have not yet gotten any that are willing to testify. There is a possibility—we are meeting with a couple more at lunch. So I don't have any names." I looked at Eddie and gave him a wink. I winked too soon. "I do have one additional witness's name to endorse who will be testifying to impeachment material of Miss Pring's direct examination. He will be a very short witness."

He gave the man's name. I'd never heard of the guy.

Judge Brimmer said, "Be more specific than that."

Cooper sounded as matter-of-fact as a bishop reporting to the cardinal. "He will be testifying that he overheard a conversation at the coffee shop Friday morning before Kim Pring got on the witness stand. The evidence is admissible despite the fact it was conversation between the client and attorney on two bases: One, it was obviously not meant to be a confidential communication by the circumstances under which it took place. Second, there is an exception to the attorney-client privilege for conversations which could result in the commission of torts or crimes, and on both of these grounds it would be admissible."

"What torts and crimes?" I asked, cold as steel. I couldn't believe it—they were offering to bring in someone who had overheard my conversation with my client? Nothing is sacred? Not even to another lawyer? And now they were suggesting I had suborned perjury—all this they would do in the defense of *Penthouse?*

"They're really desperate," Eddie whispered. "Take it easy. Be careful."

"Whatever was said would have been said in an attorney-client relationship and would be privileged," I said.

"In a crowded restaurant where people can overhear?" the judge asked. Lawyers aren't supposed to consult with their clients in a restaurant? For the judge to hold such testimony admissible he must also conclude that both Kim and I intended to publicly publish our conversation and thus to waive the attorney-client privilege. It was crazy. It was just another fever dream. I'd have to get on the stand and testify what I remembered of the conversation.

"The question is not what you remember," the judge said. "It's what *she said.* And I think she has got a right to testify as to what she said, and I think the person who heard her has a right to testify."

Eddie's Irish finally exploded. "Your Honor, I was there and I know *exactly* what she said. If they are going to be allowed to do this type of thing, I am going to ask the Court's permission to take the stand and testify because I know *exactly* what was said."

The judge said, "I presume you have the right. I am loath to have the attorneys take the witness stand."

"Your Honor, look what they are doing to us!" Eddie shouted.

"If the defendants want to recall Miss Pring, you may," the judge said to Cooper and Kelley.

"I tell you, Eddie, no one will ever be satisfied until Kim Pring is finally screwed over for good one way or the other." I said to the judge, "There's no reason to recall her. It was about that damnable Peruvian magazine, *Gente*. She's taken the position she didn't see *Gente*."

"Give her another chance," the judge said. Chance at what? Another chance on the rack? Another opportunity to confess?

"She doesn't need another chance," I said, but the *Malleus* made it clear: "Finally, if he [the judge] sees that she will not admit her crimes, he shall ask her [the accused witch] whether, to prove her innocence, she is ready to undergo the ordeal by red hot iron. . . ."[3]

"He has a right to recall her." The judge was correct in his ruling. It has always been the law, even in the days of the *Malleus*: "And note that she is to be continuously questioned as to the depositions which have been laid against her, to see whether she always returns the same answers or not."[4] The judge is bound by the law.

Now, instead, Cooper called Chenco Rodriquez, an instructor of foreign languages at Laramie County Community College in Cheyenne, to translate *Gente*. He read from Spanish to English very fluently. "It says: 'The beautiful North American baton twirler who stole the heart of Trujillo at the spring festival is the incomparable Kim Pring. Her boyfriends can write to her at the house of Richard Fiore, 1151 Dove Street, Suite 170, Newport Beach, California, zip code 92660, USA. And if they wish to call her by telephone, Kim is at 714-833-8184. Wow!" That was not her number, of course—not even a Wyoming prefix. Then Cooper recalled Kim Pring.

Nothing I could do.

One More Time.

Kim walked to the stand, stiff, mechanical, her face reflecting a patient pain one sees in the eyes of a woman who has succumbed to the ceaseless onslaughts of seasons past. The price of justice was too high.

I let her go.

"Directing your attention to the Friday morning before you testified, did you have a conversation at the Little America Coffee Shop with your attorney?" Surely a good case hadn't finally come down to what some snitch had supposedly heard me say to my own client at breakfast. The jurors were waiting.

"I had breakfast with Mr. Spence, yes."

"And do you recall saying that during the course of your trip in Peru you received a copy of *Gente* magazine?"

"No, I never did say that. I think whoever heard whatever you are asking me about—it's hard to hear the full story when you're eavesdropping—I told Mr. Spence I had never seen that magazine just as I told you in my testimony I had never seen that magazine before I had that picture taken, and that is why I trusted my chaperone, and that is not my telephone number. It was not even in the state of Wyoming."

"You didn't in any way indicate to him that you had seen a copy of a magazine before?"

"I had *seen* a copy—I had never looked through the magazine, never. I had never seen a copy of that magazine. Before I left I was shown the front cover of it. "This is the magazine that you are going to be on, Kim," but I have never looked through that magazine. I have never thumbed through it. I did not know what kind of magazine that was, just as my testimony stands."

"And you just looked at the cover and that is all?"

"Yes."

I should leave well enough alone. But no.

I gave Kim a reassuring smile. She smiled back.

"Kim, I told you not to be late that morning we had breakfast?"

"Yes."

"And what, just in your own words, did we talk about there?"

"Well, I have never been in a lawsuit before. I did not know how difficult it was going to be or what kind of pressure I was going to be under and I needed you to tell me these things—to calm me down and even when I got up here, you could see I was *still* nervous and I know I talked too fast." She looked over at the jury apologetically.

"Kim, don't worry about it, because I do that with every witness and every client and if I didn't I wouldn't be doing my job."

"Right," she said.

"But it was an open, public place?"

"Yes."

"Were we whispering?"

"No."

"Well, how were we talking?"

"In just a normal conversation as anyone would talk over breakfast."

"Was there any effort on our part to hide it?"

"None."

"Did I ever say to you, 'Be quiet because the man in the next booth might hear us'?"

"No, you never did."

"Was there any difference in what you told me then and what you told me now?"

"No, as I stated, my testimony is still the same."

"Apparently somebody overheard something and told Mr. Cooper something. Do you have any idea of who was around?"

"No."

"Did you care?"

"No. And I fully concentrated on what you wanted to talk about. We even read the paper together!"

"Just a minute," I said slowly, giving her a big grin. "Now don't get excited. Did you care who heard?"

"No. I have nothing to hide."

"Well, since the whole subject was opened up, is there anything else that you can remember that we talked about?"

"Objection, Your Honor."

"Sustained." The judge's ruling saved Cooper. She would have said, "Yes, you told me to look at the jury and tell them the complete truth. I would have anyway."

Then Cooper called Dr. Herbert Clark back to the stand from the night before.

"Where the hell is their big secret witness?" I whispered to Eddie. "I mean where is this son of a bitch who's supposed to tell the jury Kim lied and I suborned perjury?"

Dr. Clark settled himself down in the witness chair, tugged up his trouser legs to save the crease, and waited for Cooper's first question. I checked out my jury. I was still worried about the juror in the back row on the end. Once I tried to smile at him, but he tossed his head back like he was tossing me out, and now he had taken to staring at the ceiling again.

Cooper cleared his throat and asked Dr. Clark, "Were you able to form an opinion as to the effect of the story in question on a reasonable or average reader?"

The professor smiled over at the jury once more in advance of his answer. "Let me state it in this way," the professor began. "An ordinary reader of the kind I'm thinking about would think this is straight fiction and that the people referred to in the story are fictional characters. I mean it is just as simple as that." He smiled. "When Bob Newhart was playing the role of the president in *First Family*, we just thought he was playing a person in the role of the president. In that sense, that is exactly what Miss Wyoming is in this case. It's a title you put a person in—but it isn't intended to refer to any particular person—certainly not Miss Pring." Baton twirling was only symbolic, a stereotype, he said, and the use of actual places in the story was simply verisimilitude, i.e., Sherlock Holmes does not exist even though London and Baker Street do.

The professor said, "Imagine a novel about a Stanford University professor who trains a gorilla to talk. It turns out that I'm on the faculty at Stanford University and in some way I fit the description of the person in this novel." He gave one of the ladies in front a little nod and a smile. She smiled back.

"Now everybody, all of my friends around the country, know I'm not this person. Nevertheless, I get these calls and people will tease me about being this person who is training this gorilla to talk and whatever else happens in this novel."

When the professor had finished, he looked once more at the jury, gave them all, each of them alike, another smile, and Cooper turned him over to me.

I hit him straight on. "Have I been really hearing you right? That you came all the way from good old Stanford University to tell ordinary Wyoming people what they think when they read this article?"

"Yes. May I explain?"

"No. I just want the question answered, because the speech time was over as soon as your counsel sat down. I have to have the right to ask some ordinary questions about ordinary people." The judge struck my comments, and admonished the jury. I thanked the judge and pressed on.

"Well, Dr. Clark, you think you know how ordinary people think?"

"In the sense that the research tells me that I do, I do."

"When we talk about ordinary people, Dr. Clark, aren't we talking about old people and young people as well?"

"Yes."

"Do old people think the same as young people?"

"Not exactly."

"Are we talking about men and women?"

"That's right."

"Do men think the same as women?"

"Not necessarily."

"Are we talking about farm boys like Eddie and me and city boys like Mr. Guccione. Do we think alike?"

"No, not necessarily."

"Even a couple of brothers who are raised on the same farm may think differently?"

"Possibly."

"Are we talking about different areas of the country?"

"That's right."

"People down in Nantucket are going to think differently than folks here?"

"That's right."

"Now, Doctor, have you ever published any work devoted to determining what is or is not seen as fiction by an ordinary person?"

"I have not."

"Thank you."

"And you are not a treating psychologist?"

"No, I'm not."

"You are somebody who writes books?"

"That's right."

"And you teach."

"That's right."

"Now, Doctor, we do recognize that words are dangerous?"

"Some can be."

"As a matter of fact, words are sometimes as dangerous as the sword, isn't that true?"

"That is sometimes true."

"You can kill, and you can maim, and you can hurt with words, is that right?"

"That is probably true."

"And so a person who has the ability to spread words—maiming, hurting, injuring words—throughout the nation, throughout the world, has a responsibility not to hurt with words, isn't that true?"

Cooper objected, but the judge overruled.

"People ought to be careful with the words they use."

"As a psycholinguist you recognize that an accusation that Kim Pring committed oral sex in public would be an outrageous accusation, don't you?"

"Yes, it would."

"Is there any question in your mind that if it was your daughter who had been charged with giving oral sex, whether it was a joke or whether it wasn't, that it would hurt her?"

"I think that is true."

"And you don't have to be a professor of psychology at Stanford or any place else to know that, do you?"

"Nope." He wasn't smiling and the jury wasn't smiling either.

"Now, as an expert on how words affect people, I want to ask you a few questions—do you think 'blowjob' is an outrageous word that would affect and hurt someone if she were charged with being a 'blowjob artist'?"

"Yes, I would think it would."

"Even by people who don't believe it?"

"I believe that is true."

"Now stop a minute. I'm going to ask you for a minute to imagine in your mind the picture of Miss Pring 'blowing' Tito. Do you have it in your mind?"

"In some respects, yes."

"Is it outrageous?"

"It is not very pleasant."

"Let this language create an image in your mind: 'She drew his flesh into her, not with her mouth alone, but with her entire body, the deepest most remote parts of her uniting in common effort, calling to him . . . crying . . . for nourishment.' Do you have the picture?"

"I have the picture."

"Do you have the picture that an ordinary person would have reading that?"

"Probably something very much like it."

"Would it hurt if they said something like that about you?"

"That is true."

"Did you like the article?"

"Not particularly."

"Since we recognize that words are as dangerous as bullets, can hurt as bad as poison, can cause world wars and destroy nations, then don't you also agree that a minimal, reasonable kind of care is required to make certain that words don't carelessly and recklessly hurt people?"

"I'm sure there must be a minimal care."

I took the "Code of Ethics" of the Writers Guild and marked it as an exhibit. "I'm not talking to you now as a writer. I'm talking to you as an expert in the field of psycholinguistics, which would include writers because they use words, don't they?"

"They certainly do."

I read aloud from the "Code of Ethics": " 'The writer shall recognize that the constitutional guarantees of freedom of expression and freedom of the press imply a responsibility not to abuse those freedoms.' Do you agree with that?"

Cooper objected, but the judge said it was on the borderline of relevancy, and let him answer.

"It's a very reasonable thing to say," Dr. Clark said.

I read again from the code: " 'The writer shall check carefully for accuracy and verification of all facts used when writing both *fiction* and nonfiction.' " I emphasized the word with my voice. "Do you think that is a reasonable thing to require of a writer?"

The judge overruled Cooper's objection.

"That is a perfectly reasonable thing to require."

I read some more: " 'The writer shall not use the writing profession for the purpose of defaming, libeling or maligning others.' Do you think that is a correct limitation on the use of words?"

"Yes, I do."

"Do you have children?"

"Yes."

"Where would you hide *Penthouse* in your house if it were there?" The juror in the back row on the end threw his head back in disgust at my question. Cooper asked that that question be stricken and the judge agreed. The juror shook his head.

"You realize that when we are talking about twenty-five million people across the country that we are talking about every kind and character of person from psycholinguists like you to the dirtiest, crawling scrud in the world, isn't that true?" He agreed. "Do you recognize that many people believe that 'where there is smoke there is fire'?"

"I'm sure that is true . . . but I'm talking about a *reasonable* person—whether or not they will believe this story is about a fictional person."

"Do you believe that *unreasonable* people will read the article?"

He looked down. He spoke his answer to his hands, as if he were examining them for flaws. "I'm sure that some will."

"Do you think that stupid people will read it?"

"I'm sure that some will."

"Remember your novel about a talking gorilla. Let's assume the professor has sex with the gorilla. Now we have a problem, don't we?"

"I'm sure I would be teased about it. I'd know my friends would still know that it is fiction and it was not referring to me. They would not be imputing anything about my actual character."

"Do you think it might hurt you?"

"I might feel bad. I might feel uncomfortable."

"What if they called you night and day?"

"It's one of the things I have to put up with being a public figure—they already do call me up."

"Do they say to you, 'Do you really do it to a gorilla?' "

"That, they haven't done, no."

"Do they say to you, 'Is the gorilla really as good as it says in the article?' " The professor frowned. I gave him time to reconsider. "I'm trying to ask you if you have the sensitivity as a professional psychologist to recognize how deeply things like that may cut?"

"I have a lot of sympathy with exactly that sort of problem."

"Do you recognize Kim Pring may be quite different from you?"

"I'm sure Miss Pring is different from me."

"And that she may hurt where you may not?"

"I'm sure that's true."

"Do you recognize she may have a personality structure that may require support from the outside world?"

"No question, all these things are possible."

"And, Doctor, hurt or not, the story of the gorilla could have been changed so that you would never have been teased in any way had they made the professor from a fictional university—by changing one word you could have been saved?"

"The simple answer is yes."

I said, "Thank you," because, as Judge Brimmer said, thank yous are always nice to say.

Then Cooper said, "Counsel asked you if there was a sense in which words were like bullets—recall?"

"Yes."

"Are there many senses in which words are quite different from bullets?"

"Of course. Words must be interpreted by the people they are aimed at. A word by itself has no lethal effect."

"A word doesn't tear flesh?"

"No, it doesn't."

Then the judge interjected, "Ladies and gentlemen, today, as you recall, it being Wednesday, is Rotary day, so we are going to have a little longer recess than usual, principally because the speaker is a friend of mine, so I don't want to walk out in the middle of his talk." It was the first noon I could eat. I had a bowl of soup. Eddie was happy. After Rotary I continued with the cross-examination of the professor.

"Do you think even though the average reader might see this *Penthouse* writing as fiction, she might still get calls?"

"Oh, sure."

"Would the fact that the average reader saw it as fiction stop the dirty remarks to her?"

"They may not."

"Would it stop them from pointing at her?"

"May not."

"Or writing on the back of her car?"

"May not."

"Or calling every hour on the hour all night?"

"May not."

"Or hurting her?"

"May not."

"Don't you think that about any ordinary six folks from Wyoming would be as well equipped to decide what an average reader might think as you?"

"In certain respects, yes. In other respects, no."

"Do you remember telling Mr. Cooper that a word, different from a bullet, doesn't tear flesh? Do you remember that?" The professor nodded. "But a word can tear a soul, isn't that right?"

"I suppose you're right," the professor said, and I thanked him again.

When I was through with the questions, I came back to counsel table and Eddie was gone. I felt like I was in the middle of a barroom brawl and the pal I had depended on to keep them off my back had disappeared. "Where'd Eddie go?" I whispered to Kim.

"I don't know," she said. "He just got up and left."

Then Cooper said the words: *"The defense rests."*

No more witnesses? Where were these lawyers, these so-called officers of the court who would come forward and tell the court about Kim's bad reputation? Where was the secret witness who would implant that evil picture in the minds of the jury to magically transform Kim Pring to a wanton slut performing her "unique talent" on all who would offer themselves as the object of her depravity. Where were the seventeen members of the football team? Where were these witnesses?

Truth is a defense.

Penthouse had no defense.

And where the hell was Eddie?

27

You can always tell when a judge is ready to announce an important decision. A certain dull glaze falls over his eyes. It is the look of one who has fiddled with the future, one who has altered the unknowable forces of fate, like a small child who has tossed a pebble into a quiet pool, causing his puny energy to be transmitted ring on ever-expanding ring into eternity, which, some say, is only a silly giant ring rolling back on itself.

What massive reverberations occur as a product of our slightest deed—say, the mere raising of an eyebrow at a passerby! Even that inconsequential act, multiplied to the borders of the infinite, can create such a monstrous, blazing, blinding fulmination that to comprehend its totality would explode the mind to madness, and from which mankind's poor eyes and piteous brain have been shielded, lest otherwise we should perish from the horror of it. We have become, therefore, those strange creatures who see all and, except for the moment, forget all as simultaneous acts. There is, nevertheless, that one telltale sign, that unmistakable momentary haze that clouds over the eyes of a judge who has made his decision, that trace that tells us the eyes have seen it but the mind has failed to record the unspeakable that was seen—for no matter how seemingly niggling and dinky, all decisions irrevocably alter the destiny of the universe. Now in Judge Brimmer's eyes I could clearly see what I have come to call the "gloomy gaze."

To begin with, Judge Brimmer spread a small judicial smile among us equally: "The record may show that the Court will give a punitive-damages instruction as to the defendant, Penthouse International, because I think that the evidence shows that the editors of the magazine were skilled and capable persons—Mr. Hofler's testimony was that he assumed that there are people in the world who would associate the article with Miss Ping, and the *Penthouse* contract gave them the right to change the article, and they did, in fact, use that privilege. The Wideman testimony indicates that it was easy to avoid the identity issue and that in his opinion there was a flagrant disregard for basic human responsibility. There was a lack of fictional label, and most important to me"—and thereupon the judge stopped and looked at each of us with a very distressed look upon his face, which I also heard in his voice—"the very subject matter of this article itself places on the editors of such a magazine a high duty of care to act in a responsible manner so as not to inflict harm." He said he thought we had established a cause of action based on outrage, and that punitive damages were appropriate.

Judge Brimmer peered at Cooper for a long moment, as if considering whether he would say it or not, as if remembering what judges can never forget, that everything a judge says during a trial is recorded forever on the unforgiving judicial record. Finally Judge Brimmer said it. "There is a definite possibility that he was there at the Miss America Pageant and saw her perform—and even Professor Clark admitted this morning that the accusation that the plaintiff did such acts would be outrageous and portray her in a false light."

I thought Cooper acted very calmly under the circumstances. He leaned back in his chair as if preparing to have a pleasant conversation with the judge, but his voice betrayed him. He spoke through his teeth.

"I think it's a mistake to say that merely because it's explicit sex that somehow creates a higher duty. I don't know where that comes from! I've never heard of that before!" Cooper stared at the judge accusingly as if the judge had then and there made up the law out of whole cloth.

"I haven't seen any cases like that either," the judge admitted. "But neither have I ever read a case that dealt with public fellatio." Then the judge stuck out his own chin and leaned forward. "But I am firmly of the belief that since man first learned to talk, one of the vilest names one man has ever called another dealt with fellatio, and this is something that is generally known," the judge said, seemingly taking refuge in what he must have considered the authority of natural law. Cooper looked away but the judge did not.

"It seems to me," the judge continued, "that a reasonable publisher dealing in a delicate area, knowing, as he admitted, that there would be persons in the world who would associate the article with her, would then have a high duty of care to avoid the association. This just seems to me to be a matter of justice and fairness under the circumstances."

I looked over my shoulder and there was Eddie standing, grinning at me. I was damn glad to see him. He motioned me over to the corner.

"I've been gettin' the witness ready for you. She's scared, but she's ready. She'll testify." Now I knew where he'd been.

"Good!" I said. I turned to the judge. "I asked a woman, a schoolteacher, to come here as a rebuttal witness. I was talking to her at noon preparatory to her taking the stand, and she mentioned that she taught in the same high school here in Cheyenne as the juror in the back row on the end."

The judge raised his eyebrows, and waited.

"And she commenced to talk about this juror," I said. Cooper whispered something to Kelley. I said, "She and that juror in the back on the end are friends, and before the trial she talked with him about the case and that juror told her, 'I have heard from the Wyoming football team that everything they say about Kim Pring is true.' "

The judge stared in disbelief, his mouth half open, his eyes squinted.

I continued. "These jurors were questioned about that on *voir dire* by Your Honor. To me, if a juror sat there believing Kim Pring was guilty of all of those things he had heard from the Wyoming football team, then we can't get a fair trial with that juror and he should be excused and the alternate juror seated in his stead."

Cooper jumped up, pointing and hollering: "I think *they*," meaning Eddie and me, "were investigating jurors beforehand because it's obvious *he*," meaning the said juror in the back row on the end, "is not buying *your* whole act and *you* are trying to get him off the jury."

I said to the judge, "I represent to the Court I got this information at noon today for the first time. I brought it to your attention because I think it's my duty to do so." Then I felt the rage coming, and I didn't give a good goddamn—just let 'er go. "And I'm tired of being accused by counsel of lying, of stating things in public to my own client that are not true"—I was blowing. Eddie watched—"and the numerous other allegations he has made about me without any foundation during the course of this trial!" I jumped up. Cooper got up. Eddie got up. The judge pushed his chair back from his desk.

"Your Honor, I think I have an obligation as an officer of this court to call that matter to your attention in chambers," I said. Eddie walked over very nonchalantly between Cooper and me.

"I think if anything is done we should declare a mistrial," Cooper said.

The judge was suddenly very quiet, thoughtful. "I don't recall that I asked them specifically if they had heard anything about Miss Pring that indicted sexual misconduct with anyone. I'm sure I didn't ask about the Wyoming football team." What had happened was proof of a very simple fact—judges ought never to engage in the business of lawyering, and good jury selection is part of good lawyering. Yet in the federal courts most judges take over the questioning of the jury, the *voir dire*, and with all due respect to the great and skillful judges of this nation, one of whom is Judge Brimmer, the best *voir dire* I've ever heard a judge conduct would be malpractice had a lawyer done the same for his client. Judges, as lawyers, have all they can do to develop the skills of their own profession.

Judge Brimmer said, "I did generally ask them, 'Is there any other reason known to you why you couldn't be a completely fair and impartial juror?' "—a question judges should be barred from asking, because what juror will jump up and admit to a courtroom full of people he cannot be fair and impartial?

Eddie said, "Well, I think you did ask, 'Do any of you know anything about this case or have you discussed this case with anyone?'—words to that effect."

"I'm not going to embarrass that juror if I don't have to," the judge said. "You may bring the witness in."

"Could somebody neutral get her?" Cooper asked, clearly implying we might influence her on the way into chambers. I eased a step in Cooper's direction, but Eddie, making it look almost like an accident, stepped in front of me.

"Excuse me," he said. Then he said out of the side of his mouth, "Take 'er easy."

"Go get her yourself, Mr. Cooper," I said and then Judge Brimmer had the clerk bring in this scared-looking young schoolteacher.

Judge Brimmer looked her over. Then he began his own questions. She said she had discussed the case with the juror in the back row on the end, calling him by name. It had been some four weeks previously when she asked him if Kim could use the gym to teach a student. Kim had been her student and later they had become friends. The woman was almost stiff with fear.

The judge paused, studied her most gravely, and said, "Now I'm going to ask you exactly what it is that you said to him and he said to you. I want you, as nearly as you can recall, to say the *exact* words, and I want you to bear this in mind: First, what I've heard are serious charges; second, if I find that there is any real substance to them, I am then going to bring in the juror and we are going to go through it all again. And, of course, the accusation of a juror lying to the court is not only juror misconduct, it also carries the possibility of felony charges for perjury."

I whispered to Eddie, "He's got her so scared she'll never say anything now."

"So do you understand the seriousness of this matter?" the judge asked.

"Uh-hum," she said, too scared to even say yes.

"All right. Now just tell me exactly what was said, and I don't want guesses! I don't want paraphrases. I want *exact* words."

Nobody can give exact words.

"Okay," she said, suddenly blurting it all out. "I came and said, 'Can Kim Pring use the gym?' And he said, yes, he didn't have any qualms with that and then something to the effect about according to the football team in Laramie, all of what is said about her is true." There it was!

The disease of libel had spread into the heart of the justice system itself!

"What was said then?" Judge Brimmer asked.

"And I said, 'No way,' you know. Kim is one of the straightest people that I know."

The judge had no choice. He called the juror into chambers and the attorneys left the chambers while the judge questioned him. His version of what had been said was this—I read it later in the record: "Now I didn't say that the football team said it. I said I had *heard* that there was something to do with the football team, and I didn't say that it was true. I have no way of knowing that it was."

The judge asked, "Do you believe it to be true?"

"I have no way of knowing it," the juror answered. "This is just hearsay and there is no way that I would even have any idea."

Then the judge asked, "Would this have any influence upon your decision in this case one way or another?"—a question no juror finding himself under these circumstances would answer except as he did.

"None whatsoever," the juror said. What else could he say?

"Well, why didn't you mention to me before what you had heard about the football team and Miss Pring?"

"Well, I think *everybody* on the panel or anybody who lives in Cheyenne has heard things." I had no doubt that what the juror said was true. The defamation had spread to all the jury members—they were all infected.

"What you mean is that these are just rumors?" the judge asked.

"Just like reading the paper."

"And you don't consider them as evidence?"

"No," the juror had said. "Not until you heard all the facts can you come to the real conclusion."

"Let me ask you this: Do you feel that in view of that statement, that this affects your partiality in any way in this case?"

My partiality? Am I prejudiced?

"No. I really don't believe so. In fact, I'm positive it doesn't from hearing both sides of the story and by sitting on the panel as I have for the past two weeks—there is no way that I'm swayed by either side."

Then the judge told the juror that this information against him had originated from our side of the case and, of course, the juror denied any resentment against us. Of course he wouldn't be prejudiced! When the judge read us the transcript of his questions and the juror's answers, I thought, Christ! We've had it now. By bringing him in like this and the judge not excusing him, we'd poked the bear in the ass. It was all over.

Back into his chambers, the judge said, "Gentlemen, I don't think that the juror is prejudiced in this case, and I think the sum of what he said is that it was a rumor to which he gave no credence, and that is the reason he didn't mention it. I think it would have been highly prejudicial had he mentioned it. In fact, it might have tainted the whole panel."

I found it hard to understand how this one juror might taint the whole panel without himself being tainted. I argued with the judge. Why should we take the chance? Even if he wasn't prejudiced, what about the very *appearance* of justice? If my client lost the case, how could she ever believe she got a fair trial with such a juror?

Suddenly Judge Brimmer whirled and pointed his finger straight at me. "Are you moving for a mistrial?" If I answered yes, maybe he'd grant it, and we'd have to try it all over again in six months, a year— whenever we could get another trial date—just what Cooper wanted. Now it sounded like the judge was of the same mind. Or was he bluffing me? Perhaps he had asked the question so that my saying no, no, I didn't want a mistrial would be deemed a waiver by me of any claim for error later, on appeal.

And there is a limit to a judge's patience. He resented like hell being wedged into a position where no matter how the jury decided the case, the losing side could claim error for the appeal. He'd tried to give both sides a fair trial, but this was finally too much. I thought the judge was on the brink of throwing the case out. For days Cooper had urged him to do so—even had the judge half convinced he had committed error somewhere. Now I was at the judge, too.

"Careful," Eddie whispered.

Except for that one juror, we would never be in better shape with another jury, and so far as I saw it, the record was solid. There really hadn't been any substantial error committed against *Penthouse* that could justify a reversal by the Tenth Circuit. In fact, if there had been any error, I thought it had been against us. I didn't want a mistrial. But I wanted that one juror off.

I said to the judge very quietly, "The reason we have an alternate juror is for situations exactly like this. It would be a no-lose proposition for the court to seat the alternate. Unless you do, I'll feel uneasy. I won't feel like I got a fair trial and I don't think my client will either. I saw that juror walk out of this office. He was stamping, and I said to Eddie, 'There goes an angry man.' "

Judge Brimmer rushed to support his record. "I watched him walk out, and I don't think he was. Before he left the room, he said he would withdraw if it created a problem. I think he is a very fair man."

"If he is willing to withdraw, I ask that you grant it," I said.

The judge refused.

"I've been watching this juror," I said. "This morning when I asked Professor Clark where he would hide his *Penthouse*, the juror looked at me in utter disgust, and a few minutes after that, I discovered what I discovered and I brought it to the Court's attention."

The judge said, "If in the course of trial one alienates a juror, I don't think that we have got the right to get him off."

"I have done nothing to alienate that man," I said.

"I don't think you have either," the judge said.

"I think he was alienated when he came in, and if he isn't going to keep his word with the Court, I don't think that I should trust my client's case to him. If he is showing the Court a willingness to withdraw, I'm going to ask the Court to grant it. In my heart I believe we are entitled as parties and lawyers to at least think we got a fair trial. I have been in many cases in which jurors have been disqualified for one reason or another during the course of the trial—sickness—because they've found out that there was some reason why they shouldn't have been seated in the first place. That is why we have an alternate juror. I say this—I say here is an intelligent man who sat through those questions and over and over again failed to respond to the Court in any way, and now he claims he doesn't remember—"

"You have misstated it," the judge said. "He said it was a mere rumor to which he paid no attention, and it was of no consequence. That is what he said."

"He brought it out. It was he, Judge, who said, 'What they say about her and the football team is true.' We don't know how many people he talked to. Did he talk to one or ten members of the football team?"

"He said he had not talked to any one of them," the judge answered.

Eddie saw I was losing and tried to rescue me. "Your Honor, may it please the Court"—which was his lawyer way of pleading, and you could hear it in his voice—"it was an expression of an *opinion* from the juror to this other teacher."

Suddenly the judge was angry. "Now listen! I know that man and I know he is a fair, honest man, and I know he sat here and told me that it wouldn't make any difference to him in deciding this case, and I don't believe it will!"

"Well, I don't know the juror," I said.

"Well, I do! He is the husband of one of the girls in the Probation Office. And I believed him when he said that."

My God, I thought. The Probation Office! I looked at Eddie. He'd turned pale. We had further information. What should we do with it? During the trial we'd heard a second- or thirdhand rumor, presumably originating from one of the women who worked in the Probation Office, that this juror was a *Penthouse* fan and kept the magazine in his house. I decided to tell the judge what I'd heard. When in doubt, lay it out.

"Now what I heard from the Probation Office is that he has and keeps *Penthouse* magazine at his house."

The judge didn't want to hear any more. "I've decided I'm not going to discharge him. Now that is that!" The judge slammed his file closed.

It wasn't closed with me. "I want the record to show I am facing two problems: First, a juror admits he heard things, and secondly, he has been questioned by the Court and knows the problem came from our side. It's obviously embarrassing to him. It questions his integrity. It's going to put me in a position where I can't even look at him— can't even talk to him."

"Then why did you bring it up?"

"If it were the other way around, you would have thrown me in jail if I hadn't!"

"I think it's a tempest in a teapot," the judge said.

"Are you saying to me I shouldn't have mentioned that to you?" I asked. Suppose I had learned that this juror had been whispering around that he'd heard Guccione was a member of the Mafia. What was my duty then?

"The defense have their rights in this thing too," the judge said. "I find there are no grounds for the discharge of this juror. I feel that the man can be a fair juror. In the alternative, the defendants have pending their cumulative motion for mistrial. Are you saying you want me to grant it?" He was egging me on again.

"No," I said.

"I have come just that far"—the judge held his fingers measuring a hair-sized space—"from granting a mistrial in this case. I think that the conduct of counsel in the case has, cumulatively, been very, very close."

The judge had beaten me. And more. If we won the trial, Cooper would quote to the Circuit Court of Appeals what the judge had just said. I could hear it: "Even His Honor found that Spence's conduct was very, very close to prejudicial. Even the judge came within a hair of granting a mistrial."

I said softly, "You have my word this is the last time I will mention a matter about a juror to you, Judge. I thought it was my duty to do so, and I don't appreciate you punishing me for having done my duty." Eddie was still pale. Cooper and Kelley waited silently.

"I'm not punishing you," the judge said. Then he gathered up the financial statements of *Penthouse* he said he would allow the jury to see in determining what sum would justly punish *Penthouse*.

You can't punish a corporation making millions by requiring them to pay the same as the local Jackson Hole newspaper. A thousand dollars might be too much for it and ten million not enough against *Penthouse*. How much would it take to adequately punish such a publication? Cooper was objecting now to certain footnotes in the *Penthouse* profit and loss statement. He said, "There are Rainbird products advertised in the magazine. It would prejudice the jury," referring to the notes on the Evelyn Rainbird Company owned by Guccione.

"What does Rainbird have to do with it?" the judge asked.

"They sell artificial penises and vibrators," I said.

"They are advertised in the magazine," Cooper said.

"I thought they sold lawn-sprinkler supplies," the judge said.

Everybody laughed except me. Then the judge struck the Evelyn Rainbird reference from the record as irrelevant.

While the judge was going over the remaining financial statements, I leaned over to Eddie. "We can never win this case. We've got nothing to show the jury," I said.

"Yes, we can, Gerry. The judge is just protectin' us. If we win, they can never in all hell get it reversed, and the judge knows we're gonna win."

"I'm glad he knows it," I said. "He's the only one who does."

I told the judge I wanted to read to the jury from Guccione's deposition: "What do you get for a half-page ad like this one called 'Arouse Her,' for a product called Protex Arouse?" It was an advertisement for a French-tickler condom. Guccione had answered, "I can only give you an approximate idea. Probably something like thirteen or fourteen thousand in black-and-white." But the judge sustained Cooper's objection to the question and answer because, he said, "I think it's an attempt to inject sexual references into the trial."

"The sexual references came from this *actual* magazine," I argued. Guccione had injected the ad for these sex products into *Penthouse*, not me. But the judge was going to keep everything out that could possibly give *Penthouse* grounds to reverse the jury's verdict. The only problem would be getting the jury to hold for us in the first place. After all of those witnesses and exhibits that had been ruled out, and now these rulings from the judge, we would go to the jury with only a fraction of the case we had originally planned. Then the judge even ruled that although he would allow the jury to read these censored financial statements, he wouldn't let me read them out loud to the jurors. Nor would the judge permit me to read another of Guccione's answer to one of my interrogatories—that his time was worth $40,000 a day. It was true, as His Honor pointed out, that we had not sued Guccione personally, but he was, after all, the sole owner of *Penthouse*, its alter ego, I argued, and his earnings, his wealth, like his ownership of those paintings by Picasso and Chagall and Degas and Matisse, ought to be considered by the jury. But the judge said no, and he was right. I knew it. Finally he did agree that I might read several small parts from Guccione's deposition, and when court finally took up again I looked at the man in the back row on the end, and I read to him alone. For the first time in the trial, he looked back at me.

I read: "Well, Mr. Guccione, give me an approximation of your gross revenues from *Penthouse*," which included sales of the magazine and advertising. "Gross revenues," Guccione had said, "are in the region of one hundred twenty-five million, I suppose." His net for all magazines in his group, including *Omni, Forum, Variations, Viva*, and *Photo World* was fourteen million. I was also permitted to read from his deposition about *Penthouse* being in the nuclear-energy business, and involved in the licensing of publishers in other countries, such as Germany, Spain, Italy, France, Switzerland, and Austria.

The juror in the back on the end listened to me carefully now.

Maybe before he was only tired and had been saying to me, "Spence, get on with this case. Let us decide it. Trust us," and when I had asked one question beyond his ordinary human endurance, he had tossed his head at me in disgust. God, I hoped that was it.

I read another of my questions to Guccione that the judge had permitted, and his answer: "We own a club called the Penthouse Club, which is an ordinary social club. We are in the hotel business in Atlantic City. We own two major sites." Then Interrogatory 61. "Are you planning a sixty-million-dollar-plus casino hotel?" and the answer was "Yes." That was it.

"Plaintiff rests," I said,

"Defense rests," Cooper said.

No more witnesses.

A couple of the jurors smiled happily at each other. Eddie scooted his chair back. "It's all over, Kim, all but the hollerin' and the shoutin'," he said. "And they ain't gonna bring in that mystery witness."

She looked tired. I put my arm around her and gave her a squeeze. I wondered how she had made it this far. How had we? And it was over—all but the judge's instructions to the jury and the attorney's arguments—and the jury's verdict.

* * *

In his chambers Judge Brimmer took off his robe and his suit coat, pulled out a large folder, and rubbed his hands together. He was ready to go to work on the instructions. He wanted the attorneys' input, but after he'd heard the arguments on both sides, he would decide how to instruct the jurors on the law. We gathered around the table—put me in mind of my Grandpa Spence pouring out a little milk into one big old tin milk bowl around which the cats and dogs alike would congregate. There was a lot of sneaking and growling and snapping, but all the cats and dogs had to get whatever milk they were going to get out of that same old bowl, and whatever advantage we'd get from the judge's reading of the law would come from this one set of instructions we were getting ready to fight over.

Right off he read a proposed instruction that sounded as if he was putting the burden of proof on us to show that Kim was *not* a public figure. I thought *Penthouse* had to prove she *was*. How could we prove a negative? I tested the water.

"Who do you think has the burden of proof on the public-figure issue, Your Honor?" I asked.

"I think you have the burden if you want to get her in as a private figure," he said.

"You mean she is *presumed* to be a public figure?" I couldn't believe it. He really meant it? Nobody is presumed to be a public figure! That she's a public figure is a matter of defense, and the party raising the defense, *Penthouse*, had the burden to prove it.

"We're in fucking trouble again," I whispered to Eddie.

"I say the burden is yours," the judge said. "If I'm wrong, you can show me on the appeal." He went on to the next instruction.

I felt helpless. The judge decides the law. He can play the game any way he damn well pleases, and what pleases any judge the most is not to have the appeals court reverse him. If there's a close question on an instruction, the judge will often word it to satisfy the party he thinks is going to lose so that the loser has nothing to complain about when he appeals.

Then the judge read us a proposed instruction on the definition of a public figure: "While an individual may achieve such persuasive fame or notoriety that he or she becomes a public figure for all purposes, it is also possible that an individual has voluntarily injected himself or herself into or is drawn into a particular public controversy and thereby has become a public figure for a limited range of issues. In either case, such persons have assumed special prominence in the resolution of public questions and are public figures." The judge held Kelley in his gaze, whom he now seemed to accept as the expert on the technical law for the defense, and said, "Now that is nearly the exact language of Justice Powell, modified only to fit this occasion." I thought the instruction was well drafted, except what "particular public controversy" had Kim ever injected herself into? All she did was spin her baton. How could she be required now to *prove* she was a private person?

"Don't worry, Gerry," Eddie said. "The judge is just protectin' us."

"Yeah," I whispered. "But we've got to win first." People say juries don't follow the judge's instructions and decide cases as they please, but that's also a myth. I've seen jurors come in with tears in their eyes, trying to explain to the losing party that they wanted to hold for him but they couldn't—it was against the judge's instructions. A good case can be lost on the instructions.

We argued about every damned word of every damned instruction, back and forth, until I was nearly exhausted. Both sides took the words and held them up and inspected each like a jeweler examining a stone through his glass for flaws and fakery. We hollered and yelled about the words, pounded the table, and slammed the books. But the judge was mostly preoccupied with the arguments of Cooper and Kelley. They were on him like gnats in fly time. Later, if they lost, they'd argue to the appeals court, "We told Judge Brimmer that this wording was wrong. We objected to the instruction he gave. It was error. It prejudiced us and we are entitled to a new trial." But I couldn't get the judge to listen much to me.

Finally, frustrated beyond my threshold, I said, "Do you want me to say anything? Because the way I get it, either you don't hear me or you don't care what I have to say, and if you don't want me to say anything more, I won't." I started to get up to leave.

That got his attention. That was in the record, too.

"Yes, I want you to say—"

I interrupted. "I am feeling pretty helpless," I said, which I was. I couldn't get up to the milk dish.

"I want your comments," he said. He was a kind man, caught up in this miserable battle. The judge was at war, too—it was his time. Both sides were after him, attacking, pulling, manipulating him, and the record, in order to get the instructions they wanted or to twist things around so that the record would be to their advantage, even in small ways, in the event they lost. None of the lawyers were blameless. It *was* war.

We had to prove malice, the judge said, by "clear and convincing evidence." That is the law. Then the judge defined "clear and convincing" for the jury: "Clear, precise and indubitable and unmistakable and free from serious or substantial doubt." Jesus!

"That sounds like even a greater proof than 'beyond a reasonable doubt,'" I argued, and proof "beyond a reasonable doubt" is never required of a plaintiff in a civil case—and only the State must meet that burden in a criminal case. But the judge said that was right out of the *MacGuire* case, a Wyoming case, and he was going to give that instruction, and that was that!

Then the judge read his instruction defining invasion of privacy as "the unwarranted appropriation of an individual's personality—"and Kelley argued that there was no claim here that *Penthouse* had appropriated Kim Pring's personality, and I said, "You're damned right there was. They took a woman, Miss Wyoming, and used her commercially." But the judge said he would strike from the instruction the words about appropriating Kim's personality.

There was a pile of other instructions the judge said he was also going to give. I'd glanced through them. I was convinced we couldn't possibly win if he gave them all. I was tired. I felt beaten, not by the case nor by Cooper and Kelley, nor by the witnesses, but by this process I finally had no control over, and I felt beaten by the judge.

If the judge was actually going to give that pile of instructions to the jury, we'd lose. There was no way to pull the case out—even with the best final argument ever delivered in the history of jurisprudence. I'd rather try it again and hope for better times at some later instruction conference than to lose it now with that pile of instructions against me going to the jury. I got up and put my things in my briefcase. Eddie watched, shock on his face. The judge watched curiously.

As I closed my briefcase I asked, "Are you intending to give all these instructions, Judge?"

"Yes."

"This pile?" I asked incredulously.

He nodded.

"Why don't we save you the trouble. *I join the defendants in moving for a mistrial!* I've looked through these. They are defense instructions. They are cumulative. They are confusing. There is no possible way we can get a fair trial with these instructions. You wanted us to move for a mistrial on the basis of that juror. Well, I am happy to do that now. I don't think there is any way we can get a fair trial on these instructions and with that juror."

Under his breath I heard Eddie say, "Oh shit, no, Gerry!" That's all I heard Eddie say.

28

Then the judge motioned me back to my chair and said, "Forget it," almost like he hadn't heard me. Christ. I was such a great lawyer I couldn't even win a dismissal of my own case. Two hours ago, if I'd blinked twice he would have thrown the case out and me with it. But I, too, had made my record, and the arguments went on like nothing had happened, the battle over every word, every lawyer knowing the law better than his opponent on the other side of the table. The arguments were vehement and mean and long and loud and disgusting and finally the judge threw his pen down on the desk and hollered, actually hollered, like a man in terrible agony.

"You guys are the damnedest bunch of nitpickers I have ever seen! Now I will tell you frankly this is the longest and the worst instruction conference I have ever had. I haven't submitted even a stock instruction that you haven't objected to. This is a new experience to me in my five years on the bench."

"I hear your exasperation," I said quietly.

"I am not only exasperated by the way you are nitpicking, I am exasperated by the fact none of you submitted a good instruction to me in the first place." The judge had rights, too, and he was going to let it all hang out. "And in the second place, none of you are willing to submit a reasonable compromise or a reasonable suggestion. You are hanging on to picky, picky, picky things that don't mean a damn! Now, gentlemen, the conference is adjourned! I will see you at nine-thirty in the morning. Each side gets an hour and a half to argue. The plaintiff can divide her time in any manner she wishes, but you must tell the clerk your decision and she will give you a one-minute warning and you will be *cut off* at the end of that." He gave me a long, knowing look. I have never lived by any principles of brevity.

Thank God, the judge would only read the instructions to the jury, and they wouldn't have the damn things in their hands in the jury room to haggle over. If lawyers couldn't agree on what they meant, how could jurors? Then, I thought, I'd better check anyway. "You're not going to send those instructions to the jury, are you?"

"I am sending those instructions to the jury," the judge said.

"All forty of those?"

"All of them go."

"You've never done that before," I said.

"This is such a complicated case I think I have to."

Cooper looked satisfied. Kelley looked just like Cooper. Reading the instructions again in the jury room would only confuse the jurors more, and they had that complicated special verdict form with its numerous interrogatories they had to complete and answer correctly before we could win. They'd either hang and we'd have to try it again anyway, or finally the jurors would throw up their hands and some would look sad and a couple would have swollen eyes and I'd know when I saw them come filing slowly, sadly into the courtroom that they'd found against us—that's what confused and tired juries usually do—find against the plaintiff who has the burden of proof. Well, it had been a good fight, I thought.

"Come on, Eddie," I said. "Let's get the hell out of here."

I didn't sleep much that night—fought the fever dreams again, argued the case over and over, and no matter how I argued the case, the judge did not hear me. I argued to the wall, and the wall did not hear me, and finally I couldn't hear myself because the words were meaningless words and all there was was an empty anxiousness that echoed back on itself, and I couldn't run because I was in a steel closet.

When the hotel operator gave us our wake-up call, Eddie didn't say good morning.

He said, "Well, today's the day we're gonna win this case," and laughed. Eddie leaped out of bed. It was 5:00 A.M. We skipped breakfast. Eddie stayed with me. "Just in case ya wanna bounce somethin' off of me." I reorganized my notes and went over the scores of exhibits, putting things together as best I could. It is always a question of what to leave out—how to frame the story, the compelling argument out of that massive body of evidence.

When we got to the courtroom, Kim was sitting at our table looking exhausted, and now her mother, who had loyally sat through the entire trial, mostly alone in that miserable, windowless witness room—just in case we needed her—sat down in the front row. She, too, looked exhausted. This mother and this daughter, these almost sisters, had been consumed by this civilized process we call a trial, this ordeal by fire. Then Judge Brimmer burst into the courtroom at nine sharp, looking bright and ready. "Let's go to work, gentlemen," Judge Brimmer said.

I got up to begin the first of my closing arguments. The courtroom was packed. I felt the pervasive excitement that oozed out of the people, that leaked even from the objects in the room, that rose from the podium where I plopped down my notes, that steamed up out of the floor, that flooded the room and stiffened my knees and froze my breath solid. I coughed.

I looked my jury over, trying to be calm, to convey my confidence. The man in the back on the end stared down at me. He seemed angry. I felt small. The others had their arms folded again. The women had their legs crossed, and once again the message was clear—we've heard about this fancy-talking lawyer's final arguments, and he is not going to do it to us. You may get to all those other juries. We've heard about you and your famous cases, but now we have the power, and we aren't going to give any of it to you.

I felt afraid—always do. I had no excuse for still being afraid after almost thirty years in these pits. But fear is a permanent emotion. I looked down at my boots and felt it, felt it in the lower belly where I had no protection. And now I felt it in the middle of my chest, too. It was spreading on me. The jury was watching, but they could wait while a man told himself it was all right to be afraid.

I *was* all right. I spoke kindly to myself. The fear I felt meant I was alive, that I cared, and my job was to pass that feeling on to those six people so they felt the caring like I felt it. That was my job. But some might say the man standing before them looking at his boots was only praying.

Tell the jury the truth. That is the only trick a lawyer needs to know—tell them the truth, because they'll know the truth when they hear it, and to hear it is such a rarity they will cherish it.

I began in a conversational tone. "You know, folks, I think I'll start this morning by talking a little bit about me, not very much, but I am a part of this lawsuit and I suppose that some of you have seen me during this trial as this big, pushy lawyer and I guess I am. But it's a big job to be a lawyer in a case as important as this one, and no matter how big you get or how old you are, or how often you've been involved in lawsuits—and I've been involved in them all my life—you just never get over being who you really are inside. Sometimes you'd like to cover that up. You don't like to admit to people that that is the way you are. But I lie awake, stay awake at night, wondering what I'm going to say to you."

Right off, Cooper started objecting. "Counsel's personal opinions are not material. I object." And the judge sustained. So was that the way it was going to be? His objections were intended to destroy my argument, like a man dumping a bucket of paint on my canvas after each stroke of my brush. I pushed on. "So what I want you to know is that if I've been pushy, it's because of the burden I carry, a burden that soon you will carry." Cooper objected again, but the court overruled. "I want to tell you that I think about this case in this way—"

"What he thinks is immaterial," Cooper hollered. I never blinked. Push on. "I think you will remember when Mr. Cooper got up, the first thing he told you was how difficult this simple case would be." I needed to silence Cooper. I walked over and stood looking down at him. He'd look silly if he jumped up now and objected and I began to mount my argument again.

"It is not a difficult case. It is a simple case, and the defense is simply a 'no defense.' There isn't a defense except to confuse and to *interrupt*"—I stopped and looked down at Cooper a long time, and the jury watched—"and to cause innuendo and slur." I waited for Cooper to get up and object again, but with the jury watching he stayed glued.

"Sometimes I worry that I haven't said enough, asked the right questions—done my job as I should." He came unglued.

"Object to his worries, Your Honor."

"Sustained." But I was all right now. I was feeling good, and the juices were flowing. I began to realize that nobody could destroy my argument. The price he'd pay in further interruptions would be too high. Let him object. Pray he objects!

"Now I heard Mr. Cooper tell you you need to watch out for Mr. Spence, because he'll carry you off in his emotions. Well, this case would stand if we had a first-year law student in here. I don't change the facts. If I died dead in my tracks, the case would still be here. But I am a person. And I'm a particular kind of person, and Mr. Cooper criticizes that—that people should feel. But I say that a substantial part of this case is the sadness of it, the injury and the hurt. A great part of the case, folks, is the pain and the misery and the anger that ordinary people should feel, and I feel that, and that is who I am. If I don't share that with you accurately and honestly, then I too have lied to you.

"How can I tell you the truth if there is anger and I don't display it? Or sadness and I don't show it? That is my job. Kim depends on me to do it. I hope you will understand that and permit me to do my job during my closing argument this morning.

"I've talked about me—now I'd like to talk about you a little bit. You have been a wonderful jury." I paused and gave each of them a quick nod of gratitude. "It has not been easy for some of you. But as you sit there I know you must have a sense of your awesome responsibility just as I too have that responsibility." The jurors were opening to me. I was all right with all of them, all except for the man on the end in the back. He was gazing at the ceiling again. Then I stopped and waited for him. Would he ever look down, for Christ's sakes? This was the time I had to say it to him, or never, and I waited longer, just a little too long. Then he glanced down over his nose and when he did, I said to him, "And some of us have been victims in this case that shouldn't have been. And that has been hard, and I'm sorry." He looked back up at the ceiling.

"This case involves a constitutional issue. I doubt that the framers of the Constitution who met in that little brick building in Philadelphia, a plain old shabby building we later called Independence Hall, knew the importance of that moment. In many respects they were ordinary people—and folks, I need you to hear something from me right now—whenever we need something important done, we don't go to the so-called big people, but to the ordinary people in the country. I think of the ordinary people who have saved this country, who have spoken out, who have fought for it." I stopped again.

The man in the back on the end looked down to see why I had quit speaking. I said to him, "Stonewall Jackson was one of the great generals in our history. He'd been a schoolteacher for fifteen years—done his work faithfully, been a good citizen, but when history called upon him he was able to stand up and do what destiny demanded of him, and I know he didn't understand the importance of his task, as the framers of the Constitution didn't, and as you may not at this moment. The defense wants this to be a nothing case about a nothing person—a nothing case worth nothing. But the important things are done by the little people in this country."

I told the jury a story about a caravan crossing the Sahara Desert.

The water bags of one particular camel driver who owned many camels grew fuller as the journey progressed, and the people wondered why, since theirs, of course, grew rapidly empty. Then one night someone caught the camel driver stealing small amounts of water from each of the water bags of the people, and the chieftain said to the thief, "I hereby order you to return not only the water you have stolen but also a second bag to each. A lesson must be learned—that to survive it is necessary for each of us to respect the other."

"And although there was loud crying from the thief and pointing and lame excuses and *interruptions*"—I paused again and looked at Cooper—"and wailing, the decision was just and the caravan survived."

I walked back to the jury, rested my hands on the rail, and spoke to them quietly. "This is a case of an empire builder who has abused our sacred rights under the Constitution to a free press by selling and shocking and seducing a nation of young men for money. We have a right to speak freely in this country, and it's an important right, and that is why this case is so important. You have to hear that. But you know it isn't a right that permits us to betray innocent people for fun and for entertainment and for humor and for profit." I backed away from the jury so I could raise my voice.

"They don't care." I pointed to the empty places previously occupied by Guccione and Cioffari. "Where are they now? We are looking at empty seats. They are in New York, laughing!"

Cooper, red-faced, jumped to his feet shouting, "Object and ask that that be stricken. It's not evidence!"

"The phrase 'they are laughing' may be stricken," the judge ruled.

"They wanted *you* to laugh at *her*. That is malice. They wanted you to see her with scorn and ridicule and for you to hold her up in a false light. Why not just run her down, and let her eyes pop out, and let her baton burst through her body. It would have killed her in a different way. She will never be the same. She may look the same. She may sound the same. But she isn't the same—and to them that was funny, and they want you to laugh and to drag off her bloodied and butchered soul and to jump in joy to the laughter you can hear all the way back to *Penthouse* in New York!" I stopped and surveyed my jury. I was shaking.

"We are not permitted to run over a person in the street and say, 'Well, we were doing it to entertain. We were doing if for fun and for profit.' If we run over people negligently, we pay. If we run over people negligently, *we pay*," I said again like a refrain. I spoke with my hands striking at the places, chopping and slicing at the images my voice created in the deep sounds of rage. "If we run over them reckless-*ly* and knowing-*ly* and purpose-*ly* and malicious-*ly* and intentional-*ly*, the law requires us to be punished!" The rhythms and sounds I had played to myself ten thousand times on the lonely roads and in the empty hotel rooms came singing out.

"Ladies and gentlemen, we have a right to bear arms. It's an important right to all of us, but we are not entitled to kill our neighbors for sport or for entertainment or for money. We are a free people, but the other side of our freedom is a grave responsibility not to abuse our freedom by injuring innocent folks. It's that simple, and I think you know the case *is* that simple.

"They claim that this was fiction. Who cares whether it is or not? Because the bottom line is—as you will remember from Professor Clark—it still hurts. The worst kind of libels are fiction. And the monstrous thing was to hear a man from one of our great universities say, 'It doesn't make any difference because nobody knew her.' Nobody knew her! Well, she knew who raped her. She knew she was raped emotionally not by one person but by twenty-five million people across the breadth of this land. 'We didn't mean to hurt her,' they said. That is sad and that is hollow. It is as meaningless as one who goes to church and points a gun at the congregation, and when somebody falls dead they say, 'We didn't mean to kill.' They knew what they published would hit somebody named Miss Wyoming, whether it was Kim Pring or not—they knew that when they pulled the trigger of publication. Cioffari made the bullet, but *Penthouse* pulled the trigger. It was plain, uncaring, calloused malice.

"And their formula works. They intended that people see this as real—to let the reader in on some depraved dirty joke about a real person. Take a look at the magazine—the 'Forum' letters, supposedly real—that is how they sell. Something secret, ugly, dirty that they will let the people in on."

I turned to the standing-room-only audience. I spoke to them, not the jury. "Does anyone in this room think they have the courage that this young woman has had—to deal with this—the courage to bring this litigation for purposes I think are just, and fair, and beneficial to this country?" I waited. Not a person stirred. Not a sound. Not even the sounds of breathing. It was as quiet as the forest just before the thunder. Then the thunder came.

"They said they didn't mean to hurt her! What did they *mean* to do? They really meant to sell five million magazines at two-fifty apiece, which amounts to twelve million dollars a month!

"A month!

"A month!

"A month!

"A month!

"Plus advertising at thirty-five thousand dollars a page must make a gross of about twenty million a month or gross sales of about two hundred forty million dollars a year. They admit to one hundred twenty-five million gross. That is what they meant to do! And they will publish *any* picture, *any* art, and *any* advertisement, *any* vileness to *shock* and to *seduce* and to *sell*!

"Verisimilitude! Simply—the appearance of reality. Isn't that right?" I waited for confirmation from the jurors. A couple of them nodded yes. "And they were successful! And now that they have been successful, they want out."

I walked over to the empty place once occupied by Guccione— pointed at the place. "They want to confuse"—I pointed at Cooper now—"and *interrupt*, and *slur*." Then I came back to the jury again. "But they don't want to pay the bill.

"The ultimate test of whether they were successful with their ver- iss-i-militude are the calls she got. 'Do those services to *me*.' 'Are you really as good as they say?' 'Give me head!' it said on the back of her little car—calling, day and night—calling—pointing. That is the test, ladies and gentlemen, of this ugly thing, and it isn't proved or disproved by fancy people who come from Stanford University to tell you and me how we think or how we read. I will tell you who the average people in the world are. They are you and me." I spoke al- most in a whisper now. "That is why we have juries. We don't need him to come here and tell us that."

I went over to the jury box again and spoke very softly. "The real weaponry, ladies and gentlemen, is the half-truth. It's the *half*-truth. It is like a half brick." I looked at the man in the back on the end, the coach. "We all know that you can throw a half brick twice as far as you can throw a whole brick. He"—I pointed to Guccione's empty spot—"gets a lot more mileage out of the half-truth. He creates a lot more excitement for people who read his magazine and say, 'Oh, boy! What is he going to give us next?' "

The jury waited.

The people were crowded together in the courtroom, their bodies heated by the bodies of all the others, and they breathed in what had already been exhaled and in that and other ways they soaked up each other and became one. This crowd had its own feelings, a deep unreleased yearning for violence that runs in the blood of all mobs, the same unison urge of bees in a swarm or wolves in a pack, and every person in the courtroom vaguely knew of it, felt the excitement of it. I could feel it. I retreated from it now and spoke to the jury calmly, slowly, like a good teacher.

"I am not a Miss America Pageant fan, to be honest with you, but millions are, and I knew what the pageant meant to Kim Pring—something she had worked for all her life. She wasn't Miss America—never really hoped to be. She was just proud to be Miss Wyoming and to have been there. But after that August issue she would never again be known as the best baton twirler in the United States. She wouldn't even be known as just plain Kim Pring. As long as she lives she will be known as the one they held up in infamy—as the best blowjob artist in the world—so good she could levitate men."

I walked over behind Kim and put my hands on her shoulders. "You know I love her. But, with the Lord's blessing, when I see her thirty years from now, the first thing I will think of is not that she was the greatest baton twirler in the United States, not that she was this beautiful, struggling, courageous young woman, but that damnable article will come to mind." I looked down. Kim was weeping silently, and the tears came to my eyes also. "And I tell you, ladies and gentlemen, it hurts. I have been victimized just as you have been—as everyone who knows anything about that article has been. We are all victims. Why shouldn't we be able to see her as she is, see her beauty first—see her as this decent young woman, this all-American girl? Instead we will see her as these people at *Penthouse* have portrayed her.

"Is she a public figure? They claim Miss Wyoming was a *fictional* character. But if Kim Pring is a public figure, she is a *real* person, isn't she? Fictional characters aren't public figures. Mickey Mouse isn't a public figure."

Cooper objected, "That is a misstatement of the law."

"Overruled. It's within the bounds of fair argument," the judge said.

"Tom Sawyer isn't a public figure. He doesn't walk into a courtroom, and Sherlock Holmes doesn't walk into a court and say, 'I am a public figure. I have been libeled.' Only real people walk into courts, and when they claim she is a public figure"—I pointed to Cooper and started walking toward him—"they have to admit, and it *is* an admission, an *ultimate admission* that she is a *real person* and that it was a *real person they wrote about!*"

Cooper jumped up. "I object!" he shouted. "We haven't admitted any such thing and he knows it!"

"Objection overruled." Cooper slumped back down in his chair, and began writing wildly on his yellow legal pad. I glanced at Eddie. He gave me the smallest nod that meant big things to me. Then I gave a patient look in Cooper's direction.

"Counsel will have an opportunity to answer everything I have said in just a little while. He is going to have an hour and a half to do that, and I'm splitting my time, using an hour to start with and a half an hour to close. So we both have the same amount of time.

"You know, if Kim Pring is a public figure, then every single little girl who goes to Job's Daughters and is in the national finals is a public figure—every DeMolay"—I looked at the Masons—"every kid who wrestles and becomes an AAU champ. I would hate it if this case stood for the proposition that every time one of our children succeeds, every time a Little League player goes to the nationals—all our champions also become public figures, and we are free to smear them. What great constitutional right is being preserved to permit us to smear Kim Pring and call her a public blowjob artist?"

Suddenly I asked, "What should we award in this case?"

"I have asked you if one hundred million dollars would be enough." I waited for the jury to catch up with me—to think of $100 million. I wrote the figure on the blackboard.

$100,000,000. White on black.

"I can't tell you how much Kim Pring is injured inside. We can't give her back her personality—her soul as it was. We can't remove the scars. Ladies and gentlemen, there isn't anything we can do. Every day she is going to be raped again. Usually when some careless driver runs over us and smashes us, we can recover. But every day she walks out into the world, she is smashed again—every day, all new again, over and over. Every time somebody says, 'You should do *something* for me,' every time somebody points at her and says, 'That's the one,' every time somebody stares at her, talks about her, it is no longer Kim Pring. It is an emotional rape every day of her life. If she were raped once, maybe we could talk about a million dollars. I have had people look at me and say, 'Are you crazy? Who do you think you are kidding?'

"But the question is, does it seem unreasonable that I should ask for enough money to cover the rest of her life for every one of the rapes that will occur from now on? And what of the twenty-five million emotional rapes that have already occurred? If I asked for two dollars a rape that would be fifty million dollars. Would you be ashamed if I were standing here asking a jury for that for your daughter? Would you think me unreasonable? Would you point your finger at me and say, 'That man should sit down. Nobody is entitled to that'?

"When you were chosen as jurors, the judge asked you if large sums would intimidate you, and you said under your oaths they would not. I believed that, and I heard Kim say to you that she would give back one hundred million dollars just to be like she was before, and I believed her too."

I heard a small sobbing behind me and I turned to see Kim crying. "Kim," I said. "I'm sorry I have to do this." I walked over and put both hands on her shoulders again. She continued to weep quietly with her head down. "How many of you have ever looked at other people you knew were dead inside, who looked good on the outside? Have you ever looked at a loved one in a casket? They look good on the outside.

"A part of Kim Pring is dead inside. She will never get it back. That is unrefuted in this case. I can't tell you how much that is worth and the law doesn't require me to. We know how much a car is worth or a building is worth. I say that Kim Pring is worth more than any building in this country. I wouldn't trade her for Rockefeller Center. And yet, I'll tell you this. If we ran into Rockefeller Center with a big bulldozer and knocked it down, they would want every penny of it *paid for in cash.* So I am not ashamed to ask you for substantial damages of this kind."

The man in the back on the end was listening to me carefully. I spoke to him now. "The second kind of damage in this case is punitive damage. It is to say to *Penthouse,* 'You can't do this anymore.' It's to say not only to *Penthouse* but to all publishers alike, 'You cannot do this, or you will have to pay.' "

I argued that a fine of 20 percent charged against our yearly income might be reasonable had any of us done to Kim what *Penthouse* had done—that if the paper boy made five dollars a week and ran over the little girl next door on purpose, a dollar fine against him might be just. What is a reasonable sum for an empire grossing $240 million a year? How much must be levied against *Penthouse* to stop this?

"Well, it is up to you. What's happening right here in this court-room today is about the whole publishing industry—the whole cara-van crossing the Sahara. Will we survive? Can we survive? Can our great freedom survive this kind of attack?

"What will you do to stop it?" I waited.

"Do you have the courage to stop it?" I waited again.

"Well, I think you have plenty of courage. Ordinary people have always had plenty of courage to do what must be done.

"Will your verdict be seen as a courageous act of a jury saying 'No. Not again. Never. We will not permit the abuse of our people, of our Constitution. We will not permit even the abuse of the smallest among us'? Will your verdict stand for a cautious slap on the hand—five million, ten million? 'We gave a cautious slap, yes, a timid tap to Mr. Guccione. We will plug our ears when he laughs.'

"I have no doubt about what you will do. I trust you. That is why you are here.

"And Kim Pring trusts you and a nation trusts you." I sat down.

Cooper jumped up and rushed to the podium. His face was red. He began to talk before he had his notes spread out, eager to get on with the battle, to say his say now that he had his chance. He didn't bother to check the cowlick. He began without the slightest fanfare, not even a smile, not a thank you to this jury who had been in the clutches of the law, trapped these many long and heavy days and forced into this listening so alien to them.

He said, "Counsel—ladies and gentlemen. Just another *average* closing argument in another *average* case by *average* Gerry Spence." His voice was sour and strained.

"Yes, I did indicate that there has been an emotional appeal or would be throughout this case. It's difficult to avoid bias and preju-dice against a party in this case. It's difficult to avoid sympathy for a party in this case. It's difficult to avoid the attempts to pit New York versus Wyoming. It's difficult to avoid being aware of the titters of the crowd. It's difficult to avoid all the various attempts to influence your verdict by something other than the evidence in the case. That is what makes it difficult." He was a handsome man. Now he began to sound like a man who was almost asking for the jury's understand-ing of his task.

"It's easy to do as counsel suggests." He pointed at me. "Easy to see something you don't like, to see somebody who is hurt, and say here it is—here is one hundred million dollars. That is easy. It is easy because it will make you loved by Mr. Spence. But he is right. You did take an oath to decide this case on the evidence and to ignore all of those attempts to influence you, and to decide this case with calm deliberation on the facts." The jury was listening, holding on to his words as if they had suddenly become precious. It frightened me. I wrote a note to Eddie.

"What's going on?"

He wrote back, "The jury is trying to be fair. They want to hear his side of the case. Don't worry so much. Love, Eddie."

Damn the Irish forever. Cooper was undoing my work, changing the emotional lighting in the place with his first few words, stirring up different feelings in my jury—covering up my canvas, changing the good sounds, destroying the entire mood of the trial I had taken these three weeks to build. And the Irish, sitting calmly over there, relaxed, tell me the jury is trying to be fair and I should keep the faith. Damn the Irish.

I glanced at Kim. She looked like a small girl who had just been hauled in half frozen from a blizzard, and I could hear the ever-blowing wind of winter beating on the cornices of the building.

I heard the sounds of Cooper's voice. I listened as much to his sounds as to his words. The meaning is not always carried in the words, and as I listened I suddenly heard a change. The tone went dead, dull, as if the sounding board had been split and half the strings cut, and what was left was a lumbering noise, like the slow, non-rhythmical beating against the back door in the night. If you listen, you can hear the argument being made in the sounds alone, and in the beat, and the sounds speak the truth despite the words, and when the words and the sounds and the beat of the sounds do not harmonize, when they each speak a different message, then we do not believe the words anymore because the meaning of the sounds is different from the words, and what the sounds tell us always prevails.

Cooper said, "I will start by assuming that you are going to award a sum, for the purpose of argument at this point, and I'll talk about the type of calm deliberation I think is needed under our system of justice. It doesn't mean that I grant you she is entitled to damages—I will cover those reasons later." He said that as for punitive damages, *Penthouse*'s profits were only $14 million, and out of that has to come income tax. "Punishment sounds like a crime," he said, and $25 or $50 thousand is what oil and gas companies are required to pay for punishment. "Let's talk about the so-called compensatory or actual damages. There is no question that there can be substantial damages for nonphysical harm just as there can be damages for physical harm when it is actually suffered and when it's not caused by your own acts.

"We have heard a lot in this case about permanent scarring of the soul, and I think it's necessary to calmly deliberate and keep things in perspective. There are a lot of people in the world who are born without Kim Pring's assets, don't have her good looks"—he spoke to the women in front, this very handsome man—"who don't have a mother who will make it so she can pursue her individual goals to the extent that she doesn't have to do housework. There are a lot of people who are plain-looking"—he still spoke to the women—"who clean house and work hard, who suffer all kinds of embarrassment and humiliation, who suffer all kinds of things with kids in college, emotionally unpleasant things without any stories being written about them in *Penthouse*, and who still live full lives and never recover money from anyone." Would he take the women with his argument?

He claimed Kim had caused much of her own damage. "You will recall when she got off the birth-control pills, the emotional problems seemed to calm down." He had to get that in. "And the prescription for Tagamet wasn't refilled." He claimed she had not seen Dr. Howdeshell for treatment, and she hadn't obtained an unlisted phone number as suggested by her own physician, and she herself had been guilty of spreading the story.

"Was this done to help the lawsuit so that a year later she could say, everybody is talking about me? Or was it done because of the emotional needs that counsel implies? Does it matter? No. She can't recover for her failure to minimize her own damages," he said, as if everyone understood the clear justice of his position. "It's not reasonable to spread the word to other people and make the identification of yourself in a fictional story and then come into court and ask for one hundred million dollars." His words carried the sound of disgust. And disgust invaded his own handsome face.

He argued the plaintiff had to prove something other than a dislike for *Penthouse*. The Constitution required that, and he said it made him angry when I had made fun of Professor Clark's testimony and turned my back on him. He said, "If it's a test of imagination in coming up with the similarities between the story and Miss Pring, then I guarantee I lose. Mr. Spence has a tremendous one." He recited my list of similarities—They were, after all, what one would expect in any writing about a baton twirler, about that stereotype, and then he emphasized the differences.

"And remember, this large number of copies that are sold—they are all bought by people, not delivered to the front door, not shoved down anybody's throat, but to people who go out to the newsstand and buy them. They don't purchase them to read in a courtroom, or on television in the public glare. They purchase them for reading in the locker rooms, if you will, or in the barbershop. It's just a little perspective and context that needs to be kept." Now his sounds matched the words when he said it was obvious that Kim had enjoyed being in the pageant and had a right to enjoy it. "But it wasn't her right to impose her values on everyone.

"Now I've written some things up on the board, since Mr. Spence has talked about one-hundred million dollars." Cooper argued that $35 to $70 thousand would be a more than adequate sum *if*, and only *if*, anything had to be awarded. "I would suggest that those are top amounts. If you analyze what one hundred thousand dollars is, at ten percent, that is ten thousand dollars a year, forever! And you still have one hundred thousand left to give to your children at the end." He spoke to one of the women in the front—the one on the end.

He argued that the instructions of the judge would require proof that *Penthouse* had a "high degree of awareness that the article would be understood as portraying real events about real people" and that it would have to be proved by "clear and convincing evidence." Then he said, "You don't have to be a politician to be a public figure. If you go out and voluntarily attract public attention to yourself, you accomplish two things: You become widely known, and you get certain access to the channels of communication."

Outside I could hear the wind gusting at the cornices of the courthouse, a cold wind blowing.

Cooper reviewed the evidence of Kim's public appearance right down to her applications for the National Miss Black Velvet contest. She had access to the press if she wanted to complain about the *Penthouse* story. She'd gotten herself on the front cover of *Rocky Mountain Magazine*, hadn't she? "Mr. Pierson testified he doesn't know who the governor of Wyoming is. Does that mean he isn't a public figure?"

Finally he spoke of Cioffari. "If he had been malicious, he could have written about her boyfriend who committed suicide or sexual relations at age nineteen or things of this type." Cooper was arguing to the women again. "There are a lot of private facts that are not in that story."

The most the plaintiff's case showed was that the people at *Penthouse* hadn't made a phone call to find out if Miss Wyoming was a baton twirler. "That is not outrageous. It might be negligence," he admitted, but added, "There is no evidence to support this case other than the loud voice and gestures and facial actions of Mr. Spence. Voltaire, who gave rise in many ways to the American Declaration of Independence, said, 'I may disapprove of what you say, but I will defend to the death your right to say it.' The First Amendment applies to everyone, not just *Penthouse*. The right to say what we please, even with bad literature, is something, which if lost, leads to what we've seen in this trial. Only one set of values is permitted. If it isn't all favorable, if it isn't all caring about Miss Pring, then it's outside the set of acceptable values." He sounded sarcastic again, and he looked to the women, and they looked back at him.

"What's going on?" I wrote to Eddie.

"They're listening," he wrote back. For Christ's sakes, I knew that. But was he getting to the women?

"What about the woman up front on the end?" I wrote Eddie.

"She's listening," he wrote back. Goddamn it. I looked at Kim. She was listening.

Cooper didn't need all the jurors to vote for him—not even a majority. If he could convince one woman, just one—if the man on the end in the back voted against us, *Penthouse* would win because the verdict had to be unanimous.

Cooper argued on and I lost the thread in the tangle of words and in the flat sounds that no longer carried any message to me. I thought how strange—this was a case about a woman and women's rights—about the unabated persecution of women down through the evil ages and into this very courtroom—and here we were, this strong man defending against the claim of a good young woman, not even a confessed witch, and he was laying odds that the older, plainer women would hold against their own sex, perhaps out of envy, perhaps out of the alleged pettiness that women exercise against themselves because pettiness has always been exercised against them. I thought he relied on his own obvious appeal to the women, this strong, muscular man with the square jaw and fortunate features. Perhaps they would follow him the way the herd follows the dominant young bull. What part of justice is in the glands?

He argued that Kim Pring had denied ever telling anybody she had "finally made *Penthouse*," but when Mrs. Cenedese came in, Kim suddenly remembered, and then Spence had made it look as if Mrs. Cenedese was only reaching out to a friend. "Do you remember the emotion and the smokescreen?" Cooper asked. "And *Gente*—she had never seen an issue of *Gente!*

" 'Are you sure?' 'No, I never saw one.' But when she was faced with a witness who had overheard her and her attorney, then she admitted seeing the cover of the magazine." He said the words "the cover" with disdain, and, with disdain again, he said, looking at me, "and there was an examination by her counsel about that *darn eavesdropper.*"

The psychiatrist didn't bring in her reports, "and counsel was very critical of me pointing out this one passage in the notes. It says, '1975, nineteen, first sex,' and then four names and dates, and you will remember initially that she had her first sex at nineteen"—there it was again—"and had indicated these *four.* Then under cross-examination you will recall that the statement was made that this was only the first time she ever *learned* about sex!" He gave a haughty shake of his head and looked at the women in front again. "I'm pointing to these things not to embarrass anybody, including Miss Pring, but to talk about the way in which you have to analyze the credibility of witnesses in a case where they are asking for this kind of money.

"What psychiatric significance would there be in a person learning about sex for the first time at nineteen in today's world? And why weren't these notes brought in in the first place?" He was still going to make me eat those damned notes. "Would a person who was first learning of sex at her age know the language she has used during the course of this trial?"

The testimony about the seating capacity of the pageant was a "neat little trick" to make it look like Cioffari was there on an earlier night. She wouldn't have noticed. She would have been watching what was happening on the stage. "One of the things you have to consider in analyzing credibility is motivation—even one hundred thousand dollars is a lot of motivation, and if you lose the pageant, one hundred million is more than any of the winners got." The big money was getting talked about.

"Why the colors? Why the stretching from powder-blue to turquoise?" he asked. Cooper walked over and picked up the dress and displayed it to the ladies like an anxious store clerk. Was it really blue? I'll admit there was a greenish cast to her chiffon evening dress.

Kim whispered, "That looks blue to me." Her eyes were so tired.

Eddie drew his doodles. One of the women up front watched him, fascinated.

Cooper said he thought Dr. Cline's testimony that Kim would never be able to pick up a baton again was only the reflection of a man who saw things differently from most, accounting, no doubt, for his having been with the minority on the committee that reported to the president on pornography, "because he has a rather singular view of people and their sensibilities." Cooper looked down at his notes.

"And Professor Wideman was a well-qualified man who testified to the theme of the plaintiff's case, namely, that you must avoid gratuitous harm, but I finally got him to admit that literature often is intended to *do harm* and it's still good literature." Cooper surveyed the jury as if he had made the big point. I could hear the occasional coughs from the audience, the movement of bodies, the slight sounds that tell of a restlessness. I looked at their faces, faces reflecting the flat sounds they heard. "Professor Wideman thought it was all right to go after bigshots and white cops, but not after people who were important to him, like a University of Wyoming student," Cooper said.

"Many people live sheltered lives. As people grow up and go out in the real world we all are forced to accept the adversities that go with us in life and still go about our daily lives. But the desire for public acclaim plays an important role in this case." I began to draw doodles of my own.

"The people who made the calls might have done so for the reasons suggested by Dr. Clark, not because of the story but perhaps students were jealous of her as they watched her perform in front of the crowds.

"It's a pretty simple factual case," he finally admitted. "Whether or not you like that magazine, you have to decide this case on the *issues*. This is not a situation where we all get on Mr. Spence's team and get even with somebody because we are all victims of the magazine." The sounds in Cooper's voice turned mean. They were malicious sounds, like a dog snarling at small rabbits. Then Cooper fell back again to calling it a case with "complicated factual issues that have been made more complicated by emotion, and which can be solved solely by calm deliberation, cool analysis, and the answer of no to Question Number *Two*. Thank you for your attention and your consideration," he said, and sat down.

Judge Brimmer called the noon recess.

Kim's mother brought us all sandwiches. I swallowed mine in huge bestial gulps, like a ravenous dog, but I wasn't hungry. I swallowed whole unchewed mouthfuls, washed them down half a sandwich at a time with half a can of apple juice to the swallow.

"I'm gonna kill him," I said. Kim was over in the corner of the room, looking first exhausted, then frightened. Her mother still had that pleasant smile on her face.

"Here, Mr. Spence," Mrs. Pring said. "You have to eat. You worked very hard, and you have more work to do yet." She put another sandwich on my plate and I tore into it. "You have to keep up your strength."

"I'm gonna kill him," I said, chewing, pacing.

"You don't need to kill 'em," Eddie said, also chewing. "He's already dead."

"I'm gonna choke the last breath out of him," I said. "Watch me." Kim gave Eddie a worried look.

"He's all right," Eddie said. "He's just gettin' himself up for his closing argument." Then Eddie came over and pulled up a chair and looked up into my face.

"Gerry, all you have to do is go in there and bring home the money. Sweep it up in baskets. Fill up all the sacks. Only problem is we ain't got enough bags to put all the money in you're gonna get. He's admitted there's money due. He tried to confuse the jury, but they're not gonna be confused. He figures if he can get off for one hundred thousand he's won the case—if he gets off for two hundred he's happy as hell. He's opened up the safe door. Go in there and sweep out all the money. We got 'em."

I looked at Eddie for a long minute. He was serious.

29

"Are you feeling pretty good?" I asked the jury right after lunch—my stomach was fresh gut stretched over a drum, my expression pleasant enough for a man who wanted to kill. Then I began quietly, like a man swimming at sea who was calmly working a deadly cramp out of his belly.

"I want to know if you noticed that during Mr. Cooper's final argument I didn't object at all? I thought he should be given a fair opportunity to talk to you about his case without interruptions, which really stop the flow of thought and feeling. I have thirty-three minutes to talk to you about something that has to last Kim for the rest of her life. I trust that Mr. Cooper will show me the same courtesy for my last minutes with you.

"This *is* a simple case. Never once did we hear him say 'Ladies and gentlemen, I deny that Kim Pring was libeled' or 'We deny there was an invasion of privacy' or that this was outrageous. Do you know why we didn't hear that? Because his own witnesses admitted it all, and so there was nothing left for him to do but confuse and interrupt and to make his slurs against Kim Pring." I could feel the power coming back, the blessed power. The juices were beginning to flow again.

I walked over to Cooper's table and stood behind him, both of us facing the jury now, me standing, Cooper sitting in front of me. His head was turned down. I said, "I don't want to imply that Mr. Cooper here isn't a nice young man, because Mr. Cooper is a nice young man, and he has done a good job, and, indeed, Mr. Cooper is going to have a good case someday, and when he does, he will win." The whole courtroom burst into sudden laughter. I could see Cooper's neck in front of me growing red against the white collar.

"I don't mean to be funny," I said, "nor to make fun of Mr. Cooper. He is a good trial lawyer brought in from Denver, Colorado,

386

with his partner here to represent these people. He has done an
excellent job throughout this trial, and he needs to be congratulated and not made fun of. He is an honorable colleague of the bar,
and I have been proud to be involved in this litigation with him. So
I want to be sure that you hear me say that. What I'm saying is that
had Mr. Cooper sat over here at this table representing Kim Pring,
the results would be the same. Our styles are different, as you can
see. I get criticized for mine because I speak out of my feelings, because I think I have a right to feel about this case and share those
feelings with you, and you have a right to feel. Anytime somebody
says to you that you shouldn't feel, that you are not entitled to be
whole, that you are not entitled to be a human being, that you are
not entitled to understand hurt and pain, that you are not entitled to
communicate it, or think about it, or feel—then I guess they are saying you are not entitled to be alive." I walked back in front of the
jury box. The jurors calmly watched me come. They were open to
me.

"Now I heard Mr. Cooper say he thought *Penthouse* acted innocently. I wonder why he said that? People can say about anything
they want to in a courtroom. Let's look at the conduct of *Penthouse*
that is claimed to be innocent. What did they really sell here?

"They sold her.

"They sold her to twenty-five million people. Was that an innocent sale?

"They sold her so that those twenty-five million people believed it.
They call it verisimilitude—the appearance of reality. Does that
sound innocent?

"They sold her body.

"And her morals.

"They sold her to cause laughter, and Guccione on this witness
stand"—I walked to the witness chair and sat where Guccione had
sat—"Guccione said from here that he laughed, even knowing in his
own mind that there was a *real person* called Miss Wyoming."

I sat looking at the jury, and then I said from the stand, "They sold
her privacy, ladies and gentlemen." I spoke quietly to them now.
"That is something that belongs to each one of us. It belongs to you,
and to you and to you and to you and to you and to you." I looked at
each juror. "It belongs to you! It isn't for sale.

"They sold her dignity," I said in a whisper.

Then I got down from the stand and walked back to the jury box and I said, "We try to teach our young people—put them in sports, teach them to compete, to be courageous. We give them dignity to be solid human beings and then *they*"—I pointed to the empty place where Guccione had sat—"*they* sell it! I'm not supposed to get emotional about that, but it hurts me. They sell it to twenty-five million readers who pick up that magazine and say, 'Well, let's see what Miss Wyoming did,' and they laugh and guffaw. I never heard anyone say, 'We're sorry.' I only saw them point their fingers at her, and when she picked up her head two or three times in this case, they struck at her again. To see Mr. Cooper do that hurt me.

"Did you see how he just happened to mention about the birth-control pills? It was a prescription given during the time she was expecting to be married. There is no evidence that the prescription was ever filled. But I guess that means she is a bad woman. Was that just to further embarrass her?" I turned to Kim, and pointed at her. "Don't you dare raise up your head, Kim. Don't you dare say a thing against Mr. Guccione. Don't you dare say anything because we will knock you down.

"Suppose Kim Pring was the most immoral woman in the world—that she had slept with the entire football team." I looked up at the judge. "Does that make any difference? Her reputation was good. We are all entitled to our privacy, isn't that true?

"It hurts me when they take things like this." I held up the psychiatrist's notes. " 'First sex, nineteen.' I'm not going to suggest to you that she is or isn't a virgin. That isn't an issue. It's none of my business. What kind of a person would I be if I asked her and what kind of persons are they to go into it?

"But these notes don't say she had sex with four boyfriends. The notes say, '*Dated* Dave, Bill, Bob, and Charlie.' She dated Dave a year. She dated Bill three years. Bob was the one who committed suicide. And her current boyfriend is Charlie. Now that is the last five years, folks, but that isn't the way it was told to you. When she lifted her head up and provided the notes, they said, 'Look! It's dirty!' And when we didn't provide the notes, then it was 'Look! You are hiding something!'

"If you go to a friend for comfort, as she did to Mrs. Cenedese, then you are guilty of spreading the rumors. If your friend embraces you, as Mrs. Cenedese did Kim as she left this court, then it's a show. Is that fair?

"If you are libeled and you sue, then you hurt yourself. If you don't

sue, then you are still hurt, and you have given up your right to justice. Do you think that is fair?

"If all your witnesses say what you say, then you all must have
gotten together and made up a story. But if your witnesses don't
agree with you, then obviously you must be lying. *Either way you
lose.* Interestingly enough, that is the name of a story authored by
Mr. Cioffari.

"If you are a person who is well known, then you are a public figure and we can smear you unless you prove malice, and if you are not
a public figure, no one is interested in you, no one heard of you, and
therefore, how could you be hurt? *Either way you lose.*

"If you claim we were talking about you when we said you committed public oral sex, we will say, 'It wasn't you. It was only fiction.'
And if you say it sure wasn't me—I didn't do such a thing, then they
argue you weren't hurt. *Either way you lose.* These are the arguments counsel made. He made them skillfully and I congratulate
him. But I don't think he believed them and I call them to your attention because I don't think you do either." I stopped a moment,
turned my back to the jury, and looked at Cooper. He stared back,
waiting.

"And you know, they want us to put all the blame for twenty-five
million emotional rapes on one poor little boy who five years ago
committed suicide." The words were sad words. I asked my jury—
they were *my* jury—they had always been *my* jury—"How does that
grab you? How does that make you feel? Do you think that is fair?

"She was on the cover of *Gente*. There it is." I held the magazine
up. "She is good enough for me. She is good enough for Wyoming—
her picture there with the consent of her chaperones. Now they want
to say that she is a bad woman. And counsel mentioned that he
wanted you to answer Interrogatory Number Two, 'No.' It asks the
question: 'Is Kim Pring the person referred to in the article?'—well,
if it wasn't she, then she didn't get all those telephone calls and she
didn't get hounded and harassed and pointed at—none of that happened and they didn't recognize it was her, and all of this has been
for nothing and we should all just go home."

I told the jury that *Penthouse* was using poor Cioffari, that if they
hadn't used him, they would have used someone else. He made the
bullet, I said, and he should pay for it, but "I'm not going to tell you
how much. You should be humane. You don't punish Cioffari to the
same extent as you do a person who is making one hundred twenty-

five million dollars a year gross or who builds sixty-million-dollar motels and casinos and can produce sixty million over and over as long as the wheels churn and suckers come to that Penthouse casino. And so I ask you to be just, just with Cioffari, just with Guccione, and if we are talking about being just, let's look at whether or not counsel has been fair. He thinks you should give Kim thirty-five to seventy thousand dollars for her damages." I turned to the audience. "Is there anybody here who would, as humble as we may be, trade their reputation for seventy thousand dollars?"

Cooper jumped up. "Objection. That is not a proper measure of damages."

"Sustained," the judge said.

I looked at Eddie. He made a little scoop with his hand and moved it on the table—the safe is open.

"Does that strike you as being fair and just? He wanted to say maybe give her one hundred thousand dollars. Then guess what he did? He forgot punitive damages. Based on the twenty-five million people who read that magazine—figure it out—it took me half the noon hour to get the decimal point right—one hundred thousand dollars amounts to four tenths of a cent per rape. That's pretty cheap rape nowadays, folks. Pretty cheap rape he wants." I began filling the money bags. "My request to you is for four dollars a rape. That's pretty cheap, too, but it amounts to one hundred million. A hundred thousand dollars? I would like to just walk over here with the hundred thousand dollars they have offered to us and give it to Mr. Guccione." I walked to the empty spot in the courtroom and held out both hands with the supposed money. "Here, Mr. Guccione, is your hundred thousand dollars. Don't give us one hundred thousand dollars," I said to the imaginary man seated in front of me. I turned back to the jury. "It would belie the dignity of that human being to do that." I pointed to Kim. "It would be a license to Mr. Guccione to go out and do it over and over again. It would be an invitation—like with Reverend Falwell—Guccione sort of thought these lawsuits helped—and what is twenty million dollars?

"It is about one month's gross revenues from that magazine. Would twenty million stop him? That is one month's pay from just the magazine alone—not from the gambling casinos, not from anything else, just from that magazine. If somebody docked you a month's pay for having done what *Penthouse* did, I think maybe we could agree that under the circumstances that would be inadequate."

Then I stood behind Kim and put my hands on her shoulders again.

"Well, folks, this is like a time-release pill for her. It's like a huge capsule that she takes and inside are those little pills and when she starts to get well somebody points at her or somebody calls, and then another pill begins to dissolve and her stomach is filled with the poison again. It happens over and over.

"Guccione says, 'We can do what we want to. We can destroy people.' He will say after a jury accepts the position of my colleague, Mr. Cooper, 'Yes, the jury says, we approve.' He'll say, 'Yes, the jury says, we agree.' Yes, Yes, Mr. *Penthouse*, you can do that. Yes, you can smear and you can sell for money. Yes! *Penthouse!* Yes!"

Then I moved back from the jury and let all of the power come rolling out that had built up during these months of fury and fighting and frustration. "They understand just one thing—nothing about marriage, and family, and decent humble sensitivity, and plain old-fashioned rightness. Theirs is an empire built on mon-*ey*—that lives for mon-*ey* and breathes mon-*ey* and longs for mon-*ey* and sleeps and eats and cries for mon-*ey* and digests mon-*ey* and loves only mon-*ey*. It is a false empire that can be stopped only by awarding mon-*ey*—substantial mon-*ey*. This empire will not hear the cries, nor listen to the smashed souls. It won't listen to anyone. It will do nothing. And when somebody raises her head, it will strike back at her, and if Kim Pring says anything more, they strike at her again!" I filled the room.

"Money will stop it! You take the money of that corporation and you take its life and its love and its purpose for being, and it will finally listen, and it will hear, and that is what punitive damages are all about!"

I stopped. It was time to end the battle, to go home, to leave these good people whom I had grown to respect. I felt sad. "I am about to leave you, folks." Then I smiled at them. "I have good news for you. Very good news. If you get confused by lawyers and legal talk, remember there is one wonderful thing that God gave us all, and he gave it particularly to a jury—the greatest thing any person has—common sense.

"Now I'm closing." I waited like a man about to say his last good-byes. "Great things don't happen in marbled halls and in rich palaces and in penthouses. They happen in humble courtrooms like this one. I know, folks, you have a great commitment to do the right thing, and I know you feel uncomfortable with this terrible power, but you have been given enough power by the law—enough to stop this—here and across this country.

"And the wrong? Well, somebody has to stop the wrong. You've sworn to do your duty and I know it isn't going to be easy for you. It hasn't been easy for Kim Pring and it hasn't been easy for us. We've carried this burden and we've all done our jobs. And—" I waited. I walked up to the jury. I looked at each of them. They were my friends. Suddenly I felt great love for them, and then I said, "And now in this courtroom in Cheyenne, Wyoming, at twelve minutes till two, I pass that torch on to you."

I sat down and put my hand over Kim's for just a moment. Her hand was wet. Eddie reached over and gave me a small squeeze around the shoulder, and that was it. Cooper and Kelley sat as stiff as strutting pigeons, their eyes hard and bright. They would have fought on had they been given the chance. They were men with strong wills, men who would not give up. They were good fighters.

Then the judge did his duty and read his instructions on the law to the jury, which sounded vaguely relevant, I admit, but I was too exhausted to hunt for their meaning, and my mind was washed away with the sounds, and the message from the sounds of the judge's voice was clear—that the law is solemn, overriding, omnipotent, that the law is as sacred as the word of God. The jury listened carefully, and the jurors looked like they understood every word, but I understood nothing of what the judge read. I only heard the sounds of God.

Afterward the bailiff took the jury away to begin their deliberations.

I can no longer remember clearing the courtroom of our things, the dozen boxes the size of apple crates with the files and exhibits, the television, the briefcases and books that were stacked on and around the table, even on the floor. But we always did that miserable chore then because we were afraid that if we lost the case, we wouldn't have the courage or the strength left to do our packing later. Perhaps we would have only the bare energy to run like any beaten warrior runs away from a place of blood.

I can remember pacing the floor in my motel room sometime later, waiting. I remember mostly the sleepless, unrelenting pain of my exhaustion. I couldn't sit. I was too tired to pace. I can remember that ceiling in the room, a heavy lifeless eternal swirl above, in which I was only an empty speck sucked up and crushed into the grist of an endless, mindless, soulless universe of plaster and sparkle where heaven was a cheap reproduction of a painting of some soft romantic forest scene with flowers and two butterflies. And as I looked up into my space, I counted the glass crystals on the small chandelier hanging over the table—fourteen and two missing. Who would steal two cheap glass crystals, for Christ's sakes? I felt sick, but I was too tired to be sick.

I remember Eddie trying not to pace, trying to be genial, Irish, and optimistic, trying to bring good humor into that dreary room where we told the clerk she could find us when the jurors had their verdict.

"Why haven't they come in yet?" I said. "Christ, it was a simple case. Did Cooper get them confused? I mean, that was his only defense."

"It was a long trial," Eddie said. "Lotta evidence to go over—lotta exhibits."

Kim said, "Well, you did good, Mr. Spence, and no matter how it comes out, you did just right. I felt so proud that you were my lawyer." What the hell could I say back? I couldn't even feel the pleasure of the compliment. I felt helpless again.

I said, "Thanks," and then to myself I said, God, if I can just win this one I won't take any more cases like this, I'll clean up my act, I'll—I said out loud, "Why doesn't this jury come in?" Then the phone rang, but it wasn't the clerk of court. It was the newspaper wanting to know why the jury hadn't reached a verdict yet, because it was long past suppertime and that ought to be enough time for them to come to a decision, and did I think the jury was hung?

I said, "Some of them are hung and some of them aren't."

And the press man said I was being a smart bastard, and I said for him to go fuck himself, too.

Then the phone rang again, and it was the clerk saying that the jury was going to go home and they'd start deliberations again in the morning. Kim went home too. I can't remember when Mrs. Pring had left, but I think early. She had her family responsibilities.

Eddie and I went to bed, but I couldn't sleep. I argued the case over and over like the waves washing a rotten body ashore, the waves pounding out the arguments, wave on wave, endlessly, world without end, amen.

God, let me win this one.

Why do you want to win?

It hurts too much to lose. I don't want to win to win. I just don't want to feel the pain of losing. Just let me win this one. Just let me win a little. Give us the hundred grand. I'll take it. Give us the thirty-five to seventy thousand Cooper offered. I'll take it. I'll take the thirty-five. But don't let me lose. Even let the jury hang—I'll try it again. But don't let me lose. I can't stand the pain of losing.

Well, you told the jury the truth. You told the jury that he who lives by the word dies by the word—and the "he" is you.

I know, I said. But let it be later—not now. Later. Please. Not today. Not this case.

Before you can become a whole man, you will have to learn to lose. Only a half a man has learned just to win. Winning is only half.

There's all kinds of freaks in the world. Let me be a winning freak.

You are a coward.

Let me be a winning coward.

You are disgusting. Everybody loses.

It doesn't hurt everybody like it hurts me.

It hurts everybody.

They're more used to it.

Then you're overdue.

I don't deserve to lose. I had the best case. We were right.

You're not the judge of that.

"I'm a terrible loser," I said to Eddie the next morning first thing before we were even out of bed. "I can't stand it—I'm not even a good sport."

"You know the old saying," Eddie said, and he looked like he'd wrestled with the devil all night himself and like the rats had sucked on his hair and gnawed on him at secret places under the covers. He looked beat. He gave me a platitude: "Show me a good loser and I'll show you a loser." He tried to laugh, and later he tried to get me to eat.

Then Kim met us again for the agonizing wait, and as the time went on our chances worsened, as the passage of time mounts against the patient in the operating room.

"Jesus Christ, why isn't the jury in?" I asked anyone who would answer. It was half past noon of the second day. Eddie wasn't laughing much anymore. Kim was looking drawn, aged as if by witchery, her eyes faded a full shade lighter, her hair hung like old hemp, her shoulders slack, her head sagging, her one foot turned in. She hadn't slept. Her voice was empty. She plopped down on the bed. She had been raped, I thought. They could have asked her that question now.

Finally Kim spoke to the ceiling. "It's just that if we don't win, then everybody will think what they said about me was all true." She didn't say anything more for a long time, and when I looked at her, she tried to smile and I tried to smile back. She wasn't used to losing either. "Well, I believe in the jury," she finally said like some dying person reaffirming her faith in God.

"You all act like we lost the case already," Eddie said. "We're not gonna lose it."

"Well, the longer the jury deliberates, usually the worse it is for the plaintiff," I said. I should start preparing Kim. "The jury gets hung up and the more they argue, the more it costs us. The longer it takes, the smaller our chances—and if we win at all, it probably won't be very much. The big verdicts come in fast because everybody's clear on the justice of it, and clear on the money too. I think we're in trouble," I said.

"No," Eddie said. "We're not in trouble. *They* are. The jury hasn't decided this case for *Penthouse* yet and they've been deliberatin' all this time. There's a lot of instructions and they're complicated and the trial took a long time. This is a good, thorough jury. They're sincere. You gotta give 'em time to do their job."

"Big verdicts—short time," I said again.

"That makes as much sense as big feet, big peter," Eddie said. Kim tried to laugh. "It's okay," Eddie said. "You heard Cooper. Kim doesn't know any words like that. That's right, huh, Kim?"

"What words?" Kim said. Then she did laugh.

"No," Eddie said. "The jury was out for three days in the Silkwood case, remember? We thought we'd lost it for sure. They have to agree on the answers to every question unanimously—every question on that verdict form! And the amount too. That takes a lot of time, and everybody has to talk. They got a lot to say to each other."

Then the phone rang again and I jumped. But it was the hotel clerk wanting to know if we were going to check out today or tomorrow, and I said we were going to stay here forever and hung up.

"I wish you didn't worry so much," Kim said, and I wished so, myself, and I wished I could take the pain of waiting better. I wished I were as selfless as this young woman who had a better sense of things, a better balance than I. I thought, Jesus Christ, why can't she just be a raging bitch for once? I'd feel better. Why can't she be a mean, sniveling, selfish slut so I could tell her to go to hell, that I didn't give a shit whether she won or lost.

"I wish you weren't so nice," I said to Kim. Then I laughed it off. And she laughed too, like a nice person would. She understood me, I thought. I was just a big little boy. I said, "I wish you had never been

Miss Wyoming and gone to the pageant and learned how to be so sweet and good."

She smiled again—her big Miss America smile.

"Well, damn it," I said. "This is the worst part of every trial because it's the time I finally have to let somebody else decide my client's fate—and my fate, and I don't like that," I said. I began pacing again. Time always creeps when it drags so much misery behind it.

Time crept and Jesus wept.

Then, sometime later, I can't remember how much later, the clerk of court was on the phone. They had a verdict.

"At least they aren't hung," I said, rushing out the door to the car. I suppose Kim was right behind. I didn't look.

I can't remember the drive to the courthouse the way I can't remember other terrible times in my life. I can't even remember walking into the courthouse. I saw Kelley's face. I remember he looked like a fraternity boy who had just hazed the shit out of some freshman. Cooper was there. He still looked like Superman. The judge came in. He wouldn't look at me. I always suspected he had some secret line to the jury—maybe through the bailiff who listened at the door or something. He probably knew it was going to be bad for me and he couldn't bear to look at me.

We took our places at counsel table. Maybe we could survive it. I didn't know. I couldn't think. Then the jury came in. I was afraid to look at their faces because there is always a clue in them. If they decide against you they won't look at you. Can't. Finally I saw the man in the back row on the end glance at Cooper. My heart stopped. He wouldn't look at me. The women in the front row wouldn't look at me either. Then, when the judge asked if they had reached a verdict, the *other man* in the back row got up. *He* was the foreman! He was a surprise to me. I hadn't paid much attention to him during the trial. My God! I had practically ignored this man and now he was the foreman! He held the verdict in his hand. He seemed calm enough. Why didn't he scream it out?

"Yes, we have reached a verdict," the foreman answered. He was younger looking than his years, I knew that. He had nicely combed black hair. He handed the verdict to the clerk, and the clerk handed the verdict to the judge, and I could feel my heart pounding away, and I thought, this is how I will die some time for sure—waiting for the verdict to be read. The judge turned the pages deliberately, slowly. He was inscrutable. He wouldn't look at me—not even a quick blink, and I sat practically in front of him.

He handed the verdict back to the clerk. "The clerk will read the verdict," the judge said very coolly.

The clerk cleared her throat.

Now she began to read ever so slowly—beginning first with the caption of the case. I thought of running up there and snatching the verdict out of her goddamned hands. I'll read it myself. Get to the questions. The questions! Then I heard the answer to the first question, and the second. Yes, the article was about Kim Pring! They were answering the questions right. Yes. Yes. Yes. There was an invasion of privacy. Yes. They found the outrage. They found it all. All of it for us! And the money?

The clerk read, "And we do find for the plaintiff and against the defendant Cioffari in the amount of ten thousand dollars and for the plaintiff, Kimerli Jayne Pring, and against Penthouse International in the amount of one million five hundred thousand dollars and we assess punitive damages against Philip Cioffari in the amount of twenty-five thousand dollars and assess punitive damages against Penthouse in the amount of twenty-five million dollars. Signed, Foreman."

Our table erupted. Kim hugged me and was crying, and Eddie and I were pounding each other on the back like we were trying to hurt each other, and Eddie was crying, and the crowd burst through the bar and filled the courtroom with cheers, like in the movies, and then and there, when I needed to the most, I found out I couldn't cry— not a single tear.

"I can't cry," I said to Eddie, who was weeping away.

"Well, then laugh," Eddie cried, and so I laughed, and then Eddie stopped crying and laughed, too, and Kim laughed until it was all out of us.

But these were not the last laughs.

No. Not the last laughs at all.

30

Kim Pring grabbed hold of my arm, thereby transforming us into that strange-looking couple, both in high heels, she with her blond hair done up loosely on top of her head, and mine, not nearly so blond and with gray at the edges, leaking out from under my Stetson. Overnight she seemed to have magically recovered, a young woman now as wholesome and healthy as milk and honey and, except for the way she walked, she looked like a sweet Mormon miss holding onto some derelict old enough to be her father. Up close I could see the transformation had been mostly the magic of brush and powder. Then she grabbed Eddie by the arm, Eddie who also wore his boots and hat, and we boarded the plane as a strange-looking threesome.

At Denver we took a direct flight for New York City. I glanced at Kim, who with vacant eyes gazed out the window across the uninteresting patterns below I knew to be the eastern plains of Colorado, that godforsaken place where my Grandpa Pfleeger struggled against the wind that hated his hard eyes, that beat at them with gales of dust, that hated the land and blew the dust to the tops of the fence posts. And Grandpa Pfleeger stood up against the wind and fought the jackrabbits that ate every shoot of every crop he tried to grow, that ate every last sprig of grass from the dying prairies and let the cattle starve. They shot the jacks by the hundreds, my grandpa and my uncles. At night when their bones were aching, they went out killing in Grandpa's old Buick, one of my uncles sitting on each front fender, and as Grandpa drove they blasted the damned jacks with their shotguns by the light of the headlamps, and made half a sport out of that which was wholly desperate.

They hauled in the carcasses to a small, quiet, kind-eyed woman, my Grandma Pfleeger, whose voice was like an angel's voice with a heavy German brogue. She put the rabbits—heads, guts, hides, and all—into the pressure cooker and built up a hell of a fire on the old woodburner, and the heat and the hissing of the pressure cooker and the stink drove everybody but her out of the kitchen. Then after she'd cooked up the night's kill, there was enough chicken feed for a week.

They lived off of the chickens and squeezed milk out of a few old Herefords, a cup at a time. Everything came hard. When some old cancer-eyed cow got too bad, they butchered her before she died, and Grandma cooked up as much of the meat as she could in that pressure cooker of hers and canned the rest.

Then I was a small boy, walking close to the ground, with my eyes squinted almost closed against the blowing dust. The only flowers I saw, or that were to be seen in fifty miles, were Grandma's moss roses growing along the walk to the front door of the house. Three times a day she watered them with the rinse water from the dishes. The lilac bush in the front yard was dead in the drought, and years before all the cottonwoods had also died and stood like brazen, silvery skeletons. I remember the long spaces of silence in the place except for the sound of the wind that occasionally carried back the distant cursing of Grandpa, epithets in German and broken English hurled against skinny horses in the upper forty where they pulled and stumbled and dragged the cultivator through what was, allegedly, a bean field. Later I followed behind my mother with a hoe, and we chopped the weeds away from the tender plants that the cultivator had missed. There were precious few beans that came up, and those that did were dying like starving babies in the street.

As Kim Pring gazed out over those desolate plains with distant eyes, I could see the solid green circles of new pivot irrigation systems that spread the precious water over the soil 160 acres at a time. I never wanted to go back. I looked away.

"Don't spend any of that money, Kim," I said. "We haven't got it yet."

She nodded her head and spoke very seriously. "We never have had any money," she said, as if she knew she'd never get it. "I really never wanted the money. I just wanted justice."

"Money is all the justice we can get," I said. "We can't put *Penthouse* magazine in jail. It's a big verdict. I'm afraid the judges won't let us keep it."

Then Eddie said, "Those judges up on the Circuit Court of Appeals ain't got a choice. They may not like big verdicts for little people, but like I say, they'll never get in bed with *Penthouse*. See, all we gotta do is show 'em that magazine once, and it's all over. All over!"

Kim stared out the window again and after a while she said, "We're not really going to get the money."

"Why do you say that, Kim?" Eddie asked.

"Well," she said, "Guccione says the verdict won't hold, and he's right, isn't he?"

I didn't want to build up false hopes that would later be smashed by the appeals court. Maybe Guccione was right. After the verdict he had told *The Washington Post*: "The Wyoming decision isn't worth the paper it's written on. It is the product of misplaced passion and prejudice, not of reason or law." The *Wyoming State Tribune* said Guccione "scoffed at the verdict" and said, "Because of the chilling effect on the normal constitutional protections of the press neither we, nor our legal advisers, have any doubt that it will be reversed on appeal." The press hadn't asked Guccione what chilling effect his own libel verdict of $40 million against *Hustler* had on the said "normal constitutional protections of the press," but that verdict had also been set aside on appeal as the product of passion and prejudice.

Maybe Guccione knew what he was talking about. In the long history of American jurisprudence, no libel verdict the size of ours had ever survived in an appellate court; 93 percent of libel cases were finally decided for the media.[1] Juries most often found for the plaintiff, but those awards were almost uniformly set aside by the courts. An organization supported by the media, the Libel Defense Research Center, studied the results in leading libel cases and reported: "Media defendants have significant, indeed, dramatic success in reducing large damage awards and in reversing unfavorable verdicts or judgments, post-trial and on appeal. Thus to date, of the 47 awards entered in the LDRC study, only 7 awards against the media defendant have been affirmed on appeal,"[2] and they were small awards— $35,000, $50,000, $60,000, $69,500, $150,000, and $400,000, the last being the famous *Gertz* case. All other large verdicts against the media, without exception, had been set aside on appeal.

What was omitted from the LDRC statistics is that in those few cases in which the plaintiff recovered anything, plaintiff's out-of-pocket costs usually exceeded the amount the plaintiff was able to collect, so that actually the plaintiff ended up being punished for having sought justice in the first place. Martin Garbus, a New York attorney who defends libel cases for major publications, confessed in an article published in *The New York Times Magazine*: "But the often overlooked result of the libel law revolution has been that networks and major publishers have hired sophisticated attorneys who know how to run up litigation costs on the plaintiff, and drive him from the courthouse."[3]

In one way or another, the injured have gone without justice. Even though it appears that for all practical purposes, the media owns the First Amendment, the game is still played; and suckers play the slots in Las Vegas hoping for the big payoff, but the game belongs to the house. People still yearn for justice. People cannot accept the truth that justice in libel cases is not available in America—that it is not really a serious possibility in a media case. But the people keep pounding at the doors of the courts. Of course, the doors are open. The juries still respond. The jurors have not lost their sense of justice nor their willingness to deliver it, and they struggle away and sacrifice their time and the good energies of their lives hoping that they may give justice, but the courts dump out their verdicts with the rest of the morning's judicial garbage. Nobody wins big, and, finally, nobody wins at all.

Cioffari told the Associated Press from his home in New Jersey: "I'm certainly surprised and disappointed at the jury. My story was a fantastic story of imagination. I still can't believe anyone could accept it as a story about a real person. I have every hope and conviction that an appeals court will see it differently." He said more to *The New York Times*, stoutly maintaining his innocence and protesting the effect of the verdict on all writers of fiction. "As a result of the verdict I feel more inhibited as a writer now. How could I have protected myself, even if I wanted to? How could I possibly have researched every character who might have twirled a baton?" In *The New York Times* there was a picture of Cioffari sitting at his rolltop desk with his typewriter in front of him and his shirt unbuttoned halfway to the navel like Guccione's. "The implication for fiction writers is potentially horrible. It could open the floodgate for every opportunistic person trying to make a buck on something somebody wrote," he said. "The life of a fiction writer is a struggle as it is. It now appears that on top of the difficulty of continual rejections, of getting stories placed and getting a little bit of money, you will also risk losing all that you've made—and more." He advised other writers: "Be as careful as you can. It may get to the point that you have to take out insurance." He didn't tell the *Times* that *Penthouse* had provided him his defense.

It was "Spence's theatrical tactics that swayed the jury," Cioffari said. "The West against the East. The plaintiff's lawyer was defending the rights of the little individual with pioneering spirit against the encroaching danger of the East, which is responsible for all the crime, sin, drugs and war in the world." I didn't remember saying anything quite like that, but then Cioffari was home now, speaking to the East against the West. "I don't think the jury acted in a reasonable manner. I think it was influenced by their own prejudices, and by the way the case was presented."

Kim had talked to the press in the courtroom right after the verdict. She was standing there holding a small bouquet of pink roses given to her by a woman spectator who had faithfully sat through the trial from the first day. When the trial was over and the crowd had dispersed, the woman came up to Kim and said, "These are for you. You were very brave to take on *Penthouse*," as if Kim had fought for all women, and she had. Then the woman said, "I am very proud to know you." She had tears in her eyes and shoved the flowers out to Kim, and Kim took them and started to cry all over again. I asked Kim later who the woman was, but she said she didn't know her.

Kim had faced the reporters. She said she thought the jury's judgment was more than fair. "I don't have any animosity towards *Penthouse* magazine. I just think it was really unfortunate the way things happened. They should be more careful." She smiled at the reporters. "I am just really pleased that we won. No matter what the figure, it is important that Mr. Spence stood up against the abuse of the First Amendment," as if I had been fighting for the Constitution first and not for her, and then I thought, yes, the Constitution is for people; it's not just a legal abstraction that should be preserved for itself alone, or a mere business tool. It's a sacred right and should be respected. I mean it is kind of like your Bible, I thought. It is your Bible. You can do with it what you want, but even so, it is a sacred book. You wouldn't take the Bible to the outhouse for toilet paper— the Monkey Ward catalog, maybe, but not the Bible. I'm not the really religious kind, and I didn't say any of that to the press, of course, because I didn't want to get religion mixed up in this thing. The First Amendment purists are religious enough.

"The thing I am most happy and relieved about is that I am again an ordinary private person," Kim told the press. The jury had, indeed, specifically found that Kim was not a public figure.

I, too, had held forth for the press. Kirk Knox of the *Wyoming State Tribune,* whose talent as a professional scold could lead him to find something sour and sinister to say about a Sunday school picnic, observed that "Spence literally held court for the press in an empty courtroom." Knox portrayed me as so egotistically eager to speak to the press that I was being videotaped by two TV crews at once. I said the case stood for the proposition that you can't exploit innocent people. "They were selling her life and her soul. This sort of thing has to be stopped, and I think this will go a long ways toward stopping it." Knox got that much right. Then he had me talking away insatiably to yet another TV crew in the foyer of the Federal Building when a reporter asked me if I thought I could win such a verdict in any other state but Wyoming, to which I answered, "There are decent people everywhere." I don't remember Knox ever asking me any questions himself.

I had tried to say something that would counteract the media's horror at this record libel verdict, to explain that this wasn't the end of the First Amendment. The First Amendment never had and never should immunize libel. It was as though the media was protective of every flea and every tick that sucked on the dog's back for fear that, in killing fleas and ticks, we would kill the poor dog himself. But we've been killing fleas and ticks a long time to save our dogs. I thought I should say something to reassure the press that all we had done in this case was to jerk one of these bugs with a bloody mouth off the back of the First Amendment.

I said, "This is a great victory for the First Amendment, for freedom of the press. I hope it stops the exploitation of the First Amendment because if we abuse it, we'll lose it. Anybody who criticizes this verdict is not aware of the meaning of this case. It means that you can't wrap yourself up in the American flag and smear people anymore." But the press would never believe it. So far as the press was concerned, I had attacked the dog and not the ticks and the fleas.

Grutman wasn't available for comment, and Cooper and Kelley got the hell out of Cheyenne and made their statements to the press from the safety of their Denver offices. Cooper told *The New York Times* that the verdict was an assault on the First Amendment, that it meant "you can't write fiction anymore." The press went crazy.

They saw it as the beginning of the end of the First Amendment.

I told the UPI, "I am proud a Wyoming jury had the courage to make that decision," and I said to *The Washington Post* that "this case starts to set limits that people like Guccione must abide by. I think Mr. Guccione can hear this verdict all the way back to New York."

"Spence obviously inflamed the jury," Cooper said. Of course, he himself hadn't inflamed the jurors against *Penthouse*. It was I who prejudiced them, I, the trickster who put his evil spell on juries, the wizard who would do anything to win his case. The *Malleus* knew how to deal with those who successfully defended witches. They . . . are more damnable than the wizards themselves."[4] That was me all right. Cooper had me dead to rights.

Knox reported that Cooper had moved for a mistrial several times during the actual trial "because of Spence's conduct." Cooper told Knox, "I think this system is going to have to learn how to handle Gerry Spence. Obviously this is the result of his appeal to the prejudices and passions of local jurors." The *Malleus* prescribed the remedy against those who "will do all in their power to protect such wizards (or other heretics) from trial and punishment at the hands of the Judge acting on behalf of the Faith."[5] The punishment was clear: "It is enough now to say that these are by law excommunicated, and incur the twelve great penalties. And if they continue obstinate in that excommunication for a year, they are then to be condemned as heretics."[6] Death at the stake. Cooper told the press the jury's verdict would stand "over my dead body. We will file motions to set aside the verdict before we appeal." The verdict had been stolen by the wizard. The witch had been spared, and the verdict must be nullified.

But what of Guccione's magic? What of his magic used against this new necrophilic man in those dark rites of passage into the New Church; what of his demonology beginning with a first flaunting of the pubic hair like some witch doctor dangling that erotic enchantment in the eyes; what of his further casting of the spell, the spreading, sprawling, stretching of the thighs, the unfurling of vaginal lips, their distention, their distortion, their dilatation to expose the gaping, luring, leering vault? What of that magic? What of his conjuring up the weird and the wild, the wicked, the loutish demons, the maddened spirits, the capturing of the clitoris; what of his photographic dissections, the severing of whole women from themselves, or parts

of women cut up by the camera into objects by which such bewitch-
ment is accomplished—the vagina (the lucky piece), the breasts
charmingly excised from the whole body by the knife of the lens,
breasts of every size and shape and color, pointing, praying, pouting,
pleading as pretty amulets until we are dumbfounded; what of his
dragging the poor eyes so close to it they ache? What of his propping
and posturing whole bodies as his tantalizing talismans, posed and
pink, and soft like suckling, mindless babes, adorned with snakes and
dildos, racked up and spread out, exhibited from gaping mouth to
puckered rectum as enchanting charms; what of these women, his
property, his severed parts, his objects sold and consumed like any
commodity; what of the bewitchments of all of this, his magical vi-
sions performed with lights and camera transforming men into voyeurs and women into objects, women dead as the pages themselves,
in mechanical coitus, past coitus, past women in cunnilingus, past
everything, until we are finally numb, finally dumb? Nothing has
been seen. Nothing at all. The new men lonelier than before, more
impotent than their empty dreams, are separated from themselves
and from their women because a spell has been laid upon them, the
magic of the pornographer.

"What are they going to do to us when we get to New York?" Kim
asked.

"Don't worry about it," I said. "They're going to do nothing.
Nothing. We're the ones who are gonna do."

"What are you going to say?"

I thought for a while about that, and then my mind slipped away
like the warlock who by his very will can transmigrate. By my own
magic, I, the war chief, was before the roaring fire, before the dancing flames that lighted the small clearing in the forest, casting wild
shadows on my warriors painted in red and yellow. The drums beat
to the rhythm of the flames and we, the victorious dancers, danced
our wild dances after the great fight, contorting, weaving, jumping,
crying out in savage sounds like wolves over the kill, and then on one
beat the drums ceased and the dancers froze, as the heart itself beats
its last without warning, and there was only silence and fresh scalps
dangling from bright, beaded belts. There was a new bloody scalp
hanging from mine. The eagle feathers shivered on my head. I was no
longer afraid, for we were the victors.

We should celebrate, for Christ's sakes. I had learned to fight, but
never to celebrate.

I sat crowded up in the aisle seat next to Kim. My shoulders hung over and the stewardesses bumped against me as they passed, and passengers headed for the lavatories bumped me also. My legs were too long for the space ahead, a precise measurement provided for the composite person. The seats fit no one, because the composite person never existed. The man ahead of me pushed his seat button and lurched backward against my knees and I actually hollered at the pain. "Jesus Christ!" He looked around at me like I was a fool.

The stewardess supplied us one small pack each of peanuts done up in sterile foil, and we all said we wanted a Diet Pepsi. I toasted Kim. "Well, here's to the best baton twirler in the world—and to as good a client as any lawyer ever had."

"Thanks," Kim said and she touched plastic cups half full of diet drink with Eddie and me—three cups to the can, the official airline portion. The Church serves forty-seven from the communion chalice. Neither the Church nor I knew much of celebration. I toasted a $26.5 million verdict.

"Here's to you, Eddie—the best partner a man ever had. You did most of the work and I get all of the credit."

"Thanks," Eddie said. "I didn't do nothin'."

"We'd better celebrate when we get to New York," I said.

"Yeah," Eddie said.

Kim was suddenly quiet. I glanced at her. She was staring out over the plains of Nebraska with the same distant look in her eyes.

"Well, where do you go from here, Kim?" I asked.

"Don't know," she said. "I'd like to get a good job. Maybe in business or something."

"How about modeling?"

"Nope," she shook her head. "Not interested. Modeling isn't for me. I'd just like to have a good job and," she added, "I'd like to get closer to my dad." She looked back out into space. "I spent all those years twirling, which really didn't mean very much to him. It was my mother's thing and mine. It was girl's stuff, and he just made room for us to do it and kinda stood back and watched is all, but it was hard for him to get into it. And I grew up without him. I'd just like to go fishing with my dad, and do some things with him—maybe help him fix up an old car or something. Maybe if we won I could buy him some things he's always wanted, maybe a new car." For having just won the largest standing libel verdict in America, I thought Kim was acting pretty down.

"What's the matter?" I asked.

She shrugged her shoulders. Then she said, "I don't know what I'm going to do with my life. I feel kinda trapped in Cheyenne. I mean, I don't know how to get out—my mother and my boyfriend and all. I love 'em but, you know—" She didn't know what more to say.

"We all have our traps," I said. "The best trap breaker is to get acquainted with ourselves. Your trap might be like a bud on a tulip," I said. "A bud is a trap to the flower, and the flower bursts out by blooming, and I think you're going to bloom, all right." Then we didn't talk anymore until we were over Missouri.

Finally she said, "It was sure nice winning. I like to win."

"It'll be a long time before we really know anything about winning," I said. "First we've got to convince Judge Brimmer to let us keep the verdict." I had a hard time explaining to her that the judge could set the verdict aside if he wanted to and make us try the case again, or he could reduce the verdict. Justice was his business and he could tailor it to suit him. He was the judge.

"What do we have juries for if judges can mess with what they do? Why don't we just let the judge try the case in the first place?" Kim asked.

"I don't know," I said. "I guess it's because we hope the judge will respect the jury's verdict. But he doesn't have to."

"You mean to say that those poor people had to sit there all those weeks and listen to that testimony and try to figure out the law, and the judge can just throw it out if he wants to?"

"Yes," I said. "Cooper and Kelley will file motions to throw it all out."

"How can that be?" she asked.

When we were over the green hills of Indiana, Kim finally asked, "What will Judge Brimmer do?"

"You know what men like to say about the predictability of a woman, don't you? Well, they ought to be talking about the predictability of a trial judge instead."

"I don't think this will ever be over for me." When I didn't reply she asked, "Mr. Spence, will it ever be over for me?"

We landed at LaGuardia where a limousine driver stood at the door of the arrival gate with the name SPENCE written on a big white piece of cardboard, and I said to the man, "That Spence fella is me," and then he drove us in an old black Cadillac about half a block long to the Berkshire Place, which isn't as fancy a place as its name, and I took myself to bed, still exhausted, still dreaming those fever dreams, still arguing the case to the jury, and then at five in the morning we got our call to get up for our television appearance on *The Today Show.*

We went to the twentieth or thirtieth floor of Rockefeller Center where some young woman met us who had learned to smile at that hour and thereby got the job. She led the three of us to a small windowless room with pink wallpaper, a few chairs, and a television set blasting away against the far wall. They called it the "green room" because it was the place where you wait, and wait, and turn green—reminded me of the parlor in a Mexican whorehouse. Tom Brokaw filled the screen, as cold and crisp as the South Dakota wind that blew him all the way to New York. Hard to believe he was in the next room. Looked the same as he did in Jackson Hole, Wyoming.

They wanted to put makeup on me, and I let them put a little on to cover the wet nose and forehead—to cover the green—nothing on the lips, for Christ's sakes! I knew the whole procedure. I'd been there once before after the Karen Silkwood trial. Pretty soon the smiling young woman would come after us like a nurse hauling you to the operating room when your time had come.

Then our time did come, and they took Kim and me into the studio and wired us. And like I told Eddie, it's in the partnership agreement—black-and-white—he does all the work and I get all the credit. And the money. Eddie always laughed. Partnership agreements are for clients, not trial lawyers.

Brokaw came over, said good morning to us, and without more ado, NBC turned on its magic, its long lenses into which Brokaw spoke as if the glass were alive. He smiled at the glass a little, like a boy who'd been told to smile a lot. He had a teleprompter in front of him with all the questions written down so that as he talked it looked as if he were very smart and very articulate, which, of course, he is. We didn't have any answers written down. We didn't even know what the questions would be. Guests aren't supposed to look as bright as the host—that's in the agreement, too.

"Well, here is Kim Pring, the former Miss Wyoming, who has just won a twenty-six-and-a-half-million-dollar verdict against *Penthouse* magazine. Good morning."

"Good morning," Kim said. I nodded. I didn't smile either. I didn't have to.

"Well, Kim, how does it feel to be such a big winner? Twenty-six million?"

"I'm very happy we won," she said.

Brokaw shook his head in disbelief. "What are you going to do with all that money? I'll bet it's going to take you quite a while to spend it all."

They claimed we were talking to millions of Americans and now it had all come down to just another game show—how will you spend the money? I wanted to talk about libel, what the case stood for—that little people can't just be used up like fodder, like fuel and supplies to be dumped into Guccione's money machine whenever he pleases. People are not things. Women are not things. Women are not parts. They are people, and the First Amendment protects them too and I wanted to talk about Guccione's New Church.

"And here is Gerry Spence, her attorney. Mr. Spence, you get a big chunk of that money, don't you?"

"Well, I don't mind talking about the contingency fee," I said. "But wouldn't you like to know why the jury gave us all that money?"

"That would be very interesting," Brokaw said. "I'll bet it was an interesting trial, all right, and so there you have it folks—twenty-six million dollars, the largest standing libel verdict in America. Thanks for coming, Miss Pring, and thanks to you, Mr. Spence." That's how I remember it, and then the smiling woman came and led us off and told us we were "magnificent," just "tremendous," just "marvelous." If you can smile at five o'clock in the morning and know those three words, you can go a long way in television.

We had breakfast in some little crowded joint. I watched Eddie sop up his eggs with toast and make it all come out even again. Later we went to the Associated Press and had our pictures taken, this cowboy and this pretty blond maiden, after which the three of us went to the top of the Empire State Building, and I said, by God, we should finally celebrate. I stood up as close to the edge of the railing as I could get, and let out a war cry.

The people stared.

Eddie grinned. Then Eddie let out a long cry of his own in his high Irish.

Kim laughed.

I let out another, like a yapping coyote, like an Indian dancing with red and yellow paint on his face, and I let the cry come out until my face shivered, and my hat shook on my head, and I cried like a warrior with a fresh, new, dripping scalp dangling from his waist, and I cried once more, so that even Guccione could hear it all the way to his place.

The celebration over, we left for home—for a damned good place called Wyoming.

31

"This verdict is the result of passion and the presentation of prejudicial matters to the jury," Kelley almost whispered. "The size of the verdict is extraordinary, and flows from the conduct of counsel." He wagged a finger at me. I felt like a criminal who had stolen millions from his client, that good company, Penthouse International. Kelley leaned against the podium as if in search of support in this sparsely populated courtroom with only a handful of reporters and a few of the curious. Among the courthouse people there were wagers that Guccione was right—this verdict wasn't worth the paper it was written on—and if Judge Brimmer didn't set it aside, the Circuit Court would.

Judge Brimmer eased back in his reclining chair to listen. Occasionally he would pop the chair forward, make a note, and then ease back again. Sometimes he would scowl as if in deep thought. He had the power to set the verdict aside and grant a new trial. Or if he chose, he could grant a remittitur, an order requiring Kim to agree to a lesser sum than the jury had awarded, and should she fail to so agree, then the Court would also order a new trial. Or he could leave the verdict undisturbed. It was his decision. He was the judge.

The judge leaned forward again to hear Kelley. "Mr. Kelley, might I suggest that you put that little microphone on your lapel. Some of the reporters listening closely to your words might be having trouble hearing them all." Maybe Kelley didn't want the reporters to hear. I looked over at the audience once more. There was Kirk Knox. I glanced at Kim. She looked like someone revisiting a chamber of torture from which she had been once miraculously delivered. Her eyes were blank again. I could hear her heavy breathing

"Are you okay?" I whispered.

She nodded, but I didn't believe her.

411

"If I recall the Court's statement correctly," Kelley said, "Your Honor once stated that you were within an inch of granting a motion for mistrial." And now he claimed the judge should set aside the jury's verdict and grant a new trial because I had violated every ruling the Court had made: I talked about obscenity when this wasn't an obscenity trial; I talked about the pictures in *Penthouse* as involving "deviate sex and pornography," and my very first witness, Bill Storms, the man who cleaned sewers, had called *Penthouse* "pure smut."

Kelley said my final argument contained the most aggravated instances of misconduct. "How prejudicial does conduct of counsel have to be before there are grounds for a mistrial? How deliberate, how prejudicial?"

There were only sixty dollars' worth of medical bills in the case, and "no demonstrable weight loss suffered by Kim Pring," he said. She sought no treatment for her alleged injuries, but the jury awarded her $1.5 million in damages—that was evidence of a verdict based on passion. Moreover, there was that disparity between what the jury found in actual damages against Cioffari and what they found against *Penthouse*. That was inconsistent, and inconsistent verdicts cannot stand. Everybody knows that. Even Mr. Spence.

The judge asked, "You are really speaking on behalf of Cioffari at this moment?" The judge understood the potential conflict of interest between Cioffari and *Penthouse* when both were being represented in court by a single voice. "Are you saying that the compensatory verdict against Cioffari should have been greater? Isn't that an inconsistent position?"

"I think I am saying that the verdict against *Penthouse* should have been lesser. Otherwise it is inconsistent and cannot stand as to either party," Kelley said.

Kelley argued there was no actual malice to support the punitive damage award—that the $26 million in punitive damages had to fall. "I think even Mr. Spence and I can agree," Kelley said with great stress on the word "even," "that we live in a society of orderly liberties where we have a criminal justice system that fixes punishment to fit the crime." I did agree, but then men have always formed corporations to do what they themselves would never dare do as persons—to personally ravage the land, to pollute, to poison, to cheat the poor, to foist their plenteous horrors on mankind—and when a corporation commits its crimes, it can hardly be locked in the stocks in the town square or sent to prison. When a corporation kills, it is not subject to the death penalty. You cannot kill a "nothing." A corporation's only capacity to feel is its inherent feeling for money—its passion for money. And that is how you punish a corporation. You take its money.

Kelley thought that $26 million was outlandish, ridiculous. "Discussing Mr. Spence's favorite topic, the suit by Mr. Guccione against *Hustler* which resulted in a verdict of twenty-six million dollars' punitive damages against Mr. Flynt, the publisher, and eleven million against the magazine; before that case left the trial court, the twenty-six million was reduced to two million, and the eleven million reduced to eight hundred fifty thousand. To my knowledge nowhere in this country has an award left the trial court in a media defamation case any higher than that."

Then Kelley warned Judge Brimmer—one must acknowledge he warned him fair and square: "The Tenth Circuit has taken a very circumspect view of punitive damages," and a new trial, because of the many errors committed by both Mr. Spence and Judge Brimmer, was the only remedy. He looked up at the judge for a long moment to be sure his message got through. Then satisfied, he sat down.

The authority for a new trial went back to the *Malleus*, and before. The *Malleus* provided that the judge "must diligently examine and discuss the causes" and the "alleged grounds of objection" and if he "sees that he has unduly and unjustly proceeded against the accused by refusing him permission to defend himself, or by exposing him to questions at an unsuitable time, or for any such reason; when the appointed time comes let him correct his mistake carrying the process back to the point and stage where it was when the accused asked to be defended, or when he put a term to his examination, etc. For by the removal of the grounds for objection, the appeal, which was legitimate, loses its weight."[1] Fix things up right if they were wrong so the later appeal to a higher court cannot be successful. That was the sage advice of the *Malleus* to the trial judge.

I took the podium and began without the microphone. "May it please the Court," and I hoped to God I could please him today. Millions were on the line—a single word represented thousands of dollars. May I please, please the Court.

I started by telling Judge Brimmer the first truth on my mind. "I wish Eddie were here today," I said. "He does a much better job arguing these kinds of things than I. I don't feel very adequate sometimes in arguing the law, because I have so often been cast in the role of someone who continually violates it in the courtroom. Eddie is trying a case up in Jackson, Your Honor, in Judge O'Brien's court, and he asked Judge O'Brien for leave to interrupt his trial and come here, but Judge O'Brien said that if I couldn't argue this case to you I didn't deserve to keep the money, so here I am without Eddie."

The judge smiled.

"The first fact we have forgotten is that we are dealing with a private person. The jury found she is not a public person, not public property, not somebody who can be smeared and sold. She has greater rights."

I told His Honor that this jury had understood the case—exquisitely so, I thought. I apologized to Judge Brimmer for my lack of faith in the jurors. "I can remember a time when we were sitting in chambers, and you had forty-two of those damned instructions out there, half of which I couldn't understand myself (which is no reflection on anybody excepting me, Your Honor) and counsel was moving for a mistrial as he did every other minute—which was his game in this case—and I looked at those forty-two instructions and suddenly had this overwhelming need to just say 'Me, too!' Nobody can understand those instructions, and nobody, surely not me, could understand those interrogatories the jury had to answer. Not one person could do that without an error, much less six persons.

"But Your Honor kept the faith in the jury. I have been proven wrong so many times, and I was proven wrong again by Your Honor and by the jury who did understand. And the jury found Kim Pring was a private person."

I moved several steps nearer to the judge. "Counsel points at me and says I have been wrong, that I have misconducted myself; I have prejudiced the jury against the defendants and the court has prejudiced the jury with its instructions. And I just want to say that these *Penthouse* people have been the most arrogant conglomerate of human beings I have ever encountered in the course of almost thirty years of practice. They don't and didn't have an honest defense in fact or in law to what they did. The way they undertook their defense in this case wasn't to come into court and say to you or to me, or to a jury, 'We did wrong, and we're sorry that we have hurt her, and we wish that we could make some amends.' Had they said that simple thing I think the jury might have responded in kind.

"Instead they charged that everybody else did everything wrong.

They attacked me, filed a complaint against me before the Wyoming State Bar that had nothing whatever to do with the merits of this case, that had for its only purpose an attempt to intimidate me, hoping that under attack I would falter and fail.

"Then they filed a motion to recuse Your Honor, which was insulting, and arrogant and ill-founded, and they knew it was based upon the worst kinds of fabrications and half-truths. They hoped by that method to intimidate Your Honor, and when they didn't exhibit enough good faith to even file the affidavit that was the basis of their recusal in the Circuit Court of Appeals, that Court summarily threw it out.

"Now they admit their magazine was obscene by complaining today that we talked about the content of their magazine—'You were talking about the contents of our magazine; therefore you were talking about obscenity; therefore you were violating the Court's order; therefore you were being prejudicial to us.' Those are the kinds of circular arguments they have made here. Every day before we went to the jury, Mr. Cooper dutifully trudged into chambers and made his morning motion for mistrial. There wasn't any real effort on the part of these people to defend—they attacked the judge instead, and they attacked me. I have never seen a Court who, having been slapped first on one cheek and then the other, was so patient.

"They had no right to introduce any of the expert witnesses they brought to court. Mr. Pierson hadn't been listed as a witness in time, according to the rules of court. The evidence they elicited from these witnesses was in violation of *Smith* v. *Ford.* The Court simply set its own rules aside to give them a fair chance to defend. That's what it amounted to." Judge Brimmer popped forward in his chair and wrote something on his pad. Was I making points against my own case? I pressed on.

"They complain in their motion that they were not permitted to introduce evidence of Kim's sex life." I glanced at Kim. She was looking tense and tight again. "They claimed, 'We have evidence that she has misconducted herself sexually,' and the Court invited them to bring that evidence before him. They didn't bring anybody. They didn't subpoena anybody. Nor offer to subpoena anybody. And so it went.

Now they attack the jury, and after this was all over, after forty-two instructions and sixteen interrogatories the jury answered correctly, after a verdict that seems fair and just and was intended to teach these people a lesson, to stop them once and for all, what do we hear Mr. Guccione say publicly and to the press? That 'this verdict isn't worth the paper it's written on.' And what does Mr. Grutman finally tell the press? 'This girl,' he says, 'won't receive a penny from *Penthouse*.' "

"And we hear Mr. Guccione say in effect, 'I will do as I please, and I will publish as I please, and I will attack whomever I please—I will attack lawyers, and I will attack the clients, and I will attack the judges, and I will attack juries, because the verdict is worthless." My voice was banging up against the walls of the courtroom.

"We never heard them say, 'What we did was to take a private person and subject her to the view and laughter and scorn of twenty-five million people. We called her the worst thing you can call a human being, in print, not once but many times, and we laughed about it.'

"And then besides that, if anybody was offended, they were supposed to have the intelligence of flatworms or their brains were tainted! I apologize. I should be talking to you as a student of the law but we are human beings—I am, and you are, and we all are, everybody here was, the jury was, the plaintiff is, and Mr. Guccione is. Everything we did here had some relationship to the honest efforts of real human beings trying to do what was right and just. This was as sincere and honest a jury verdict as I ever saw."

I explained to His Honor that what Cioffari did was different from what *Penthouse* did. Cioffari wrote an article. Unpublished, it would have done little damage. Published in the Pine Bluffs paper it would have done very little damage. Published in the Cheyenne paper, more. In the Denver *Post* more still. But it was published in *Penthouse* with its twenty-five million readers. That's where the damage was done. So the jury had the right to apportion the damages between Cioffari and *Penthouse*. Had they not done so, Kelley would have been complaining they should have.

"Was the verdict too large? They wouldn't be hollering about any so-called 'error' if the verdict had been ten dollars or ten thousand. What they are really saying is, 'Don't take so much money away from us.' But ask Mr. Kelley this question: 'If I would remit some of it to you—if I would give you back a million or two, would you promise me you won't appeal?' No. They want it *both* ways. And if you give them some back they will go to the Court of Appeals and argue, 'You see, Judge Brimmer knew this was a prejudicial verdict, because he gave back a million dollars. It is another Catch Twenty-two proposition. They want a license signed by this court and ultimately by the Circuit Court of Appeals that says, 'We can do whatever we want to.' " I stepped over by Kim to complete my argument. A lawyer ought not let the Court forget that the case is the client's. It didn't belong to the judge or the lawyers. It was Kim's case.

"Does this verdict shock the conscience of the Court? If the jury had done as Mr. Cooper requested and given four tenths of a cent per reader—would that shock the conscience of the Court? Would you have added money to our verdict then?

"Corporations demand that they be treated as ordinary human beings. They say, 'We have the same rights as you.' Well, if they have the same rights, they also have the same duties, and I know many a man who has been fined a total year's gross income. Why should a corporation be treated any differently?"

I saw the judge glance over my head into the audience. I addressed the man the judge was looking at. "Now there is a reporter sitting here whom I have become fond of in my own way. He is listening to my voice. His name is Kirk Knox. He hears my words, if he is paying attention to me, but sometimes his writings indicate that he doesn't pay all that much attention," and I smiled at Knox who only gave me a rancid stare back. "And I think he should. But supposing his paper, with let's say twenty-five thousand readers had done this, and the jury returned a punitive damage award of twenty-five thousand dollars. Would that shock anyone's conscience? For twenty-five *million* readers it seems to me this was a reasoned result. Maybe not perfect. Maybe you would have exercised your discretion differently, Your Honor, but then, why do we have jury trials?

"There are things you are always happy to have a jury decide." We use juries to decide hard cases, life-and-death cases. "We shouldn't make them do the dirty work and then play around with the cream on the top. We ought not have them paint a painting and then strike out some part of it and put our name to it.

"*Penthouse* can charge fifty cents an issue more for their magazine in the future. Sometimes they charge fifty cents more when they include that life-sized naked centerfold, and for fifty cents over a year's time, paid by the readers who raped Kim Pring, an additional thirty million dollars will be realized from which they can pay this judgment, and they'll make a few extra million besides. Twenty-five million is very little more than a month's gross from that magazine—only a *month's* gross.

"Now, Judge, I know you are not supposed to signal the jury, but if the jury said to you, 'Could you give us a little wink if what we have in mind is correct—would it be all right to charge them only one month's gross—maybe that would teach them a lesson?'—well, I don't think that if the Court gave the jury his sign of approval it would be unreasonable, and that's what I want the Court to do today—give the Court's signal of its approval to what this jury did.

"This jury wants this stopped, and I don't know how else to stop it. The jury wants to make sure that what they did was effective, that it would be heard. So what, that it is the biggest verdict to come down? That just makes me proud of this jury. I brag about them to anybody who asks. I hope you won't hold that against me, and show me up for a fool later on by taking it away."

I sat down.

"Thank you, Mr. Spence," the judge said, and then Kelley sauntered back to the podium with this long yellow pad in his hand to make his last remarks.

"Well, Your Honor, we heard Mr. Spence's closing argument again, an argument largely calculated to inflame, which I would think the Court at this stage would find close to insulting." But Judge Brimmer gave no indication that he felt insulted. He listened and waited. Kelley told him the evidence was "scant" concerning the state of mind of the defendant. I wondered how a corporation without a mind could have a state of mind.

He quoted from certain cases he thought to be controlling. He talked some more about the inconsistency between the verdicts against *Penthouse* and Cioffari, which seemed to bother him considerably, and then he said thank you, and that was it. That was all. It was that clear to Kelley. It must be that obvious to the Court, to the press, to everyone.

Now the judge's decision was at hand—on that single sheet of paper with the small pencil scrawls that meant millions for the parties. Judge Brimmer cleared his throat. "Thank you, gentlemen, for your splendid arguments." I loved the judge. He was kind. He was a Wyoming man. He had courage. Kim grabbed my arm and held on.

He began with the sound of a man who knew whatever he was about to say was right, and indeed it was, for he was the judge. "The law is shifting sand at best. There are nineteen of us that may eventually have something to say about this, and it starts with me at the bottom, and there are nine members of the Court of Appeals above me to look over me, and there are nine members of the Supreme Court beyond that which, as I count, would be nineteen.

"I basically feel these instructions were fair." Eddie was right, of course. Now that we'd won, all the losses we'd suffered by the judge's adverse rulings during the trial would come rushing in to support our verdict. "I also believe that Mr. Spence's view with respect to causation is realistic, namely that the jury could and did consider that what Mr. Cioffari did was different from what *Penthouse* did. After all—if the story had been only shown to one of his neighbors, it wouldn't have caused much damage. So there is a difference in the damage caused by the actions of each of the parties.

"With respect to the pretrial rulings, particularly those with regard to the past conduct of Miss Pring, it was, and still is, the view of the Court that examination of the plaintiff as to specific instances of her sexual experiences, if any, in an effort to prove lack of good reputation, is not permissible. I believe that to be the controlling law and I have followed it."

Judge Brimmer, to his everlasting credit, had finally, irrevocably thrown out five hundred years of putrid precedent. He had disavowed the *Malleus Maleficarum!* Cooper looked very mean. Kelley sat in shock. I thought of the faces of "our dear sons, Heinrich Kramer and James Sprenger," and I could hear their droning denunciations based upon the reasoning of Saint Augustine himself: "None save great men have been the authors of great heresies."[2]

Out, utterly out with the *Malleus!* I thought I heard the angels singing. I looked at Kim. She was glowing. She looked healed.

"With regard to the conduct of counsel in the course of the trial, my recollection is that I admonished the jury from time to time—it seemed to me almost as if it were a broken record—to the effect that the statements of counsel were not to be consiered in any way by the jury. I have no reason to believe that the jury did consider anything said by counsel. Every time I gave that admonition, they nodded rather knowingly, and I just cannot believe that they didn't follow my instructions in that regard as well as in other regards." The judge had protected my record, and his.

"The defendants have contended they had no time to adequately prepare. The fault for that lies squarely at the doorstep of Norman Roy Grutman who asked for a continuance on the grounds that he had to be in a trial in Long Island, but the Court discovered by the media that he wasn't in any trial at all in Long Island, and instead he was appearing on behalf of *Penthouse* against Reverend Falwell in Lynchburg, Virginia, at the time he told me that he was going to be in a trial in Long Island. I think that Mr. Grutman didn't appear because he just didn't want to.

"I think the motion of Penthouse International for a new trial should be denied, *except* as I am about to state."

I heard it! Everybody heard it—that word *except.* Jesus Christ, I knew it had all been too good to be true. Now the *except* had been spoken. The *except* could destroy us—the case, the trial, a life, justice, destroyed in one word. Goddamn that word. It was the single word that could take everything back that had ever been given.

"With regard to the twenty-five-million-dollar punitive-damage award against Penthouse International, the plaintiff's agrument is very, very persuasive, and yet, as I said, when dealing with such amounts that seem so large as to be almost beyond the comprehension of us ordinary mortals, I believe that we have got to be guided mostly by the court *precedents.* After all, that's the principle on which our courts operate."

Precedent?

Precedent! I'll tell you what precedent is. Precedent is the rule that holds that little people never get big justice. Precedent is the rule that holds that little people get little justice. I'll tell you what precedent is! It holds that the great and the powerful non-people, the corporations, the nonbreathers, pay small penalties, and suffer little punishment. We put people in dark prisons while corporations pay piddling penalties for the same crimes.

Precedent! The *Malleus* is precedent. Precedents contaminate us, plague us, as if every blank page on which the law will ever again be written must forever be stained by the blood of the past.

Precedent! We are all married to the dead past, and always we return to the same old and rotten places with a lust for what we reverently call *Precedent.* We contaminate the present by shrouding it in foul garments dug up out of the moldering graves of history, as if ancient germs are not as deadly. Don't speak to me of precedent!

"It is precedent," Judge Brimmer said. "The *Malandris* decision would indicate that they [the Circuit Court of Appeals] considered a reduction by two-thirds of the punitive damage award as proper. However, the files disclose in this case that Continental Casualty Company wrote *Penthouse* a liability policy at an annual premium of ninety thousand dollars in the amount of five million, and a supplemental liability insurance policy of five million, written by Employers Reinsurance Corporation for a premium of twenty thousand seven hundred and fifty dollars.

"Now the Court is well aware of the general view of the judiciary that the existence or nonexistence of liability coverage is irrelevant to litigation. However, we live in a practical world in which it is unrealistic, I think, for the judiciary to hide its head from the realities of the business world. It is obvious here, when I have this information in the file before me, that the jury, in making the award of twenty-five million punitive damages, meant to punish Penthouse International for its misconduct or to deter any such future conduct.

"Yet if the Court reduces the punitive damage to less then eight and a half million, *Penthouse* will merely demand that Continental Casualty and Employers Reinsurance Corporation pay their policy limits, and *Penthouse* will have suffered no punishment at all for its actions. And that, too, would be a result that would shock this Court's sense of fairness.

"Since the jury of six, I believe, impartial persons, after hearing the evidence decided against *Penthouse* on every single issue in the case, and that fact can't be ignored, I think the jury expected *Penthouse* to pay a part of this judgment as punishment.

"Now I am inclined to believe that the amount of twenty-five million is excessive. It is such a large figure that it does shock the conscience of the Court, and I believe that it would be unjust and inequitable to allow the judgment in that amount to stand.

"For these reasons the Court has concluded that the punitive-damage award of twenty-five million dollars should be reduced by fifty percent or to the amount of twelve and a half million, which will make the plantiff's total award fourteen million thirty-five thousand dollars."

Kim looked as if she didn't understand. "That means we just lost twelve and a half million dollars, just like that," I whispered. The judge was still talking. Her face was vacant. She gazed up at the judge as if she didn't hear me.

Twelve and a half million lost in less than five minutes! It had taken us years, and the sweat and tears and the agony of a long trial, and the jury had struggled with us, six good men and women true, and now half of it was gone—half of justice—just like that. The magic of the judge was the supreme magic of all, the power of God.

God can give or take that which no man can ever comprehend—that which man has labeled with his feeble word, by calling it "justice."

Judge Brimmer said, "If a remittitur of twelve and a half million is filed by the plaintiff within twenty days from this date, the Court's order denying the motion for a new trial will stand. However, if a remittitur is not filed in the sum of twelve and a half million reducing the punitive-damage award against *Penthouse* to twelve and a half million, then the motion for a new trial on all issues shall be granted.

"I might further point out that the Court does not believe that the jury's verdict was the result of passion or prejudice and the Court does not find that the Court erred or the jury erred or abused its discretion, either on the issue of damages, or on the issue of liability.

"Any further problems, gentlemen?"

I knew the judge had done what he must do if justice was to prevail and any part of the jury's award was to stand. He had to reduce the verdict to a sum that stood at least some chance at surviving the scrutiny of the Circuit. Otherwise he thought the Circuit would throw the *whole* verdict out as being excessive and the product of passion and prejudice. Even now, what was left was the largest standing libel award in the country. His reasoning was sound. He had given credence to the jury's intent. He had done what he thought was right. Now it was up to eighteen other judges to also be right.

Judge Brimmer, like any man who had done his best, and whose work was over, and who felt the heavy burden lift from his shoulders, was in a jovial mood. He said to me from the bench, "I think, Mr. Spence, that you have kidded me about when, many years ago, you and I were trying a case against each other, I got a remittitur from Judge Kerr of one hundred thousand, and I think you say to this day that I still owe you one hundred thousand dollars. I guess you can now say the amount I owe you is twelve million six hundred thousand."

"That's right, Your Honor," I said.

"Thank you, gentlemen." The judge left the bench, left us holding whatever it was we were holding. It was no longer whole—whatever it was had been sliced in two by the deft judicial slicer, the steel of the judge's remittitur. But what we had, we had.

Kim and I just sat there. The reporters rushed up to Cooper and Kelley.

"You just made twelve and half million for *Penthouse*," a reporter said. "How does that feel? Will you appeal?"

"We will appeal," Kelley said.

"Mr. Spence, you just lost twelve and a half million. How do you feel?" I saw Kirk Knox listening in the background. I nodded at him.

"It's like getting kicked in the guts by a friendly boot," I said.

Kim said she understood, but I didn't think she really did. She shrugged her shoulders. "You do whatever you think we have to do. I never expected to get any money anyway. We aren't moneyed folks. It would probably just be a lot of trouble to us." We walked down the street to her little yellow bug one more time. We passed where the bitch in heat had been smashed in the street and the dogs had been fighting over the dead body. The blood had been washed away by the winter's snows. She got into her car, and before she closed the door she said, "When the judge takes away half of it, does that mean that I was half bad?"

Eddie and Schuster were sitting around the table with me in the atrium, and we didn't know whether to cry or to laugh. How does one lose twelve million and not cry, and how does one keep fourteen million and not laugh?

"It's your fault, Eddie," I said. "If you'd been there you would have saved the twelve and a half for us."

"It's Judge O'Brien's fault. He wouldn't let me outta my trial." Eddie had won his case.

I asked my warriors for counsel. "What shall we do?"

"Nothin' we can do," Eddie said. "We gotta agree to give the twelve and a half back or we gotta try it over and then if we get twenty-five million the next trial, he'll just give it back again. We ain't got a choice."

"He's right," Schuster said.

"Well," Eddie laughed. "The judge did us a favor. He gave us an insurance policy. The Circuit can't mess with the jury's verdict now. It cost us twelve and a half million for an insurance policy against the Circuit reversing the verdict on us." He laughed. "We got 'em. This time we got 'em for sure."

"Yeah," I said. "That's pretty expensive insurance."

"It's the best thing the judge could have done," Schuster said. "He helped us."

"It's hard to feel helped by losing twelve and a half million dollars," I said.

* * *

Then we filed the remittitur, a simple single sheet of paper that said we agreed to the reduction of the verdict. "The plaintiff does hereby *sadly* remit $12.5 million to the defendant Penthouse International." It bore my signature.

"We still got the fourteen," Eddie laughed. "That ain't half bad for a bunch of country lawyers."

"Yeah," I said. "Now this bunch of country lawyers has to keep the Circuit Court from taking the rest."

In the mountain country, spring is ignorant of calendars. I stood in the road with the snowbanks to my ears, shaking my fist at the naked aspens, hollering, "Come on spring! Come on, damn you! I've had enough of this." The snow had buried bush and beast— buried all but me. I had no business here this time of year. My breath puffed out in frozen clouds, and then, by God, it began to snow again—

The flakes as white as smother
The sky as dark as dreary

and a bitter wind from the south bit to the bones. Winter was eternal, and my calendar had fooled me again—it was the first of April.

I had argued against the remittitur and come home again.

One day I glimpsed a small patch of barren sky, like an incorrigible crone in dismal dress flashing for the fun of it, flashing her old faded fanny, and the snow began to melt in small valleys under certain sagebrush, and I saw the wet black earth again in places no larger than a witch's thumb. But to the easy eye spring had not come. Tiny tips of sagebrush poked up through the blanket of snow where once the surface of the prairies was white and smooth and perfect, except for a mouse's track, and the brush marks of wings descending for a winter dinner. If not alert, one could by sheer negligence miss the arrival of spring in Jackson Hole, miss the first sagebrush buttercup, yellow as a yellow-varnished baby's button, hugged yellow to the Mother Earth like a suckling child for small warmth.

Up in the fork of an old cottonwood yonder in an untidy pile of sticks, the great gray owl hatched her eggs, and the rock chucks were awakening, yawning. You could hear their chirping in the morning and maybe twice more when the sun was high, as if they chirped and stretched and then rolled over for one last catch of sleep, as if they, too, were willing to let springtime come and go without even having said hello.

In the lower valleys the pheasant cocks crowed, marking their territory with voice, not bombs, and in the mountains that sagebrush buttercup made small talk with the grizzly, saying such friendly things as, "I'm glad we both got through the winter," and the bear, of course, stepped on the flower in reply, and went on looking, sniffing under log and bush for bugs and beetles peeking out to test the sun, but soft paws do not squash small things. To the easy eye that took the white world at a glance, we were still in the middle of winter—although by my calendar's insistence, it was already the first of May.

Then like a curtain rapidly rising to an impatient audience, the snow lifted up along the mountainsides, followed by dancing grasses green as young girls, and the sky was bright as new love, and wild delphiniums made the prairies purple as passion—larkspur, we call it, poison to the cattle but joyous to old winter eyes—and the *Balsamorrhiza*, the prairie sunflower, bloomed in tribal clumps as effortlessly as yellow-shirted Indian boys running down the mountain. It was the first of July and time for warriors to do battle again, time to pick up spear and shield and move out, time for war again, not in the bloody pit but in a high and holy place, in a sanitary place far from the sweat and blood of people, away from the sounds of people in pain, in the safe and sacred sanctuary of the high court, the Tenth Circuit Court of Appeals.

Within a few days after the appeal had been filed by *Penthouse,* Kelley, back in Colorado, took to the press. No one had filed a complaint against him with the Colorado Bar; Norman Roy Grutman should have reminded me.

With his client, the Denver *Post,* covering what he said, Kelley spoke to the Boulder Press Club: "When you work for the news media and your case goes to a jury, you're in trouble, whether you work for *Penthouse* or *Good Housekeeping."* Kelley also knew how to put *Penthouse* in respected company. He told the gathered group that when Guccione and his editor arrived for the trial, "Cheyenne, needless to say, was a culture shock for them and they were a culture shock for Cheyenne." He said no one seated on the jury admitted ever having seen a copy of *Penthouse* magazine," and when the judge "allowed the entire magazine, not just the Miss Wyoming piece, to be entered in evidence, it was passed around the jury box like a hot potato. Even the man we thought was on our side [the one in the back on the end] declined to look at it in front of everyone else. When the jury did look at the magazine in private, the jurors found a lot of things that don't sell well in Cheyenne, Wyoming," he said, "including a photo layout of lesbianism and letters to the editor about various sexual escapades."

With the Denver *Post* reporter hanging to his every word, Kelley continued, "In Wyoming, things like this might be discussed on a male-only hunting trip, but certainly not in mixed company, and this was a trial in mixed company." Things must be different in Boulder, Colorado, I thought. They must be very sophisticated there in that small town less than a hundred miles south of Old Cheyenne. This was the attitude that this alleged Victorian Wyoming jury had been perfectly capable of detecting, and was probably, more than anything else, responsible for the size of the jury's verdict. Kelley told the press club, "It would have been much easier to present the sexual material to a jury in Denver or Boulder." But I thought that jurors everywhere know what's right and decent and what's justice.

Kelley was making news for the Circuit Court judges to read before they made their decision in our case. The Court sat in Denver and the judges presumably read the Denver *Post*. If the judges missed it in the *Post*, they could read it in the *Rocky Mountain News*, and if they missed it in the *News*, it was carried in most other little papers in Colorado and Wyoming. Kelley told the reporters that anyone reading the *Penthouse* piece would know right away that it was "fantasy and fiction," exactly what he would argue to the Circuit Court judges after they'd read it all first in the papers. I could still hear the high howling of Grutman to the Grievance Committee concerning my profile in *Rocky Mountain Magazine*: "If Mr. Spence had done in England what he has done, or caused to be done in this article, he would be in prison and probably stripped of the right to practice law." And again I heard Grutman exclaim, "This is no mere peccadillo or trifle lightly to be disregarded."

Next Kelley filed his brief in the Circuit Court. The briefs were bound with baby-blue covers so that the judges could tell immediately, without even reading the title page, that this was the brief of the appellant. I held this one innocent-looking document in my hand, and examined it with wonder. It stood for $14 million. It should have been bound in green. The tone of the language was sacrosanct—the First Amendment protected them—the very pages of their brief seemed to transmogrify into old parchment and ancient calligraphy. I could smell the musty pages soaked in history where the enemy of the courts was the poor, the squatters driven from their forest homes by the closure of the land, where the midwives and the women who healed (the so-called witches) were condemned by the physicians.

Kelley raised all kinds of legal hell—claimed the article was about a fictional Kim Pring although the jury had found differently. He claimed that works of fiction were constitutionally protected—complained about the instructions of the Court to the jury, cried about the judge's refusal to grant a continuance, objected to the court's jurisdiction in Wyoming, and argued that plaintiff was a public figure. In effect, he was asking the Circuit Court to try the case anew without the benefit of the witnesses—to try it on the cold dead record and to substitute their findings for those of the jury.

But his big argument was that everything I had said was prejudicial, from my opening statement to my last breath before the jury—every matter previously ruled on in those every-morning sessions when Cooper made his motion for mistrial was now rehashed before the Circuit Court in Kelley's brief. He attached an appendix with ninety-five examples of my claimed improprieties.

"Schuster," I said, pacing, "how do you get a bunch of judges to understand Kim Pring? Or even want to? How do you get judges to feel what she felt, to see it as the jury saw it—to see it as a case about a human being, not just a case about the law?" Schuster didn't answer. "Kelley ignored the jury's findings." I threw his brief halfway across the room. It lit with its silly baby-blue face staring up at the ceiling. "He picks and chooses the facts and quotes whatever law he wants. Kelley's case never existed." I gave the brief a kick. It rolled over and collapsed. "It's like tearing your house down and rebuilding a different one out of the same materials and calling it home. Kelley's case has nothing to do with Kim. It has nothing to do with her injury—it has nothing to do with her at all!"

"But we've got to meet the legal issues," Schuster said. He had books stacked all over the atrium so you could barely walk through the damn place. "We've got to show the judges the other side of the legal hand."

"Fuck the legal hand!" I hollered. "This case is about the right of an ordinary woman to be protected by the law. If the law isn't for the people, and by God, women are people—that may come as a surprise to the judges"—I was shouting—"then the law should be outlawed, and lawyers should be outlawed and judges should be outlawed!"

Yet Schuster was right. When our case came before the judges, they saw the pretty-colored briefs and the cold legal words stacked in proper paragraphs with correct margins and type size. And they saw the citations to precedent, to blessed precedent! Life in the law is not of people but of the jurisprudential baby that bursts stillborn on appeal from the judicial womb and replaces the living. The living are only names in the title of the case.

Some appellate lawyers insist that appellate judges, cloistered in those high places, in those judicial monasteries where the citizens never tread—where living people never dare enter—don't really care about people. How could they? They've never seen the people. Nor are they passionate about justice. How could they be? They've never looked into the empty eyes of those justice has forsaken. The judges, they say, are in love with the law, embrace it, surround themselves with it, roll in it like hound dogs in something dead.

Yet even under the law, the Circuit Court of Appeals was not permitted to retry the case. The law bound them to accept as true the jury's findings of fact unless there was no evidence to support their findings. Every presumption of correctness was, under the law, to be given to the jury's verdict and the judge's rulings. Yet we all knew the Circuit judges would do whatever they damn well pleased with the case. They were the judges. Mere jurors do not bind judges.

Schuster and I labored for weeks over our brief, a good brief, bound in red as required by the Court rules so the judges could tell at a glance it was the appellee's brief—the scarlet brief. We told the Court of Kim's life, her struggle to become a champion, her pride in being Miss Wyoming, and how, in a few pages in *Penthouse,* she had been destroyed and how that had caused her to slink away and hide—that the libel was a perpetual, lifetime rape. If they'd just read our brief. But the judges read what they wish if, indeed, they read at all, and those desperate words we had inserted to make Kim Pring alive to the judges—well, that was all irrelevant anyway.

So far as I knew, nobody up there on the Circuit Court gave a damn about Kim Pring. That is called impartiality. None had ever laid eyes on her, ever looked in her face, ever heard her voice, ever tried to understand her hurt, ever saw the sneer on Guccione's face or heard the sound of utter disdain in his voice. They had seen nothing. They were, indeed, blind justice. The plaintiff had a name, but her name meant nothing, like a name scratched in the sand at low tide.

In our briefs we included reproductions of the actual article—told the judges Cioffari had actually attended the pageant—quoted Goode when he said he wouldn't have published the article at all had he known of all those similarities in the story to the real Miss Wyoming—explained how *Penthouse's* own expert, Pierson, admitted he would have consulted a lawyer before publication had he known of those similarities, and how Guccione thought it was all so very funny—and about his "flatworm testimony." We quoted their witness Clark that the story was outrageous and John Wideman, who was astounded at the flagrant disregard for basic human responsibility. We explained to the judges that Judge Brimmer had found that both parties had received a fair trial and quoted the actual findings of the jury that "a reasonable man reading the article would understand that Miss Pring *was* the person referred to therein"—that "both *Penthouse* and Cioffari published a false and defamatory statement *concerning the plaintiff*"—that "the article unreasonably placed *Miss Pring* in a false light before the public" and "that both defendants had acted in reckless disregard of whether the published matter *would be understood by a reasonable person to convey statements of facts about the plaintiff.*"

The jury had also made a special finding that our case had been proved by "clear and convincing evidence."

We quoted the United States Supreme Court in *Gertz*:

> But there is no constitutional value in false statements of fact. Neither the intentional lie nor the careless error materially advances society's interest in "uninhibited, robust and wide-open" debate on public issues.

Fiction, too, can libel. We all know that. Every first-year law student knew that. Every lawyer in the case knew that. Judge Brimmer knew that. Everybody had always known that. Libel is libel whether it comes from fiction or nonfiction.

Then we cited precedent—blessed precedent, the celebrated case of *Burton* v. *Crowell Publishing Co.*, in which a man was depicted in an actual untouched photograph holding a saddle, but the cinch, hanging loosely between his legs, gave the obviously false appearance that he was endowed with a penis of inhuman proportions. Professor Eldredge recounts that during a luncheon at the Harvard Club, Judge Learned Hand pulled the advertisement out of his briefcase and without any comment passed it around the table. His companions burst into roars of laughter. "That settles it," said Judge Hand. "It's defamatory." And in his now famous opinion he wrote:

> Everybody would at once see that it was the camera, and the camera alone, that had made the unfortunate mistake. . . . It is patently an optical illusion, and carries its correction on its face. . . . It would be hard for words so guarded to carry any sting, but the same is not true of caricatures, and this is an example; for notwithstanding all we have said, it exposed the plaintiff to overwhelming ridicule.

This was no First Amendment case. It was a case of libel, pure and simple. "We do not believe that we nor this Court has any bent on regulating *Penthouse*'s choice of material for its magazine. This case does not question *what* may be said. It only specifies against whom it *may not* be said recklessly and wantonly. It simply precludes *Penthouse* from committing the equivalent of emotional rape through its 25 million readers behind the cloak of the First Amendment. It is a case where no real First Amendment issue exists, but only the intimidating assertion that the First Amendment is somehow involved."

We took head on Cooper and Kelley's contention that we had been guilty of misconduct: "The trick, of course, is to combine, in one place, all of the questions objected to by *Penthouse* during a two-week trial covering 2,288 pages of testimony in order to create the illusion of misconduct. It is like gathering all the dandelions in the lawn, dumping them in a small pile and claiming the whole yard is yellow." We commented on each—defended each—pages of them.

Then Cooper and Kelley had called on the Libel Defense Resource Center in New York City for help, a corporation supported by the insurance companies, including such giants as C.N.A. Insurance Company and Employers Reinsurance Corporation, which wrote the insurance for *Penthouse;* and by the Association of American Publishers, which represents most of the major book publishers in America; the Authors' League of America; the American Newspaper Publishers Association; the Association of American University Presses; Doubleday and Company, the corporation that published my first two books; and the Magazine Publishers Association. It included the National Association of Broadcasters, which counts among its membership the major TV networks of the country. Its partisans also included Time, Incorporated, *The Washington Post*, the Times Mirror Company, the Writers Guild of America, both East and West, Dun and Bradstreet, and many other major organizations. In short, the supporting members of the Libel Defense Research Center control the media of this nation.

LDRC immediately reported the plight of *Penthouse* to its many powerful members. LDRC admitted: "A letter from counsel for *Penthouse* requesting *amicus curiae* assistance and describing his case [*Pring v. Penthouse*] and the issues presented on appeal was circulated to LDRC's supporting organizations." "Special alerts," as they are called, were sent to supporting members for *amicus curiae* assistance in the Pring case. Early on, LDRC reported in its newsletter, "It is understood that three organizations, the Association of American Publishers, the Authors' League of America and the Reporters' Committee for Freedom of the Press, were planning separately to file *amicus* briefs which were due on July 27, 1981. Copies of the various *amicus* briefs in *Pring* will be on file with LDRC."

Kim was no longer just a Wyoming woman seeking justice. She was *Pring*, the name of a case known across the land. She stood for the enemy of the organized media, and, as promised, they filed their *amicus curiae* briefs in the case—briefs filed as "friends of the court." The best appellate attorneys in America spoke to the Court, not as friends but as new litigants who, themselves, had their own axes to grind. They weren't Kim's friends.

The Association of American Publishers, representing over three hundred of the major book publishers in the United States advised the Court, "To permit the punitive damage award to stand in the face of such a clear effort to punish expressions of unpopular views would 'unnecessarily exacerbate the danger of media self-censorship' and, in the process, would undermine the most fundamental principles underlying the First Amendment." That a Wyoming woman had been maliciously libeled wasn't even an issue they addressed. It sounded as if the media were reaching for some new right, some new power without limits, a new power that would vest the absolute ownership of the First Amendment not in the people but in the media, which were, in major part, corporate America.

The Reporters' Committee for Freedom of the Press, an association of reporters and newspaper editors from the print and broadcast media, which by its own admission "provided representation, information, legal guidance, or research in virtually every major press-freedom's case that has been litigated since 1970," argued that the obvious goal of Kim Pring was to win the Miss America Pageant, that she had sought publicity all her life and had thereby become a public figure, making it all right, I guess, for *Penthouse* to transform her into the greatest cocksucker in the world.

The Authors' League of America, "whose 10,000 members write books, plays, and magazine stories and articles," simply ignored the jury's findings altogether and told the judges of the Circuit that Kim was not libeled because the story was fiction, that her privacy was not invaded since the story did not refer to her or use her name. The award was excessive and violated *Penthouse*'s constitutional rights. The Constitution was the sole property of the media, their exclusive business tool, and Kim Pring had interfered with that tool.

No one filed an *amicus* brief for Kim Pring. Who cares about the sparrow? No one would criticize the judges for throwing out the case of one ordinary sparrow. And if the judges held for the pornographer, their decision would be celebrated for having courageously upheld the First Amendment. The politics of the decision was therefore clear. I could never make the Court understand that this was not a First Amendment case because I could never make the *amicus* people believe it, and the Court would listen to them, to the ten thousand snarling voices of the leopards echoing across the jungle in the night. Guccione was right. The verdict wasn't worth the paper it was written on.

The summer had gone, the chokecherries had ripened and were stripped from the bush by the bears, and the chokecherry seeds were scattered in the droppings of the bears. Small flocks of gentle geese flew over the house of a morning—geese mated for life, flying over the exact southernmost peak of the roof—and the brave blooms of late wild asters fought against the frost. In the high country on a timbered mountainside I had heard the perfect bugle of the bull elk in rut. Its pure sound struck a joyous shiver in me and I saw my toddling granddaughter in the yellow light of early fall, gold on gold.

Then the elk had been driven down from the high mountain pastures by fresh fall snows, and the elk trampled on the bear dung in these lower places and ate the scrub along the creeks and the seeds of the chokecherries were shoved down into the soft soil by the sharp, planting hooves of the elk. The snows had followed the elk on down the mountain and covered the ground as high as the shanks of the elk, and the seeds and the bears would slumber all winter and bring forth new life in the spring.

But in November the elk were hunted and the geese were hunted. The elk hid in the timber shivering, the deep snows behind them blocking their retreat to the high country, and the hunters in front of them barring their escape below. The crack of the hunters' guns fractured the clear fall air, and geese fell out of the sky, and I saw one goose circling and circling where its mate had fallen, and I heard the long cry of the goose, and there was fear and sadness in the air in Jackson Hole.

In the late fall of 1981, on November 18 to be exact, the lawyers appeared before the Circuit Court in Denver to argue the case. The courtroom was packed with the lawyers from the offices in the Federal Building where Cooper used to work and with the judges' clerks, and the court personnel. I saw a young lawyer I knew.

"What's going on?" I asked. "I've argued here a lot of times and the place is usually empty."

"They came to see the so-called 'flamboyant' Gerry Spence get his comeuppance," he said. He grinned like he was only kidding

"You kidding?" I asked.

"No," he said. "They want to see the judges get you."

"How come?" I asked. I felt like a scared kid left alone in a strange place. "Why would they want to get me?"

"You're the big-time country lawyer, aren't you?" He laughed. "I tell 'em, 'Country lawyer, my ass.' They know you're a slick talker, but they figure that you can't slick talk the judges." I tried to walk away from him and started down the aisle to my table. He followed after me. The people gawked as I walked by. I nodded to them, but they didn't return the nod. "They say, 'This guy Spence is supposed to be good in front of a jury, but he can't keep a verdict once he gets it. Courts always take 'em away from him.' And I tell 'em, 'Don't count this guy out too soon. He may surprise you.' But they figure their judges will handle you, and they want to see it. The clerks have got bets going that as soon as you open your mouth, they'll get you."

"Thanks," I said. "That's just want I needed to hear. Really makes me feel good and warm and secure."

I left the bastard at the bar of the court and went over to my table.

Then I could see it all. There was Kelley, all hunkered down at counsel table in front of the bench where the three judges of the panel assigned to hear this case would sit. And next to him sat Norman Roy Grutman, in his black coat and gray striped pants and the head of his red farmer's kerchief bobbing out just right from the chest pocket of his coat. I walked over to Grutman and extended my hand. He took it with a curt bow and said nothing. I sat down at a small table provided for the appellee. The courtroom seemed dark like a forest and the high ceilings were a gray and gloomy sky, and I could feel my fear. The bailiff was crying that the court was in session, as though he were announcing the opening of this year's hunting season on people's lawyers and he prayed that "God save this Honorable Court." I prayed a little myself.

Then the three-judge panel marched in single file to their seats, their black robes flowing, each wearing his own particular judicial countenance. The judges peered down on the lawyers. Each judge, in turn, peered down at me, and when they did they offered no sign of human recognition. I smiled up at them but it is unjudicial for judges to return a lawyer's smile. I felt like running out of there, but the scowling judges, like deep winter snows, blocked any escape and the hostile audience behind me waited for the kill, and I thought of the elk at home shivering in the timber.

Kelley sat across from me with Cooper and Grutman at his table, his briefs and files stacked up in neat piles in front of him. In the audience I recognized the insurance man for *Penthouse* wearing his pinstriped three-piece suit, and there were other men sitting next to him with similar suits, pallbearers, I thought. I was wearing my own pinstripe, goddamn it, my Sunday best, for weddings and funerals— pants too damned tight. Going to throw up. Needed to pee. I couldn't leave. Chief Judge Seth was speaking to the lawyers. Each side would have half an hour and a yellow light would come on to warn when our time was about up, and we would be stopped on the exact second—probably even between syllables.

Kelley rose to his feet and began: "If it please the Court."

I heard him say that the article was obvious fantasy—heard Kelley's words droning on, words without music, sounds without any trace of human emotion so that the judges would not be riled—the story, Kelley said, was so inherently fantastical, so preposterous that no reasonable person could connect the contestant in the story to Pring—it was that simple, and the verdict was a result of passion and prejudice caused by the highly improper conduct of Pring's lawyer. Moreover, the verdict would threaten humor that identifies *real people* or places, such as Art Buchwald's fictional conversations or the *Doonesbury* comic strip. Hadn't he just assured the court that the article was about a fictional person, *not a real person?* "It is a matter of common sense that there has to be protection for statements in the form of humor, satire, and burlesque," Kelley said, and then he sat down.

I wished I could tell the judges how I felt, that I was afraid of them. Why shouldn't I be afraid of them? They could make this country lawyer pop and jump and dance like a dunce. They had the power of $14 million piled up on the bench in front of them, the power to do with it as they chose, and if they were displeased with this fool they could give it back to *Penthouse* and to the insurance-company men sitting there waiting for it, or they could dump it back into the pit and make me fight for it all over again.

They glanced blankly out over the audience but they couldn't see Kim Pring. At least look at the live person in the case, for Christ's sakes—she's the blond woman sitting in the back row on the end. See her? I tried to be calm, to look confident. They were human. Surely they could hear me. Two of the judges were thumbing the pages of the briefs in front of them. Chief Judge Oliver Seth ordered the timer set on me. Justice is borne by the clock.

"Well, Your Honors," I began in a very friendly voice. "My partner Eddie said I shouldn't talk to you like jurors—that I shouldn't argue the facts of my case. But I need you to know my client, Kim Pring. This case is not just about law. It is about a human being who was hurt. She was libeled. The jury said so." Their faces clung to the bone.

"She was a little girl who was born with a clubfoot who wanted to become a champion. Her mother helped her. She sold Avon products door to door to earn the money to—"

Then Chief Judge Seth interrupted me. "Counselor," he said in a low voice that sounded like God speaking down through the universe, "you'd better adhere to the advice of your partner and keep to the legal arguments in this case." There were snickers from the audience, then laughter. My face turned red. I couldn't stop the goddamn blushing. I was that choirboy again who had forgotten my lines, and all I could do was hum the tune and go "la, la, la," but afterward my mother said I had done very well, that nobody knew. I needed my mother.

Now I had my notes. Thank God for my notes. I grabbed them, and then I looked up and I said, "I thought perhaps you wanted to know first about the *people* in the case." I was surprised at the timid sound in my voice.

"We'd like to know about the legal principles in the case," one of the other judges said. He sounded more friendly. Perhaps he had a concern for people too. Then he said, "Mr. Spence, if we let this verdict stand, what would happen to *Doonesbury?*" The audience laughed. "Would *Doonesbury* not be endangered from suits such as yours?"

I remembered Kelley had mentioned *Doonesbury* in his argument. Was that merely by chance or had he known the judge was a fan of that comic strip? My God, surely the Court was able to make the necessary distinctions between fair comment and purposeful satire on the one hand, and a vicious, purposeless libel on the other. I tried to answer as best I could. I must answer. I was losing the case already. I could see $14 million emptying into the waiting sacks of the insurance men who had come to take it home again.

And I also forgot to argue to the Court: "The media wants freedom of the press? I want freedom of the press, Hitler and Goebbels wanted freedom of the press, and they had the power of the press behind them and so libeled a whole group of humans that the Holocaust was born. Goebbels used the free press to depict the Jew as 'racially and morally subhuman, a monster, a poisonous bacillus that had to be destroyed.'[1] Goebbels laughed with glee at having libeled his enemies with the monstrous joke until they were laughed out of existence. 'We dragged one [of the Jews] from among their midst and set to work on him. . . . We exposed him to the public without charge, nicely tamed for the people to look at, and we did this with wit and gall, anger and malice, and a piercing laughter already sounding the day of doom. . . . The laughs were on our side.' "[2] Why did I forget? Perhaps I knew the chief judge wouldn't give me the extra twenty seconds to make such an argument.

Ah, you judges! You complain of the incompetents of the Bar, but do you know how you frighten us? Next to you sit only your brothers, but to us, looking up, they are those near gods looking down with their terrible judicial faces and their deadly voices that stifle thought and choke the mind and drub into near helplessness these already frightened men, these men who would wish to stand proudly before you but who only blither and bumble and are rendered dumb like stagestruck children.

"This case involves a magazine, *Penthouse*, hiding behind the claim that this was fiction, not satire about real people, as in *Doonesbury*." For Christ's sakes, this wasn't a case about *Doonesbury*, but a case about a woman who had been libeled. What a pity *Doonesbury* was more real to the judge than Kim Pring. I said, "*Penthouse* has never claimed this article was about a *real* living person. *Penthouse* has steadfastly maintained this is fiction, and that fiction is protected by the First Amendment no matter what is said—even if the person in the fiction can be easily identified as a real person, and is libeled. That has never been the law." I was convincing no one.

"Sometimes it is the absurd that hurts the worst, the monstrous joke. Kim Pring is entitled to protection from libel. Fiction can libel. No one has ever doubted that. *Doonesbury* is entitled to great latitude as the author writes about public figures, but Kim Pring was a private person—the jury so found. So did the judge. The satire in *Doonesbury* is not libelous, not malicious. The jury found this *was* libelous and *was* malicious." I saw no change on the three faces of the law.

Then I just said it: "If *Doonesbury* ever calls a private person like Kim Pring 'the best blowjob artist in the world' to twenty-five million people and causes the damage that was caused to this young woman, and if a jury finds damages against *Doonesbury* who then comes running to this court for protection, well, with all due respect, I hope you throw *Doonesbury* out!"

The jury's award was excessive, was it not? An award that size was prima facie evidence of the jury's passion and prejudice, was it not? How could I begin to justify a punitive-damage award the size of this one? Their questions fragmented my presentation. I gave them my quick arguments about corporations being responsible in the law the same as we are, that they should be punished to the same extent that we are punished—$14 million, twelve and a half of it punitive damages—do you see it there in a pile, Your Honors? The jury says that sum represents justice—that is the sum necessary to punish *Penthouse*. And the jury said *Penthouse* should be punished.

But I could hear their answer, as clearly as if they had rendered their decision that very moment. I could hear it—twelve and a half million—yes, we see it there in that pile. That is the sum the jury wants to give to one ordinary person. That is too much for one ordinary person to receive—it would be unjust enrichment, and unjust enrichment is immoral.

They would never hear my response—that to permit *Penthouse*, the wrongdoer, to keep money it had been ordered by the jury to pay in punishment is unjust enrichment of *Penthouse*, for the money does not rightly belong to *Penthouse*. It was awarded by the jury to the injured. To take the corporation's money, its blood, is the only way to punish it. Surely you care about the living, about justice for people, more than you cherish preserving the corporate coffers.

But the judges would have only said: We care about the law, and when, in the law, the issues are in conflict, the controlling principle will decide.

What is the controlling principle?

The controlling principle is as it has always been: *Little people do not receive big justice.*

I didn't make my best arguments, I admit it, and when the damned yellow light went on, I struggled for a way to close gracefully. I don't remember what I said.

Then to my surprise Norman Roy Grutman got up. Kelley had left him only three minutes of the thirty allotted to *Penthouse*. His voice was melodious and high flying and he wasted no time in getting started. He was in his usual good form, and his words flowed.

"This is a grotesque verdict," he proclaimed. He revealed to the Court a judicial freak of monstrous proportions. "The article was so preposterous and outlandish that Miss Pring herself said no one in his right mind would ever have believed it." He quickly attacked "the mundane and rather maudlin attitudes of the 'heartland,' " referring to the Midwest, as compared to the more sophisticated views of the East. This was a case of the heartland against the East. "Mr. Spence has exploited the 'heartland' area morals to win," Grutman said.

"Let's not talk about 'the heartland,' " the chief judge said. "I'm tired of hearing about it." The chief judge's abrasive admonition didn't appear to faze Grutman. He argued right on, right on up to the closing bell. He was in the midst of a crescendo when the chief judge told him his time was up. Later I heard the judges said they were very impressed with him.

With the sound of our voices fresh in their ears, the judges had gone to their cloaking rooms, and they had probably laughed and joked with each other as they hung up their robes, about that Spence who had been put in his place, that's for sure, and how Grutman had been, too. The "heartland"! Imagine! Nobody could claim the judges hadn't been evenhanded. Then they had decided the case in half an hour, no more, maybe less, and one had been assigned to write the opinion.

The arguments of the judges are secret and unpublished. What was said by the judges vanished into the walls forever. The notes they made were secret, of course. Whether they read the actual trial record, whether they considered, even knew, even cared to know, the evidence the jury considered will never be known, because that is not for us, below, to know. The judges cannot read the whole of each record before them—thousands of pages to a case. Even they admit that. Their clerks are said to read the briefs we so assiduously labor over, these briefs in which we test and taste each word, and the clerks, these lawyers fresh out of law school, prepare a short summary of what they conclude we said in the briefs. How would I know if the judges read even their clerks' summaries? We only presume. We trust, as Schuster says, but it is not for us to know.

When I walked out of the courtroom, I could see that the lawyers and the clerks in the audience were grinning, and as I walked by them they stopped talking. I knew I hadn't done well. Nobody came up and said, "That was a great argument, Mr. Spence." They were honest by their silence. Then I saw Kim waiting for me at the door.

"Let's get out of here," I said.

She seemed happy. "You really did good," she said. But I knew she didn't know, and the lawyers stared at us as we walked out—got the hell out—into the late fall sun of Denver, Colorado.

We grabbed a cab to the airport. Kim still seemed happy enough. Maybe she knew the way women know. Maybe she knew and had become resigned to it. Maybe she was only glad it would soon be over. She didn't say.

But I didn't tell Kim Pring what I knew.

It would never be over for her.

33

The winter came and settled in at forty below and only the chickadees and the magpies and the mountain ravens dared stay, those brave birds black as aspen knots or white as aspen bark or both black and white as aspens with black-twigged fingers twisted, cramped in patient prayers. The moose ate away at last summer's new growth on young trees and then stood defiantly in my drive as if they owned the place. I stepped aside, and I also conceded to the chickadees their territory in the upper reaches of the trees, even at my window, for they sang on the bright days of winter and staked their claims by song, and I could enter no defense to such assertions. The magpies and the ravens squawked and scolded at each other and at me, and filled the winter full of racket. It was against them that I hollered back like lawyers holler at each other, and all winter both sides thought they'd won the argument.

Then came spring and also new birds to the aspens, the yellow warbler, the calliope hummingbird, the western tanager—birds of red and yellow and green like new flowers, like the Indian paintbrush and the yellow dogtooth violet and the wild geranium. We were not forgotten after all, except by the Tenth Circuit.

We heard nothing from the Circuit. Every morning I argued the case again and had better answers to offer up to the judges, and my arguments came to sound like faithful praying, for the judges held my case in their hands the way God holds one's fate and one's soul, but God had never been as silent as the Circuit, nor as careless with a man's life, which is his time. Had we been a day late in filing our brief, we would have lost it all; but no such restraints are placed on the judges to exhibit equal timeliness in rendering their decisions.

Summer came—still nothing. Then one day I received a call from that same lawyer I'd talked to in the Circuit Court just before I'd given my argument. He'd been right, of course. The audience did enjoy that new spectator sport called "getting the country lawyer." Now he offered further predictions.

"Well, I'm sorry to tell you this, Gerry, but you're going to lose." He didn't sound sorry.

"Oh, yeah, how do you know?"

"Well, I haven't been wrong in three years. I shouldn't tell you, but I will, because you are a friend."

"Thanks," I said.

"Yeah. The philosophy of the chief judge is well known. He appoints the panels to hear the case." I knew that. The chief judge assigns each case to a panel of three. "He appoints the people to the case who will see the case like he sees it. He knows his own judges. He appointed himself to this case. Right?"

"Right," I said.

"This is going to be the decision of Judge Seth's panel and the panel is gonna decide it for *Penthouse*."

"Why would they do that?" I felt weak. I felt sick. His logic seemed so correct and he sounded so sure of himself. He had been right before.

"I just say it," he said. "I'm a court watcher. You get so you can predict these creatures." He laughed. "The rest of it's my secret."

I told Schuster what the guy said, and Schuster said I should keep the faith. Eddie was more blunt about it. "I don't give a damn. That guy is full of shit. Those judges ain't gonna pat *Penthouse* on the ass and let 'em get away with that shit."

"Schuster," I hollered. He came popping out into the atrium. "This case is going to be decided by some judge's clerk. Who are the clerks?"

"Dunno," Schuster said. "They aren't going to decide this case any more than Rosemary makes your decisions." But my secretary decides a lot of things for me, a lot more than I admit.

"You've been worrying too long. You're getting paranoid."

"Yeah," I said, "and if you need to know what the law is or should be, just ask some kid who's never had a client and never been in the pits, some pansy ass who's never worked a day—just ask one of them—and they'll give you the answer every time."

"You're really on one again," Schuster said. "You ought to try some potassium. They say it helps calm the nerves."

The longer I waited, the worse I got. The Court was undoubtedly having trouble with the case. The judges couldn't agree and were haggling—that was the problem, I thought. There would probably be a dissent and we would probably lose, all right, just like the son of a bitch said. I decided we'd better settle the case. Eddie didn't think so, and Schuster didn't think so either, but I thought if we could pick up a couple of million we ought to take it and let the rest go. A bird in the hand—little people don't get big justice—the Baboon Rule—I argued them all.

"Two million is just fifteen percent of the judgment," Schuster said, after a quick calculation.

"We shouldn't give this verdict away," Eddie said. "We worked too hard for it. You're just gettin' too nervous."

I said, yeah, I was getting too nervous all right. I trust people, juries, ordinary men and women who understand how it is to be helpless and afraid. Juries are drafted and wield their power involuntarily. History has proven the supremacy of the collective judgment of laymen over the decisions of judges who exercise power out of choice, perhaps out of some deep craving. Power is a dastardly potion.

Judges exercise the power of God—it is they who take away the babies from their mothers, who yawn at the receiver's report and extinguish a man's lifetime work with a single word—who condemn men to those hellholes called penitentiaries where human beings are stacked up like corpses in the toilets because there is no other room—who sentence men to choke and gag and die in the name of justice, in the name of revenge—that is the daily work of judges. Oh, Your Honors! You have such power over all of us! You can, with the ease of emperors, of gods, transform brave men to grovelers and proud men to obsequious fools.

The Circuit Court was silent. We had better settle, I thought, before the decision comes down against us.

"The law is *for* us," Schuster said. "Take it easy."

"It makes no difference how you read the law. It's how the judges read the law," I said. The judges of the Circuit had their libraries brimming with books, and the books were laden with endless cases, any kind of a case they needed to support whatever decision suited their fancy on any particular day. I thought of my mother sorting through her button jar to find the buttons she wanted to sew on my shirt, and the buttons usually didn't match at all. She picked the buttons. I didn't. But it was my shirt and I had to wear it.

I called Kelley. Could he get everybody together for a settlement conference? Maybe. Could they come to Jackson? No. He would have to bring in the insurance people from Chicago and New York and the insurance lawyers would have to be there too. It would be hard for everybody to get to Jackson. I agreed to come to Denver and in the early fall of 1982, we finally met.

The Circuit was still silent.

We gathered in the offices of Cooper and Kelley in Denver. We filled their plush conference room, Eddie and me and Cooper and Kelley and the insurance men from the two companies and their lawyers. They still wore their pinstriped suits and their neat little loafers with the thingamabobs that flopped when they walked. We wore our jeans and open-collared western shirts and hats, which didn't impress them either.

Cooper shoved a paper under our faces. "Read this and sign it, or we're not going to have a meeting," he said.

Everybody stared at us, waiting to see what we would do. Among other things, the paper said the meeting would be confidential and that "we will not repeat, discuss, comment upon or in any way communicate any acts of or statements by persons attending this meeting." We should have gotten up and left.

"Let's get the fuck out of here," I said to Eddie.

He thought a moment. "Yeah," he said. "But it's their problem. They're as uptight as a bull's ass in fly time. Let's sign it. We're not agreeing to anything we wouldn't do anyway." Eddie was right. Settlement conferences are treated as confidential by ethical lawyers. It was an insult, but I wanted the insurance men to hear our evaluation of the case. Up to this point they had heard only from Cooper and Kelley—and maybe Grutman. We signed. Then I gave a good final argument, I can say that much. I performed for them, but there was no settlement.

On the way home I said, "Eddie, these guys have to know something we don't know. We didn't even come close. Our case isn't that bad. If the Circuit affirms, Grutman will sue those insurance companies for not settling within the policy limits, because *Penthouse* will have to pay out of its own pocket the four million that isn't covered by insurance, plus interest, and the insurance companies could have settled and saved *Penthouse* the overage. They've got to know something we don't."

And no sooner had we returned home than another call came in from my court-watching friend in Denver.

"Sorry to tell you this, but you lost the *Penthouse* case."

"Nobody told us that," I said. "How do you know?"

"I know. Everybody in the Federal Building in Denver knows. It's all over. It's been the topic of conversation for weeks—you lost two to one."

"What's the deal?"

"You aren't going to get a damn cent," he said.

"Nothing?"

"Nothing! They aren't even going to send it back for a new trial or cut the verdict or anything. You get *nothing!*" he said.

"Jesus," I said. "I sure hope you're wrong."

"I'm not. I haven't missed in three years."

I guess I'd forgotten. This was the case of a woman who had been charged by *Penthouse* with possessing certain magical powers, the powers owned only by a witch, and the witch had come to court to defend herself, to defend against the charges of *Penthouse,* and she had been tried. Nothing changes. It *was* the trial of a witch and the law of the *Malleus* applied. How could I forget? The *Malleus!*

I opened the ancient document: "If he [the judge appealed to] sees that the reasons for the appeal are frivolous and worthless, and that the appellant only wishes to escape or to postpone his sentence, let his apostles be negative and refutatory."[1] Let the burning begin.

"Eddie! Schuster!" I hollered. "We're gonna lose!" God, I couldn't stand the pain of it!

Eddie didn't believe me. Schuster didn't. They were the faithful sons of the law. For the rest of the fall they did not believe it. As the Angus steers across the fence on my neighbor's ranch grew sleek on green grass, shiny as wet muskrats, as they grew soggy, as they say, ready for the fattening pens, they still did not believe it. Nor did they believe it later on in the fall when the geese were flying again over the south gables of my roof, nor did they believe it when the peaceful mountain air was shattered once more with the sounds of the hunters' guns, and the geese and the elk and the moose were dying, and the hunters were jubilant with their killing. They did not believe it until something made me call Rosemary from our plane that late afternoon on November 5, 1982.

We were headed through a storm. The *Spirit of Wyoming* was bucking, and the ice was popping from her propellers and wings, and the propellers were chopping through a sky as gray as gloom and air heavy and dreary as doom.

"I have bad news," Rosemary said through the static. The radar was bright red ahead. "Please don't kill the messenger."

"What's the bad news?" Imaging? One of the kids, my father, for

Christ's sakes? "It's the *Penthouse* decision—we lost," she said. "That's all I know. You better call the AP." I tried frantically to get the AP on our in-air phone and when I couldn't make the damn thing work I asked our pilot, Glen, to get the AP for me. I couldn't think. I could only hold on. I thought I would throw up. I never got airsick. Then Glen said he had the AP, and some dead-voiced reporter asked what comment I had on the Circuit Court's decision.

"What decision?" I asked. I felt my heart in my throat. I choked.

"The Circuit Court has ruled that the *Penthouse* story was not libelous," the reporter said. "What is your comment, Mr. Spence?"

"I don't understand," I said. "Of course it was libelous. The jury said so. You must have misread the finding."

"No, I have it right here on the wire. 'Miss Pring will get nothing.' "

"Well, I don't believe it," I said. "I'll have to see it to believe it."

Then the reporter read the wire story to me. It included the glowing comments of Kelley: "This is the first case that has unequivocally recognized that the First Amendment precludes recovery of libel from an author of fiction who does not intend to depict real events. Heretofore, authors have been in an extraordinary state of uncertainty."

Kelley, not Miss Wyoming, had saved the world.

When I read the newspaper account the next day, I still did not believe it. There had to be a horrible mistake. I had to see the decision. Dan Paul, a distant lawyer, gloated to *The New York Times* that the ruling "would clear the air and restore a proper balance.... It [the decision] shows the importance of adequate appellate review of jury verdicts."

Finally the decision came, and finally I spoke to the press. All I could think to say was the truth—that when I learned of the Court's holding, I wept. "Weeping is the reaction somebody has who puts his heart and soul in a case for a client and the jury gives justice, but the Court throws it all out." There was nothing else to say.

I called Kim. She had already heard. I choked up, but Kim's voice was clear and strong over the phone. "That's all right, Mr. Spence. You did your best. We did the best we could. I'm not ashamed of what we did."

"You remember when we talked a long time ago in the Hitching Post, and I told you we'd go all the way to the United States Supreme Court? Well, that's where we're going to go now."

And Kim said, "You bet."

The Tenth Circuit's decision was split, the majority opinion having been written by Chief Judge Seth and joined in by Judge Logan. Judge Breitenstein had dissented. Judge Seth said the question was "whether the story must reasonably be understood as describing *actual facts* about the plaintiff." If the story wasn't to be understood by a reasonable person as describing *actual facts*, then there would be no liability, which, of course, gave complete immunity to the monstrous joke that could so injure, injure even worse than any facts a reasonable person might actually believe were true. Maybe *Doonesbury* was what it had all come down to after all. It was the *Doonesbury* Decision.

The judge cited the *Greenbelt* and *Letter Carrier's* cases where the courts had held that the words in question could not be taken literally; therefore it followed that no factual representation was present. He accused Judge Brimmer of refusing to submit to the jury the question of "what was reasonably understood," although he found that Cooper and Kelley had offered such an instruction. He said, "It is simply impossible to believe that a reader could not have understood that the charged portions were pure fantasy and nothing else. It is impossible to believe that anyone could understand that levitation could be accomplished by oral sex before a national television audience or anywhere else. The incidents charged were impossible. The setting was impossible." He had taken the defendant's argument, hook, line and sinker. Since everybody knew that you couldn't levitate by fellatio, there was no libel. It was that simple.

The decision recognized no rights for Kim Pring or any other human being injured by the vicious lie—the more vicious the lie, the more the lie got protection because no one could take the monstrous lie seriously, even though it could devastate the victim. The monstrous lie was now fully shielded by the courts. It was a simplistic view that if no one believes such a lie, then there is no right to redress for libel, even if the lie might destroy an innocent person.

Judge Seth wrote, "The story is a gross, unpleasant, crude, distorted attempt to ridicule the Miss America contest and contestants. It has no redeeming features whatever"—but if it had no redeeming features whatever, then wasn't it obscene, and being obscene, was it now entitled to constitutional protection? The words of the judiciary suggested no human being, no living person, no blond, breathing, real Wyoming woman ever existed. There was no living victim. There was only the law.

I agreed with Judge Seth when he said: "The First Amendment is not limited to ideas, statements, or positions which are accepted; which are not outrageous; which are decent and popular; which are constructive or have a redeeming element; or which do not deviate from community standards and norms; or which are within prevailing religious or moral standards. Although a story may be repugnant in the extreme to an ordinary reader, and we have encountered no difficulty in placing this story in such a category, the typical standards and doctrines under the First Amendment must nevertheless be applied. The magazine itself should not have been tried for its moral standards. Again, no matter how great its divergence may seem from the prevailing standards, this does not prevent the application of the First Amendment." I agreed, but I didn't need the lecture since the lecture wasn't to the point. *Penthouse* was not tried for its morals. It was tried for libel, and what the judge had failed to recognize was that the Constitution does not immunize libel in fiction or in any other writing. No, it does not. It should not. It never has.

Judge Breitenstein dissented. He said the question was whether *Penthouse* can escape liability by the claim that the article was fiction and fantasy—and that the article contains both fiction *and* fantasy. He wrote, "The article says that Miss Wyoming performed fellatio with a male companion and caused him to levitate. In her appearance at a national Miss America contest, she thought that she might save the world by similar conduct with officials. She manipulated her baton so as to simulate fellatio. She performed fellatio with her coach in view of television cameras. I consider levitation, dreams, and public performance as fiction. Fellatio is not. It is a physical act, a fact, not a mental idea. Fellatio has long been recognized as an act of sexual deviation or perversion. Numerous decisions place fellatio within the crime of sodomy, which civilized people throughout the world have long condemned. In *Hunt* v. *State*, 10 Cir. 638 F. 2d 1305, a conviction for sale of a movie 'graphically depicting a woman performing fellatio,' Id. at 1307, was affirmed. The statements in the *Penthouse* article that Miss Wyoming, identified by the jury as plaintiff Pring, engaged in acts of sexual deviation and perversion, is a defamation of character which no decision of which I am aware has placed within First Amendment protection.

"*Penthouse* cannot escape liability by relying on the fantasy used to embellish the fact. *Penthouse* did not present the articles as fiction." Then the judge said, "Responsibility for an irresponsible and reckless statement of fact, fellatio, may not be avoided by the gratuitous addition of fantasy." If that is not obvious, then no person is safe from libel since to protect from it, all that must be done is to add a little fantasy. It would be like saying, Do you see that pile of dung?

Yes, I see that pile of dung.

Watch me put this dab of fantasy whipping cream on top. Now watch me put this pretty fantasy cherry on top of that. What we now have, of course, is no longer a pile of dung. What we now have is something that has been transformed, by the wizardry of the judiciary, and whipped cream, into something other than dung, something entitled to constitutional protection.

"This is not the law!" Schuster shouted. "We'll file a motion for the whole Court to hear this case. The majority of the Court could never concur in this decision."

"For the majority to disagree, they've got to go against the chief judge who gives them their daily bread of cases," I said. "The tribe won't banish the chief."

"The hell they won't, if the chief is wrong," Schuster said.

We had no other choice. There was no other move to make. We were in a desperate place. We had lost. We hadn't even been given the right to a new trial. It was all over, unless we could get the full Court to hear us. Oh, we could still apply to the United States Supreme Court to take the case, but our chances there were nil. Who would hear the plea of a baton twirler in far-off Wyoming?

We labored over our brief. We wrote: *"The effect of the decision is staggering.* It plainly holds that all fiction and fantasy is protected no matter how private the plaintiff may be, no matter that the plaintiff is plainly identified or identifiable, no matter how maliciously the writing was published, and no matter how grossly obnoxious the libel may be. If it is fiction or fantasy, or even partly so, the whole of the writing is immune, and no remedy exists for innocent citizens so injured. This cannot be the law of this land."

We pointed out that Judge Seth was "just plain wrong" when he found that Judge Brimmer failed to submit to the jury the question of whether this publication conveyed statements of fact about the plaintiff. "The trial court instructed the jury in this regard *in two separate instructions,* and the jury made a special finding of fact 'that the published matter could be understood by a reasonable person reading it to convey *statements of fact* about the plaintiff.' By overlooking the specific findings of the jury and the Court's instructions in this regard, the majority substituted its own contrary findings of fact for that of the jury."

We asked the Circuit judges: "Well, then, does the insertion of a fantasy immunize the remainder of the factual material contained in the writing?" That was the question. Had the court adopted the Whipped Cream and Cherry Rule as the new law of the land?

We said to the Circuit judges: "No court in this land has ever ruled that libelous material may be immunized by the inclusion of fantasy. No court in this land has ever ruled that fantasy and fiction itself is immune from libel if it maliciously injures an identifiable person. As a matter of fact, the contrary has always been the law of the land."

Schuster said, "I'll bet they just needed to save *Doonesbury*."

"No," I said. "The same old principles of the law are still at work. If this case had been the case of a man libeled—if they called him a cocksucker—and if the jury had only returned a small verdict for the man, and if the entire national media hadn't descended on the court at once, the decision would have been different. The *Malleus* is still alive, Schuster."

But Schuster was a legal scholar, and no student of the law could give serious credence to the *Malleus*. We are an enlightened age.

Schuster shook his head in disbelief. "You're a strange man," he said. But his eyes were kind and his voice was soft.

I said, "Even Judge Seth couldn't help but mention it in his decision—about how Kim had amended her complaint to avoid answering *those questions*. The rule that little people aren't entitled to big justice is still the law."

Schuster nodded.

"And that decision was the only way the Court could deal with fourteen million dollars. It gave them a way out. They didn't know what to do with fourteen million dollars, especially the twelve and a half million in punitives. They've never really known how to handle punitive damages. One little Wyoming girl sure wasn't going to get that much money. I always thought they couldn't stand it that the kids of Karen Silkwood might get ten million in punitives—and they reversed that case too, remember? That is the controlling principle behind these decisions—little justice for little people—so they give the money back. That's my *opinion*."

"Well, you're still entitled to your *opinion* in this country," Schuster said.

"They gave the money back to *Penthouse* because we can never overcome the Little People–Little Justice Principle," I said, "It is just too much money."

"We'll try," Schuster said.

"Yeah, we'll try," I said. "Steers try." I was feeling impotent.

We wrote another brief. "One could now claim that a named, revered judge committed fellatio on his fellows during argument to pursuade them to his point of view. It could detail his sexual acts with the other members of the court, actually naming them, all of which acts might be factually possible, but the whole story would be immunized by claiming that he also committed the act publicly underneath the bench during the argument of some famous case. The outrageous claim of public fellatio immunized the entirety of the defamation."

We covered every base in the brief—even *Doonesbury*. We said, "When this case was up for oral argument, one of the justices asked, 'But if this is libelous, will we lose *Doonesbury?*' In the first place, *Doonesbury* doesn't deal with private persons, is immune under the fair comment doctrine, and deals with an editorial matter, not so vile and unworthy that it has no socially redeeming value at all, as the majority depicts this *Penthouse* article. To save *Doonesbury*, we need not sacrifice the good names, lives and privacy of the American public."

We wrote: "The present holding of this Court leaves naked and unprotected the constitutional right of private persons to their privacy. As important as the First Amendment is, it must not give license to the irresponsible to defame and injure private citizens without remedy." We pointed out that even *Penthouse*'s senior editor admitted that if the jury saw the article as being about a real Miss Wyoming, it certainly held her up in a false light, and "a celebrated witness for *Penthouse* [Pierson] said even fiction is capable of holding persons up in a false light and invading their privacy. The pain and agony of being emotionally raped by twenty-five million readers is no less painful because part of it, yes, even all of it, could be seen as merely fiction." We filed our petition for rehearing in the Tenth Circuit Court of Appeals on the twelfth day of November, 1982.

Then before the Court could decide, Cooper and Kelley hit us again in the Denver *Post*, the paper the judges would most likely read. A reporter called me on the fifteenth of November. He said, "Kelley says you're unethical. He says you don't represent your client's best interests. He says all you're interested in is big verdicts. He says you misconduct yourself so badly it's little wonder your cases get thrown out. *Silkwood* got thrown out. Now *Pring.* What do you have to say."

I couldn't believe what I was hearing. While the Circuit was considering our petition, Kelley was attacking again in his client's newspaper. I should have kept my mouth shut, but I have a weakness. I replied, "Well, I think these people are a little premature to sit there clattering their teeth about how Gerry Spence is really a dummy. Neither of these cases have been finally disposed of. The United States Supreme Court has agreed to hear the Silkwood case and the Pring case isn't over yet." I told the reporter he ought to check with Kelley before he printed what Kelley had supposedly said—I thought it was libelous.

The article came out with the language somewhat softer. Kelley said that the record in both the Silkwood case and the Pring case revealed that "Gerry Spence doesn't play by the rules laid down by the appellate courts." He wanted the world to understand that I was unethical, but he carefully chose his words. Yet Kelley knew as well as I that although he had complained bitterly and profusely to the Court about my alleged misconduct, the Court in neither the Silkwood case nor in the Pring case even so much as made mention of such allegations.

I said, "You see, it works like this: *Penthouse* says, 'We print ugly things about you because it sells magazines. Now, if you want to say anything back, if you want to take us to court, we'll make you sorry for it—we'll claim your lawyers are unethical. We'll attack you further!"

And the *Post* wasn't through with me yet. It reported: "But Kelley's main criticism of Spence—who, with the heavy publicity and the recent publication of his autobiography, is one of the country's best-known and most sought-after lawyers—is that he's too interested in the flourish of a big jury judgment and not interested enough in whether his clients ultimately win on appeal." I didn't care about winning on appeal? I didn't care about Kim? That hurt the worst. Maybe I should ask Schuster if that was libel—to subvert my client's interests in favor of my own, which is, is it not, a charge of unethical conduct?

Then for the finishing touches, the *Post* got Dan Paul into the act again. The story said: "As far as Spence's trial tactics are concerned,

Paul, who is critical of him on other counts, called them 'nothing short of brilliant.' " How the hell would he know? To my knowledge he'd never seen me in court. "It's just that they [Spence's trial tactics] were used for the wrong purpose," Paul said. I guess the correct way for a man to use his talent was to represent Corporate America against the people—against the Kim Prings of America.

I wished I had kept my damned mouth shut. It made it all look like a terrible brawl. The headlines in the *Post* read: LAWYERS SQUARE OFF. OPPONENT DISPARAGES SPENCE'S FAMOUS TACTICS. Perhaps it was an intentional brouhaha fomented in the local press just when the judges were about to decide our petition for rehearing. The timing was too exquisitely coincidental, and before the *Post* article had concluded, Kelley spoke once more to the Tenth Circuit judges on their favorite subject. "If the original judgment stands, satirical cartoon strips such as *Doonesbury* and numerous other parodies could be deemed libelous." There it was again—*Doonesbury!*

On the twelfth day of January, a divided Court refused our petition. Four of the nine judges voted to rehear the case. The chief was not banished nor his decision reconsidered.

Another long winter passed and another season came, a time again for new life, for new growth on young aspens where moose had fed all winter, a time for the buttercup to poke out its tiny, shiny yellow face from under the banks of melting snow. Then on April 4, 1983, we filed our petition for writ of certiorari in the United States Supreme Court.

The *Malleus*, too, explained that one last appeal to the highest court of the Church might occur, should the "Most Holy Lord," the pope, allow it. But such appeals were reserved for only the few and the mighty, and the *Malleus* warned the judges even then "against engaging in litigation [in taking part in such appeals]" so that they should not become "sorely troubled with fatigues, misery, labour, and expense in Rome. . . . Other heretics, seeing the judges fatigued and detained in the Court of Rome, will exalt their horns and despise and malign them and more boldly proclaim their heresies, and when they are accused they will appeal in the same way," and other judges "will fear lest they may be troubled with miseries and fatigues arising from similar appeals. All this is more prejudicial to the Faith of the Holy Church of God."[2] Nothing changes.

Our petition to the High Court was our humble request that a lowly citizen be heard. It was only a request for a hearing—that's all—just hear us, please. It was an important case we told the justices, and it raised crucial questions deserving a hearing: "Is fiction a complete defense to a libel action under the First Amendment? Does the insertion of fantasy immunize the article as a whole from libel?" We were beating at the gates—please take this case. Please hear us.

We told the Court that, simply stated, the rule of the Circuit was that *a little fantasy immunizes a lot of libel*. We wrote, "It is time to reject the effort by *Penthouse* to wrap this conglomerate of indecencies in the fine, luxurious silks of the First Amendment. It was not right for *Penthouse* to transform Kim Pring into a hussy, to pluck her out of the Wyoming plains like some kind of bauble they could play with in their New York corporate offices, painting her falsely with whorish and brazen colors, dangling her in front of millions of men to leer and gawk at as they flip through pages of descriptions of fellatio, intermixed with photographs of lesbian lovers who reach sexual climax with the aid of water from a garden hose. It is not right that Kim Pring is used in this manner, and it is not right that others in the future may be so used by *Penthouse* or other publications when they decide to make more money by dangling another young bauble before their readership.

"It is time for common sense to prevail," we said. "If the *Penthouse* argument is approved and the ruling of the Tenth Circuit Court of Appeals is permitted to stand, then all citizens—public figures and private, obscure people alike—will be without remedy against the vilest defamations and the most outrageous false-light invasions of privacy. Publishers will be permitted to escape liability simply by inserting an obviously fictional segment into the offensive, and otherwise actionable, article. This publishing expedient will thereby serve to immunize the article from redress, and to wrest from all citizens the rights that this Court has painstakingly decreed."

Kelley wrote a brief opposing the High Court's hearing of our case. He said, "We also think it is time for common sense to prevail. If petitioner's unprecedented theory of liability were sustained in the present case, it would bring to a virtual halt the publication of satirical writing that is inspired even indirectly by real events and real people participating herein." He spoke again of *Doonesbury!* Well, I thought, why should private persons become mere fodder for writers? Why are the rights of writers superior to those of ordinary persons? Why is libel no longer a rule of law available to protect the citizens' reputations? Had the baboons finally given it all away to the leopards?

"They'll grant our petition," Schuster said. "They'll give us a hearing. The questions are too important to ignore. The Court can't let that decision stand. Besides, we lost both the decision and the motion for rehearing by just *one* vote—just one! It was that close!" Schuster pounded the table. "And the decision wasn't just!" His face was red. "The Court has to hear it."

Then I reminded Schuster what all lawyers and judges know of the United States Supreme Court—it is not a court of last resort for the people. It is a court that establishes policy and interprets the law and, in fact, makes the law. It does not render justice. Juries render justice, but where has the jury system gone? In civil cases, juries are only vestiges of the past. The civil law has been taken over by the judges and is now their exclusive property. The civil law is business. And people will not be allowed to meddle in something as important as business. Yet, even now, the people have not yet discovered they have been disenfranchised. Even lawyers can't stand to admit it. In any nation in which the people's rights have been subordinated to the rights of the few, in any totalitarian nation, the first institution to be dismantled is the jury. I was, I am, afraid.

"We no longer have a jury system," I told the great court. The Circuit had substituted its own findings for those of the jury. Yet they often had—whenever they pleased, whenever that Court was not in agreement with the jury's verdict. The press printed up my lamentations and thought it was just the sour grapes of a losing lawyer from the sticks.

Another season passed, and on the first day of summer in the year 1983, with Colter's daisies just beginning to show their light purple and the new water pipits peeping cautiously from their nests along the mountain streams, white with roar, and the young of the white-crowned sparrows hatching in the greenly willows, the Supreme Court of the United States threw out our plea without comment, and let stand the Circuit Court's opinion against Kimerli Jayne Pring.

I called her on the phone.

"It's all over, Kim."

"I know, Mr. Spence. I heard on the news. I'm sorry," she said. "You worked so hard."

"Well, at least it's all over."

"No," she said. "It's still happening to me. They still call me 'that *Penthouse* girl.'"

"The rape is still going on."

"Yes," she said. "Every day."

"And you're in season all year long, aren't you?"

"Yes, I guess," she said.

"We only kill the geese and the elk in the fall."

"But there's five seasons of rape," Kim said.

"What do you mean?" I asked.

"A woman can be raped in the spring and the summer and the fall and the winter." She waited. Her voice wasn't sad. She didn't sound bitter. She didn't sound hurt. I couldn't hear the sounds of feeling anymore. I heard the dead sounds of the intellect. She sounded like a judge. "And a woman can be raped in a fifth season," Kim Pring said. "Whenever she's in court."

34

A law of nature I'd learned watching the chickens in the chicken house is that nobody loves a loser. When a chicken gets a small sore on its head, the other chickens start pecking at it until the wound is open and bleeding, and the others peck at the poor chicken until it's dead. When the alpha male among the wolves, who rules the pack, and who towers over them and has led them through many a battle, is hurt and goes down, the others descend, ripping and tearing until he's nothing but a bloody spot in the snow. And when you go down you better grab your ribs and cover your head because the kickin' is just gettin' started.

People took after Kim unmercifully. Their weapons were phony solicitous smiles and words that bit from insincerity. "Oh, isn't it too bad that you didn't get to keep all that money" and "Well, it was a good go for the dough while it lasted. You were rich on paper" and "You got your money's worth in publicity, you gotta admit that." Someone began a whispering campaign that the real reason she didn't win was because everybody knew that what they'd heard about her doing it to the football team four times a day, or whatever, was true. They still called her "Penthouse," and men gawked and panted when she walked by, and some still hollered out of open car windows, "Hey, Penthouse, how about a little?"

Kim tried for months to get a job. She had her application in numerous places but, as one prospective employer said, they didn't need a woman with her particular talent. While another was leering at her in a way that made her sick, he admitted that his wife wouldn't let him hire her. "But I'm sure in favor of having a girl around the office who's got talent like you got!" And he laughed. Kim didn't go to any more interviews.

One day she called me. "I just can't get a job," she said. She was almost hysterical, sobbing. "What am I going do?"

"I don't know, Kim," I said.

"Well, then, I'm going to join the army," she said. "My dad made a good career for himself. Maybe they'll take me."

"I'd sure think so," I said. "They'd be lucky to get you. But I wouldn't join out of desperation."

"I'm not desperate," she said. "I just have to get out of here." She began crying again. I felt guilty—like I was the one who had helped kill Kim Pring.

I felt down too, I'll admit it, and sure enough, the Denver *Post* began pecking again, this time in a gratuitous editorial. They said I was going into show biz, which I wasn't, and that I had become a favorite subject of newspaper and magazine articles because of my "self-promoting style—jet-setting from courtroom to courtroom, broad-brimmed cowboy hat, leather jacket, Indian jewelry, blue jeans and long hair." I was a deluxe coxcomb who, they claimed, "is fond of bragging on radio talk shows that he has never lost a trial by jury," which I'd never said. Then they went on to make me look like a full-blown, unethical bullshitter: "However, he conveniently neglects to point out that many of those victories have been overturned on appeal and some clients will never get a dime from their original multimillion-dollar jury verdict."

The *Post* was just getting started. "The most recent example of Spence's hollow victories comes from Wyoming, where he persuaded a hometown jury to give the outrageous sum of $26.5 million to a former Miss Wyoming who claimed she was defamed by a satirical article in a porn magazine. The verdict was widely publicized, and Spence parlayed the case into another round of radio talk-show appearances and magazine interviews." Then they really pecked hard. "Any first-year journalism student could have predicted that the verdict wouldn't stand, and—sure enough—the woman ended up without a penny after the case was taken all the way to the U.S. Supreme Court and arguments of law superseded arguments of emotion." I wondered if Kelley wrote part of that editorial—it seemed to me I'd heard that song before.

I called the *Post* and talked to the editor; we had a nice long chat about libel and being fair and all, and I told him Kim and I were tired of being pecked at in the chicken house, and he said he didn't know what the hell I was talking about, but that if I insisted, which I did, he'd give me equal space on the editorial page of the *Post* for a reply which, of course, would prove once and for all that the Denver

Post was fair. At least it proved they knew how to sell newspapers. I wrote:

> We don't get the *Post* out here in the sticks, so I didn't know what my friends were so excited about until I finally got a copy yesterday. I'll admit it was a regular full-blown diatribe about what a rascal I am—a no-good-publicity-seeking-low-life-kind-of-a-fella who tricks juries out of huge verdicts just so he can get his name in the paper. It didn't even hint I might actually work hard for ordinary folks—said my cases were big sideshows, not to help my clients, but to make me famous.
>
> I got to wondering—how come the *Post* is so put out at me? I mean, what did I ever do to the *Post*? I've never even met the fella who wrote the editorial, and I find out later that all he knew about me was that he heard me on a Denver radio show once when I was trying to sell my book, *Gunning for Justice* (thanks). So why is the *Post* so huffy about this country lawyer who lives over 300 miles away in little old Jackson, Wyoming, and who tries to mind his own business representing his clients, one of whom was Miss Wyoming, against that 'porn magazine,' *Penthouse*?
>
> Then the next morning in the shower, which is where I always do my best thinking, it came to me—I'd sued the Denver *Post* once for a fella the *Post* had called a gunrunner and a crook when, in fact, he wasn't either, a pretty decent sort who'd been staying home minding his own business, too. All I ever did to the *Post* was represent my client. Everybody's entitled to a lawyer, wouldn't you say—even if you're suing the *Post*—or *Penthouse*?
>
> Now that editorial of yours said, at least as I read it, that I was guilty of using the legal processes, not for the benefit of a decent Wyoming woman whom *Penthouse* said some really despicable things about—but instead to get publicity for myself. Why should the *Post* be siding with *Penthouse* against me and a nice woman from Wyoming whom the *Post* had never met either? Well, I thought, it might also be because the lawyer who represented *Penthouse* in the Miss Wyoming case has represented the *Post* for years. I figured I shouldn't be too peeved; if I had to choose up sides, with all due respect, I'd rather be on the side of a good Wyoming woman any day than on the side of *Penthouse* or the *Post*—not suggesting it's 'birds of a feather.'
>
> You said some pretty careless things, too, like, 'any first-year journalism student could have predicted Spence's verdict against *Penthouse* wouldn't stand.' That statement doesn't give much credit to the jury, to Judge Brimmer, who sustained the verdict,

to former Chief Justice Breitenstein who declared in his Tenth Circuit opinion that the *Penthouse* article was libelous, not to mention a divided court, 5 to 4, on my motion for rehearing.

In any event, since I'd never met the fella who wrote this nasty editorial I thought, how come he gets off being so mean against somebody like me without having talked to any of the thousands of people I've represented, or anything else, when he could just as well say something good about me if he wanted—how come he chooses to say something just plain hurtful? Then, this morning in the shower it came to me: The kind of person who's that way is usually one who was accused by his dad of doing something naughty in the bathtub (which he was innocent of), and he must have never gotten over it, and so he's been accusing other innocent folks the same way ever since. It's that kind of bathtub journalism which gives the press even a worse reputation than lawyers.

Kim finally had to give up teaching baton. The students dwindled and dropped one by one. Her mother told me Kim was reluctant to go out in public, even for a show or dinner with her boyfriend. I lost contact with her for a long time. I was trying other cases, writing, lecturing across the land, mostly trying to teach young trial lawyers their skills. It isn't technique, I'd explain. It's being who you are. It's all right to be who you are. It's all right to be afraid. This is frightening business. It's all right to be honest about being afraid and angry, and it's all right to care. You can't expect the jury to be honest with you if you aren't honest with them, and you can't expect the jury to care if you don't care. You can't fool the jury.

Once in Atlanta I was on a panel of lawyers sitting before the American Bar Association, for a program titled "Trying the Big Libel Case." With me on the panel was this fellow, Dan Paul, and also Floyd Abrams, who represents *The New York Times*, and Don Reuben of Chicago, and Arthur Miller of Harvard Law School, whom I'd known from other mutual outings; and when I looked down the table there also sat one Norman Roy Grutman as prim and pretty and pious as you please in his black jacket, his red farmer's kerchief bobbing. I said, "Hi, Roy," and he said, "Hi, Gerry," and then he was the first to speak to the all-lawyer audience.

He said the *Penthouse* case involved a story that "attributed certain bizarre sexual abilities to a fictitious Miss Wyoming to which the real Miss Wyoming took offense. Enter counselor Spence," Grutman said. The audience laughed. I sat there in my buckskin jacket and jeans and listened. "The entire state of Wyoming was mobilized and it was led by the Lone Ranger." He pointed at me and the audience laughed again. I smiled. "Even the plaintiff, Miss Wyoming, said no one in his right mind would believe that fictional story in *Penthouse* magazine.

"But after *Sixty Minutes* did that broadcast on Gerry, the chief justice of the Wyoming Supreme Court wrote them that Gerry was a Lone Ranger fighting for the underdog. I almost wrote the chief justice, 'If you think Gerry Spence is the Lone Ranger, you must be Tonto—because Tonto, when translated, means crazy.'" They all laughed, and I had to laugh too. Then Grutman explained to the audience how he masterminded the defense.

When it came my turn I told the lawyers, "I can tell you how to get justice for your client from a jury, how to get those big awards for the rape and desecration of your client's good name, which is as devastating as a rape of the body, but I can't tell you how to keep what the jury gives you. You'll have to get advice on that from my brother, Norman Roy." He hadn't had any better luck keeping Guccione's award against *Hustler*. That was nothing against Grutman. Nobody could keep big libel awards on appeal. I told the lawyers, "Kim Pring was raped all right, raped by twenty-five million readers, and thereafter raped every day, four seasons of the year. She continues to be raped every day. She is being raped as a result of that article—and, brothers and sisters, she was raped one more time—by a blind lady.

"She was raped by a lady named Justice. All the jury gave me was a dollar a rape, but that shocked the conscience of the Court.

"The point I want to make is this: That between two of the great evils in this world—one being pornography, evil because it is destructive of women, and the other being the evil of giving a little Wyoming woman twenty-six and a half million dollars, the latter is the worst of these two evils. It shocks the conscience of the Court to its very core, this giving of big money to little people."

I said to the lawyers, "I have no tricks to offer you. You have to be straight with the jury. The pit is no place for the fancy dans of our profession. You have to speak to a jury as a *person* if you want the *persons* on the jury to speak back favorably to you."

The Denver *Post* carried the story and reported, "Gerry Spence brought his Jackson Hole, Wyoming, style of lawyering to the American Bar Association convention last week, but he was trumped again by the attorney who knocked him out of a $26.5 million verdict in Cheyenne."

After the conclusion of the panel, I went over and spoke to Grutman. "Well, Gerry," he said, "do you remember when you wrote me that there'd come a time after our case was over when we could sit down and get acquainted—and that we might enjoy it? What do you say we give it a try?"

"I'll buy a cup of coffee," I said.

"I'll buy," Grutman said. He won that one too.

He brought his wife along, a very handsome lawyer who seemed as real and solid as Grutman was bright and charming, but in our company she deferred to her husband. Grutman and I let our hair down, and as we did, I could see he was a man who was a lot like me, besieged by the same demons, lured by the same sirens. He was a trial lawyer who bled in the pits, but who tried to cover the fear of it with great grace, and an inimitable grand style of his own. It was better to attack than to run—I could understand that—better to be arrogant than to snivel and whimper. He was a marvelously articulate man, his great brain having been fine tuned by a very correct education in the best schools. As we sat there talking quietly about our lives, I'll admit I found myself beginning to like the man. Perhaps I had always known I would. I get impatient sometimes at the short life-span of my grudges. Try as I may, I'm never able to hang on to them as long as I'd like. Despising one's adversary is such a luxury and, like all riches that are wasted, soon depleted.

I had long ago learned one must finally come to distrust that seemingly most dependable of all feelings—anger—that lovely will to kill that creates the propelling fuel of every decent trial lawyer. I say you must distrust anger, because on the other side of it is caring, and that feeling you can trust. I have never been angry at a cipher. Roy Grutman had been my enemy, but I would never have an enemy unworthy of me, one for whom I could not care.

I told Grutman he should come to Jackson some time for a visit, and he said, "Indeed," and then one day, by God, here he came. I couldn't believe it. We sat out in the yard listening to the songs of the warblers and the yellow finch and we gazed up at the Tetons on a bright warm day, and I could see that his face was pale from having battled too long in those places in which he was shielded from the sun but not the sword. He was weary. Only our enemies truly understand us, for if one could only get into those soft secret places of one's enemies, and look closely, one could see himself.

We talked of our cases and we traded war stories and we were like boys fantasizing the great battles we might fight together, cases we could take for the betterment of the human race that would be fun instead of frightening. He was a man who was caught in his own traps, of course, and I thought that *Penthouse* might be one of them. Every man must first survive before he can be noble.

I took him to meet my friends, the mountain climbers, those strange people who communicate better with huge slabs of vertical rock and tiny buds growing in wayward crevices than with men, and I introduced him to the poets and philosophers of Jackson Hole, who were also my friends, and Roy Grutman was at home with them because his friends, those certain books, those certain great authors, were also theirs, and there was that divine moment between them when they were happy because they were not lonely, and there was much laughter and lively conversation, and we ate together, which was the final proof we were no longer enemies because enemies do not eat out of the same trough.

Some months later, when I went to New York to see my publisher, I visited the Grutmans in their country home in Connecticut, and they were gracious and charming, and their beautiful home was filled with good music and wonderfully tasteful appointments. Roy and I went riding one day, he on his English saddle in his eastern getup with that funny little black cap with the cute little bill and his formal jacket and those silly jodhpurs and black boots to the knees, and me in my cowboy outfit, the big hat and boots with an underslung heel, looking equally ridiculous on a western saddle he'd found for me to ride. We must have made quite a pair. A man who rides an English saddle must mount from a platform, for Christ's sakes. Imagine! I couldn't figure out what the hell would happen if he had to get off his horse and pee. Then we rode into the amiable woods on a well-worn riding trail, and I loved his gentle land, green and tender-looking, and I wondered how such a brave and stalwart man as this could have come from such sweet places. Later he introduced me to his friends, the books of Nabokov, which I had known somewhat, and the writings of Edmund Wilson, which I hadn't. Both proved to be great gifts.

Hustler magazine had given Grutman the dubious honor of being its "Asshole of the Month," a monthly column illustrated with a full-in-the-face view of the male buttocks with the testicles hanging down and the picture of the recipient of the award superimposed in place of the rectum. It was a libel its publisher, Larry Flynt, bestowed every month on some unfortunate against whom he held some personal rancor and gleefully dispensed to his million monthly readers. Grutman had undoubtedly been chosen because he had previously represented Guccione against Flynt in that contentious litigation in which Guccione was portrayed in *Hustler* as being engaged in "buggery," as Grutman always called it. The attack on Grutman was vulgar and defamatory to the extreme. No one seemed willing to take Flynt on, and we talked of the law of libel, and of the First Amendment. A person is not entitled to say anything he chooses. As Oliver Wendell Holmes had said from the High Court: "The most stringent protection of free speech would not protect a man in falsely shouting fire in a theatre and causing a panic." We saw many things alike and I thought Roy Grutman probably agreed with me that the unrestrained abuse of this most important of all freedoms could cause its demise.

Then, sometime later, Schuster came bursting into my office with a copy of the latest *Hustler* in his hands. "Look what this bastard has done! Goddamn it, it's just like we told the Circuit Court of Appeals! We told them their fucking decision would bring on this kind of shit! Now the whole country has to live with this." He dropped the magazine in front of me opened to what appeared to be a full-page, full-color ad for a liqueur called Campari, and there smiling out to the reader alongside a bottle of the liqueur was the pious face of Jerry Falwell. The headline read: JERRY FALWELL TALKS ABOUT HIS FIRST TIME.

> **Falwell:** My first time was in an outhouse outside Lynchburg, Virginia.
> **Interviewer:** Wasn't it a little cramped?
> **Falwell:** Not after I cleaned the shit out.
> **Interviewer:** I see; you must tell me all about it.
> **Falwell:** I never really expected to make it with Mom, but then after she showed all the other guys in town such a good time, I figured, 'What the hell!'
> **Interviewer:** But your Mom? Isn't that a little odd?
> **Falwell:** I don't think so. Looks don't mean that much in a woman.
> **Interviewer:** Go on.
> **Falwell:** Well, we were drunk off our God-fearing asses on Campari. . ."

The "interview" went on, finally ending with Mom passing out, and the "shit and the flies being too much for a second try," and with

Falwell asserting he always "gets sloshed before he goes out to the pulpit" since he couldn't "lay down all that bullshit sober." Barely visible to the careful eye in the smallest print at the bottom of the page were the words "Ad parody—not to be taken seriously."

Well, it was protected, was it not? Wasn't this the darling child of the Tenth Circuit, which had decreed that when a writing is obviously not factual, it is protected under the Constitution?

Schuster said, "I want that case! I want to take that up to the Circuit and hold it under their noses. Is this what the First Amendment has finally come down to?"

Falwell had shown his Christian beneficence. He had forgiven Grutman, this man who had laughed him out of court when Falwell had tried to stop the publication of his interview in *Penthouse*, this lawyer who had beaten him so soundly again when Falwell had later sued *Penthouse* over the same matter, beaten him so badly that he had had to dismiss his own case. Now Falwell offered his case against *Hustler* to Grutman, and Grutman took it. I also thought Falwell's olfactory sense for the coin was extraordinary. Some claimed that standing on the pulpit he could smell a dime in the back row of a large church.

Now Grutman would argue that the Tenth Circuit decision in *Pring* v. *Penthouse* really didn't apply after all. This was a case of libel—clear libel and invasion of privacy and also outrage. I agreed. I also must say that the sign of a good lawyer is that he can argue, at will, either side of a case with equal force, and the sure sign of a great lawyer is when those he has opposed in previous cases want to hire him. But the lawyer who is truly blessed is the lawyer who is free to choose his cases and match them to his personal principles.

"This is a pitched battle between the forces of good and evil," Grutman proclaimed in his Moses voice, sounding more like Falwell than Falwell. "I'll be wearing a white hat. Ask Mr. Flynt what he'll be wearing." Now Grutman would finally have his own shootout at the O.K. Corral. Falwell took after Flynt on television. He asked the jury to clear his name and punish Flynt for "besmirching the memory of my dear mother."

Flynt claimed he had made Falwell a lot of money with his little parody in *Hustler*, that Falwell had mailed the *Hustler* "ad" to thousands and had been able to raise $800,000 to fight this legion of darkness. Flynt claimed Falwell himself had spread the defamation for personal gain, for money and for money's sake. Falwell replied that he couldn't bring this litigation to defend himself against this outrage without the lawsuit also bringing the public's attention to the matter. Kim Pring knew all about that.

The press set up the contest as one between Falwell, 50, who "leads a $70 million national electronic congregation from his base at Thomas Road Baptist Church in Lynchburg, Virginia, and who preaches against abortion, homosexuality and pornography, against Flynt, 41, a Kentucky farm boy who built a multimillion-dollar sex empire." The press said the question would be whether the disclaimer at the bottom of the so-called "ad parody" that it was "not to be taken seriously" was sufficient to save Flynt and *Hustler*. Since Falwell is a public figure, the press believed he would have to prove malice in order to win.

Now with my white hat on, Grutman also borrowed my speech, even saying it a little better, I thought. "It is time to draw the line against those who seek to cloak vile and unspeakable obscenity and character assassination behind the constitutional guarantee of a free press." He sued for $45 million.

At the beginning of the trial, the federal judge permitted the lawyers to question the individual jurors behind closed doors so as not to embarrass the jurors by a public interrogation about how each prospective juror felt about certain sexually explicit matters that would be seen in the magazine. Falwell came to court with his wife, Marcel, and two of his three children. He said the publication "has created the most difficult year of performance, personally, mentally and emotionally that I've had in my whole life."

Grutman told the jury that Falwell, the founder of the Moral Majority, suffered "unspeakable inflictions" as a result of the ad. I was sure he had. It hurt me to read it, and I didn't think you had to be a fan of Falwell's, which I wasn't, in order to feel that way. Falwell said, "I think I have never been as angry as I was at that moment. If Larry Flynt had been nearby when I first read it I might have physically reacted. I really felt like weeping." He said the allegation of incest was especially painful because his mother, who died in 1977, "was the closest to a saint that I have ever known." I understood.

No one would believe the ad to be true, *Hustler*'s attorneys countered. It was obviously pure fantasy, pure parody. It was satire, like *Doonesbury*. And what would happen to the likes of *Doonesbury* if this were not protected?

The publication was not factual, nor did it appear to be factual.

Even Falwell's friends didn't believe it; therefore, since no one could believe it, it was not actionable and was fully protected as fiction under the Constitution. "Anyone who ever believed that kind of absurdity would never send money to Falwell," *Hustler's* attorney argued—probably had the educational level of a flatworm. The parody was so unbelievable the disclaimer at the bottom wasn't even necessary. "The whole idea is that it is incredible."

"If you really want to hurt someone, you put down things that are believable," Flynt said. "Readers know it was not intended to defame Reverend Falwell or any member of his family, because no one could take it seriously. No liquor company is really going to use that kind of language to advertise their product." I'd heard it all before.

Grutman countered: "People who believe in him have not accepted the filth, but the Reverend Falwell is reaching for those who have not yet heard the message. Without his reputation, where is he? His reputation is the jewel of his soul." And so was Kim's.

Falwell told the press, "This case really doesn't relate just to Jerry Falwell, but to whether a publisher can maliciously attack an individual without any recourse. The case will be watched carefully by all Americans who have been mistreated by the media."

Grutman took a video deposition of Flynt who, like Guccione, put on quite a performance. The deposition was taken while Flynt was hospitalized. He was shown wearing his hospital gown, yelling an assortment of obscenities at Grutman and claiming that what was said in the ad about Falwell was all true. He said he had affidavits from three residents of Lynchburg to prove it. He said he could prove that Falwell committed unnatural acts with his mother, young girls, animals, and famous people. He refused to produce the evidence and gave conflicting answers as to his sources. He said he had run the full-page ad to "settle the score, to assassinate Jerry Falwell." When Grutman questioned him more closely during the deposition, Flynt insisted he knew what he was saying. "I am under oath, Mr. Grutman," he shouted, "and I am not crazy—I was telling the truth [about the ad]." Flynt called David Kahn, the president of *Hustler,* a liar and repeatedly told his lawyer to shut up when he objected to Grutman's questions. But at the trial, Flynt's lawyer told the jury that Flynt had no such proof, that Flynt was emotionally ill at the time of the deposition and was trying to destroy himself.

Grutman called Senator Jesse Helms, a Republican from North Carolina, to testify to Falwell's reputation. Helms said he had known

Falwell for fifteen years and spoke with him regularly, and "In my judgment there is no finer citizen than Jerry Falwell. He is easily one of the most dedicated men to this country." Under cross-examination Helms said that he had never heard Falwell's morality or temperance questioned before or *after* the ad. Now *Hustler* would argue that no one believed the material contained in the ad and, therefore, there was no libel; therefore, no one was hurt, and, therefore, there should be no money awarded Falwell as damages.

They were familiar arguments, except one thing was missing. The defense did not ask *those questions*. No one wanted to know any details about Falwell's sex life. Falwell never went up on the rack—this was not a witch's trial. This was the trial of one of the sons, the favored sons, who are not put on the engines of torture to extort their confessions.

Flynt said he had no strong resentment of Falwell, proving, of course, that he had no malice. But he said, "I don't respect him, because he's a hypocrite." From his gold-plated wheelchair Flynt said, "Obviously Falwell would like to be president of the United States. He should identify himself as a politician, not as a preacher."

In contrast to other court appearances at which he had appeared wearing an American flag as a diaper, Flynt wore a conservative gray three-piece suit and a nice Burgundy tie. He looked like a gentleman. Falwell was dressed in red, white, and blue with a gold JESUS FIRST lapel pin. Asked what he thought of Flynt, Falwell said, "Oh, it's what I expected, but I expected him to have a Bible under his arm." And he said, "He isn't crazy. He's dumb like a fox. He's a master actor." I thought the Right Reverend should recognize one.

Grutman hammered away at Flynt on cross-examination, and once Flynt revealed its shattering effects by exclaiming to Grutman, "You may have been the very person who triggered much of my behavior," referring to his conduct in the hospital during his depositions.

Then Grutman closed his case and Flynt's lawyer asked the judge to dismiss the case, saying a reasonable reader wouldn't believe the parody was factual. "It was incredible," he argued. Earlier the judge dismissed Falwell's claim for invasion of privacy. It had no application in the case, the judge ruled, since the parody had not actually been used for advertisement.

Grutman attacked without mercy in his final argument. "This man is a Dr. Jekyll and Mr. Hyde," he said. "That man"—he pointed, and his indignation vibrated through every fiber in his body—"that man is exactly what his magazine is called, a hustler. The leopard doesn't change his spots. The three-piece suit isn't going to conceal the black rot that comes out of his magazine." Grutman said Falwell had suffered continuously. "His reputation is the touchstone of what he does. And without it, he's finished. The scar will be with him forever." I thought Grutman's argument for damages was nothing short of brilliant. He asked for one dollar in compensatory damages for each copy of the magazine sold.

Flynt was very excited over the puny verdict—only $200,000. The jury had awarded only $100,000 to compensate the plaintiff for his injury and $50,000 each against both Flynt and *Hustler*. The jury had found that Falwell had not been libeled. They had followed the Court's instruction on the law of this case, the law of Judge Seth, the law of *Pring* v. *Penthouse*, that had come back to haunt my friend Norman Roy Grutman.

But the jury found that Flynt had been guilty of intentionally inflicting emotional harm on Falwell and hence their verdict. The media's champion, Alan Dershowitz of Harvard Law School, said, "If it [the verdict] was against Harvard *Lampoon* or *The New York Times*, I have no doubt that the Court would throw out this verdict," he said. "But since it's against *Hustler*, an extremely offensive and unpopular magazine, there's just no predicting how the court will respond. The Court of Appeals may very well bend the law to express their outrage at *Hustler*." But I thought that if *The New York Times* had published such a parody, the courts would probably be harder on the legitimate press than on the *Hustler* ilk.

Marc Franklin of Stanford University Law School said, "The ease with which a plaintiff could say he was upset shows the danger of creating this kind of category [intentional infliction of emotional harm on a public figure]. The public figures in our society can't be as thinskinned as Falwell appears to be," which meant, I suppose, that a principal qualification for being a public figure is that you mustn't get upset if someone calls you a motherfucker.

The media was curled up under the covers again, embracing its own sumptuous stools as if they were the precious stuff of Jefferson, Madison, and the Constitution. It was as if the legitimate press could not distinguish what was responsible from what was not, what was right from what was wrong, and having failed to pass the test by which the worst of the criminally insane are judged, the legitimate press stood in a catatonic trance, too impotent to perform its principal function in a democracy—to speak the conscience of the people. It had forgotten the admonition of its mentor, Felix Frankfurter: "Freedom of the press is not an end in itself but a means to the end in a free society."

I thought of my own angel mother who wanted me to be a preacher, and sometimes I thought she'd gotten herself a preacher, all right. If I were going to preach a sermon to the media I'd start with Luke 12:48: "Unto whomsoever much is given, of him shall be much required," and I might end it with Proverbs 22:1: "A good name is rather to be chosen than great riches."

Even though the award was minimal, Flynt said he would appeal. It was the principle of the thing. He would fight to the death, he said, for the right of a free press. My friend Grutman was equally adamant: "Giving Flynt freedom of the press is like giving matches to a pyromaniac." Grutman, too, said he would appeal.

35

One evening in the late spring, the song of the purple finch was interrupted by the sound of the telephone and the voice of Moses. It was my friend Roy Grutman.

"My spirits are elevated to hear the good sound of your voice," he said, and then he told me about a case he wanted me to try for a poor woman "who has been miserably butchered by a group of quack-salvers"—surgeons, I supposed. I watched the clouds roll in fierce winds at the top of the Grand Teton. "You are the best trial lawyer in America, and this woman deserves you," he said.

"She's already got you. And you're the best," I said.

"No, she's entitled to both of us. We will try this case together, and you will be chief trial counsel, and I will sit at your side." Roy Grutman knew how to flatter a man. Then we talked about other cases, and finally I had to know.

"Roy," I said. "Do you remember somebody in the Pring case who was supposed to have called you in New York while the trial was going on who told you that Kim had performed fellatio on him?"

"Of course," he said. "The guy said, 'It was the first date I had with her and it was the best blowjob I ever had in my life.'"

"He said that?" Jesus Christ!

"Yes, sir! And wait until you hear the rest of the story—I said, 'Would you be willing to testify to that?' He said, 'Yes, but I'm in business, and if I lost any money, bla, bla, bla,' and I said, 'We'll pay you and make up any losses you have if you'll testify,' and things go along, and Cooper's trying this case and I'm busy trying my little case in Nassau County and trying at night to organize both ends, and we're trying to subpoena this guy, and he lights out of Wyoming, and goes off to Idaho or some place or other and has a number of telephone conversations with me, and then he calls up Guccione."

"Oh, you're kidding," I said.

"I kid you not. And he's willing to come and testify. I think he started out at two hundred thousand or two hundred fifty thousand. I remember negotiating with him when he was down to one hundred thousand."

"You're kidding!" was all I could say again.

"No!" Grutman said. "And this guy said, 'She did. She did! She did it to the whole football team. She did it regularly!' "

There it was again, except this time somebody wanted to sell the libel for a quarter of a million.

Grutman said, "This guy kept reducing the price and I kept saying, 'We cannot pay that to you. It's utterly unreasonable, and if it ever came out, nobody would believe it,' and he said, 'Well, fuck you then; I'm not testifying,' and he disappeared."

"I'll be damned," I said. I reflected for a moment. The idea that somebody would actually try to peddle such testimony for a quarter of a million dollars scared me.

"So you see, Gerry, I made a remark to you one time that that lady wasn't what she represented herself to be." Grutman laughed.

"Well, when somebody is willing to testify about something for a quarter of a million dollars, I don't know how much reliance you could put on that, do you?"

"I don't know," Grutman said. "But he mentioned that to a lot of people," and then Grutman began to name a long list of people to whom this slander was communicated. The man had been willing not only to sell it, but to spread it.

"You have a remarkable memory, Roy," I said.

"Gerry, I have had few experiences with anything quite as bizarre as that, and that is why it stuck in my memory. And that is why, as this case was being conducted, I said to myself, 'Gerry Spence has to be the most temerarious lawyer that exists.' "

"Now what the hell does that mean?" I asked.

"Nervy," he said. "How you could have the cheek to hold up a fallen woman like that!" Grutman began to laugh again. "That's the story, and it certainly is a great footnote to the famous Miss Wyoming case."

I was silent, still feeling stunned.

"Well, I'll tell you this," Grutman continued as if to make his proof. "There are tape-recorded conversations between Guccione and this guy in which he asserts that that event took place and he wants the money to testify, which he asked for, and which Guccione told him we couldn't pay."

"God Almighty," I said sadly.

"As a matter of fact, Gerry, now that I remember it, we took that matter to the U.S. Attorney's Office for the Southern District of New York, and sought to have this man prosecuted for extortion and obstruction of justice, and they considered the case and decided that it was too lurid, and it didn't involve New York as much as it did Wyoming."

"What was your motive for that?"

"Well, Guccione was put on the short end of a twenty-six-million-dollar judgment at the time." Grutman laughed again. "And he had those tape recordings, and that evidence was presented to the U.S. attorney."

Grutman had nothing to hide. He used the man's name as we talked. I said, "I'm going to call this guy and see if he will admit all of that."

"Gerry, I don't know what he will tell you, but if he won't admit it, take it from your friend Roy Grutman that what he said to me is exactly what I have just told you."

"Well, I'll tell you one thing. They can say all the things they want to about Roy Grutman, they can call him—"

"Pompous—" he offered.

"Yes, and say that he attacks the judges, that he'll kill you in a hundred ways, but one thing—at least one—he never lies. He has yet to lie to me," I said.

"That's the truth. You got it," he said.

Right after that, I did call the man—caught him at home on a Sunday afternoon having a cookout. He was impatient, suspicious, and vague. He tried to be cagey with me.

"I don't remember anything about it. It's been a long time ago," he said.

"Well, Penthouse's lawyer told us you had called him to tell of your experiences with Kim, and I just want to know if he was telling me the truth or not."

"No, I have no comment, you know. I have nothin' . . . I don't think I have anything of any value to anybody."

I told him Grutman accused him of talking both to him and to Guccione, requesting $100 thousand for his testimony.

"That's not true—let me explain it to you. I did not want to testify for them. I felt I had nothing to do with it—they tried to subpoena me—tried to force me into an uncomfortable situation. . . . I was in business and it would be damaging to me, and there would be no reason for me to be involved. They completely ignored that I would have to be off work. I would have to go through all this crap testifying against Miss Wyoming, and I have no interest in it. But I'd do anything to help." You bet—for a price.

"Did you—"

"No! It would be damaging to me. All I'd get is witness fees. Why should I do them a favor?"

"Well, did you ever ask them for money?"

"I never said anything. I just told them it would be a problem for me financially, because it would hurt my business and my time and I didn't want anything to do with it. I didn't ask them for anything."

"You didn't ask them for money?"

"I'm uncomfortable with the situation. I surely am at the moment. I would help any way I can, but I'm busy at the moment."

"Grutman told me that if you had been paid the right price you would have testified that she gave you a blowjob."

"No. No! I was partners with one of the Cheyenne lawyers in a deal, and it was joking conversation, and they wanted me to testify, and it was just a bunch of bull. There's no truth in that, and then they tried to subpoena me anyway and I didn't want to testify. I hope I've helped you."

"You never told them she gave you blowjobs?"

There was a long silence. "No comment. They joked a lot," he said. "It just all got misconstrued. Maybe you can talk to her about those type facts," he said. "I was only out with her once in my life and then this lousy thing happened, and like I say I'm kinda busy right now."

I told him Kim said he was a nice person and that there was nothing he would or could say about her, and he said, "That's exactly true," and then he admitted that he had heard all that talk about her having made it with the football team and all, and that that had hurt her.

I mentioned Guccione's tapes and that Guccione had gone to the U.S. attorney with them. Then his story seemed to expand.

"Well, I had conversations with them," he admitted, "and he can construe them to do that. The conversation mighta got deep. But it was never that I was trying to do anything wrong. I was just telling them that I had damages, and I didn't want to testify for them." He said that because the attorneys in Cheyenne had been trying to subpoena him, he ended up calling Grutman and Guccione.

"Did you really talk to Guccione?"

"Yeah, I talked to him," he said. "Anyway, you ruined my day."

I said I was sorry I had ruined his day, but this had to be straightened out, and surely he wasn't the kind of person who would go around asking for $200,000 to testify.

"Well—there was no way it was in those kind of terms," he said, whatever that meant.

Then he asked, "Is the case out of court?"

"Absolutely, and all the appeals are all over," and when he wanted to know what happened when Guccione took his tapes to the New York authorities, I told him the U.S. attorney had turned the criminal prosecution down.

"Thank God, there's somebody in this world who has a right mind," he said. "Well, it's a real privilege to talk to you, if you want to know the truth, and I think Kim had a right." He never would admit to the exact amount of money that had been talked about, but he insisted throughout that the money was to compensate him for a ruined business. "I would be testifying against Miss Wyoming, and I make my living here, and all the people here will think I am a bad guy associating with *Penthouse* and helping them against our Miss Wyoming. And like I said, I still basically believe *Penthouse* was in the wrong."

"Did the figures ever get as high as a hundred thousand?"

"Oh, yeah, they mighta got there. It was all hearsay talk." Then he said he thought I should have won the case.

To me the incident was just one more injury Kim had to bear, the insufferable indignity that there always have been and always will be those who, for a price, will come into court and swear in the public record and who, for the green-paper blessing, would testify against the witch.

Early in 1984, Kim finally joined the army. She sent me a clipping headlined KIM PRING OUTSTANDING ARMY TRAINEE. The article said: "Miss Wyoming 1978 has exchanged her beauty queen title for an Army rank and was selected as 'Soldier of the Cycle' after her basic training. Kim recently completed basic training at Fort Dix, N.J., and was selected from among some two hundred trainees for the honor. Pring told the publicity office she left Wyoming and joined the Army 'out of a sense of patriotism, for job security, travel, and a chance to do something on my own.' " She's sprung herself out of at least one trap, I thought.

Later I talked to her on the telephone. She was in Germany, "seeing the sights," and she seemed enthusiastic, even happy, and optimistic about being selected later on for officers' training.

"Your dad is really proud of you," I said, which was true. I had heard it in the soft voice of this retired air force sergeant when he spoke of his daughter.

"I hope so," Kim said. "This thing was really hard on my parents. I think my dad always wanted a son to sort of follow in his footsteps, but he never did say so. You know how quiet he is."

"Well, you got away from it, didn't you, Kim?"

"No. I'm never going to get away from it. I just have to learn to live with it. I never knew people had such memories. I was walking down the streets of Salzburg one day and some guy from the base hollers, 'Hey, Penthouse,' and some of the guys still say that same dirty stuff to me. I can't get away from it."

"I know."

"The chaplain says I just gotta learn to live with it," Kim said. "I'm an assistant to the chaplain, and I'm learning about counseling people. A lot of people have it worse than me. I learned that much." Then she laughed and I could tell by her laugh she was trying to be all right, and after that she sent me a cheerful Christmas card posted from Germany. She was still hoping to get into officers' school.

"I hope Kim's going to be all right," I said to Schuster.

"She'll get over it," Schuster said. "Someday people will forget. People only remember what they have a need to remember."

One Sunday afternoon in late September of 1985 when that sure curtain of snow had already closed over the peaks and was slowly descending the mountainside to lay claim to the greenly willows and to the grasses, easy and golden as the aspen leaves, and also to the fireweed, as ragged and scarlet as the cry of the half-grown coyote pups—when the elk were holding back against their own descent into the hell of winter and the guns of the hunters, and the geese were still unmolested in their grazing fields of late clover, I spoke with that blond mother, and she told me Kim had fought through it all right. She said, "She learned she had to let go of it. And she did."

"What's she doing?" I asked.

"She won her competition again," she said. "She beat everybody in Germany for the All-Army Show. There's representatives from

Korea and Japan and from all over. We're so excited. We're so proud. She's in Virginia and they're practicing every day, and on October twelfth they're going to perform at Constitution Hall for President Reagan, and—"

"That's great," I said.

"And we have six tickets," she said. "I expect somehow we'll find a way to get there."

Nothing changes.

And Schuster never lost his faith in the system. He was like any man of religion who refuses to denounce God merely because God has forsaken him—always gives Him another chance. God gave Schuster his great brain to perform that miracle of the species called logic, and Schuster labored away on our new cases, and as he had grown older, he gathered a new handsome wisdom that people respected, especially me. And Eddie had fought new battles in the courtroom by himself, and he had won big. He would become a great trial lawyer. Plenty of his peers said he already was and that I, like any father, would be the last to know. But he still said his sweet aphorisms like "The justice system may not be perfect, but it's the best system ever devised by man."

I said, "Yeah, Eddie, I agree with you that this is the best system ever devised by man. Maybe that's what's wrong with it. It was devised by men. It sure isn't a system that works very well for women." And Schuster, hearing that and sticking with Eddie, said I was just messing around with my pronouns.

Then Eddie said, "The system isn't as quick to learn as we are—it takes time. You gotta be patient with the system. Look, we damn near made it—we came within one vote up there on the Circuit— one vote! That's pretty good for an old system like ours. They say ya can't teach old dogs new tricks. Well, we got this old dog's attention anyway."

"We taught the old dog wrong tricks, Eddie," I said.

"Well, Gerry, it's gotta get worse before it gets better. You can't win 'em all," Eddie said, happy with his old sayings and his new battles, and he laughed, and his laugh seemed to make it better.

Finally, before I put the case away, I wanted to say good-bye to the jurors. I hadn't spoken to any of them since my final argument, and that had been over three years ago. Judge Brimmer told me it would be all right, that his rule against lawyers talking to the jurors was for lawyers, not writers. He laughed. "You have First Amendment rights, too," and the jurors seemed happy enough to talk to me.

We were still friends. One of the jurors said, "We jurors did wrong."

I was surprised. "Why?" I asked.

"We give her too much. We should have stayed below their insurance. They fought it too hard."

"Well, if you put it below their insurance limits, *Penthouse* wouldn't have to pay anything, and you wanted to punish them, didn't you?"

"I did then and I still do. I've always said myself that for a million dollars you can call me a cocksucker." He laughed.

"How did you folks come to the twenty-five million?" I asked.

"Ah, we was listening to her lawyer—and you're it. You mentioned twenty-five million in the trial. You put the figure in our minds. But that wasn't the whole reason we came to it. We figured two months of his advertisements, and it came out approximately to twelve and a half million dollars in advertisements in that magazine."

The women later told me they held the verdict down and that if it hadn't been for them, the men would have given a lot more than the twenty-six and a half.

More? Even more!

Yes, the men wanted to give even more.

"What did you think of Kim Pring?" I asked the juror.

"I thought then that she looked like a pretty good young lady, and I still think so. I didn't realize it all the way through the trial, but I knew Kim as a kid—lived six houses from her on the base, and your first witness—Bill Storms—I knew, too. I told the bailiff about it on our first coffee break—didn't recognize the name—hadn't seen him for about six or seven years, and I didn't recognize him until he got up in the witness stand. Never been close friends with him. The bailiff, he says, 'If you've never been close friends, he's not going to influence you at all.'" He stopped. Then he said, "And I've seen her half a dozen times since the trial, and I'd say that today she's still a beautiful young woman. But I think we done her wrong. We went way above the insurance and that forced them to fight harder.

"And you know how I looked on that fantasy end of it," he said, "where they said you couldn't levitate? Right?"

"Right," I said.

"Well, if you get a blowjob, you're on cloud nine anyway. You've been levitated—the way I looked at it. That *is* fantasy. But then again, it isn't." He laughed.

"How did you feel when the Circuit Court of Appeals threw the case out?"

"Made me feel like I just wasted my time—completely. 'Why should we have a jury?' I said. 'Why have the law?' You put a jury up there and put them through that, and believe it or not, it is torture to sit through that."

"I'll bet," I said.

"That girl went through hell and back. She earned every bit that she would have got. Then to have the Court throw it all out, in my mind, all that is is a bunch of lawyers just pulling on loopholes, paying no attention to the law at all, and I don't even mind telling a lawyer that."

"I don't mind you telling me that either," I said.

"I couldn't understand *Penthouse.* For crying out loud, when you got *Penthouse* up on the witness stand all they did was contradict themselves. And when you got the author up there on the witness stand, he can't remember what he wrote under whatever name he wrote under and made money from it. I can remember almost everything I've done for making money. But he couldn't remember writing for *Hustler.*"

"Why do you think those judges threw the case out?"

"I don't know. I haven't been able to understand that at all. But I think it's a good waste of taxpayers' money that they put us through up there. They know the law better than I do, let's face it. But I don't see right to this day any reason for throwing out our decision on it. I can see the judge cutting it down. It didn't bother me that bad when Judge Brimmer cut it down. I said, 'What the hell.' "

He continued, "If you find them guilty, you assess punitive damages to the point that it will hurt them." He should have argued the case to the Circuit judges.

"Oh, you know, it didn't bother me that she was going to get that much," he said. "Let her have it. Between the two, I'd much rather see her or you get it."

Then I asked him, "Did you folks have any trouble arriving at your verdict? You took plenty of time. You went all of that night and then you came back the next morning."

"We had no trouble on the verdict. We said *Penthouse* was guilty in the first five minutes in there. We was just arguing how to hit 'em. That's all we were arguing on. We was well aware in our minds, every one of us, that they were guilty. We was just fightin' over how much she was gonna get, and how hard we oughta hit the author. As you know, we didn't hit the author too awful hard."

Then I needed to know. "If you were going to give me some advice as a friend on how to be a better lawyer, what would you advise me?" A man can learn a lot from an honest juror.

"Not to try for quite such big sums. I think you impressed the jury too hard with it—even though—let's face it—*Penthouse* made money on this trial. We weren't gonna hurt them no matter what we assessed them. The advertisement of the case helped *Penthouse*. I really feel it. The people buy more magazines. So twenty-five million wouldn't hurt *Penthouse* if they had paid it."

"You got that exactly right," I said.

"I feel I do. But I've put a lot of thought on that case after we got done with it. It never does cease to amaze me that the Supreme Court threw it all out. I knew you was sincere about the case. I also knew you were a big fancy lawyer. But you didn't strike me as just puttin' on. You know, I've understood for quite a while that you don't take just any case. You've got to believe in a case to take it."

"Thanks," I said.

"To me that means a heck of a lot. You believed in her or you wouldn't have took the case. What her morals are, I don't know. Don't care. It's just the fact that someone did her wrong. They did libel her in my mind. In fact, I don't think she's ever going to live it down here."

"How did you know it was her for sure in the article?"

"The way she does that mouth roll with the baton—when she demonstrated how she worked that baton right there in front of us, I could see where the author got the idea. It just didn't strike me as his right to put it in there."

I asked him about the juror on the end in the back, and he said that the juror said that "even if she had done it with the football team, that was her business." I asked about one of the women jurors and he said, "One was one of them little ol' ladies down there—never even knew what any of these terms were."

"Is that right?"

"It was way over her head. She never knew about a blowjob. She was asking what some of these words meant. I said to one of the younger ladies, 'Why don't you take her into the ladies' room and explain what's up.' You wouldn't a believed how that ol' lady come out of that restroom! And when she come out, she was just as red as a beet from head to toe."

"Was she mad?"

"No, but she says, 'I don't believe it. I don't believe it. Nobody would do that.' Course, now, she's of the old school. We had a lot of fun in the jury room—things like that takin' place."

"What do you remember about the trial that stands out strongest in your mind?"

"It was the look on Kim's face all the way through it—it was the look of her hurtin'. She was suffering all the way through it."

"What did you think of Guccione?"

"I thought his morals was just as low as he thought we were. He thought we was dumb enough to have the mentality of flatworms and I thought his morals were just about that low—oh, I can remember his high-heeled boots and his suede pants. I can remember him. He was an arrogant son of a gun, I can tell you that."

"Did you think the judge's rulings were okay?"

"No, I don't. I don't think you was able to bring out enough. I've always felt in a case of that type, nothing's barred. You're trying to prove they did wrong, and they are trying to save themselves. I really believe that should have been left to the jury."

"We had to fight the country's whole publishing industry, you know that, don't you?"

"I can see that—the right to freedom of speech is what it comes out to," he said. "I can see we should have it too, but not to the point that you libel anybody. I don't care how big they are, why should anybody be able to ruin a person's life through their speech and make their private life public like that?"

"Absolutely," I said.

"And I can see where someone like *Time* magazine would even fight against you, which doesn't print smut as such, but still, I think *Penthouse* stepped over the line on what they could write—and tried to call it fantasy."

"Yes."

"They were making money on a story and that's all. It did have an appeal in a way—for everyone here in Wyoming, it damn sure had an appeal. Especially if anyone watches the Miss America Pageant, which most of us watch it for that swimsuit." He laughed and finally so did I. "Well, you know, Kim Pring was on there. A local girl. You watch to see how they do."

"Sure."

"The Miss America Pageant is a good way to get to the normal person. The whole thing's set up."

"That's exactly right," I said.

"And winning it is just mentally a heck of a boost. A story like that cuts all that work to hell." The man understood. I have always believed in the wisdom of the common man. "She had a hard life working up to it," he said. "To get that far in life is a hell of a lot to accomplish. She had a hell of a job making that climb the first time. And I just feel that *Penthouse* didn't have the right to knock that hill right out from under her. That's what they did."

"Well, you tried to give justice," I said. "You did the best you could, and we tried to get justice, and we did the best we could, and I guess that's the way it's gonna be," I said.

"Yeah, it gives you a hell of a new outlook on justice. I'm wondering if there really is any," he said. Later the other jurors echoed the same thing. Even Clarence Darrow had said as much: "The litigants and their lawyers are supposed to want justice, but, in reality, there is no such thing as justice, either in or out of court. In fact, the word cannot be defined."

Nothing changes.

Once when I was a little boy, my father brought me home a snapping turtle from one of his fishing trips. I'd watched my father coming, the turtle dangling from the end of a stick my father had put in front of the turtle's face, a stick the turtle had snapped at and locked to. I could see the stick and turtle swinging back and forth like the pendulum to some primeval clock in cadence with my father's easy stride. He sat the stick and the turtle down in front of me. I picked up this curious thing, shook it, twisted it, even put my foot on its back and pulled until I was afraid I'd pull off the poor turtle's head.

"That's a snappin' turtle for ya," my father said, sitting his fishing pole down. "You could cut his head off and he'd still be clamped down on that stick. Dumb reptile would rather hang on and die than let go and live." Then he said something kind like he usually did. "It's hard for snapping turtles to let go—that's their way," he said.

I put the turtle under the front porch, and dug him some worms, and laid them beside his wrinkled old head, and I talked to him for quite a while, and went to bed. In the morning the turtle was gone, and so were the worms. I ran to my father.

"My turtle's gone," I cried. "He let loose of the stick and he went away."

"Well," my father said, "Even a turtle's got enough sense, when he's got all night to think about it, to know when to let go."

"It's hard being a snapping turtle," I said one day to Schuster. He looked at me, and then smiled his kind smile again and he said, "You're a strange man, Gerry." But I thought he knew what I meant.

One day I met Andrea Dworkin. My literary agent, the beloved Elaine Markson, my friend, my mother when I chose, had invited me to dinner, and next to me at the table sat Andrea Dworkin—this woman whom I had quoted with reverence so often, this woman who fought the exploiters of women, who hurled herself into causes against pornography because "pornography is the material means of sexualizing inequality," and because pornography "is the central practice in the subordination of women." Her great anguish for her sisters, for herself, escaped in her essays, sometimes in logic as hard, as clear, as cold and pointed as icicles, and sometimes in the unmuzzled screams of every woman who had ever twisted and wrenched and burned at the witch's fire. She was, I thought, the spirit of every revolutionary—angry, true, unreasonable, committed to her very corpuscles, a woman out of whom emerged a certain chastity of purpose that was frightening. She was a woman with kind eyes and the voice of a forest thrush, and it is hard to argue with that kind, but I had argued, of course, and I had carried away from that evening a precious gift, a new insight into the spirit and the rationale behind the fight this woman waged against pornography.

About a week later I received an envelope from Elaine Markson. In it were some pages, obviously from *Hustler* magazine. As I examined them I felt a sudden, painful stab. There was a cartoon of two immensely ugly lesbians, one sitting on the bed, the other between her legs coming up for air with the vaginal juices dripping from her mouth, and the caption, "Edna, you remind me of Andrea Dworkin. It's a dog eat dog world."

I couldn't believe my eyes.

Then came five pages from the next month's edition of *Hustler*, in full color, containing numerous photos of women engaged in lesbian sex, and again, Andrea Dworkin was identified, obviously quite erroneously, as one of the women, and the captions also included a vicious slur against her Jewish ancestry. The last page was from a still later edition of *Hustler*, a photo of a man performing cunnilingus while masturbating—the woman in the photo was identified by *Hustler* as the mother of Andrea Dworkin.

"Schuster," I hollered out in the atrium. "Come here and look at these! Eddie!" I hollered. I shoved the packet of pages to them.

"Jesus!" Schuster said.

"Jesus!" Eddie said.

I said, *"Hustler* is punishing this woman for her fight against pornography." I explained how Andrea Dworkin was the co-author of the Minneapolis Ordinance, a newly created piece of legislation that gives standing to women to sue pornographers in certain defined cases where women are presented graphically by sexually explicit pictures or words as dehumanized sexual objects or commodities to be raped, mutilated, hurt, humiliated, or degraded. The ordinance was seen by pornographers and their numerous allies in the legitimate media as a threat—a business threat, I thought.

"Well," Eddie said, "she sure as hell has a constitutional right as a citizen to work peacefully for those kinda laws. She's got a constitutional right to her own free speech without being assaulted for it like this." He threw the pages on the table and said, "That's a hell of a case."

Schuster joined in. "How can *Hustler* claim the use of their First Amendment rights to attack this woman who is only exercising hers? The Circuit hasn't gone so far as to allow the use of the First Amendment for plain old verbal assault and battery. I like the case—a lot," Schuster said.

"Well, you know how these cases come out," I said. "You know what the courts do. You know the law of these cases." I looked hard at Schuster. "The law isn't in your books. It isn't *New York Times* v. *Sullivan!* It isn't *Gertz!*" I was pacing back and forth in the atrium. "It's the Little People Rule and the Baboon Rule and Whipped Cream and Cherry Rule—that's what these cases are about. We'll just end up making things worse again like we did in Kim's case. *Hustler* wouldn't have dared publish this crap if the Circuit hadn't made that holding in her case. Look what *Hustler* did to Falwell after *Pring.* We hurt the people. Getting in these cases is like getting in quicksand. The more we fight the deeper we sink. The country was better off before we took the Pring case."

"You should have a little more faith in the system," Schuster said. "Give it a chance to correct itself."

"Yeah," Eddie said. "It'll come around. It always does." He stopped and looked as serious as an Irishman ever looks. "I'll tell ya one thing. This time we can win for sure." He was excited. His words got jumbled, and they tumbled and fell over each other. He stopped and started over. "Those judges, well, we got 'em this time, because when you finally get to the bottom of the stinkpot, there ain't any place to go but up."

I heard the tormented cries of women. I could hear the Church's holy proclamation—"All wickedness is but little to the wickedness of a woman." This vicious plague had diseased the nerve roots of the law, and I could hear the women weeping. Blackstone himself had decreed at the time of our Constitution: "To deny the possibility, nay, actual existence of witchcraft and sorcery is at once flatly to contradict the revealed word of God in various passages of both the Old and New Testament." Our great father of the law saw women as the pornographers see them—as mere property of men: "the very being or legal existence of the woman is suspended during the marriage," he once ruled.

I heard the mourning of women that in this land of the free and enlightened, at the time of this fledgling government itself, we should witness the Massachusetts Bay Colony providing in its founding document, the Body of Liberties, that witches "shall be put to death," that there the good women of Salem should be hanged for their abominable sins of witchery, and I heard the horrid choking and gagging as the women dangled at the end of the ropes of justice, which Cotton Mather had called "logical, and the dear fruit of reason."

And I could hear Andrea Dworkin's clear voice again: "Pornography is women turned into subhumans, beaver, pussy, body parts." I could hear her crying, "It is women converted to genitals, buttocks, breasts, mouths opened and throats penetrated, covered in semen, pissed on, shitted on, hanging from light fixtures, tortured, maimed, bleeding—"

"For Christ's sakes, spare me," I said out loud. "I'll take the case."

Schuster looked surprised. Then he said, "We have a new Supreme Court case. It will make things easier. Listen to this." He picked up a printout from our computer of the latest enunciation from the United States Supreme Court—*Dun* and *Bradstreet*, he called the case. Schuster began reading. " 'For as Mr. Justice Stewart has reminded us, the individual's right to the protection of his own good name reflects no more than our basic concept of a decent system of ordered liberty. The protection of private personality, like the protection of life itself, is left primarily to the individual states.' And listen to this," Schuster said, as excited as a man dipped in Yale and toasted at Harvard can get. " 'It is speech on matters of public concern that is at the heart of the First Amendment protection.' " He picked up the *Hustler* cartoon of the bestial lesbians. "No one can ever argue that this is a matter of 'public concern.' "

"That's right," Eddie said.

And through it all, I could hear Andrea Dworkin still speaking for women, her voice as sweet as an angel. "The pornographers turn us into objects that are disemboweled, and killed. The scissors are poised at the vagina—we are being raped, gang raped, fucked by dogs, and horses and snakes. We are tortured in pornography for the pleasure of men, and we are presented as if we adore it, and we are begging for more." She was reading a bill of charges. "Pornography is women, kept a sexual underclass, kept available for rape and battery and incest and prostitution. It is what we are under male domination; it is what we are for under male domination."

"Spare me," I said aloud once more. "Spare me. I'll take the case."

"Good," Schuster said. "I like this case a lot."

Eddie was happy.

I looked out. I saw the birds of a past season, striplings freed from the bluebird's nest, gangly brothers and sisters alike, each with identical rights to fly.

"Bluebirds are a lucky sign," Eddie said.

The Irish.

Once more I began to smell the musty odor of old books, and I could feel the heavy cloak of Precedent, laden with its filthy diseases of the past, clinging to me as if I had been robed by the devil. I could not rip the dastardly cloth from my body. Then I heard the voices of "our dear sons, Heinrich Kramer and James Sprenger," chanting their holy dictum from the *Malleus:* "For common justice demands that a witch should not be condemned to death unless she is convicted by her own confession."[1]

And I heard the rattle of the executioners preparing their engines of torture, and I heard their first question, as if the question itself had been burned into my genes as a lawyer, a question they asked as a clear matter of right.

"Are you a virgin, Ms. Dworkin?"

SOURCE NOTES

INTRODUCTION
1. T. A. Larson, *History of Wyoming* (Lincoln: University of Nebraska Press, 1965), 86.

CHAPTER 1
1. Heinrich Kramer and James Sprenger, *Malleus Maleficarum*, translated and introduced by Rev. Montague Summers (New York: Dover Publications, 1971), vii.
2. Ibid., 222–223.
3. Ibid., 225.
4. Ibid., 230.
5. Ibid., viii.
6. Ibid.
7. Rosemary Radford Ruether, *New Woman, New Earth: Sexist Ideologies and Human Liberation* (New York: Seabury Press, 1983), 89, 111; and Matilda Joslyn Gage, *Woman, Church and State*, 2nd ed. (New York: Arno Press, 1972), 247. In Mary Daly, *Gyn/Ecology: The Metaethics of Radical Feminism* (Boston: Beacon Press, 1978), 183.
8. Norman Cohn, *Warrant for Genocide: The Myth of the Jewish World Conspiracy and the Protocols of the Elders of Zion* (New York: Harper & Row, 1966), 17. In Reuther, 19.
9. Kramer and Sprenger, *Malleus*, 228.
10. Ibid., 225.
11. From Johann Matthaus Meyfarth, quoted in Henry Charles Lea, *Materials Toward a History of Witchcraft*, arranged and edited by Arthur C. Howland, with an introduction by George Lincoln Burr, 3 vols. (New York: Thomas Yoseloff, 1957), Vol. II, 735. In Daly, *Gyn/Ecology*, 200.
12. Kramer and Sprenger, *Malleus*, 226.
13. Ibid., 228.

CHAPTER 2
1. *Touch the Earth: A Self-Portrait of Indian Existence*, compiled by T. C. McLuhan (New York: Promontory Press, 1971), 12.

487

CHAPTER 4

1. Michael Korda, *Power! How to Get It, How to Use It* (New York: Ballantine Books, 1975), 52–53.
2. "The Place of Pornography: Packaging Eros for a Violent Age," a forum in *Harper's,* Vol. 269, No. 1614 (November 1984), 38, 33.
3. Ibid., 31.
4. Ibid., 34.
5. Andrea Dworkin, *Woman Hating* (New York: E. P. Dutton, 1974), 149–150.
6. *Harper's,* "The Place of Pornography," 32.
7. Ibid., 32–33.
8. Kramer and Sprenger, *Malleus,* 47.
9. Marquis de Sade, *Juliette,* translated by Austryn Wainhouse (New York: Grove Press, 1976), 269. In Andrea Dworkin, *Pornography: Men Possessing Women* (New York: Perigee, 1981), 100.

CHAPTER 5

1. Jerold S. Auerbach, *Unequal Justice: Lawyers and Social Change in Modern America* (New York: Oxford University Press, 1976), 51.

CHAPTER 7

1. Kramer and Sprenger, *Malleus,* 114.
2. Ibid., 233.
3. Ibid., 225.

CHAPTER 8

1. Jackson J. Benson, *The True Adventures of John Steinbeck, Writer* (New York: Viking Press, 1984), 31.
2. Marquis de Sade, *The 120 Days of Sodom and Other Writings,* translated by Austryn Wainhouse and Richard Seaver (New York: Grove Press, 1967), 701. In Dworkin, *Pornography,* 100.

CHAPTER 9

1. *Harper's,* "The Place of Pornography," 34.
2. Erich Fromm, *The Anatomy of Human Destructiveness* (New York: Holt, Rinehart & Winston, 1973), 350.
3. Ibid., 343.
4. Ibid., 350.
5. Ibid.

CHAPTER 10

1. Kramer and Sprenger, *Malleus,* 43.
2. Ibid.

3. Ibid., 46.
4. Ibid., 47.
5. Andrea Dworkin, "Against the Male Flood: Censorship, Pornography, and Equality," *Harvard Women's Law Journal*, Vol. 8 (Spring 1985), 19.
6. Kramer and Sprenger, *Malleus*, 228.
7. Ibid., 223.
8. Ibid., 229.
9. Ibid., 225.
10. Ibid., 226.
11. Ibid.
12. Ibid., 227.
13. Ibid.
14. Ibid., 228.
15. Ibid., 46.
16. Ibid., 44.
17. Ibid., 45.
18. Ibid., 8.

CHAPTER 11
1. Kramer and Sprenger, *Malleus*, 92.
2. Ibid., 97.

CHAPTER 12
1. Anthony Polk, "The Lady and the Lawyer," *Rocky Mountain Magazine*, Vol. 2, No. 7 (November/December 1980), 30–31.
2. Ibid., 31.
3. Ibid.

CHAPTER 13
1. Kramer and Sprenger, *Malleus*, 198–199.

CHAPTER 14
1. Kramer and Sprenger, *Malleus*, 208.
2. Ibid., 242.

CHAPTER 15
1. Kramer and Sprenger, *Malleus*, 219.
2. Ibid.

CHAPTER 20
1. Larson, 202.
2. Ibid., 44, 53.

3. Lola M. Homsher (ed.), *South Pass, 1868* (Lincoln: University of Nebraska Press, 1960), 19. In Larson, 52.
4. Larson, 196.
5. Ibid.

CHAPTER 24
1. Kramer and Sprenger, *Malleus*, 241.
2. Ibid., 219.
3. Ibid., 213.
4. Ibid., 241.

CHAPTER 25
1. Kramer and Sprenger, *Malleus*, 215.

CHAPTER 26
1. Kramer and Sprenger, *Malleus*, 216.
2. Ibid., 218.
3. Ibid., 231.
4. Ibid., 213.

CHAPTER 30
1. "Franklin Follow-up Study Will Assess Impact of Hutchinson and Wolston," *LDRC Bulletin*, No. 1, July 31, 1981, 2.
2. "Defamation Trial and Damage Awards—More and Larger Awards Entered Against Media Defendants: But Few Upheld on Appeal," *LDRC Bulletin*, No. 4, Part 1, Aug. 15, 1982, 3.
3. Martin Garbus, "New Challenge to Press Freedom," *The New York Times Magazine*, January 29, 1984, 41.
4. Kramer and Sprenger, *Malleus*, 269.
5. Ibid.
6. Ibid., 270.

CHAPTER 31
1. Kramer and Sprenger, *Malleus*, 271–272.
2. *The Great Thoughts*, compiled by George Seldes (New York: Ballantine Books, 1985), 26.

CHAPTER 32
1. Viktor Reimann, *Goebbels: The Man Who Created Hitler*, translated by Stephen Wendt (New York: Doubleday, 1976), 97.
2. Ibid., 96.

CHAPTER 33
1. Kramer and Sprenger, *Malleus*, 271.
2. Ibid., 274–275.

CHAPTER 35
1. Kramer and Sprenger, *Malleus*, 222–223.

BIBLIOGRAPHY

Auerbach, Jerold S. *Unequal Justice: Lawyers and Social Change in Modern America.* New York: Oxford University Press, 1976.

Benson, Jackson J. *The True Adventures of John Steinbeck, Writer.* New York: Viking Press, 1984.

Cohn, Norman. *Warrant for Genocide: The Myth of the Jewish World Conspiracy and the Protocols of the Elders of Zion,* New York: Harper & Row, 1966.

Daly, Mary. *Gyn/Ecology: The Metaethics of Radical Feminism.* Boston: Beacon Press, 1978.

Dworkin, Andrea. "Against the Male Flood: Censorship, Pornography, and Equality," *Harvard Women's Law Journal,* Vol. 8, Spring 1985, 1–29.

———. *Pornography: Men Possessing Women.* New York: Perigee, 1981.

———. *Woman Hating.* New York: E. P. Dutton, 1974.

Fromm, Erich. *The Anatomy of Human Destructiveness.* New York: Holt, Rinehart & Winston, 1973.

Gage, Matilda Joslyn. *Woman, Church and State.* 2nd ed. New York: Arno Press, 1972.

Garbus, Martin. "New Challenge to Press Freedom," *The New York Times Magazine,* January 29, 1984, 34 ff.

Homsher, Lola M., ed. *South Pass, 1868.* Lincoln: University of Nebraska Press, 1960.

Kaufman, Henry R., ed. "Defamation Trial and Damage Awards—More and Larger Awards Entered Against Media Defendants: But Few Upheld on Appeal," *Libel Defense Resource Center Bulletin,* No. 4, Part 1, August 15, 1982, 1–17.

———."Franklin Follow-up Study Will Assess Impact of Hutchinson and Wolston," *LDRC Bulletin,* No. 1, July 31, 1981, 1–4.

Korda, Michael. *Power! How to Get It, How to Use It.* New York: Ballantine Books, 1975.

Kramer, Heinrich, and James Sprenger. *Malleus Maleficarum,* translated and introduced by Rev. Montague Summers. New York: Dover Publications, 1971.

Lapham, Lewis H., ed. "The Place of Pornography: Packaging Eros for a Violent Age," a forum in *Harper's,* Vol. 269, No. 1614, November 1984, 31–45.

Larson, T. A., *History of Wyoming.* Lincoln: University of Nebraska Press, 1965.

Lea, Henry Charles. *Materials Toward a History of Witchcraft,* arranged and edited by Arthur C. Howland, with an introduction by George Lincoln Burr. 3 vols. New York: Thomas Yoseloff, 1957.

McLuhan, T. C., comp. *Touch the Earth: A Self-Portrait of Indian Existence.* New York: Promontory Press, 1971.

Polk, Anthony. "The Lady and the Lawyer," *Rocky Mountain Magazine,* Vol. 2, No. 7, November/December 1980, 27–32.

Reimann, Viktor. *Goebbels: The Man Who Created Hitler,* trans. Stephen Wendt. New York: Doubleday, 1976.

Ruether, Rosemary Radford. *New Woman, New Earth: Sexist Ideologies and Human Liberation.* New York: Seabury Press, 1983.

Sade, Marquis de. *Juliette,* trans. Austryn Wainhouse. New York: Grove Press, 1976.

————. *The 120 Days of Sodom and Other Writings,* trans. Austryn Wainhouse and Richard Seaver. New York: Grove Press, 1967.

Seldes, George, comp. *The Great Thoughts.* New York: Ballantine Books, 1985.

INDEX

Abrams, Floyd, 460
Actual malice, definition of, 176–177
American Cancer Society, 247
American Nazi Party, 102
American Newspaper Publishers Association, 431
American Scholar, 294
Anatomy of Human Destruction (Fromm), 124
Armstrong, Flo, testimony of, 213–214
Associated Press, 409
Association of American Publishers, 431, 432; amicus curiae brief in *Pring* v. *Penthouse* appeal, 432–433
Association of American University Presses, 431
Attorney-client privilege, in *Pring* v. *Penthouse*, 341
Authors' League of America, 431, 433

Baboon Law, 30, 33
"Best of *Penthouse*, The," 71–73
Bindrim case, 333, 335
Boteen, Bernard, 101
Boulder Press Club, Kelley's speech to, 426–427
Bread Loaf Writers Conference, 291
Breitenstein, Judge, 447, 448–449
Brenner, Bob, testimony in *Pring* v. *Penthouse*, 264–265
Brimmer, Clarence A., 80, 136, 140, 142, 477; and arguments on setting aside verdict in *Pring* v. *Penthouse*, 411–423; on Cline testimony, 184; and conflict over instructions to jury, 363–366, 367–368; and Cooper's motion for continuation to hear new information on Pring, 312–316; and Cooper's motions for mistrial, 204–205, 317; on Cooper's right to recall Pring, 342; on cross-examination of Guccione, 215–216; and defense in

Pring case, 175–176; and determination of sum for just punishment of *Penthouse*, 360–362; Grutman loses suit against, 170; and Grutman's absence from court, 174–175; and Grutman's efforts to withdraw from *Pring* v. *Penthouse*, 189–192; on Grutman's motion for his disqualification, 157–161; on Howdeshell's reports, 326–327, 330–331; instructions to jury, 352–353, 392; and list of witnesses in Pring case, 178–181, 182–184, 186–188; and motion to dismiss *Pring* v. *Penthouse*, 100–113; and motion for new depositions, 93–99; at opening day of Pring trial, 193–207; on "outrage" issue, 176–177; and possibility of setting verdict aside, 407; and prejudiced-juror issue, 354–360; pretrial requirements, 184–185; and *Pring* v. *Penthouse* appeal decision, 447, 449; on punitive damages, 177–178; and questioning of jury, 195–197; refuses withdrawal of Grutman and Daichman, 170–171; ruling on Cioffari's *Hustler* article, 285; ruling on Guccione's deposition, 74–77; rulings on pending motions, 160–161; on showing of Miss America Pageant film, 257; and *Smith* v. *Ford*, 185; and Spence's interrogatories to Guccione, 145–149; sued by *Penthouse*, 161–167; and virginity issue, 128, 150; on witness overhearing Pring-Spence conversation, 341. *See also* *Pring* v. *Penthouse*
Brokaw, Tom, 408–409
Brownmiller, Susan, 123
Bruce, Harry, 289
Burton v. *Crowell Publishing Co.*, 430–431

C.N.A. (insurance company), 189; relationship to *Penthouse* and Grutman, 191
Caligula (film), 84–88, 149, 155

Cardona v. *The University Hospital,* 174

Carlson, Dr., 179

Carmichael, David, 170, 192

Carter, Jimmy, 172, 173, 246

Cenedese, Barbara J., 383, 388; testimony in *Pring* v. *Penthouse,* 336, 337–339

Cenedese, Tammy, 337

Censorship, 14, 65. *See also* First Amendment; Libel cases

Cheyenne, Wyoming, 18, 45, 46, 47; description of, 257; history of, 255–257; Kelley on, 427. *See also* Wyoming

Cheyenne Kiwanis Club, 264–265

Chic magazine, 90, 119, 274

China Syndrome, The (film), 334–335

Chisholm, James, 256

Cioffari, Philip, 45, 107, 108, 187–188, 192, 205, 214, 221–222, 223, 248, 259, 260–261, 430; at Atlantic City Miss America Pageant, 120–121, 180; attitude toward Spence, 267–270; Cooper's motion to separate out of *Pring* v. *Penthouse,* 316; in Cooper's summation, 381; culpability distinguished from *Penthouse*'s, 416, 418–419; deposition of, 89–91; income, 288; liability of, 289–290; motion for default judgment against, 284; at opening day of *Pring* v. *Penthouse,* 203; Pring's attitude toward, 114, 121; second deposition of, 114–121; Spence's attitude toward, 280–281; testimony in *Pring* v. *Penthouse,* 266, 269–277; verdict against, 412; on verdict in *Pring* v. *Penthouse,* 401–402. *See also Pring* v. *Penthouse*

Clark, Dr. Herbert, testimony in *Pring* v. *Penthouse,* 339, 344–350, 353, 373, 380, 384, 430

Cline, Dr. Victor, testimony in *Pring* v. *Penthouse,* 182, 183–184, 301–302, 384; Cooper on testimony of, 316

Congressional Record, 96

Cooper, Paul, 170, 174–177, 182, 210, 250, 285; and "actual malice" issue, 177–178; and Armstrong's testimony, 213–214; asks Brimmer to control cross-examination of Guccione, 215–216; and Brimmer's instructions to jury, 353; on Cioffari's liability in *Pring* v. *Penthouse,* 289; and Cioffari's testimony, 271–277, 284–291; cross-examination of Brenner, 265; cross-examination of Cline, 302; cross-examination of Guccione, 245–250; cross-examination of Hofler, 222–224; cross-examination of Howdeshell, 325–328, 329–330; cross-examination of

Pring, 308–310, 318–320; cross-examination of Wideman, 298–299; on defense in Pring case, 175–176; and determination of sum for just punishment of *Penthouse,* 360–362; final summation, 378–384; and Goode's testimony, 257–264; on Grutman's absence, 184; and Guccione's press conference during trial, 226–227; and Hofler testimony, 216–222; informs Brimmer of new information on Pring, 312–316; and leading questions, 224–225; and Libel Defense Resource Center, 431–432; and list of witnesses, 187; motion to separate Cioffari from *Pring* v. *Penthouse,* 316; motions to dismiss, 333; motions for mistrial, 204–205, 257, 277–278, 280, 283–284, 316–317; objections during Spence's summation, 370, 372, 376, 390; objects to psychologist's report offered into evidence, 330–331; at opening day of *Pring* v. *Penthouse,* 193–198, 199, 201, 202, 204–207; on "outrage" issue, 177; and prejudiced-juror issue, 354–360; questioning of Cenedese, 337; questioning of Clark, 344–345; questioning of Pierson, 333; questions Pring on use of birth-control pills, 318–319; re-cross-examination of Pring, 318–320, 322, 343; requests continuance of pretrial conference, 189–192; rests case, 351; at settlement conference, 443; and *Smith* v. *Ford* requirements, 184, 186; and Spence's questioning of Guccione, 231, 233, 234, 237; statement to press after decision in *Pring* v. *Penthouse,* 403–404; statements to press during decision on rehearing *Pring* v. *Penthouse,* 450–451; and Storm's testimony, 208–210, 212; and use of secret witnesses, 339–341; and virginity issue, 180–181; and Wideman's testimony, 294, 298–299; and Wilson's testimony, 300–301; on witness overhearing Pring-Spence conversation, 341. *See also Pring* v. *Penthouse*

Daichman, Jeffrey, 105, 113, 118, 119, 121, 141, 142; asks for contempt-of-court ruling against Pring, 139–140; at opening day of Pring trial, 194; and questioning of Pring, 17, 19–23; requests permission to return to New York, 299; and retaking of Cioffari's deposition, 115, 116; and retaking of Goode's deposition, 122–123; and retaking of Hofler's deposition, 125–127; takes Brimmer to court of appeals on writ of mandamus,

161–167; and virginity issue, 127–131, 133–138, 139–140, 145. *See also Pring* v. *Penthouse*

Denver Post, 426; article on lawyers' panel on libel suits, 461; articles on *Pring* v. *Penthouse*, 451–452, 458

Dershowitz, Alan, 469

Digby, James P., 264

Dog Day Afternoon (film), 333, 334

Doonesbury (comic strip), 437, 438, 451, 453, 466

Doubleday and Company, 431

Drum Majors magazine, 308

Duff, Rick, testimony in *Pring* v. *Penthouse*, 323

Dun and Bradstreet, 432

Dworkin, Andrea, 67, 134; Spence meets, 483; suit against *Hustler*, 483–486

"Either Way You Lose" (Cioffari), 117

Eldredge, Laurence, 104–105

Ellis, Albert, 72

Elshtain, Jean Bethke, 67

Evelyn Rainbird Company, 61, 124, 149, 361

Falwell, Jerry, 184, 258, 390; Guccione and, 170–174; *Hustler's* sham interview with, 464–465; suit against *Hustler*, 465–470; suit against *Penthouse*, 170–174, 215–216, 221, 238–239, 246

First Amendment, 14–15, 145, 176, 177, 183, 223–224, 235, 333–335, 370–371, 382, 431, 433, 484; Guccione's use of, 127; libel and, 65; and *Penthouse* appeal, 428; pornography and, 14, 63–65; and *Pring* v. *Penthouse*, 29, 100–101, 102, 103, 105, 194, 403–404; and *Pring* v. *Penthouse* appeal decision, 426–427, 447–448, 448–449; Spence-Moriarity discussion on, 280–283; and women, 409

Fleischli, Gus, 179, 318

Flynt, Larry, 68, 413, 463–464. *See also Hustler*

Ford Motor Company, 153. *See also Smith* v. *Ford*

Forever Amber (film), 109

Franklin, Marc, 469

Freedom of speech. *See* First Amendment

Fromm, 124

Frost, Robert, 291

Gale, Kenneth W., 166

Gallery, 90, 118, 274–275

Gente magazine: article on Pring, 103, 206, 304–305, 309, 342–343, 383, 389;

Pring's conversation with her attorneys on, 343–344

Gertz v. *Welch*, 101, 430, 484

Goebbels, Joseph, 437

Goldstein, Al, 67

Goode, James, 192, 269, 430; deposition of, 91–92, 122–123; testimony in *Pring* v. *Penthouse*, 257–264

Graham, Billy, 246

Greenbelt, 447

Griesa, Thomas, 166, 167

Grutman, Norman Roy, 45–46, 49–50, 128, 142, 145, 196, 238–239, 319, 340, 403, 419–420, 426, 427, 444; ability as lawyer, 154–155; absence from *Pring* v. *Penthouse*, 170–175, 228; appearance before Circuit Court, 439; attacked by *Hustler*, 463–464; attempts to prevent taking of Guccione's deposition, 74–77; and Cioffari's deposition, 89–91; description of, 78, 100; efforts to withdraw from *Pring* v. *Penthouse*, 189–192; and Falwell's suit against *Hustler*, 465–470; and Falwell's suit against *Penthouse*, 171–172; and Goode's deposition, 91–92; and Guccione's deposition, 79–83; and Hofler's deposition, 92; influence on *Pring* v. *Penthouse*, 312–314, 315; on lawyers' panel on libel cases, 460–462; legal talents of, 167–168; lodges complaint against Spence with Bar Association Grievance Committee, 151–155; loses suit against Brimmer, 170; motion demanding gynecological examination of Pring, 110–112, 156; motion to dismiss *Pring* v. *Penthouse*, 100–113; motion to disqualify Brimmer as presiding judge in *Pring* v. *Penthouse*, 157–159; motion for new depositions, 93–99; and Pring's deposition, 49–57; relationship with Spence after *Pring* v. *Penthouse* trial, 462–463; requests continuance, 162–163; role as *Penthouse* attorney, 220; speaking style of, 102; and Spence's efforts to reach settlement, 169; and Spence's interrogatories to Guccione, 145–149; suit against Gale, 166; takes Brimmer to Court of Appeals on writ of mandamus, 161, 162–167; tells Spence about "secret witness" in *Pring* v. *Penthouse*, 471–473. *See also Pring* v. *Penthouse*

Guccione, Robert C., 29, 32, 192, 200, 202, 203, 296, 297; attitude toward sex, 59–60; attitude toward women's rights, 59; business enterprises of, 61, 62; and *Caligula*, 84–87; career of, 58–68; con-

Guccione, Robert C. *(continued)*
tents of publications, 60–61; Cooper's
questioning of, 245–250; cross-examination of, 215–216; deposition of, 79–83,
361–362; Falwell and, 170–174; financial worth of, 148–149, 361–362; and
First Amendment rights, *see* First Amendment; Grutman's attempt to prevent
deposition by, 74–77; and Grutman's
motion to disqualify Brimmer as presiding judge, 157–159; on *Hustler,* 68; on
influence of *Penthouse,* 132; interviewed
by Safer on *60 Minutes,* 62–63, 65–66,
68, 71, 235–236, 461; and laws on pornography, 64; libel suit against *Hustler,*
79–80, 461; meets with press during
Pring v. *Penthouse,* 226–227, 283; motion for mental examination of, 156; at
opening day of *Pring* v. *Penthouse,* 194,
199; on *Penthouse,* 127, 247; on power,
62; reaction of jurors to, 481; and "secret witness" in *Pring* v. *Penthouse,*
471–473; Spence's interrogatories and,
146–149; and Spence's motion for new
depositions, 94–99; Spence's reexamination of, 248–250; starts *Penthouse,*
58–59; subpoenaed by Spence, 192; suit
against *Hustler,* 92, 96, 97, 147, 413;
suits against, 61; testimony of, 228–241,
242–245; on verdict in *Pring* v. *Penthouse,* 400. *See also Penthouse; Pring* v.
Penthouse

Hefner, Hugh, 59. *See also Playboy*
Helms, Jesse, 467–468
Herschler, Governor Ed, 179
Hitler, Adolf, 65, 437
Hofler, Robert, 192, 352–353; cross-examination by Cooper, 222–223; deposition
of, 92–93; retaking of deposition of, 123,
125–127; testimony in *Pring* v. *Penthouse,* 214–215, 216–224
Hollander, Xaviera, 234
Holmes, Oliver Wendell, 464
Howdeshell, Dr. Angela, 380, 383; Cooper's cross-examination of, 325–328;
329–333; records on Pring, 328–329; testimony in *Pring* v. *Penthouse,* 323–328,
330–332
Hull, John, 318, 322
Hunt v. *State,* 448
Hustler, 68, 241, 271–272, 275–277, 291,
400, 413, 461; attack on Grutman in,
463–464; cartoons on Dworkin in,
483–486; Dworkin suit against, 483–486;
Falwell's suit against, 465–470; Guccione's suit against, 79–80, 92, 96, 97,
147

Innocent VIII, pope, 18, 139
Invasion of privacy issue, 176–177, 365

Jefferson, Thomas, 65
Jong, Erica, 66
Judges: and monetary awards, 185; power
of, 103, 143, 168, 188–189, 231, 352,
429, 443
Jury in *Pring* v. *Penthouse:* attitude of,
344, 348; Brimmer's instructions to,
352–353; deliberations, 392–396; and
determination of sum for just punishment of *Penthouse,* 360–362; discussion
with Spence after *Pring* v. *Penthouse*
trial, 477–482; and Falwell's suit against
Hustler, 469; Kelley on, 426–427; and
prejudiced-juror issue, 354–360; selection of, 193–197; verdict, 396–397. *See
also Pring* v. *Penthouse*

Kahn, David, 467
Kelley, Tom, 170, 174, 181, 182, 192, 250,
275, 278, 285, 313, 328; and "actual
malice" issue, 177; appearance before
Circuit Court, 435–436; arguments for
setting aside verdict in *Pring* v. *Penthouse,* 411–413, 418; and discussion
with Brimmer on cross-examination of
Guccione, 216; files brief in Circuit
Court, 427–428; and Libel Defense Re-
source Center, 431–432; at opening day
of *Pring* v. *Penthouse,* 196, 197,
203–204; on *Pring* v. *Penthouse* appeal
decision, 446; on reputation issue, 316;
at settlement conference, 443; speech to
Boulder Press Club, 426–427; statements
to press during decision on rehearing
Pring v. *Penthouse,* 451–452. *See also
Pring* v. *Penthouse*
Khomeini, Ayatollah Ruhollah, 239
King, Martin Luther, Jr., 294
Kinsey report, 60
Knox, Kirk, 403, 404, 411, 417–418, 422
Korda, Michael, 62
Kraft, Joseph, 221, 223, 323
Kramer, Heinrich, 132, 181, 313

La Costa case, 247
"Lady Chatterley's Last Stand" (Cioffari),
119–120
Lady Chatterley's Lover, 109
Laramie, Wyoming, 47–49
Lawrence, D. H., 267
Lawyers: censorship of, 283; compared
with matadors, 116; fears of, 103–104
Letter Carrier's case, 447
Libel case, 30, 65; decisions in, 400–401.
See also Pring v. *Penthouse*

Libel Defense Research Center, 400; and *Penthouse* appeal, 431–432
Life magazine, 259
Logan, Judge, 447

McCarthy, Joseph R., 105
McClellan, George B., 255
McIntosh, Rosemary, 151
Magazine Publishers Association, 432
Maliciousness issue, 182–183
Malleus Maleficarum (The Witches' Hammer), 10–11, 70, 132, 133, 134, 135, 136, 137, 138, 139, 145, 165, 178–179, 181, 303, 311, 313, 315, 325, 340, 342, 404, 413, 419, 420, 445, 450, 453, 485, 486; comparison with *Pring v. Penthouse* trial, 17–23; influence on judges and lawyers, 132, 190; misogyny and, 132–133; and virginity issue in Pring case, 111, 112
Mansfield, Judge Walter, 168
Markson, Elaine, 483
Mather, Cotton, 485
Media: and libel suits, 31, 400–401; and Libel Defense Research Center, 432
See also Press
Michigan Quarterly, 115, 291
Miller, Arthur, 460
Miller, Henry, 87, 267
Miller v. California, 63, 72
Milton, Chad, 189
Miss America Pageant, 41, 53, 307, 353, 375; film shown to jury in *Pring v. Penthouse*, 250, 254, 257, 309; jurors on, 481; in *Pring v. Penthouse*, 218–219, 239, 240
Miss USA contest, 308
Moral Majority, 172–173. *See also* Falwell, Jerry
Moriarity, Eddie, 29, 31, 34, 35, 40, 96–97, 100, 108, 110, 111, 122–123, 170, 174, 184, 186, 187, 189, 192, 224–225, 227, 246, 250, 271, 272, 289, 299, 316, 335–336, 340, 344; and "actual malice" issue, 177–178; advice during *Pring v. Penthouse*, 242–243, 244, 245, 258, 260, 274, 277, 290, 292, 317, 321, 379, 382, 385; after Pring case, 398, 477; awaits jury decision, 393–395; background of, 31–32; on Brimmer's ruling on witnesses, 180, 182; celebrates verdict, 409–410; and conflict over Brimmer's instructions to jury, 363, 364; on Cooper's stalling cross-examination of Pring, 310–311; and decision in *Pring v. Penthouse*, 397; discusses *Pring v. Penthouse* with Spence, 280–283; and Dworkin's suit against *Hustler*, 483–486; and

Grutman's complaint against Spence to Bar Association Grievance Committee, 152–153; on Grutman's motion to disqualify Brimmer, 159; and Howdeshell's reports, 326–327; inability to attend hearing on setting aside verdict in *Pring v. Penthouse*, 414; on law and pornography, 63–65; leaves courtroom at end of trial, 350–351; motion for default judgment, 284; at opening day of *Pring v. Penthouse*, 195, 197, 207; personality of, 32; and prejudiced-juror issue, 354–355, 358, 359, 360; on *Pring v. Penthouse*, 163–164; and *Pring v. Penthouse* appeal decision, 445; reaction to Brimmer's lowering damages, 423; and retaking of Goode deposition, 122–123; and rumors about *Pring v. Penthouse* appeal decision, 442–443; at settlement conference, 444; on verdict in *Pring v. Penthouse*, 399–400; and virginity issue, 180; on witness overhearing Pring-Spence conversation, 341–342. *See also Pring v. Penthouse*
Morris, Esther Hobart, 12–13
Mulhaver, Minnie, 264

Nabokov, Vladimir, 267
National Association of Broadcasters, 432
Nazi Germany, freedom of press in, 437
Necrophilic personality, 124
Newhart, Bob, 345
New Jersey Gaming Commission, 62
Newsweek, 246
New York Bar Grievance Committee, Grutman's complaint against Spence to, 77, 151–155
New York Times, 96, 401, 403, 446, 460, 469
New York Times Book Review, 294
New York Times v. Sullivan 104, 183, 484. *See also* Public-figure issue
Nizer, Louis, 165

O'Brien, Judge, 414
Oh! Calcutta! (musical play), 109
Omni, 61, 362
Orlando (Fla.) *Sentinel Star*, 62
"Outrage" issue, 176–177

Parks, Bert, 41, 250–254
Parsons, Salley Mae, 264
Paul, Dan, 446, 452–453, 460
Pauling, Linus, 104
Penthouse, 10, 17; article on Kim Pring, see *Pring v. Penthouse*; attitude toward writers, 267–269; contents of, 66–67, 71–73; and determination of sum for

Penthouse (continued)
just punishment of, 360–362; effects of,
404–405; first issue of, 58–59; income of,
374; and Miss Idaho, 179–180; payments
to writers, 118; popularity of, 139; and
private investigators of Pring, 192; Rancho La Costa suit against, 165–167, 168,
247; reasons for growth of, 148; subscriptions and newsstand sales of, 62,
248; suit against *Playboy*, 166–167; suits
against, 147; and U.S. Supreme Court
definition of obscenity, 63. *See also* Guccione, Robert C.; *Pring v. Penthouse*
"Penthouse Forum," 60–61, 63, 66, 71–72,
96, 124, 234, 362, 373
*Penthouse International, Ltd., and Philip
Cioffari, Petitioners, v. Clarence A. Brimmer, United States District Judge for the
District of Wyoming, Respondent,* 162
Penthouse International, Ltd. v. *Playboy
Enterprises Inc.,* 166
Photo World, 362
Pierson, Frank, testimony in *Pring v. Pent-
house,* 333–335, 382
Playboy, 58, 59, 173; *Penthouse* suit
against, 166
Polk, Tony, 152–153, 155
Pomeroy, Dr. Wardell, 60
Pornography: defenders of, 67; Dworkin
and, 483, 486; effects of, 66–67,
404–405; First Amendment and, 14;
legal status of, 62–65; opponents of,
67–68, 68–69; and tensions between the
sexes, 66, 123–125; victims of, 68–71
Powell, Justice Lewis, 363
President's Commission on Pornography,
182, 301, 302
Presley, Elvis, 259
Press: on Falwell suit against *Hustler,* 466,
469–470; Guccione and, 226–227; and
Kelley's pre-appeal speeches, 427; and
Pring v. Penthouse appeal decision, 446.
See also Media
Pring, Kimerli Jayne, 10, 36; affidavit, 107;
and arguments on setting aside verdict,
411–423; attitude toward Cioffari, 114,
121–122; attitude toward virginity issue,
127–131; awaits jury decision, 394–396;
background, 46, 49; career of, 101,
205–206, 304–305, 308–309; celebrates
verdict, 409–410; childhood, 26–28;
Cooper informs Brimmer of new information on, 312–316; cross-examination
by Cooper, 17–21, 308–310, 317–320;
and decision in *Pring v. Penthouse,* 397;
deposition of, 131, 133–140; first meeting with Spence, 23–28; impact of ques-

tioning on, 141–142; impact of trial on,
242, 243, 245, 279, 302, 368, 377; information on sex life of, 329–332; interviewed on *Today Show,* 408–409; joins
army, 475–477; learns about *Penthouse*
article, 51; in Miss America contest,
120–121, 251–254; physical appearance
of, 24; on picture in *Gente,* 304–305;
plans for future, 406–407; and possibility of Brimmer's setting verdict aside,
407; preparations for deposition, 49–50;
problems after defeat of case, 457–458,
460; psychiatric testimony on, 323–328;
reaction to Brimmer's lowering punitive
damages, 421, 422–423; reaction of jury
to, 303–304; reaction to *Penthouse* article, 37, 43, 52, 214, 305–308, 349; reaction to *Pring v. Penthouse* appeal
decision, 446–447; reaction to Supreme
Court refusal of rehearing, 455–456; reexamination by Spence, 320–322; relationship with mother, 43, 210–211;
requestioned on conversation with attorneys, 343–344; *Rocky Mountain Magazine* article on, 152–155; and ruling on
virginity issue, 150; and suicide of boyfriend, 327, 329, 332; testimony of,
303–310, 317–320; after trial, 398; on
verdict, 399, 400, 402–403; victory in
Miss Wyoming contest, 24. *See also
Pring v. Penthouse; Pring v. Penthouse*
appeal
Pring, Mary Jayne, 23–28, 36, 37, 50, 206,
305, 385, 393, 476–477; impact of *Penthouse* article on, 43, 208–209; impact of
trial on, 368–369; at trial, 210–211
Pring, Norman, 27–28, 50, 208
Public-figure issue, 176–177, 196, 200, 240,
265, 375–376; and Brimmer's instructions to jury, 363–364
Pring v. Penthouse: and "actual malice"
issue, 177–178; arguments on verdict in,
411–423; Armstrong testimony, 213–214;
attorney-client privilege in, 341; Brenner's testimony, 264–265; Brimmer's decision on verdict, 422; Brimmer's
instructions to jury, 352–353; Brimmer's
rulings on pretrial motions, 160–161;
Brimmer's rulings on witnesses,
178–181, 182–184, 186–188; Cenedese's
testimony, 336, 337–339; and Cioffari's
deposition, 89–91; Cioffari's testimony,
266, 269–277, 284–291; Clark's testimony, 339, 344–350; Cline's testimony,
301–302; compared with *Malleus, see
Malleus Maleficarum;* conflict over
Brimmer's instructions to jury,

363–366, 367–368; costs, 157; damages asked in, 377–379, 381; defense, 175–176; depositions conflict, 74–77; and determination of sum for just punishment of *Penthouse*, 360–362; discussed by lawyers' panel, 460–461; Duff's testimony, 323; editorial after decision on, 458; efforts to reach settlement, 169; and Falwell's suit against *Hustler*, 466, 469; final summations, 368–392; and Goode's deposition, 91–92; Goode's testimony, 257–264; Grutman's efforts to withdraw from, 189–192; and Grutman's motion to disqualify Brimmer as presiding judge, 157–159; and Grutman's request for physical examination of Pring, 110–111; Guccione on verdict in, 400; Guccione's testimony, 228–241, 242–245; hearing on Grutman's motion to dismiss, 100–113; Hofler's deposition, 92–93; Hofler's testimony, 220–224; Howdeshell's testimony, 323–328; impact on Prings, 476–477; information on Pring's sex life in, 329–332; invasion of privacy and "outrage" issues in, 176–177; jury in, *see* Jury in *Pring* v. *Penthouse*; jury selection for, 193–197; list of witnesses in, 186–188; Miss America Pageant shown to jury in, 250–254; opening of, 193–207; pending motions in, 156; *Penthouse* motion for continuance denied, 174–175; and *Penthouse's* suit against Brimmer, 161, 162–167; *Penthouse* witnesses, 184, 186; and petition for writ of certiorari to Supreme Court, 452–455; Pierson's testimony, 333–335; and prejudiced-juror issue, 354–360; press on outcome of, 401–404; pretrial conference, 174–192; Pring's testimony, 303–310, 317–320; and "public figure" issue, 176–177; reactions to verdict in, 401–404; and reputation testimony, 311–312; and retaking of Cioffari's deposition, 114–121; and retaking of Goode's deposition, 122–123; and retaking of Hofler's deposition, 123, 125–127; Rodriguez's testimony, 342; Schuster-Spence discussion on, 142–145; secret witnesses in, 339–341, 344, 351, 471–475; Spence-Moriarity discussion on, 280–283; Spence's decision to take, 29–44; and Spence's motion for new depositions, 93–99; Spence's reexamination of Guccione, 248–250; Storm's testimony, 208–210, 212; trial date set, 113; verdict in, 396–397; virginity issue,

127–131, 133–138, 140; Wideman's testimony, 293–300; Wilson's testimony, 300–301. *See also Pring* v. *Penthouse* appeal

Pring v. *Penthouse* appeal, 426–440; *amicus curiae* briefs filed in, 432–433; arguments before Circuit Court, 434–439; decision in, 444–449; petition for rehearing on decision, 449–451, 453; rumors on decision in, 441–446; settlement conference prior to decision on, 443–444

Rancho La Costa, suit against *Penthouse*, 165–167, 168
"Rat Hunting in the Bronx" (Cioffari), 115, 116, 117
Reagan, Ronald, 477
Reporters' Committee for Freedom of the Press, 432–433
Reputation issue, 311–312, 318–321, 325–332, 354–360, 388–389, 418–419, and Cooper's motion for continuation for new information on Pring, 312–316
Reuben, Don, 460
Rockwell, George Lincoln, 101–102
Rocky Mountain Magazine, 152–155, 158, 160, 427
Rocky Mountain News, 427
Rodriguez, Chenco, testimony of, 342
Rogers, Will, 208
Roth, Dr. Howard R., 264
Rufinus, 138

Sade, Marquis de, 72–73, 117, 119
Safer, Morley, interviews Guccione on *60 Minutes*, 62–63, 65–66, 68, 71, 235–236
Salem witch trials, 10–11
Schuster, Robert, 29, 31, 32–34, 40, 61, 452, after Pring case, 477; background, 33–34; brief on suit against Brimmer, 168; discussions with Spence on Pring case, 156; and Dworkin's suit against *Hustler*, 483–486; files brief in Circuit Court, 429–431; on Grutman's motion to disqualify Brimmer, 159; on Guccione's rights, 183; on *Hustler's* sham interview with Falwell, 464–465; on impact of *Pring* v. *Penthouse* on Pring, 476; on law and pornography, 63–65; and *Penthouse* appeal, 428–429; and petition for writ of certiorari to Supreme Court, 454–455; and *Pring* v. *Penthouse* appeal decision, 442, 445, 449–451; reaction to Brimmer's lowering damages, 423; and ruling on virginity issue, 142–145, 150; and Spence's interroga-

Schuster, Robert (*continued*)
  tories to Guccione, 145–149. *See also*
  Pring v. *Penthouse*
Screw magazine, 67
Seth, Chief Judge, 436, 439, 442, 447–448,
  469
"Shattering" (Cioffari), 119
Shellow, Jim, 10–11
Shockey, Gary, 128; and Pring's deposi-
  tion, 50, 53–57
Silkwood case, 197, 355, 450, 452
60 Minutes, Guccione interview on, 62–63,
  65–66, 68, 71, 235–236, 461
Smith, Jack. *See Smith* v. *Ford*
Smith v. *Ford*, 179, 184–186, 415
"Snuff movies," 65
Society of Witches, 18
Socrates, 132, 138
Spellman, Percy P., 264
Spence, Gerry, 191; appearance before
  Circuit Court, 434–435, 436–438; argues
  against Cooper's request for continuation of pretrial conference, 189–192;
  argues against setting aside verdict
  in *Pring* v. *Penthouse*, 413–418; attitude toward Cioffari, 267–270; attitude
  toward Grutman, 167–168; attitude
  toward jury, 292; attitude toward Miss
  America Pageant, 218; attitude toward
  New York City, 82, 83–84; attitude
  toward winning and losing, 36; awaits
  jury decision, 392–396; and Brimmer's
  rulings on witnesses, 178–181, 182–184;
  childhood, 482; Cioffari's attitude
  toward, 280–281; and conflict over
  Brimmer's instructions to jury, 363–366,
  367–368; and Cooper's motion for continuation for new information on Pring,
  312–316; on Cooper's stalling cross-
  examination of Pring, 310; cross-examination of Cenedese, 338–339; cross-
  examination of Clark, 345–350;
  cross-examination of Pierson, 333–335;
  on damaged-reputation issue, 181; and
  decision in *Pring* v. *Penthouse*, 396–397;
  decision to take Pring case, 29–44; and
  determination of sum for just punishment of *Penthouse*, 360–362; discusses
  Pring v. *Penthouse* with Moriarity,
  280–283; discussion with Brimmer on
  cross-examination of Guccione,
  215–216; discussions with *Pring* v. *Penthouse* jurors, 477–482; and Dworkin's
  suit against *Hustler*, 483–486; editorial
  in *Denver Post* on, 458; education, 33;
  efforts to reach settlement in Pring case,
  169, 189; family background, 398–399;

and feminism, 11–14; files brief in Circuit Court, 429–431; files suit against
  Penthouse, 45; final summation in *Pring*
  v. *Penthouse*, 369–378, 386–392; first
  meeting with Pring and her mother,
  23–28; and Grutman's complaint to Bar
  Association Grievance Committee,
  151–155; and Grutman's request for
  continuance, 162–163; and Grutman's
  request for physical examination of
  Pring, 110–112; and Guccione's deposition, 79–83; and Guccione's press conference at trial, 226–227; and
  interrogatories for Guccione, 145–149;
  interviewed on *Today Show*, 408–409;
  on judges, 143; as lawyer for insurance
  companies, 37–40; and leading questions, 224–225; on libel suits, 484–485;
  and motion to dismiss Pring case,
  100–113; moves for mistrial, 365–366,
  367; at opening day of *Pring* v. *Penthouse*, 193–207; on panel on libel cases,
  460–462; and *Penthouse* appeal,
  427–429; and possibility of Brimmer's
  setting verdict aside, 407; on precedent,
  420; on public-figure issue, 176; questioning of Brenner, 264–265; questioning of Cioffari, 269–277, 284–287,
  290–291; questioning of Goode,
  257–264; questioning of Hofler,
  214–215, 216–224; questioning of Pring,
  303–308, 343–344; questioning of Wideman, 293–300; reaction to Brimmer's
  lowering damages, 423–424; reaction at
  end of case, 9; reason for writing book,
  10–11; reasons for taking Pring case,
  43–44; reexamination of Guccione,
  248–250; reexamination of Howdeshell,
  331–332; reexamination of Pring,
  320–321; relationship with Grutman
  after *Pring* v. *Penthouse* trial, 462–463;
  reply to *Denver Post* editorial, 459–460;
  rests case, 333; and retaking of Cioffari
  deposition, 114–121; and retaking of
  Hofler deposition, 123, 125–126; on role
  of pornography, 123–125; and rumors
  about *Pring* v. *Penthouse* appeal decision, 441–446; and "secret witness" in
  Pring v. *Penthouse*, 471–475; sees *Caligula*, 85–88; at settlement conference,
  444; and *Smith* v. *Ford*, 184–186; subpoenas Guccione, 192; takes Cioffari's
  deposition, 89–91; takes Goode's deposition, 91–92; takes Hofler's deposition,
  92–93; talks to press after decision in
  Pring v. *Penthouse*, 403; and virginity
  issue in Pring's deposition, 128–131,

133–138, 139–140; and Wilson's testimony, 300. *See also Pring* v. *Penthouse; Pring* v. *Penthouse* appeal
Sprenger, James, 132, 181, 313
Stars of Tomorrow, 264, 265
Steinbeck, 115
Stewart, Justice Potter, 485
Storms, Bill, 412; testimony of, 208–210, 212
Supreme Court, 62, 63, 103, 104–107, 430, 449, 452; Dun and Bradstreet case, 485; on free speech, 282; petition for writ of certiorari in Pring case to, 453–456

Tenth Circuit Court of Appeals. *See Pring* v. *Penthouse* appeal
Theis, Judge, 198
Time, Incorporated, 432
Times Mirror Company, 432
Today Show, The, interviews with Spence and Pring, 408–409
Tomorrow Coast to Coast, Guccione and Falwell on, 173
Turk, James C., 171–172, 173–174
Twirl magazine, 308

Ulysses (Joyce), 109
Underwood, James, 137
United States Supreme Court. *See* Supreme Court
UPI, 404

Valerius, 138
Variations, 60, 66, 362
Variety, review of *Caligula* in, 87
"Vegas Dreams," 284–285
Vidal, Gore, 84
Virginity issue in Pring case, 17–23, 54–55, 110–112, 127–131, 133–139, 140; Brim-

mer rules on, 150; Daichman and, 145; and effort to disqualify Brimmer, 157–159; and Grutman's suit against Brimmer, 164–165; impact on Pring, 141–142; Schuster's reaction to, 142–144. *See also* Reputational issue
Viva, 61, 259, 362

Wahl, Dr., 318–319
Wall Street Journal, on Falwell, 173
Washington Post, 307, 400, 404, 432
Where Do You Draw the Line? An Exploration into Media Violence, Pornography, and Censorship (Cline), 301
Wicked Wanda, 94
Wideman, Dr. John Edgar, 353, 384, 430; testimony of, 293–300
Wideman, Robbie, 295
Wilson, Tracy, testimony of, 300–301
Witches' trials, 18–19, 133, 136–137, 485
Woman hating, 69–71, 138–139
Woman Hating (Dworkin), 67
Women: burned as witches in Middle Ages, 10–11; crying in court, 138; Guccione and Falwell and, 172–173; Guccione's attitude toward, 59; lack of equality under law, 22; in Wyoming, 12–13. *See also* Woman hating
Women Against Pornography, 67
Worell, Larry, 189
Writers Guild of America, 432; "Code of Ethics" of, 348
Wyoming: history of, 255–257; woman suffrage in, 12, 13. *See also* Cheyenne, Wyoming; Laramie, Wyoming
Wyoming State Tribune, 308, 403

Zappa, Frank, 308